LORD PALMERSTON
VOL. II

LORD PALMERSTON IN 1861

LORD PALMERSTON

BY

HERBERT C. F. BELL

IN TWO VOLUMES
VOLUME TWO

WITH ILLUSTRATIONS

32496

ARCHON BOOKS
HAMDEN CONNECTICUT
1966

FIRST PUBLISHED 1936
LONGMANS, GREEN AND CO., LTD.

REPRINTED WITH PERMISSION 1966
IN AN UNABRIDGED AND UNALTERED EDITION

LIBRARY OF CONGRESS CATALOG CARD NUMBER: 66-14604
PRINTED IN THE UNITED STATES OF AMERICA

CONTENTS OF THE SECOND VOLUME

CHAPTER XX

THE REVOLUTIONS OF 1848, AND PALMERSTON'S CONFLICT WITH THE QUEEN—II

CHAPTER XXI

PALMERSTON'S DISMISSAL FROM THE FOREIGN OFFICE, 1850–1851

CONTENTS

CHAPTER XXVI

1856–1857

CHAPTER XXVII

1857–1858

CHAPTER XXVIII

PALMERSTON AGAIN PREMIER

CHAPTER XXIX

1859

CHAPTER XXXIV
1864

CHAPTER XXXV
1865

* Guide to Citations is printed in Volume I, p. 448.

ILLUSTRATIONS IN THE SECOND VOLUME

LORD PALMERSTON

In the autobiography of the eighth duke of Argyll, there are some rather striking passages on Palmerston's reaction to the German nationalist movement of 1848 and the developments which it produced.[1] First, on his general attitude :

> Chevalier Bunsen . . . Prussian Minister . . . in London . . . had an intense love of the Fatherland, and . . . eagerly believed that . . . the Revolutions of 1848 would somehow end in a consolidated German Empire. . . . Of course, . . . he desired above all things that this union should be effected under the leadership of the Prussian monarchy. At one moment it seemed about to be accomplished, for the Imperial Crown was offered to the King of Prussia. Bunsen was in the highest state of excitement. He mounted the German tricolour upon the Embassy ; he decorated his carriage with its rosettes, and even mounted one on his own breast. Of course, he was made the laughing-stock of political society in London, . . . Palmerston, . . . was the very incarnation of ridiculing disbelief. But more than this : he hated Prussia, and had the worst opinion of the motives of Prussian statesmen. They were playing a game for the hegemony of Germany, and not at all for the establishment of constitutional liberty amongst the German people. . . . Palmerston . . . was detested . . . by the German Unionists.

Then, on an incident which occurred in 1850, when the hopes of a spontaneous union had vanished, and Prussia

B

was making a futile attempt to effect a partial consolidation
on her own terms :

> I well recollect standing with Bunsen outside his Embassy at
> Carlton Terrace when a procession was passing by along the Mall
> below us.   When Palmerston passed there was some cheering of the
> spectators ranged on each side.   Bunsen turned his eyes away slowly,
> saying, half to himself, half to me : ' He has no principle, and he has
> no heart.'

Finally, Argyll's comment on Bunsen's reproach :

> In the sense in which these words were spoken they were founded
> on truth ; but they were wrong in the sense they conveyed in our
> language.   Palmerston was not, in the ordinary meaning of the word,
> an unprincipled politician.   He was honest in his purposes, and
> truthful in his prosecution of them.   That ' honesty is the best policy '
> was his favourite adage in diplomacy ; but what Bunsen meant was
> true—he had no high ideals for the future of the world, and had a
> profound distrust of those who professed to be guided by such
> ideals.   To them he seemed to be, and he really was, heartless and
> unsympathetic.

Certain it is that the very idealistic and intellectual Germans
who tried to realise their liberal aspirations just at the
middle of the century were treated by the foreign secretary
in a manner bordering on contempt.

It is a curious fact that, while Palmerston showed almost
no interest in the formation of a united German state, he
could argue most convincingly the advantages of close
friendship between England and Germany.   This came
out in a memorandum which he presented to Prince
Albert in September 1847, while he was discussing with
Bunsen the renewal of a commercial agreement between
Great Britain and the Zollverein.[2]   England and Germany,
he pointed out, had no interests which were likely to conflict ; whereas they were both menaced, potentially at least,
by Russia and by France.   Since an united Germany
would certainly have been a far more valuable ally to
Britain than the existing Bund, it might have been expected
that he would go on to express some hope that unity would
be achieved.   All he did in that direction was to bless
the Zollverein as ' uniting Germany by one common

national feeling.' And, as Theodore Martin, the Prince's biographer and co-worker for German unity, pointed out, the remainder of his argument proved him hostile to the Zollverein itself :

> But the Zollverein maintained . . . prohibitory duties against English manufactures, . . . Accordingly, . . . [Palmerston's] Memorandum expands into an elaborate dissertation on the futility of all restrictive duties, . . . All consideration of the gain to Germany, to Europe, or to England, from a strong and united Germany, in intimate alliance with England, drops out of view, and Lord Palmerston sums up his argument by the conclusion, ' that any English Ministry would be thought to have much neglected its duty, and to have sacrificed the commercial interests of the country, if it did not make every proper effort to persuade the States of Northern Germany, who have not joined the Zollverein, to continue to refrain from doing so.' [3]

Prince Albert, who was spending much time with Stockmar and Bunsen in working out plans for a new Germany, received no support from the Foreign Office, where he might confidently have expected to find it.

It was so unlike Palmerston to give commerce precedence over national prestige and national security, that only one explanation seems possible : he did not take the German unification movement seriously. This conclusion is borne out by his letters.[4] Thus to Bloomfield at St. Petersburg in August 1848 :

> As to German unity that vision seems fast dissolving but probably the efforts made to realize that phantom may lead to a reconstruction of the Confederation in some form better adapted to the present state of Germany.[5]

On one occasion he wounded Bunsen by remarking that, while the formation of a real German state would be beneficial, and very much in accord with British policy, the ' tendency ' toward it ' appeared merely good as a plaything.'[6] To Prince Albert he was more tactful :

> I confess, Sir, that for my part I have never yet been able to see clearly through these complicated matters and for that reason among

others, I have abstained from pointing out to the British diplomatic agents in Germany any course or any language on these questions, lest from mistaken views, we might do mischief instead of good.[7]

But Palmerston was not the man to remain in ignorance or doubt where he saw any object in securing information and making up his mind on it. Thus, one returns to the same conclusion : he refused to support the movement in any way because he did not consider it worth his while. But why this apathy ? It is true that he never showed much appreciation of continental nationalism *per se* ; but he had been quick enough to perceive the advantages to be drawn from the development of a stronger kingdom in northern Italy, quick enough to suggest that England and Germany might make common cause against Russia and France. Argyll found the answer in his ' hatred ' of Prussia, his ' ridiculing disbelief' and his 'lack of high ideals of the future of the world.' That he disliked the Prussian government at this time is altogether probable ; that he rightly saw its policy as a selfish one is quite certain.[8] But that need not have deterred him from showing some sympathy to the Frankfort parliament. Argyll might have done better to suggest that he was influenced by his annoyance at the part played by the parliament in the question of Schleswig-Holstein. The other two suggestions call for more comment.

The ' ridiculing disbelief' of Palmerston was scarcely to be wondered at. When Prince Albert, Stockmar, and Bunsen all presented different schemes for achieving German unity ;[9] when the Prince was at one time for the inclusion of Austria, and at another for a confederation in which Austria was to have no place and Prussia the fullest measure of control ; when the intellectuals at Frankfort took a long time to agree as to whether the new Germany should be a republic or an empire, and as to whether Austria should be allowed to bring in her non-German territories ; when the Prussian king now paraded in the tricolour, now refused contemptuously the crown which the delegates at Frankfort offered him, it was not strange that Palmerston dismissed the movement as too ' complicated.' In point of fact, its very nature offended

him. He believed in states organised from above, not
from below ; in constitutions granted by wise sovereigns
who appreciated the inestimable advantages of the British
form of government, not constitutions extorted or even
framed overnight by revolutionists.[10] He could sympathise
with a movement headed by a ruler of Sardinia, but not
with one in which any irresponsible German enthusiast
might have his say.

His highest ' ideal,' in that period at least, was the
one he had carried with him and offered to Europe for so
long : the British form of government administered in
the British way. Various despatches to the Prussian court,
and especially his comments on the constitution which
Frederick William IV granted in February 1847, offered
further testimony to his sincerity in that. Thus to Russell,
at the time when the nature of the Prussian king's concessions was first disclosed :

> The new Prussian constitution need not so much have alarmed
> Austria and Russia, except in as far as it must be looked upon as only
> a first step ; for, certainly, no representative assembly ever had their
> teeth drawn and their claws cut more completely. There are so
> many things they are not to do, that one is almost puzzled to find out
> what it is they are to do. . . . But Prussia has now cast the die, and
> she must go on, for retreat is impossible. *But if she does go on,
> Germany will follow her, and sooner or later her example must be
> followed by Austria.*[11]

For some years he had realised Prussia's growing leadership. During his visit to Berlin, in 1844, he had been
much impressed with the ' great intellectual activity ' of
the Prussians. ' Prussia,' he had written, ' is taking the
lead in German civilisation ; and as Austria has gone to
sleep, and will be long before she wakes, Prussia has a fine
career open to her for many years to come.'[12] Whether
or not he was desirous of furthering this leadership, he did
his best to persuade the Prussian ruler to grant a constitution of what he regarded as the proper sort.[13] Westmorland, his minister at Berlin, was very tactfully to suggest
that ' the King having made up his mind to give a constitution . . . would act most wisely by making that
constitution a practical reality and that all attempts to

nullify in fact that which has been granted in words can only lead to embarrassing and dangerous difficulties.' Reverting almost to the very phrases which he had used in parliament more than fifteen years before to justify his change of attitude toward parliamentary reform, he went on : ' Concessions which to-day would be accepted with thankfulness may at no distant period be considered a very insufficient satisfaction.' At Berlin, as at Madrid and St. Petersburg, he called attention to risings elsewhere in order to give his admonitions weight. Had he shown half so much attention to the plans of the ill-fated parliament at Frankfort, the German unionists might have regarded him in a very different light.

But the reason why the German unionists ' detested ' Palmerston was not so much his general attitude, as the fact that he opposed them on the question of Schleswig-Holstein.[14] That bugbear of mid-nineteenth century diplomatists (and of those who would chronicle their activities) may really be surveyed without extreme discomfort if one is satisfied with a very general and therefore none too accurate view. The difficulty of understanding it arises from the complicated relations of the duchy of Schleswig and the duchy of Holstein to one another, to Denmark, and to the German Bund. In the first place, each duchy had for its duke the Danish king, but was determined to resist any incorporation with Denmark. In the second place, the duchies clung together, partly for mutual support, and partly because the association of centuries had created between them a strong *de facto*, in addition to a very weak *de jure*, bond. And lastly, Holstein, a state that was German in everything save its sovereign, was a member of the German Bund. Curious as the situation was, it might easily have endured had the Danes and the Germans been content to have it so. But the spirit of nationalism, reinforced as usual by considerations of self-interest, stirred both nations to action as the century wore on. The Danes, in view of the fact that the population of northern Schleswig was predominantly Danish, pressed their king to incorporate the duchy in the monarchy ; the Germans, inspired by the spirit of nationalism and the desire for an outlet to the sea, urged that Holstein's supposedly inseparable twin should, in consideration of the very German character of its more southerly districts, be brought into the Bund. And neither was at any loss for arguments, as Palmerston pointed out :

> The former history of Denmark and the two Duchies seems to be so confused and to be so full of irregular transactions, that some events may be quoted in support of almost any pretension.[15]

There was one disagreement of an especially threatening kind. Was or was not the succession in the duchies, or in Schleswig at least, governed by the Salic law ? In view of the fact that Frederick VII, who became king-duke of Denmark and Schleswig-Holstein in January 1848, was almost certain to die without heirs, and to be succeeded by a prince whose personal claim was very disputable, but whose wife was descended from an elder female line, both Danes and Germans exhausted themselves in searching for documents and elaborating arguments.

Frederick's accession, and his public endorsement of an outline constitution left by his predecessor, brought to a head a situation which had been growing more ominous for several years. Since 1842, the king of Denmark had been preparing unmistakably to separate the duchies and incorporate Schleswig ; while the Germans had been agitating for a closer union between Schleswig and Holstein, and the inclusion of the former in the German Bund. Moreover, the Powers had been ranging themselves on either side. Russia, France and England, for various reasons and in varying degrees, all gave their sympathies to Denmark. Frederick William of Prussia emphatically ranged himself with the Bund ; and Metternich seemed inclined to do the same. Hence, with the accession of the new Danish king, and the example of revolution offered by all the discontented elements on the continent in the spring of 1848, there existed all the conditions needed to produce a European crisis of the first magnitude. And it came, in fact, with great rapidity. In March, the inhabitants of Schleswig-Holstein rebelled : at the beginning of April, they renounced allegiance to the King-Duke.

The Danes easily crushed the revolutionary troops ; but were almost immediately driven back by a German army, despatched by Prussia, endorsed by the Frankfort parliament, commanded by General Wrangel, and consisting in the main of Prussian troops. Excitement ran high in all the Baltic states. Sweden prepared forces for the assistance of the Danes, and the Tsar sent a fleet to cruise protectively along their coasts.

Palmerston found himself in northern, as in southern Europe, playing the unaccustomed and exacting rôle of a non-interventionist. He summarised his difficulties in a private letter which he sent Lord Bloomfield, his ambassador at St. Petersburg, on May 19, 1848 :

> I am labouring hard to bring these people to terms but it is difficult when one has to deal with Copenhagen Berlin Frankfort and Genl. Wrangel ; I hope however that with the assistance afforded by the declarations of Russia & Sweden we shall at last succeed. I must say I think the Prussians have acted in this matter with unjustifiable violence.[16]

What he wanted was to secure assistance in bringing the Germans to a halt while there was still time to prevent a general war ; and essentially to preserve the *status quo*. He had no idea of allowing the duchies to escape from the king of Denmark's rule. England was to some extent bound by treaty in so far as Schleswig was concerned ;[17] and there were both economic and political considerations to be thought of. It would not suit him to see the German Zollverein pushed up into the peninsula, or the Danish government rendered too weak to guard the entrance to the Baltic Sea. And there might be a disastrous upset of the balance of power if Russia and Prussia came to blows. Later on he had other reasons for wishing the termination of the conflict. He could hardly enter the House of Commons, he wrote the Queen, without encountering complaints of the damage inflicted on British trade and shipping by the Danish blockade of the German ports.[18] For all these reasons, and perhaps also because British public opinion was strongly with the Danes,[19] his despatches enjoined prudence on both sides, but bore down especially upon Germany.[20] He warned the Prussians not to go beyond Holstein, and the Danes to keep their forces in Jutland. He suggested to the German national parliament at Frankfort that it had better compose its quarrel in the north, and keep its strength to meet dangers from the east and west. At times he even took a threatening tone. He reminded the Prussian king that England was under treaty engagements with Denmark, and had quite as good a right to fulfil them as Germany had to make good its obligations to Holstein. And he threw himself into the work of mediating and helping to arrange an armistice. It may be true that by carrying an unopened despatch in his pocket for two or three days, he hindered negotiations at one juncture, and caused an unnecessary loss of lives and ships ;[21] but no one in Europe was working harder to keep the peace.

He was not only playing an unaccustomed rôle, but taking an unaccustomed attitude by opposing the liberals of Germany and Schleswig-Holstein. It was not that he entirely failed to sympathise with them. In his letter to Bloomfield he expressed hopes of setting up a principle for the ' final arrangement ' of the whole affair :

That principle being a division of Sleswig [sic] according to national character. The German part becoming a member of the confederation under its Duke as Holstein now is ; the Danish & northern part being incorporated with Denmark.[22]

And he, who disliked revolution hardly less than Metternich, and who ' never could understand . . . the ground of right, upon which the Frankfort Assembly and Govt. endeavoured to justify their attack,'[23] admitted to Victoria that the inhabitants of the duchies had had much excuse :

Both in Hungary and in Schleswig the sovereign who is also sovereign of another country published a decree ordering a change in the constitution and a practical incorporation of the country with the other state over which the sovereign reigned and those edicts were published without the consent of Sleswig [sic] or of Hungary, in both cases much may be said as to the right of the nation to resist. . . .[24]

But the people of the duchies and their German friends

were the aggressors at a time when the need for peace and for the *status quo* was paramount. Hence, while he was afraid that the Danes might ' become . . . too cock a hoop from their powerful backing and indisposed therefore to reasonable terms,' he was willing to risk this in opposing the ' violent overbearing oppressive, disingenuous, shuffling & tricky ' conduct of Baron Arnim, the Prussian minister.[25]

His attitude was disconcerting to some of the London world. While England as a whole was entirely with the Danes, some of the foreign secretary's admirers among the radicals grieved at his lapse from grace. More striking was the fact that both the Princess Lieven and Brougham wrote to Aberdeen in praise of his conduct.[26] Brougham was especially struck with the fact that he had had to fight not only the Court but certain of his colleagues who wanted to play up to the radical ' knaves.' Aberdeen found it ' strange to hear ' that the government was ' right in anything ' ; but he had his own views as to Palmerston's motives :

. . . with respect to the Danes, the feeling of England is so strong that I do not think it would be possible for any minister to take an open part against them.   Had we spoken to Prussia at the commencement, as we ought to have done, we might have prevented the continuance of this war ; but our hatred of Austria made us unwilling to oppose the aggrandisement of Prussia, and there was no objection to a little coquetting with the rebels at the same time. . . .[27]

For so really good a man, Aberdeen had striking ability to see his rival's acts in the most unfavourable light.

Palmerston's disagreement with the Court over the Schleswig-Holstein question did not reach its height until the danger was practically past, and the time to consider a final settlement had come. This was in the summer of 1850, when, after two years of incessant negotiation and British mediation, after three spells of fighting and three armistices, the king of Prussia signed a treaty with Denmark leaving things very much as they had been before. The treaty was highly distasteful to the Queen, who felt that the Germans had been entirely justified in intervening on behalf of the duchies, and that the ' independence ' of

Schleswig would have to be secured. For Palmerston's
mediation she showed nothing but contempt. The
threats by which he had attempted to impose moderation
upon both combatants had elicited the sour remark that
'the mediating power merely watches which of the two
parties is in the greatest difficulties for the moment, and
urges it to give way.'[28]   Matters were made worse by the
fact that Palmerston, despite all his wife could do, seemed
to glory in arguing.[29]   But what most stirrred Victoria's
wrath was Palmerston's successful effort to secure the
signature by the five great Powers, and by the Scandinavian
governments, of a protocol recording their opinion that
the integrity of the king of Denmark's possessions should
be preserved. This the Queen regarded as 'a direct
attack upon Germany,' and as 'repugnant to all feelings of
justice and morality' in disposing of 'other people's
property' without their consent.[30]   Palmerston was so
nettled as to inquire of Russell, in a letter immediately laid
before the Queen, whether her Majesty was not requiring
that he should be 'Minister . . . for the Germanic Confederation.'[31]   He might really have abstained from such
impertinence, especially at a time when he could con-
gratulate himself on such success.

For, although the actual settlement was not achieved
until after his expulsion from the cabinet, he had already,
in 1850, realised his aims. Peace, the balance of power
and Britain's commercial interests had all been preserved.
It was true that the potential dangers of the situation were
as great as they had been before ; and that a greater
statesman might have secured better provision for the future.
But when one considers the difficulties which accompanied
his every move, and the incessant demands upon his
attention in those years, it is hard to be critical.

If Palmerston's liberal and radical admirers were disappointed in his attitude toward the Frankfort parliament
and the Schleswig-Holsteiners, they must have suffered
still greater disillusionment in observing his apparent
indifference to the struggle which the Hungarians were
carrying on against Austria.[32]   To anyone who understood
and sympathised with the spirit of the time, this struggle

could not but have great appeal. No nation in Europe was able to present more convincing claims to autonomy than the Hungarians—claims not only ethnological and cultural but historical. And their case was greatly strengthened by the developments of the spring of 1848. In March, the Austrian government, temporarily paralysed by revolution at its own capital, conceded to Hungary almost complete autonomy and responsible government. Had the Magyars not made the sad mistake of refusing to show any consideration for the national feelings of the Serbo-Croats and Roumanians who lived under their own rule, it is possible that a dual monarchy would have been established then and there. But, as the year wore on, these Hungarian Slavs attacked their oppressors with some success. Austria, heartened by this, by news from Italy, and by a revulsion of feeling at Vienna which assisted the Austrian generals in re-establishing ' order ' and installing Schwarzenberg, took up the Slav cause in Hungary. In October they made actual war, and prepared to retract the concessions which the Magyars had won during the spring. Confession of an open breach of faith was avoided by the claim that Francis Joseph, installed as emperor at the beginning of December, could not be bound by the undertakings of the feeble-minded uncle who had been forced to make way for him. The Hungarians, after vainly insisting that they must have self-government, and showing extraordinary valour in the field, declared their country an independent republic in April 1849. Their failure to consider the dislike of republics, and the regard for the carefully balanced territorial arrangements of 1815 common to all the Powers but France, was perhaps almost as rash as their refusal to concede anything to the claims of their subject nationalities. But, whatever their mistakes, their heroism and misfortunes in the struggle which ensued were enough to touch any generous heart. In spite of the rebellion of the Slavs within their gates, in spite of errors and quarrels on the part of their leaders and generals, they more than held their own. Only when the Tsar, glad to strike at revolutionists, and to teach a new lesson to the Poles, sent troops to attack the Magyar forces from

the direction of the Roumanian principalities, were they
overwhelmed.   On August 13, 1849, their principal army
surrendered to the Russians at Vilagos.   A few days later
some five thousand refugees, largely Poles, and including
Kossuth and several other of the principal leaders, fled
across the frontier into Turkey.   They were fortunate to
escape.   Civilian insurgents, including women, were being
flogged under the orders of the Austrian general, Haynau ;
and the more important of the refugees had been marked
for death.

Palmerston, as has been said, long seemed indifferent
to the whole struggle.   It has been shown that Hungarian
emissaries, sent to appeal for aid, were turned away from
Downing Street with the answer that England had ' no
knowledge of Hungary except as one of the component
parts of the Austrian Empire.' [33]   It has been pointed out
that for the whole year 1848 only two despatches relating
to the Hungarian revolt—and those displaying no more
sympathy than the answer given to the Hungarian envoys—
were offered to parliament.[34]   When the Russian intervention was projected and carried through, the foreign
secretary, usually quite ready to lecture Nesselrode,
abstained from all comment.[35]

But his official conduct cannot be taken as a sure guide
to his private sentiments.   He confessed to Ponsonby, of
all persons, that he was fully in sympathy with the
Hungarians ; [36] and on one occasion he argued their cause
to Russell in a manner which could hardly have been
improved upon by Kossuth :

. . . right and justice was on the side of the Hungarians. . . . The
Austrian cabinet wanted to alter that constitution [the Hungarian
constitution of March 1848] entirely, to abolish the independent
legislative powers of the Diet, to incorporate Hungary with the
aggregate mass of the Austrian Empire. . . . Instead of endeavouring
to persuade the Hungarian Diet to agree to this . . . the Austrian
Cabinet determined to carry it by force. . . .[37]

And what a pretext, to claim that the substitution of the
new emperor for the old justified them in forsaking their
undertakings, and insisting that Hungary should accept
a new constitution designed for the whole empire !

... if this leaves him [Francis Joseph] free in regard to the Hungarians, it must equally be held to leave the Hungarians free in regard to him. If he is not bound to observe the laws and constitution of the country, the public cannot be bound to observe allegiance to him. ... The Austrian Government had no right to employ force to impose the ... constitution on the Hungarians, and force having been employed with that view, the Hungarians were fully justified in resisting force by force and in declaring the forfeiture of the Crown by the Emperor and his family.

Seldom did Palmerston condone revolution in this way, and never in public. But his sympathies seem to have been no secret in the summer of 1849. ' I have not seen the Palmerstons,' wrote Charles Greville, after news of the Hungarian *débâcle* had been received, ' . . . but have no doubt they are provoked to death at the overthrow of the Hungarians.'[38] It is true that these evidences of his sympathy date, whether by accident or not, from the time when Hungary's resistance was nearing its end ; but the whole career and character of the man offer strong presumptive evidence that his feeling was spontaneous and of long standing.

It is not difficult to reconcile his official indifference with his personal sympathy. He explained it on various occasions, but never more clearly than in answering one of the Hungarian envoys. He greatly disapproved of Austria's policies, but a strong Austrian empire was indispensable to the balance of power :

. . . if it did not already exist, it would have to be invented ; . . . it was an European necessity, and the natural ally of England in the East ; he therefore counselled us [the Hungarians] to reconcile ourselves with Austria, because in the frame of the European State-system it would be impossible to replace Austria by small States.[39]

He explained the same idea with greater elaboration to the House,[40] pointing out that Austria stood in the centre of Europe, ' a barrier against encroachment on the one side, and against invasion on the other.' For this reason he believed that ' the political independence and liberties of Europe ' were bound up with ' the maintenance and integrity of Austria as a great European Power.' Lest he should be misquoted or misunderstood, he did not forget to remind his hearers that Austria's government had, ' in the opinion of a great part of the Continent, been identified with obstruction to progress.' Even Schwarzenberg was fully enlightened to the same effect as parliament, and, almost needless to say, enjoined not to make Hungary ' a source of weakness,' ' a political cancer,' by refusing to satisfy her ' national feelings.'[41]

What outcome did he then hope for when the great struggle was in progress ? Not complete success for either side, but what has lately been called ' peace without victory.' He explained this clearly both to Russell[42] and to parliament :

> . . . if the war is to be fought out, Austria must thereby be weakened . . . if the Hungarians should be successful . . . such a dismember-ment of the Austrian empire . . . will prevent Austria from continuing to occupy the great position she has hitherto held among European Powers. If . . . Hungary should by superior forces be entirely crushed, Austria . . . will have crushed her own right arm.[43]

No wonder he was ' provoked to death ' at the capitulation of Vilagos.

The only satisfaction that he had in the days immediately following was in preaching—to Schwarzenberg of all people !—the wisdom of showing clemency to the defeated Hungarians and the Poles who had assisted them, and giving the Hungarians a free constitution after all :

> The thing evidently to be done is to re-establish the ancient Constitution of Hungary, with the improvements made in it last year. . . . If Austria wishes for a legislative union with Hungary, it should be proposed in a legal way, like our unions with Scotland and Ireland. . . .[44]

Even with his remarkable optimism, he must have found this rather a discouraging task ; but he relieved his feelings in a private letter to the no doubt scandalised Ponsonby :

> The Austrians are really the greatest brutes that ever called themselves by the undeserved name of civilised men. Their atrocities in Galicia, in Italy, in Hungary, in Transylvania are only to be equalled by the proceedings of the negro race in Africa and Haiti. . . . I do hope that *you* will . . . maintain the dignity and honour of

England by expressing *openly* and *decidedly* the disgust which such
proceedings excite in the public mind in this country ; and that you
will not allow the Austrians to imagine that the public opinion of
England is to be gathered from articles put into the 'Times' by Austrian
agents in London, nor from the purchased support of the ' Chronicle,'
nor from the servile language of Tory lords and ladies in London,
nor from the courtly notions of royal dukes and duchesses. . . .[45]

Even Schwarzenberg should be able to understand that a
favourable public opinion in England would be of some
value to Austria,

if for nothing else, at least to act as a check upon the illwill towards
Austria, which he supposes, or affects to suppose, is the great actuating
motive of the revolutionary firebrand who now presides at the Foreign
Office in Downing Street.

To write like this was really good fun ; but it produced
no sense of things achieved. Surely he longed for a
chance to deliver some real stroke.

If so, Providence was extremely good to him. At the
end of September he learned that Austria and Russia,
with some assistance from Stratford Canning, once again
British ambassador at the Porte, had given him an exceptional opportunity. The two imperial governments, em-
ploying a strained interpretation of certain international
treaties, had demanded that the Sultan should deliver up
the Polish and Hungarian refugees. Compliance being
refused, they had threatened war by breaking off diplomatic
intercourse. Stratford Canning had done his part by
assuring the Sultan that Britain would support him in
resisting the Russian and Austrian demands.[46] Palmerston
was equally sure. Tales of the public flogging in Hungary
even of ladies, and of the sentence of strangulation first
passed on the distinguished Count Batthanyi had aroused
such horror among Englishmen that any move to help the
refugees was almost certain to be popular. And the foreign
secretary had some small share at least in working up public
sentiment, as appears from a letter he sent to his new friend,
Peter Borthwick, of the *Morning Post* :

There can be no objection to the publication of this . . . and
you may say that in addition to the ladies therein mentioned it is

understood that the Austrian Govt. have imprisoned . . . the mother
of Kossuth, aged 72 . . . and you might make such observations
as may suggest themselves upon this unmanly war waged against
Hungarian women and children by those Austrians who were unable
to stand up against the Hungarian men until they had called in to
their assistance an army of 150,000 Russians.[47]

There was another aspect of the matter which was sure
to count heavily with the cabinet and with parliament.
Russia's attempted coercion of Turkey seemed to be one
of a succession of threatening moves. Making use of
the excuse offered by revolutionary disturbances in the
Roumanian principalities, she had gradually installed a
large army there. In spite of all protests, she had attacked
the Hungarians from Turkish soil. In England the old
fears for Turkish independence, for British trade in the
Levant, for the routes to India and for the balance of
power revived.

So convinced was Palmerston of his colleagues' willingness to support the Turks, that he wrote immediately to
Normanby at Paris, outlining for Normanby's private
information what in his personal opinion should be done.[48]
Friendly representations should be tried at Vienna and
St. Petersburg ; but, at the same time, British and French
squadrons should quietly take position outside the Dardanelles, with orders to proceed to Constantinople in case
of actual necessity. The cabinet, rapidly assembled,
entirely justified his hopes. Hardly had its decision been
rendered, when three separate messengers were hurried
off, to inform Canning and the Turkish government at the
earliest possible moment that Turkey would have support,
both ' moral ' and ' material,' from Great Britain and from
France.[49] One of them, having accomplished an almost
incredible record for speed and endurance on horseback,
became, thanks partly to Palmerston, the hero of ' Townley's
ride.'

But there was no trace of reckless chauvinism in
Palmerston's attitude. As usually occurred, the seriousness
of a really great issue steadied him. He was determined
as man could be that Russia and Austria should give way,
and quite ready to go to extremities if they did not. But

he took the utmost precautions to see that they were neither threatened nor otherwise provoked.[50]   The joint action of the British and French governments was represented as inevitable in view of Turkey's simultaneous appeal to them ; no word was uttered to any Austrian or Russian minister or representative concerning the movement of the squadrons to the Dardanelles ; the Turks were warned not to bring the ships up except in case of dire necessity, and the British commander to confine his operations to purely protective ones.   Ponsonby was directed to assume an argumentative, not a threatening tone to Schwarzenberg :

> What could Austria hope to gain by a war with Turkey, supported, as she would be, by England and France ?   Austria would lose her Italian provinces . . . and she never would see them again. What she might gain to the eastward I know not. . . . At all events, I cannot conceive that, in the present state of Germany, it would suit Austria to provoke a war with England and France. . . . Pray do what you can to persuade the Austrian government. . . .[51]

Palmerston explained his caution in a latter to Canning :

> The example [of sending vessels to Constantinople] might be turned to bad account by the Russians hereafter ; and it would be too much of an open menace, and the way to deal with the Emperor [of Russia] is not to put him on his mettle by open and public menace. In this affair we are trying to catch two great fish, and we must wind the reel very gently and dexterously, not to break the line.   The Government have indeed resolved to support the Sultan at all events, but we must be able to show to Parliament that we have used all civility and forbearance, and that if hostilities ensue, they have not been brought on by any fault or mistake of ours.[52]

There really was a suggestion of the angler in all this.

As it proved, the fish were brought in with unexpected ease.   Although the Tsar was mainly responsible for the whole crisis, he soon lost heart.   Bloomfield was informed in ' strictest confidence ' that the Russian government and people ' regretted deeply the wholesale butcheries in Hungary,' and that the matter of the refugees would almost certainly be arranged by a mere exchange of notes with the Turkish government.[53]   On the evening of the very day on which Nicholas received the Turkish envoy, he informed Nesselrode that the demand for extradition would be given up.[54] And there is no doubt that it was England's firmness which really won the day. Nesselrode frankly confessed as much in a letter to Baron von Meyendorff, his special envoy at Berlin :

> Certainly I hate Palmerston as much as Prince Schwarzenberg can hate him, and my feeling goes back of his ; but Palmerston is not eternal, and a war with England would be the worst of all wars. It is out of our power to inflict damage on her, and it is we who should have to pay the costs. God preserve us from that ! [55]

It was left for the British Foreign Office only to see that such refugees as did not receive amnesty from Austria were as comfortably interned and as rapidly released from internment as possible.[56] Palmerston, however, took occasion to revert to his old policy of fortifying the Turk against the day to come, by offering all possible British assistance in the strengthening of his defences against the Russian power.[57]

The crisis being over, he allowed himself to do a little crowing to Canning :

> All things however have turned out well. The English Government and nation have shewn a spirit, a generosity, and a courage which does us all high honour. We have drawn France to follow in our wake. . . . We have forced the haughty autocrat to go back from his arrogant pretensions ; we have obliged Austria to forego another opportunity of quaffing her bowl of blood ; and we have saved Turkey from being humbled down to absolute prostration. All this will be seen and felt by Europe . . . but all this *we* ought not to boast of, and on the contrary we must let our baffled Emperors pass as quietly and as decently as possible over the bridge by which they are going to retreat.[58]

There were few in England who did not feel that his whole conduct of the affair had been most creditable. One of the exceptions was, as usual, the Queen.

She was naturally aggrieved ; for her wishes had been overridden and her protests treated-with something very like contempt. She had been unwilling that the Sultan should be urged to refuse surrender of the refugees, or that his refusal should receive anything save ' moral '

support from the British government.[59] ' What business
have we to interfere with the Polish and Hungarian Refugees
in Turkey ? ' she had demanded of Russell on September 12.
Palmerston's answer to the prime minister, a copy of which
apparently reached her,[60] was anything but calculated to
appease her wrath.   It contained, not only his justification
of the Hungarian revolt, and of Hungary's refusal to accept
the rule of the new Austrian emperor, but a passage which,
to the Court, must have seemed gratuitously impertinent :

. . . the Hungarian leaders may certainly be called revolutionists,
but they are revolutionists in the same sense as the men to whose
measures and acts at the close of the seventeenth century it is owing
that the present Royal Family of England, happily for the nation, are
seated on the throne of these realms . . .

This letter was written in September, 1849, at a time when
the Queen's determination to secure his removal, although
twice balked, was particularly strong.
    From that time on, her determination to oust him from
his place became, if possible, more fixed.   It was not so
much his manner of treating her, or his occasional lapses
from the truth that made her so resolved : it was the
fact that, in all sincerity, she felt it her duty to combat
both his policies and his methods.   She believed that he
was doing great injury by his attempts to promote the
extension of constitutional government on the continent,
and the formation of a strong kingdom in northern Italy :
she was appalled by his incessant disputes with other
governments, and the rebuffs which they brought upon
her court.   Her indignation seems to have robbed her of
all ability to judge calmly.   She had worked herself into
a frame of mind where she could declare that ' the *whole*
movement on the Continent ' was ' *anti-Constitutional, anti-
Protestant, and anti-English.*' [61]   Prince Albert was of
opinion that since Palmerston's return to power England
had not had a ' single success,' save perhaps in Switzerland,
where Stratford Canning had been responsible.[62]   In
February 1850, the Queen ' exploded ' at Windsor to
Clarendon ;   and Prince Albert ' poured forth without
stint or reserve all the pent-up indignation, resentment, and

bitterness' with which he and Victoria had 'been boiling for a long time past.'[63]   They could not think that the Queen's constitutional position required her to submit to the 'inconceivably mortifying and degrading' position of having to endorse measures which 'the world' knew she disapproved, when those measures represented the will neither of the nation nor the cabinet.   On Russell's part there was nothing but 'weak connivance': and Palmerston, 'always . . . easy, good-humoured, very pleasant to talk to,' was so obstinate and unreliable that neither the Queen nor the Prince had spoken to him for a year.   In this mood the Court commenced negotiations with Russell for a change of foreign ministers.

The negotiations dragged on from March to May.[64] Russell, unwilling that 'a most agreeable and accommodating colleague,' who had 'acted . . . in the most spirited manner on all political questions,' should be handed over to the protectionists or radicals ('both . . . ready to receive him as their Leader'), was determined to keep Palmerston in the cabinet.   But from the beginning there was fair agreement.   At the end of the parliamentary session of 1850 Russell was to take over the Foreign Office and go to the House of Lords : Palmerston was to accept the Home Office and the leadership of the Commons, 'the highest position a statesman could aspire to.'   The royal couple agreed to Palmerston's leadership in the Commons most reluctantly.   If the Whigs went out of power, might not Palmerston break with Russell and 'force himself back into office as Prime Minister'?   This, Victoria declared, really could not be allowed.[65]   Prince Albert, informing Russell of a most scandalous incident that had occurred at Windsor some ten years before [66] (and had apparently been allowed to remain in oblivion until Palmerston aroused the Queen's intense hostility), explained that no one so debased in private character could be entrusted with the responsibilities of a prime minister.   Russell 'admitting that danger, thought Lord Palmerston too old to do much in the future (having passed his sixty-fourth year)'!   Palmerston himself, informed of the suggested changes almost from the first, seemed quite resigned.   Until the session was over the arrangement was to be held in ' the *utmost secrecy.*' As things turned out, it never became operative. And one of the persons responsible for its failure was a Portuguese Jew of shady reputation, born at Gibraltar, later resident at Athens, and known to history as Don Pacifico.

It has always been recognised that the dramatic element in Palmerston's career reached its ultimate climax through his championship of this unpleasant person's claims. Within the interval of a day or two, one saw him exhibited to the country at his very worst, and threatened with political disaster that might conceivably have been permanent in its effects : then, in a flash, he was exhibiting himself at his very best, and achieving a political triumph rarely paralleled. Never, before or afterwards, did he give so amazing a demonstration of his reserves of strength.

The details of the Pacifico affair itself would be scarcely worth retailing did they not show what a bully Palmerston could be, and how utterly he could lose his head.[67] For years he had been in a state of increasing irritation with respect to the Greek government. The more the British Foreign Office insisted on reform and sound finance, the more anti-British the Greek sovereign and his ministers became. Financial claims made by real or alleged British subjects were ignored ; and the claimants, of whom the most vociferous was Don Pacifico, turned to Palmerston. This happened to be at a time when the British squadron which had lain off the Dardanelles for the protection of the Turks against Austria and Russia, found itself unemployed. Without warning, the settlement of all outstanding claims, including Pacifico's, was demanded from King Otto's government at the cannon's mouth. It was a curious way of fostering British ' influence ' in Greece,[68] especially since Pacifico's claims were notoriously exorbitant. Palmerston could not justify such harshness by complaining of the Greek government's refusal to admit the justice of Pacifico's demands ' in principle.' Still less could he do it by inveighing against King Otto as ' the spoilt child of absolutism.'[69] And, apart from this, the propriety of his action was more than questionable. Russia

and France, appealed to by the Greeks as co-guarantors
of Grecian independence and a large Greek loan, claimed
that England had been under obligation to consult them
before coercion was applied.[70] Nesselrode, anxious to
pay off recent scores, charmed at the opportunity of
strengthening the waning Russian influence at Athens and
appearing as the defender of the weak, inquired in very
Palmerstonian language whether England intended to
repudiate all obligations, and make brute force the principle
of international policy.[71] The French republic, anxious
to preserve at once its dignity and the advantages of the
new entente, offered to mediate. Palmerston reluctantly
accepted ; and terms of settlement were soon agreed upon
at London. But, disdainful of the fact that he was already
under fire for his bullying tactics, the foreign secretary
proceeded to pile offence on offence. By delay in notifying
the British minister at Athens of the agreement concluded
in England, he allowed coercion in Greek waters to proceed,
and a second agreement to be concluded, without French
mediation, at Athens. It may be, as Clarendon seemed
anxious to believe, that he was guilty only of procrastination
and discourtesy.[72] But the French had much justification
for concluding that he was determined to settle the matter
independently, even by an act of bad faith and deliberate
insult toward England's one friend among the Powers.
For only under the strongest pressure from the cabinet
and the Court would he allow the London arrangement
to go into force.[73] Even then the sum total of his misdemeanours was not reached. When France withdrew
her ambassador, Drouyn de Lhuys, and threatened an actual
diplomatic break, Palmerston told the House that the
French envoy had gone to Paris ' in order personally to be
the medium of communication between the two Governments.'[74] On the following day he wrote Bloomfield that
Drouyn had been ' ordered back to Paris as a mark of the
dissatisfaction of his Government,' and that his letters of
recall might reach the Foreign Office at any time. So
childish an attempt at deception (for the true state of the
case could not even momentarily be concealed) shocked
his best friends. And when it was remarked that the

French, Russian and Bavarian courts (Otto, it will be remembered, was Bavarian) were not represented at the diplomatic celebration of the Queen's birthday, men naturally commenced to ask whether Palmerston would leave England a single friend.

Realisation of the discredit and even danger which he had brought upon England stirred his critics and adversaries to unprecedented efforts. The Peelites, although still fearful that they might bring about the re-establishment of protection by overturning the Whig ministry,[75] decided that an effort to alter the country's foreign policy was worth some risk. The protectionists were quite ready : and the men of the new ' Manchester school ' (*i.e.* the ' economic ' radicals who followed Cobden's view that British foreign policy should subserve nothing save economic internationalism) were, if anything, more ready still.[76] Thus the Queen could hope that the ' some day ' which she had prophesied in September 1848, had arrived at last. ' There certainly never appeared to be so good a chance of getting the Foreign Office out of Palmerston's hands as now,' wrote Charles Greville.[77] Just what understandings may have existed between these elements of opposition to the foreign secretary it is difficult to say. Disraeli later spoke of a plan made by Aberdeen ' under the inspiration of Madame Lieven and Guizot,' favoured by the Court, and subscribed to by Stanley [Lord Stanley of Bickerstaffe, later the 14th earl of Derby] on behalf of the protectionists.[78] Lord Beaumont, speaking in the House of Lords, referred to the attack on the foreign secretary as ' of foreign origin, dictated by foreign influence, intended for foreign purposes.' [79] Palmerston himself wrote of ' the shot fired by a foreign conspiracy, aided and abetted by a domestic intrigue.' [80] It was not unnatural that he should suspect something of the sort ; but there is no evidence that he took the idea very seriously. What he probably meant, and what indeed was true, was that the ' Tambour Major ' of Paris (the Princess Lieven's latest sobriquet), and her friend Guizot were warning Reeve and Greville of the dangers brought on England by the foreign secretary's policies ; and that the influence of these four persons was brought to bear successfully on *The Times* and Aberdeen.[81]   But whoever did the originating and whoever the subscribing, Stanley, speaking in the House of Lords on June 17, opened the coalition's attack on Palmerston's handling of the Greek affair.[82]   The interest was intense,—so intense that great ladies were willing to sit on the floor of the peeresses' gallery rather than miss hearing the debate.   Thanks to Peelite aid, the protectionist leader carried a vote of censure by thirty-seven votes.   ' *Wie gerecht endlich ist der Wahrspruch*,' wrote a German diplomat from Vienna, when he had read the next day's *Times*.[83]   He was, of course, mistaken if he believed that the vote involved the fall of Russell's ministry ; but such action by the upper House placed it in actual danger.   The prime minister thought it worth while to justify his continuance in office by an appeal to precedent.[84]

A greater struggle was soon to come.   Russell, embarrassed by the condemnation of the peers, and not daring to accept Palmerston's immediate offer to resign,[85] needed endorsement from the lower House.   But the Peelites and protectionists were too discreet to offer battle where Palmerston's policy would receive the half-reluctant endorsement of the Whigs and the enthusiastic backing of a large group of radicals.[86]   Hence it was decided by the ministry that the war should be carried into the protectionist and Peelite camp, and that the attack should be commenced by a radical, the famous Mr. Roebuck.   He was to demand approval, not of Palmerston's indefensible conduct in the Don Pacifico affair, but of the government's foreign policy in general.[87]   In truth, Palmerston's opponents had gone too far.   As Greville was quick to see, the attack upon him, and therefore upon the government, in the upper House had brought Russell back to his support :

> All his indignation against Palmerston, his determination to endure it no longer, his bold resolution to take the labour of the Foreign Office on himself . . . are as a dream.

Forced to assail the foreign minister, the Peelites, protectionists, and Manchester free-traders did it ruthlessly. Peel, Graham, Herbert, Gladstone, Cobden and Disraeli were among the leaders of the van ; and Herbert, at least, had been provided with weapons by Aberdeen.[88]   Palmerston's foreign policy was assailed from every possible angle.   Graham went to the limit of imaginativeness by charging him with direct responsibility for the overthrow of the Orleans dynasty ;[89] Peel to the limit of comprehensiveness by the accusation that in his hands the Foreign Office, instead of ' soothing resentments ' had operated ' to fester every wound.'   Russell and the other ministers defended the Foreign Office loyally and shrewdly, making full use of the danger to free trade that the defeat of the ministry would involve.   On the whole they felt quite confident.   But it was, of course, Palmerston's own defence that made the debate unforgettable.   His speech was designed to save, not only the ministry, but his own reputation as a foreign minister.   Like all of his great efforts in parliament, it had been composed with the most laborious care.   According to Hertslet's none too perfect memory, its preparation involved the use of between two and three thousand volumes of Foreign Office manuscripts.[90] A copy was presented to each Foreign Office clerk, presumably as a guide to his footsteps.[91]

The very acme of political drama was reached when, at a little before ten o'clock on the evening of June 25, Palmerston, the most feared, the most hated, and the most admired statesman in Europe, rose before the world's greatest court to plead for his political life.[92]   A crowded House watched him tensely as he stood, with a half sheet of paper, jotted with headings, in his hand.   Were they to hear new levities and impertinences, new accusations and defiances flung recklessly at adversaries in England or abroad ?   They heard nothing of the sort.   Instead, they listened to a calm and reasoned defence of all his foreign policy from the time of Canning's death to the day of Don Pacifico, to a flow of facts perfectly marshalled and arranged, punctuated by explanations and justifications of his principles.   More than that, the speech was faultless in point of taste, saved from monotony by changes in address and style, and lighted here and there by fine examples of pure oratory.   The oratorical periods naturally caught the attention of most of his audience, and have given the speech its place in history ; but it was the temper of the whole which called forth most remark from the cooler commentators at the time. Note, for example, the dexterity and discretion with which Palmerston met Graham's bitter attack :

It was my dislike to M. Guizot, forsooth, arising out of these Spanish marriages, which overthrew his Administration, and with it the throne of France ! . . . what will the French nation say when they hear . . . it stated that it was in the power of a British Minister to overthrow their Government and their monarchy ? Why, Sir, it is a calumny on the French nation . . . if they had thought that a foreign conspiracy had been formed against one of their Ministers . . . that brave, noble and spirited nation, would have scorned the intrigues of such a cabal ; and would have clung the closer to, and have supported the more, the man against whom such a plot had been made.

At last came the peroration—this alone, it seems, actually memorised—with the resounding *leitmotiv*, ' *Civis Romanus sum.*' The House found itself cheering until it seemed that the cheering would never stop.[93]   And Lady Palmerston, who thought her husband had spoken for an hour, discovered that it was after half-past two.[94]

It would be difficult to exaggerate the effectiveness or the effects of this amazing speech. Neither was to be measured by the government majority of forty-nine. Among the superabundant testimonials to both which still survive, one may, almost at random, select those of Lord and Lady Clarendon.[95]   The former who, be it noted, was ' not disposed to quarrel with the Lords for the result they arrived at,'[96] thought that the foreign secretary's great effort for ' mastery of the subject . . . order and lucid arrangement . . . well-sustained interest . . . varied style . . . and the good temper and good taste with which he handled such a legion of bitter assailants, can never have been surpassed anywhere.' Like everyone else, Clarendon marvelled at the exhibition of ' physical and mental power almost incredible in a man of his age.' As for the effect :

It will place him on a pinnacle of popularity at home, whatever it may do abroad, and completely settle the question about which I never had a doubt, that no change at the F.O. is possible, and that Lord John must either go *on* with him or go *out* with him.

And Lady Clarendon, lamenting ' the triumph of a *wrong* cause,' wrote in her diary :

He has triumphed over the great mass of educated public opinion, over that mighty potentate the *Times,* over two branches of the Legislature, over the Queen and Prince and most of the Cabinet he sits in, besides all foreign nations !

The minister whose downfall had been so carefully pre-pared had become, as Grey told Greville, 'the most popular man in the country.'[97] Cobden and Bright wondered whether their votes against him would not cost them their seats in Yorkshire and Manchester.[98] Greville, who, on June 21, had believed that he was 'proving the ruin of the Govern-ment,' decided ten days later that he had made it strong.[99] He himself was so modest as only to claim the greatest measure of popularity enjoyed by a foreign secretary ' for a very long course of time.'[100] But he might have been tempted to regard himself as the most popular man, not only in England, but on the continent. Hertslet's well-known story of the Austrian officials who refused to allow the cutlery of ' Palmer & Son ' to enter their country, and Turgeniev's tale of the Russian peasant who crawled from the bushes of a swamp to ask, 'Who is this Palmestron ? '[101] may be exaggerated, not to say apocryphal. But they contain a very strong element of truth. According to Bunsen, his speech of July 1849, on the struggle between Austria and Hungary, had 'made him in a few days the idol of the Radicals in England, and the most popular and most powerful Minister in Europe.'[102]

CHAPTER XXI

PALMERSTON'S DISMISSAL FROM THE FOREIGN OFFICE, 1850–1851

AT the end of June 1850, Palmerston seemed to be standing on a pinnacle of success ; but there was considerable question as to his future. What, above all, were to be his relations with the Queen ? She, at least, was quite unaffected by the *civis Romanus* speech. Prince Albert confessed to his brother that the Court was ' weakened ' by ' the unhappy combinations of circumstances that granted our *immoral one for foreign affairs* such a triumph in the Commons ';[1] but the Court was none the less resolved that the ' *immoral* ' one should give up his portfolio.[2] Palmerston was equally resolved to do nothing of the kind. Since the spring, when he had consented to take the Home Office and the leadership, he had been attacked and vindicated before the whole nation. Clarendon, Greville, Reeve and Delane, urged on by Mme. de Lieven and Guizot, had plotted against him, so he charged, and had been confounded in their plot.[3] He had no intention of allowing his assailants to triumph after all.[4] Hence, a struggle between sovereign and minister lay ahead, and a struggle which would not be merely personal. The Queen, to put it bluntly, intended to have the final voice in shaping British foreign policy. No doubt she felt justified in this. Her experience with Palmerston had persuaded her that foreign secretaries, if not checked, were apt to harm the country's interests. But this was not the only reason for her attitude. She and Prince Albert were dissatisfied with the prevalent ideas of cabinet government. It was only a little later that the Prince endorsed ' every word ' of a memorandum by

Stockmar on the proper position of a British sovereign.[5]
According to this, the detachment of the sovereign from
politics was a 'constitutional fiction' and a dangerous one.
The king or queen, being in a position to exercise
'independent judgment,' should be 'the permanent
Premier, who takes rank above the temporary head of the
Cabinet, and in matters of discipline exercises supreme
authority.' The sovereign might even 'take a part in
the initiation and the maturing of the Government
measures.' And in nothing, thought Prince Albert, did
British ministers so need a guiding hand from Windsor as
in foreign policy. Canning, in 1826, had adopted the
unfortunate idea of showing sympathy to revolutionaries :
Palmerston had adhered to it with dire results.[6]   To all this
the Court must put an end. What lay ahead of Palmerston
was conflict, not merely over foreign policy, but over some
important principles of British constitutional practice.

Had Palmerston desired to take stock of his forces, a
presentation and a banquet which celebrated his triumph
in the House would have shown where his shock troops lay.
The presentation [7] was made by a 'hundred of the most
Liberal members' ('radicals' of that bygone-day) ; and
consisted in the bestowal on Lady Palmerston of a portrait
of her husband and hero. The artist, Partridge, had made.
the hero look quite mild ; but a bust of Canning peered
out from the background. Apparently men of the 'most
Liberal' type were also responsible for the banquet.[8]
Perhaps the honoured guest had fears that the affair would
be too radical ; for he declined a dinner at Covent Garden
of a thousand plates, before accepting one at the Reform
Club of a fifth that size. Even at that not a minister was
to be found among the banqueters. Russell had refused ;
and it had therefore been thought better not to invite the
rest. Greville called the diners a 'rabble' ; and damned
them utterly by adding that he did not know one in ten of
them by sight.[9]   But just because of this, perhaps, the affair
went off with remarkable spirit. Patriotism and poetry ruled
the evening. Great cheers accompanied the singing of :

> Confound their politics,
> Frustrate their knavish tricks,

as the audience, looking on its hero, remembered that :

> If severe in aught,
> The love he bore to freedom was in fault.

And as for disputes with other governments :

> This proved his worth ; hereafter be our boast—
> Who hated Britons hated him the most.

The guest of honour's speech was not especially fiery ; but it showed him quite impenitent. Once again he declared his determination to throw England's weight into the scale (whatever that might mean) against foreign governments interfering with ' the development of liberty ' : once again he declared his conviction that ' no other country is a bit more desirous . . . of going to war with England, than England can be of going to war with it.' The ' most Liberal ' banqueters applauded him as usual.

It may seem a puzzling thing that a man so conservative as Palmerston should, even in that day and age, have been a hero to men classed as radicals. But so it was. Graham flung the taunt that he truckled to the ' radical ' element in a manner treacherous to his colleagues.[10] Apparently the foreign secretary's foreign policy, his understanding of a crowd, and his possession of qualities which the mass of Britons loved made the strange alliance possible. Witness the manner in which he captured the radical element among the burgesses of Tiverton in the election of 1847.[11] His contest was watched with special interest, and drew reporters from all the great dailies. For he was facing Jacob Harney, the editor of the *Northern Star*, a Chartist, and a man ranked in radical circles as a great authority on foreign policy. For two hours he was under Harney's fire. His career and his policies were raked fore and aft. He was ' devoid of true patriotism, a breaker of pledges, and a foe to the liberties of the people, whose dearest rights he would trample in the dust.' He was a disciple of Canning, that ' talented buffoon ' : he was responsible for a reform bill that had done nothing for the people, and for a poor law that had set up a Bastille ' big enough to hold the whole country.' He remained quite unperturbed. In a long reply, he took flattering pains to justify his foreign

policy ; but he made little concession to the feelings of
real radicals concerning parliamentary reform. True, he
claimed to be ' a decided advocate for reform . . . effected
by reason and by argument,' and not promoted 'by the
agitation of physical force.' But Chartist proposals on
reform he tore to shreds. The outcome was curious.
Harney seemed victorious on a general show of hands ;
but the actual polling did not give him a single vote. The
ministerial candidate's understanding of his audience must
have contributed, along with local pride and local influence,
of course, to produce such unanimity. The duke of Bedford found his speech undignified ; but Harney was
delighted with his sportsmanship and geniality.

So, too, were the men who reported his speeches.[12]
His affability and genuine kindness warmed their hearts ;
his playfulness in telling amusing anecdotes, even when
times were critical, brightened up tedious and anxious
hours. Best of all, he filled the reporter's greatest need,
the need for accurate and early news. Men believed, at
least, that he timed his speeches with reference to the hours
when the great dailies went to press ; and, when such
timing was impossible, provided outlines which could be
embellished in his well-known style. He would have had
an incomparable press if the reporters had had their way.

But with the editors it was another thing.[13] Most of
them had to consider the behests of financial or political
magnates who wished to see the foreign secretary well
dressed down. Tory and Peelite papers attacked his moves
relentlessly, whether conviction or mere partisanship moved
their masters. Delane of *The Times* still followed Aberdeen
as his first great patron, his tutor in foreign policy, and
the source of valuable and exclusive news.[14] Reeve, who
wrote most of the leaders on international affairs,[15] treated
them from the same angle. And Aberdeen, be it remembered, regarded Schwarzenberg as the champion of ' good
order and good Government ' in Europe, relied upon the
Tsar to ensure stability in Germany, and rejoiced ' that
revolt should have been successfully repressed, both in
Naples and Sicily.'[16] Like him, the ' Thunderer ' was as
antagonistic to the foreign secretary as it was friendly to

the cabinet as a whole.[17]   The *Chronicle*, long fervently
Palmerstonian, adopted much the same attitude after its
passage to new owners, in 1848.[18]   When its sale was
first mooted, Palmerston seems to have planned its purchase
by the ministry ; and its proprietor, Easthope, when this
project failed, desired to make its sale conditional on its
continued support of its old favourite.   But only the
Peelites seem to have offered a satisfactory price.   Stockmar,
within a few months, found that the policy of both *Times*
and *Chronicle* was inspired,

if we except occasional whiffs from the Continent, by Lord
Palmerston's Tory opponents, and it is often edifying to see how on
the one and the same day, both papers chant forth to the world the
same tune which they have just been taught.[19]

The *Globe* was in the closest touch with the Foreign Office [20]
and gave it warm support ; but it lacked sufficient influence
to make any appreciable headway against Delane's abuse.
Palmerston was badly in need of an organ.

And then, in 1850, Peter Borthwick was engaged to
revitalise the declining *Morning Post*.   With much foresight and apparently with some conviction, too,[21] Borthwick
decided that the *Post*, Conservative in all else, should be
Palmerstonian in foreign policy.   Immediately the foreign
secretary found the paper ' much improved,' and ' not
indisposed to view with candour the conduct and course of
the Government.' [22]   Three months later, Clarendon was
talking of Palmerston's ' " Morning Post " articles.' [23]
There was growing up a very suggestive intimacy between
Palmerston, Borthwick and Borthwick's son, Algernon
(later Lord Glenesk), at this time the *Post's* Paris representative.   Before the year was out Palmerston was
' warmly applauding ' Algernon's letters, and expressing
the wish that he would ' bite the [Paris] Embassy and give
them some youthful impetuosity.' [24]   About the same time
Algernon's parents became frequent attendants at Lady
Palmerston's soirées.   There was a very piquant side to
the relationship.   Thus, Peter Borthwick to Algernon in
March 1851 :

Every day I have intended to answer at length your most able and valuable letter on the State of Parties in France, and on their various possible and impossible relations to England. I read it literatim to Pam: who said that he had never had the good fortune to peruse any document which indicated so large and so accurate a sweep of observation—nor one which was more cleverly expressed. It certainly, he added, is a masterpiece of diplomatic statesmanship. . . . Mama and I go to Lady P.'s soirée this evening.[25]

And this from Mrs. Borthwick in the following month :

Lord P. says if the Protectionists come in, you are the only man— next to himself—fit to be Foreign Secretary. . . . I said to your Papa Lord P. ought to give you some good appointment himself. Your Papa says wait a little.[26]

While the Peelite *Chronicle* is said to have cost its backers £200,000 before it was resold in 1854,[27] the *Post*, backing protection, Palmerston and Louis Napoleon, soon had a larger circulation than any rival save *The Times*.

In any reckoning with the Court, Palmerston could count on great general popularity, the support of parliamentary ' radicals,' and the commendation of the *Post* and *Globe*. Within limits he could even count on his party. As usual, he seldom supported his ministerial colleagues in debates, unless the objects of his great solicitude, foreign affairs, the slave trade and defence, were up. But he was in fair agreement with them on the leading issues of the time. He had unusual sympathy with the Irish, but his position was quite orthodox.[28] As a free trader he denounced all compromise, even at times when union with the protectionists must have tempted him :

I myself am of opinion, that when the party who still call themselves by the antiquated name of Protectionists come to consider calmly, and free from the irritation of former disputes, the freetrade measures and their results, they will come round to our opinions on the point of justice as well as on that of expediency.[29]

Neither was he much at odds with the party on Russell's last two ventures as prime minister : an attempt to block the re-establishment in England of a Catholic hierarchy, and a mistimed effort to amend the Reform Bill of 1832.

The story of Russell's fight against ' papal aggression ' makes strange reading nowadays.[30] The papal plans had

long been known to the premier and at least some members
of the cabinet ; but the people were quite unprepared.
In the autumn of 1850, earnest Protestants, alarmed already
by the Oxford Movement among Anglicans and the
numerous conversions to the Catholic Church which went
with it, were horrified to hear that a papal bull had made
Cardinal Wiseman archbishop of Westminster. They
learned, too, that the twelve bishops of his province were
no longer to be known under the foreign titles of bishops
in partibus, but were to govern dioceses which took their
names from English places, as in pre-Reformation days.
The bull, framed solely in accordance with Catholic claims
to spiritual rule, sounded menacing in English ears ; and
Cardinal Wiseman was more exultant than tactful. There
were even prominent English Catholics, such as Lord
Camoys, who took offence.[31] Popular irritation grew into
excitement, and excitement into something like panic.
There were cries of ' no popery ' ; there was anti-Catholic
rioting. Petitions rained upon the government. The
Pope's temporal and spiritual authority were confused.
Englishmen, Russell said in the Queen's Speech, were
acquiring titles by authority from ' a Foreign Power ' :[32]
English towns, the solicitor-general declared with great
solemnity, were being made cities in being designated as
the seats of Catholic bishoprics.[33] Could anyone deny
that this involved the exercise of ' territorial jurisdiction
and authority ? ' The Queen was being ' insulted,'
' humiliated ' and ' debased.'

Catholicism in Ireland was treated by the government
as a useful if not too pleasant growth ; but Catholicism in
England was regarded as a rather noxious weed. More
than two years before, Russell had drawn up, and Palmerston
warmly endorsed, a plan by which the Irish Catholic clergy
were to have been given stipends and also allowances for
the maintenance and repair of places of worship.[34] A year
or so later Palmerston had spoken passionately for the
continuance of the government subsidy to Maynooth.[35]
The Whigs in general, and the prime minister in particular,
had been rated as the best friends of the Irish Catholics
among the three great parliamentary groups. But the

papal bull which regularised the English hierarchy seemed
to cloud the vision of most of the ministers. Unable to
distinguish between spiritual and temporal power, they
decided that ' papal aggression ' must be stopped. Russell
introduced a bill forbidding the Catholic bishops to assume
the titles conferred on them from Rome, or, having assumed
them, to perform their administrative functions in such
matters as the management of church finance. The bill
was argued, amended and re-amended through interminable
and passionate debates. Members of every parliamentary
group, but in particular the Irish members and the leaders
of the radicals, pointed out the confusion in the minds of
those who drew it up, the obvious impossibility of enforcing
it, and the danger that it would cause trouble, especially
in Ireland. In the end, it was placed upon the statute
book, ignored by the Catholics, and conveniently forgotten
by the government.

Palmerston, for all his long devotion to religious liberty,
for all his friendship with the radicals and the Irish, stood
squarely for the bill. In parliament he was relatively
moderate, although he spoke of ' aggression by a foreign
authority . . . on the independent sovereignty of the
country,' which it was the ministry's ' bounden duty to
repel.'[36]   But his letters were couched in a very different
tone.[37] He was by no means sure that the Pope was not
claiming jurisdiction over Protestants :

. . . he might as well claim jurisdiction over the waves of the
Channel, or the winds that raise them, or the tides that sweep round
our shores as over the Protestants of England.

It was ' childish folly ' for Cardinal Wiseman to announce
his enthronisation to Catholic governments :

A cardinal has no business in England, and as long as he is here
there will be no peace or charity between Protestant and Catholic.

He wanted ' a return to the system of vicars apostolic ' ; and
hoped that the praemunire statute of Richard II's time
could be invoked.[38] His seeming inconsistency is comprehensible. He had always been an ardent nationalist ;
and his son-in-law, the philanthropic and passionately

Protestant Lord Ashley, was at his ear. One must even pay some tribute to his willingness to engage himself in a dispute where he had nothing in the world to gain, and the support of Irish and radical members to lose. But in one respect his tactics are difficult to condone. If one may judge from a letter which he sent to Peter Borthwick of the *Post*, he was guilty of helping to stir up religious prejudice, even within the English church :

> As to the Pope's new Bishops in England, it is a piece of foolish impertinence . . . but we ought not to be surprised if the bigoted and ignorant Cardinals who now govern Rome have been misled by . . . the progress of Puseyism in England. . . . It is a curious instance of the weakness of human intellect to see a Pope, whose authority within the walls of his own capital is maintained only by the presence of foreign bayonets, pretend to govern the people of England.[39]

Even in this he was with his premier. Russell's similar but even more inflammatory letter to the Bishop of Durham was sent to the press only a fortnight afterwards.[40]

But when it came to parliamentary reform, Palmerston agreed far better with the ministry as a whole than with Lord John.[41] For two years he and what was apparently a majority of the cabinet had been attempting to persuade their chief to leave the bill of 1832 untouched.[42] And when, in the autumn of 1851, Russell refused any longer to be held in check, Palmerston had plenty of support in objecting to the proposed bill. Lansdowne in particular would have resigned rather than countenance it in any way, but for his unwillingness to break up the government.[43] Russell's suggestions were comparatively mild. They called for sizeable reductions in the county and borough franchises, and establishment of the principle that no borough with less than 500 electors (according to the qualifications fixed in 1832) should have a seat in parliament. At that, the extinction of small boroughs was to be avoided by the device of joining them for electoral purposes with neighbouring towns. The only important novelty lay in the suggested abolition of any property-holding qualification for members of parliament.

But these suggestions were far too much for Palmerston.[44]   Why could not Lord John leave well enough alone until there was some real demand for change ?   Why take away the property-holding qualification for members, and, worst of all, so alter the franchise as to change the relative representation in parliament of England's two great economic groups ?

. . . no one can justly say after the Repeal of the Corn Laws and the alteration of the Navigation Laws, to say nothing of other changes, that the commercial and manufacturing interest has not effective weight in the House of Commons ; and it seems to me that in making changes in our Constitution we ought to look to the great and permanent interests of the country rather than to momentary considerations or individual opinions.[45]

Perhaps he would have come to some agreement with the premier in the end ; for he was ready as usual to accept a compromise.[46]   But long before the bill was ready for parliament he had been ' kicked out ' of the cabinet.   Even at that, he had, in one respect, the better of the argument. He had laid some stress upon the point that the premier had not been anticipating any real demand.   And it was very clear that no one save Lord John felt much regret when the reform bill died, along with Russell's ministry, early in the session of 1852.[47]

It could be said, then, that Palmerston was on satisfactory terms with his party regarding everything but his diplomacy.   Even as to that, the Whigs, like Stockmar, could find fault with his actions only ' *in concreto.*'   They seldom complained of anything save his methods : his arrogance, his offensiveness to other governments, his frequent exhibitions of indifference to the wishes and feelings of his colleagues and of the Court.   Most of them believed with him that the existing order in Europe, though very useful on the whole, was by no means sacrosanct. They disagreed, as he did, with Conservatives and Peelites like Aberdeen, who saw in the co-operation of the three eastern courts the bulwark of European stability against ' sentimental ideas of nationality and self-government.' They saw it rather as a dangerously unyielding wall against

the advancing spirit of the time.   They knew their
foreign secretary's value, too : the popularity which he
won for them, the votes for which he was responsible in
parliament.   In spite of the anxiety and resentment which
they felt from time to time, they would have been willing
to put up with him had it not been for the Court.

The Queen adopted new tactics against the foreign
secretary after the Don Pacifico debate.   Finding that
Russell would not, indeed could not, remove Palmerston
from Downing Street as he had promised in the spring,[48]
she set about devising some new method of control.   Hence,
in August 1850, she demanded his acceptance of a
memorandum in which his official obligations to his
sovereign were explicitly defined.[49]   Though Stockmar
was almost certainly the real author of this famous document,[50] it was sound enough as an exposition of British
constitutional practice.   The Queen had, as it stated,
every right to be informed both of the facts and of her
foreign minister's policy regarding them in every issue
that arose.   She was entitled to approve despatches before
they were sent off ; and to hold the foreign secretary guilty
of a breach of faith if he subsequently altered them without
consulting her.   There was, indeed, something disturbing
about the bald statement that in such case she might
' exercise . . . her Constitutional right of dismissing that
Minister ' ; but it was not technically unsound.

On the other hand, the presentation of the memorandum as a virtual ultimatum was no ordinary step.   So
humiliating was the rebuke which it involved, that
Palmerston was justified in believing that Victoria expected
him to resign.[51]   Instead, he kissed the rod.   With every
expression of surprised regret, even with tears (supposedly
of contrition) in his eyes, he bound himself to obey the
memorandum in every particular.[52]   Perhaps for the
moment he was actually contrite ; but, as he later pointed
out, there were compelling reasons why he should give
way.   He could not resign on such an issue without
bringing the sovereign into politics, and exposing her to
very disagreeable comment.   And he really felt that after
the vindication just given him in parliament his resignation

would be unjust to the nation, to the party and to himself.[53] Believing that no one except the few persons actually concerned would ever hear of the affair, he swallowed the affront and promised to offend no more.

Exitus acta probat ! Within six weeks he had not only violated his undertakings to the Queen, but had done so in a manner particularly calculated to hurt her sensibilities. This was in connection with the General Haynau incident.[54] The hero of Austria's war against the Hungarians, known all through Europe as the man responsible for the atrocious floggings even of women which had followed Hungary's defeat, paid a visit to Barclay's Brewery in London, and was recognised by the workmen. Belaboured with brooms and besmeared with dirt, the valiant general fled through the streets to the shelter of a public house, and was probably saved from serious injury or death by the police. The apology to the Austrian emperor which Palmerston drafted seemed perfunctory in the extreme.[55] It was even offensive in suggesting that a person with the reputation of Haynau would be well advised to avoid exposing himself to public indignation in England. When the Queen and Russell demanded its alteration they found it had already gone. So much for Palmerston's tearful penitence. Again the Queen longed for the fulfilment of Russell's promise of the spring.

Her hopes must have revived at the end of February 1851, when Russell's cabinet resigned.[56] Suffering from the chronic Whig complaint of inability to produce acceptable budgets, the government was further weakened by its war against the Pope. The Irish and those ' most Liberal ' members who admired Palmerston had caused its defeat by joining with the opposition on a minor issue. Victoria had to face the trying task of finding a combination of parliamentary groups which could command a safe majority ; but she had the comfort of expecting to see the Foreign Office placed in different hands. During a period of ten days five separate attempts to find a stable government were made ; and Palmerston appeared somehow in all of them. To begin with, the protectionists were tried. Their leader, Stanley, frankly said that scarcely anyone save Palmerston

or Aberdeen seemed fitted to be foreign minister.[57]   But
Stanley so soon requested Victoria to investigate other
possibilities before urging him to take control, that
Palmerston's position did not become a matter of dispute.
It was different when the Peelites were called on to form
a junction with Lord John.

It would be difficult to think of anything which could
better have revealed the strength and, still more, the dangers
of Palmerston's situation in 1851 than this abortive attempt
to anticipate Aberdeen's famous coalition government of
1852.   Of course, all parties were agreed that his return
to the Foreign Office was not to be thought of.   Prince
Albert informed Aberdeen and Graham that the Queen
would not allow it to take place ; and Russell assured all
three of them that ' Lord Palmerston ought to form no
difficulty.'[58]   According to the Prince, Aberdeen and
Graham objected to having him in the cabinet at all :

> One subject seemed uppermost in the minds of Lord A. and
> Sir James, viz. :—the impossibility to have Lord Palmerston in the
> Cabinet and the House of Commons.   Sir James said he would prefer
> seeing him as leader of the Protectionists opposite to him to having
> him on the Treasury Bench next to him, after his having seen him
> (Ld. P.) play falsely to his former colleagues, intriguing with the
> Radical and Irish fraction of their supporters, detaching that party
> from them and using it and his influence over it as a means of coercing
> his colleagues.[59]

And Aberdeen would not consider what seemed to Russell
the only practicable plan for persuading Palmerston to
give up his favourite post :

> On my saying that Lord John had thought of the possibility of
> giving him [Palmerston] the lead in the House of Lords Lord
> Aberdeen looked very black and assured me that the House would
> never submit to that.   They thought the Lord Lieutenancy [of
> Ireland] with a peerage was the right thing to offer him.

In view of what occurred two years or so later, when
Aberdeen's ministry dealt with the preliminaries of the
Crimean War, the ' noble thane's ' further objections were
significant :

> Lord A. declared he personally had no objection to sit with him

in the Cabinet but well remembered that, when he had been in office with him under the D. of Wellington, the constant disputes with him (who was then only Secretary at War) on the foreign Policy was anything but pleasant. I am afraid that Lord Aberdeen himself looks for the Foreign Office again, which we know Lord John will not agree to.[60]

Russell was in a desperate quandary :

> He had seen Lord Palmerston, who was not willing to give up the Foreign Office—spoke of retiring from business at his age, of his success in conducting Foreign Affairs, and of its being a self-condemnation if he accepted another Office. Lord John told him that he did not agree in this view, that the Lord-Lieutenancy of Ireland was to be maintained, and thought it best to leave it there.[61]

The negotiations soon broke down, largely because of Peelite objections to Russell's fight against the Pope. But the two parties had reached an understanding which threatened unpleasant consequences for Palmerston. It was expected that Stanley would after all come into power ; for he had promised to attempt the formation of a ministry in case the Whig-Peelite coalition proved impossible. Hence it was agreed that, once ' papal aggression ' had been relegated to limbo, Whigs and Peelites would combine in putting Stanley out and dividing up the cabinet offices.[62] And the Peelites were more than ready to dispense with Palmerston. Graham and Aberdeen, at least, asked nothing better than that he should go over to Stanley and the protectionists. Such change of allegiance, they assumed, would so affect his popularity as to make him almost innocuous.

Similar hopes were apparently cherished at Windsor when the Queen, after vainly requesting Aberdeen to construct a ministry, asked the protectionist leader to live up to his promise. How else explain the following passage from one of Prince Albert's memoranda on his discussions with Stanley on the distribution of cabinet offices ?

> Lord Palmerston had often so much secret understanding with Disraeli that he might be tempted with the bait of keeping the Foreign Office, particularly if personally offended.[63]

Victoria was apparently willing that Palmerston should

become a protectionist foreign minister.   If so, it could
only have been in expectation that he would retire discredited after Stanley's government had run its inevitably
brief course.   He would certainly not have returned to
the Foreign Office save by her express consent.   Witness
her declaration that she refrained from ' passing a sentence
of exclusion ' upon Disraeli as a secretary of state only
out of regard for Stanley's difficulties, and on condition
that Stanley should be ' responsible for his conduct.' [64]

   But royal and Peelite hopes concerning Palmerston
were all in vain.   On February 27, Stanley reported that
his difficulties in forming a government were insuperable.
What could the Queen then do but ask Russell to return ?
After all, she had his promise that Palmerston should not
go back to Downing Street, and Wellington's opinion that
his return would be ' a terrible misfortune.' [65]   Bitter
disillusionment awaited her :

   The Queen . . . reminded Lord John of . . . his promise that
Lord Palmerston should not again be thrust upon her as Foreign
Secretary.   Lord John admitted to the promise, but said he could
not think for a moment of resuming office and either expel Lord
Palmerston or quarrel with him.   He (Lord John) was in fact the
weakness and Lord Palmerston the strength of the Government from
his popularity with the Radicals. [66]

The removal of the radical idol from Downing Street
would be looked upon as due to ' a personal objection ' on
Victoria's part ;   and the resentment so aroused would
render the reconstructed Whig-Liberal government still-
born.   All Russell could do was to promise that he would
remove Palmerston during the Easter recess, or submit his
own resignation in case the ' difficulties ' should prove too
great.   It was on the strength of this undertaking that
the Queen empowered him to proceed ;   but in a short
time he was explaining that its execution was impossible. [67]
Palmerston's expulsion from the Foreign Office was indefinitely postponed.   Aberdeen more than once assured
the Princess Lieven during this year that it would soon
occur ; [68]   and, all things considered, his prophecy was
safe enough.   But the doomed minister was not disturbed.

He continued serenely on his way through the late spring, the summer and the autumn. If anything, he grew even more reckless.

In fact, the rashness of his conduct in the autumn of 1851 is almost incomprehensible. Stockmar went so far as to declare that he must be insane : [69] Russell and Fox Maule, the secretary at War, suspected him of trying deliberately to provoke a break.[70] Very possibly he was. Even he must have wearied of his eternal struggle with the Court and of all the annoyance and hindrances which it entailed. Confident in his popularity and his indispensability to the Whigs, he may have wished to test his strength against the Queen's.

The first real crisis in their continuing conflict came, toward the end of October, with the arrival in England of Kossuth. This hero of the Hungarian and British radicals announced his intention of visiting the foreign secretary to express his thanks for the protection given two years previously to himself and his fellow refugees. Had he gone at once, objection to the interview could scarcely have been made. But the visit was postponed ; and in the meantime Kossuth's denunciation of Austrian cruelty and tyranny had given his activities in England the appearance of a political crusade. Fearful of fresh complications with the Austrian court, and urged on by the Queen, Russell demanded that Palmerston should not receive Kossuth even unofficially.[71] When Palmerston proved obstinate the premier grew peremptory :

I must therefore positively request that you will not receive Kossuth.[72]

Palmerston's reply, dashed off while Russell's messenger waited, was beyond measure provocative :

. . . there are limits to all things. . . . I do not choose to be dictated to as to who I may or may not receive in my own house ; . . . I shall use my own discretion on this matter. You will, of course, use yours as to the composition of your Government. . . .[73]

Russell, reluctant to take up the challenge, begged Victoria to interpose a royal command.[74] She consented, on con-

dition that Lord John would see to it that Palmerston obeyed.
But the premier and ministry managed to avert so dangerous
a clash.[75] At a meeting of the cabinet on November 3,
Russell, without mentioning the Queen, presented his
own case. The ministers decided that Kossuth should
be requested not to call on Palmerston. Lord John was
immeasurably relieved ; and Charles Greville bemoaned
the fact that the evil-doer had once more eluded punishment.
But Prince Albert knew that Palmerston was not so easily
quieted. ' On my life,' he wrote, ' he'll see him [Kossuth]
yet, or he'll do something still worse.' [76] The second
part of the royal prediction was justified without delay.

At least, Palmerston's next escapade was regarded as
still worse. That he intended to misconduct himself
would be difficult to prove : for he offended by imprudent
action in an affair that was not of his making.[77] Radical
delegations from Islington and Finsbury called on him to
present addresses expressing gratitude for his services to
liberty in general, and to Kossuth in particular. In these
the sovereigns of Russia and Austria were referred to as
odious and detestable tyrants. Palmerston, glowing with
pride and popularity, thanked them for their compliments,
and repeated most of his well-known convictions with
regard to British foreign policy. He added that he
could not be expected to subscribe to their animadversions
on foreign sovereigns ; but he administered no real reproof.
Later, he admitted that he should, perhaps, have asked to
see the addresses in advance, and to have made some
inquiry into the status of the persons who presented them.
For one of these was a reporter (a ' trading penny-a-liner,'
Palmerston called him) ; and, as pressmen will, he wrote
a highly coloured version of the interview.

' The storm-compelling Jupiter Anglicanus of our
Foreign Office,' as young Borthwick styled him, was quite
living up to the designation in so far as domestic weather
was concerned. At London and Windsor his reception
of the delegations was denounced as an insult to two
friendly Powers, an act of deliberate defiance to Victoria,
a breach of his understanding with the cabinet, and a
shameless bid for radical support. The Queen's dis-

pleasure had never been more evident. Even Lady Palmerston was treated in a manner which, if it had not been permissible under the rules of royal etiquette, would have been considered grossly rude.[78] The Court at once demanded that the foreign secretary should be removed. But, galling though it was to her, the Queen relinquished the demand when Lord John pointed out that compliance would involve an immediate change of government.[79] Both the chaotic party situation in England and the disturbed conditions on the continent made a cabinet crisis extremely undesirable. And then, of course, there was the old danger in removing Palmerston on an issue of this kind. His dismissal would be bound to bring a storm of popular indignation on the heads of those regarded as responsible, and to make the culprit even more popular than before. He and his ' rabble ' seemed to have the Court and cabinet in chains. The Queen's cup was particularly full. For Schwarzenberg, the Austrian chancellor, saw that Palmerston's reception of the radical delegations gave the Austrian government a new opportunity of working up her indignation against her foreign minister.[80] Lord Westmorland, who had just arrived in Vienna as her ambassador, was forced to wait an utterly unprecedented time before obtaining the customary audience with the Emperor. Nesselrode condemned this action as an affront to Victoria rather than to Palmerston.[81] He did not realise that to wound the Queen was exactly what the Austrian chancellor desired.

The Court was finding the situation quite intolerable when Palmerston, according to Prince Albert's views, exemplified the adage that a rogue will hang himself.[82] On December 3, he commented approvingly to Walewski, the French ambassador in London, on the *coup d'état* by which Louis Napoleon seized absolute power in France.[83] Walewski had explained that Napoleon's relations with the French assembly had became impossible ; and that, menaced by its activities, he had decided to strike first. Palmerston, speaking, as he always insisted, personally and unofficially, expressed his belief that Napoleon had acted in the best interests of France. He was perfectly sincere.

It was not in him to respect a constitution such as that under which France had been ruled since 1848—a constitution established by revolutionists to set up republican and very democratic government. Moreover, all predilections of this sort aside, he realised that its provisions made orderly constitutional government well-nigh impossible.[84] The president and assembly were so evenly balanced in power that neither could prevail by legal means :

. . . As to respect for the law and Constitution, . . . it is scarcely a proper application of those feelings to require them to be directed to the day-before-yesterday tomfoolery . . . invented for the torment and perplexity of the French nation. . . .[85]

It was better that the constitution should be overthrown, and that, of the two powers, the president should prevail. What could the assembly offer France save, perhaps, an attempted restoration of the Orleans dynasty, hence .civil war and probably anarchy ? The Orleanists, if not actually engaged in plots, were certainly alert to seize on any chance.[86] It seemed better by far that Napoleon should have full opportunity to restore order and prosperity in France. Such were the thoughts which lay behind his unprepared and unofficial statement to the French ambassador.

The statement might never have led to trouble had he not been on bad terms with the British ambassador in Paris, Normanby. A difficult and haughty man (so unsuited to his post that Palmerston's successor, Granville, lost no time in recalling him), Normanby had been nursing for five years the feeling that Palmerston had abandoned him in his bitter quarrel with Guizot.[87] And the two men were at odds in policy. Normanby, in common with *The Times* and Aberdeen, was notoriously hostile to Napoleon : Palmerston was exactly the reverse.[88] He later boasted of having ' detected and thwarted ' Normanby's ' intrigues ' against Napoleon in the period just before the *coup d'état*. At any rate, he ridiculed one of the ambassador's despatches and condemned his partiality.[89] Normanby, unable to retaliate officially, did so behind the scenes. His wife, a

former favourite with the Queen, retailed his grievances
and his tormentor's sins in voluminous letters to Normanby's
brother, Colonel Phipps, then secretary to Prince Albert.[90]
Her letters were cleverly designed to please the Court,
and to place Napoleon and Palmerston in the worst light
possible.   While Normanby was in this vengeful frame
of mind, he learned of Palmerston's statement to Walewski
from Napoleon's foreign minister, Turgot.

The propriety, indeed the constitutionality, of the statement was open to some argument.[91]   There were those,
like Wellington, who denied that any expression of opinion
by a minister could be given unofficially.   Palmerston,
with vastly more experience than the Duke, maintained the
opposite doctrine throughout his life.   Was he likely to
forget how, in the Near Eastern crisis of 1840, his colleagues
had freely expressed disagreement with the official policies
of the cabinet, even to the envoys of foreign Powers ?
And in this very affair Palmerston claimed to possess
conclusive evidence that other members of the cabinet,
including the prime minister, had acted just as he himself
had done.   His case seems very strong.[92]   He made his
charges, not only in the House when on his trial, but
privately and a year later to the duke of Bedford, Russell's
elder brother.   And to the Duke he cited Walewski, still
French ambassador to England at the time, as his witness.
He had Walewski's word, he said, that Russell had
unofficially approved the *coup d'état* not once but twice.
The first alleged occasion was at Palmerston's residence,
on December 3 : the second was during a dinner given
by the premier two days afterward, a dinner at which
other ministers were present.   Walewski also told him,
Palmerston went on, that notification of the premier's
approbation was sent to Paris by despatch ; whereas his
own expression of opinion had been transmitted only in
a private letter to Turgot.   But apparently no one investi-
gated the indiscretions of other ministers at the time.
Palmerston's was the word that counted most ;   and
Palmerston's comment was in clear conflict with the official
pronouncement adopted shortly afterwards by the cabinet.
According to this, England's detachment from French

political dissensions was complete. Normanby was instructed to abstain from doing anything 'which could wear the appearance of an interference of any kind in the internal affairs of France.' [93] He was not instructed to communicate his orders to Napoleon's government ; but he did so on his own account. It was then he heard from Turgot that Palmerston had expressed his 'entire approbation' of the *coup d'état*.

Palmerston might have avoided trouble had he been willing to take any pains. But he acted with the utmost nonchalance both before and after learning that he had again come under fire. When Normanby asked an explanation of the discrepancy between the cabinet's instructions and the foreign secretary's comment, Palmerston allowed some days to pass without troubling to reply. Normanby, whose exasperation had reached boiling point, wrote haughtily that the Paris embassy had been placed in a situation of great embarrassment.[94] This time Palmerston answered. He denied, with a convincing exhibition of logic, that he had contradicted himself in any way. And he took the opportunity of reiterating his private opinion of the *coup d'état*. As in duty bound, he sent Normanby's despatch and a copy of his reply to Russell and the Queen. But he did not send them until after his reply had been sent off to Normanby. He had the right, he claimed later, to answer directly a personal attack.[95] Nor did his nonchalance stop even there. Victoria, outraged at his indifference to her famous memorandum on constitutional practice, and angry, too, that he should repeat his justification of the *coup d'état* in a despatch, had demanded through Russell an immediate explanation of the whole affair. Palmerston, after delaying far longer than regard for courtesy and respect should have allowed, had complied by sending a fresh exposition of his views.

He had been guilty of more serious lapses ; but never, or so his critics thought, had he so delivered himself to them. At last, it seemed, the premier and the Court would be actually applauded for removing him. Had he not endorsed the destruction of 'constitutional government,'

and the establishment of a blood-stained dictatorship ?
The radicals, of all people, might be expected to approve
his punishment. It is true that Russell, who undertook
the punishment without reference to the Court, could
offer an excellent excuse to Clarendon :

> I have had for five years a most harassing warfare . . . as umpire
> between Windsor and Broadlands . . . my patience was drained to
> the last drop.[96]

But it is strange if he overlooked the fact, quite patent to
others,[97] that he was taking advantage of an unequalled
opportunity. At any rate, he wrote Palmerston briefly, on
December 19, demanding that he should immediately
resign. It is worth noting that he accused himself in later
years of having been ' hasty and precipitate.' [98]

Certainly the dismissal had all the effect of an unfore-
seen event. The Queen was almost incredulous in her
delight.[99] Palmerston, of course, was exceedingly angry.
He felt, as he told Disraeli later on, that he was not turned
out of the cabinet but ' kicked out.' [100] Of course a
solatium was offered him, the lord-lieutenancy of Ireland
and a British peerage. It was, as Graham pointed out,[101]
rather a curious commentary on the political customs of
the time that such honours should be tendered to a man
accused of insulting his sovereign and playing false to his
colleagues. Nor was the offer of the least avail. Palmerston
had only one thought—to bide his time. There was little
else that he could do. Though Russell took action without
even notifying the cabinet,[102] the dismissal was unanimously
approved. It is true that some of Palmerston's friends
were not present at the time. But Lansdowne was ; and
for no one in the ministry did Palmerston, before and
afterwards, show more deep regard.[103] There was a
general feeling that the foreign secretary's last offence,
though not especially heinous in itself, was ' the drop
which made the cup overflow.' [104] There was also a general
appreciation of the fact that the Queen had been trying
to free herself from Palmerston for years. Her exact
motives were probably less understood.

That one of her motives was to secure increased control

of foreign policy was evident enough when the choice of Palmerston's successor was discussed. The members of the cabinet, with the exception of Russell, were unanimously for Clarendon. But the Queen and the premier decided upon Lord Granville. He was young and inexperienced, but so suave as to be designated ' Granville the Polite ' by the prime minister,[105] and as ' Puss ' even by his family.[106] Victoria claimed ' the unfettered right to approve or disapprove ' the choice of the new foreign minister ; and wrote that the cabinet's objection to Granville on the ground of inexperience did ' not weigh much with the Queen.' When the cabinet's decision was announced, and Russell decided to concur in it, she ' protested against the Cabinet's taking upon itself the appointment of its own Members, which rested entirely with the Prime Minister and the Sovereign, under whose approval the former constructed his Government.'[107] Russell showed himself not only timid but disingenuous. His colleagues and the world in general were allowed to believe that an offer was actually made to Clarendon.[108] In point of fact, Russell wrote him privately that he and the Queen thought it best to give Granville the place.[109] Clarendon had no deep regrets. He was glad to escape any possible suspicion on the part of Palmerston that he schemed to get the post, and glad to avoid ' the *guerre sourde* . . . waged so long from Windsor against the F. O.'[110] Yet he who had made the House of Lords ' a bed of roses ' for Aberdeen when Peel was premier ; he, on whom the Queen had relied in 1846 to keep things smooth abroad, wrote bitterly of the Court's resolve to dominate the conduct of foreign policy :

The Queen and Prince are wrong in wishing that courtiers, rather than ministers, should conduct the affairs of the country ; but they were quite right in thinking I should not be a subservient tool nor prepared to sacrifice my own opinions to theirs. They labour under the curious mistake that the F. O. is their peculiar department and that they have a right to control, if not to direct, the foreign policy of England. I make some allowance for their objections to me, as they have suffered such deep humiliation from Palmerston that they now fear an independent-minded man as a scalded dog does cold water.[111]

'Granville the Polite' anticipated 'no trouble in any
quarter.'[112]   He assured Victoria and the Prince that 'it
would be as easy to him to avoid Lord Palmerston's faults
as difficult to imitate his good qualities'; that he would
establish better communications with other governments,
avoid connections with the press, and 'give evening parties,
just as Lord Palmerston had done, to which a good deal
of his influence was to be attributed.'   He had learned
from an Englishman just returned from the continent that
'the only chance one had to avoid being insulted was to
say *Civis Romanus non sum.*'

The Court was all happiness and confidence.   Prince
Albert shared his feelings with his brother in Coburg :

> And now the year closes with the, for us, happy circumstance,
> that the man who embittered our whole life by always putting before
> us the infamous alternative of either approving of all his misdeeds in
> all Europe, or of raising the Radical party here, under his guidance,
> to a power which would bring about open war with the crown . . .
> cut his throat himself. . . .[113]

With Granville safely installed, the Queen felt that she
could make provision for the future.   Striking while the
iron was hot, she immediately demanded that the foreign
secretary should draw up 'a regular programme' on
foreign policy, and that, after revision by Russell and
herself, it should be made a matter of record.[114]   Thus she
could be assured that the policy of her foreign ministers
would 'be in conformity with the principles laid down and
approved.'   Lord John's reply suggests that he may have
been wondering whether the change at the Foreign Office
was going to prove an unmixed blessing after all ; but
Granville was not at all disturbed.   He produced a
memorandum laying down principles so incontestable that,
as his biographer points out, they could equally well have
been subscribed to by either Palmerston or Aberdeen.[115]
Granville was a courtier ; and Victoria was content.

But the Queen's triumph was by no means so complete
as it had seemed at first.   Palmerston's admirers had not
deserted him by any means ; and his bearing in public
compelled some admiration from his critics.   True, he

THERE'S ALWAYS SOMETHING

" I'm very sorry, Palmerston, that you cannot agree with your Fellow Servants ; but, as
I don't feel inclined to part with John, you must go, of course."

Punch, January 10, 1852

wrote bitterly to his brother, attributing his dismissal to
'a weak truckling to the hostile intrigues' of the Orleans
family and of various foreign courts, which had
'poisoned' the Queen's mind.[116] He even encouraged
Borthwick of the *Post* to make insinuations to the same
effect, until the Russian and Prussian envoys felt it
incumbent upon them to protest.[117] But, outwardly, his
behaviour was for the most part irreproachable. He was
very cordial and helpful to Granville, and spoke warmly
of the Queen's 'sagacity.'[118] Of his former associates it
was only Russell and Normanby whom he greatly blamed ;
and even of the premier Lady Palmerston was able to
write airily :

> Ld John has certainly behaved very ill to Palmerston but I think
> it is still more from weakness than from bad intention—though I
> think there was a good deal of jealousy besides in his breast which he
> perhaps hardly avowed to himself.[119]

She dwelt on the fact that he was possibly jealous :

> . . . if so he will be very much annoyed now to feel that he has
> raised up the rival he meant to run down—for the feeling of the
> public is all with P.—& there is no end to the letters & Newspapers
> which we have received from all parts of the Country full of praise &
> approbation whilst John is abused in no measured terms. We hear
> the same of the talk in London . . . & a general belief that the
> Government cannot go on. . . .

What she said of popular sentiment was quite true. Nor
was there any doubt that the government had lost a very
valuable asset. 'His good nature, courtesy, and hospitality,'
wrote Clarendon, 'made him many friends, and he was
able to turn away the wrath of opponents as no other member
of the Government can do.'[120]

And now he was widely regarded as a martyr. In
vain *The Times* announced that he had adopted a cause
which 'extinguished all freedom among the most advanced
nations of the Continent,' and challenged the radicals to
reconcile their admiration for him with his acts.[121] In vain
Bright sneered at the 'many simpletons' who had 'fancied
him a great friend of freedom abroad.'[122] His radical
admirers were not inclined to take the side of so reserved

and Whiggish a person as Lord John,[123] and a cabinet so aristocratic as to be called 'the Dukery.'[124] Nor were they beguiled by the lip service which the Manchesterites paid to liberalism on the continent. They, and much more conservative persons, such as the earl of Malmesbury, believed that Palmerston had been the victim of a plot.[125] They caught at the indiscreet admission of the 'Thunderer' that one of Palmerston's chief sins had been his unpopularity with the 'elder statesmen' of Europe. Considering all of this, they refused to wax indignant over his approval of the *coup d'état*. Like Clarendon, they felt that 'L. N. put an end to a system that everybody knew was a fraud, and could not last.'[126] Nor did they believe that the charges levelled at their favourite were the actual cause of his disgrace. Like Lady Palmerston, they waited confidently until he should vindicate himself in parliament, and until the Whigs should try to maintain themselves without his aid. Though Lady Granville's 'Wednesdays' were running in rivalry to Lady Palmerston's 'Saturdays,' no one but Victoria could profess to doubt that Russell's government was in grave danger.[127] There was really evidence enough in Russell's unsuccessful overtures to the Peelites to accept places in his government.

Great was their disappointment when, on February 3, Palmerston's dismissal was argued in the House.[128] Russell, put on his defence, proved effective and once again disingenuous. He knew quite well that Palmerston had not given the 'moral approbation' of England to the destruction of 'parliamentary government.' He knew it was absurd of Normanby to inquire whether he was to disregard instructions sent officially for a third-hand, verbal account of Palmerston's conversation with the French ambassador. But the real feature of his speech was his reading of the Queen's memorandum of the preceding August on her relations with her foreign minister. This was a hard blow, and, according to Palmerston, an unexpected one. He had refused to believe that Russell would actually deliver it. Everyone noted its effect. Palmerston, his face covered with his hands, seemed crushed. And no wonder. The whole world was suddenly informed that he, who had been

so independent and self-confident, had submitted to an
unparalleled rebuke in preference to giving up his post.
The private explanation which he gave to shocked friends
afterward—the quite convincing explanation that he could
not resign on such an issue without coming publicly into
conflict with a lady who was his sovereign—could not be
offered to the House.   Russell had really enraged him now ;
but for the moment he could not retaliate effectively.

His reply bore little resemblance to his Don Pacifico
defence.   He seemed to have no fire.   He insisted that
he had talked to Walewski unofficially, and that the interview had been ' highly coloured ' in the report sent by the
ambassador to Turgot.   He defended his views on the
grounds of common sense, and explained his apparent
disrespect to Crown and sovereign by press of work.   He
insisted that other members of the cabinet, including the
prime minister and Sir Charles Wood, the chancellor of
the Exchequer, had expressed opinions on the *coup d'état* in
no wise dissimilar to his own.   But once again discretion
hampered him.   He could not make much use of Walewski's
evidence.   He ended with an appeal :

. . . at all events, that ' firebrand of revolutions,' as I have been
called, that individual who has been accused of having embroiled the
relations of England with all other countries, after having found the
country involved in difficulties, has left office with no question of
serious difference between this and other nations, but with amity
subsisting between this and all other countries.[129]

But even this seemed limp—the rather pitiful effort of a
beaten man.

Palmerston appeared to have blundered from his
pinnacle into a crevasse.   This time the House was cold,
even to unfriendliness.   Two or three friends rallied to
his support, suggesting that, if it had been ' necessary to
offer up . . . the late Foreign Secretary as a sacrifice to
the evil genius of foreign despotism,' the other members
of the cabinet would have done well to share his fall.[130]
They stressed the rejoicings of the despotic governments
at his fall, and suggested repeatedly that some poisonous
plot, in which foreign courts were very much involved, lay

beneath the surface of the whole affair. Disraeli, his mind set as usual on the political seduction of Russell's 'strongest' minister, suggested that, however wrong the government's foreign policy, it had been better administered by Palmerston than it could be by any other of the Whig-Liberals. But the impression prevailed that Russell's action had been a natural one. On the accusation that other members of the cabinet had been equally guilty, Russell quoted Walewski as having 'only a vague recollection' of their discussion on the subject, and a willingness to state only that Russell ' might have said ' that he hoped the President would triumph over anarchy. When Lord John went on to say that the chancellor of the Exchequer could not remember having commented on the *coup d'état* at all, Wood endorsed the statement with a loud ' Hear ! Hear ! ' Russell was apparently believed : Palmerston seemed rejected, humiliated, well-nigh done for. Disraeli may have been half in earnest when he exclaimed ' There *was* a Palmerston ! ' [131] Who then could guess that Stockmar would one day pay tribute to Palmerston's foresight in publicly approving of the *coup d'état* ? [132] Who then could dream that in little more than three years' time Napoleon would arrive at Windsor to receive the Garter from the Queen, and Palmerston would be there, as premier, to welcome him ?

CHAPTER XXII

PALMERSTON'S POLITICAL MANŒUVRES, 1852, AND HIS WORK AS HOME SECRETARY, 1852–1854

'PALMERSTON,' wrote the future marquess of Dufferin, after the debate of February 3, ' is completely floored, and people seem to think he is not likely to rise again.'[1] He did not see that Palmerston's humiliation would serve him in good stead after all. The sight of such abasement in a man of whom even Peel had said that he had made every Englishman feel proud of him, a man who had been regarded by Englishmen and foreigners alike as the symbol of resistance to European autocracy and of British influence in world affairs—this was no pleasing spectacle. And the public asked themselves who was responsible. Not the cabinet ; for the cabinet, as all men knew, had been taken unaware. Not Russell, solely and individually ; for nothing had happened personally between the two, either as individuals or as ministers, which could have brought summary expulsion on Palmerston. Who then ? Well, certainly, in considerable degree, the Court. And what was the Court ? The public, not without some justification,[2] believed it was coming more and more to be personified in the Queen's husband. And to them he was still a petty German prince, un-English in habits, ideas, and above all, interests. Was influence such as this to overthrow a Palmerston on the pretext that he had been rude and negligent in doing a thing which sound English common sense could hardly disapprove ? Was it manly, was it proper, that colleagues who had shared his policies and profited by his popularity should leave him at the mercy of the Court ? Indeed, many believed that he had been the victim of a foreign plot, in which Austria had borne a leading part. At any rate, Schwarzenberg had

placarded the news of Palmerston's dismissal in the streets
of Vienna, and given a ball to celebrate the happy event.
None of this squared well with British public sentiment.
The fallen hero acquired a distinct halo of martyrdom ;
and Ellice was soon recording (lamenting might be a better
word) the existence of a ' Palmerston fever ' even in the
higher circles of society.³   Less than a week after Russell
had explained the dismissal to the House, Wellington,
Disraeli, Gladstone and the duchess of Bedford were
noticed at one of Lady Palmerston's parties.⁴ The ' *immoral
one*,' in falling, had landed on his feet.   And he was quick
to undertake the task of upsetting the man who had brought
him down.   The session of 1852 had been in progress for
little more than a fortnight when he dislodged Russell by
what he called his ' Tit for Tat.'

There was something in the triviality of the phrase
which befitted the event.   The fatal blow which Palmerston
levelled at the ministry was really a *coup de grâce*.   Everyone
had agreed that the government was almost sure to be
defeated on reform, or in a debate on conditions in South
Africa.   Palmerston preferred to strike in a cause dear to
his public and his heart.   The question was one of national
defence.   The fact that France was obviously on its way
to become once more a Napoleonic empire (the mere
word ' empire' was enough) set England ' cleaning . . .
old rusty cannons and . . . building fortifications,' and
Prince Albert to begging that his brother would send him
' a Prussian needle-gun.'⁵   Russell proposed to meet the
danger (or perhaps, to speak more correctly, the popular
demand) by providing a local militia, relatively ineffective
but quite cheap.   Palmerston, convinced as ever that
only the more mobile and more expensive ' national ' militia
would be of real use, moved to amend.   Carrying the
protectionists and some Peelites along with him, he beat
the government, on February 20, by thirteen votes in an
unusually slim House.   In a letter to Clarendon, he showed
that he had no illusions about his victory :

. . . the cabinet were glad to make use of the militia question as a
convenient parachute to avoid a ruder descent and a more dangerous
one in Table Bay. . . .⁶

But his friends were charmed. His lady, who had drunk in from the gallery the applause which greeted Russell's fall, rushed home to open up her drawing-rooms and receive a throng of congratulatory visitors.[7] ' One would think,' wrote Shaftesbury in his diary, ' that he had saved an empire, or that he was mounting a throne.'[8] Of all the happy faces that were to be seen that night there was none happier than Disraeli's. Malmesbury, going to visit him on the following day, learned that he ' felt just like a young girl going to her first ball.'[9] He had gone into the same lobby with Palmerston, Gladstone and Herbert on the division which drove out the Whigs, and he anticipated a bright future.

Russell's resignation left confusion worse confounded in the House. The one tendency observable in all parties was a tendency to disintegrate. The Whigs, indeed, had so far stayed with Russell almost to a man ; but a Whig schism was a very obvious possibility. The old-fashioned and conservative element, well typified by Lansdowne, found Lord John too pliant, not to say advanced ; while another group was very sensible of the attractions and the popularity of Palmerston. The Peelites, now reduced in number to three score or less, were still a unit, but could not be relied on to remain so. Of the heads, Aberdeen and Graham, as befitted Scots, were usually inseparable, even in thought, and were reputedly becoming more liberal in matters of reform. Gladstone and Herbert were as conservative as ever, and seemed detachable from Scotch leadership. Moreover, the one issue that had originally separated all of them from other Conservatives, the issue of free trade, was rapidly ceasing to be a question of practical politics. Though the Peelite leaders as a whole had reached an understanding with Russell in the crisis of February 1851, there was no real reason why some or all of them should not form a junction with Stanley's followers as soon as protection was decently buried. The protectionists seemed more united ; but under the surface they were divided between the die-hards, or ' cannon-balls,' and a much larger group who were ready to forswear protection whenever they could do it without too much loss of face.

Among the so-called radicals there was almost no organisation or discipline, save in the Manchester group. And this frequently held itself apart. Lastly, came the Irish Roman Catholic ' brigade,' accustomed to act with the Whigs and radicals, but now bitterly resentful toward Russell. These troubled waters promised good fishing for Palmerston. The sport began when, on February 22, Stanley, now the earl of Derby, accepted the Queen's commission to form a ministry.

Thanks to Wellington's deafness, and to his consequent difficulty in catching the relatively unknown names of eight of the eleven men whom Derby summoned to his cabinet, the protectionist government of 1852 has come down to history as the ' Who-Who ' ministry. It has been well described as ' a stop-gap Government without a majority and without a policy.'[10] Its very appearance was greeted with a mixture of horror and hilarity. Graham shook his head over ' the novel precedent of a whole cargo of the rank and file being carried down to Windsor to be made members of the Privy Council, before they could receive the seals of office ' ; [11] and Henry Greville wrote of the ' volley of jokes ' to which Derby's cabinet-making had given rise.[12]

But it was not Derby's fault, nor Disraeli's either, that Wellington did not hear the name of Palmerston. The new premier obtained the Queen's consent to make him chancellor of the Exchequer. For he had pointed out that Palmerston seemed to be planning a party of his own ; and that, if not included in the cabinet or at least propitiated, he ' might in fact force himself back at the head of a Party with a claim to the Foreign Office.'[13] But, let him accept another post, and his claim to be the guide of England's diplomatic destinies would be waived. Derby apparently intended, too, to make him leader in the lower House. Disraeli, who had been ' coquetting . . . with Palmerston ' for some time, readily offered to be a ' loyal lieutenant.'[14] And Palmerston allowed them both to hope. Derby's foreign minister-elect, the third Lord Malmesbury, looked from the windows of the Carlton Club, on February 22, to see Lord Palmerston ' passing

. . . with his jaunty air, towards St. James's Square.'[15]
Why Palmerston chose to offer his services,[16] or at any rate
to respond to Derby's call remains somewhat of a mystery.
Negotiations between the two men immediately came to
a halt on Palmerston's refusal to admit ' the expediency
of the imposition of any duty, under any circumstances,
upon foreign corn.'[17]   Yet Peter Borthwick, after seeing
him before the interview, expected him to take office ; and
neither Borthwick nor Derby was sure afterwards that
Palmerston might not still be amenable to argument.[18]
It is possible that he expected Derby to renounce protection
in order to secure him as a recruit ; but it seems by far
more probable that he was keeping his options open, and
giving the Whigs something to think about. It was
pleasant, and even useful, to be wooed.

At any rate, he showed marked benevolence to the
Who-Who government throughout its ten months of
precarious life. He began by giving the benefit of his
knowledge and experience to its foreign minister, Malmesbury.[19]   No doubt he found particular pleasure in doing
this from his remembrance of the lessons in diplomacy he
had received from Malmesbury's grandfather, almost half
a century before. The ' pith ' of his advice was that
England should ' keep well with France.' On the other
hand, he pointed out that the two countries, in their desire
for preponderance in the Near East, were ' like two men
in love with the same woman ' ; and that Napoleon might
desire ' to avenge his uncle's fate.' He made various
suggestions on technique (Malmesbury was ' to insist on all
official correspondence being written in a plain hand with
proper intervals between the lines ') ; and he offered a
general admonition that was as essentially Palmerstonian :

You have no idea until you know more of your office what a
power of *prestige* England possesses abroad, and it will be your first
duty to see that it does not wane . . . take care you yield nothing
until you have well looked into every side of the question.

It would be amusing to know how this advice accorded
with what ' Puss ' Granville offered on the basis of his two
months' experience.[20]   But one does know that Malmesbury
found it very similar to Wellington's.[21]

Palmerston's manifestations of good will to Derby's cabinet threw into relief the detached and resentful attitude which he showed at the same time toward Russell. The amenities were carefully preserved through a call of personal reconciliation paid by Lady Palmerston to Lady John, and the appearance of Lord and Lady John at a Palmerston party. But both the master and mistress of Broadlands talked to any willing listener of Lord John's unfairness in reading the Queen's memorandum to the House without warning, and of Palmerston's resolution never again to take office under him. They were very censorious concerning the love of popularity and the tendency toward vacillation and impulsiveness which were certainly his most patent faults. During the following autumn, Palmerston summarised his ideas about Russell's position in a letter to Lansdowne :

My belief is that justly or unjustly John Russell is, as the French would say, *tellement deconsidéré* that a Government formed by him at the present moment would not be backed by public confidence. . . . In office under a discreet chief he may recover his lost ground ; in opposition, clutching to the right and left every floating straw of fancied popularity, he is more likely to sink lower in the opinion of moderate & right thinking men ; and though he may draw closer to him Graham Cobden & Bright, he will widen the breach of opinion between himself and many other liberals.[22]

Russell's attempts at political reconciliation were steadily repulsed. Palmerston treated Lord John's action in inviting him to a Whig meeting which took place in March as almost impertinent.[23] Russell had given him his freedom, and he intended to make full use of it.[24] One of his methods of doing so was to see that the *Morning Post* did not overlook the shortcomings of the late premier.[25]

One particular opportunity for doing this, and at the same time showing 'benevolence' toward the ministerial bench, occurred at the middle of April. The government introduced a militia bill which, though falling short of Palmerston's desires, accorded in general with his views. On the second reading Russell, who had kept still at first, joined the Manchester group in attacking it. Disraeli reported the sequel to the Queen :

Your Majesty's Government, about to attempt to reply . . . gave way to Lord Palmerston, who changed the feeling of the House, and indeed entirely carried it away in a speech of extraordinary vigour and high-spirited tone.[26]

Russell, so he charged, was allowing party feeling to shape his attitude with respect to the defences of the realm. Herbert gave similar testimony :

Palmerston handled him [Russell] very severely, and with a very general concurrence from the House.   The Government, I think, got a good lift last night. . . .[27]

Russell had sustained a rebuff which he could not afford. More than one person had already noted or suspected 'a great attempt . . . to throw the little ex-premier overboard.'[28]   Matters were by no means improved by the report that he had invited John Bright to dine with him.[29]   It seemed a very dubious action on the part of one who could be accused by the duke of Newcastle of adherence to ' the spirit of Whig Oligarchical Cliquery.'[30]

' I have for the last twelve months,' wrote Palmerston, at the end of 1852, ' been acting the part of a very distinguished tight-rope dancer & much astonishing the public by my individual performances & feats.'[31]   This was not an empty boast, as observers could well testify.   During the spring, his attitude in parliament and his connection with the *Morning Post* suggested that he would go to Derby after all.   But no one could accuse him of sacrificing his convictions to the Derbyites.   He did not hesitate to wax sarcastic in the House about the 'amicable Arcadian dialogue which . . . passed between the Austrian Government and the present Ministry ' ; nor even to state his conviction, anent a note from Malmesbury to Schwarzenberg on the harsh and arbitrary expulsion of certain British subjects from Austria, that ' a despatch more submissive in its manner, more abject in its tone and substance ' it had never fallen to his lot to read.[32]   Again, he expressed full concurrence with the prevailing view that Derby should appeal to the electors on the question of a new corn law as soon as the ' necessary ' legislation for the year was passed.[33] But this did not make for reconciliation with the other side. Instead, it brought him full tilt against Russell's Manchester friends, who would not admit that ' necessary ' legislation would include a militia bill. Palmerston's tight-rope performance was trying to political leaders of all groups ; for they all realised his power. His popularity in the country was remarkable. The Princess Lieven wrote to ask whether he was really ' *l'homme le plus considérable et le plus populaire de l'Angleterre.*' [34] And he was certainly coveted by the Conservative party. Richard Monckton Milnes no doubt exaggerated grossly in stating, a few months later, that, if excluded from Aberdeen's cabinet, he would be ' at the head of three hundred men ready, like the Duke's army at Bayonne, " to be led anywhere and do anything " ' ; [35] but he had ' army ' enough to be of great importance to party managers.

The summer found the party situation still more complicated, and Palmerston's ' performance ' still more difficult. In May, Evelyn Denison, using the nautical phraseology so fashionable among politicians in those years, wrote Aberdeen : ' Lord Derby's ship is gradually going down.' An effort to save the ill-constructed craft was made, on July 1, by the long expected dissolution of parliament ; but it emerged only a little more seaworthy than before. The Derbyites were still in a distinct minority, though they had divided with the Whigs and radicals some two-thirds of the former Peelite seats. But neither were the Whigs and radicals combined sufficiently numerous to command a safe majority. Hence a number of combinations were proposed ; and Palmerston figured somehow in all of them. In one important respect he was freer than before. Derby privately admitted that any duty on corn had become impossible ;[36] and his party could drop the protectionist label, and once more call itself merely Conservative. Thus, as Sidney Herbert pointed out, Palmerston had ' two strings to his bow.' [37] He fingered both during the summer and autumn.

Palmerston's first and favourite plan was for a Whig-Peelite ministry, in which the Whigs would play the dominant part, and absorb such Peelites as Gladstone and Herbert.[38] The door was, of course, to be open to

converted Derbyites ; and proper consideration was to
be given to the radicals. Since he knew that the Queen
could still avoid making him her premier, he decided to
have for chief his friend and mentor, Lansdowne. True,
Lansdowne was old and tired, even somewhat infirm ; but
he was honoured everywhere, and his views were very
close to Palmerston's. His ministry would be stout about
free trade, conservative though not necessarily quite in-
transigent concerning parliamentary reform, and liberal
in its views of continental politics. The difficulty was to
persuade Lansdowne to undertake the task, and, having
done this, to bring Russell into line. When Lansdowne
pleaded age and infirmity Palmerston grew eloquent :

. . . I can easily understand that you should after many years of
ministerial labour & confinement prefer freedom, to constraint ; but
' when Honour calls, where'er she points the way, the sons of Honour
follow and obey.' and if the course of events should render a sacrifice
on your part necessary, that sacrifice will undoubtedly be made.[39]

His optimism seems to have carried him very far. On
October 22, Herbert reported that he quoted Lansdowne
as saying : ' Give me a majority of a hundred and I am
ready ' ;[40] while, on that very day, the Marquess wrote
Palmerston that he ' remained unshaken ' in thinking that
Russell, after the lapse of a few months, would be the best
premier of the projected government.[41] At the same time
he admitted that Lord John, in consequence of a conversation between Bedford and Palmerston, had offered to serve
under him. Palmerston, convinced as usual that his
wishes must be realised, was charmed : ' I now for the
first time begin to see daylight through the mist which has
of late obscured the political horizon.'[42]
    But all the time he had the second string—the possi-
bility that he might join, and in joining quite transform,
the Derby government. The cabinet consisted, so he told
Herbert, of ' three men and a half.'[43] With eight members
who were replaceable, it might become ' quite another
affair.' He allowed it to be well understood that he would
never think of enlisting under Derby by himself[44] (Gladstone and Herbert were reputedly the two men whom he

would especially have desired to take with him), or without coming to a very definite agreement as to policy. But it is very doubtful whether he seriously considered the possibility of using this second string, save as a means of strengthening the first. If at any time he consented to negotiate with the Conservatives, the evidence is not yet accessible. Aberdeen and Graham, who would no doubt have liked to break his hold upon liberals of all shades, were apparently in hopes that he would go over to Derby. In August, Graham described to Aberdeen his unsolicited efforts to put Palmerston in the place of Spencer Walpole, Derby's home secretary :

I talked this matter over with Goulburn [chancellor of the Exchequer in the last Conservative government] about a week ago. He is intimate with Walpole and when I suggested that Walpole would act wisely if he sought timely shelter on the bench, the reply was ' but who is to be Home Secretary ? ' I answered that if I were Lord Derby, I should not hesitate to offer the Seals to Lord Palmerston. . . . This course would cover the frank abandonment of Protection in the speech from the throne ; would place the management of the militia in the competent hands of its great champion ; and by superseding d'Israeli without offence, in the lead of the Commons, might facilitate the junction of Gladstone and other useful recruits. . . .[45]

The reason for Graham's apparently disinterested efforts becomes still more clear when one considers the efforts he and Aberdeen were making to prepare for the advent of an Aberdeen instead of a Lansdowne ministry.

The difference between the two plans was not in leadership alone. Palmerston's desire was for a Whig-cum-Peelite ministry : Aberdeen's for a Peelite-Whig coalition, in which the Peelites should have at least half of the power and the glory, perhaps a little more. And the policies which the Peelites had in mind were different, too : at home, some concession to Russell's ideas of reform ; abroad, as friendly an attitude as possible toward the defenders of ' order ' at Berlin, Vienna and St. Petersburg. Thus, a new ' Liberal ' party would come to birth.[46] The Peelite duke of Newcastle even suggested that the names of Whig and Peelite should be consigned forever to oblivion. Graham found it necessary to point out that to ' un-Whig

Lord John Russell is like the unfrocking of a parson, or stripping the buttons from a soldier's jacket.' The adhesion of Russell was, of course, the *sine qua non* of success.

The Peelite plan ripened slowly through the summer and autumn of 1852.[47] In July, the Peelites made advances to Russell.[48] Lord John reciprocated by writing Aberdeen that he had no sympathy with Palmerston's recent advocacy of a north Italian kingdom, ' bounded by Genoa on the one hand, and Venice on the other.'[49] Before the end of August, Lord John had promised support in case Aberdeen should be called upon to form a ministry. True, he later gave the same assurance to Lansdowne : but there was no reason why he, too, should not have a second string. There were times when he hindered negotiations by changing his mind, regarding it as ' personal degradation ' that he should be anything less than premier.[50] But Aberdeen, whose admiration for him was profound, and who could be as tactful as anyone, always succeeded in keeping touch.

In early November, when parliament met, Palmerston was still optimistic concerning his first string. Lady Palmerston, writing her daughter, Lady Jocelyn, summed up the situation as she saw it :

> There are many speculations afloat in London—one is that if Lord Derby should not stay in, Lord Lansdowne might form a government, with Palmerston Home Office and leader in the H. of Commons, Lord John, Foreign Affairs and going up to the H. of Lords . . . but I am all for Ld Derby's Governt. remaining if they do well.[51]

Graham described the situation as a whole : ' The ball will open with a country-dance in which no one has secured a partner.'[52] As the manœuvring for office approached its *dénouement*, the situation became more complicated still ; but one must follow Palmerston as well as possible through the last two developments. Early in November he was working with the Peelites to secure a reprieve for Derby's government : a little later he was concerned with the question as to whether he should enter it.

Palmerston's action in coming to the Conservatives'

rescue again suggests that he wished to keep open every possible option. His opportunity to do fresh service to Derby came, when all sections of the opposition decided that the premier must be forced to admit that the free trade question was a *chose jugée*, or to resign.[53]   Since the great bulk of the Conservatives had already made submission in everything but words, the passage of a mild resolution, merely affirming the benefits of free trade, would have been satisfactory to almost every section of the House.   But the high priests of Manchester, somewhat contemptuous of the chivalric manner in which parliamentary proceedings were usually carried on, presented a resolution which the Conservatives could not have accepted without admitting categorically that they had been wrong in 1846.   The matter was, as Palmerston said truly, ' an affair of words ' ; but the attempt to make the cabinet and its supporters bite the dust turned it into a serious political issue.   The resulting alignment was curious.   Russell, whose complaisance to the Manchester leaders was, for a good Whig, quite remarkable, backed their resolution and brought nearly all of his party into line.   On the other hand, almost all of the Peelites took the stand that simple affirmation would be quite enough.   And with them stood Palmerston.   He personally moved an amendment which no one save a few irreconcilable protectionists could oppose.   It was carried by 468 votes to 53, after the original resolution had been rejected by a comfortable majority.

' I . . . brought together, the largest majority that ever voted on any question, to affirm in the strongest terms the doctrine of Free Trade,' wrote Palmerston.[54]   In precisely how far the boast could be justified, it is difficult to say.[55]   He was acting in conjunction with Gladstone and Herbert when he secured Disraeli's preliminary endorsement of his amendment ; and the actual wording seems to have been decided upon by the Peelites.   But it is certain that he forwarded to Gladstone a draft resolution that was in all essentials identical.   Moreover, he had made appeal to a spirit which most members of parliament still held dear :

Sir, we are here an assembly of Gentlemen—and we who are Gentlemen on this side of the House should remember that we are dealing with Gentlemen on the other side ; and I, for one, cannot at all reconcile it to my feelings to call upon a set of English Gentlemen unnecessarily, for any purpose that I have in view, to express opinions they do not entertain, or to recant opinions that may be still lingering in their minds.[56]

He had the pleasure of defeating Russell, and even, perhaps, of depriving him of the pleasure of being called upon to form a ministry : but his own position was hardly better than before. He had won some gratitude from the Conservatives ; and he had worked shoulder to shoulder with Gladstone and Herbert, who figured largely in his hopes of using either of his 'two strings.' But the Court was not in any way appeased ; and the Court was very much in evidence when the last development occurred—when there arose the question of the reconstruction of the Derby government.

This question was under consideration even while the free trade resolution was before the House. It was evident that Derby's days were numbered unless he could find strong allies ; and there was a prevalent feeling, especially after he intervened to save Derby, that the Warwick of the next few months at least would be Lord Palmerston. The Court was quite convinced that he intended to be leader of the House, either under Derby or under some Whig peer. This would make him the *de facto* premier ; and the Queen was determined to prevent such a ' calamity ' at all costs.[57] On the whole, she would probably have preferred that Palmerston should enlist with Derby, provided he did not obtain the leadership. For Stockmar, who was in the thick of the discussions, dined with Cobden ; and Cobden pointed out that nothing could so ruin the people's idol, and help the righteous to unmask his liberal pose, as would his junction with the Conservatives.[58] It was probably with this in mind that Victoria empowered Derby to open negotiations with Palmerston and his Peelite friends, always on the condition that the '*immoral one*' should not receive the leadership.[59] Stockmar, now the Court's great authority on the British constitution, pointed out that to make this condition was rather venturesome.[60] In view of the fact that the constitution knew nothing of leadership, the Queen's

action was scarcely constitutional. And it was likely to
create some popular feeling if disclosed. Nevertheless,
he went on, Victoria could manage in an emergency ;
for she could forbid Palmerston's appointment to any
ministerial post.

It has been asserted that the Queen, in refusing to
allow Derby to offer Palmerston the leadership, prevented
his junction with the Conservatives. But so conflicting
were the reports concerning his attitude which reached
Derby and the Queen that they themselves were never sure
that he would join the ministry on any terms.[61]   Disraeli,
who attempted to open the negotiations with him in a personal
interview, gave up all hope when Palmerston stated that
neither was he acting in agreement with Gladstone and
Herbert, nor had he reason to believe that either of them
would consider serving in the Derby government.[62]   As it
was fully understood that he had no intention of enlisting
unless they should do likewise, his answer was apparently
a tactful way of closing the negotiations then and there.

Moreover, a letter written to his brother, a few days
previously, shows that he was still pinning his hopes on a
Lansdowne ministry.[63]   It is notable, too, that Aberdeen,
well informed through a man so sharp of ear and eye as was
Graham, could never be convinced that Palmerston would
cross the House.[64]   When, on December 17, the ' Who-
Who ' government, defeated on the budget, gave up the
ghost, Palmerston was not in the House. It seems to have
been illness which kept him away ; but there was a suspicion that he preferred being absent to contributing to
Derby's fall.[65]   His friends were insistent that he would
have voted with the majority, had he been there.[66]

The ministerial crisis of December 1852 immediately
broke the first of Palmerston's ' two strings.' Although
the Queen summoned Lansdowne simultaneously with
Aberdeen, she seems to have had no intention of asking him
to form a cabinet.[67]   Apparently, she sent for him in order
to have the benefit of his knowledge and judgment, to
placate the Whigs, and possibly to please Derby. At any
rate, she lost no time in asking Aberdeen to form a ministry.
Apart from her personal preference, she could scarcely

WHAT EVERYBODY THINKS

Young Palmerston (a sharp, clever boy) : " Oh, crikey ! What a Scotch Mull of a Prime Minister ! "
[That may be ; but it is not Pretty to say so.—*Punch.*]

Punch, October 8, 1853

have done otherwise. She was doubtless informed that a Peelite-Whig coalition had been agreed upon in a meeting at Woburn Abbey during the preceding week ; [68] and she knew that Aberdeen could be particularly useful at this time. His qualifications were summed up by a journalist :

. . . the dispassionate, cool head always learning, always observing, is, after forty years of work and watching, full of wisdom. . . . Of all men known to the public, he is especially fitted for the task . . . of being the centre of a combination of parties : for with ' all the talents ' in one Cabinet, amenity is preferable to genius in the chief. Mediocrity with sixty-eight years is sublimity.[69]

The Queen was quite comfortable as to the policy which the coalition would pursue. Aberdeen admitted that ' the door could not be closed ' against parliamentary reform ; but he added that ' it might be postponed for the present, and there was no real wish for it in the country.'[70] As for the Foreign Office, that was to be in Russell's hands. The Queen was now persuaded—how, it does not quite appear—that ' Lord John's views were very sound and moderate, and that the line of Foreign Policy he had formerly had to pursue had been forced upon him by Lord Palmerston.'[71] If she had expressed confidence that Russell, with Aberdeen for premier, would be amenable to royal ' guidance,' one might be more convinced of her clear-sightedness or her sincerity.

But Lord John was a problem for all that ; and his exhibitions of temperament were destined greatly to influence the fortunes of Palmerston.[72] At first, he apparently wished to be leader in the Commons and foreign minister. For this, as Aberdeen pointed out, ' made him virtually as much Prime Minister as he pleased,' and enabled him to follow ' the precedent of Mr. Fox.'[73] In the days that followed, he changed his mind so frequently as almost to distract the premier. In the end, he returned to ' the precedent of Mr. Fox,' but on condition that Clarendon should relieve him of the Foreign Office at an early date. After just two months, that arrangement was put through ; and Lord John, in defiance of precedent and the wishes of the Queen, was allowed to lead the House without the cares of a portfolio. And he succeeded in imposing two more conditions on Aberdeen. He was to have ministerial support in promoting parliamentary reform ; and he was to become prime minister whenever the time seemed ripe.

Once Aberdeen had been commissioned to form his coalition ministry, Palmerston had to decide whether or not to accept a post in it. For Aberdeen, Russell and the Queen all felt that it would be 'imprudent to leave [him] to combine in opposition with Mr. Disraeli.' [74] And, in Graham's mind at least, there was another reason why he should be brought in :

> John Russell and Palmerston will balance each other, and it may be possible with skill to pull between them. [75]

He was not only invited to join the cabinet, but treated most considerately. Aberdeen began by suggesting that he take the Admiralty, but ended by offering him any post (he was known to have renounced the Foreign Office for all time) which he might choose. [76] The first invitation to join the coalition he declined, pointing out that he and Aberdeen had been so fundamentally and so long opposed in policy that their union could scarcely benefit the country, or fail to provoke unfavourable comment. And, if Graham was correct, ' he added that, if there were no other objection, his reluctance to agree to any further Reform of Parliament, would be an insuperable one.' [77] But he showed his appreciation of Aberdeen's friendliness in a manner which caused great merriment at Windsor :

> . . . nothing could have exceeded the expressions of his cordiality ; he had even reminded him [Aberdeen] that in fact they were great friends (! ! !) of sixty years' standing, having been at school together. We could not help laughing heartily at the *Harrow Boys* and their friendship. [78]

Coburg was, perhaps, deficient in providing episodes so *lächerlich*. Two days later, Palmerston, having agreed to let Lansdowne decide for him, gave in, and selected the office of home secretary. The Court was satisfied. ' If he is in a department in which he has to work like a horse, he cannot do any mischief,' wrote Prince Albert. [79] More-

over, the Queen and Prince had noted that he looked
' excessively ill,' and that he 'had to walk with two sticks
from the gout.'[80]   It was his friends who were troubled.
Shaftesbury shook his head over the ' mortification '
which he would have to undergo.[81]

If ever those who accused Palmerston of clinging to
office at any cost seemed justified, it was in this case.
He was joining what Aberdeen described as a ' liberal
Conservative Government in the sense of that of Sir Robert
Peel,' a government which would find no favour with the
' radicals.' [82]   Contemporaries who looked for his reasons
found them in his love of power, his lack of means, the
urgings of his wife, or the fact that he seemed ' transformed
. . . suddenly into an old man.' [83]   But it is unnecessary
to go beyond the defence he made to his brother-in-law,
Laurence Sulivan :

> Now I should like to know what other course you would have
> had me follow and what object & end you would have had me aim at ?
> Perhaps you will say, to be Prime Minister myself ; but that is not
> a thing a man can accomplish by willing it.   He must first find
> himself the head of some large party, and then must be chosen by the
> Sovereign ; I could fulfil neither of those conditions.[84]

Decision of some sort he was compelled to make :

> I have for the last twelve months been acting the part of a very
> distinguished tight-rope dancer & much astonishing the public by my
> individual performances & feats.   First I turned out the Minister
> who had dismissed me.   Then I mainly assisted in carrying measures
> for national defence which I had in office for several years vainly
> urged upon my Colleagues.   Then in this Session I saved a Govt.
> from premature defeat . . . & I thus saved the Hs. of Cns. from
> the discredit which the course they were going to pursue would have
> brought upon them.   So far, so well ; but even Madame Sacqui,
> when she had mounted her rope and flourished among her rockets,
> never thought of making the rope her perch, but prudently came down
> again to avoid a dangerous fall.

Supposing he had persisted in his refusal to join Aberdeen :

> . . . what would have been my position ?   I must either have been
> left alone between heaven & earth with the imputation of nourishing
> implacable personal resentments, and from my new position have

lost much of my influence in the Hs. of Cns., or I must have accepted
the invitation which the 310 Derbyites were preparing to make to
me, to place myself at their head as Derby's Lieutenant & Disraeli's
chief.

Should he have gone over to the Derbyites ?

If I had been a reckless adventurer, without principles to restrain
one, without friendships to care for, without character to lose, such
a course would have been a clear one.   I might have become a factious
Conservative and, unscrupulously attacking all the Party with which
I have been acting for two and twenty years, and the men with whom
I have been sitting for the last twelve months, I might possibly . . .
have brought Derby in again & have become the Leader of his
Government in the House of Commons.   What would the great
Liberal Party, not in the House of Commons nor at Brooks's nor at
the Reform Club, but in the United Kingdom, have said of such a
course ; nay, to come to particulars, what would that party at Tiverton
by whom I have so long been returned have said, & how should I have
been sure of not having to go a-begging like Graham from one place
to another ?

There is really no ground for speculation save, perhaps,
as to how many men of equal vigour and ambition would
have taken a different course.   He was looking to the
future ; and he could not, at the age of sixty-eight, waste
time ' between heaven & earth.'

It is almost impossible to think of Palmerston as home
secretary without being reminded of one of the most popular of all stories concerning him.   The Queen, being
alarmed by reports of strikes in the north of England,
asked her home secretary whether he had any news.   ' No,
ma'am,' Palmerston is said to have replied, ' I have heard
nothing, but it seems certain that the Turks have crossed
the Danube.' [85]   So excellent a club anecdote is suspicious
in itself ; but, if it may be assumed that men's private
letters deal with the matters closest to their hearts, some
confirmation may be found.   Palmerston's pen was as busy
as ever in 1853 and 1854 ; but the letters pertaining to
that part of the public service which was peculiarly his
own are few indeed as compared with those on foreign
affairs or even on parliamentary reform.   One might feel,
too, from looking at the parliamentary debates, that Palmer-

ston was very willing to allow others both to introduce
and to defend bills for which he might properly have
made himself responsible.   On the other hand, only long
investigation would make it possible to say that he neglected
his duties.   Shaftesbury, though he at one time accused
Palmerston of taking up the easy things and neglecting
the difficult, remembered no other home secretary ' equal
to Palmerston for readiness to undertake every good work
of kindness, humanity, and social good, especially to the
child and the working class.' [86]   True, Shaftesbury was his
affectionate son-in-law.   But, for this very reason, he had
better knowledge of the home secretary's attitude than most
men.   And it is hardly to be supposed that a minister so
humanitarian and so competent in administration would
be as great a failure in his office as was sometimes alleged. [87]
One thing is sure : he entered on his duties in the most
characteristic fashion possible.   He sent a clerk to the
Foreign Office to master the technique of folding papers
properly, and gave orders that the ribbons used for tying
them should be blue instead of green ! [88]

Like all home secretaries, he had to give his attention
to a great variety of things.   Religion and public morals ;
sanitation and penology ; labour legislation and the regulation of trades unions ; the abatement of the smoke
nuisance in London, and the establishment of winter assizes ;
national defence (in so far as the militia was a part of it),
and the supervision of political exiles who had taken refuge
in England—these were some of the matters which most
engaged his time.   He must have found them rather irk-
some at a time when the situation in the Near East was so
full of interesting possibilities.   And he must have missed
the joy of giving battle to Metternichs and Guizots and
Schwarzenbergs.   But he did manage occasionally to be
his pugnacious self.

All of his accustomed breeziness came out in his dealings
with religious authorities.   If he did not, as the wits said,
treat God as a foreign Power, he addressed the Almighty's
representatives in terms not a little reminiscent of his
despatches to foreign ministers.   Firm supporter as he was
of the Anglican establishment, he reverenced it only as an

institution that was highly useful to the state. He did not hesitate to refer in parliament to the 'Augean stable' of its venerable courts.[89]   When he was importuned to permit exceptions in favour of the clergy to a new law concerning burials in churches, he declared his inability to see any special relation 'between church dignities and the privilege of being decomposed under the feet of survivors.' Nor did other denominations escape. The grave presbyters of Edinburgh, on asking the proclamation of a day of fasting and humiliation to check the progress of the cholera, were reminded that God bestowed His blessings on those who showed obedience to His laws. When Edinburgh had freed itself of the 'gaseous exhalations' arising from overcrowded dwellings and undisposed-of filth, it would be time to ask the Maker of the Universe to interpose.[90]   And, although he was ready to show consideration for Catholicism in Ireland as the religion of the great majority, he was violently opposed to its extension in England. Only Aberdeen's restraining hand, it seems, prevented him from taking measures against the 'masquerades' of monks and nuns appearing publicly in conventual dress.[91]   Yet it must be said that he was more ready to do justice to non-Anglicans than many others of his time. It was partly thanks to him that the Anglican clergy were no longer permitted to monopolise appointments and stipends as chaplains in the jails.[92]   He had doubtless heard complaints that they used their monopoly and their power of giving or withholding good conduct reports to proselytise the prisoners. And he introduced into his 'Burials beyond the Metropolis Bill' of 1853 a provision that Catholics and dissenters should have their allotted shares in new burying-grounds.[93]

For the morals of the populace he showed notable concern. He, a *bon vivant* of parts, he, who by every report conformed to Victorian standards only in the preservation of appearances, was as concerned as any temperance advocate of later days about the effects of public houses on the working class :

The Beer Shops licensed to have the Beer drunk on the Premises, are a Pest to the Community. They are haunts of Thieves and

Schools for Prostitutes. They demoralize the lower Classes. I wish you would turn your mind to consider Whether this Evil could not be abated.

That Beer should be Sold like anything Else, to be taken away by the purchaser to be consumed at Home is most reasonable and the more People are enabled so to Supply the labouring Classes the better, but the words ' licensed to be drunk on the Premises ' are by the common People interpreted as applicable to the Customers as well as to the Liquor, and well do they avail themselves of the License.[94]

But, to be sure, intemperance was not among his sins ; and men were probably wont to exaggerate his gallantries.

More significant than Palmerston's concern for the morals of the working class was his attitude toward legislation on the hours of labour, and on the activities allowed to trades unions.[95] In these matters the friend of the radicals was again the cautious reformer, the man of compromise. He would give no countenance to a bill that would have limited the hours of labour for women, ' young persons ' and children alike to ten for ordinary days, and seven and one half for Saturdays. He pleased the manufacturers by substituting a measure which merely forbade the employment of young children between the hours of six and six. His main argument, as stated to the House, placed him in the dwindling band of those who still paid homage to the principle of *laissez-faire* :

It was a matter of considerable delicacy to interfere by legislation with the employment of those who, being of age to determine for themselves, were to be considered as free agents, and therefore ought to be at liberty to work as long or as little as they should think fit to do.

With regard to trades unions, he took a stand that was conciliatory but extremely cautious. As the law had stood for nearly thirty years, working-men who combined to raise the rate of wages by inducing employed men to quit their work were liable to punishment.[96] A decision of the court of Queen's Bench, rendered some six years before, had made this doubly plain. In 1853, a bill was brought into parliament which was allegedly a mere re-affirmation that workmen might voluntarily combine to secure better conditions as to wages or to hours. But it was interpreted by some as permitting the peaceful persuasion of employed men to stop their work, and thus repealing part of the act of 1826. Palmerston, subscribing to this view, opposed its passage :

It appeared to him that it [the bill] would legalise that system of quiet and peaceful intimidation by which poor men, who were in great distress, and were willing to work at the smallest wages by which they could maintain themselves and their families, were sometimes prevented from so working, in order to be driven into combinations with other persons which they did not wish to join. . . .[97]

But, working with the law officers of the Crown, he offered parliament an amended version, which, though forbidding even such 'molestation' as was involved in picketing, would have been pleasing to the workers as a re-affirmation of their rights.[98] The upper House, under the arguments of the chancellor, rejected it as superfluous if nothing more.

In general, he seems to have followed the conservative principle of showing consideration for the welfare of the people, so long as the people showed due respect for order and the authority of the law. Questions of penology concerned him a good deal, and elicited declarations of principle which, if not especially original, were eminently sound.[99] He pointed out that all ideas of vengeance on an offender, of making the punishment really fit the crime, were irreconcilable with the spirit of the age. Punishment should have a deterrent effect on other actual or potential criminals ; but 'the great object,' in all save the worst cases, was 'the reformation of the criminal.' It was very important that there should always be an 'element of hope . . . in prison discipline.' With children, above all, the attempt at reformation should be the guiding principle. Nor did he content himself with principles. Acting, apparently, on the inspiration and with the aid of Shaftesbury, he put through the 'Youthful Offenders' Bill' of 1854, thus providing for the establishment of reform schools where young delinquents might be sent on the expiration of brief terms of imprisonment.[100] This measure is supposed to have reduced in marked degree the alarming juvenile delinquency which had prevailed. For older offenders, too, he did something. Up to about this time such of them as were transported to Australia had enjoyed the incentive to better conduct offered by a ticket-of-leave system. But the Australian colonies having, with one exception, refused to receive any further shipments of convicts, the incentive could be offered in few cases. Hence Palmerston, collaborating with the premier, framed, introduced, and secured the passage of a bill establishing a ticket-of-leave system to be effective in England. His interest in reformation was again exhibited in a scheme for assisting pardoned convicts to start life afresh in the Falkland Islands.[101] And he seems to have formed some of his conclusions on first-hand evidence. He visited at least one prison, and wrote a memorandum, which might still be read with profit, on the lack of ventilation in the cells.

The preoccupation with sanitary measures, which came out so strongly in his dealings with prisons and Presbyterians, was equally evident in other affairs. He protested against having the ' zeal and activity ' shown by the Board of Health replaced by ' the jog trot routine of a government office.'[102] To check the smoke nuisance in London, he was ready to incur hostility from the owners of soft coal mines. To close burying-grounds in the interests of good health, he was ready to go in the face of public sentiment. And it is not difficult to imagine the opposition which would have arisen eighty years ago had he been able to carry out his wish that no unvaccinated child should be admitted to any school receiving public aid.[103]

Most of his departmental activities were calculated to keep him at least on easy terms with his ' most liberal ' admirers in the House ; but he came to a sharp break with them over his attitude toward political refugees. England was giving asylum to men such as Kossuth, Mazzini and Ledru Rollin, who wished the overthrow of most of the governments on the continent, and who frequently lent active aid to plots undertaken by their friends at home. Constant complaints came in from foreign courts ;[104] and with some of these the Home Office was really forced to deal. Palmerston's attitude gives room for thought. He had never approved of violent revolutions ; and it was his duty, especially in an Aberdeen cabinet, to see that foreign governments had no basis for complaint. But he showed real eagerness to pursue one of Europe's greatest revolutionists in the most spectacular charge of plotting which came to the attention of the Home Office in his time. Information was received that powder and ammunition, far in excess of what the law allowed, were stored and packed for export in a small factory in Kent. It was a factory which had formerly supplied munitions to the Hungarians; and Kossuth was reputedly involved. Palmerston ordered, not only that a seizure should be made, but that the offenders should be prosecuted vigorously. He could put forward as excuse the need to rob foreign governments of all pretext for demanding that England take strong measures against political exiles in general. But there were aspects of the affair extremely difficult to reconcile with his straightforwardness, or his sympathy with the Magyars' great leader. When the matter was brought to the notice of parliament and the public by the radicals, one point obscured all others in interest : was Kossuth personally involved ? As often as the point was raised, Palmerston evaded it.[105] He directed that Kossuth's name should be kept out of the trial, but that all evidence tending to inculpate him should be introduced. His private letters place all this evasion in a most unpleasant light. Legal evidence against Kossuth, he admitted, there was none. But it was his hope that the public, in reading of the case, would believe, as he and Clarendon believed, in Kossuth's complicity. Aberdeen, who knew this, thought his conduct 'straightforward' and 'judicious' ;[106] but the radicals, who found him evasive and flippant in parliament, were disgusted and perplexed.[107] The satirical Mr. Whitty of the *Leader* wrote of 'the liberality of the Liberal Lord Palmerston, when foreign refugees have to be annoyed and tortured to please Absolutist courts,' and of 'Lord Palmerston's anxiety to introduce a Viennese police system.'[108] It might well have been asked how long the home secretary's popularity would survive. Yet Henry Greville wrote, in August 1853 : 'People begin to prophesy that he will be Prime Minister before the next session is over.'[109] The reason for this was that a storm was rapidly blowing up in the Near East.

CHAPTER XXIII

THE HOME SECRETARY IN FOREIGN AFFAIRS, 1852–1855

THERE was a good deal of irony about the prelude to the Crimean War. At Christmastide, 1852, when the message of the herald angels was being chanted at Bethlehem, angry disputes about the custody of the birthplace of the Prince of Peace were threatening to involve Europe in war. Three days previously the Turks had, under French pressure, handed over the keys to the Roman Catholic patriarch ; and the Tsar, incensed by an act which so testified to the decline of his influence at the Porte, was not only preparing to resist, but was turning over in his mind a favourite scheme for making Russia dominant in the Balkans. The project was an ambitious one ; but he reflected with satisfaction that Aberdeen was now prime minister of the country which would ordinarily erect the greatest obstacles. Not only did Aberdeen dislike Napoleon and detest the thought of engaging England in a war : in 1844 he had agreed that England and Russia should negotiate the partition of the Sultan's apparently moribund empire whenever its dissolution should be clearly in sight.[1] Hence, in January and February 1853, Nicholas tried to strike a definite bargain with the British government. Maintaining that the Turkish empire's disintegration was now imminent, he suggested that the Turks be driven from Europe, the Balkan nations organised as Russian protectorates, and Egypt and Crete handed over to England. But Russell, Aberdeen's foreign secretary *pro tempore*, refused even to admit that Turkey's case was desperate ; and Nicholas in his disappointment fell back on an alternative. He decided to try for a general protectorate over Turkey's Greek

G

Catholic subjects by bringing direct and immediate pressure on the Porte. The letters of Count Brunnow, his ambassador in London, encouraged him to believe it would be safe.[2] His advisers informed him that it would be proper. Hence, at the end of February, a blustering Russian envoy, Menschikoff, arrived at Constantinople to require (under the proper diplomatic camouflage) that Turkey should admit the Tsar's possession of treaty rights which entitled him to interfere between the Sultan and his Greek Catholic subjects. Later on, he even demanded a new alliance with Russia. Greatly alarmed, but realising that their very independence was at stake, the Turks as usual played for time. In May, Menschikoff, finding that mere threats did not produce results, launched an ultimatum at the Porte. But the Sultan's ministers, almost panic-stricken three months before, had been growing steadily more confident. In March, Napoleon's interest in their cause had been evidenced by the appearance of the Toulon fleet at Salamis : in April, Stratford Canning, their old friend and champion, had arrived back at the British embassy. Even the Austrian and Prussian envoys would not advise submission. Hence, before May was out, a very angry Menschikoff departed for St. Petersburg ; and a very angry Tsar announced that, if Turkey delayed submission to a new ultimatum for longer than eight days, Russian troops would occupy Moldavia and Wallachia, Turkey's Roumanian 'principalities.' By the end of June the occupation had begun. The Tsar explained rather disdainfully that this invasion was not to be looked upon as war ; and the Turks, on the urging of the British government, professed to take him at his word. This left Nicholas somewhat nonplussed, and gave the governments of all the Powers a breathing space. Their foreign ministers had been much occupied with the question for some months. And so had England's home secretary, Palmerston.

In surveying the diplomatic exchanges, the naval and military operations, which accompanied and followed these events,[3] one is tempted to apply the dictum that it is better to ask not who, but what, should be held responsible in any case for war. Yet he who is interested in Palmerston cannot ignore the fact that he has been accused of wishing ' war at any price.' First indicted for his warlike proclivities by that sincere and statesmanlike master of oratory, exaggeration and partisanship, John Bright, he has been charged with organising a ' war party ' in the cabinet, stirring up a war mania in the public and the press, and bullying a too gentle premier into unwilling adoption of a war policy. His accusers can cite much circumstantial evidence.   They can point to his rejection of Aberdeen's policy of keeping peace at almost any price, of avoiding all offence to Nicholas, of accepting whatever settlement the great Powers might agree upon, and of constraining the Turks to make whatever concessions this settlement might involve.   Whether British public sentiment would have allowed the ministry to hold this course is decidedly doubtful ; but certainly Palmerston would have none of it.   In his view, England's especial task was to resist Russia, both as the aggressor against the weaker Turks, and as the great menace to the European balance of power.   Nor did he think that effectual resistance could be made by words alone.   Too often had he found the Russian government quite prodigal of reassuring language at London and St. Petersburg, the while her agents were pushing forward in the Near and Middle East.[4] In so dangerous a crisis as that of 1853 her aggressive acts could be met only with acts.   The Tsar might take offence ; but the use of force was the only language he would understand.   It was to be expected, and greatly to be hoped, that if resisted he would agree to reasonable terms.   If not— well, peace might prove impossible.

Palmerston's policy, his old policy of preserving Turkish independence at almost any cost, had a very realistic side. True, he talked of a ' progressively liberal system '[5] at Constantinople, which certainly did not exist.   True, he wrote of the superiority of the Turkish empire over the Russian ' in many points of civilisation,' and of the greater advantages with respect to ' security for person and property ' enjoyed by the Sultan's Christian subjects over the population of Russia.[6]   But he had always enjoyed labouring an argument ; and he may have had some satisfaction in teasing Aberdeen, who was shocked by any comparison between the Christianity of Russia and the 'fanaticism and immorality' of the Turks. When occasion required, the 'storm-compelling Jupiter Anglicanus' could discard imaginative generalities and produce realistic argument :

> To expel from Europe the Sultan and his two million of Mussulman subjects . . . might not be an easy task ; still, the five Powers might effect it, and play the Polish drama over again. But they would find the building up still more difficult than the pulling down. There are not sufficient Christian elements as yet for a Christian state in European Turkey capable of performing its functions as a component part of the European system. The Greeks are a small minority, and could not be the governing race. The Sclavonians, who are the majority, do not possess the conditions necessary for becoming the bones and sinews of a new state. A reconstruction of Turkey means neither more nor less than its subjection to Russia, direct or indirect, immediate or for a time delayed.[7]

He feared seeing Russia 'bestriding the Continent from north to south—possessing the command of . . . the Baltic and the Mediterranean, enveloping the whole of Germany, embracing regions full of every natural resource.' For then 'she would become dangerous to the liberties of Europe, and her power would be fatal to the independence of other States.' And what would become of England, her commerce and her eastern empire ?

As the months went on he decided that Russo-Turkish relations should not even remain as they had been. He demanded that the Russian government should be compelled to give up the stipulations of former treaties on which it had founded its demands.[8] He later gave reasons for this position to the House :

> Better far would it be for Turkey to have one of her limbs cut off, than to have infused into the whole body politic a poison which would destroy her vital energies and lay her prostrate at the feet of her powerful neighbour. That, Sir, which Russia demanded was nothing less than right of sovereignty over 12,000,000 of the subjects of the Sultan, which would have the effect of rendering the Sultan the nominal, and not the real, sovereign of his country.[9]

He was really an effective advocate. When he argued the whole matter out with Aberdeen, Clarendon, who had replaced Russell at the Foreign Office before the end of the winter, was impressed with the ' very good case ' which he had made.[10]   Unless Russia were turned back, England would 'always be on the eve of war,' since Constantinople would always be in danger of falling into Russian hands.

Needless to say, Palmerston was unwearied in efforts to secure the adoption of his policy by the cabinet.   He was always among the ministers who urged that the British and French navies should give greater and greater protection to the Turks ; and usually, though not invariably, he led the group.   Unfortunately, each event which postponed settlement made his policy more dangerous to peace.   The Tsar became increasingly incensed, the Turks increasingly reckless, the British government increasingly committed to their support.   The first orders given the Mediterranean squadron were to undertake a movement which would merely warn the Russians and hearten the Turks ; but, long before England and Russia went to war, the squadron's commander had been authorised to seize Russian ships in the Black Sea.   Thus fresh irony entered in.   Palmerston's policy, had it been wholeheartedly adopted at the start, might quite conceivably have brought ' peace with victory.' Those who made it increasingly dangerous and at last fatal to all hopes of peace, were the peace lovers who insisted on delays.   And the first of these was Aberdeen, who, by his policy and his pronouncements both, gave great encouragement to the Tsar.[11]

Through most of 1853, Palmerston was straining at the leash.   In March, when Menschikoff commenced bullying the Turks, and the British chargé at the Porte wished to move the Mediterranean squadron to the neighbourhood of the Dardanelles, Palmerston and Russell urged ' violent measures' against the successful opposition of Aberdeen and Clarendon.[12]   At the end of May, when news of the Tsar's threat to occupy the principalities reached London, the home secretary demanded that the squadron should be sent up to the Dardanelles, and Stratford Canning (who had now been made Lord Stratford de Redcliffe) given power to summon it to the Bosphorus in case an attack on Turkish territory should seem imminent.[13]   If England, he wrote haughtily, was to be precluded from taking protective measures merely by fear of displeasing Nicholas, she ' had better at once acknowledge the Tsar as the dictator of Europe.' For once Palmerston's policy received a trial. Aberdeen was prolific in arguments for delaying all action;[14] but the cabinet, apparently swayed by public sentiment, forced his hand.[15] On the other hand, Canning was expressly requested not to make use of his new power.[16] But Russian forces immediately seized the principalities ; and, early in July, Palmerston was making fresh demands. ' Acts should be replied to by acts ' was now his great motto.[17] The squadron should be sent up to the Bosphorus, with permission to enter the Black Sea if needed for the protection of the Turkish coast.[18] It was intolerable, he wrote, that England and France should be in the position of ' waiting without venturing to enter the back door as friends ' while the Russians had taken ' forcible possession of the front hall as enemies.' And the moving up of the allied squadrons would actually make for peace, by stimulating Austria and Prussia ' to increased exertions to bring the Russian government to reason.' When Aberdeen declared that such ' empty bravado ' was calculated to make peace impossible, Palmerston seemed momentarily to give way ;[19] but the issuance of a haughty and threatening Russian circular soon drew from him the renewal of his last demand, together with an angry outburst against the members of the cabinet who were thwarting him :

If the two Powers had acted with that energy, decision, and promptitude which the occasion required ; if when Menschikoff began to threaten the two squadrons had been sent to the neighbourhood of the Dardanelles, and if the Russian Government had been plainly told that the moment a Russian soldier set foot on Turkish territory, or as soon as a Russian ship-of-war approached with hostile intentions the Turkish coast, the combined squadrons would move up to the Bosphorus, and, if necessary, operate in the Black Sea, there can be little doubt that . . . things would not have come to the pass at which they have now arrived. But the Russian Government has been led on step by step by the apparent timidity of the Government of England, and reports artfully propagated that the British Cabinet had declared that it would have *la paix à tout prix* have not been sufficiently contradicted by any overt acts. The result

now has been that the cabinet of St. Petersburg, not content with
bullying Turkey, threatens and insults England and France. . . .[20]

But the ministry preferred the cautious attitude of the
premier. Palmerston had to wait until September, until
Aberdeen could square his conscience by reflecting that
there was fear of an outbreak against even British Christians
at the Turkish capital,[21] before the fleet was ordered to the
Bosphorus. In the following November, Clarendon confessed to Aberdeen how much he regretted the delay :

> We are now in an anomalous and painful position, and, although
> I shall admit it to no one but yourself, I have arrived at the conviction
> that it might have been avoided by firmer language, and a more
> decided course five months ago.[22]

Clarendon's ability to steer between premier and home
secretary has perhaps been over praised.

Yet, for all his insistence that England should meet
Russian force with force, Palmerston was, as he wrote the
premier, ' prepared to share in the responsibility of submitting even to insult,'[23] rather than interfere with the
negotiations which were going on. When the representatives of the four Powers, in the ' Vienna note ' of July 28,
produced a scheme of pacification very similar in appearance
to the text of Menschikoff's demands, he seems to have
raised no objection to its endorsement by the cabinet. By
September he was 'coming reluctantly to the conclusion'
that Russia and Turkey would come to blows, and that
England should ' manfully assist ' the Turks ; but he was
still ready to exhaust the resources of diplomacy. The
Russians had accepted the Vienna note ; but the Turks,
suspicious as to the interpretation which the Tsar might
place on it, had demanded that its text should be so altered
as to contain a categorical denial of Russia's right to
' protect ' the Sultan's Greek Orthodox subjects. When
Nicholas refused to consider any change, and when a Russian
indiscretion revealed the fact that Turkish suspicions as to
Russian interpretation were amply justified, a British statesman with a taste for war might well have found excuse for
declaring that the Tsar had closed the way to peaceful
settlement. Palmerston emphatically took Turkey's side ;

but he readily agreed with Aberdeen and Clarendon to
break the deadlock by proposing ' that the four Powers
should declare that they adopted the Turkish modifications
as their own interpretation of the note.' [24]   In fact, according to the premier, the agreement was ' in great part
written at his [Palmerston's] dictation.' [25]   Surely he was
no war-monger then.   Not, at any rate, so much as Russell,
who threatened resignation because a step so ' degrading
Turkey ' had been resolved upon.[26]   Indeed, it was not the
first time that Aberdeen had found ' Palmerston . . . not
so warlike as Lord John.' [27]   But the home secretary received
the lion's share of the blame.   Unlike Russell, he was always
determined and steadfast ;   and he was a dog with a bad
name.

In October he had the best of opportunities to show
just how dangerous he was.   By the middle of the month
the Vienna note had been discarded ;   the Russians were
marking time in the Roumanian principalities ;   the allied
fleets had been ordered to the Bosphorus ;   and the Turks
were preparing to despatch their armies to the north.   But
even a Russo-Turkish war was not inevitable yet.   It still
seemed possible that the fears of energetic action in the
Euxine by the British and French fleets would bring
Nicholas to terms, or that the continuing negotiations at
Vienna would bear fruit.   Even more hopeful seemed the
fact that Canning was preparing a new note for presentation
by the Turks to the great Powers.   This juncture was the
most critical so far reached ;   and, for this reason, it offered
a conclusive test of Palmerston's bellicosity.

To Aberdeen his attitude must have been trying at this
time.   He would be satisfied with nothing less than a very
rash attempt to frighten Nicholas.   And he exhibited what
the premier called ' a morbid desire ' [28] to see negotiations
transferred from Austrian to British soil.   On October 7,
he placed his suggestions for coercing Nicholas before the
cabinet.   No doubt he relied upon support ;   for Russell,
' more warlike than ever,' [29] had given previous notice of
his own belief that unless the Tsar gave way the British
would be bound to ' appear in the field as auxiliaries of
Turkey.' [30]   Palmerston, just before the cabinet met, had

made the same demand in more explicit terms. Orders should be sent out to the British and French fleets, he thought, to enter the Black Sea, ' detain ' all Russian warships cruising there, and to hand them over to Turkish authorities. In general, the British and French governments should offer all assistance requisite for Turkey's actual defence, on condition that the Sultan consulted them in making peace.[31] He still maintained that to threaten a European war was the best way of rendering Nicholas less warlike.[32] When the cabinet convened, he urged his views ' perseveringly, but not disagreeably.' Finding, however, no concurrence save some ' faint ' support on Russell's part, he agreed that the fleets should move only when Turkey's coastline was in obvious danger of attack.[33] Even Aberdeen supported this, feeling that ' perhaps it was impossible to do less.'[34] On the matter of continuing negotiations at Vienna, Palmerston again gave in. He complained of the ' political miasma ' of the place, and added characteristically : ' A Vienna conference means Buol, [the Austrian foreign minister] and Buol means Meyendorf [Russian ambassador to Austria] and Meyendorf means Nicholas.' But he was apparently won over by his belief that concurrence by Austria and Prussia in such proposals as France and England might put forth ' wd increase the chances of success both at Constantinople & afterwards at Petersburgh.'[35]

Perhaps he came nearest to incurring direct responsibility for the eventual outbreak of war when the cabinet was discussing Canning's note. Aberdeen's idea was that the Turks should be required, on pain of sacrificing British aid, to accept the note *totidem verbis*, and to suspend hostilities so long as England continued to negotiate, and the Russians to refrain from new offensive moves.[36] But Palmerston, working as usual with Russell, demanded that the cabinet should modify this plan.[37] The Turks should be threatened only with the loss of *some* British support ; they should be required to suspend hostilities only for a ' reasonable ' time ; and they should be at liberty to ask for alterations in the text. He made his arguments in the name of peace :

If we send them a draft wh. they must either take as it is, or reject, we may have a rejection wh might have been avoided, & we may lose by our own pertinacity an invaluable chance of a peaceful arrangement.

It is a perfectly tenable hypothesis that Palmerston and Russell destroyed the chance of ' peaceful arrangement ' by their successful insistence that the Turks should be required to suspend hostilities only for a ' reasonable time.' For the Sultan, eager to make war with Anglo-French support, delayed only a fortnight in opening hostilities. But even the acceptance of the hypothesis as fact would scarcely justify Bright's reference to ' the 50,000 Englishmen who died to make Palmerston Prime Minister.' [38]

It is very significant that the home secretary's colleagues found little reason to complain of him.   True, he engaged in brisk exchanges of letters and memoranda with the premier now and then, the briskness being mainly on his side.   But Argyll, Aberdeen's lord privy seal and special confidant, a member, too, of the so-called ' peace party ' in the cabinet, has pointed out that credit for the harmonious manner in which foreign policy was handled in the ministry by no means belonged solely to the premier :

. . . there was not even one single heated discussion. . . . As to Palmerston, he was singularly silent, and when he did discuss, it was always frankly, always with perfect temper, and always acquiescing without any show of irritation in the general sense of the Cabinet. . . . When Palmerston felt strongly on any step which he thought ought to be taken, he generally explained it fully to Aberdeen in a letter, and gave notice that he would raise the question in the next Cabinet.   This was a straightforward method, and an excellent one for securing an adequate discussion . . . much has been said and believed about the Aberdeen Cabinet and the causes of the Crimean War which is absolutely untrue.   Spencer Walpole's story about it is almost pure fiction. [39]

But the best evidence is that left by Aberdeen himself.   To like or trust the man who had accused him of displaying ' antiquated imbecility ' he found impossible.   Moreover, he was grieved to see what influence Palmerston had on Russell and Clarendon, not to speak of the cabinet as a whole. By the autumn of 1853 he had come to the point of wishing to get rid of him.   But his letters disclose no feeling on his part that he was being bullied and overborne.   His nearest

approaches to complaint were in writing that the home
secretary argued ' perseveringly ' and was not ' unreasonably
pugnacious.'[40]   Indeed, for all his bitter grief that his
cabinet brought England into the Crimean War, Aberdeen
was too honest to condemn this action utterly.   He always
doubted whether it was necessary or even wise ; but he
felt, too, that it could be defended as disinterested and just.[41]
Gladstone considered it not only just but sensible.[42]

There remains the charge that Palmerston coerced the
cabinet by conjuring up war sentiment, by stirring the
public through his speeches and his influence with the press.
For this suggestion, too, there is circumstantial evidence.
The ministry was undoubtedly sensitive to the prevailing
Russophobia ; and Palmerston's speeches were often music
to the Russophobes.   The press at large enthusiastically
backed his policy.   Conservative papers praised every
move against the Tsar ; and so, to Bright's and Cobden's
grief, did some of those in favour with the radicals.[43]   But,
if Palmerston fostered that curious eagerness for war which
took possession of his countrymen, it would be hard to prove
that the action was deliberate.   His speeches were of the
old familiar kind, blasting tyrants as typified by Nicholas,
and appealing to British honour and prestige, to the sturdi-
ness and independence and invincibility of Englishmen.   As
read by an angry public they were inflammatory without
doubt.   But one wonders in how far they were intended to
be so.   Their tone appears identical with that of their
author's private letters to the premier ; and even Palmerston
would scarcely have hoped to make Aberdeen a chauvinist.
It would need much proof to establish that he tried to force
on war while the cabinet in which he sat was attempting to
preserve the peace.   As for his influence with the press,
it has recently been shown that his only journalistic connection was with the *Morning Post*.[44]   *The Times*, after
playing both sides, became as warlike as the best ; but how
far it submitted to his influence may be judged from a
letter written in November 1853 by Lady Palmerston :

> I saw the account of your Mansion House Festivities in the
> papers, . . . & the *Morning Post* as usual gave the best account—
> for that brute of the *Times* always tries to cut short anything flattering

to you . . . The *Times* says Ld Aberdeen & John Russell were cheer'd by the Spectators. The *Morning Post* says you were all three Cheer'd—and I dare say, You were the most so.[45]

The ' Thunderer ' was in most respects as close to Aberdeen as it had ever been ; but, like the country, it was ' drifting into war.' No group or person in the cabinet had been dominant enough to give one policy a thorough trial.

Whatever Palmerston's responsibility or lack of it for the approach of war, Aberdeen was extremely anxious to get rid of him. Hopes that ' Jupiter Anglicanus ' was past the dangerous age and ' safely tethered within the peaceful pastures of the Home Office '[46] had vanished speedily. Graham might talk of his loss of energy ; but he showed far more vigour than the premier. And the strength of his position, both in the cabinet and outside, was greater than the premier and the Court had counted on. The Tsar, in creating the menace of war, had unconsciously been very kind to him. With all there was at stake, ministers could not ignore advice from the country's greatest specialist on continental politics. Nor did they dare. ' The Palmerstonian stocks have gone up immensely,' Prince Albert had written ruefully in October.[47] His resignation on Near Eastern policy would be bound to cause a storm. The Conservatives supported him because his policy ' quite agreed ' with theirs,[48] the radicals because he was opposing Europe's greatest autocrat. The Whigs themselves had not ceased to feel a certain pride in him, or to realise his value at election times : and there were Whigs and Peelites, both, who thought he was quite right about Russia.[49] His influence was greatest with some of the most influential members of the cabinet. In Clarendon's case it seemed increasingly pronounced.[50] Grey believed that the home secretary ' had the correction of nearly all Clarendon's notes ' ; and Palmerston showered Clarendon with compliments. Russell, no longer obliged to consider how Palmerston's aggressiveness and Palmerston's relations with the Queen affected his own position as prime minister, could once more give hearty endorsement to his policies. With such backing the aged prisoner at the Home Office bade fair to shape the government's foreign

policy almost as much as he had done in the ministries of
Melbourne and Russell.   In popular estimation he was
commencing to overshadow his colleagues.   Readers of the
Leader, who had learned at the beginning of the year that
he was likely to become ' " master of the situation," arbiter
between Whigs and Peelites and Radicals,' were informed
during July that he had ' seized a predominance in the
Cabinet.' [51]   People were predicting that he would soon
be premier.[52]   He was rather inclined to agree with them.[53]
     This was a most grievous prospect for the Court.   In-
deed, the existing situation was very hard to bear.   Once
more the ' *immoral one* ' had to be tolerated, not to say
humoured.   The Queen, on Aberdeen's suggestion that he
could best be checked through gentleness, reluctantly
entertained him at Balmoral, in September, 1853.[54]   But
scarcely was this piece of royal self-abnegation at an end
when Palmerston interfered, not only with foreign policy,
but with the private and sacred concerns of the royal
family.   Anxious as usual that England should enjoy all
possible influence at the Tuileries, he had the unheard-of
presumption to suggest that the Princess Mary of Cambridge, a Protestant spinster of Victoria's own blood,
should marry that nominally Catholic rake, that disreputable
member of an upstart dynasty, Prince Jerome Bonaparte.[55]
Worse still, he intimated that the Princess was, to say the
least, willing.   Aberdeen was scandalised, Victoria outraged.
Let it be known, she announced to her distressed and
apologetic premier, that she would ' visit with the highest
displeasure ' (one wonders just how much the phrase meant
to Palmerston) anyone who should so presume to interfere
with royal concerns.[56]   Aberdeen, after an interview with
the delinquent, reported that he refused to disclose his
reasons for presupposing the Princess Mary's willingness,
but would be unlikely to interfere again.[57]   But by this
time the situation at Windsor and at Downing Street was
similar to what it had been two years before.   Court and
premier were longing to free themselves from Palmerston ;
but both realised that he must leave the ministry for some
reason which would tend to diminish, not to accentuate,
his popularity.   His attitude on the Near Eastern crisis

was one of the principal reasons for getting rid of him ;
but it was the last issue on which he could safely be
permitted to resign.

While Court and premier were wondering what could
be done, Russell opened a possible avenue of escape. He
demanded that the cabinet should support a new bill for
the reform of parliament, thus raising the one issue on
which Palmerston had made reservations when entering
the government. No popular demand existed at the time ;
and the ministers as a whole, becoming more and more
engrossed in deciding how much pressure should be placed
on the Sultan and how much on the Tsar, had no great
desire to argue about boroughs and franchise.[58] But Lord
John had Aberdeen's promise. His project, almost identical in essentials with that which he had offered to his own
ministry two years before, was referred to a committee of
cabinet for study and report. Palmerston served on the
committee with Russell, Granville, Newcastle and Graham.[59]

Considering the attitude of Aberdeen and the Court,
political expediency dictated that Palmerston should exhibit
sympathy with Lord John's proposals, for the time at least.
Instead, he immediately reverted to the hostile attitude he
had assumed in 1851.[60] As then, he objected that Russell,
in offering a bill at all, was going in advance of any real
demand. As then, he protested against any upset of the
existing balance in the representation of economic and social
' interests.' If the ministry regarded itself as pledged to
a reform measure of some sort, he would agree that a score
or so of boroughs should lose their seats to counties,
and that the property qualification for voters in the counties
should be lowered. And he really approved of ' fancy '
franchises, i.e. of provisions by which persons whose professional or economic circumstances offered presumptive
evidence that they would make proper use of votes, would
be registered, despite their failure to qualify by owning or
occupying real estate. But any great reduction of the qualification for voting in the boroughs he would not have.
It would be particularly unfortunate at a time when ' the
vast additions annually making to the quantity of the
precious metals ' was producing a reduction automatically.

To lower the qualification would be to ' overpower intelligence & property by ignorance and poverty.' Voters too ignorant to see through agitators, or too poor to resist bribes, would send undesirable representatives to the House. And it was certain, he felt, that members would ' insensibly and unavoidably adapt their language their tone and their votes to the lowest class of electors.' He saw ' daily in the United States the lowering effect of this dependence of members upon the lower orders of the community.'[61]

It is difficult to question his sincerity, as some of his opponents were very soon to do. Not only did his private letters ring with conviction : his action in fighting a project adopted by the cabinet involved him, under the circumstances, in some risk. He seems to have sensed this when, on December 8, he stated in writing his refusal to support Russell's projected reform bill. For he announced his refusal in a letter, not to the premier, but to his lifelong friend, Lansdowne, then serving as a minister without portfolio.[62] Two days later, he sent to Aberdeen copies of his letter to Lansdowne and of Lansdowne's reply, together with a covering letter of some length. In this he asked that the copies should be returned.

His letter to Lansdowne seemed instinct with the frankness and determination which were so much a part of him. It set forth with some vehemence his objections to the details of Russell's scheme, including the incautious words that the lowering of the borough franchise would ' overpower intelligence & property by ignorance and poverty.' And it presented new reasons for his uncompromising attitude :

> I have told Aberdeen that I am persuaded that the measure as proposed by John Russell & Graham will not pass through the two Houses of Parliament without material modifications, and that I do not chuse to be a party to a contest between the two Houses, or to an appeal to the country for a measure of which I decidedly disapprove and that . . . in short I do not chuse to be dragged through the dirt by John Russell. I reminded Aberdeen that on accepting his offer of office I had expressed apprehension both to him & to you that I might find myself differing from my colleagues on the question of Parliamentary Reform.

There was nothing so very unusual about this. Offensive as

the phrase regarding Russell seemed, it was not especially out of keeping with its author's style and temperament. But a later paragraph of the letter was more significant :

> I should be very sorry to give up my present office at this moment, . . . I have matters in hand which I should much wish to bring to a conclusion, moreover I think that the presence in the cabinet of a person holding the opinions which I entertain as to the principles on which our foreign affairs ought to be conducted, is useful in modifying the contrary system of policy which, as I think, injuriously to the interests & dignity of the country there is a disposition in other quarters to pursue, but notwithstanding all this I cannot consent to stand forward as one of the authors and supporters of John Russell's sweeping alterations.

It is difficult to decide how this paragraph should be interpreted. He was not making so direct a threat as Lansdowne had done two years before.[63] In view of his strength both in the House of Commons and without, and of the fact that his other letters gave no indication that he expected to resign,[64] his challenge looks very much like bluff. He may very well have thought that he could bluff the premier and cabinet out of making unwise submission to Lord John.

The covering letter which he sent the premier [65] appeared to be, and quite likely was, a guileless document. There was a friendly statement of his desire to have ' no concealment of his correspondence with Lansdowne, a temperately worded justification of his refusal to concur in Russell's reform plans, and an extensive exposition of his views on the Russo-Turkish quarrel. He was merely taking the opportunity, he wrote, to repeat opinions on England's attitude toward the crisis which he had offered more than once before. There could be no proper settlement until Nicholas would ' *renounce some of the embarrassing stipulations of former treaties* ' ; and it was greatly to be hoped that the protection of the principalities, of Servia, and of the Sultan's Greek Catholic subjects in general would be provided for in a treaty between the five great Powers. But how could Nicholas be brought to any reasonable terms ? Only, it seemed, if no Russian warship in the Black Sea were allowed by the British and French navies ' to show itself out of port ' until all Russians had retired from Turkish soil. Under this condition the Turkish army could probably ' make in Asia an impression that would tend to facilitate the conclusion of peace.'

Did Palmerston, in writing these two letters to Lansdowne and Aberdeen, cherish ulterior designs ? Argyll, who was extremely well informed, referred to him later as having been ' eminently straightforward, quite honest, outspoken ' [66] in his relations to the cabinet. But at the time Aberdeen felt that the home secretary had delivered an unscrupulous and clever stroke. He had ' stolen a march by combining the Eastern Question with Reform.' The premier added, half admiringly : ' Truly he is a great artist.' [67] Aberdeen was certainly in a quandary. Was he to quarrel with the hypersensitive Russell on the question of reform, or was he to risk having Palmerston resign and the public attribute the resignation to disagreement on Near Eastern policy ? In either case there would be grave danger to the ministry. He was, by his confession, ' at a loss what to do.'

Some of his friends, however, were at no loss at all ; for they were convinced that Palmerston was determined to wreck the government. They found a clue to his desires in the fact that he had addressed his letter to Lansdowne, the ' greatest objector' to reform among all the members of the ministry.[68] They deduced that Palmerston was hoping to persuade Lansdowne to resign with him, and expecting thus to upset the ministry, revenge himself on Russell and the Court for his dismissal in 1851, and open the way for his own elevation to the premiership.[69] It does not seem impossible that they were right ; but, if so, it is hard to see why he pursued his strategy so openly. He had given warning to Aberdeen before sending him a copy of the letter to Lansdowne.[70] That he made his definite refusal to support Russell's bill in a letter to an old and trusted friend need suggest no more than fear that it would be used against him if a break should come.

And to use it was just what some of his opponents immediately resolved to do. The Queen and Prince Albert had already pointed out how wise it would be ' to let him go at once,' how important that he should go ' on the *Reform question*,' which was ' unpopular ground,' and how useful it would be to have a statement of his objections ' *in writing*.'[71] Hence Aberdeen almost certainly wished to keep a copy of the letter to Lansdowne.   But its return had been specifically asked for ; and the premier was an honourable man. Graham had to encourage him in taking a step which must have gone against his principles :

> We have a crafty foe to deal with ; but these very clever men sometimes outwit themselves.   The letter to Lord Lansdowne contains nearly all that we want, or that we could have hoped to extract in black and white.[72]

Sir James went on to suggest that Aberdeen should have copies made of the letter and of Lansdowne's reply, and should inform Palmerston of the fact.   Whether the copies could actually be used, he was not sure, but their very possession would enable Aberdeen to deal with his refractory minister.   In any negotiations that ensued the premier would, of course, stress reform and keep foreign policy in the background.

Thus encouraged, Aberdeen immediately pressed matters to an issue.   He notified Palmerston that he was keeping a copy of the letter to Lansdowne ; and offered the excuse that he had been on the point of requesting a written statement of his objections to reform, ' with a view to ascertaining by communication with the Queen and with our colleagues, how far it might be possible to remove or to modify the opposition ' which Palmerston was ' disposed to make.'[73]   But, whether he feared or whether he took for granted the cabinet's attitude, he consulted only three other ministers.[74]   Two days later, he wrote in the most formal terms to say that he, Russell and Graham considered it impossible to make alterations in the reform project with which Palmerston would be satisfied.[75]   His letter, as he informed the Queen, was drafted with the expectation that Palmerston would resign immediately.[76]   He knew his man. Though Lady Palmerston begged her husband ' not to be in such a hurry,'[77] Palmerston lost no time in despatching to Argyll House as curt a letter of resignation as it was possible to frame.[78]   If he had really ' stolen a march by

combining the Eastern Question with Reform,' he did not
persist in his tactics.   It is true that, three days before, on
hearing of the 'massacre' of Sinope, he had written Lansdowne that he felt 'ashamed as an Englishman & á minister'
of the part his government was acting.[79]   And he had
demanded from Clarendon an expedition against Sebastopol.
But his valedictory letters to Lansdowne and Clarendon
spoke of his resignation as occasioned only by the cabinet's
attitude on reform.[80]   In well-informed Whig circles he
was taken at his word.[81]

In after years Lord Stanmore, who was one of Aberdeen's
sons, and, in 1853, one of his secretaries, explained to Reeve
that Charles Greville had never succeeded in finding out the
truth about this strange affair :

He was kept specially in the dark about the real history of Lord
Palmerston's resignation in 1853. . . . Hardly anybody does know
what lay behind, though the difference about Reform was a very
real one, so far as it went, and quite sufficient to justify—at all events,
ostensibly—Lord P.'s virtual dismissal.[82]

And again :

I have never known a secret better guarded than the fact . . .
that Lord P.'s resignation . . . was *not* voluntary, and that he was,
in fact, extruded.   But, to be sure, half the Cabinet did not know
this. . . .

The real reason for the 'extrusion,' according to Stanmore, was that Palmerston 'had given great offence to the
Queen,' and that his 'more important colleagues,' Clarendon
in particular, believed that he was carrying on 'intrigues.'
The statement seems quite plausible.   Victoria was exceedingly annoyed with him.   The groundless story of his secret
communications with Stratford Canning [83] was in circulation
even then; and, what is more, Clarendon professed to have
received his confession that he meditated 'breaking up the
Government.' [84]   Considering Stanmore's intimate knowledge ;   considering the tone of the letters which passed
between the three 'most important' ministers who enjoyed
the premier's confidence';[85] and considering that Lansdowne,
the 'greatest objector' to reform, was urged to retain office
and expected only to refrain from attacking Russell's bill

until it reached the House of Lords,[86] there is every reason to believe that Palmerston's ' extrusion ' was a fact.   The whole incident was unpleasant ; but it had its humorous side.   Russell, in approving Aberdeen's action, scarcely realised, perhaps, how ardently both premier and sovereign hoped that Palmerston's downfall would ' tend greatly to the improvement of Lord John's Foreign Policy.'[87]

But the important thing was the reception which the cabinet, the House of Commons and the public would give to the announcement, on December 16, that Palmerston had resigned.   Aberdeen's allies, *The Times* and *Chronicle*, worked hard.[88]   If any hint of ' extrusion ' came to them it was carefully concealed.   With some indifference to fact, they assured their readers that Palmerston had resigned rather than sanction *any* measure of reform, and that he had been guilty of wantonness and frivolity in retiring from the ministry.   *The Times* even declared that he was acting precisely as Wellington had done almost a quarter century before.   What was more, they claimed ministerial authority for part at least of their charges.   Since constitutional usage sealed the accused's lips until parliament should meet, this seemed unfair even to his critics.   True, the *Morning Post* quite outdid *The Times* in misstatement, claiming that Palmerston had resigned on account of the ministry's foreign policy.[89]   But it did not claim authority.   It was, in fact, forbidden to make such claim even for the moderate statement which Palmerston sent to it—a statement that he had resigned, not because he was opposed to all reform, but because he considered Russell's proposals as ' inexpedient,' and as going beyond ' the necessities of the time.'[90]   The general upshot of the press battle was that sympathy came to Palmerston from all quarters.[91]   The ' radicals ' refused to desert him : the Conservatives' praise was louder than ever.   Even pure Whigs considered him ill used.   Lord Grey, still among the most severe of his critics, protested against the ' *disgraceful*' attacks of the ministerial organs, and pointed out that ' the anxiety thus to forestall him with the public ' had ' the natural effect of making everyone doubt the truth of the reasons assigned by *The Times* for his withdrawal from the Govt.'[92]   Gradually it became

apparent that Palmerston would again reverse the Humpty
Dumpty rhyme.   All the queen's horses and all the queen's
men could not keep him from his wall of popularity and
influence.

The cabinet itself would not endorse his fall.   True,
Russell had become 'decidedly conciliatory and con-
siderate ' ; and the other members seemed at first inclined
to accept the *fait accompli*.[93]   But, as the dangers of the
situation became more evident, some of them raised 'rather
a storm.'[94]   Six, half Whigs and half Peelites, demanded
that their departed colleague should be brought back again.[95]
The premier reported mournfully to the Queen :

> All the people best conversant with the House of Commons
> stated that the Government had no chance of going on with Lord
> Palmerston in opposition, and with the present temper of the public,
> which was quite mad about the Oriental Question and the disaster
> at Sinope.[96]

In vain the Queen begged for deliverance.[97]   Times had
changed sadly since the second Henry's time.   No one
would rid her of the pestilential minister.   Though the
premier and Lord John denounced the 'cowardice' and the
'shabbiness' of the colleagues who demanded his return,[98]
they could do no more than make the return a little difficult.[99]
It was decided that Palmerston would have to make
first overtures ; and, while he would be allowed to raise
objections to the details of Russell's bill, no important
alterations should be conceded him.   Just one week after
his resignation had been announced, he was brought back
to the fold by Newcastle and Lansdowne.[100]   Once again
Prince Albert was in the bitterness of despair :

> Now Palmerston is again in his seat and all is quiet.   The best
> of the joke is, that, because he went out, the Opposition journals
> extolled him to the skies, in order to damage the Ministry, and now
> the Ministerial journals have to do so, in order to justify the recon-
> ciliation, (?) . . . I fear the whole affair will damage the Ministry
> seriously.   Palmerston gulps down, it is true, all his objections to the
> Reform Bill (which is to be altered in none of its essentials), but he
> will lead the world to believe that it is to *him* concessions have been
> made.[101]

It was proving very difficult for a British sovereign to be
' permanent Premier ' with ' supreme authority ' in ' matters
of discipline.'

It was not even true that Palmerston ' gulped down '
his objections to the Reform Bill.   He stood uncommitted
as to its ' details.'[102]   Even *The Times* admitted that his
reconciliation with the cabinet involved no sacrifice of
principle on either side.[103]   And he had reason to hope that
Russian guns had sunk the bill when they had sunk the
Turkish ships at Sinope.   Reform is seldom popular in time
of war; and the prospects of war were now greatly increased.
The Russians, though acting quite within their rights, had
annihilated a weak Turkish fleet and taken four thousand
Turkish lives at a time when Turkey was relying upon
British and French aid.   British public opinion had flared
up ; and the cabinet, even in Palmerston's absence, had
resolved at last that British ships, along with French,
should enter the Black Sea.   There seems no question that
the cabinet's decision was a factor in Palmerston's apparent
surrender on reform.   Not only did he say so in the letter
to Aberdeen which asked that his resignation be cancelled,
but he took care to secure confirmation of the cabinet's
action *from the French ambassador* before writing Aberdeen
at all.[104]   Why did it count so much with him ?   Perhaps
he was merely anxious to make sure that there should be no
drawing back, and to have a hand in war if war should come ;
but he may well have gambled that the imminence or outbreak of war would make the passage of a reform bill
virtually impossible.   At any rate, he lost no time in opening a fresh attack on Russell's proposal for reduction in
the borough franchise.[105]

The session of 1854 gave him opportunity to show that
his opposition to Russell's reform proposals was inveterate.
Despite the impatience of the cabinet, the almost pained
surprise exhibited by the House,[106] and the ' apathetic
indifference throughout the country,'[107] Russell attempted to
secure a second reading for his bill in April.   By this time war,
inevitable from the beginning of the year, when the fleet
received orders to allow no Russian vessels to show themselves in the Black Sea, had been declared.   Palmerston flatly

C. Wood   W. Molesworth   Lord Clarendon   Lord Granville   G. Grey
                Duke of Argyll   Sidney Herbert
                    Lord Lansdowne   Lord J. Russell Lord Aberdeen Lord Cranworth Lord Newcastle
J. R. G. Graham W. E. Gladstone   Lord Palmerston

THE ABERDEEN CABINET AT THE OPENING OF THE CRIMEAN WAR

refused beforehand to vote for the bill,[108] thus extinguishing the last faint hope that ' the bugbear of the Session, the secret dread of Ministers and Opposition, the skeleton at the Parliamentary banquet '[109] might be allowed to pass. He was able to make his refusal with impunity ; for more than ever was he indispensable. When Russell resigned, and Palmerston courteously offered to leave the cabinet in order that Lord John might stay, no one seems to have thought of taking him at his word.[110] He was safe even in announcing his intention of opposing Russell's bill if and when it should again be introduced.[111] For the nation thought of nothing but the war, and turned to the members of the cabinet who seemed fitted to bring it to a victorious issue.

Once more he grew in popularity and influence. Now freed from all restraint, he could belabour the Russian autocracy in the way the English loved. And he could enjoy equal pleasure and profit from turning his oratorical guns against the pacifists. Bright soon gave him a rare opportunity. At a farewell dinner for Sir Charles Napier, who was departing to command the Baltic fleet, Palmerston's speech was so rollicking and indiscreet[112] that Bright charged him in parliament with a grievous departure from the canons of good taste.[113] His contemptuous and insolent reply[114] was far below the standards of parliamentary comity; but he could claim some justification in the example Bright had set for him. And, in a second attack upon his foe, he struck home at the materialism which muddied the ideals of the Manchester group :

The hon. Member for Manchester (Mr. Bright) asks, ' What is our interest in this war ? ' and he also asked me to explain the meaning of the expression ' the balance of power.' . . . ' Balance of Power ' means . . . self-preservation . . . The hon. Member, however, reduces everything to the question of pounds, shillings, and pence, and I verily believe that if this country were threatened with an immediate invasion likely to end in its conquest, the hon. Member would sit down, take a piece of paper, and would put on one side of the account the contributions which his Government would require from him for the defence of the liberty and independence of the country, and he would put on the other the probable contributions which the general of the invading army might levy upon Manchester, and if he found that, on balancing the account, it would be cheaper to be conquered than to be laid under contribution for defence, he would give his vote against going to war for the liberties and independence of the country, rather than bear his share in the expenditure which it would entail.[115]

When Bright opposed a bill forbidding British subscriptions to a Russian loan, Palmerston compared him to a Dutch admiral who sold powder to his adversaries in the morning in order that they might continue hostilities in the afternoon.[116] He was beginning to win approval in unaccustomed places. Even Prince Albert's courtly biographer admired the speech about the Dutch admiral when taken as a whole.[117] And the public decided that England had found a great war minister.

To this even the Court soon agreed. Prince Albert had grown quite warlike by the first weeks of 1854, rejoicing that the 'wand' by which Nicholas had 'ruled Central Europe' would be broken, and that the German governments, forced into constitutional reforms and 'alliance with the west,' would be delivered from 'the tyranny of revolution and demagogy.'[118] The *immoral one* was at last regarded as useful by the Court. 'Sir Charles Napier, Lord Stratford, and Lord Palmerston are the three persons who alone could carry on the war,' Prince Albert told Napoleon at the beginning of September 1854.[119] The Prince even complained of Aberdeen's inability to adapt himself to war; and Victoria begged her dejected favourite not to be too complimentary to Nicholas in the House of Lords.[120] The Court had not developed any love for Palmerston; but it depended on him as a man in whom the English masses placed their trust, whom Napoleon regarded as almost his one friend in the ministry,[121] and who possessed sufficient energy and decision to grasp the situation and make the best of it.

He was determined not only to make the best of it, but to get the utmost out of it. To the eager Poles, whose proferred assistance could not be accepted in view of the impression it would make at Vienna and Berlin, and on whose discretion he knew better than to count, he explained that he had no desire to cripple or 'make an enemy of Russia.'[122] He wished only to compel the abandonment

of her designs on Turkey and the Black Sea generally.
But to Russell he wrote that merely to expel the Russians
from the principalities and leave them in full strength,

would be only like turning a burglar out of yr house, to break in
again at a more fitting opportunity. The best & most effectual
security for the future peace of Europe would be the severance from
Russia of some of the frontier territories acquired by her in later
times, Georgia, Circassia, the Crimea, Bessarabia, Poland & Finland . . . she wd. still remain an enormous Power, but far less
advantageously posted for aggression on her neighbors.[123]

For the achievement of these modest aims, attack might
be made at four different points. The Turks, aided by a loan,
some European commanders and a little naval help, should
account for Georgia and Circassia. The British and French
fleets, with 50,000 or 60,000 troops, should take the Crimea
and Sebastopol. The clearing of the principalities could be
effected by the Turks, with such co-operation as Austria
might be willing to offer in her own interests. Finally,
the allies should be able to master the Russian ships and
arsenals in the Baltic by giving subsidies and other assistance to the Swedes, and by allowing them to hope (without
definite promises, of course) that they might retain so much
of Finland as they could take.[124] But, of course, as he
assured the Poles, there was to be no conflict à outrance !
Yet he was practical enough in some respects. Gladstone
congratulated him upon being the first man in England
to suggest the Crimea as the main point of attack.[125]

CHAPTER XXIV

Palmerston becomes Premier, 1855

On a day in January 1855, so cold that 'the frost on the rails delayed the express train' (for the winter was bitter in England as well as in the Crimea), the Saxon minister, Count Vitzthum, went down to Windsor, to dine with the Court, the premier, and other members of the government. Later he committed to his diary the reflections to which the events of the evening had given rise, beginning with his impressions of Aberdeen :

> As I looked at that excellent old gentleman, and saw how he sat there in the icy apartment shivering and chattering his teeth, I involuntarily asked myself whether he was the man to battle with the storm, and lead England safely through the dangers of a European war.   For a storm there was, which was shaking the British Constitution to its base. . . . The British Constitution is no mere piece of paper . . . It is a labyrinth to which a knowledge of public opinion affords the only clue.   But this very public opinion is . . . a kite which rises or falls with every breath of air, and which none can fly but those who understand the game to be a game.[1]

Disillusionment and depression arising from reversals suffered by the army and the fleet had caused an outcry against the government at a moment when no other government seemed possible :

> The ship of State ' Britannia ' had sprung a leak, and was rolling almost without a pilot in the trough of the sea.   Men's eyes were opened to the magnitude of the war, which had been so recklessly begun ; after the fever came the cold fit.   Sir Charles Napier had slipped away from the Baltic ice with his task unaccomplished.   In the Crimea the gallant armies had won desperate battles, but, so to speak, not a foot of land . . . a cry of indignation arose, and, as always happens in such cases, the blame was heaped on the men, not

the system. . . . At such a moment, there was nothing too absurd
to pass muster as probable. Thus, a silly report was spread that the
Prince was willing to sacrifice the army in the Crimea out of love
for his German relatives. . . . Lord Raglan, Lord Hardinge, and
the Duke of Newcastle, and in the last instance the Premier, Lord
Aberdeen, were the men who were loaded with contumely of every
kind. . . . A direct attack, the success of which could not be doubted,
would have morally obliged the Conservatives to form a Government.
But where were the materials for that Government to be found in the
midst of such a storm ? . . .

The Count, it will be seen, was given to some exaggeration
as well as to rhetoric ; but his painting of the situation
remains substantially true. And, to some minds, there lay
in it another danger, which in retrospect one feels tempted
to scorn, but which may well have appeared quite real in the
winter of 1854–1855. On the very day, curiously enough,
which was to see a fatal blow dealt to Aberdeen's regime,
Alexis de Tocqueville pointed out this danger to Nassau
Senior, the English economist :

I hear, as you do, with great satisfaction of the mutual good
feeling of our armies in the Crimea . . . But I am not equally
pleased with your management of the war. The English ought to
know that what has passed and is passing there has sensibly diminished
their moral force in Europe . . . I have been struck by it peculiarly
in a late visit to Paris, where I saw persons of every rank and of every
shade of political opinion. The heroic courage of your soldiers was
everywhere and unreservedly praised, but I found also a general
belief that the importance of England as a military Power had been
greatly exaggerated ; that she is utterly devoid of military talent,
which is shown as much in administration as in fighting ; and that
even in the most pressing circumstances she cannot raise a large army.
Since I was a child I never heard such language. You are
believed to be absolutely dependent on us ; and in the midst of our
intimacy I see rising a friendly contempt for you, which if our
Governments quarrel, will make a war with you much easier than
it has been since the fall of Napoleon.[2]

It was under such remarkable conditions that Palmerston became prime minister for the first time : but the
conditions were hardly more remarkable than the combination of forces through which his ambition was achieved.

Russell, who was determined to head the government himself, quite unintentionally opened the way : the British people, inclining more and more to regard Palmerston as a new Chatham who alone could lead his country to success in war, propelled him towards the goal ; while the Queen and Aberdeen, who would ordinarily have preferred almost any other statesman alive, exerted themselves to remove the final obstacles.

Russell made his unintentional contribution by resigning his own place in Aberdeen's administration in the most unexpected fashion.[3] ' Lord John,' wrote Aberdeen's son, Arthur Gordon, on January 22, ' is the one source of trouble and weakness . . . it is impossible to imagine what he may or may not do next.' Within a day Russell had made further imagining quite superfluous. On the evening of the 23rd, Gordon, having heard the radical and aggressive Mr. Roebuck give notice of a motion for a committee to inquire into the condition of the army before Sebastopol and the departments of the government charged with the conduct of the war, and Lord John one for a bill on education, ' went home to dinner to report a quiet opening of the session.' Strolling at ten o'clock into his father's library to see what the day's boxes might contain, he found in the first one a ' bombshell' from Lord John. Unable, Russell wrote, to see how the ministry could repel Roebuck's censure of some of its members, his one course was to resign. The letter was read with some amusement, and even with relief. For Lord John had exhausted the premier's patience. But the bombshell had inflicted on the ministry so dangerous a wound that Graham, the tried consultant, was soon being dragged from his dressing-gown and hurried through the snow to make his diagnosis and prescribe. He could give little hope. With so prominent a member of the administration as Russell admitting even tacitly that Roebuck's censure of Aberdeen and of Newcastle, the secretary for War, was well deserved, how could Disraeli's jibes be answered and the impatient Whig supporters of the government be held in line? At the Queen's insistence, the ministers consented to make what fight they could :[4] but a week later, when Roebuck's motion came to a vote, the

BURSTING OF THE MINISTERIAL PIPES

Old Lady of the House : "Dear! Oh dear! We might have expected this change of weather,
and ought to have provided for it."

Punch, February 10, 1855

government was defeated by a majority which, as Gladstone said, ' sent us down with such a whack that one heard one's head thump as it struck the ground.'[5]

Though Palmerston must have seen what possibilities for his own advancement Russell's action opened up, he not only condemned it, but sought to rob it of effect. In a scathing letter to the offender, which won warm approval from the ministry and the Court, he pointed out that some such motion as Roebuck's had been anticipated before the meeting of parliament, and that Lord John should have declared himself at the time. He might thus have avoided paralysing England's executive and alarming her allies in the midst of a great war, to say nothing of sparing the ministry ' the appearance of self-condemnation by flying from a discussion which they dare not face.'[6] In parliament, where he now spoke as leader of the House, Palmerston was curiously ineffective ; but he left no doubt as to his attitude.[7] And as though to place his disinterestedness beyond question, he offered to accept the War Office under Aberdeen, if Newcastle's retirement would induce Russell to stay on.[8] It is not at all impossible that Palmerston, shrewd as he was impulsive, fond of power as he was loyal, perceived that righteous indignation and attempts to save the ministry were exhibitions of virtue that might bring their own reward. Even so, Russell had opened the way to virtue and to opportunity.

For Lord John, all unknowingly, had killed two birds with one stone. He had closed the doors of Downing Street to two statesmen hitherto preferred to Palmerston : to himself as well as Aberdeen. All supporters of the coalition ministry, save Russell's most indulgent friends, condemned him just as Palmerston had done. Thus, while Aberdeen, in deep humiliation and morbid self-condemnation, withdrew from public life, Russell, branded even by the Queen and his Whig associates as unstable, timid and devoid of patriotism, could hope to lead no ministry until he had purged himself of his offence.

But neither the close followers of Aberdeen nor those of Russell would at once recognise them as disqualified. It was only by degrees, in the days of endless consultations

and royal memoranda which followed the coalition's fall,
that the figure of Palmerston as the one possible prime
minister emerged.   A great element in his favour, quite
obvious from the outset, was his position as the people's
choice.   Little enough this would have counted for in
ordinary times.   But with impatience and exasperation
rising daily over reports of mismanagement, misery, and
waste of life at the theatre of war, there were strong arguments for fixing responsibility on the nation's favourite.⁹
The Queen's notorious dislike of him became in some sense
an asset when it was felt that even suspicion of royal discrimination against his claims might raise a ' storm.'¹⁰
On the other hand, the popular will could not suffice to
make him premier.   It could fortify his claims, assure him
a fair chance ; but it could not stop the party leaders and
the Court from testing every possible alternative.   And
there were few who saw in him the capacity of a wise and
strong prime minister.   Peelites and Whigs together shook
their heads at mention of his name, fearing a war pushed
on relentlessly for ' ulterior ' aims agreed upon in secret
with Napoleon III.   Friends and foes together pointed out
that he could count upon no party, and upon no element of
society effective in the House or at the polls.¹¹   ' He has
not,' wrote one of Arthur Gordon's friends, ' the country
gentlemen like Derby, the Whigs like any scion of the
Bedfords :   the independent Liberals like your Father's
government.'   Even Shaftesbury lamented that his father-
in-law lacked ' even two or three able and friendly adherents.'
Finally, the Queen, exhausting her ink-well in underlining
her determination to ' think of *nothing* but the Country and
the preservation of its Institutions,' even though her ' *own*
personal feelings would be sunk,'¹² retained some hope of
being spared the final sacrifice of calling Palmerston to
power.
    Constitutional practice was at first entirely on her side.
Nothing could have been more proper than that she should
apply to Derby, late leader of the Conservative opposition.
And nothing, as it happened, could have placed Palmerston
in a position of greater embarrassment.   The Conservative
leaders, considering him as indispensable on account of his

popularity, his grasp of current affairs and his intimate
connection with Napoleon, offered him every inducement
to enter their projected cabinet.[13]   Although some regarded
him as unfitted by age and by the failure of his sight and
hearing to assume the leadership of the House,[14] Disraeli
agreed to relinquish it to him.   He was commissioned to
invite Gladstone and Herbert to accompany him to the
Treasury bench.   Derby, after tendering these bribes, drove
from Palmerston's house in Piccadilly, during the early
afternoon of January 31, in a hopeful frame of mind.   For
Palmerston had seemed distinctly receptive.[15]   He had said,
it was true, that he would have difficulty in joining a
ministry in which Clarendon did not have charge of foreign
affairs ; but the Conservative leader did not take this very
seriously.   He failed to realise that Palmerston found himself in a dilemma, and was looking for a way out.   To
Gladstone the late home secretary frankly admitted his
embarrassment.[16]   If he refused the Conservative invitation
' it would be attributed to his contemplating another result,
[his own accession to the premiership] which result he
considered to be agreeable to the country.'   Gladstone
acted as the candid friend :

> I then argued strongly with him that though he might form a
> government, and though if he formed it, he would certainly start it
> amidst immense clapping of hands, yet he could not have any reason-
> able prospect of stable parliamentary support . . . He argued only
> rather faintly the other way, and seemed rather to come to my way
> of thinking.

But Palmerston again expressed his feeling with respect to
Clarendon.   Though in all probability this feeling was
sincere enough, it served him well in his embarrassment.
For Clarendon, interviewed immediately after Gladstone,
declared that he would refuse any offer from Derby.[17]
Palmerston, after seeing Lansdowne, ' that noble Friend,' as
he told the House, ' whose opinion will guide me in every
important transaction of my life,' [18] informed Gladstone,
Herbert, and Derby that all prospect of his joining the Conservatives was at an end.   So was his dilemma ; for Derby
almost immediately gave up hope.

With Derby's failure ' another result ' began to appear
most probable.   Some result had to be reached immediately.
' No one can remember,' wrote Greville on February 4, ' such
a state as the town has been in for the last two days.   No
Government, difficulties apparently insurmountable, such
confusion, such excitement, such curiosity.' [19]   The Queen
and the Whigs had hopes of Lansdowne.   But Lansdowne,
old and none too well, decided, after various ' soundings,'
to do no more than join Prince Albert in giving his
sovereign advice.[20]   The three were substantially agreed.
Application must now be made to Russell and Palmerston.
Russell, ' long accustomed "to sit attentive to his own
applause," ' would fail almost as certainly as he would
consent to try.   But he should have first choice, partly for
the constitutional reason that he had contributed so greatly
to the fall of Aberdeen, and more, perhaps, because no
incoming prime minister would be secure until Lord John's
tormenting ambition was stifled by the realisation of his
impotence.   The realisation was rapid and complete enough
to have satisfied the most resentful of his late associates.[21]
News that Russell had been commissioned, on February 3,
to form a ministry, produced an ' uproar ' in coalition
circles generally ; and Lord John's confident advances to
his old associates brought him a shower of refusals, of
which some were nothing if not frank.   In contrast stood
out the seemingly magnanimous consent of Palmerston to
continue at the Home Office and lead the House—provided
Clarendon remained in charge of foreign affairs.[22]   Actually,
his consent involved no magnanimity at all.   For not only
did his position as the almost certain alternative to Russell
make it impossible for him to refuse, but the known attitude
of Clarendon and the Peelite leaders left it scarcely doubtful
that Lord John would fail.   ' After twenty-four hours of
humiliation, such as hardly any English statesman has ever
undergone,' [23] Russell threw up his commission.   Palmerston's chance, for whatever it might be worth, had come
at last.

It is one of the ironies in the life of each of the three
persons concerned that Palmerston was finally assisted in
achieving the premiership by Victoria and Aberdeen.   But

the reasons were compelling ones. The ministerial crisis
had to be ended at the first possible moment ; and, though
Palmerston was backed by the majority of the Whigs, by
the British public and by Britain's chief ally, he was apparently in need of Peelite votes to secure a safe majority.
Here was reason enough why the Queen should urge the
Peelite leaders to serve under him. But she had another
reason quite as good. Responsibility, she judged, would
place some check on Palmerston's exuberance ; but only
the Peelite leaders, Gladstone, Herbert and Graham (she
could scarcely hope for Aberdeen), would apply a really
trustworthy curb.[24]   And Aberdeen, though most reluctantly, supported her efforts.[25]   Against personally taking
office he rebelled as a ' painful sacrifice ' and a ' gratuitous
indignity,' worse than death itself ; but he consented to
use all his influence with his followers. Thus, on February 4,
Palmerston went searching for a cabinet, with his sovereign
and, eventually, his late premier at his back.

   ' Palmerston,' wrote his wife to Shaftesbury four days
afterwards, ' is distracted with all the worry he has to go
through.' [26]   No one who has looked at the letters and
memoranda of those days will doubt her word. At first
the prospects seemed utterly discouraging.[27]   Russell
refused office ; and the Peelites followed suit. Gladstone
loftily expressed distrust of the foreign policy of a Palmerston cabinet without Russell or Aberdeen : Graham went
about declaring that he would not see the fleet placed under
French command. But Palmerston proved as persistent a
wooer in politics as in love ; and he had excellent auxiliaries.[28]   Aberdeen brought increasing pressure on his
friends ; Lansdowne and Clarendon co-operated vigorously ; and Herbert, who had wavered from the first, soon
used shrewd arguments for acceptance on his fellow Peelites.
Their refusal would not only bring them extreme unpopularity, but might cause the formation of the very kind of
government which they feared, and expose the country to
the very perils against which they were so much on guard.
For it might drive Palmerston to recruit among ' wilder
and more dangerous men.'   He went on, writing to
Aberdeen :

We hope for peace, and, if he chooses to try for it, there is no one who could make peace so easily as Palmerston. Terms would be accepted from him here in England which would be hooted at from you. I do not believe in the ' iron will ' and the inflexibility of Palmerston. On the contrary, I never saw a man so pliable. . . . And on foreign policy, though he has occasionally talked about Poland, he has never embodied any of his ideas on the map of Europe in a proposal to the Cabinet. . . .[29]

Palmerston himself did not disdain to lull the Peelite fears. Thus to Gladstone, February 6 :

If by a Stroke of the wand I could effect in the Map of the world the Changes which I could wish I am quite sure that I could make arrangements far more conducive than some of the present ones to the Peace of Nations, to the Progress of Civilization, to the Happiness & Welfare of Mankind, but I am not so destitute of Common Sense as not to be able to compare Ends with Means. . .[30]

On this date Gladstone and Graham, reluctant and distrustful still, consented to retain their former offices ; and Palmerston kissed hands. He was prime minister of England by grace of party anarchy and of the confidence of a people that he would lead them out of danger, discouragement, and distress. He summed it up himself : ' I am, for the moment *l'inévitable.*'[31]

But his troubles were scarcely half over. The inevitable was not accepted with the best of grace ; and cabinet-making would have been a troublesome task for anyone at this time. So Prince Albert realised :

. . . in the present disruption of Parties, the difficulty of obtaining any strong Government consists, . . . in the over-supply of Right Honourable gentlemen produced by the many attempts to form a Government on a more extended base. There were now at least three Ministers for each office, from which the two excluded were always cried up as superior to the one in power. . . .[32]

The Prince's opinions were stated to Gladstone, who quite agreed, and pointed out the country's need for the old system of two parties, distinct and firmly organised. Yet it was, of course, precisely Gladstone and his Peelite friends who, in their perpetual wavering between the two sides of the House, made every incoming premier's task so difficult.

In February 1855, they showed their inextinguishable and aggressive party consciousness by demanding that half the posts in the new administration should be theirs. Jealous and irritated, the Whig-Liberals exerted counter-pressure on the premier.[33]   No wonder that he was 'distracted,' or that Gladstone complained of the new coalition ministry, as even more 'acephalous' than the old.[34]

But relief came soon in unexpected form.   Hardly had the Peelite triumvirs, Gladstone, Graham and Herbert, settled back into office under Palmerston, than they did him the great favour of deserting him.[35]   Once again it was Roebuck, that invincible invalid, who brought an unpleasant situation to a head.   The new ministers, Peelites and Whig-Liberals alike, had hoped that he would be content in having helped to give the country a new premier and a new secretary at War. Pending improvements, he might relinquish his demand that a committee of inquiry should be set up and set to work. Palmerston did his level best to persuade the House into giving the new ministry a chance.   Fearing that mere argument against the encroachment of the legislature upon the functions of the executive would not suffice, he tried the effect of humour on the discontented liberals.   Would they not take him for their leader, for their Richard II, in place of the Wat Tyler (Mr. Roebuck) who was leading them against the Crown ?   They would do nothing of the sort. The House was out of hand, and the popular clamour for investigation serious.   Either Wat Tyler would have his moment of triumph, or a new ministerial crisis would ensue. Palmerston chose the more sensible and patriotic alternative of allowing Roebuck a bloodless and a barren victory.   Not so the Peelite triumvirate.   Impelled by loyalty to Newcastle and to Aberdeen, by constitutional scruples, by dissatisfaction with their position in the cabinet, and perhaps, as Palmerston suspected, by a 'secret aversion to the war,' they resigned in protest against the surrender of the ministry. Palmerston was again in luck.   The defection of the Peelite leaders, condemned on every side, left him with a ministry that was homogeneous and intensely popular.   It took away that curb which the Queen had helped to place on him ; and it opened the way to a reconciliation with Russell.

Palmerston's handling of Russell at this juncture was quite worthy of his diplomatic skill.[36]   Scarcely had he taken office as prime minister when he sent Lord John to Vienna to discuss peace terms with the Russians.   True, Clarendon suggested this, but in any case it was a master stroke.   It removed Lord John from parliament while the ministry was getting on its feet ;   it greatly pleased his followers ;   and it gave what seemed to the public, both in England and abroad, a guarantee of Palmerston's desire for peace.   The dowager Lady Dufferin, attending one of Lady Palmerston's receptions on an evening when Russell's acceptance was in doubt, found ' all England sitting with its hair on end and its mouths open waiting for events.'[37]   Before ' all England ' sought its homes a telegram from Russell had dispersed much of ' the thick yellow fog ' which obscured the political atmosphere.   The air was further cleared when Russell's chief enemies of the moment, the Peelites, resigned.   For Lord John, mollified, humbled, and possibly contrite, consented not only to accept the Colonial Office but actually to occupy only the second place on the ministerial bench.   This, as the premier wrote gleefully, would ' beyond   measure   strengthen   the   government.'[38]   Of course, Palmerston's difficulties in forming a satisfactory government were by no means at an end.   Witness the explanation given by his son-in-law, Shaftesbury, of the withdrawal of Palmerston's offer to Shaftesbury of the chancellorship of the Duchy of Lancaster :

Lord Lansdowne took the lead against me, stimulated, in part, by many of the Whig party, who wanted the place for a Whig . . . Palmerston was terrified, and gave way.   I do not blame him. . . . He had to get the machine of Government into motion, and he was anxious for anything that might grease the wheels.   He yielded, therefore, for a Whig.   When Lord L. had brought him thus far, he waited a bit, and then asked for Carlisle.   Palmerston protested against such an appointment as ridiculous, useless, enfeebling ; but, as usual, he gave way, and Brookes' prevailed . . . I much doubt whether he has, since he became Premier, been able to do any one thing according to his own judgment and preference. . . .[39]

Yet the prospect for the future had brightened more, probably, than anyone at the time perceived.   The eclipse of the Peelites as a party was to prove permanent. Already lesser members of the group had broken away from the great leaders to remain with Palmerston.[40] The reversion to a two-party system, desirable alike for the country and for its first minister, had, though almost imperceptibly, begun.

Palmerston as prime minister was so arresting a figure that diarists, letter-writers, and journalists delighted to portray him. In fact, delight in authorship led Disraeli to paint a portrait so false in general effect that it deserves preservation mainly as presenting the opposite of the truth :

. . . Palmerston . . . is really an impostor, utterly exhausted, and at the best only ginger-beer, and not champagne, and now an old painted pantaloon, very deaf, very blind, and with false teeth, which would fall out of his mouth when speaking, if he did not hesitate and halt so in his talk. . . .[41]

For full value this delineation must be displayed in proximity to a picture of one of the little breakfast parties at which the premier entertained such men as could give information which he needed. William Howard Russell, the great *Times* correspondent, who on at least one occasion was the principal guest, records that his host ' rather bounded than walked ' into the room, explaining that he had not invited Delane because Delane was not an early riser.[42] Russell was subjected to a severe grilling, and treated to an astonishing display of knowledge concerning the army, before he left. After breakfast, in case there was no morning session, the premier conducted ' business ' until three, dined at half-past, and left for the House (sometimes if not customarily on horseback) at a little after four.[43] How he appeared in parliament may be judged from the probably partial but lively account of the door-keeper, William White, who happened also to be a journalist :

Those strangers who cannot get into the House, and who wish to see the Noble Lord, should place themselves in the lobby. About five o'clock any day, when the House sits, he may be seen crossing from the members' staircase to the House ; but the strangers must keep a sharp look out, or he will be gone before they catch a glimpse

of him—for the grass never grows near the feet of the Noble Lord—
he always moves at a quick pace. When he arrives at the door, his
messenger, waiting there, hands him his despatch-box ; he then
swings through the door, and passing along the left division-lobby
enters the House at the back of the Speaker's chair, and takes his seat
about the middle of the Treasury Bench ; and there he sits with
his hat on, his face in deep shadow, looking as though he were fast
asleep through the whole sitting, excepting for about half an hour,
when he adjourns to the refreshment rooms, or when he rises to
address the House. But, as the proverb says, ' Catch a weasel
asleep ' ; the Hon. Member who may fancy that the Noble Lord
is napping, and takes the opportunity to say something smart touching
his Lordship, will certainly very soon discover his mistake. We
believe the Noble Lord seldom sleeps in the House, and when he does
he sleeps as the cats are said to do when they watch at a mouse-hole.[44]

Still more vivid was another passage in White's pen-
portrait :

> Lord Palmerston is, we should say, about five feet ten inches in
> height, looks about fifty-five years old—not more, albeit he is turned
> seventy—walks upright as a dart, and steps out like a soldier. He
> always, in the House, wears a surtout coat, buttoned up close, dark
> trousers, and black necktie. His Lordship does not affect preciseness
> or fashion in dress, like his opponent Disraeli, or his colleague
> Mr. Vernon Smith. We have seen Cabinet Ministers frequently
> in full dress on the Treasury Bench, but Palmerston never. Indeed,
> from the opening of Parliament to the prorogation, he seems to us to
> eschew all pleasure, sticking to the House as a diligent tradesman
> sticks to his shop. Further, after the day's labour, even though the
> House sat far into the morning, we have heard that he generally
> walks home. We passed him ourselves one morning, in broad daylight,
> last session in Parliament Street ; he was chatting away as briskly as
> if he had freshly risen from his bed ; and yet that day there had been
> a morning sitting, and he was in his seat soon after one p.m., and then
> it was past two a.m.

There is plenty of real evidence concerning his vitality.
Sir George Grey, the home secretary, broke down under the
burden of adding Russell's duties as colonial secretary to
his own while Lord John was at Vienna ; but Palmerston
added the direction of the Colonial Office to his other
cares, and kept its business entirely up to date, without
apparent detriment to his health.[45] When an opportunity

for the curtailment of his hours of labour came, he would
have none of it.[46] In February 1856, a resolution was
offered for the regular adjournment of the House of Commons at midnight. An enterprising member claimed to
have counted twenty-six other members, including the
premier and three ministers, in peaceful slumber at an early
morning hour. He drove home his point with a parody
of Cowper :

> Sweet sleeps the Chairman in the chair,
> Sweet the tired members on the bench behind
> And sweet the clerks below.

The prime minister was on his feet :

> Sir, I should be the first person to do ample justice to the benevo-
> lent intentions of my hon. Friends who have proposed and seconded
> this motion. To exempt Ministers from the effects of old age—to
> guard them against the gout—these are undoubtedly very great
> temptations held out to us to accede to the proposition of my hon.
> Friends. But, nevertheless, I feel that it would not be consistent
> with our duty as servants of the Crown, charged with the business of
> this country, to agree to their proposal.

Nor would he hear of the limitation of debate in that ' great
and important machine for legislation . . . assembled to
deliberate on great interests.'[47]

He had good need to keep long hours and remain on the
alert ; for his power was menaced from all sides, and constantly. No doubt Bright voiced a sentiment common to
others than his group in telling the House that he preferred
to see Palmerston and Russell, as the two men most responsible for the war, held responsible for its further
prosecution and its close.[48] But what general support the
premier might expect from the Manchesterites was shown
in Cobden's vituperative words :

> Could any people not in its dotage look to such a quarter for a
> saviour ? However, it is a consolation that we shall soon see the
> bursting of that bubble which the Cockney clacquers have been so
> industriously blowing for the last few years.[49]

Nor, it may be judged, was the cabinet too popular in
certain other ' radical ' circles. The ' outcry against aristo-

cratic Government,' which was a feature of the time, produced a significant piece of doggerel :

> Cease ye rude and boisterous railers
> Do not dare our crew contemn
> Manned with such patrician sailors
> Our good ship the tide must stem.
> A jaunty Viscount is our skipper,
> A Duke and Marquis are her mates
> Three Earls do serve on board the clipper
> Four Sirs and all of them first-rates,
> Two Barons and another Viscount
> Duke Bedford's brother and therewith
> One single commoner can I count
> The lord-like looking Mr. Smith.[50]

Where then was the premier's real support? Not in the
departed Peelites most assuredly, nor in the Conservatives;
though both groups would be at least as forbearing as Bright
until the war should end.   There remained the Whigs and
Liberals, merging groups, the former distinguished by surviving reverence for ducal houses and adherence to the
institutions of 1832.   But even they were not entirely
dependable.   For one thing they included too many Right
Honourable or would-be Right Honourable gentlemen, such
as A. H. Layard, archæologist and diplomat, who considered the War Office his speciality, found it full, and soon
discovered some amazing shortcomings in the government
and its head.[51]   Gladstone, as the candid friend, had been
quite right.   The prime minister, in securing majorities,
would have to be a fisher of men.   ' I am told,' wrote Lord
Lonsdale, ' that the House of Commons is becoming more
unmanageable at every session, that no division can be
calculated upon, that so many of the town members owe no
allegiance and vote for popularity.' [52]   But surely, if popularity was to be the basis, the *civis Romanus* could hope for
some success.

Especially justified seemed this hope in view of the
fact that the premier's first and outstanding duty was to
bring about a more vigorous and efficient prosecution of
the war.   No one could deny his exceptional qualifications
for the task : his long training at the War Office and as

foreign secretary ; his capacity for methodical and incessant work ; his dislike of half measures and red tape ; and the courage, pride and optimism which impelled him to meet a threat with defiance, a reverse with a shrug.   To the less hardy he seemed reckless.   Herbert, for example, complained that ' he always wishes to play double or quits.' [53] But an alarmed public and a discouraged army were none the worse for observing how lightly the most responsible servant of the Crown could bear the burden of the war at the age of seventy-one.   It was a great responsibility and as great an opportunity.   The effects of military reforms instituted by the coalition ministry, though becoming perceptible in the Crimea,[54] were as yet invisible in England ; and *The Times* had recently ' opened fire ' on the commander of the expeditionary force, Lord Raglan, and on the general staff.   So much was wrong that it seemed as though the surging energy of the prime minister could find outlet in relation to every line of activity involved in the prosecution of the war.

On the other hand, it would be impossible to understand Palmerston's position, or to estimate the credit which properly accrued to him, without remembering that, individually, he possessed no actual authority.   In relation to all lines of military activity he could, if he so chose, exert considerable influence: in relation to none could he do more. Hence the extent to which his influence could fruitfully be brought to bear depended largely upon both the ability and the amenability of other persons ; in particular of Raglan, and of Lord Panmure, the secretary of state for War. Unfortunately for Palmerston, neither was, with respect to his particular position, too greatly endowed with either quality.   The weight of testimony seems conclusive that Raglan, for all his popular reputation and prominent career, lacked the energy requisite for the performance of his task.[55] Nor was he, as the premier pointed out, ' much of a hand at forming opinions or inventing plans.' [56]   Equally noticeable was the fact that he gave way most gracefully to the French, but stubbornly resisted his own government.   Panmure, though certainly not without experience and ability, was pronounced by Lewis, his colleague in the cabinet, ' one of

the dullest men he ever knew . . . as bad as possible as
Minister of War—prejudiced, slow and *routinier*.'[57]   He was
considered quite capable of having issued the general order
that ' the men of the working parties in the Crimea should
be stripped and put beneath blankets on their return.'[58]
And as for obstinacy !   Granville, contemptuous of this
' Scotch divinity,' pointed out that he alone of all the members
of the cabinet could ' defy the Prime Minister, all his
colleagues, excepting perhaps Charles Wood, and the Court
itself.'[59]   When Panmure, his head apparently turned by his
temporary importance, announced an increase of pay for
the expeditionary troops before consultation with the
cabinet, Palmerston was not sparing in reproof ; but Panmure's resignation would have proved so dangerous that the
premier went to the limits of conciliation to keep him.[60]
Hence Palmerston set about to save his country under a
decided handicap.   Raglan he had of course inherited from
the preceding ministry.   Panmure was apparently the
premier's own choice; but the fact that he was one of the
' Scottish Whigs ' who hung about Russell, and the contemptuous references to ' Whig placemen ' in the War Office
which circulated at the time suggest that the choice had
not been an unfettered one.[61]

The ideals of clean-cut organisation, speed, and practical efficiency which Palmerston set for himself and others in
the prosecution of the war carry one back immediately to
his own War Office days.   From the first week of his
advent to power the reorganisation of the administrative
departments in charge of military affairs, which had proceeded slowly under Aberdeen, was pushed forward with
despatch.[62]   In fact, when the cabinet was formed, the post
of secretary at War was left unfilled, so that the duties of
the office could be at once assigned to the new secretary of
state for War.   On a decision reached at the first meeting
of the cabinet, so it is said, the sacred Ordnance Department,
which claimed the great Burghley for its progenitor,
Wellington for one of its greatest protagonists, and Raglan
for its existing champion and head, was subjected to the
authority of the new secretary.   Changes in personnel were
made as determinedly ; and the Army Medical Board,

criticised but left undisturbed for many months, soon found itself under a new head. But the measures to which the prime minister gave himself heart and soul were those which promised immediate and practical benefits to the combatant troops. A letter to Panmure shows his attitude:

> It is also very likely that some regiments are encamped or hutted upon ground known to be unhealthy, and, if so, they ought to be removed without listening to the ' military considerations ' which officers commanding brigades or divisions may urge. The most important military consideration is to keep soldiers alive and in good health.[63]

That solicitude for the troops was an impelling motive from the first, a cabinet memorandum, written in Palmerston's own hand just six days after he took office, proves.[64] Some of the suggestions for reforms which it contained seem to have originated with a certain Dr. Gavin, and to have reached Palmerston through Shaftesbury; [65] but at least the premier won the credit of adopting them immediately, and of putting them into operation with all speed. They were very imposing in their comprehensiveness : the formation of a marine transport corps (communicating daily with the War Office) to deliver supplies to Raglan's army at the base, and of an improved land transport corps to rush them to the front : the employment of a band of Turkish scavengers to clean the camps : the sending of one special commission to supervise sanitation in the camps and hospitals, and of another to inquire into and regulate the workings of the commissariat : finally, the appointment of a chief of staff (an innovation in itself) who should investigate Raglan's staff officers and suggest such supersessions as might seem desirable.

Most of these improvements were carried through successfully, with Palmerston always prodigal of advice, assistance or reproof.[66] He could write in a most peremptory tone, as in directing Raglan to act ' in the most peremptory manner ' against those who resisted the reforms. He could tell a pompous colonel of militia in the House that ' his influence in his own circle at home might be attended with greater advantage to the nation ' than his service in the field.

Sometimes, as in the selection of sanitary commissioners, he performed notable service. Sometimes his well-intentioned interventions must have seemed superfluous, if not ridiculous, to the dry and practical Panmure. At one moment he was suggesting how fresh beef and mutton might be procured; at another, urging that the issue of beer and wine instead of spirits might save the troops from 'fevers' and a 'bad habit of body.' As the weather turned warm he advocated the issue of peaked forage caps, of white parasols for the officers, and of 'gypsy' tents to serve as awnings in the trenches. When the cholera grew more menacing he pressed Panmure to investigate the 'sulphuric acid' method of treatment, and insisted upon tent-to-tent visitations twice a day. All this was done in private letters to his ministers, unknown to the public or to parliament.

But there were times when Palmerston found his driving energy and insistence on results at any price checked by the firmness, or obstinacy as one may prefer, of Raglan and Panmure.[67] In Palmerston's view (a view which history only to a moderate extent sustains) Raglan's quartermaster-general, his adjutant-general and, in particular, Filder, his commissary-general, were all 'unfit for their respective situations' and due for summary removal from their posts. Raglan, he admitted, might object; but Raglan was 'a creature of habit,' without sufficient energy to make the necessary changes if left to himself. It proved that Raglan had sufficient energy to resist the changes advocated by the premier; and Panmure took his side. Moreover, the two found an ally in General Simpson, appointed as the first chief of staff. The nature of Simpson's duties had called for an officer exceptionally energetic, courageous and alert. Instead, contemporary estimates show 'an elderly gentlewoman' or 'a sensible old man,' reputed to walk twenty miles a day to keep off the gout. Sensible or not, he had no fault to find with Raglan's staff, not even with the commissary general. In vain the premier pleaded the demands of public opinion and the impossibility of defending Raglan's staff officers in the House. In vain he insisted that he could not leave the troops to the mercies of Filder, 'that most respectable incapacity, whom you are determined to keep on in a situation for which he is wholly unfit.' Not until after Raglan's death was the ' respectable incapacity ' recalled.

By early summer the troops in the Crimea were reasonably healthy, comfortable and content ; but their numbers were too small. For this Palmerston's optimism was apparently in part to blame. In December, he had defended the coalition ministry against a charge of failure to provide reserves by an empty boast that the ' reserve upon which Her Majesty's Government had counted was the British nation.'[68] Two months later, as premier, he had declined to use any recruiting measures more forceful than an increase of bounty. ' The militia,' he found, ' had had its ranks filled by voluntary enlistment to a most satisfactory degree.'[69] But, in fact, there never were enough recruits —not nearly enough. Lack of men as well as of ships made offensive operations in the Baltic an impossibility,[70] and the chances of an early victory in the Crimea very slim. By June, Palmerston was thoroughly alive to his mistake. The boaster and the optimist now showed himself a practical statesman, determined at any cost to meet a threatening emergency. The minister who had always been intolerant even of the use of words of foreign origin was now ready enough to use the troops of foreign governments in the sacred British army :

We are forty thousand men short of the number voted by Parliament, and we shall be without the shadow of an excuse if we do not resort to every possible means and every possible quarter to complete our force to the number which Parliament has authorised ; let us get as many Germans and Swiss as we can, let us get men from Halifax, let us enlist Italians, and let us forthwith increase our bounty at home without raising the standard. Do not let departmental, or official or professional prejudices and habits stand in our way ; we must override all such obstacles and difficulties. The only answer to give to objections on such grounds is, the thing *must* be done. We *must* have troops.[71]

Little did he realise that the attempt to ' override all such obstacles and difficulties ' would shortly threaten to involve his country in a new conflict. It was enough that the fortunes of war in the Crimea soon commenced to turn.

From the intense absorption of the ministry in the prosecution of the war one scarcely would have guessed that peace negotiations were proceeding at Vienna from March to June.   But, indeed, these negotiations were as half-hearted and unpromising as peace negotiations could well be.   From first to last the prime mover was Austria, that mother of troubles for nineteenth-century Europe. The part she played was hesitating and cautious.   Desire to play a leading part in European politics, and to increase her influence in the Balkans at Russia's expense, impelled her to make common cause with the allies.   Poverty, the fear of insurrections in Hungary and Italy, and dread of that which might ensue were Russia and Prussia to become her declared enemies, all held her back.   The policy which emerged was that of using armed neutrality to influence the terms of peace between the combatants; in other words, to make them pull her chestnuts from the fire.   The British and French governments, which long believed that she would join them in the field through mere self-interest, had reached an understanding with her concerning the ' Four Points ' on which the peace treaty should be based, during the summer of 1854.   The Powers, instead of Russia, should exercise protection over the Roumanian principalities, Serbia and the Christian subjects of Turkey ; navigation of the mouths of the Danube should be free ; and treaty arrangements which gave the Russians preponderance in the Black Sea should be cancelled.   Needless to say, the last-named provision, distinguished as Point III, was the one which England was most eager to obtain and Russia most reluctant to concede.

As the autumn of 1854 advanced, and the western armies suffered greater and greater discouragement and misery, the British and French governments had grown increasingly insistent that Austria should join them in the war.   Austria, plausibly enough, declared that she must first despatch an ultimatum summoning Russia to negotiate on the Four Points.   Francis Joseph, it was understood, would regard a Russian refusal as a *casus belli*.   Distrustful as they were of Austria's designs, the French and British governments dared not incur the risk of re-cementing the

'Holy Alliance' Powers, and exposing themselves to accusations of having neglected an opportunity to make peace. Their bargain with the Austrians was recorded in a treaty concluded at the beginning of December 1854.

Palmerston had no heart in the affair. He, even more than most of the coalition ministers, had consented reluctantly to the bargain with the Austrians. How could one negotiate a satisfactory peace 'in the middle of a battle upon the issue of which the conditions of peace must depend'? [72] And he was more than suspicious that both the Austrian and Russian governments would use the projected negotiations to postpone Austria's active participation in the war. It would be well, he suggested, to find out in advance whether the allies were agreed with Austria as to actual peace terms. [73] The suggestion was a good one ; since points, principles and bases are very different things from terms. In particular, the interpretation of Point III could be developed in half a dozen ways, from the Russian suggestion of opening the Straits to the ships of all nations alike, to the British plan of neutralising the Black Sea, or at least reducing the Russian naval forces there almost to vanishing point. Clarendon, who apparently thought he had bound the Austrians to support the allied terms or fight, was later to find out his mistake. [74] When Palmerston became prime minister the conference had been arranged, and England was, as he said ruefully, ' bound in honour to go into it *bona fide*, come of it what may.' [75] The matter for his immediate decision was the rejection or acceptance of Clarendon's nomination of Russell as negotiator. Acceptance, as has been shown, was almost a political necessity, and was apparently given as such. For the premier was uneasy about Lord John's ' habit of acting upon sudden impulse,' ' his aptitude to be swayed by others.' [76]

By the time the conference assembled, on March 15, Palmerston found his scepticism already justified. It was clear, as he wrote Russell on that very day, that Austria would press on Russia no conditions which Russia would refuse, and that Russia, still holding Sebastopol, would have peace only on her own terms. [77] Within a week it was equally plain that the French negotiators were taking no firm stand, and, worst of all, that Russell was proving as impulsive and impressionable as Palmerston had foretold.[78] On March 20, he suggested that England concur with France and Austria in requiring only that Russia should not *increase* her naval forces in the Euxine—concur, in other words, in perpetuating and legalising just what England was fighting to destroy.   His suggestion being disapproved, Russell characteristically threatened to resign.   But Palmerston, foreseeing fresh trouble in the House, played upon his envoy's vanity.   ' As to giving away the seals that would be giving away the apple of our eye,' he wrote.[79]

In the midst of all the ' devilries ' at Vienna, as the disgusted Clarendon called them,[80] Palmerston reverted to his old practice of using the House of Commons as a tribune from which to distribute threats and blandishments among the Powers.   To Vienna he repeated the fortifying assurance that he considered the Austrian empire, including Hungary in particular, ' as an aggregate body in the centre of Europe, to be an essential element in the balance of power of Europe ' ;[81] to Prussia and the German states he delivered a message more suggestive still :

I have no hesitation in stating my own opinion that the kingdom of Poland, as at present constituted, and at present occupied, is a standing menace to Germany.   It is for the Powers of Germany to determine . . . whether under circumstances which may lead them into war with Russia, they will think it for their interests to endeavour to change that position of affairs.

Russia and the dreaming Napoleon were not forgotten:

. . . no stipulations in regard to a new arrangement of Poland form part of those points upon which Her Majesty's Government are now, in concert with the Government of France, negotiating in Vienna . . . but the two Powers have reserved to themselves the right, . . . of adding in the future to these Four Points any other stipulations which they may think essential for the future security of Europe.

Fruitless words, of course, they were ; but the prime minister felt safe in relieving his pent-up feelings.   His cabinet was behind him, and so, apparently, was his friend Napoleon. The French emperor not only ordered his envoys to demand that the Euxine should be neutralised, but sent his foreign

Rischgitz

LORD JOHN RUSSELL

secretary, Drouyn de Lhuys, to Vienna to ' stiffen ' their resistance to Russia and Austria. Drouyn, visiting England on his way, signed an agreement that, unless either neutralisation or the strict limitation of Russian naval forces in the Black Sea were agreed upon, negotiations should be broken off.[82] Such an outcome Palmerston could regard with perfect equanimity.

But he was to receive a new lesson in the reliability of French diplomatists. Just as he was congratulating himself that by Anglo-French co-operation ' the treacherous game of Austria and Russia ' would be exposed ; just as Lord Cowley, the British ambassador at Paris, was writing that Drouyn hoped to ' shame the Austrian Government into active co-operation with the Allies,' [83] it became apparent that shaming or exposing Austria was the last thing that Drouyn had in mind. Whether, as has been asserted, he definitely disliked the English alliance and was fatuous enough to hope for a combination between France, Austria, and the German states which would keep England in her proper place ; or whether he merely succumbed to agile diplomacy, he and Russell were soon adopting an Austrian solution of the Black Sea question which was a mere variant of that with which Lord John had shocked his government a month before.[84] Even yet, however, the British cabinet had a trump card, and the premier was using it with marked success.

France, after all, held firm. For Napoleon could always control French foreign policy ; and the British government was able to bribe him effectively. The Emperor, who, as a parvenu among sovereigns, had longed for the cachet which he would acquire by his reception at a first-rate European court, was received at mid-April as an honoured guest by Queen Victoria. The visit gave great satisfaction to Lady Palmerston in more respects than one :

How curious it is to remember all the resentment the Q. showed to P. only for advocating the French Alliance at the time of the Emperor's accession—and now he is the only Friend we have now [*sic*] to depend upon ; however, she is very friendly and courteous now to P. as in olden times and he is to stay at Windsor all the time the Emperor remains.[85]

The visit to England of ' the only friend ' quite justified the
rosiest hopes.[86]   The meeting of the two sovereigns not only
created between them a real, if somewhat ephemeral, friendship, but fortified the Emperor in his belief that he would
be wise to keep British support in his foreign policy.   The
English mobs who cheered the ally of the moment, as all
mobs will, were helping to confound the diplomatists in
session at the Austrian capital.   For Napoleon, impressed
and flattered, was held, though none too easily, to the English
side.   On April 21, before he had returned to France, the
Congress at Vienna had adjourned without definite result.
Three days later Drouyn was informed that his adoption
of the Austrian project was disapproved.[87]   There were
anxious moments yet.   It required Palmerston's thrice
repeated ' entreaties ' to keep Russell in the ministry ; [88]
and not only his efforts but those of Cowley to hold the
Emperor, after his return to Paris, steady in the faith.[89]
But, before the summer came, France was committed to a
continuance of the war, and Austria to a further extension
of her neutrality.

   Having stimulated, sustained and directed the generals
and diplomats in the Crimea and in the Vienna conference
with something more than reasonable success, the premier
had personally to fight the war in parliament.   During
May, June and July, attacks came thick and fast.   Tories
and radicals alike abused the government, now for failing
to make peace, now for ambiguities in utterance and in
policy which the cabinet could not, without hopelessly
alienating France and Austria, explain.   At one time a
coalition of Conservatives, malcontent liberals and radicals,
appeared to threaten the government's very life ; and once
Palmerston escaped defeat by the uncomfortably narrow
margin of three votes.   But the prime minister well knew
how to rally at need both those who thought first of England's
glory and those whose affections turned first, perhaps, to
ledgers and securities :

   I say that the intention of Russia to partition Turkey is as manifest
as the sun at noonday, and it is to prevent that we are carrying on
the war.   The object of the war, . . . is not only to protect Turkey
—to protect the weak against the strong, and right against wrong—

but to avert injury and danger from ourselves. Let no man imagine that if Russia gets possession of Turkey, and if that gigantic Power, like a Colossus, has one foot upon the Baltic and another upon the Mediterranean, the great interests of this country will not be perilled— let not the peace-at-all-price imagine for a moment that their trade and their commerce would not be deeply injured . . . trade would . . . soon disappear, were the Mediterranean and the Baltic under the sole command of a Russian naval force, and that Power exercising a dominant control over Germany.[90]

Ultimately, out of these debates some bad and some good emerged. Russell, once again as warlike in utterance as the best, was driven from office under a torrent of condemnation, when the Austrians exposed his inconsistencies.[91] But, if the departure of Russell was to be counted for a loss, the attitude of the Peelites brought to the ministry compensatory gains. For they, and Gladstone in particular, now attacked the government bitterly for failing to make peace at almost any price. Thus, as Prince Albert mournfully observed, they not only diminished still further what influence remained to them, but made the reconstitution of the old Conservative party more than ever impossible. In England, as in the Crimea and Vienna, the prime minister had made headway.

CHAPTER XXV

1855–1856

WITHOUT delay Palmerston had established himself as a great ' war ' prime minister ; but making war is not a normal activity with Englishmen, and the premier's hardest tests were yet to come. What attitude would he and his aristocratic cabinet take on everyday affairs ? Would they understand and meet the demands of a country in which the influence of prosperous business men was becoming every day of more and more account ? And how far would they go to satisfy the ill-defined but increasingly influential groups of those holding ' advanced ' views ? There were ' political ' radicals, intent on the passage of some extensive measure of parliamentary reform, and even on the introduction of the dreaded ballot ; there were ' economic ' radicals of the Manchester school, not only extreme free-traders but rigid non-interventionists, anti-militarists and tax reformers ; and finally there were the ' religious ' radicals, resentful of all the special advantages enjoyed by the established church. What particularly irked them was the obligation laid upon non-members of the church to assist in financing both its services and its ' fabric,' *i.e.* its churches and churchyards. Two or all three kinds of radical were often to be found in the same man ; but the government had to encounter three separate categories of demands. And again, how would the ministry conduct itself when it came to making peace ? Here again the premier, to whom, personally and politically, public opinion meant so much, had reason to beware. Pacifism, and perhaps business interests as well, would create pressure for an early and easy settlement : national pride and desire for recompense, to say nothing of jingoism, would bring demands for a harsh peace, even though purchasable only

through continued war. Nor would settlement with
Russia leave the Foreign Office with a clean slate. Several
difficult problems were evolving overseas—in particular, a
dispute with the United States. And neither in domestic
nor in foreign affairs could the ministry afford to make
serious mistakes. ' In no period of our history,' wrote
Clarendon about this time, ' has party warfare been carried
on with the same recklessness of consequences ; men like
Disraeli, Roebuck, Bright and Layard . . . are banded
together for the sole object of mischief.'¹ The cabinet's
strength was to be thoroughly tested within the two ensuing
years.

Even during the parliamentary session of 1855 it was
possible to see that Palmerston's attitude toward domestic
questions was to be that conveniently designated as ' liberal
conservatism.' The old institutions—church, throne, and
hereditary aristocracy, were obviously dear to him still.
A bill was introduced to abolish the compulsory levy of
church rates. No one, as his son-in-law, Shaftesbury,
lamented at this time, could call the premier a devoted
churchman :

He does not know, in theology, Moses from Sydney Smith. The
Vicar of Romsey, where he goes to church, is the only clergyman
he ever spoke to, . . . Why it was only a short time ago that he
heard, for the first time, of the grand heresy of the Puseyites and
Tractarians !²

Yet he was outspoken in his defence of a compulsory levy
for the maintenance of the ' fabric.'³ The system of pro-
motion in the army by the purchase of military commissions
was attacked. Palmerston, whom the Queen regarded as
the most troublesome of all her ministers, was quick to
remind the House that the control of the army was vested in
the sovereign.⁴ A bill was offered for equal division between
the heirs of intestates. The prime minister opposed it as
a defender of ' the hereditary peerage and the constitution.'⁵
As for the introduction of the ballot, it seems impossible
to do justice to his attitude save in his own words :

. . . my objection to the ballot is that . . . publicity or responsibility for public opinion is an essential principle of our representative constitution . . . the right or privilege of election is a

trust confided by law . . . for the benefit of the community at large . . . every person who is invested with a public trust ought to discharge that trust in the face of the whole country. . . . Sir, the majority of the electors would evade the law and give their votes in public ; and it would be only the few who would go sneaking to the poll for the sake of screening themselves, from some personal inconvenience, but who would thereby become objects of obloquy and degradation in the eyes of their fellow-countrymen.[6]

There was something besides conservatism there.

A conservative he was, certainly ; but, as certainly, a liberal conservative. Provided the framework of England's institutions stood, he was willing to make alterations for comfort—for space to move in, for light, for air. Both political expediency and his natural inclination to tolerance moved him to make or consent to alterations readily. He avowed himself prepared to consider a measure for relieving dissenters from the payment of rates applied to the support of Church of England services ; [7] and he used church patronage in a manner to delight even the religious radicals.[8] Each of his early episcopal nominations was ' an insult to the Church ' in Bishop Wilberforce's eyes : but these nominations won him thanks and support in Yorkshire and Lancashire. Early in the session of 1855 he stood shoulder to shoulder with Cobden in supporting a deceased wife's sister bill, on the grounds that the existing ecclesiastical ban on marriage with a deceased wife's sister was set up by parliament, not by the law of God, and that ' *nil prosunt leges sine moribus.*' [9] To administrative reform he was usually friendly, admitting that the purchase and sale of military commissions was entirely wrong in principle,[10] and extending the system of examination for civil servants.[11] In the realm of economic legislation, he showed himself not only alive to the need for a new limited liability act, but ready to threaten parliament in order that the needed relief should not be postponed :

There is . . . a great quantity of small capital locked up, which, if these Bills were passed, might be employed for the benefit of those who possess them, and also for the advantage of the community at large. It is a question of free trade against monopoly. [*Cries of* ' No, no ! '] I don't say it offensively, but that is the real fact. . . . I tell the House that I feel so strongly on this question that I will urge the House to go on day by day, and morning after morning, with these Bills, and if it is attempted to talk the Bills out, and to consume time by long speeches, the country shall at least see with whom the fault rests . . . the consequence may be that we shall have to sit, perhaps, into the month of September.[12]

To handle the House of Commons in such fashion required some assurance on the part of a new premier who lacked a really safe majority.

Yet, as the session progressed, there were evidences that liberal conservatism, backed by successes in the Crimea, was proving acceptable. There were some complaints that the premier was apathetic in the matter of reform, and that his party were ' democrats in opposition but oligarchs in office ' :[13] there were assertions that the cabinet was kept in office only by the continuance of the war, and could not long survive in any case.[14] Disraeli was at first quite scornful about its ' majorities collected God knows how, voting God knows why.'[15] But Palmerston well knew why ; and Disraeli's paper, for all its jokes about the ' Parliamentary grandpapa,' was soon confessing that he was ' a Triton among the minnows.'[16] In meetings of his supporters, designed, as he wrote the Queen, to operate as ' safety valves,'[17] he was already showing some of that skill in the management of his supporters which in later years was to become proverbial. Only the ' peace party,' inspired by the Manchesterites, resisted all his blandishments. Bright especially roused his ire by the use of ' bitter personalities, vehement invective and vituperation, heavy jokes and commonplace pathos ' in parliament.[18] The great free-trader, infuriated at Palmerston's elevation to the premiership, had become if possible more inveterate in his dislike, unrestrained in his abuse, and incorrigible in his misrepresentations than before. This was the time when he spoke of ' the 50,000 Englishmen who had died to make Lord Palmerston Prime Minister.' And Palmerston, to whom such action was ordinarily alien, more and more yielded to the temptation to ˒reciprocate.[19] The invective he might have overlooked : he forgave as great abuse from other men. But Bright's ridicule of, and constant opposition to, his schemes for making England great—those constituted the unpardonable sin. The two men had become enemies for life. On the whole, however, Palmerston was doing well. He was certainly stronger when the session closed. Of course, the credit was by no means all his own. ' In the last days of May and the first ten days of June,' wrote Argyll, ' . . . our capture of Kertch, which opened the gateway into the Sea of Azof, . . . gave new life to us as a Government, in the country and in Parliament.'[20] Not only the Russians but Disraeli had been put to rout.

On the other hand, though he did not realise the fact, he was making no progress whatever with the Court. Clarendon, who as foreign secretary, a friend of Palmerston's, and a person high in favour at Windsor, could speak with great authority, outlined the situation to Granville :

I think they are unfair about Palmerston, and are always ready to let their old rancour against him boil up and boil over, tho' he has done nothing to justify this since he has been in office, and I have given them abundant reasons to be satisfied that he is moderate and amenable. Like everybody else, he requires to be dealt with after his own fashion, and he won't bear to be *brusqué*, or put down by *authority*. They don't bear in mind the total change that has taken place in P.'s position. He has no colleagues to fear or to upset ; he has attained the object of his ambition ; he can't act upon his impulses at the F.O. ; he is more immediately responsible to Parliament than he ever was before, and he is proud of having, as he thinks, overcome the repugnance of the Court. The Queen, therefore, must not persist in thinking him the Palmerston of old. He has put off the old man and has become a babe of grace with his altered position. . . . This evening I got a letter from him which pray show the Queen, as I trust it will convince H.M. that Palmerston is open to reason and is not violently addicted to his own opinion.[21]

For the time being, however, the Court's hostility did not matter much. During the weeks which followed the rising of the House, the Queen and her consort were en-grossed, and for the most part happily engrossed, in matters which involved no friction with the premier. They visited Napoleon, were enchanted with his hospitality, and said hearty *au revoirs* in a blaze of rockets and salutes.[22] Soon afterwards they were rejoicing at Balmoral in news of the fall of Sebastopol, and in the betrothal of the Princess Royal to the heir presumptive to the Prussian throne. There was some dissatisfaction over the failure of the French and British generals to follow up their victory ;[23] and there were anxious consultations over the choice of a new British commander in the field.[24] But neither matter called for, or even allowed, much actual exertion on the part of Court or premier. The truce between them even held when peace negotiations were taken up once more.

The resumption of peace negotiations was being forced upon England ; and, what was more serious, she was in danger of having to accept terms quite unsatisfactory from her point of view. Austria, profiting by the fall of Sebastopol to resume the rôle of mediator, framed a new ultimatum which enlarged on the Four Points by calling for the neutralisation of the Black Sea, a change of frontier in favour of Moldavia, and other possible benefits for the allies. And her move was greatly welcomed by the French government.[25] To have chastised Russia and garnered such military laurels as operations in the Crimea could afford was enough for France. To fight for the attainment of the wider aims which the British had in mind ; to assist, perhaps, in building up British prestige ; and to wound Russia beyond hopes of forgiveness, did not enter into the calculations of her statesmen, still less of her financiers. Napoleon did sometimes talk of continuing the war to achieve aims so wide as to alarm the British ministers— such as the resurrection of Poland.[26] But as usual they were more dreams than aims, and dreams not to be realised when public opinion stood clearly in the way. Hence the Tsar was soon being sounded on peace terms by emissaries both from Vienna and Paris ; and the British government was facing the alternative of letting France and Austria call the tune, or of dragging out all by herself a maritime and probably an inconclusive war.

Once again Palmerston's reputedly fire-eating attitude seems in point of fact to have corresponded with that of most of his colleagues and of the Court.[27] Decidedly, he —and they—would have preferred to give the British army time and opportunity to gather more laurels of its own, and to thrust back, rather than merely to check, the Russian 'colossus' in its advance. Yet, as he had assured Gladstone, he was 'not so destitute of common sense, as not to be able to compare ends with means.' That his hopes of forcing Russia back into more limited confines had been shrinking for some time is shown by a letter sent to Clarendon in September, concerning a treaty (actually concluded two months later by the British, French, and Swedish governments)[28] for the defence of Sweden against Russian encroachments :

> We went to war not so much to keep the Sultan and his Mussulmans in Turkey as to keep the Russians out of Turkey : but we have a strong interest also in keeping the Russians out of Norway and Sweden and if we can do so by ink shed instead of by bloodshed surely it is wise to take the opportunity to do so.[29]

The treaty should serve to deter the Russians not only from attacking the Swedes, but from demanding exchanges of territory :

> The treaty we propose would be a *part of a long line of circumvallation* to confine the future extension of Russia even if the events of the war should not enable us to drive her outposts in at any part of her present circumference. . . .

It would be interesting to know how far the idea and the initiative were the premier's own.

Though Palmerston could no longer hope to drive in Russia's outposts, he was still resolved to hold out against the efforts of other Powers to deprive Great Britain of such advantages as the military situation entitled her to claim. But this resolution involved him in a struggle which in one respect recalls his difficulties in the Belgian question a quarter century before. Once again he had simultaneously to co-operate with, and resist, the French ; once again he was dealing with a French ruler appreciative of a British entente, but divided between the counsels of a pro-English ambassador at London (Persigny) and a very tricky[30] and anti-English foreign minister at Paris (Walewski). True, Clarendon, not Palmerston, ruled at the Foreign Office ; but there were times when even Clarendon had to be opposed.

Time and again, as the negotiations pursued their slow and devious course, the premier lashed out against the opponents of British policy in his familiar style. When Austria and France coolly presented for British endorsement an ultimatum to the Russian government, defining peace terms as arranged between the Tuileries and the Ballplatz,[31] the Queen, after inclining to acceptance, pointed out to Napoleon the British objections to such procedure in friendly though rather cutting terms.[32]   But Palmerston used language which his friend Napoleon did not soon forgive :[33]

La nation anglaise serait enchantée d'une bonne paix qui assurât les objets de la guerre ; mais plutôt que d'être entraînée à signer une paix à des conditions insuffisantes, elle préférerait continuer la guerre sans d'autres alliés que la Turquie. . . .

Clarendon did not like the tone, but confessed himself ' in better humour ' with it as proofs accumulated of Walewski's ' insolence.'[34]   When Walewski stated to Cowley that he was the virtual author of the supposedly Austrian ultimatum, and threatened the withdrawal of the French troops from the Crimea if England did not adopt it as it was,[35] the premier's language became even more that of old times.   Walewski was capable of anything ; but his attempts to ' bully ' could be defeated by ' passive firmness,' and, if need be, by an appeal to public opinion on both sides of the Channel ! As usual, Palmerston's own ' firmness ' rested on confidence, and confidence on calculation :

The French government will not dare to leave us in the lurch or to bring away from the Crimea more men than may well be spared from their force there during the winter.[36]

Nor did Austria by any means escape the premier's wrath. ' Palmerston is very rabid,' wrote Clarendon, in December, when the Ballplatz was amending the British amendments to the peace proposals, ' and his feelings about Austria are so savage that he almost compels me to take her part.'[37] Perhaps Clarendon was a little piqued by the fact that on the day he wrote of Palmerston's rabid attitude, he was

worsted by the premier in cabinet council. Clarendon had
suggested that Turkey should grant autonomous institutions
to the Roumanian principalities ' with the consent of the
guaranteeing Powers.' Palmerston's successful insistence
on the substitution of that phrase ' in concert with the
contracting Powers,' was a matter of some significance.[38]

From mid-December to mid-January, when the time
limit set by the Austrian ultimatum expired, the prime
minister found himself in the familiar and congenial position
of the defender of British honour and British interests
against the wiles and weaknesses of the continental Powers.
Austria, having failed to win British endorsement for a
clause in the ultimatum which was understood as giving her,
in Russia's place, a protectorship over the Roumanian
principalities,[39] haggled over the British supplements to the
ultimatum, and, in spite of all urgings, delayed sending them
to St. Petersburg. That was of course discouraging ; but
Palmerston was apparently far more distressed by a fear
that the French and Austrian governments would make
concessions regarding the ultimatum itself. His numerous
letters during these weeks were like variations on one refrain :

> We must not let Walewsky and Buol drag us into the mire.
> If we hold out the French government must stand by us.[40]

In the end Napoleon held firm ; and the Tsar, influenced
by an appeal from the Prussian king, gave way. An entry
in Henry Reeve's journal shows what happiness and credit
this brought the premier :

> We went in the evening to the French Embassy. The Palmer-
> stons . . . were there. Palmerston in great spirits, and proud of
> the success of the firm and consistent language his Government has
> held. Persigny assured me that it was the energy and prevision of
> the British Cabinet which had mainly, if not solely, brought about
> this result ; for that Walewski and most of the Emperor's advisers
> in Paris would have given in half a dozen times over.[41]

The premier himself characteristically pointed out that
since ' holding out ' had worked so well thus far, no other
policy for the immediate future was thinkable.[42] But it
proved unfortunate that, during these early days of 1856,

he decided to stand out against the United States on ground that was much less tenable.

The heart of the trouble lay in the difference of interpretation placed by the British and American governments upon that clause of the Clayton-Bulwer treaty by which the two countries bound themselves neither to colonise nor exercise dominion over any part of Central America save British Honduras. The American government held that the clause was retroactive in effect ; while the British, rejecting this interpretation, not only held their right of protecting the Mosquito Coast as unabridged, but proceeded, on the basis of alleged prior possession, to claim direct sovereignty over the strategically important ' Bay Islands,' north of Honduras. As both the British interpretation of the treaty and the claim to prior possession of the islands admitted of doubt, American opinion, stimulated by congressional oratory hardly less flamboyant than the accompanying press diatribes, became inflamed. On the other hand, the United States government had not shown itself at all tender of British susceptibilities. It was hard for Englishmen to accept with equanimity the formal adoption of the Monroe Doctrine, Secretary Everett's announced conviction that it was the ' manifest destiny ' of European possessions in America to come ultimately under the control of the United States, or the tacit approval frequently extended by the authorities in Washington to American filibustering of a clearly anti-British sort in Nicaragua and the Mosquito Coast. For some time both governments had been amply occupied elsewhere. But the president and senate of the United States were looking forward to a reckoning with England when the Kansas-Nebraska trouble had quieted down ; while the British government was hoping to enjoy the luxury of more freedom of expression if not of action after the close of the Crimean war.

As events fell out, the Crimean war itself produced a new issue which made restraint on both sides infinitely more difficult. For Palmerston's government, in its determination to ' override all obstacles and difficulties ' in finding troops, attempted to secure them even in the United States. In July 1855, James Buchanan, the

American minister to England, complained of this contravention of American law. And he was still in ignorance of the fact that Crampton, the British minister at Washington, and certain British consuls were personally involved. Clarendon, whose *bête noire* during the Crimean war was his fear of trouble with the Americans, offered soothing assurances ; and for the time being American complaints were stilled. But when, in the autumn and early winter of 1855–1856, it was discovered that Crampton had not only been personally responsible, but had later adopted the disingenuous device of inducing would-be recruits to go to Nova Scotia for enlistment there ; when, too, it was noted that the British fleet on the American station was being strengthened against ' Russian privateers,' the American government lost patience. It demanded that Crampton's activities be publicly disavowed by his recall ; announced its determination to stand its ground in the dispute over Central America ; and made military preparations, not too ostentatious but quite perceptible, for a possible collision.

Palmerston, tied still by the Russian war, and none too sure that British public opinion would be on his side, sputtered and blustered in impotent wrath. To increase his irritation came what seem to have been false reports concerning the *pourparlers* of the Persian-American treaty of the December following.[43] The ' Yankees,' he heard, were to send ships to protect the Persians. What was this but ' impudent intermeddling ' in affairs with which America had no concern ? And of course the intermeddling had had its real origin in St. Petersburg.[44] For Central America he scarcely cared at all. Sceptical of the practicability of canal-building across the Isthmus, he was willing to relinquish the Mosquito Coast to ' one of the neighbouring republics,' or to consent to a joint Anglo-American protectorate. Concerning the Bay Islands, he wrote on January 26 : ' If we wanted to recede with dignity, a reference to arbitration, the verdict of which would probably be given against us whatever the merits of our case, might be the easiest way out.'[45] But in the Crampton affair, where to recede with dignity was difficult, and in which the honour of the country, as he conceived it, was involved, he showed himself not only unyielding but truculent.[46] If Crampton received his passports, so should Buchanan too. After all, the Americans were merely trying to 'frighten the commercial men.' In writing Clarendon he fairly exploded, on January 29:

. . . we will not allow these blackguards to bully us. The course you propose to follow is the right one. Tell Buchanan that we entirely approve Crampton's conduct and that we shall certainly not recall him.

And in dealing with blackguards gentlemen need not be scrupulous :

Bulwer ought to send you Clayton's private and confidential letter in order that it may be placed on record in the Foreign Office and made public if necessary. We need use no delicacy towards such fellows.

Fortunately the premier's record of many years shows that this suggestion may be taken as a measure of his irritation rather than of his character.

It was one thing for Palmerston to pour out his indignation to Clarendon, but it was quite another for him to handle the same question in parliament in such manner as to conciliate all shades of liberal opinion.[47] His first speech on the subject, in early February, expressed nothing so much as gentle consideration and good will in so far as the Americans were concerned. His government, he said quite truly, stood ready to arbitrate on Central American matters at any time. As for the recruiting controversy, orders had in the first place been given by the Aberdeen government that nothing should be done to offend the Americans ; and when Buchanan, in July, had made complaints, the foreign secretary had been able to tell him that, on the mere report of dissatisfaction in America, all further recruiting had already been forbidden. Later complaints from Washington he could not discuss in parliament until investigations had been carried on. He made no reference to Crampton's complicity or to the recently received demand for his recall. But when, a week later, this discreet silence was broken by the indiscreet Mr. Roebuck, the premier's urbanity deserted him.[48]   Roebuck, speaking on the authority of a pamphlet of American origin documented with Crampton's own letters, asked whether the House could believe ' that when we made an apology we were attempting to evade the laws of the United States, which we promised to observe ? '   Palmerston betook himself to the last refuge of public speakers, that of outraged patriotism:

> The hon. and learned Gentleman . . . rising in his place, and holding in his hand the brief of the antagonist of his own country, he makes himself the mouthpiece of calumnies which have been uttered by interested parties in the United States against Her Majesty's officers . . . neither the spirit of party, the vehemence of opposition to any Government, nor any other motive, would induce me to take a part of which I should feel ashamed . . . to call upon Members ignorantly and without information to pronounce a judgment against my country. . . .

The two speeches were not especially statesmanlike ; and, what is worse, they were disingenuous.   In both it was stated that Buchanan had expressed his satisfaction with Clarendon's explanations of July, and his conviction that his government would ' entertain a similar feeling.'   This was Buchanan's comment :

> Had Lord Palmerston . . . been careful to consult accuracy, he would have said :—' When the communication to which I have referred was made to the American Minister in London he expressed the satisfaction he would have in communicating it to his Government ; but having subsequently learned that the British Minister at Washington was implicated in the transaction, he informed Lord Clarendon more than once that he did not know the fact when he expressed this satisfaction.' [49]

Save under the unlikely supposition that Clarendon deceived his premier, the incident gives some justification for Henry Adams' bitter words :

> If Palmerston had an object to gain, he would go down to the House of Commons and betray or misrepresent a foreign Minister, without concern for his victim. . . .[50]

Here, for the time, this somewhat trivial but very revealing episode may be allowed to rest.   It was, in fact, distinctly punctuated by Buchanan's return to the United States, and the arrival of George Dallas to take his place. Palmerston found the new envoy ' a respectable-looking elderly gentleman with a pleasant and rather open countenance very unlike his predecessor in looks.'[51] To Dallas he seemed decidedly friendly, going to some pains to move the Admiralty to make search for a missing American vessel.[52] But he had already advised Panmure to look to the defence of Canada, and expressed a happy confidence that the progress being made at Paris by Clarendon in peace negotiations with Russia would ' lower the political barometer at Washington.'[53] Delay in acting upon the American demand for Crampton's recall could be excused on the ground of Clarendon's absence.[54]

Throughout the six weeks of intricate diplomacy which elapsed between the Russian surrender to Austria's ultimatum and the formal opening of the peace conference, Palmerston was still standing fast. The matter of his particular concern at the moment was the fate of those English peace terms which Austria had failed to present : undertakings on Russia's part to leave the eastern coasts of the Black Sea unfortified and open to commerce, and not to restore certain demolished fortifications of the Aaland Islands from which she had threatened Sweden in pre-war days.[55] It was the clear duty of the French, the premier maintained, to inform the Tsar that they were united with the British in insisting that Russia concede these points before peace preliminaries providing for actual negotiations should be signed, and an armistice arranged.[56] The French, objecting that they were too deeply committed to the Austrian ultimatum to take this step, offered instead their secret promise to treat the English terms as *sine quibus non* to the final signature of peace.[57] But Palmerston saw in this answer only an attempt to ' trap ' England into an unsatisfactory peace ; for who, he argued, could suppose that ' these men ' would ever recommence war once the preliminaries and armistice were in force ?

We stand on the brink of a slope . . . if we allow ourselves to be dragged down at the tail of Walewsky we shall be drawn into the mire at the bottom.[58]

Better to let the French alliance go, and the public judge which country was at fault.　When the Austrian government attempted to put on pressure, the premier sent word informally to Buol that he apparently ' quite forgot whom he was addressing such language to.' [59]　But it was impossible even for Palmerston to stand fast against all Europe, including his own foreign secretary, his cabinet and the Court.　Prince Albert intervened with a long cool memorandum, urging that it was better to trust to French good faith than to risk seeing the Crimean army ' left prisoners in the hands of Russia,' and an almost defenceless England faced by a hostile continental league ' in which no one will doubt America also taking a prominent place.' [60] So felt the cabinet ; but, ' in order to meet the views of Lord Palmerston,' it was decided that France should be urged to inform the Russians of her promise to the British government.[61]　Such reward for steadfastness seems slight indeed ; but it is not certain that the effects of the premier's stoutness can be measured merely by tangible gains.

And now Clarendon set off for Paris, where England had consented that the conference be held, in order that a flattered Napoleon might keep an Anglophil eye on his plenipotentiaries.[62]　Palmerston, for reasons not too difficult to surmise, would have preferred to keep Clarendon at home, and send that breezy sailor-diplomat, Sir Edward Lyons, in his stead.[63]　Being overwhelmingly overruled, he enjoyed the arduous consolation of acting as foreign secretary once more, and instructing his envoys, Clarendon and Cowley, privately as well as officially, at every turn. Just how much Clarendon owed to these instructions it is hard to say.[64]　Since many of them at least were never seen even by the cabinet, only the writer and the recipient could leave trustworthy evidence ; and they, unfortunately, have left too much.　For Palmerston, on the one hand, instructed Clarendon constantly and opposed giving him much discretion ; and, on the other, assured him that he was too skilful to need suggestions from home.　Clarendon wrote contemptuously to Granville of the premier's earlier exhortations, and boasted to Greville that he was able to achieve success by ' taking on himself to disregard any instructions or recommendations from home that he did not approve ' ; yet he more than once acknowledged his chief's letters to be ' of the greatest use and comfort.' These contradictions, the results of vanity, tactfulness and impulsiveness on both sides, make any conclusion well-nigh impossible ; but one of Clarendon's letters to his chief seems to throw genuine light on a related aspect of the relations between the two men :

> I know by long experience that your support may always be relied upon by the agent or the colleague who does his best under difficult circumstances.[65]

And perhaps that was the most important aspect after all.

As the negotiations advanced, it became clear that Palmerston had not parted with his old habits of demanding everything which it seemed within the bounds of possibility to secure, and of using arguments one-sided to the point of absurdity in justifying his claims. Cornewall Lewis (Sir G. C. Lewis), his chancellor of the Exchequer, may have been right in thinking that he often made demands ' with the expectation of being refused,' [66] but he seems rather to have been obsessed with the dread of being ' dragged at the tail of Walewski' or someone else down the ' slope ' of concessions :

> It is very easy to argue in a case of this kind that each separate condition, taking the conditions one by one, is not of sufficient importance to justify a continuance of the war for that particular condition, but such a mode of arguing would lead step by step to an abandonment of every condition essential to future security.[67]

His one-sidedness could scarcely find better illustration than in his disgust at perceiving a similar tendency in the Russian envoy, Orloff.[68] Orloff was ' deeply impregnated with Russian insolence, arrogance and pride. . . . He will stand out for every point which he thinks he has a chance of carrying.' In fact, he was ' like a housebreaker who tries every door and window in succession.' Thus, while the British envoys were to stand out for a promise by Russia not to fortify the Aaland Islands, it took ' Russian impudence ' to suggest that England should give a similar undertaking with respect to Heligoland.

The premier found ample occasion to display his methods during the first two weeks of the conference, when the envoys were discussing the question of Kars,[69] a great stronghold of Asiatic Turkey, which had fallen to the Russian armies in late November. The Russian government naturally wished to use it in barter, and especially in evading a demand which Austria had placed in the ultimatum on her own account : a demand for the cession of part of Bessarabia to the Roumanian principalities. Palmerston, who supported the Austrian demand with enthusiasm, as a means of keeping the Russians away from the Pruth and Danube rivers, and making more difficult the advance of their armies in any future Balkan war, almost outdid himself in arguing his own and the Austrian case. The Russians must and should carry out the terms of the ultimatum point for point, and had no right whatever to bargain over the restoration of Kars. They would be well paid for its surrender in securing peace, and in saving Cronstadt and Georgia from allied attacks. And how could they talk of conquest when the place (after five months' siege !) ' fell into their hands merely by the accident of the garrison not having enough to eat ? ' What was more, considering that the fortifications consisted of earthworks, it was ' therefore to be considered as so much territory occupied and not as a place like Mayence or Cambray or Ehrenbreitstein ' ! But once again he found himself upon the slope of concession. At first the Queen and the cabinet, who may have been spared his arguments, supported his conclusions ; and Clarendon was instructed in that sense.[70] But when the foreign secretary, protesting that he was ' not faint-hearted ' but was walking on a diplomatic mine, declared some abatement of the demand for the cession of Bessarabian territory unavoidable, the premier, ' after a row in the Cabinet,' gave way.[71] One reason may have been that he was now mainly interested in coaching his envoys as to the limitation of Russian naval forces in the soon-to-be-neutralised Black Sea. It was hard for Clarendon to receive in silence such information as that ' the deck [of any vessel] is always from stem to stern much longer than the keel ' ;[72] but his contempt for such tutoring may have been tempered by appreciation of the fact that Palmerston's original suggestion as to the amount of naval force that Russia should be allowed to maintain in the Euxine corresponded surprisingly with that decided upon at the conference.[73]

With respect to the other terms of the Treaty of Paris Palmerston proceeded in easy agreement with his colleagues and envoys,[74] showing himself, as Lewis said, ' moderate and reasonable.' In his humanitarianism he lamented his inability to help his old friends the Circassians, and showed great concern for the Polish refugees who had fought in the Turkish ranks. But he gave Clarendon ' the credit of having obtained very good terms,' considering the military situation and the yielding attitude of the French. His calm acceptance of what from his point of view was an unsatisfactory compromise, brought him praise and blame from quarters from which he had seldom received them. The Queen, while assuring Clarendon that the government's success at Paris and the upholding of England's dignity were due ' to *him* alone,' conferred on her prime minister the first Garter bestowed on a member of the House of Commons since the time of Castlereagh. But the British people who had so firmly trusted him now felt that they had been let down. It was not enough for them that the Four Points had been more than realised ; that Russia had been forced to consent to the neutralisation of the Black Sea, and to return southern Bessarabia to Moldavia. They had expected something more spectacular. Dallas reported that the peace was ' very generally regarded as . . . a botchery and a sham,' [75] and that when the illumination of London in its honour was decreed, the diplomatic corps were in doubt whether they ran more risk of having their windows broken by lighting them or by keeping them dark. Granville noted that the heralds who proclaimed the peace were hissed at Temple Bar.[76]

What the Londoners who hissed the peace or broke diplomatic windows lighted in its honour did not know, was that they would ere long be cheering frantically for developments in Italy which must at least have been long years delayed if the despised deliberations at Paris had

not taken place. They were aware, of course, that the
king of Sardinia had placed his troops beside those of
England and France at a critical juncture, and that the
Sardinian contingent had done some excellent fighting.
They must have known, too, that Sardinian representatives
had played a minor part in the negotiations at Paris. Perhaps
they had even noted that the Austrian delegates had failed
to prevent some discussion of the griefs of Italy, in particular the occupation of part of the central portion by foreign
troops. But of course they could not know that Sardinia's
super-diplomat, Count Cavour, had engineered Sardinia's
participation in both war and peace negotiations in order
to obtain French and British sympathy for his country ;
or that the British premier had not only made a particular
point of his admission to, and good treatment in, the
negotiations at Paris,[77] but was full of plans for helping
him. With respect to later developments, no part of Palmerston's diplomatic activities in the spring of 1856 have
greater interest than his exposition of the nebulous schemes
he and Napoleon were cherishing for a revision of the map
of Italy. Napoleon took the lead.

Napoleon's favourite plan, worthy of Elizabeth Farnese,
and presented to Palmerston some time before the opening
of the Paris conference, was to give the Roumanian
principalities to the duke of Modena, Modena to the duchess
of Parma, and Parma to Sardinia.[78] Palmerston was
attracted. ' As far as England is concerned,' he wrote
Clarendon, ' it would I should say be our honour, interest
and wish to increase the territories of Sardinia in Italy and
the addition of Parma would be a great acquisition.' [79]
But although he presented the Napoleonic scheme to the
Queen as deserving of consideration, and played with it
longingly for a while, he was shrewd enough to see not
only its immediate impracticability but its implications for
the future. Austria, he pointed out, would certainly
object, not merely because she believed herself to have
reversionary rights in the Italian duchies, but ' because the
Moldavian Wallachia [Roumanian] state would look upon
itself as the foundation of a snowball to be enlarged by
additions, some of which would come from the side of

Austria.'[80] Perhaps, then, ' the easiest way of adding to Piemont [*sic*] would be to give the [papal] Legations or part of them to Austria and give Lombardy to Piemont.'[81] Considering that Austria had no wish to part with Lombardy, and that French and Austrian troops were occupying the papal states for the protection of the Pope, it is hard to see how this scheme could be regarded as ' easier ' than the other.

So long as the general peace terms were under discussion the British representatives at Paris could take no step with respect to Italy. For they found Austria's diplomatic co-operation more and more indispensable to England as that of France was gradually withdrawn. But when signatures had been set to the treaty, Palmerston had new solutions for the Italian question to propound.[82] Might it not be possible ' to buy out the Duchess of Parma and her son ' ? But hardly, he thought, answering himself ; for the duchess was ' a highminded though low statured woman,' and would probably not care to sell her child's inheritance, even though ' she must poor woman live in daily dread of the stiletto.' But why not this scheme of glorious possibilities : to marry the duchess to the prince of Carignan (distant cousin to the king of Sardinia), establish the newly-married couple in Greece by the forcible intervention of French and English troops, give Parma to Sardinia, and secure from the Sardinian government an annual allowance for King Otho and his wife ? ' The very idea of such a change,' wrote Palmerston, ' does one's heart good.' Clarendon agreed. ' Your plan about Mr. and Mrs. Otho makes my mouth water, but I fear it is not good for realisation—however it shan't be lost for lack of trying.'[83] Try Clarendon certainly did ; but Napoleon, while professing his high approval of the project, could see no possibility of executing it.[84]

Palmerston, forsaking regretfully these enticing schemes, reverted to a broader solution of the whole Italian question which he had had in mind all along. The main source of trouble in the peninsula, he explained in a despatch to Clarendon, lay in the French and Austrian occupation of the misgoverned Papal States. If the Pope was incapable of governing properly, the Powers should leave him to settle with his own subjects ' in the way in which differences between nations and their sovereigns are usually adjusted, or else do that which nothing but the most extreme case could justify, namely, to interfere forcibly between the parties and to remodel the central part of Italy.' Personally, he stood ready to remodel the whole peninsula :

> I should like to see the Pope reduced to the condition of the Greek patriarch of Constantinople and Romagna made into a republic or the different states of Italy re-arranged so as to form three self-supporting kingdoms, north, middle and south.[85]

Nor had he misgivings for a self-governing Italy :

> To say that the Italians of the present day are just what the Italians have been from the earliest historical periods, and yet that they are incapable of being governed more or less constitutionally is to call history to the witness box and to shut one's ears to its testimony.[86]

The first step in giving the Italians their chance would be to call a conference at London of representatives of the five Powers and Sardinia, for the purpose of setting a definite term to the occupation of the Papal States, and of admonishing the Pope and the king of Naples in the matter of internal government. But the most practical of all the premier's schemes was still impracticable. When Napoleon, in fear of offending the French clericals, declined to endorse any measure more drastic than the joint expression of ' a hope that the occupation of papal territory by foreign troops should cease,' this suggestion, like all its predecessors, fell to the ground.

Disappointed in all hopes of immediate action, the prime minister looked to the future. Thus to Clarendon :

> Buol like all Austrians is fond of *Buollying*, but he must be made to understand that in the next war between Austria & Sardinia, if it is brought about as it will be by the fault of Austria, Sardinia will not be left alone as she was last time.[87]

Clarendon was no doubt too cautious to convey any such threat. But Cavour, who visited England at the end of

April, seems to have carried back with him to France an
astonishing assurance :

> I told Cavour that he might say to the Emperor that for every
> step he might be ready to take in Italian affairs he would probably
> find us ready to take one and a half.[88]

Though Cavour was, of course, far too much the realist to
attach undue importance to a statement so unauthorised
and indiscreet, he must have been delighted to have such
evidence that the premier intended to be faithful to the
rôle he had played so long as foreign secretary.   And, on
the other hand, Italian affairs were now almost sure to
become an issue in British domestic politics.

CHAPTER XXVI

1856–1857

It might, perhaps, seem that the signature of the Treaty of Paris should have constituted a punctuation point in Palmerston's activities in 1856 : but a moment's reflection will show why it did nothing of the sort. Through all the time that Clarendon was in Paris the dispute with the United States was hanging fire, and a rather humdrum session of parliament pursuing its slow course. Nor were the negotiations over peace terms by any means at an end when the treaty was signed. The working out of its terms was to be a long process, involving the same intricate diplomacy which had been necessary for agreement on their general form. This process was, in fact, to occupy the government until another year had dawned, a year bringing new problems as difficult and dangerous : a war with China, a parliamentary crisis great enough to demand an appeal to the electorate, and finally the great Indian mutiny. Seldom, if ever, was Palmerston, in all his busy career, busier than in the months which followed the proclamation of peace at Temple Bar.

The dispute with the United States hung fire while Clarendon was in Paris ; but the foreign secretary, on his return to England, found that in one important respect its aspect was now changed. English public opinion was veering to the American side. George Dallas, who replaced Buchanan in March, noted at once that America's ' well-wishers ' were ' becoming loud and more numerous hourly,'[1] and lost no time in establishing confidential relations with Aberdeen.[2] At a Mansion House dinner, where the new American minister made his initial speech, Edward Cardwell, a rising Peelite, went so far as to say that he ' could almost pledge the Commons of England to

sustain the American Minister in the assertion of his
country's international rights against any ministry whatever.' And 'all the members present stood up as ex-
pressive of their adhesion to his views.'[3] In parliament
the opposition, with Roebuck and Gladstone in great
prominence, used the American issue almost as much as
the peace treaty for an avenue of attack.

For a long time Palmerston, quite confident of peace,[4]
tried to bluff the matter out. He had begun by telling
Dallas that it was for the United States to choose between
peace and war, and to remember that they, not England,
would be 'the greatest sufferer' if war occurred.[5] In his
irritation he had even stiffened his attitude on the Bay
Islands, claiming that their ownership had nothing to do
with the Clayton-Bulwer Treaty, since the treaty related
only to Central America, while the islands lay thirty miles
off the coast![6] When, however, the public and parliamentary opposition grew more formidable, the ministry
temporised. On the one hand, it strengthened the
garrisons in Bermuda and Canada, and invited Dallas (with
suspicious insistence, and quite unavailingly) to attend a
great naval review;[7] on the other, it demanded more time
to consider the evidence in Crampton's case. Dallas was
by turns pessimistic and hopeful. Late in April he was
wondering whether cotton, a 'pretty good bail for the
peaceful behaviour of this country, as a general thing,'
could be relied upon in all 'epochs and circumstances.'[8]
But a fortnight later he saw through the premier's bluff:

> Lord Palmerston just at this moment seems to be in as victorious
> an attitude as any British premier has ever held. He has . . .
> boldly carried the peace through. . . . His majorities are large, and
> his party is full of exultation. Still, there is that thorn of America
> in his side, *haeret lethalis*, and if it do not bring him to the ground,
> it will be because you may come to his relief, or he may suddenly, by
> the indications in France, discover the expediency of greater con-
> ciliation in his relations with us. All men of opinions worth any-
> thing agree in saying (I should not be surprised to hear it from his
> own lips) that a conflict with the United States is the only thing he
> could not stand for six months, or even half that time. His power is
> immense, but that is a rock on which, if he touch, he founders.[9]

The only question was how long Palmerston might hold out.

But Palmerston held out surprisingly long—long enough to destroy for a time Dallas's new-found confidence. His anxiety was revealed by his efforts to avoid debates on Anglo-American relations in the House ;[10] but even when, early in June, news arrived that Crampton had received his passports, the premier was all for returning the compliment. England would be 'dirt-eating' if Dallas did not go home too.[11] Was she to submit to hints at commercial distress on the part of visiting Americans ?

Moreover they resort to the hackneyed formula of saying that I am thought particularly hostile to the United States in order to induce me to do some act of servility in order to disprove the assumed imputation. This is just on the same principle on which a man reproaches a woman with being cold when he sees that her passions are on the point of breaking loose.[12]

Argument was piled on argument. America must and would sell her cotton to England in any event ; and it was only the 'refugee Irishmen' there who wanted war.[13] For a moment Dallas wondered whether he would be 'the last minister from the United States to the British Court.'[14] But the premier's was a losing fight which ended suddenly. 'The dread of a war with the United States' was 'very general' ; 'the two great interests, manufacturing and mercantile,' were 'beginning to bestir themselves to prevent it' ; while 'the Opposition in Parliament took an attitude not to be mistaken.'[15] The cabinet, with the full assent of its head, agreed that British claims to a protectorate of the Mosquito Coast should quietly be given up ;[16] and on June 16 Palmerston announced that he was 'most anxious' to prevent a diplomatic break with the United States.[17] Herbert felt that it was 'most discreditable' to the government to 'take a reversal of a peace and war policy from the House of Commons';[18] but 'the commercial people' were not lightly to be resisted by a Whig-Liberal government. Palmerston, having submitted, was at pains to win them back. When he defended his policy in the House, Gladstone admitted that he scored a great success : ' He not only made the House of Commons drunk, but made them drunk on ginger beer.' [19]

If one were to judge from the letters of the patriotic Dallas, he might suppose that Palmerston came successfully through the session of 1856 merely by wooing the industrial and commercial classes in his conciliation of America. But it is impossible even to glance at the records without realising that middle and even lower class support had been studiously solicited in other ways ; that party discipline had been applied ; and that a cautious policy, well calculated to avoid dangerous conflicts in the House, had been the general rule. A few examples will serve. The *Manchester Times* was delighted with ' the proper appreciation of the merits and position of manufacturers ' shown in the elevation of a mill-owner to the upper House' ;[20] and the 'manufacturers, clothier-workmen, Methodists, and Dissenters ' of the diocese of Ripon, were gratified by the appointment, as bishop, of the very low church Mr. Bickersteth.[21] A subscription list, opened with the object of presenting the troublesome but popular Roebuck with a thousand pounds, was headed by the premier. And who but he reminded the humblest voters that,

> Noble actions may as well be done
> By weaver's issue as by prince's son,

when thanks were offered to the returning troops ?[22] In all probability, too, there were a good many of his humbler fellow citizens who heard the story of a shoemaker in the Strand who manufactured ' elastic ' heels, and was aggrieved at the lack of interest in his invention displayed by the army. What solace it was when the prime minister himself rode to the shop, bestowed sympathy and an order for a pair of heels, and even quoted the toast :

> Here's to our friends : as to our foes—
> May they have tight boots and corns on their toes.[23]

What must the Whig grandees have thought of tales like that ? Not, of course, that their interests were forgotten by the popular premier. At just this time he gave assurances that the official candidate for a vacant parliamentary seat was one ' who would not try to establish in the borough any personal interest at variance with that of Lord Lansdowne's family.'[24] He urged the advancement in the peerage of Lord Ward, who had an income of £100,000 and ' considerable influence bearing upon the return of members for two or three seats.'[25] But the public did not have to be informed of that. Neither was it necessary to publish the fact that the comptroller of the Queen's household was removed for missing 70 out of 111 government divisions, while Palmerston had been present at all but 14.[26]

Something of the same regard for various classes was of necessity shown by the premier in conducting the legislative business of the session. When Russell, a few decades ahead of his time, attempted to provide his country with primary schools locally supported and controlled, and partially non-sectarian, Palmerston, though professedly warm to the principle of practical, moral and religious instruction for the working class, prudently left Lord John's measure to a chilly death.[27] In the famous affair of the Wensleydale peerage, when the premier proposed, in the interest of law reform, to revive the royal prerogative of creating peers for life, he showed that his devotion to the principle of ' standing fast ' did not apply in domestic as it did in foreign policy.[28] A convinced believer in the physical and moral benefits of Sunday band music for the masses in the parks, he was brought, figuratively of course, ' plump on his knees before the Archbishop of Canterbury,' when his Grace became spokesman for outraged and influential sabbatarians.[29] He even agreed against his principles that London's sabbath calm should not be broken by the opening of the British Museum and the National Gallery.[30] Once again the demand for abolition of the purchase and sale of military commissions was shelved, though the premier's openly declared opinion was ' in the abstract, against the system. [31] This session certainly gave some justification for Disraeli's sneers at the conservative leader of a party of liberals. Yet Palmerston could claim to be at least the better liberal of the two. Disraeli, for example, would not allow that it was a function of the state to educate the working classes either for trades or for the cultivation of the soil ; while the prime

minister, defending appropriations for instruction designed
' to qualify them to support themselves and their families,
and to struggle through life in that position in which their
lot had been cast,' maintained that ' there could not possibly
be a better application of money ' than to the education of
the Irish peasantry in agriculture.[32]   His plea for the Irish
seems almost worthy of the Gladstone of a later time :

> Every man must know the unfortunate state in which Ireland
> had for ages been placed, and how Ireland had been the victim of
> misgovernment on the part of this country . . . they knew that that
> country was comparatively poor, because in former ages it had been
> misgoverned, because its resources had not been brought forth, and
> because it had been made the victim of oppression and the object of
> class legislation. . . . For many years past a more enlightened
> policy had prevailed. . . . But even now . . . they were . . .
> bound, in justice, to make Ireland an exception from the general
> rules of legislation.

But Palmerston lacked not merely Gladstone's settled conviction and determination on the question, but Gladstone's
opportunity.   Only constitutional and diplomatic questions
seemed to have the power of rousing the parliament of 1856.
' Nothing remains to keep one awake,' wrote Dallas of it
in July, ' but the drowsy hum of the Italian question.' [33]

The legislative record of the session of 1856 was far
from a brilliant one ; but Palmerston and his ministry
emerged not only safe but apparently stronger than before.
As Argyll later pointed out, the prime minister was obtaining
a new hold on his countrymen :

> His older popularity was entirely founded on foreign affairs, in
> which the British public are rather fond of games of bluff.   But now,
> when in the multifarious transactions of his office as Prime Minister
> his moderation and good temper came to be often felt, he was becoming
> more and more a universal favourite.[34]

Russell believed that he reached intellectual maturity only
when he had exhausted the biblical span of life : and *The
Times* in one of his obituary notices, made almost the same
suggestion :

> Had he died at seventy he would have left a second-class reputa-
> tion. . . . It has been his great and peculiar fortune to live to right
> himself.[35]

Nor, in Argyll's judgment at least, had he much to fear
in 1856 :

> In truth, the Opposition was completely broken up. It had no
> name to conjure with. Lord John Russell was entirely discredited.
> So was Gladstone, because of his violent pro-Russian speeches, . . .
> His continued animosity to Palmerston after the peace, on every
> question on which opposition could possibly be raised, did not tend to
> rehabilitate him in the public estimation.[36]

And all the time Palmerston seemed to be earning fresh
laurels in the field of diplomacy.

For, if the session proved a drowsy one, the prime
minister and the Foreign Office were kept very much awake
through the late spring, summer and autumn of 1856, by
disagreements concerning the execution of the Paris treaty.
The Russians, taking advantage of every loophole which that
rather hastily concluded agreement seemed to afford, were
still trying to defeat some of the war aims of the British
government.[37]   The new frontier between Russian Bessarabia and the Roumanian principalities had been defined
partly in relation to the small town of Bolgrad.   But there
were in fact two Bolgrads ; and the acceptance of the Russian
contention that the treaty referred to the more southerly
would largely have defeated the British purpose in backing
Austria's demand for an alteration of the old frontier, by
conceding to Russia a good strategic line and easy access
to the Danube.   Again, the Russians, who were supposed
to have relinquished the Isle of Serpents at the mouth of
the Danube, now proceeded to reoccupy it.[38]   Apart from
these and other instances of Russian enterprise, there arose
a difference of opinion between the Powers as to whether
the Roumanian principalities should be allowed to form
a single autonomous state under Turkish sovereignty, as
most of their inhabitants desired, or whether they should
be compelled to remain separate.[39]   Engrossing as these
matters were in themselves, they gained a new significance
through being accompanied by, and in part the occasion for,
a partial realignment of the Powers.   The French government, though wavering as usual between the conflicting
policies of its sovereign and his strange band of advisers,

showed an unmistakable inclination to transfer at least part of its diplomatic support from its late allies to its late enemies ; while England, Austria and Turkey evinced an increasing sense of a community of interests. Before the British government lay a wide choice of policies ; but questions of concession or resistance to Alexander and Napoleon stood first.

Palmerston regarded the whole situation with the eye of the opportunist. The time of the French alliance, he had pointed out early in the spring, was a season of fair weather in which England should make what harvest she could. The sun was Napoleon's conviction that the alliance was an almost essential element of his policy. But Napoleon, he found, was ' liable to sudden changes of purpose.'[40] One should be prepared for all eventualities :

> When people ask one . . . for what is called a policy the only answer is that we mean to do what may seem to be best upon each occasion as it arises, making the interests of one's country one's guiding principle.[41]

As for Russia, England must hold out for the exact fulfilment of the treaty, offering friendship but no concessions of any kind.[42] Such was Palmerston's approach to the problems of the Near East. He might have blessed the union of the principalities if a strong young state, under a sovereign preferably Italian but certainly not susceptible to Russian influence, could thereby have been born.[43] This seeming impossible, he determined that the Roumanians should remain disunited and weak, dominated by Turkey and closed to Russian influence. After his experience of the last quarter century he had no desire for ' the creation of another Greece on the North of Turkey and in immediate contact with Russia.' And had it not been ' one of the first objects of the war ' to keep the principalities under Turkish rule ?[44] Austria and Turkey naturally agreed with him ; but France, Russia and Sardinia all advocated the union of the principalities. Napoleon was even ready to support the Tsar with respect to Bolgrad and the Isle of Serpents.

More opportunist still was the premier's professed

attitude toward the Franco-Russian rapprochement.[45]   To
most British statesmen of the time it must have seemed an
obstacle if not a danger : but the premier pretended, at
least, to welcome it as affording an opportunity for teaching
a few much needed lessons to the governments at Paris and
St. Petersburg.   England, forced by 'peculiar circumstances' to 'play second fiddle' to France in the Crimea,[46]
had so far enjoyed French support only by the personal
favour of Napoleon.   True, she had asserted herself at the
Paris conference, had 'prevented many bad things thereby
and carried several good things' ; but it was now time for
her to give the alliance greater value in French eyes by
showing that she felt strong enough to 'act as well as
negotiate' on her own account.

> There is no danger of our losing France.   The only question is
> whether we shall drag her into stoutness or whether she shall drag us
> into weakness.[47]

The Russians, too, should learn.   Believing England to be
'tied like a kettle to the tail of France,' they had been courting the French in the manner of racetrack touts who bribe
the trainers to drug the horses before a race.[48]   But they
would drop that game when Admiral Lyons had forcibly
removed their detachment from the Isle of Serpents, and the
Admiralty had despatched the home squadron to Kiel.

> I am ready to take upon myself the whole responsibility of re-
> moving these Russians from Serpents' Island, but I cannot take on
> myself the humiliation of allowing them to remain there . . . we
> ought to telegraph Lyons to remove the detachment and take it to
> Odessa.[49]

Chreptovitch, the new Russian envoy, on threatening to
leave England because of Palmerston's language concerning
the conduct of his government, was told that the sooner he
did so the better, unless he was prepared to let the premier
have his say.[50]   Some of this bluster may be put down to
the frayed nerves of a man, who, as the summer and the
session of 1856 drew to a close, complained of being 'hunted
morning, noon and night' ; [51] but the policy of implacable
resistance which it revealed had nothing to do with parliamentary duties or with weariness.   Indeed, much of his

weariness must have come from his determination to hold
the Foreign Office firm. In a single month he sent Clarendon eighty-one holograph letters and memoranda on foreign
policy.[52] And many a memorandum bore Clarendon's
pencilled direction to some clerk : ' Write accordingly.'
Nor was this all. Occasionally, at least, he wrote directly
to Napoleon's foreign minister.[53] ' Never hesitate about
sending me boxes and messengers,' he admonished Clarendon, ' if people cannot give time and take trouble with
things before hand they are sure to be forced to give much
more time and to take much more trouble and more disagreeably with those things afterwards.' [54]

The early autumn brought some leisure, the welcome
news that Napoleon had come to the English way of thinking
in so far as the Isle of Serpents was concerned, and the
abatement of some of the prime minister's truculence.[55]
The Russian ambassador was the recipient of his congratulations on the extraordinary valour shown by his master's
troops in the Crimea, and Clarendon of the information
that the premier hoped that a bridge could be built, over
which the Tsar and Napoleon might gracefully retreat.

But what kind of bridge ? France was urging a fresh
conference. This would be all very well, wrote Palmerston,
if England, Austria, and Turkey were assured of a majority
in any voting that should take place. But were they ?
France would make her graceful retreat by voting with
Russia ; and Sardinia, to the premier's disgust, seemed
resolved to give full backing to Napoleon.[56] Hostility
towards Austria, perception that France might help him
as England neither would nor could, and perhaps some
lingering hope that the duke of Modena would still resign
his duchy in exchange for a united Roumania, placed
Cavour squarely on Napoleon's side. It was in vain that
Palmerston complained of his ' unreasonableness ' in
viewing Near Eastern affairs from the angle of Italian
interests, and suggested that he had better keep his views
on the union of the principalities to himself.[57] It was in
vain that the premier tried to promote a marriage between
that most coarse-mouthed and free living of contemporary
sovereigns, Victor Emmanuel, and Queen Victoria's maiden

cousin, Princess Mary of Cambridge.[58]   Perhaps Shaftesbury and other English Protestants would, as he hoped,
have been gratified by the prospect of the spread of Pro-
testantism in the Italian peninsula through the Princess
Mary's influence ; perhaps Italian nationalists would have
been attracted by the hope of alliance with both great
western Powers.   He never knew ; for the negotiations
soon petered out.   Hence success in a conference, being
dependent on the Sardinian vote, was dependent still on
the attitude of France.   At the end of September the prospects for settlement seemed of the gloomiest.   But
Palmerston, as Clarendon remarked almost impatiently,
did not doubt that the government would 'pull thro'
somehow, admitting at the same time that it would be very
awkward if parliament were to meet to-morrow.' [59]

The end of October found the foreign secretary more
pessimistic still :

Palmerston is very jaunty and won't hear of arbitration—says the
Emperor is sure to yield if we stand firm ; but I don't share his
opinion.[60]

Palmerston was not pessimistic ; but he was exceedingly
angry. The Turks had apparently intimated that they
would not be sorry to see the British squadron depart from
the Black Sea :

As to the application of Walewsky and Thouvenel to the Porte
to shut the Straits and turn us out of the Black Sea, besides its being
an act of impertinent folly it is the basest treachery.   I always
suspected that the impulse came from Paris.[61]

Of course the British ships would stay just where they
were :

The only thing to tell Walewsky about the Straits is that we are
in the Black Sea and that we shall like to see who will venture to try
to turn us out.

His attitude throughout was typically Palmerstonian.   So
in some ways were its effects.   Malmesbury noted that at
the Lord Mayor's banquet, on November 9, 'the Corps
Diplomatique was represented by the Mexican Minister
and the one from the Republic of Hayti, a black man.' [62]

Before parliament should meet, the government had a breathing spell of at least three months : and during this time its chief maintained his attitude, impatiently shaking off every plea for concession that friend or foe could frame. With the Austrians in the principalities and with a British fleet commanding the Black Sea, the game was, physically speaking, in his hands. Why then make any sacrifice of those British interests and that British prestige for which he stood as steward ? If, for example, Russia gave in concerning the Isle of Serpents, the British (instead of matching this with a concession concerning Bolgrad, as the French emperor wished) should merely feel encouraged to persist in their other demands.[63]

. . . don't let us fall into the bad ways of John Russell who is stout as a lion till the horizon seems to look clearer and then suddenly wheels round and gives up all he had been contending for.[64]

Arbitration was not to be thought of :

Every engine of intrigue would be set to work . . . and when France & Russia hunt in couples, they have such means of corruption that we should not be a match for them.[65]

Even Leopold of Belgium could not be trusted to arbitrate between England and the two Emperors :

. . . it would be Threadneedle Street to a china orange against us—He would give it for the Emperors as sure as eggs is eggs.[66]

Cavour's intercession brought the comment that it was ' disingenuous and discreditable ' of the Piedmontese minister to argue that England and her friends should spare France the mortification of giving up ' a wrong opinion ' by themselves relinquishing ' a right opinion.'[67] Even Persigny, reputedly the best of England's friends among the French, drew upon himself by his pleading a letter (unseen by Clarendon until after it was sent) that seemed to the Queen like Palmerston's ' worst ebullitions in the olden time.'[68] But, as the premier explained, if England yielded to Persigny's friendship, that friendship would, in effect, be more deadly than Walewski's hostility.[69]

None of the ' ebullitions ' of these weeks is more revealing than the following letter to Clarendon :

Might not Cowley point out how mean, how unworthy, how disgraceful it is for a Power whose territory stretches from the White Sea to the Black, from Behring's Straits to the Baltic to be throwing away its reputation (if it ever had it) for good faith and for a sense of honour and self-respect by haggling and bargaining for a few thousand souls (bodies they ought rather to call them, though the tyranny of the govt. is such that the poor people cannot as the saying runs, call their souls their own) and a few square miles of useless land. . . .[70]

This letter, be it noted, was penned by the critic of the ' Ashburton capitulation.'

Though such an appeal to Russian honour could hardly have been expected to bear fruit, the final outcome justified the premier's optimism and tenacity. Thanks largely to the belated good offices of Napoleon, the Sardinian vote was won, and a sham conference arranged.[71] Russia, out-voted by agreement on all essential points, obtained, with Palmerston's full consent, ' just enough to save her honour,' but not to afford her either strategic advantage or a ' tumblerful ' of the waters of the Pruth.[72] Before the year 1857 was two weeks old the government was ready to meet parliament—in so far at least as the affairs of the Near East were concerned.

The reservation is a highly necessary one ; for there were several minor matters of foreign policy on which, as Clarendon put it, members of parliament stood ' in awful array.'[73] The administration had been engaged for months in a lingering dispute with the Neapolitan government over the harshness and oppressiveness of its rule ; and had come off none too well.[74] Then there had been a complicated and unpleasant quarrel with Persia in which Russian influence, indignities to a British representative, and Persian aggression against Afghanistan were as usual con-cerned ; and from which had developed the usual kind of mid-eastern war.[75] As Palmerston, and presumably his cabinet, believed that British ' military possession of southern Persia . . . might lead to Russian occupation of northern Persia,'[76] England was not exacting in the negotia-tions for peace. Though protracted beyond the opening of parliament, they were closed early in March. In fact, the principal negotiator on the British side had been instructed that no more time could be allowed. For the government was about to dissolve parliament as a result of the Commons' censure of its Chinese policy ; and it hesitated at appealing to the electors with two wars on its hands.

But one must go back for a moment to see how affairs in China had brought Palmerston's government to defeat. Trouble between England and China was chronic and almost inevitable.[77] The most constant source of irritation —the refusal of the Chinese government to live up to its treaty obligations by admitting foreigners to Canton—was merely a phase of the Son of Heaven's persistent policy toward Europeans. They were still and always to be regarded as barbarian rebels of low commercial status, whose claims to courteous treatment as equals of the celestials were preposterous, and whose superiority in the barbarian art of making war was properly met by falsehood, evasion, and, in emergencies, assassination. Considering this, it seemed to Palmerston that the European Powers should make common cause for the protection of their citizens in the Far East. When, in the autumn of 1856, news arrived of the murder of a French missionary by the Chinese, he suggested that a British naval force should cut off supplies from Peking by seizing the junction of the Yangtse river with the great canal.[78] How much more then was the champion of Don Pacifico, the steady and warm supporter of British representatives in far-off lands, prepared, in the spring of 1857, to support a British agent who used armed force in demanding reparation for a technical insult to the British flag, and compliance with the treaty stipulation relating to Canton ? He had shown much patience under the continuing provocations of the Chinese government ; [79] but the affair of the lorcha *Arrow* convinced him that he had been patient long enough. It was high time, he thought, to extract from the Chinese ' concessions . . . indispensable for the maintenance of friendly relations between China and the Governments of Europe.' [80] What he had in mind was the establishment of regular diplomatic intercourse.

But the events in China, and even the government's attitude regarding them, were of less immediate significance than the political struggle for which they offered ground. The opposition was already re-enforced, as the pessimistic Clarendon saw :

I never remember the recklessness and spite of faction to have been greater than at this moment. Gladstone's rabies for office renders him capable of anything—Dizzy and he play into each other's hands, and I grieve to say that Lord John is lowering himself every day by the increased bitterness of his tone, which everyone understands to be influenced by personal mortification. . . .[81]

Fighting on the Chinese question, the opposition leaders could be sure of wholehearted support from Gladstone, the special assailant of the ' Opium ' war, and from pacifistic radicals led by the business-like Manchester men.[82]   And Bethell, the attorney-general, shook his head over the serious case which could be made against the government on international law.[83]   But Palmerston seemed undismayed, countering Derby's meetings of supporters with a meeting of his own,[84] looking hopefully to the division that would decide the fate of his ministry, and not forgetting, one must think, to gaze beyond the House to that public which so revered him, and to which he could make ultimate appeal. He well knew that his public as a whole was not concerned with the niceties of the case.   He knew that they cared little about the exact status of the tiny vessel carrying a British flag which the Chinese had boarded, or about the proprieties of British demands and the British bombardment of Canton.   Rather, like their premier, the people were concerned with the chastisement of 'a set of kidnapping, murdering, poisoning barbarians,' with the advancement of their trade, and with the continuance of the Liberals in power.   Also, to a large though sometimes exaggerated extent, they were concerned in seeing their doughty premier retain his place.   Sidney Herbert knew this well :

. . . Palmerston . . . is the only public man in England who has a name.   Many criticise, many disapprove, but all, more or less, like him and look on him as the only man.   He has on his side that which is the strongest element in the mental organisation of all human

EARL OF D—RB—Y.   C—BD—N.   P—LM—RST—N.

THE GREAT CHINESE WARRIORS DAH-BEE AND COB-DEN

Punch, March 7, 1857

society, namely, the public's national prejudices. Some one said
' Give me the national songs, and I will rule the nation ' ; and
Canning said, ' Don't talk to me of the " sense of the nation " ; give
me the *nonsense*, and I will beat it hollow.' [85]

To put him out would be a formidable task.
And so events proved. When the Chinese question
came up in parliament, ' an unholy alliance,' which included
Disraeli, Russell, Gladstone, Roebuck, Layard and the
Manchesterites,[86] attacked the government. Palmerston,
waving the national emblem, denying Cobden the right to
be called a true Briton, and thrusting at Gladstone with the
stale taunt of defending the ' poisoning of the wells,' [87]
drew some Conservative support, but went down to defeat.
Then came the public's turn. For the Queen, about to
undergo ' the fatigue of dropping another pearl in the
jewelry casket of her devoted subjects,' [88] preferred ' *any
other alternative*' to a ' fruitless ' ministerial crisis, and
readily fell in with Palmerston's decision to dissolve
parliament.[89] A general election immediately supervened ;
and British electors, in the latter days of March, heard
opposition taunts of bullying and chauvinism answered by
ministerial taunts of indifference to national interests and
prestige. But the uncertain quantity was the attitude of the
' liberals ' ; and one of the great issues was that of national
leadership. Lady Palmerston, campaigning for her grand-
son, Evelyn Ashley, was very clear on this :

> What we want is to get the liberal party, or at least a part of them,
> and perhaps in this way he [Palmerston] may cut into both parties.
> . . . You might mention to your friends that Ashley is Palmerston's
> private secretary. This will lead them to feel that he is a real
> Palmerstonian and not a Tory in disguise.[90]

The result of the polling seems fully to have justified her
hopes ; for it was well summarised by Dallas as ' a great
accession to the incongruous strength of what is called the
Liberal party, and a decisive individual triumph to Lord
Palmerston.' [91] Indeed, it was the general impression, both
before and after the event, that ' the elections . . . turned
. . . entirely on him [Palmerston] personally.' [92] Argyll
wrote that ' there had been no such triumph for any

Minister' since 1832.[93] Not the least striking or satisfactory feature of the premier's success was the defeat of
Bright and Cobden, those radical prophets, on the basis,
as it seems, of their pacifistic attitude.[94] But, in the preceding November, Herbert had noted that Palmerston
seemed ' to have flourished much at Manchester.' [95]

Yet the new majority contained elements much too
radical to be really Palmerstonian. The prime minister's
uneasy anticipation of this result was shown by his complaints to Granville while the elections were still being
held :

I see plainly that the Ryder Street Committee have been trying
to pack the parliament with ballot men willing or unwilling. This
is a bit of treachery.[96]

And again :

What can be the use of urging candidates to declare for ballot
and other things which the present government never can agree to.
They are only storing up causes of disruption of the party and such
pledges are wholly unnecessary for success of any Liberal candidate.[97]

As results came in he could only express a hope that ' some
who have given these foolish and unnecessary pledges may
perhaps not vote when the question comes to be discussed.' [98]
But everyone knew that, for all his ' triumphs,' he would
rule a divided band ; and Dallas reported speculations as
to whether the liberals might not become ' solidified ' and
' rush into Reform ' after the ' infusion ' had ' fermented '
for a year.[99] There were already signs that Palmerston, as
a liberal-conservative prime minister, would find it more
difficult to hold members of radical proclivities than he had
in days of old, when flouting continental despots was his
special task. It was the ' country gentlemen ' on both
sides of the House who now turned to him more and more.[100]
The new parliament would require careful driving ; but
its leader was in form. Thus in early June :

. . . my lord Palmerston could yesterday mount a fine spirited
horse at Windsor, ride to Ascot, in the Queen's train, stay to the
races, and ride back again, without feeling the weight of duties or
years.[101]

And, since even the most radical of members were Britons after all, such form was a political asset.

The balance of the session afforded a better test than had previously been possible of Palmerston's domestic policy. So far, indeed, he had proved himself a very indifferent liberal. Even at the beginning of the current session he had refused to involve the cabinet in any measure of parliamentary reform, alleging that he saw no pressing need, and was one of those (what fine conservative doctrine this !) who valued the constitution too much to amend it, save as urgent necessity arose.[102]   Before the election, some excuse for such an attitude might have been found in the patent instability of his position ; but now his majorities, especially for liberal projects, seemed well assured, and his liberal supporters justified in hoping for a change.   Soon enough it became apparent that the change was to consist, not so much in any marked re-orientation of his general policy, as in a display of greater determination in putting measures through.   There was nothing new in the premier's declaration that he knew of no argument against the admission of Jews to parliament,[103] or in his approval of the wider use of qualifying examinations in the civil service.[104]   Anyone who realised his dislike of complicated and antiquated machinery could have predicted that he would find a bill for removing matters of testamentary disposition from the ecclesiastical to the civil courts ' a good and necessary measure ' :[105] anyone who recognised his large humanity could have foretold his warm support of a measure for bettering the housing of the urban working class :

The hon. and learned Gentleman said that an Englishman's house was his castle.   In this case every builder's house was his dungeon ; and it was into this unhealthy dungeon that, for the sake of private gain, they crowded a number of persons, who could not live together with safety to either body or mind.[106]

But there was a new determination in his driving through the House of a bill to make divorce something other than a monopoly of the rich.   When the opposition, headed on this occasion by the high church and therefore outraged

Gladstone, tried to ' talk out ' the bill, the premier playfully but resolutely shook the whip :

> The hon. and learned Gentleman asked me how long I proposed to keep the House sitting. Why, Sir, as long as may be necessary to dispose of the important measures before us. I remember sitting in this House until the middle of September.[107]

And again :

> Mr. O'Connell used to say, ' Don't all call out for silence, for if you all call silence there never will be silence.' In the same way if hon. Members consumed a great part of the evening in asking when the Session would be over, there would be very little chance of the Session ever being over.[108]

Before August was out the opposition had succumbed, and the ministry's legislative record could be reviewed. Taken in all, it could be regarded as highly creditable. It seems all the more so when one remembers that the premier had been to some extent absorbed in a diplomatic tangle concerning the future of the Roumanian principalities,[109] and that the Indian mutiny had been in the forefront of attention for two months.

The actual suppression of the mutiny demanded far less than did most things the personal activity of the prime minister—far less than any legislative programme or the regulation of international affairs. General oversight and responsibility devolved upon him in common with his cabinet, and that was all. On the other hand, through individual effort in matters of administrative detail ; by maintaining public confidence in England and India, and belief in England's inherent strength elsewhere ; and finally, in distributing commendation or condemnation to civil and military officials at the seat of trouble, he was able to exercise much influence. Not, of course, that he did not share the responsibility and credit for the general suppression of the mutiny. One recalls the tribute of the governor-general, Lord Canning : ' You have poured troops into India with a readiness and liberality that deserves all honour.'[110] Within five months of the time when the first news of the mutiny reached England, Canning had the support of some 80,000 white soldiers.[111]

Remembering the Crimean war, it is unnecessary to dwell much upon Palmerston's incessant personal activity in suggesting sources of man-power, and insisting that the troops should go out properly supplied.[112]   He was among the first to urge the lowering of recruiting standards (on the ground that ' if five foot four was good enough against the Russians, it is surely good enough against the Sepoys '), and the raising of black regiments in Canada to relieve the West India garrisons.[113]   But he would hear of no expedient that could be construed at home or abroad as an evidence of weakness or exhaustion.   He insisted that the guards should be kept at home, and all offers of foreign troops, even by King Leopold, refused.[114]   England, he wrote, must ' win off her own bat.'

Above all things, he was the sustainer of morale.   Many wise heads were shaken in England during the summer and autumn months, but never the jaunty head of the prime minister.   When in the first days of depression, and even panic, he wrote the Queen and Panmure that he had no fear of the results, and that the outbreak might lead ' to our establishing our power in those countries upon a firmer basis,' [115] he defined his personal attitude once and for all.   In fact, it seemed to the Court and some of the ministers that Palmerston's confidence was too absolute in so far as the safety both of India and of Great Britain was concerned.[116]   The Prince Consort wrote bitterly of the premier's ' juvenile levity.' The Queen, for all her friendships with crowned heads, for all the visit to Osborne in August of her friend Napoleon, was constantly alarmed lest England itself should lack defenders if a sudden international crisis should arise.   Her cousin, the duke of Cambridge, vastly impressed with the responsibilities arising from his recent appointment as commander-in-chief, shared her anxiety.   So did Clarendon, and so did even Cowley, the British ambassador at Paris. But Palmerston, who normally saw in every Frenchman or Russian a potential foe, for once had no uneasiness.

. . . we have no danger threatening us in Europe and at home. France is perfectly and sincerely friendly, Russia may snarl and growl in secret, but has been too severely chastised to venture as yet openly to show her teeth ; besides which . . . September is too late in the year for Baltic fleets to be put in motion . . . and as to our national reputation for strength, the best way of maintaining that, and of deterring any foreign power from presuming on our supposed weakness, will be to crush the Indian revolt as soon as can be done.[117]

There resulted a fresh misunderstanding with the Court.[118] When, thanks to the harvesting season, recruiting lagged, the Queen tried to insist that larger and larger forces of militia should be embodied in order to provide for home defence and release reserves for India. The ministry, she wrote, in following the policy of 'letting out sail by degrees' (her first minister's own phrase) were 'tempting Providence' and incurring a 'fearful responsibility' by their 'apparent indifference.'[119] Even Clarendon, 'in a state of great alarm,' accused Palmerston of believing 'all that Panmure tells him about having a reserve.'[120] It may be, as some thought, both at the time and later on, he did take the mutiny too easily ;[121] but in one respect at least he was justified by the event. Napoleon, instead of planning an invasion, was soon offering to allow British reinforcements for India to travel across France.[122]

Perhaps, in considering Palmerston's words and deeds in connection with the mutiny, one finds him at his best in his relations with the rather tactless but great-hearted governor-general of India. It was hard for Palmerston to approve of Canning. He blamed him for his shyness and reserve, his failure to show sympathy or to guide Indian opinion in the crisis.[123] His own optimism caused him to question the propriety of Canning's action in diverting to India troops embarked for service in the Chinese war :[124] his own passionate nature led him to sympathise with the rabid Anglo-Indians, and to regard Canning's 'Clemency' proclamation, aimed to prevent the execution of mere deserters from sepoy ranks, as 'twaddling' and 'ill-timed.'[125] He deeply wounded the harassed governor-general by neglecting to send him a word of approval or encouragement. [126] But when the newspapers of England and India heaped calumny and abuse on Canning's head, and Canning's friends pressed Palmerston to intervene,[127] he came to the defence of the beleaguered and discouraged governor-general with all the powers of oratory at his command.

At a Mansion House dinner he ' spat out ' a vindication
of the man for whose judgment he had such scant regard
that silenced the press attacks immediately, and earned for
him the grateful and repeated thanks of Canning and his
wife.[128]   In parliament he vigorously took Canning's side.[129]
Palmerston's chivalry, like his abusiveness and boastfulness,
was never expressed by halves.   Unfortunately, yet not
uncharacteristically, he mingled boastfulness of a most
offensive kind with the chivalry of his Mansion House
address.   He who had so lately declared the international
sky serene, the French so loyal, burst out with threats
against any nation that should dare to presume upon
England's time of adversity.   The effect was described
by the British ambassador at Paris :

> Palmerston's speech . . . has raised the indignation of these
> ridiculously susceptible people, who can see nothing . . . but an
> insult to France. . . . I cannot but see a great difference in the
> Emperor's manner as regards England.[130]

' *Il n'y a que la verité qui blesse,*' wrote the premier airily.[131]
But French irritation was, in the late winter of 1857–8,
to be a notable factor in the chain of circumstances which
brought the unconcerned statesman's period of rule to a
sudden close.

CHAPTER XXVII

1857–1858

In all the parliamentary history of nineteenth-century England it would be difficult to find any short period in which the elements of party chaos, confusion of issues, surprise and intrigue played a greater part than during the months which elapsed between the late autumn of 1857 and the early spring of 1859. Disraeli would have done better to keep for these months his reference to 'majorities collected God knows how, voting God knows why.' And yet such divine omniscience may be shared by those who have sufficient patience to peruse the letters and diaries of leading parliamentarians, and who bring to the task some understanding of political jealousies, parliamentary susceptibilities and popular caprice. Even in outline the tale is rather an engrossing one, as a story of unscrupulous warfare for high stakes. Unfortunately, the introduction, *i.e.* the analysis of the elements concerned, repels one's interest : but its omission is impossible.

Especially noticeable in the situation was that quality so often referred to by writers on parliamentary history as 'kaleidoscopic' : the existence of numerous groups, of varying political colours and shades, poised at a given moment in precarious equilibrium, but ready to fall into any one of several patterns should that equilibrium be disturbed. There were stiff Conservatives, still hoping to hand the constitution on to coming political generations without substantial change ; and there were more liberal or more opportunist Conservatives, such as Disraeli, ready to make changes where even the constitution was concerned, or to strike bargains, for mutual advantage, with almost any of the other groups. Still more unstable, and therefore more difficult to count upon, were the Peelites, led by the great triumvirate of Graham, Herbert and Gladstone, but still giving ear to Aberdeen, and reinforced by the growing prominence of Cardwell.   Rather conservative by instinct but swayed by liberal impulses, strongly moved by personal feelings (above all by Gladstone's loathing of Palmerston), ready to come to terms with almost any group or party at any time, not infrequently divided even among themselves, they made a real two-party system impossible, and were primarily responsible for the existing chaos.   As for the Whig-Liberals, they were even more at cross purposes than their name would indicate.   The Whigs who formed the core, while loyal to party ties, were hardly to be distinguished from Conservatives in their views on domestic issues.   But sharing the government benches with them were other groups, representing various shades of liberalism in relation to both home and foreign affairs, and including almost a hundred 'independent' Liberals who were more or less detachable. Still more detachable, if not quite detached, were the mutually related but distinct groups of 'radicals.'   Between them and the 'independent' Liberals a clear-cut division was impossible.   When it is remembered that the Whig-Liberals were also apt to divide along personal lines, such, e.g. as allegiance to Palmerston or to Russell, it will be seen that the possibilities of different groupings were almost infinite.

While the Whig-Liberals, acting in full strength, had a commanding majority after the spring election of 1857, it will be noted that their leader, personally, was by no means so safe.   A combination between the normal Conservative opposition, the great Peelite orators, the jealous Russell, and even a considerable portion of the radicals would be very dangerous.   If many of the 'independent' Liberals should leave him, the desertion might easily be fatal. During his whole career as premier he was to be engaged, as Clarendon put it, in holding together a 'great bundle of sticks.'[1]   His wide and gentle grasp had proved quite effective since February 1855 ; but, in the autumn and early winter of 1857–8, there were reasons for doubting whether it would continue so.

There seem to have been two reasons in particular, both a little curious : his handling of parliament as a whole, and the increasing importance of parliamentary reform as a practical issue in politics. It was curious that when he showed such consideration for the elements making up the party which he led, he should have displayed insufficient consideration for the general susceptibilities of the House. But he had taken a haughty, domineering attitude ; and, what was even worse, had ' affected contempt ' for the independent Liberals and radicals below the gangway.[2] His domineering tone had already made some members feel that he might be the better for a little chastisement : and before parliament met again he gave fresh offence by the appointment of a morally discredited nobleman, Lord Clanricarde, to be lord privy seal. Lansdowne was reported to have inquired ' if he were out of his mind.'[3] The curious feature about the increasing importance of parliamentary reform as a practical issue was that no one knew whether or not the country as a whole really wanted it. But the question, thanks largely to Russell, had been hanging fire for several years ; so that it had become ' a political game, not a public demand.'[4] The promises of radical measures which, to Palmerston's disgust, had been used to catch votes for liberal candidates in the election of the preceding spring, had made the postponement of action still more difficult. Hence a reform bill was promised by the ministry at the opening of a nine day session called in December 1857, to deal with a financial panic and a shortage of currency. ' I think,' wrote Clarendon, at the beginning of the winter, ' reform will be the rock on which the government will go to pieces.'[5] The premier, seeing the danger, was careful not to reveal his intentions in advance.[6]

By great good luck there survives in the Windsor archives a long exposition of Palmerston's personal views on parliamentary reform, as contained in a confidential letter, written in October 1857, to the Queen.[7] Besides containing a reiteration of his published convictions, it set out what guiding theories he had. In general, he concluded, the ten-pound franchise for boroughs should remain untouched, because it went ' quite as low as intelligence

and independence reach.'   Yet ' large numbers of well-
educated and independent men ' were ' shut out by the
technical test of a ten-pound house in a borough or a forty-
shilling freehold or a farm in the country.'   This could be
met by giving votes to naval and military officers, including
those of the militia, to lawyers, physicians and clergymen,
and to ' all clerks of merchants, bankers and manufacturers,
and to any other classes who might be found to come within
the same principle.'   But he was not in favour of a purely
upper and middle class franchise.   He ' would give much,'
he wrote, ' to discover some qualification which would admit
some of the best and most intelligent of the working classes.'
Hence he was ready to consider enfranchising men who
could show respectable savings bank accounts, or evidence
of having earned a stated amount of wages for a stated time.
Behind these suggestions and his other pronouncements on
reform lay political theory, strongly conservative, no doubt,
but a theory none the less : the theory that the franchise
should be conferred as a matter, not of universal and inherent
right, but of privilege, of trust ; not on the male adult
population, but on certain representative elements of the
population ; not directly on the basis of possessions or
of birth, but on the basis of the intelligence, education,
independence and responsibility presumably not found in
most of those who lack possessions or birth in some degree.
It was a theory which he had always held, and would always
hold, in common with a goodly though diminishing proportion of the statesmen of his time.   Like most of them
he would make reluctant concessions in matters of detail
to a public which naturally cared much more for details
than theories—always hoping that in some manner the
dominance of ' intelligence and independence ' would be
maintained.   The more liberal Whig-Liberals neither understood his theory nor knew what concessions he would make ;
but they understood his general attitude.   Since the introduction, not only of a reform bill, but of one to reconstitute
the system of government for India, was regarded as inevitable ; and since the resentment of parliament at the
premier's masterful manner was becoming obvious, it was
not difficult for political forecasters to predict stormy days.

Before parliament met, Brougham had warned Lady
Palmerston that her husband's position was anything but
strong.[8]

When the session of 1858 first opened it seemed that
the prophets of disaster might have been mistaken after all.
The government's India bill obtained an unexpectedly
flattering reception ; and the ministry had a working
majority of 100, something ' unheard of since the Reform
Bill.'[9]   But the premier's opponents, well aware that these
appearances might prove deceptive, were seeking an opportunity to strike.   They had apparently decided that the
Clanricarde appointment would offer the best basis for
attack, when a more tempting prospect suddenly opened
before them.   The possibility appeared of hoisting the
civis Romanus on his own petard, and impairing, if not
destroying, the nation-wide popularity which he had first
acquired as the upholder of England's dignity and prestige.
Lord Derby was substantially correct in thinking the attack
was ' the work of Lord John Russell and Sir James Graham
in the interests of the Radicals.'[10]   Had he said ' in the
interests of Russell and the Radicals,' he might, perhaps,
have been even closer to the truth.   But the original and
unconscious agents of Palmerston's overthrow were the band
of political refugees in England who hatched the ' Orsini ' plot
to assassinate Napoleon, and who had been able to concoct
their plans and procure their weapons with slight risk,
thanks to the inadequacy of the existing British law.[11]   The
French emperor and his subjects were unconscious agents,
too.   The French were not very fervently devoted to their
emperor ; but their inextinguishable hatred of the English
expressed itself under this new excuse in addresses and
demonstrations which would have been comic had not their
effects been serious.   Napoleon, anxious on the one hand
to preserve the British alliance, but fearful, on the other,
of diminishing his slender hold on the affections of his
subjects by placing himself too openly in opposition to
their chauvinism, fell back on an ambiguous policy.[12]
While he privately apologised to the British government
for the ridiculous outbreaks of his people, he allowed
Walewski to send a sharply worded despatch to Clarendon,

demanding measures to curb the activities of the refugees. Moreover, the official *Moniteur* published addresses presented to him by his officers, addresses couched in terms grossly insulting to the British people.

What were the British ministers to do ? Were they to risk the recriminations and political hostility of their excited countrymen by compliance with the not unnatural demands of the French government ; or were they to satisfy British public opinion at the probable cost of a serious breach with France ? One might expect to find that a government headed by Palmerston preferred the second alternative, and that the pacific Peelites and radicals, and perhaps even the Russellites, insisted upon the first. Instead, the positions of the leaders at any rate were exactly reversed. Palmerston from the first took the position that England must guard herself against the charge of protecting assassins and conspirators, and that the law which classed the activities of the Orsini conspirators on English soil as mere misdemeanours should be altered without delay.[13] In consequence, he introduced a Conspiracy Bill, making such activities punishable as felonies.[14] Devotion to the policy of an entente with France,[15] and confidence in his power to have his way in parliament, doubtless contributed to keep the premier firm in his resolve ; but there was something distinctly admirable in his refusal to be turned by public clamour, the tartness of Walewski's phrases, or the realised danger of a political reverse[16] from what not only he but Derby, the Prince Consort and other sensible persons regarded as the proper course. It is more difficult to understand the disgust at Palmerston's ' truckling to the strong ' (surely an unusual charge !) displayed by such men as Russell, Graham and Gladstone. That it was genuine in the case of most or all of them, and was shared by such persons as John Stuart Mill, seems incontestable :[17] that it might have been less intense had the Conspiracy Bill originated from some other quarter, one may at least surmise. In any case, they saw and treated the decision of Palmerston and his cabinet as ground for attack. Graham craftily suggested that their endeavour should be to secure a long interval between the first and second readings of the

bill, so that public excitement should have time to rise
(not a very pacific suggestion this !), and to work its effect
on parliament.[18] Derby, on the other hand, had assured
Clarendon of his full approval of the bill.[19]

On the first reading the government, with Conservative aid, secured a very large majority ; but the second
never came. For Russell and Graham now attacked by
using a most skilful device—the introduction of an amendment condemning the government, not on the basis of
the bill, but for having neglected to answer Walewski's
objectionable despatch. Crafty, too, was the decision that
the amendment should be introduced by Milner Gibson,
a man of the radical Manchester group, and therefore one
who presumably held peace especially dear. Unofficially,
the despatch *had* been answered, both in Paris and London,[20]
as many of the members of parliament must have known ;
and the government could argue with some plausibility that
the official answer had been properly delayed, pending the
verdict of parliament on the Conspiracy Bill. But the
amendment had been framed to supply an opportunity to
those members of all groups who might desire to rebuke or
overthrow the government ; and as such it was utilised.

To rebuke rather than to overthrow the cabinet was
apparently the intention of many of those who voted for
Milner Gibson's amendment when it came to a vote on the
night of February 19. Nor was it expected that even this
modest aim would be realised, until the debate had been
in progress for some time.[21] Early in the evening, the
government whips had allowed a number of supporters
to leave the House unpaired. But as the debate progressed,
Gladstone's eloquence, showing up in brilliant contrast to
the ineffective speeches of the government spokesmen,
visibly moved the House, even as Clanricarde's provocative
appearance in the galleries angered it. Palmerston, showing himself altogether too offhand and jaunty to please
his fellow-members, was ' perhaps, [for] the first time . . .
received with derisional " Oh, oh's." '[22] Suddenly Derby and
Disraeli recognised their opportunity. The latter, insisting
upon immediate division, lest adjournment should give
the ministers a chance to rally their forces, carried the

amendment by 19 votes in a House of only 449. The successful combination was the same as that which had attacked Palmerston a year before, consisting of the Conservatives, the Peelites, Russell with his followers, and nearly all the 'independent' Liberals and radicals. Some members had voted purely in deference to their constituents' indignation at the premier's ' truckling ' to the French. ' There can be no doubt,' wrote White, ' that it was "the people that did it." ' [23] Two days later the cabinet announced its decision to resign.

Thus, on a snap vote secured by political manœuvring, and through an appeal by its opponents to popular passions which it had had the wisdom and courage to defy, fell Palmerston's first ministry. Nothing, perhaps, became it better than its death. And yet, considering the particular demands made upon it since the dark days of January 1855, its achievements could be considered satisfactory. Not constructive legislation, but successes in war and in diplomacy had been the urgent necessities of the time. To round off a notable record of military successes in the Crimea, in India and in Persia, there came, at the very moment of its fall, news of what seemed a triumphant conclusion of the Chinese campaign. As for diplomacy, the premier, in reading over the confidential estimate of the foreign situation prepared by the permanent and supposedly non-partisan officials of the Foreign Office on the occasion of the change of ministry,[24] had reason to feel that he and Clarendon had shown themselves able custodians. By firmness, flattery and compromise, applied at appropriate times, the entente with the French emperor had been preserved. The problems arising out of the Treaty of Paris had been solved, or bade fair to be, in a manner quite consonant with British interests. There was a rising controversy about the construction of the Suez Canal ; but that was ' hushed for the present.' Russia, exhausted, unsuccessful in her attempts to sow discord between England and France, was assuming a more cordial attitude : Austria, save for her inclination toward interference in Turkey, and her perseverance in promoting the union of the principalities, was as accommodating as could be desired. The Sultan

was properly deferential.   Relations with the United States
were ' on a more satisfactory footing than . . . for many
years.'   Even supposing that the author of the estimate
had put the best face on affairs, the balance sheet was imposing.   What puzzled some men was that a ministry so
successful should so precipitately have retired.

For the resignation of the Palmerston cabinet created no
little suspicion and surprise.[25]   Since the House had had no
considered intention of turning out the ministers ; and since
they, in consequence, had been under no actual obligation
to resign, there were some who suspected the government
of courting defeat in order to make a *fausse sortie*, and
return to power after a reconstruction which would relieve
it of Clanricarde.   The suspicion seems to have been
groundless.[26]   The Queen and Derby were apparently
quite ready to let Palmerston return ; and it was only
when the fallen cabinet refused to allow any motion of
confidence, designed for its reinstatement, to be introduced,
that Derby agreed to take the reins.   Surprise was hardly
more justified.   That a ministry, faced with exceedingly
contentious issues, conscious that its majorities were
increasingly precarious, and justly fearful of defeat on
the Clanricarde issue, should be willing to give place to
the followers of ' the Jew and the Jockey,' a set of men
whom it would presumably be able to displace at will,
was not a matter for great wonderment.[27]   For its ageing
chief, however, the matter was more serious.

For what was really dramatic, really curious and possibly
permanent in the change that had taken place, was not at all
the defeat and resignation of the ministry, but the fall of
Palmerston.   Dallas, well posted on the London gossip of
the day, thought it was ' possibly . . . irreparable.'[28]   Its
completeness suggests such caprice on the part both of
parliament and people as seems scarcely credible.   But
witness Palmerston's admirer, the journalist-doorkeeper,
White :

. . . the ' Great Minister,' who but yesterday rode on the top-
most crest of the waves of popularity, is sunk so low that there is
hardly a man of his former friends to say, ' God save him.'   Nor do
men think of him in their speculations as to the future.   That further

DIGNIFIED POSITION

PAM (who has just been knocked over by the Foreign gent.):
"Oh, I beg your pardon, I'm sure! I didn't hurt you, I trust!"

Punch, February 20, 1858

changes are ahead every one believes, but nobody seems to imagine
that Lord Palmerston can be reinstated.[29]

The Prince Consort, writing after the session had closed,
regarded Palmerston's unpopularity as its ' most remarkable
feature.'[30]   He had frequently been hooted ; and his
advocacy of any cause seemed to insure its defeat.

> The man who was . . . stamped the only *English* statesman . . .
> is now considered the head of a clique, the man of intrigue, past his
> work, etc., etc.,—in fact hated ! and this throughout the country.

Greville found him an object of bitter aversion even to many
of his former friends and adherents ; and believed that his
political career was drawing to an end.[31]   Granville, who,
on account of ' the very bitter feeling against Palmerston,'
had assumed the leadership of the Whig-Liberal party,
dissented only in regarding ' a second reaction in his favour '
possible.[32]   Even the choice of seats by some leading
parliamentarians when the House assembled under Disraeli's leadership seemed ominous.[33]   Gladstone, Graham,
Herbert and Roebuck remained on the government (now
the Conservative) side.   Russell, after apparent hesitation,
went to the opposition benches ; but showed his independence by seating himself below the gangway.   Though
the Conservatives were outnumbered in the House by more
than two to one, it seemed to Granville that Derby's
' tolerably presentable cabinet ' might, by virtue of the
' personal hatreds ' among the liberal parties, succeed in
weathering the storm.[34]   As events proved, it was to
weather two attacks before four months were out, and
personal feelings—if ' hatreds ' be too strong a word—
were to contribute in no small measure to its success.

Attack of some sort could not be long deferred.   True,
most of the opposition leaders felt it would be unwise to
upset Derby until a Whig-Liberal fusion of some kind
had occurred ; but the rank and file, including even those
who had helped to turn out Palmerston, were soon demanding that the scandal and unfairness entailed in the rule
of a minority should be removed.[35]   Palmerston was not
the man to turn a deaf ear to such a call ; and an excellent

avenue of attack was offered when the ministry introduced its India Bill.

Almost any India bill which the Conservatives could have framed would have offered a fair target ; but that which Disraeli expounded to the House of Commons, on March 26, invited not only attack but ridicule.   Anxious to draw votes from members who would not normally give them support, the Conservative leaders proposed to erect for the government of the great dependency a council of eighteen members, of whom five were to be elected by the £10 householders of the five greatest commercial cities of the United Kingdom.   This hybrid measure was received in a manner which Palmerston did not greatly exaggerate :

> People met one another in the street, and one laughed and the other laughed, and everybody laughed.   ' What are you laughing at ? ' said one.   ' Why, at the India Bill, to be sure.   What are you laughing at ? '   ' Why, I was laughing at the India Bill, too.' [36]

Certainly the House of Commons laughed immoderately ; and the chuckles from the occupants of the opposition benches were as much over the predicament of their opponents as over the fantastic nature of the bill.   No party or group save the Conservative minority would approve the measure ; and Disraeli, on April 2, warned his chief that it would probably be rejected on the second reading. His pessimism was quite justified ; for it seemed that Russell would take the field, with Palmerston and the late cabinet at his back.[37]   Granville lamented over the prospect :

> I am sure our danger is being too impatient.   Pam has no time to wait.   The opinion, which in this case is almost as serious as the fact, is rapidly growing, that he is no longer the same man.   Johnny is impatient by nature.[38]

' Johnny ' had in fact sent word to the late ministers that he was inclined to move the rejection of the bill, and had received their promise of support.

And then Russell, with his genius for upsetting Palmerston's plans, suddenly intervened to save the government.[39]   There is no reason to suppose that he agreed with Granville as to the danger of assailing Derby's ministry too soon. The only question seems to be whether he desired to keep the government of India out of party politics, as he and certain of his friends alleged, or whether he wished to keep Palmerston out of the premiership and place himself once more in the forefront of affairs, as was much more commonly believed. In any case he sent word privately to the embarrassed Disraeli that he was prepared to offer resolutions of his own for reforming the government of India. Thanks to Disraeli's adroitness, and to the anger of the regular opposition at Russell's action, the result was even more of a triumph for the Conservatives than could have been foreseen. When Disraeli gracefully announced that he felt it incumbent upon him to give resolutions offered with such ' high authority ' the precedence over his own measure,[40] the opposition, being determined to rob Russell of the fruits of his manœuvring at any cost, insisted that the responsibility of wording and introducing the resolutions should be taken over by the government. Thus Disraeli obtained an opportunity to correct all his mistakes and enlist additional support. To Palmerston nothing remained save to jeer in his best style at Disraeli's efforts to rescue the original bill from complete obloquy :

> The right hon. Gentleman, like Antony, came to bury his Bill, and not to praise it. . . . We have been assisting at a sort of Irish wake.[41]

But more than one corpse was present. Whig-Liberal hopes of upsetting the government on the Indian question were dead.

The first attack on the Conservatives had never developed to a critical point ; but the second proved, as Greville said, a ' Marengo ' for the Whig-Liberals—an anticipated triumph changed into a disastrous rout.[42] The affairs of India again furnished a battle-ground.[43] Lord Canning, as governor-general, had issued a proclamation which on its face appeared to call for brutal and indiscriminate confiscation of land in the province of Oudh ; but which, as interpreted and explained by its author, could be considered wise and not especially harsh. A draft of the proclamation reached England in advance of the explanations ;

and the explanations when they did arrive were given in a
letter to the retiring Whig-Liberal president of the Board
of Control (*i.e.* the minister for India), Vernon Smith.
Smith failed to hand over the letter to his successor, Lord
Ellenborough, as promptly as he should have done ; but
even this delay could not excuse Ellenborough for what
ensued.   With all that intolerable pomposity which caused
him to be likened generally to a peacock, he reproved Canning in the most scathing and immoderate terms ; and, what
was worse, gave both proclamation and reproof publicity
by laying them before the House.   Here then was promising
ground for an attack—the infliction of public humiliation
on a man who had earned great thanks and praise for his
activities during the mutiny.   The fact that Ellenborough,
on discovering the seriousness of what he had done,
resigned, was not sufficient to exculpate the ministry ;
for the other members of the cabinet had had ample
opportunity to alter or suppress his inexcusable despatch.
The Whig-Liberal leaders, finding that Russell and other
fair-minded members of the House, to say nothing of
Canning's friends, could be counted on to vote with them,
decided on a shrewd plan of attack.   Resolutions of censure
on the government were to be moved by members who did
not figure as Whig-Liberals : by Shaftesbury in the Lords,
and Cardwell, the Peelite, in the Commons.   Had the
vote been taken immediately, they would apparently have
been successful in both Houses.[44]

Why, then, their rout ?   In some part it was due to the
skill of Disraeli and his henchmen in emphasising Vernon
Smith's mistake and Canning's alleged harshness. Emphasis
on the latter provided fair bait for members of humanitarian
impulses, and fair excuse for members primarily intent
on preventing Palmerston's return to power.   Roebuck,
Graham and Bright all felt impelled to go to the Conservatives' rescue ; and Granville considered that the deciding
factor in the House of Lords was the ' hatred ' felt by
Aberdeen for Palmerston.[45]   The outcome may also have
been due in some degree to Derby's luck.   For Derby (of
whom it was remarked that there was almost too much of
the stable about him for a prime minister) appears to have

benefited in this crisis from his connection with the turf. A two-day adjournment of parliament was considered indispensable, so that the members might be present at the race which bore the premier's name ; and this gave time for the arrival from India of despatches which strengthened the government's defence. But the interlude did not suffice to put an end to such tumult as even the lower House had seldom if ever experienced :

> Language almost transgressing the borders of decency was used, and it seemed at one time as if men would have come to blows. The Derby intervened . . . but the fury was renewed afterwards. . . . No one can form the least idea, from looking at Hansard, of what took place. The cheering, groaning, laughing, were beyond belief. We considered ourselves justified in using inarticulate means of rendering the eloquence of the other side nugatory. . . .[46]

In the last analysis, the factor which turned the scale seems to have been the government's appeal to the self-interest of the members of the lower House, an appeal which involved some rather questionable tactics on the part of the Conservative leaders, of Graham, and of the Court.[47] Disraeli threatened that Derby, if defeated, would dissolve, thus forcing the members of the House to go through a second tiresome and expensive election within a year. Such procedure was highly improper, not to say unconstitutional ; and the Queen at first refused flatly to lend herself in any way to it. But later she gave way, on condition that ' risk ' should be eliminated, that ' details ' should not be entered on, and that ' her honour would be safe ' in Derby's hands. Perhaps there was some measure of excuse in Derby's and Disraeli's apparently sincere belief that Palmerston was spreading the report that the Queen would not permit the premier to dissolve ; but the honesty of Graham's conduct in particular was extremely dubious.[48]

Thus came the debates remembered for Bright's unchivalrous suggestion that Liberal majorities were secured by distribution, with a ' discriminating hand,' of Lady Palmerston's ' beautifully engraved cards ' ;[49] and thus came Disraeli's first great triumph in the House. As the debate went on night after night, it slowly became clear that, instead of victory, the Whig-Liberals were in for a humiliating defeat. Disraeli's famous description of the ' earthquake ' which finally ensued [50] is less enlightening than Granville's analysis :

> I felt my tail between my legs when . . . I came into the House of Commons just in time to hear Pam advise Cardwell to withdraw his motion. We cut rather a foolish figure. I believe that a hundred Radicals agreed at the last moment that they must do everything to prevent a dissolution. . . . I have had a correspondence with Aberdeen. . . . I believe that he and Gladstone . . . were determined at all price to prevent Palmerston forming another Government.[51]

For if Derby had fallen, the Queen would almost certainly have sent for Palmerston.[52]

The end of the session of 1858 found the British party system more chaotic than ever. True, the Conservative government had become decidedly stronger. It had not only routed its enemies, but had managed to transfer the government of India entirely to the Crown, to postpone consideration of parliamentary reform, to obtain some satisfaction from Naples, and to smooth matters with the French. But its legitimate supporters were still a mere minority ; and union among its rivals seemed an impossibility. It appeared to Greville that the opposition would have to be ' completely reorganised and reformed ' before it could ' take the field again.' [53] Some of its more liberal adherents, disgusted by the party quarrels, were demanding complete new leadership, and even threatening to cross the House. As for the Peelites, they had practically passed out of existence as a group.[54] Gladstone had been deterred from accepting a post in Derby's ministry only by his failure to induce his former associates to go with him ; and it was far from certain that he would not yet emerge from his well of loneliness on the Conservative side. Graham and Aberdeen were practically out of politics : Herbert, Newcastle and Cardwell were acting more and more with Palmerston. But, for all that the Peelites were ' disjointed and unpopular,' for all that there was ' no cohesion among the Liberals,' [55] the existence of Derby's

government was precarious and even scandalous. Never
had a cabinet been so dependent on its natural enemies.
John Lothrop Motley was interested to find that ' the extreme
Liberal party ' had ' taken the present Ministers under its
protection,' and amused to see Bright ' patting Disraeli on
the head from the Opposition benches.' [56] Granville was
disgusted at the lack of principle exhibited by a ministry
' ready to give up anything that anybody asks for.' [57] The
radicals sneered at it even in giving it their votes ; while
Prince Albert described its situation with unwonted
exaggeration and humour :

> A Tory Ministry, with a Radical programme, carrying out
> Republican measures, with a Conservative majority, against a Liberal
> opposition, is a considerable difficulty for a constitutional monarch. [58]

No wonder the political prophets were much at odds.
Granville and Herbert gave Derby two or three years of
office ; Russell and most of the Whig-Liberals conceded
him six months. Palmerston decided that : ' If I was to
make a book about the govt. chances I would rather back
them in than out for next session.' [59]

It was rather a delicate matter for Russell and Palmerston
to speculate on the probable date of Derby's overthrow ; for
everyone felt that until they two had composed their differences the formation of a strong Whig-Liberal administration
would be almost impossible. But how was an understanding
to be reached ? It was not at all a question of letting bygones
be bygones ; Palmerston at least was always ready to do
that. It was not even a matter of immediate precedence ;
for Granville was acting as leader. It was primarily a
struggle as to which would be premier in a new Whig-
Liberal government. Most people felt that Palmerston's
were the better claims ; but Russell was as ambitious as he
was obstinate ; and his position was in some ways very
strong. Not only would it be almost impossible to dispense
with his support ; but he could claim to be the fitter of
the two rivals to deal with what seemed an increasing
popular demand for the reform of parliament. No persuasion was effectual to bring him to a settled and reasonable
stand. His strange and contradictory impulses had grown

so pronounced that his proud and devoted brother, the duke of Bedford, burned his letters instantly lest they should leave a record damaging to his renown.[60]   In vain Whig leaders tried to persuade each of the rivals that he would be very splendid and happy in the House of Lords, or that the Foreign Office yawned for him : in vain meetings of the two were planned.[61]   Social amenities were perfectly preserved : Lady Palmerston pointed out that her husband had ' a great affection for John,' and Palmerston declared himself quite ready for any meeting that might be arranged.[62] But when, before the second attack on Derby's government, the rivals had met on neutral ground and Palmerston had driven Lord John home, it had been noted with pain that he did not enter Russell's house, and that things remained just as they had been before.[63]

Palmerston, for all his frequent impulsiveness, could play a waiting game.   During the balance of the session he took a fling at Disraeli now and then;[64] but he delivered nothing more serious than harassing fire.   In September, Prince Albert noticed his tactics :

Lord Palmerston himself remains, outwardly at least, quite cheerful, and seems to care very little about his reverses ; he speaks on all subjects, bids for the Liberal support as before, even at the expense of his better conviction . . . and keeps as much as possible before the public ; . . .[65]

Waiting, no doubt, for the ' second reaction ' which Granville had looked upon as possible, he also kept up his old time hospitality.   Two Americans have testified to that.   He had now moved into Cambridge House at 94 Piccadilly, a mansion then carrying the glamour of former royal occupancy, but more associated now with Lady Palmerston's parties.   Motley, visiting him there, was struck with his handsome appearance, his cordial manner, and his ' very gentle, soft, and winning' address.[66]   He noted too, the famous blue coat with gilt buttons, the fashion of an earlier day.   Late in the following month Dallas went to visit at Broadlands.   He was enchanted with the beauty of the place—with the ' sparkling, murmuring' stream that formed a border to the lawn, with the magnificent timber,

and with the paintings and 'rare objects of vertu.'[67]
But he was still more delighted with his host :

> While Morphy was challenging and beating all Europe at chess
> in Paris I was following his illustrious and patriotic example by
> conquering the conqueror of Derby at billiards, and by outshooting
> him marvellously during a five hours' tramp after partridges. . . .
> Our coveys were shy and required more than usual activity in pursuit ;
> and it was glorious to see how this veteran managed to keep up his
> animation and brisk step to the very last, dressing and coming to
> dinner too in an hour afterwards as if he had been upon a satin sofa
> all day.

Palmerston's graciousness to his American guests may
perhaps have been evidence of nothing save kindly hospitality ; but his travels during these two months suggest
that politics were by no means absent from his mind.
What the Prince Consort described as ' an official tour ' of
Ireland was followed by a visit to Paris, where he dined
with the Emperor, went shooting at St. Germain and found
both Napoleon and Walewski very friendly and gracious.[68]
He wrote Granville admiringly of the French sovereign's
abilities. ' Napoleon, in beautifying his capital, merely
followed Augustus ; but he would probably do far more
than his Roman prototype for the actual prosperity of his
empire.'

One would like to know more of this visit to Paris, and
especially of the conversations with Walewski and Napoleon.
For the French Augustus was entering upon a course of
action calculated to make his relations with any English
party leader an element of importance in British and in
continental politics. The essential quality of this course of
action was well indicated by the Paris wits who remarked
that the imperial boast, ' *L'Empire, c'est la Paix* ' was
coming to sound suspiciously like ' *L'Empire, c'est l'Épée* ' ![69]
And the particular manifestations of Napoleon's *neues Kurs*
were two : on the one hand, extensive additions to the fleet
and to the fortifications on France's northern coast; on the
other, an increasingly obvious intention (especially since
the Orsini outrage) to ' do something ' for Sardinia and
Cavour.

The effects of Napoleon's policy of strengthening the

coast fortifications and the fleet were not long in making themselves felt in the domain of English party politics. It was not merely that England, for reasons geographical and historical, was the last country which could afford to be indifferent to French preparations for naval warfare at any time. The very circumstances which had brought the defeat of Palmerston's government had shown that the hostility to the English of a large and influential portion of the French, a feeling merely latent at the best of times, was now especially acute. The Emperor seemed friendly ; but the Emperor was always a little unfathomable, and was necessarily susceptible to French public sentiment. Moreover, in September of this year, he made the blunder of calling British attention to his activities in the most dramatic manner possible. Proud of his new fortifications at Cherbourg and of his growing fleet, and at the same time anxious to reanimate the declining friendship between Windsor and Versailles by one of those personal visits which had been so effective in the past, he invited the Queen and Prince Consort to witness a naval review at Cherbourg in August. The result was the exact reverse of what he had desired.[70] The Queen and Prince found him (for reasons of which more anon) suspiciously ' *boutonné* and silent.' Worse still, the review suggested French success in outbuilding the British fleet ; while the hundreds of cannon which thundered from the forts and encircling hills in a spectacular farewell salute, seemed to Victoria and Albert and their suite to be pointed with dire intention at the British shore. Nor did French humour fail to find stimulation in the review. It was pointed out that the initials of the four royal personages, emblazoned in fireworks, spelt NEVA, thus carrying a graceful compliment to the Tsar.[71]

As the autumn advanced, suspicion of France in British official circles became even more pronounced. Malmesbury, the foreign secretary, took quite seriously a secret plan for the invasion of England worked out by a French admiral the year before.[72] Even the growing realization that Austria rather than England was for the time being at least Napoleon's potential foe did little to reassure either the royal family or the Foreign Office. Victoria regarded

NAPOLEON III

Austria as a very essential part of Germany, and Germany as her own and her husband's spiritual home. Malmesbury remembered that Austria had proved herself, only ten years before, the main upholder of that settled order so dear to the Conservatives. Peace in Europe and good will to all sovereigns established by Wellington and Castlereagh, was the favourite Christmas carol of that year for the British Court and ministry.

Already, too, the British press and public were commencing to take alarm. *The Times* became more and more bitter in its criticism of the French, while the people on the south coast began to suffer from nightmares. When a highly stimulated junior officer of the navy, left in charge for an evening of a warship in Queenstown harbour, enjoyed himself by firing indiscriminate salutes, ladies fainted and officers dashed up from all directions to the cry : ' The French are come.' [73] Panics soon affect politics.

As for the other side of Napoleon's ' new course,' the planning with Sardinia of a war to expel the Austrians from Italy, the essential bargain had been concluded by Napoleon and Cavour at Plombières in July. This probably accounts for the fact that Victoria and Albert found Napoleon so *boutonné*, and makes one curious concerning his conversation with Palmerston. The matter was, of course, as secret as it could be made ; but the trend of Napoleon's policy was unmistakable. If war actually came, just what should be the British attitude ? Here again was a matter upon which British party leaders might ruminate.

As no immediate crisis was in sight, anything resembling a decision could be postponed ; yet even so early as in the autumn of 1858 a shrewd politician might have formed something rather better than a guess as to how certain political groups and politically influential individuals would react to Napoleon's activities. No group or individual of them all would favour war for England unless it were actually forced on her ; but within a neutral status there was wide latitude. The Conservatives, it could be foretold, would arm the country against the possibility of French attack, and throw all their sympathy to Austria. The ' economic ' radicals would decry, not only expenditure for

armament, but such risk of loss in international friendship
and the trade that went with it, as any diplomatic efforts
on behalf of the Italians might entail.   The other groups,
divided between dread of France and sympathy for the
Italian liberals, would probably prove susceptible to leadership.   The prospects with respect to individuals were also
interesting.   Russell's Italian sympathies, reinforced by
his marriage with Minto's daughter and a recent trip to
Italy, were as fervent as Palmerston's.   And Gladstone's
had for years been deepening.   There was at least a
possibility (it could be no more) that Napoleon might help
to tilt the British parliamentary kaleidoscope.

But where in all this picture was Lord Palmerston, the
man who had proved as resolute as Castlereagh to preserve
the balance of power and check the French, and yet had
always seemed inclined to maintain the best of relations
with the new Napoleon ?   No one could be expected to
prove more jealous of French armaments containing any
challenge to British security ; yet no British statesman
would be more pleased (in the interests both of continental
liberalism and of the balance of power) to see the Austrians
driven from Italy.   Had he not given an amazing promise
to Cavour ?   He had his own career to think of, too.
England, delivered from the perils of the Crimean war and
of the mutiny, had found it possible to dispense with him ;
but might not England, faced with the possibilities of French
attack and the incalculable dangers of a continental war,
turn back to him ?   On the whole, the prospects which
Napoleon was opening up were not altogether unpromising
from his point of view ; but any precipitate act or declaration on his part would have been very dangerous.   Public
alarm and suspicion concerning Napoleon's forts and ships
almost entirely obscured any public sympathy for the
Italians.   One thing was sure : he would have to proceed
cautiously.

He proceeded so cautiously that it is doubtful whether
anyone will ever succeed in following his steps as regards his
connection with Napoleon.   But it seems worthy of note
that Malmesbury believed the connection to be close and
most carefully concealed.[74]   Given that this was true, the

principal connecting link was Persigny, the highly emotional
French ambassador, who seems almost to have worshipped
Palmerston and the Anglo-French entente, and to have
been placed at London for this reason. Persigny's grief
at Palmerston's fall was unabated, and his indiscretions,
according to Malmesbury, astonishing. So far did he go
in seeking advice from Palmerston, and in repeating to
Palmerston all that he heard from the Conservative premier
and foreign secretary, that all important communications
to the French government were sent to Napoleon's foreign
minister, Walewski. Persigny resigned, apparently hoping
to precipitate Walewski's fall. He was disappointed ; but
his return to Paris gave Palmerston a devoted friend in
the Emperor's entourage. A second bond is said to have
been furnished by Algernon Borthwick of the *Morning
Post*. Borthwick, on visiting Paris, was not only warmly
received by Napoleon, but actually allowed to see private
despatches from Malmesbury, which furnished the *Post*
with material for attacks on Derby's ministry. On the
basis of these facts, Malmesbury and Vitzthum (the
Saxon diplomat and friend of the Prince Consort) accused
Palmerston of plotting to upset the Derby government.
The allegation is unproved if not unprovable ; and it
seems fairly certain that Palmerston warned the French
emperor, during the autumn of 1858, against counting on
English sympathy if he forced war on Austria.[75]

That the understanding between Palmerston and Napoleon was by no means perfect is suggested, ironically enough,
by the fact that the Emperor invited Palmerston and
Clarendon to visit him, in November, at Compiègne. For
the ex-premier the invitation was exceedingly embarrassing.[76]
British feeling against the French, already hostile enough,
had been reinforced by the belief that Montalembert was
being persecuted for ' a panegyric upon England,' and by
the fact that France was bullying Portugal for having
dared to capture a French slave ship.[77] Of all times in
the world for Palmerston of all men to be called upon to
avow his friendship for Napoleon ! But public opinion
was not his master yet ; and, as he wrote Clarendon, the
visit promised certain advantages :

Perhaps some of our Radical friends would rather not see us too intimate with Napoleon ; on the other hand, our being on personally friendly terms with him may be politically useful to us individually, and to the country—if we should come into office again. . . .[78]

An understanding with the French government was still called for by his foreign policy ; and he knew that in so far as the French nation was concerned the Emperor was quite justified when he declared : ' *L'alliance, je le répète, c'est moi !* '[79] At any rate, it seemed to Palmerston impossible to decline this royal command. The visit itself proved at least a qualified success. The visitors were overwhelmed with entertainments clothed in second empire magnificence : shooting parties with loaders in cocked hats, and beaters moving to the sound of a trumpet in lancers' boots and spurs ; with quadrilles on horseback, indoor football and charades.[80] Palmerston, when the party went hunting on a particularly wet day, contributed to the *décor* by appearing in a red coat, while all the rest were ' muffled up in waterproofs.' Napoleon opened his heart about Italy (though not of course about the details of his bargain with Cavour) ; and Clarendon, alarmed at his ' most strange and extravagant ' ideas, warned him of the dangers of his policy.'[81] What Palmerston said is not disclosed ; but men felt that after his return both he and the *Post* were more than ever ' French.'[82] He even asked Delane to moderate *The Times*' attacks against Napoleon.[83]

It was not, however, so much his increased ' Frenchness ' which interested his contemporaries, as the anticipated effect of the visit on his own career. The knowing ones, such as Guizot, at once pointed out that he was lending himself to Napoleon's scheme of securing England's assistance for the projected ' *coup* ' in Italy :[84] more persons, less informed, saw fresh evidence of the ' subservient predilection' as regards the Emperor of which he had been accused in connection with the Conspiracy Bill.[85] But everyone, apparently, agreed with Lady Theresa Lewis, Clarendon's sister : ' so far as Lord P. is concerned, I should think he had placed another very large nail in the coffin of his premiership.'[86]

This assumption was a trifle premature. It was yet to

be seen how British public opinion would react to Napoleon's Italian policy ; and of course the tenure of the premiership would be decided mainly on matters of domestic politics. In the forefront of these there stood the question of parliamentary reform ; and here, as luck would have it, Palmerston's position was a strategic one. The country was undecided; and he was uncommitted. He was bound to no group of reformers ; and, thanks largely to the war in 1855, the peace in 1856, the dissolution in 1857 and his own fall in 1858, had escaped committing himself to any detailed scheme. He had, indeed, publicly declared his willingness to reduce the voting qualification required for leaseholders and tenants-at-will in the counties from fifty to twenty pounds a year, opposed the assimilation of the county to the borough franchise as a measure that would lead to the disappearance of both boroughs and counties as distinct electoral units, and repeatedly rejected the suggested adoption of the ballot. But the public had not been informed of the views which he had expressed to the Queen in his letter of October 1857.

Shrewd politician that he was, he decided to play a waiting game, remaining in his safe position and allowing enemies or rivals to expose themselves. That they would do so was a certainty. The Conservatives could not avoid offering some sort of bill ; while the radicals, confident of their ability to sway the public and exact terms from the ministry, would certainly rush into the open. By agitation they would force the hands of the Conservatives as other radicals had forced those of the Whigs nearly thirty years before. Even Russell could hardly contain himself, as Palmerston pointed out to Lansdowne on October 19 :

> The Govt seem to have made up their minds to propose a Reform Bill, and I hear that John Russell means to let them play their card, and probably intends to overtrump them, and as he imagines, to win the trick—I think our course should be that of moderation, but we shall have plenty of time to discuss these matters.[87]

It was the radicals who moved first. Even as Palmerston was writing Lansdowne, Bright was embarking on a tour of the great towns of the north, where he preached the

Manchester school's ideas of reform, and attacked aristocracy and the House of Lords.[88]   But England, as Greville noted, was not yet ready for the Manchester scheme.[89]   Even Russell was apparently alarmed at the lengths to which Bright wished to go.[90]   And Palmerston still waited.   On December 19, he wrote Clarendon that the wise procedure was ' to lie quite still.' [91]   To attempt an understanding even with Russell would only be to bring out dangerous differences :

> There are many reasons which make it desirable that some Reform bill should be passed this next session, and I should not be disposed to quarrel with it for its shortcomings unless they were great and manifest.   John Russell, I hear, wants to add a million to the existing voters.   This would be very much to swamp property and intelligence. . . . He at length deems Bright a dangerous man. I suppose this means that he thinks him a dangerous ally, because he [Bright] is losing his hold upon the country by unmasking his revolutionary yearnings.[92]

No more with respect to reform than with respect to Anglo-French relations was the political future clear.

Nothing was less clear than the future of the Whig-Liberal party or that of its late premier.   Graham wrote that the fragments of the party were so shattered by personal dislikes that reunion would be utterly impossible.[93]   Lord Howden found its position as between the Conservatives and radicals ' very difficult, not to say damnable,' and cudgelled his brain in vain to save it from being ' squeezed into nothing between two wedges, or . . . obliged to live by having continually other children's pap forced down their throats.' [94]   And things looked especially unpromising for Palmerston.   The Manchester radicals would reputedly accept no leader save Russell ; and some of Palmerston's former supporters were said to have begged Broughton to persuade him to abdicate the leadership.[95] For the future of the party seemed hopeless, with ' Lord John believing that Lord Palmerston sanctions or orders articles to be written against him, and then Lord Palmerston supposing the *Daily News* pleases Lord John by attacking the Compiègne visit.' [96]   For the printing-press was one of the chief arms in the strange warfare that was going on.

Gladstone was attacking Palmerston and even the party most virulently in the *Quarterly* ; while the *Edinburgh* was too much maimed by party dissensions to return effective fire.[97] The radical press was inflicting damage, too—so much so that Palmerston had opened a subscription for the purpose of buying up the weekly *Statesman* and turning it into a penny daily in order to show ' that Bright's real wish is to assimilate our constitution to that of the United States of America, and to point out in detail the vices and faults of the American system.'[98] Perhaps the money would have come in faster if those he solicited had not been so inclined to consider his days of glory at an end. For many of his old adherents, even Clarendon, ranked at this time as the most devoted of them all, thought his return to the premiership practically hopeless. Some even ventured to tell him so. They might as well have talked to Nelson's Monument.

CHAPTER XXVIII

PALMERSTON AGAIN PREMIER

NELSON on his pillar must have received many appreciative glances from Englishmen in the early days of 1859 ; for this year, the year that was to see the Liberal party really consolidated at last and Palmerston made prime minister for life, found England in a sadly frightened and bewildered state. From New Year's day the prospect of a war deliberately provoked by France and Sardinia against Austria became imminent. To Victoria, and to most of her subjects who thought about such things, the prospect was fraught with appalling possibilities. If Napoleon were successful, he would set no bounds to his aggression ; if he failed, his imperial dominion, which had proved so stabilising an influence for France and for the continent as a whole, would be at an end. In any case, the dreaded general war and epidemic of revolutions might be at hand. There was fear in the hearts of the timorous at the thought that England, with a moribund government, insufficient defences and a fleet almost certainly inferior to that of France,[1] would probably be involved. Even parliamentary reform yielded place in public interest :

> Let your Reform for a moment go,
>   Look to your butts and take good aims.
> Better a rotten borough or so,
>   Than a rotten fleet or a city in flames ! [2]

Indignation, too, possessed a great number of the Queen's subjects—indignation against Napoleon, Victor Emmanuel and Cavour. Malmesbury could resign himself to the eternal and inalterable fact that France was 'a curse to Europe,' but not to the conduct of 'that little

conceited, mischievous State now called " Sardinia." '³
It was ' intolerable,' he wrote, ' that Europe should be
deluged with blood for the personal ambition of an Italian
attorney and a tambour major, like Cavour and his master.'⁴
Lord Cowley, the successor of Normanby at Paris, who
had always been on the most friendly terms with Napoleon,
was equally shocked. The tambour major, once suitor for
the hand of Princess Mary of Cambridge, had now married
one of his mistresses, and wished her to be acknowledged
as queen : ' And this is the man for whose sake Europe is
to be embroiled in a bloody war.' ⁵ The sympathy of the
English seemed to lie almost wholly with Austria. Aberdeen,
who was undergoing torments of self-reproach for having
allowed England to go to war with Russia, was apparently
quite ready to take up arms on her behalf.⁶ Great Whigs,
such as Clarendon, Lewis and Granville, thought only of
restraining France.⁷ The population at large was supposedly so excited against Napoleon that the ministry had
difficulty in framing a sufficiently noncommittal speech
from the throne for the opening of parliament.⁸ Hardly
anyone seemed to care much about Italian liberation ;
hardly anyone save Palmerston and Russell and, of course,
Gladstone, who was far away on a mission to the Ionian
Islands. And of these Palmerston was the one on whom
the attention of nervous and pro-Austrian Englishmen
was concentrated. His ' dicta,' wrote Charles Greville,
were infinitely more important than those of Lord John.⁹

Why this intense concentration on Palmerston ? Why
did Lewis say that ' on Palmerston's language in the House
of Commons the peace of the world might possibly depend ' ?¹⁰ It was because, as Cowley explained, there
was panic in France itself at the prospect of the war ; and
Napoleon, now hesitating about carrying out his undertaking with Cavour, was waiting for a sign.¹¹ It is easy
to infer the rest. Expressions of sympathy from the most
internationally known of British statesmen, the old champion
of continental liberalism, the man who had so well succeeded
in the past in bringing parliament and public to his views
on foreign policy, would fortify the French and Sardinians,
and create a deep impression on other peoples. And one

could add to this the probability that Palmerston would again be premier before many months had passed. Slowly but surely his political stock had been going up again. No doubt the collapse of Bright's crusade, the new dangers abroad, Russell's unpopularity, and Palmerston's steady refusal to abdicate the leadership of the Whig-Liberals all played their part. At any rate, Napoleon, who could count on him to show no favour to Austria, appeared to hang upon his words. ' You must not mind my saying,' Cowley wrote Malmesbury, ' . . . that the line that Palmerston may take will in all likelihood turn the scale.' [12] And to Palmerston himself he made a personal appeal :

> . . . I think that although out of office, you may render a great public service. . . . I fear the Emperor [Napoleon] . . . finds himself, as it were, on the verge of war, without exactly knowing how he has been brought into that dilemma. The panic, however, which this state of things has created has shown H.M. that his country is not disposed to go to war, and he accordingly hesitates what to do. . . . From many circumstances which have come to my knowledge, I feel certain that the Emperor looks very much to the opinions which you may express. . . .[13]

Apparently he also had in mind the effect which Palmerston might produce upon the members of the House : ' If our Parliament takes the line of justifying the ejection of Austria from Italy, the probability is that we shall have war in the Spring.'

It seemed at first that the appeal had been successful if not superfluous. ' Jupiter Anglicanus,' as his private letters show, agreed with the pro-Austrians at many points.[14] If he sympathised with the attorney and the tambour major and all nationally minded Italians, if he believed that both Italy and Austria would be much better off when the last Austrian soldier had been withdrawn across the Alps, he would do nothing to encourage aggression on the part of Napoleon and Cavour. He had times of doubting whether the gain to the Italians which might accrue from war would afford sufficient compensation for the suffering and loss entailed : and he was always conscious of the danger that Austria, engaged in Italy, might be dismembered by risings in Hungary and Galicia. There were other reasons, too. Without sharing the fear of immediate French invasion, he was by no means blindly trustful of Napoleon ; and he could not quite forget that England was a signatory to the settlements of 1815 from which Austria derived her rights in Italy. What was more, he had a personal motive for adopting an attitude of reserve, a motive which Clarendon pointed out :

> I dare say the Emperor is speculating upon the change of goverment, and the countenance he shall receive to his anti-Austrian policy from Palmerston and Lord John. He will be disappointed however, for at present no Minister here could stand a week who was thought to be favourable to war. . . .[15]

Palmerston had had a lesson in running athwart public opinion a year before ; and he had enjoyed little opportunity as yet of guiding it, in so far as Italian nationalism was concerned. It would hardly have been prudent to defy it, at a moment when his party was still disorganised, his great rival for the leadership was bidding for support, and the fate of all political leaders and parties was *en jeu*.[16] Hence Greville, reading some of his letters, thought him ' exceedingly sound and judicious ' on foreign affairs, and in his apparent ' lack of impatience to return to office.'[17] Hence, too, when parliament was opened on February 3, and foreign affairs brought into debate in connection with the address, Derby was able to report that Palmerston had ' maintained as strongly as Your Majesty's Ministers the necessity of adhering to the faith of treaties,' and ' condemned in no equivocal terms the conduct of Sardinia.'[18] Russell had taken the same line. Three days later, Cowley wired from Paris of ' a great change for the better ' there,[19] attributing it in considerable part to the debates at Westminster. Relieved for the moment from any great anxiety concerning events abroad, Derby's ministry turned to the favourite game of politicians at the time, the game of ' parliamentary reform.' Its chances seemed by no means bad ; for Disraeli had been flirting successfully with some of the independent liberals,[20] and the session had opened quite propitiously.[21]

The reform bill which Disraeli introduced[22] seemed

to many a ' homœopathic ' dose,[23] effecting a little piece-
meal redistribution, disfranchising the forty-shilling freeholders, virtually assimilating the county to the borough
franchise, and offering votes to special classes (' fancy
franchises,' in Bright's contemptuous phrase) on a system
surprisingly like that suggested to the Queen by Palmerston.
Naturally enough the bill was instantly assailed by the stiffer
Conservatives as opening the way for the submergence of
the upper and middle class electorate, and by the radicals
as damming up the course of democratic evolution. Bright
wrote in his diary that it was ' an insult to the country.'[24]
Naturally enough, too, the Whig-Liberal opposition,
studiously reserved at the outset, pressed its advantage as
the criticism swelled.[25] Disraeli's almost pathetic pleas that
the measure should be considered without reference to
party politics, and his offers to mould it to the tastes of the
majority of the House, were brushed aside. On the second
reading he was given a taste of the medicine he had helped
to administer to Palmerston.[26] Russell, working as usual
with Graham, moved an amendment as cunningly contrived
to catch votes from different sections of the House as that
which had overthrown the Whig-Liberal ministry a year
before. By attacking both the disfranchisement of the
twenty-shilling freeholders in the counties, and the retention
of the £10 borough franchise, the amendment drew support
at once from those who felt the government had gone too
far and those who were angry that it had not gone further.[27]
The parliamentary battle which ensued was described
delightfully by Granville :

> In the House of Commons I am told that the scene was most
> dramatic. Johnny in his best manner, holding his arm and stroking
> his elbow, expressed his indignation in the most dignified way.
> Stanley reeled, and tried to evade the question, when Pam hit him
> under the ear on the other side, and laid him prostrate amid cheers
> which rang all round the House.[28]

In the heat of battle the members had almost forgotten that
the contest was supposedly about reform.[29] On April 1,
after protracted debates, and accompanied by ' confusion
and excitement and noise ' which White could find no words

to describe,[30] the amendment was carried by a majority of 39.
No wonder members were confused. It was not every day
that the House saw Palmerston voting side by side with
Bright ! Then, like a ' bombshell ' (for bombshells seem
to have exploded rather frequently in the House of Commons
in those years) came the sequel : Derby would not resign.
Instead he demanded an appeal to the electorate. The
speaker regarded this as ' a rash and mischievous act.' [31]
The Queen, however, was ready not only to dissolve, but
apparently to pray that the Almighty would give the
majority of her voting subjects Conservative hearts.[32]
Surely He would be on the side of Austria.

According to Greville's much quoted and generally
accepted dictum, Palmerston showed himself ' very insincere '
in the reform debates.[33] And it is certainly difficult to
credit him with a desire for the ' greater extension of the
franchise in cities and boroughs ' for which Lord John's
amendment called. But it is not clear that his opportunism
went beyond that of Disraeli or certain other leaders of the
House. True, he agreed with Disraeli rather than with
Russell on redistribution, fancy franchises and the qualifications for voters in the boroughs. But the assimilation of
the county to the borough franchise, which formed the
outstanding feature of the bill, traversed one of his few
definite principles, in making for the creation of electoral
districts ; [34] while Argyll was convinced that he would
have swallowed even this, and voted for the bill, had it not
been for ' the folly of the Government in insisting on the
forty-shilling clause.' [35] And was a leader of the opposition,
recently turned out on little more than a technicality,
longing for reasons selfish and unselfish to return to power
—was he to be convicted of excessive opportunism for
refusing to extricate his successor from a scrape ? Sincere
or not, Palmerston had played a part that was cautious, and
in all probability shrewdly planned. Holding back on the
first reading, he had consented, on the second, to follow
Russell's lead. Thus he had encouraged Lord John to
incur a charge of undue eagerness to be in power again, and
had offered a subtle flattery which might later yield returns.
And Russell, as though determined to involve his party,

and to place his personal ambitions beyond doubt, had quite gratuitously explained to parliament his own projected reform bill.[36]   As between Palmerston and Russell there is little doubt as to whose chances of the premiership were improved and whose impaired when the House was dissolved by proclamation, on April 23.   But the effect of Victoria's prayers had still to be known.

The fervency of the Queen's devotions reflects the fact that the 'great change for the better' at Paris had not been maintained, and that a continental war had become more than ever imminent.   The situation was as disappointing to the Court and cabinet as it was alarming ; for Derby's ministry had done all that cautious and noncommittal diplomacy could do in the interests of peace.[37]   Late in February, Cowley, who stood in friendly relations not only with Napoleon but with the Austrian minister, Buol, had gone to Vienna on a mission of explanation and appeasement. The results, while inconclusive, had not been unpromising. But, hardly had Cowley returned to Paris at the middle of March, than Napoleon, casually putting the mission and its results aside, announced that he and the Tsar wished to submit the whole Italian question to a congress of the five great Powers.   Derby's ministry, though disappointed and distrustful, dared not object ; for Napoleon, supposedly at least, ruled the action of Victor Emmanuel and Cavour, and, consequently, the decision as to peace or war.   But the ' tambour major ' and ' Italian attorney ' were able after all to get the situation largely under their control. They had already checked the progress of negotiations by the mobilisation of their troops : they now proceeded to make the assembling of a congress difficult if not impossible.   On the one hand, they brought pressure on Napoleon by threatening an exposure of his secret diplomacy ; on the other, they goaded the Austrians to take some warlike step, by flaunting their own preparations for hostilities, and demanding that Sardinia be admitted to the proposed congress.   In vain the Derby government tried to administer fresh ' opiates and sedatives ' to the French emperor : in vain it commended Cowley for giving it as his personal opinion that if Napoleon went to war with Austria ' without reason . . . he would have both the moral and material efforts of England arrayed against him.'[38] Before April was over, or the British elections had been held, Cavour's policy had proved almost more successful than he had any right to hope. For Austria, losing patience, suddenly defeated the efforts of her friends, put herself in the wrong, and made war unavoidable, by demanding that Sardinia should disarm within three days. Italy's English friends received the news with mixed feelings. Palmerston, quite incredulous at first, reminded Granville that the gods make mad those whom they will destroy.[39] And to Clarendon he wrote :

We have, therefore, a hedge against Fate. If this squall blows over, we shall have peace, and that will be one good thing : if war ensues, we shall have Italy freed from the Austrians, and that would be another good thing. In any case we must stand aloof and not engage in the war.[40]

At least it relieved him from having to be so careful about what he said.

By this time a large proportion of his fellow-countrymen had come to share his sympathies in the continental quarrel ; for a remarkable change in public sentiment had set in during March.[41] In that month Gladstone had returned to England by way of Italy, 'completely duped by Cavour,'[42] to scandalise Aberdeen, and to reinforce the small but influential group of pro-Italians. In that month a band of Neapolitan liberals, under sentence of transportation to America, landed at Queenstown, crossed over to England, and drove through the London streets in laurel-decked cabs, preceded by a band. ' To welcome or relieve the Neapolitan prisoners,' wrote Dallas, ' . . . is the order of the day.'[43] To cap the climax came Austria's blunder. The feeling of the English public which, in their sovereign's view, had been ' all that one could desire,' was now expressed ' in the most *vehement* sympathy for *Sardinia*.'[44]

This development produced an amusing and significant change in Palmerston's plans for appealing to the electorate. As early as April 7, he had drafted the speech he was to deliver to his constituents at Tiverton, forwarding a corrected

P

copy to his friend Borthwick of the *Morning Post*.[45] At that time he was still apparently too cautious to commit himself regarding either Italy or reform. According to Borthwick's biographer, the draft contained ' no foam and fury,' and but ' little more than the constitutional question as to whether the Government ought not to have resigned rather than dissolve Parliament.' But the speech, as actually delivered three weeks later, was very different.[46] Though his seat was uncontested, the senior member for Tiverton treated the burgesses, and through the press a vastly larger audience, to an impassioned harangue on the evil doings of Austria in Italy. The Austrians, he said, might appeal to the judgment but not the sympathies of Europe :

I do not say the sympathies of Europe because unfortunately her system of governing those provinces has been such that no man can deny that the discontent which prevails among the peoples of those countries is justified by the maladministration of Austria since she has possessed them. (Cheers.) . . . Austria not content with ruling her own provinces in her own way—and Heaven knows that hers was a way that no right-minded government would have persevered in—entered into negotiations and engagements, exerted influence over and exacted treaties from all the other States of Italy from the Po down to the Mediterranean, by which in all those countries from that time to this the most abominable system of misgovernment has been supported by the confidence which their governments felt that, if the discontent of their subjects should at any time break out into open resistance Austria was there by an overwhelming military force to compel obedience. (Cheers.) . . .

There were cheers, too, for the final pronouncement that if Austria were expelled from Italy ' we shall rejoice at the issue, though we may regret the miseries which may have preceded it.'

The tone of the speech is all the more striking when compared with that which Russell delivered to his London constituents.[47] Frank in his admission of sympathy with Italy's grievances, Lord John coldly charged France and Sardinia with greed of territory, balanced French against Austrian culpability, and declared for ' open, honest and strict neutrality.' ' Lord Palmerston,' *The Times* commented dryly, ' knew very well what England would look

to find in a speech of his at this crisis.' [48]   But Aberdeen
afterwards made a far more interesting comment :

> The most brilliant stroke made was Palmerston's speech at
> Tiverton.   His declared wish to see the Germans turned out of Italy
> by the war has secured Gladstone, who is ready to act with him, or
> under him, notwithstanding the three articles of the *Quarterly* and
> the thousand imprecations of late years. [49]

'Lord Aberdeen,' wrote Gladstone shortly afterwards,
'holds me to be the most extravagant and abandoned of
English politicians.' [50]
    Whether Gladstone or anyone else would act with or
under Palmerston was a matter undetermined for another
month.   For the dissolution had proved ' a blunder and a
crime,' [51] leaving the situation little better than it had been
before.   The elections had given three hundred seats to the
Conservatives, and only some fifty more to all other parties
and groups combined.   There was great uncertainty regarding the future ; and the prospects were none too promising
for Palmerston. [52]   Disraeli, burning for office, and willing
to buy a majority of almost any sort, decided to try his
luck once more.   Writing, early in May, under excuse
of an 'ancient confidence' (which Palmerston apparently
failed to recognise), he dangled no less a bribe than the
Conservative leadership. [53]   Russell, he argued, would
probably be the Queen's next choice for premier ; and
even if Palmerston *were* preferred, he would be forced by
the desertion of advanced liberals into dependence on
Conservative votes.   Would it not be better straightway
to give himself and his personal following to Derby,
who waited only to find himself with a majority before
relinquishing the leadership ?

> . . . You would then be entire master of the situation.   The
> foreign policy of every Government of which you are a member
> must be yours, even if you might not think it expedient to undertake
> the Foreign Office.   As for domestic policy, when the occasion serves,
> you could bring in your own Reform Bill, which, with our increased
> force, may be as conservative as you please.   You could dictate your
> terms . . . what I am now proposing is only an arrangement that

I have long meditated, and more than once endeavoured to accomplish. You would receive from me, not merely cordial co-operation, but a devoted fidelity. . . .[54]

But alas for Disraeli's hopes ! Palmerston's reply was as curt as bare politeness would allow.[55] He was ready to gamble on the chance of becoming the next premier, and of ruling with the aid which, as he quite realised, the Conservatives would not refuse.[56] On May 20 he was seeking ' cordial co-operation ' from Russell at Pembroke Lodge.

The meeting of the two old statesmen, now more than ever rivals, marked, not only the closing of a breach, but the partial cementing of those foundations on which the Liberal party was long to rest secure. Prepared by Lewis and Granville in advance, preceded by a written agreement that Derby should be at once attacked, it had for object the laying of plans to be followed in the day of victory.[57] In two hours the plans were completed in all respects save one. The government was to be challenged on a motion of no confidence, and, if it fell, a ministry broad enough to include the ' best Whigs,' the Peelites, and the ' advanced Liberals ' (as the radicals were now termed), was to be formed. Palmerston, deferring to public opinion on the matter of parliamentary reform, would then accept a bill embodying such reductions in the borough and county franchises as would be satisfactory to Russell and, presumably, to Bright. In general, the prospects seemed excellent. No shadow of disagreement arose on foreign affairs. Granville had already brought the cheering news that Gladstone apparently ' wished his former score rubbed off ' ;[58] and all the other great Peelites, save Aberdeen and possibly Graham, were willing for a marriage with the Whigs under the name of Liberals. Yet in one particular, and no minor one, uncertainty still reigned. Russell had evaded any undertaking to serve in any capacity save that of premier.

Russell's evasiveness hindered the ' Liberal ' leaders in taking the next essential step to power ; but patience and pressure finally removed even this obstacle. The sacred union which the leaders were working to cement had to be accepted by the rank and file—accepted and proclaimed.

But how ?   Palmerston was ready to give a dinner at which
Russell should be a specially honoured guest ; but Russell,
seeing that this would put him obviously in second place,
refused to go.[59]   Nor, in the view of some of the party's
ablest tacticians, would anything less than a general meeting
of all those members of the House who professed liberal
sentiments suffice.[60]   Palmerston protested.   Some of the
members would be sure to say unpleasant things, and strive
to exact pledges which would later be inconvenient.   But
his associates were firm.   Better, Herbert pointed out, to
have unpleasant things said in private than in the House ;
better to face dissensions before the old government was
attacked than when the new was being formed.   Palmerston
gave way ; and the meeting was called at Willis's rooms for
June 6.   The invitations, sent in the name of the most
' advanced ' as well as in that of the most conservative
' Liberals,' drew a great gathering.   Curiosity and excitement ran high ; for no one could be certain as to the result,
and one fundamental condition of unity had apparently not
been satisfied.   Russell, in spite of protests, even by his
brother, the duke of Bedford, against his ' indefensible and
suicidal ' conduct, had not, in so far as was known, given
way.[61]

In the meantime another series of negotiations had been
coming to a head.   Since the introduction of Disraeli's
reform bill, Bright had been in closer relations with the
Whig-Liberals and Peelites.   In Russell, of course, he
found his best prospect ; for Russell was ' moderate and
liberal ' in his views, though ' not disposed to anything
positive.'[62]   When Bright discovered that the elections
had given to him and to his followers the balance of power,[63]
he determined to make use of it.   ' We have the key in
our hands,' he wrote, ' and nobody will pass into office by
us without paying toll to the people and to freedom.'[64]
It was known that he would join in an attack upon the
government, and that his friend, Milner Gibson, might
even take the initiative.[65]   He had his last meeting with
Russell on June 3, at Gibson's house.[66]   Russell was still
firm in his determination not to take second place in the
House to Palmerston ; but he and Bright discussed the

terms on which the radicals might enter the combination
to be formed at Willis's rooms. A bargain was easily
struck, when Russell gave assurances that the Liberals
would offer a reform bill providing for a £6 rental franchise
in the boroughs, and would maintain the strictest neutrality
with respect to the Italian war. On June 5, Bright and
Gibson decided that they would demand at least two seats
in the Liberal cabinet :[67] on the next day they presented
themselves at Willis's rooms.

The meeting, which justified the hopes both of the
optimistic and the curious, and set up a milestone in the
progress of Liberalism, was described by Sidney Herbert
in a manner hardly to be improved upon :

> I am just returned in a state of liquefaction from Willis's Rooms.
> There were about 280 members present, which is thought very large,
> as the Irish members are not yet come over in any number. Pam.
> first got upon the raised dais, and when he helped Johnny up by the
> hand there was a droll burst of cheering. Pam. spoke shortly and
> well, . . . and . . . said that he and Johnny were at one (great
> cheering). Then there was a pause, and a call for Lord John, who
> spoke in the same sense, and said if the vote succeeded it was necessary
> to look forward, and if the Queen sent for Pam., he, Johnny, would
> cheerfully co-operate with him in the formation of a Government
> —broad basis, etc.—and then Pam. whispered to him, and he added
> as much for Pam. Then calls for Bright, who . . . Wanted some
> clearer assurance about war, but upon the whole promised co-operation.
> Pam. gave the clearer assurance, and I got up : said I also came from
> below the gangway. . . . I preached union, . . . Then came
> Mr. E. James, Mr. Loch, Mr. Monckton Milnes, Mr. *Roebuck*,
> Mr. *Horsman*, Mr. *Lindsay* ['independent' Liberals], Mr. Ellice,
> Col. Dearing. The underlined [italicised] men *against*. Roebuck
> very ill received, Horsman only raising difficulties, and wanting it
> put off for ten days, but the rest all for. So the proposition was put
> and carried amidst loud cheers, and Lord Hartington and Mr. Hanbury
> are to move and second the identical amendment which Peel carried
> against Lord Melbourne in 1841. On the whole it was very
> successful, no one objecting who was not expected to do so, and others
> concurring who had not been reckoned on.[68]

Thus, Whig-Liberals, Peelites and radicals appeared to
have been merged into a party quite deserving of the name
Liberal.

Against this merger the ministry could make no stand. When a motion of no confidence, moved by Lord Hartington, came to a division, on June 10, after three nights of spirited debate, only Gladstone and a handful of ' independent ' liberals, led by Horsman and Roebuck, supported the Conservatives. Derby was beaten by thirteen votes in an unusually full house. Carlyle, who seems to have been a little short-sighted now and then, was quite indifferent to the issue of the ' Dizzy vs. Palmy ' fight.[69] But it was one of the decisive divisions of the mid-nineteenth century. Malmesbury wrote that the Sardinian minister and the French chargé, who had been waiting anxiously in the lobby, ' embraced and halloed in the most frantic way when Palmerston walked out of the House.' A wit announced that ' the Old Italian Masters ' had returned.[70] But they were all going somewhat too fast. The Queen could exercise some choice as to the next prime minister.

Never after 1830 did Palmerston obtain high office without encountering serious obstacles. June 1859 furnished no exception to the rule. All the world had supposed that Russell would be his only competitor, and hardly at that an equal one, for the highest office in the state. But Victoria, passing over the verdict rendered at Willis's rooms, on the specious pretext that it would be invidious to choose between her two former prime ministers, selected the smooth and pliant Granville for the place, and demanded that some one other than Palmerston should have the Foreign Office seals.[71] She was to find that the tact and guile which she admired in Granville could hardly match the craft which experience had brought to Russell and Palmerston. Urged to subordinate themselves as a matter of loyalty, they coupled compliance with conditions intrinsically reasonable, yet fatal to the formation of such a government as Victoria desired. For Palmerston, accepting at the outset Granville's offer of the leadership of the Commons, refused to give it up ; while Russell demanded the leadership for himself, and the appointment of Palmerston as foreign minister.[72] But, if the two ex-premiers contributed about equally to making Granville's success impossible, Palmerston's geniality or his shrewdness, as one may prefer to think, gave him once more an advantage over his real competitor. Without concealing his surprise that Granville had been preferred, he seemed whole-heartedly ready to accept the situation, for the good of England and his old political associates.[73]   Russell, on the other hand, stated bluntly that he might take the second place in the new ministry but not the third.[74]   The result was like that of 1855.   Palmerston, when Granville's efforts came to naught, not only received the commission to form a government, but gained credit for his attitude.[75] There was, however, an additional reason why he, not Russell, was the Queen's second choice.   He alone, as Sir George Grey pointed out, could form a government that would draw Conservative support.[76]

Even with the sacred union at his back, even with Gladstone wanting his score rubbed off and Victoria in retreat, Palmerston found the construction of a new ministry no easy task.   A provisional offer of the Foreign Office which had been made to Clarendon ' by the Queen's desire ' had to be withdrawn ; for Russell, being given first choice, would take no other post, and his support was indispensable.[77]   In the same way, Lewis had to relinquish the Exchequer to Gladstone.[78]   The Peelites, now vanishing for all time as a separate group, received, besides the Exchequer, the Colonies (Newcastle), War (Herbert) and the Irish Secretaryship (Cardwell).   Great Whig-Liberals filled most of the other posts.   Granville, leading in the upper House, was given for support besides Newcastle, two others of the ' best tried and least objectionable ' dukes, and by a ' happy hit ' the popular earl of Elgin.[79]   In the Commons, the three gifted and aristocratic baronets, Sir George Grey, Sir George Lewis and Sir Charles Wood (sometimes misnamed the new premier's ' corporal's guard ')[80] joined with Herbert and Cardwell in supporting the great triumvirate comprised of Palmerston, Russell and Gladstone.   Though the premier was willing to give the 'advanced' Liberals some representation in his cabinet, the left wing of his followers did not fare well.   Two 'hard and homely,' but not unsuitable, places were assigned them at the Board of Trade and Poor Law Board ; and these, on

Cobden's refusal to accept a seat,[81] went to Milner Gibson and Charles Villiers. Palmerston seems even to have sounded Bright ; and he was certainly ready to give his most inveterate enemy the empty (but reputedly desired) honour of a privy councillorship. The Queen would not hear of it : it was 'impossible to allege any service' Bright had rendered, and 'problematical whether such an honour conferred upon Mr. Bright would, as suggested, wean him from his present line of policy.'[82]

Palmerston's failure to do more for this group may not have been his fault, but it was decidedly unfortunate. Bright was mortified that no seat had been offered him, and scarcely mollified by the premier's explanation that his attacks on 'classes' during his autumn speaking tour had made his inclusion impossible.[83] He could see no one in the cabinet except Russell and Gibson who would not 'gladly smother' the movement for parliamentary reform.[84] Before the cabinet had settled into place the great radical had decided that, after all, it would have been better for his friends to have kept their independence.[85] He relieved his feelings by writing a sharp editorial for the *Morning Star* on the preference given to Whig placemen and 'the three Baronets.'[86] Thus Palmerston and the Queen had weakened the ministry in advance. It was all very well for Graham, the Peelite, to commend his 'forgiving temper and exemplary fairness,'[87] and for others to note the rich array of talent he had assembled around the cabinet board. To some at least of those who had cheered him at Willis's rooms, the Whig-Peelite aristocrats he had chosen, with three dukes and a duke's son in their midst, represented no very accurate embodiment of the combination on which the Liberals of the left wing had set their hopes. Witness Sir Benjamin Hall, who had expected the Home Office, and found that he was to return to his old post as first commissioner of Works :

I understand that the liberal party are very angry at the arrangement. They say that the agreement entered into at Willis's rooms was that the new Cabinet should be formed upon a broad and liberal basis and that it should fairly represent the various sections of the opposition. These were almost the words used at the meeting which

elicited a universal cheer and settled the affair. . . . Bright has expressed his sentiment in a leader in the *Morning Star* of today, and he
will I have no doubt use his influence with Cobden to induce him
not to enter the Cabinet.   He also said . . . 'I have not seen
Mr. Gibson since the division and I have not heard one word as to
the proposed arrangements.' . . . I sadly fear that we shall all be in
confusion very soon again. . . . The two men most objected to by
the Liberal Party are Gladstone and Sir C. Wood. . . . The Tories
are in high glee and bets were freely offered that the Govt. would be
upset or remodelled in 6 months. . . .[88]

It was with a slim majority, and precarious chances of
retaining any majority at all, that the new cabinet finally
settled down to work in early July.

The ' second reaction ' had occurred : the premier whose
fall had seemed almost irreparable a year before, once more
presided at the Treasury bench.   He was once more
grasping a bundle of sticks, sticks of unusually high quality,
but including not a few that were thorny or slippery.   To
begin with, there was Lord John, with his habit of resigning
and his passion for reform.   There was Gladstone, who had
voted for Derby to the very end, was reputedly ' eulogistic
of rotten boroughs as nurseries of statesmen,' [89]   and
claimed ' close harmony of sentiment ' with the premier
and Lord John only where foreign (*i.e.* pro-Italian) policy
was concerned.[90]   Even his niece wrote of the ' uproar '
which his acceptance of the Exchequer had caused, ' view
his well-known antipathy to the Premier,' and of her inability
to answer the question, ' why, if he can swallow Palmn.,
couldn't he swallow Dizzy, and in spite of him go in under
Lord Derby ? ' [91]   Then there was Sir Charles Wood,
' the Spider,' with his unfortunate unpopularity,[92] and
Newcastle with his inconvenient insistence that the cabinet
should have the last word in diplomacy.[93]   There were Gibson and Villiers, whose thoughts were partly in Manchester,
and Elgin who, discontented with the place assigned
to him, seldom took his mind from the Far East.[94]   ' There
are,' wrote Shaftesbury, ' elements of discord, rivalry,
intrigue, ambition . . . if Palmerston were removed, the
whole thing would be an agglomeration (and nothing more)
of molecules floating in various, and ever opposite, direc-

tions.'[95] Against him was a compact body of Conservatives,
who had learned at last that Disraeli was a leader well worth
following, and who might again be able to win the support
of the disaffected liberals and radicals. To make the
cabinet's position still more precarious, the election committee soon unseated seven of the men who made up its
slim majority.[96] Lastly, there were several right hon.
gentlemen who felt deeply aggrieved at receiving no invitations to join the cabinet. Palmerston's task looked if
anything more difficult than it had done in February 1855.
But the Peelites had disappeared ; and there was another
equally important difference. ' He has never been deaf to
the teachings of experience, or slow to learn the sweet uses
of adversity,' wrote a contributor to the *Quarterly* some
four years afterwards.[97]

CHAPTER XXIX

1859

OF the reinstated prime minister's ability to handle the problems which confronted him, the developments of the remaining months of 1859 gave only a partial test. In so far as his strength in parliament was concerned, they gave practically none. Certain bills had of course to be followed through ; but the necessity for disposing of the budget in the short time that remained before prorogation gave excuse for postponing every contentious measure, even to parliamentary reform. As for the budget, swelled as it was by the military and naval estimates which the fear of Napoleonic aggressiveness had imposed, Palmerston found that his chancellor of the Exchequer could both frame and carry it with little aid. This condition was eminently pleasing ; for, almost from the moment of his appointment, he had immersed himself joyfully in foreign affairs. Needless to say the Italian question claimed first place.

The situation with regard to Italy was just the sort that Palmerston loved. Once again he could buckle on his armour to lead his country in championing his own especial brand of liberalism. And more : he could exercise a guiding, perhaps a controlling influence on England's policy, and make London the real centre of high diplomacy. England raising up Italy ; England restraining France, if necessity arose, for the preservation of Austria ; England admonishing, patronising, mediating, through her Foreign Office *and* her prime minister : this was how he doubtless envisaged the developments of the coming months. Then there was Russia (reported by the Foreign Office to have an understanding of some sort with France) to be watched and manipulated ; and there was Prussia to be advised. There was certainly full scope for the use of all his powers, on the continent and even at home. The Court and most of ' society ' felt with Aberdeen that Austria was still ' fighting the battle of Europe.'[1] And, although Russell had reversed his position of earlier years and come into full agreement with the premier,[2] the majority of the cabinet leaned to ' society's ' point of view.[3] So did other leaders of the party. Clarendon, for example, was urging the British ambassador at Paris not to ' accept the *obiter dicta* . . . of Lord John without protest,' and not to ' wheel round to suit the tastes of anyone whom a party vote in the House of Commons ' might ' accidentally place at the Foreign Office.'[4] But the people, Palmerston's people when he was in his most assertive moods, shared his sympathy for the Italians as much as they did his distrust of Napoleon. It was rather like the days of '48.

The promise of Franco-Italian success given, soon after his accession, by news of Napoleon's victory at Solferino, brought him to an immediate decision concerning Italy.[5] In the first place, there must be an ' entire and absolute relinquishment by Austria of her Italian Lombardo-Venetian provinces.' For ' the honour of France, the unanimous demands of all Italy, the justice of the case would be satisfied by nothing less.' Following that, the Italians should have full liberty to reorganise the peninsula as they saw fit ; though this would not debar England from using her ' moral influence ' to support the formation of a strong, independent, and constitutional state. ' Such a state,' he concluded, in a memorandum of June 28, ' must be built up on the present kingdom of Sardinia.' Victor Emmanuel should be allowed to commence the building by annexing Parma, Modena and perhaps Tuscany at once. Two days later Russell wrote in similar terms to the English minister at Turin.[6] But Palmerston's enthusiasm for Italy did not make him forgetful of the balance of power. He wished to see Austria merely relieved of the incubus of her Italian provinces, not crushed. ' It would be very dangerous for the future independence of Germany,' he wrote, ' that a French army should be allowed

to follow a beaten Austrian army to Vienna.' [7]   And his
attitude was well understood.   The Saxon envoy concluded
that the very premise from which England's policy should
be judged was the premier's belief that Austria would be
stronger without Lombardy-Venetia.[8]   Victoria was gratified to find Palmerston in accord with her in feeling that
the French had no reason to take offence because Prussia
armed against eventualities.[9]

But to any application in the Italian question of the
Canningite spirit and methods which underlay Palmerston's
idea of ' moral influence,' the Court and the other pro-
Austrian elements in society and politics were unalterably
opposed.   No suggestions, no advice, no expression even
of personal views by persons in responsible positions
should be allowed.   Anything of the sort would be ' intervention.'   Intervention, as Palmerston rather tactlessly
pointed out,[10] had been regarded as eminently proper for
preserving peace in Europe and the *status quo* : but the
Court felt it would be eminently improper as representing
an effort to influence the final terms of settlement.   Let
the combatants arrange matters as they would and could :
England had and should have no responsibility.   The old
conflict of opinions between the premier and his sovereign
had begun anew ; and its importance can scarcely be over-
stressed.   Continuing through almost the whole time of
Palmerston's second ministry, it not only supplied the
key to the relations between the premier and the Queen,
not only left its mark continually on British foreign policy,
but gave rise to new and bitter struggles for the control
of foreign policy.   On one side the Court, on the other
the premier and foreign minister, stretched the constitution to achieve success.   The Queen and Prince
Consort sought advice outside the cabinet, received confidential information concerning cabinet meetings outside
the regular channels, and used it to bring influence to
bear on individual ministers, with the object of inducing them to resist their chief.[11]   Palmerston and Russell
attempted to override their colleagues in the cabinet by
committing themselves, both in speeches and in diplomatic
interviews, to policies in which the cabinet did not concur ;

and by sending without cabinet sanction despatches in which these policies were expressed.[12] Both ministers were offenders ; but Granville, who sent most of the secret reports on cabinet meetings to the Court, drew a distinction between them :

> Lord Palmerston is generally very communicative to the Cabinet, and it is only on some point on which he lays great stress, and is determined to carry, that he acts without them. Lord John does so from a loose way of doing business and from a dislike of submitting himself to any criticism.[13]

It is not difficult to see which of the two statesmen Granville considered the stronger.

Napoleon's policy in the summer of 1859 was an incitement both to Palmerston and to the Queen. Recoiling before the horrors of the war ; and disturbed by German military preparations, by the warnings of his generals, by the complaints of French nationalists against the creation of a ' new Prussia ' in the south, and by the protests of French clericals against the undermining of the Pope's temporal power, the Emperor decided to make peace without attempting to defeat the Austrians decisively. But to make peace thus prematurely he had to put forward a series of proposals which falsified his promises to liberate Italy ' from the Alps to the Adriatic.' Painfully conscious that he was incurring charges of irresolution, weakness, and faithlessness on the part of European liberals, and anxious to have a lever in making terms with Austria, he did his best to secure the backing of the British government. The question of ' intervention ' was thus definitely posed.

Napoleon's first request for backing, which may after all have been only a trial balloon as regards both England and Austria, was made through his ambassador, Persigny, on July 4.[14] The Emperor asked the British government to propose an armistice with a view to the conclusion of peace on terms which provided for the cession of Lombardy to Sardinia, the union of Venetia and Modena as an independent duchy under an Austrian archduke, and a confederation of Italian states. Palmerston, in a letter to Russell, immediately refused to support terms so disappointing to the Italians :

> It [the peace] would obviously fall far short of the wishes and expectations of Italy ; and if we made it, we should be accused of having interposed and stopped the allied armies in their career of victory, and of having either endeavoured or of having succeeded to [*sic*] rivet on Italy a remnant of Austrian shackles. . . .[15]

The Austrian archduke in Venetia would soon be at odds with Sardinia ; Austria would intervene ; and, through her troops in Modena, 'would again take her place in Central Italy.' The French Emperor, he concluded, would have to suggest such a peace entirely on his own responsibility. He was quite satisfied with the cabinet's decision to transmit the proposals to the Austrian government without comment.

Yet six days later he took an entirely different attitude. Napoleon, without waiting for British action, concluded an armistice with Francis Joseph on his own account, and arranged for a meeting at Villafranca on July 11, at which a preliminary peace was to be made. On July 10, Persigny requested British support for his master in proposing conditions which differed little from those suggested six days before, and received the assurance that Palmerston favoured giving it.[16] The premier, after seeing Persigny, rode out to Richmond to discuss the matter with his foreign secretary. Before the interview ended Russell had written a letter to the Queen advising strongly in his own name and that of his chief that Napoleon should receive the 'moral support' which he desired.[17] Whether Palmerston now first realised that the complete liberation of Italy had become impossible, and foresaw or was forewarned that Napoleon, if not bound by agreement with England, might concede conditions even more disastrous to the Italians, one can only surmise. At any rate, he and Russell now definitely took the stand that England should intervene. The Queen, firmly resolved that England should do nothing of the sort, demanded that the cabinet should be called to consider her letter of protest, and decide what answer Napoleon should receive.[18] It

was the opening of a long duel ; and first blood went
to the Court. While three or four of the ministers at
first appeared to sympathise with the triumvirate (for
Gladstone ranged himself with Russell and Palmerston) the
reading of the Queen's letter, together with that of a note
from the Austrian ambassador stating that his government had refused the terms suggested on July 6, produced
a 'unanimous' decision that the two emperors should be
allowed to come to an agreement without any suggestion
on Great Britain's part.[19]

Palmerston and Russell were sufferers in more ways
than one. They were not only defeated by the Queen, but
made use of, if not deliberately deluded, by Napoleon.
The cabinet's decision, rendered on the very day that saw
the conclusion of a preliminary peace at Villafranca by
the two emperors, did not, of course, affect that settlement.
But Napoleon, receiving a telegram from Persigny that
Palmerston and Russell had approved his second set of
terms, used it to impress Francis Joseph with his magnanimity in agreeing to a third set which Palmerston and
Russell were to spend months in combating.[20] Indeed, the
Villafranca settlement promised the Austrians a diffused
and legalised influence in Italy which might, had it come
a month earlier, have cheered Metternich on his deathbed.[21]
While Lombardy was to go to Sardinia, Austria was not
only to retain Venetia, but, through her possession of Venetia,
was to become a member (and necessarily the dominant
member) of a federation embracing the whole Italian
peninsula. And there was another agreement no less
repugnant to the three great English 'Italianissimi' : the
rulers of Modena and Tuscany, who had been expelled by
their subjects, should 'return to their states.' Palmerston's
promise of 'moral support' had been used to ease the way
of such a settlement as this ! It was a great triumph for
the Queen. Not only were the prestige of Austria and the
old order in Italy preserved, but Victoria was able to
point out that only her superior penetration and foresight
had saved the British government from falling into Napoleon's
'trap,' and appearing to Austria as an 'extortioner.' The
cabinet, so Russell wrote, 'concurred very much' in her

Q

feeling.[22] Palmerston, it was noted, seemed 'deeply mortified.'[23]

But, to a man of the prime minister's temperament, mortification was merely incitement to further combat. The battle was not lost. The agreement at Villafranca was only preliminary; and much might be done to modify its terms before the plenipotentiaries of the three belligerents should meet at Zurich to sign the peace. The agreement was, in fact, but two days old when Palmerston protested to the French ambassador that, in delivering Italy 'tied hand and foot' to Austria, it failed to supply any satisfactory basis for a settlement.[24] Napoleon was not unwilling to listen. Embarrassed by the difficulty of reconciling his ante-bellum promises to the Italians with the promises just made to Austria, he was hoping to shift the responsibility of final settlement to a European congress. By suggesting that the British Foreign Office should take the initiative in this,[25] he invited the British 'intervention' on which Palmerston was so bent. And there were other indications that the Villafranca agreement might not go into force. The plan for a confederation was soon repudiated by its suggested president, the Pope.[26] And just how were the rulers of Modena and Tuscany to 'return to their states'? The peoples of all the central duchies and of the Romagna were clearly desirous of union with Sardinia; and at Villafranca a verbal understanding had been reached that no French or Austrian troops should coerce them.[27] Quite hopefully, then, the British premier and foreign minister commenced to send despatches which criticised the Villafranca settlement, and even proposed the calling of an assembly in Tuscany to decide about 'the autonomy of that country.'[28] But, although they had reason to be hopeful, their course was adventurous in more respects than one. The Queen was clearly right in pointing out that if their intervention should help to bring a renewal of hostilities in Italy, the British government would have either to evade a moral responsibility or join in the war.[29] Even in the renewed struggle with the Court which their policy entailed, they ran some risk. 'In the present evenly balanced state of parties and strong anti-French feeling, the Court could ride its race its own way,' wrote Herbert at this time.[30]

Thus the battle between Victoria and her two interventionist ministers was resumed, to rage through sheaves of letters, memoranda and despatches ; through cabinet meetings, debates and diplomatic interviews ; through scenes and storms at Windsor, Osborne and Balmoral, during all the remaining months of 1859. Russell and Palmerston strove to carry the cabinet with them, not only in denouncing, but in encouraging Napoleon to repudiate, and the central duchies to resist, the preliminary treaty. The premier wrote the Queen in the admonitory tone she had always found so hard to bear :

> England is one of the greatest powers of the world, . . . and her right to have and express opinions on matters . . . bearing on her interests is unquestionable ; and she is equally entitled to give upon such matters any advice which she may think useful, or to suggest any arrangements which she may deem conducive to the general good.
> It is no doubt true that the Conservative Party, since they have ceased to be responsible for the conduct of affairs, have held a different doctrine, . . . but . . . if that doctrine were to be admitted, Great Britain would, by her own act, reduce herself to the rank of a third-class European State.[31]

And he could join with Russell in advancing other arguments. England was bound to use her influence in behalf of the Italians, not only because she might thus prevent ' a spirit of revenge and revolution ' from taking possession of the peninsula, but because assurances had been given to Cavour in 1856.[32] How he and Russell intended to use England's influence was first shown in a proposal to refuse participation in the congress on the ground that Napoleon had falsified his promises. Such condemnation proving too direct for their colleagues, they got around the obstacle by wording inquiries as to the terms on which the congress might be expected to agree in such manner as to express implicit disapproval of the Villafranca agreement in every paragraph.[33] And, before the summer was over they made real gains.[34] The cabinet, while insisting that Great Britain should be kept clear of any moral responsibility for a renewal of the war, supported them in objecting to the kind of Italian federation agreed to by Napoleon, and in protesting against any coercion of the peoples of the little duchies. ' The restoration of the Grand Duke of Tuscany and the Duke of Modena by foreign forces,' Russell was allowed to write the Austrian and French governments, 'would be to return to that system of foreign interference which for upwards of forty years ' had been ' the misfortune of Italy and the danger of Europe.'

At every step the premier and foreign secretary were reminded that the Queen was as determined as ever to exercise a controlling influence in foreign policy.[35] She was resolved that no criticism, warning or advice, direct or indirect, should be sent to Paris, Vienna or Turin until at least definitive peace had been concluded at Zurich. Her ministers were ' not the Servants of the Emperor Napoleon but the advisers of the Queen of England ' ; and what right had they to point out that the peace did not fulfil the Emperor's declared aims ? She would not sanction ' officious intermeddling ' and the sending of ' mere paper protests intended not to be followed up by deeds.' Pleas that England might regain moral leadership in Europe as well as more tangible advantages by championing the oppressed, were met by sharp rejoinders that England could not honourably advise breaches of contract (French promises to the Italians apparently having no validity whatever in her eyes) ; that a neutral could not ' upbraid ' a belligerent ; that Austria was entitled to exercise great influence over the confederation, and over the little duchies in particular, as ' compensation ' for the loss of Lombardy ; and that no English interest could be subserved by intervention of any sort.[36] Palmerston's and Russell's device of conveying criticism through inquiries does not seem to have deceived her in the least.[37] The ministerial adventurers found progress difficult. The Queen (and, incidentally, the foreign diplomatists) well knew that the cabinet inclined more to her side than to theirs.[38] And she was able to embarrass them by pointing out that the French had already shown ' the cloven foot ' by asking territorial compensation for Sardinia's gains.[39]

Moreover, Palmerston and Russell gave her the opportunity to pose as the champion of the cabinet. Growing bolder as the weeks went on, they drafted despatches which suggested territorial rearrangements for the greater part of Italy, even to the appointment of the duke of Parma as ' regent ' of the Papal States.[40] Whether the initiative in these suggestions came from Persigny, the French ambassador, as Palmerston stated to Russell ; or whether, as Granville believed, the ideas were planted in Persigny's mind by Palmerston is not clear.[41] But it is certain that the premier and foreign secretary were going far beyond anything which the cabinet would have approved, and that the Queen, in refusing to endorse despatches in which their plans for Italy were set forth, won thanks from the other ministers.[42] But Palmerston was irrepressible. Insistent as ever on his ' constitutional ' right to give his personal opinions to foreign envoys unofficially, even threatening resignation if his right should be denied, he conveyed his hopes and sympathies to Napoleon and Victor Emmanuel through Persigny.[43] He even gave his personal endorsement to a scheme for the destruction of the Pope's temporal power, and the division of the Papal States between Sardinia and Naples.[44] Only with difficulty did the Queen succeed in having Russell explain officially that the premier's views were in no way to be imputed to the cabinet.[45]

As the warfare between the Court and Downing Street went on, feeling on both sides grew intense. Despatch after despatch was returned to Russell accompanied by royal letters couched in terms of mounting vehemence, which he was ordered to submit to his colleagues. During the summer Victoria's irritation was so extreme that she could not even discuss Italian affairs with Palmerston.[46] When the session ended, when the Court went to Scotland and the ministers scattered for their holidays, things grew even worse. The Queen's visit to Balmoral was ' embittered ' by ' a paper warfare ' ; and, late in September, Charles Greville reported ' all the Ministers in London, having passed their lives during the last fortnight in the railways or in Cabinets.'[47] Granville and Sir George Grey had done their best to reduce the strain, by urging the

Queen to 'show as much kindness as possible ' to Russell, to give 'no ground for suspecting that other advice was given or taken without reference to him,' and to 'appear to communicate frankly' with Palmerston.[48] But all in vain. Palmerston spoke bitterly of the Court ; while Victoria complained of being ' in a state of constant nervousness from the fear that some trick would be played her.'[49] No doubt she found justification for her own resistance in the willingness of the cabinet ministers to rush back and forth between London and the country, rather than to be ' at the entire mercy of offhand despatches and random shots by our leader Robin Hood and his colleague Little John.'[50] But the hostility of the Court went beyond reasonable bounds. It is impossible to justify, either as to fact or to tone, a memorandum drawn up with apparent deliberation by Prince Albert on the last day of the year :

> As to Lord Palmerston's conduct . . . All his old tricks of 1848 and the previous period are revived again. Having Lord John Russell at the Foreign Office whose inefficiency in the office, love for Italy and fear of Lord Palmerston make him a ready tool and convenient ally, he tries to carry on a policy of revenge against Austria and to bind us to the Emp. Napoleon more than ever, regardless of all the interests of England or Europe, and if impeded by the Cabinet or the Queen he is violent and overbearing and if this be of no avail cheats and tricks. He . . . has again pamphlets written against me and the ' Coburg Influence ' in order to bear down all opposition. . . .[51]

Palmerston disregarding the interests of England, and for the petty gratification of having ' revenge ' on Austria ! Palmerston charged again with writing anonymous pamphlets against his sovereign ! Prince Albert, for all his virtues, was not too well endowed with understanding of, or charity towards, the opponents of his policies.

No doubt the Prince's bitterness arose in part from a consciousness that the two offending ministers had practically won their stubborn fight. The Queen had gained victories in forcing Palmerston and Russell to consult the cabinet, and in holding up despatches advocating any change of boundaries in Italy. It was doubtless due in part also to her efforts that the ministry had refused to give pledges of support to France. But she had never been able to silence her premier and foreign minister, or to prevent them from sabotaging the Villafranca settlement. Cowley, the British ambassador to France, was emphatic as to their influence. Witness a memorandum written by Prince Albert on November 24 :

> . . . Lord Cowley . . . admitted that it would have been much better to take a purely neutral and more passive position, but this has been rendered impossible by the conduct of Palmerston and John Russell up to this moment. He believes that there would have been not the slightest difficulty in carrying out the peace of Villa Franca if our Govt. had given it a lending hand and that the Duchies would have taken back their Sovereigns, if they had not been told from London to stand out.[52]

But since the cabinet as a whole endorsed the sending of despatches pointing out the rights of peoples to choose their governments, protesting the employment of armed forces in the duchies, and asserting that the former rulers there had ' lost their rights,' the other ministers were in no small degree responsible.[53]   The question of the duchies was still the most crucial feature of the Italian situation when the year drew to a close.   In November, a definitive treaty of peace had been concluded at Zurich ; but no practical method of arranging for the Italian confederation or the future government of the duchies had been arrived at.   A congress was still talked of ; and the British cabinet had gone so far as to declare itself in favour of plebiscites in central Italy.   But the cabinet had hardly settled on its plenipotentiaries when Napoleon, by the anonymous publication of a pamphlet on the Roman question, horrified the Austrian government into refusing to take any part.   Failing a conference, concerted action by the Powers bècame impracticable, and the freedom of the duchies to join Sardinia came to depend on Great Britain, France and Austria.   Palmerston and Russell soon entered into a new conflict with the Court, by insisting that if fresh hostilities occurred between the Austrians and the French, Great Britain could not honourably preserve neutrality.[54] Even Russell's argument that England's abstention might allow the French to ' get possession of Italy, mind and soul ' was quite unavailing to move the Court. Hence the ' breezy weather ' that had prevailed in high government circles during the summer and autumn carried over into the new year. And there was promise of disturbed conditions in the relations of England and France. Palmerston was already warning the French emperor that he would be unwise to take Savoy.[55]

That ' Robin Hood ' and ' Little John,' after all their disagreements, should now agree so perfectly was a matter of amazement to their contemporaries. ' Whereas,' wrote Granville, ' we all feared danger from the disunion of the two great statesmen, our chief difficulty now is their intimate alliance.'[56] And not even yet can one regard this alliance, destined to endure till Palmerston's death, without perplexity. Palmerston the overbearing and impetuous, Russell the thin-skinned and self-confident : on what terms did these two men really stand ? Was the partnership between them formed on the basis of community of views and held firm by common resistance to the Court, an equal one ; and, if not, where did the leadership reside ? Is it true, as has sometimes been assumed, that Russell should receive first credit for all that was good in British foreign policy in these years ; or should the premier receive the larger share of credit—as he has usually received the larger share of blame ? The question is perhaps insoluble ; but it is worth while to note what conclusions were drawn by contemporaries. Granville, it will be remembered, gave Palmerston credit for at least the greater determination and aggressiveness : Prince Albert spoke of Russell as the premier's ' ready tool.' Both Clarendon and Charles Greville held the same view :

> Palmerston, who is thoroughly versed in foreign affairs (while Lord John knows very little about them), in every important case suggests to Lord John what to do. Lord John brings it before the Cabinet as his own idea, and then Palmerston supports him, as if the case was new to him.[57]

Quite conceivably this may have represented the situation in 1859 : that any such relation persisted through the

INDIAN DIFFICULTY
CHINESE DIFFIC
ITALIAN D
AMERICAN DIFFICULT
REFORM DIFFICULTY
RSTONIAN POLIT

Blondin Outdone

Punch, October 8, 1859

succeeding years seems almost impossible. Yet there is no doubt that Palmerston, while careful to write at times in a way which suggested that Russell was the real architect of the government's foreign policy,[58] preserved a tutelary attitude to the end. And Russell seems to have accepted it with surprising complacency. Even Granville could not have known that a draft of Russell's not infrequently came back to its author with some such comment as that it resembled 'a newspaper article written by an irresponsible observer of events';[59] and that Russell seemed more ready than most foreign secretaries not only to swallow such reproofs, but to accept his chief's drafts outright in place of his own.[60] Did he then acknowledge Palmerston as his superior in the conduct of foreign policy? Would he have seen any justice in the verdict of Beust, the shrewd and well-informed Saxon diplomat, that he was 'quite destitute' of the qualities which had made Palmerston 'the very ideal of a Foreign Minister'?[61] It seems impossible to say—impossible in fact to go much beyond the easy friendliness of the two men. For Palmerston, on his side, was content to regard Russell as 'a strange compound . . . of talent and foolishness,'[62] and let it go at that. 'Bright and Gladstone,' wrote Shaftesbury of Palmerston after his death, 'were the only two of whom he used strong language.'[63]

If he was not using strong language about Gladstone in 1859 he was on the way to it; for already in this year he found himself at the beginning of a struggle with his chancellor of the Exchequer which was to prove hardly less acrimonious than that which he carried on with the Queen. A mutual lack of understanding created between them an atmosphere in which official disagreements, arising almost inevitably from differing views and the differing duties of their offices, became inflamed. It was not because they had felt the lashes of each other's tongues, that Gladstone had poured contempt on the *civis Romanus*, and Palmerston upon the man who justified the Chinese in poisoning the wells. They were both too experienced as parliamentarians to give thought to that. Yet these speeches revealed a gulf of temperament that lay between

LORD PALMERSTON

them—a gulf which made mutual understanding almost
impossible. The pagan *enfant terrible* of seventy-five years
could neither adapt himself, nor explain himself, to the
pious and much younger chancellor. Palmerston, jaunty,
flippant, rakish and irrepressible, would have shrunk from
explaining his devotion to England, his pride in serving
her, with the same horror as a healthy English schoolboy.
Hence Gladstone saw the bombast, the enjoyment of power
and popularity, which lay on the surface, without giving
due credit to the genuine emotion underneath : while
Palmerston, who could hardly understand that a man would
really expose his soul, was inclined to see in Gladstone's
quite sincere declarations of principle a strong element
of cant. Cant to him was evidence of weakness ; and he
thought he saw other weaknesses in Gladstone. For the
chancellor would not infrequently resist and then give way
in the face of strong pressure. Both resistance and submission were in most instances the fruit of careful consideration and of conscience. But, alas ! their alternation
made the premier both angry and contemptuous. More
fundamental still, perhaps, in holding the two men apart
was the curious fact that each regarded the other as a
dangerous demagogue. To Gladstone the premier was
a chauvinist, who worked up popular alarms and international enmities, partly because it was natural to him,
and partly because he found it popular. What Gladstone
was to Palmerston let Clarendon explain :

Lord Palmerston regarded him as combining all the elements
calculated to produce a most dangerous character for this country.
He might be called one of the people ; he wished to identify himself
with them ; he possessed religious enthusiasm, and made it powerful
over others from the force of his own intellect. His leanings were
towards Roman Catholicism—if he were turned out from the
representation of the University of Oxford he would be set free from
all trammels and might stir the country from its inmost depths.
Enthusiasm, passion, sympathy, simplicity—these were the qualities
which moved the masses ; and Gladstone had them all. He would
always be more powerful out of office than in it.[64]

Hence, in the most vital respects, the separation was
profound. Old and intimate association, or a common

struggle against some influence inimical to both, might possibly have bridged the gap. But no such bridge was found. Just at the beginning they worked hand in hand for Italy ; but, even before the Italian question had ceased to be a great issue, they were being driven rapidly apart by questions of defence and finance. Gladstone, the brilliant and conscientious financier, the little Englander, and the exponent of the pacifistic views of England's industrial and commercial middle class, could not but strive to cut down naval and military expenditures. Palmerston, the adventurer in foreign policy, who demanded that England be not only respected but feared in every European capital and on every continent, whose principles of action as much as his reputation rested on the policy of assertiveness at all times, was bound to demand for military and naval expenditure far more than his chancellor would give.

In 1859 great nervousness regarding possible developments abroad was taking possession of the British people. Napoleon was suspected of every nefarious design ; and his understanding with Russia regarded as full of direful possibilities. A march on the Rhine might lead to a fatal upset of the balance of power ; the seizure of Belgium might make it a French pistol levelled at England's head. The building of the Suez Canal, coupled with French activity in Syria, and Russian penetration through Asia, might give the French and Russians the domination of the Near East, and heighten the standing menace to India. But these fears were nothing in comparison with the dread that England itself would be invaded by the French. ' The popular expression that steam has bridged the Channel is a very insufficient description of the change that has taken place in our position,' wrote Sidney Herbert, the secretary for War.[65] And Cowley, in answering a complaint of the French emperor's regarding England's lack of confidence in him, went into greater detail :

Lord Cowley . . . admitted the existence of the suspicions to which H.M. referred. There were many causes which had given rise to them—H.M.'s sudden intimacy with Russia after the Crimean War—his sudden quarrel with Austria and the equally sudden termination of the war which made people think that he might wish

to carry it on elsewhere. The very name he bore with its ante-
cedents, the extraordinary rapidity with which the late armaments
had been made, the attention devoted to the Imperial Navy—its
increase—the report of the Naval Commission of 1858, which showed
plainly that the augmentation of the French Navy was directed against
England—all this had suddenly opened the eyes of the people in
England to the fact that within easy distance of the British shores
were five hundred thousand men with a steam fleet as powerful or
more powerful than could be brought against them—this state of
things had created a great deal of alarm. . . .[66]

Cowley himself, and, incidentally, the Foreign Office staff
did not believe that the alarm was really justified.[67]   But
the English people and the great majority of their leaders,
moved partly by fact and partly by fiction, demanded a great
increase in armaments.[68]

Fiction lay, of course, in the belief that Napoleon was
intending to attack England.   As Cowley vainly pointed
out, the Emperor desired the friendliest relations possible.
He had not forgotten the part that England had played
in the overthrow of his great uncle, or the effect which
a break with England had had on the fortunes of the
Orleans dynasty.   On the other hand, fact was represented
by the conviction of the English that Napoleon was determined to play a leading part in world affairs, even at the
cost of friendly relations with the British government ;
and to fortify himself for this by augmenting French sea
power.   He had no idea of allowing his country to take
second place whenever her interests and those of England
clashed ; for this would have damaged his hold upon
his subjects irreparably.   If the British navy was to remain
the greatest in the world (and he made no sustained effort
to rob it of this place) the British government must be
made to realise that the French navy was not to be encountered without risk : that France, perhaps with the aid of
an ally such as Russia or some satellites among the smaller
Powers, could hold her own.   The Emperor was intent,
too, on the extension of French influence, in the Mediterranean especially.   He could not permit the British to
decide just when he had gone far enough.   To be prepared for any crisis, he fortified his coasts ; was on the

watch for possible allies ; and challenged England's naval supremacy.

The naval race between the English and the French which set in at this time, and which had a great effect on the relations between Palmerston and Gladstone, has recently been treated with such insight and thoroughness that the merest generalities will suffice here.[69]   After the Crimean war, the French, impressed by the part their armoured ships had played, decided to hold back the building of new wooden ones, and develop armoured vessels as rapidly as possible. The English, reluctant to adopt principles of construction that would make their existing navy obsolete, were active in experimenting with artillery and armour plates, but very slow in putting their knowledge to use.   As a result the French acquired an early lead in the matter of iron-plated ships, while holding something like an equality in large wooden ones.   This fact had come home to the British with crushing force during the scare of 1858 ; and produced on the part of Derby's government great efforts to make up for loss of time. Naturally, too, it caused the English public to suffer from dreadful visions of French battleships and transports, stealing across the Channel in the dark, and conveying hordes of French soldiers who thirsted to indulge their instincts for rapine on English homes.   Cobden, who ridiculed these fears, and managed to produce statistics of a sort to prove British superiority, was met with counter statistics and with arguments that were unfortunate in effect.   For the speeches made by the big-navy advocates, suggesting that the French were guilty of every kind of veiled aggression and hostility, and at the same time emphasising England's alleged helplessness, offered new incitement and encouragement to French chauvinists.[70]

Such was the general situation when Palmerston, one of the greatest nineteenth-century advocates of ' preparedness,' became head of the government.   No alarmist, in so far as immediate danger was concerned, he was quite as determined to provide against eventualities as other men to guard against what they believed to be the risk of imminent attack.[71]   The ' volunteer ' movement, that

largely spontaneous attempt to create a home guard for
protection against French invaders, was just getting under
way. Palmerston and his ministry gave it encouragement
by supplying its units with rifles and with facilities for
securing instruction in the use of them.[72]   But the government's main duty, as the premier saw it, was to provide ships
and forts and guns.   And here some conflict with Gladstone
was almost unavoidable.   It was not that Gladstone was
blind to possible dangers, or ready to risk the safety of
the country in the interests of a favourable balance-sheet.
But so old and close a friend as Sidney Herbert was
annoyed to find that, in his attempts to save money, his
' interference and criticism . . . was . . . exercised on
even minute matters of purely departmental moment.'[73]
Rightly considering the danger from Napoleon as greatly
exaggerated, and certainly not immediate, he wished money
to be diverted from the building of wooden line-of-battle
ships to that of the slow and cautious construction of
armoured ones.[74]   But Palmerston, always a free spender
where armaments were concerned, and very slow to be
convinced that armoured ships were making wooden vessels
obsolete, wanted additional appropriations for the latter,
and a large sum for fortifications on the south coast
besides.[75]   A conflict of opinions existed almost from the
start.

To the end of the year it went hardly beyond that.
Though the danger to England and the means proper for
meeting it were vigorously discussed in parliament during
July, the new administration could undertake no new
measures in the few weeks of the session which remained.
However, before the year was out, Gladstone had good
warning of what lay ahead.   Herbert had secured the
appointment of a royal commission on national defence ;[76]
and Palmerston was holding meetings of a ' war committee,'
which included the commander-in-chief, the secretary for
War, and the first lord of the Admiralty.[77]   Although the
commission did not report until the following year, the war
committee knew by the middle of November that the report
would contain recommendations for the construction of
coast fortifications to be completed within four years at the

cost of some £11,000,000, and that it favoured the raising
of this sum by loan.[78]   As Palmerston and the committee
were ready to concur, and as Gladstone's general attitude
was already evident, the coming year seemed to promise
lively sessions of the cabinet.

What made the prospects even more lively was the
pretty tangle that they involved.   Palmerston, Russell, and
Gladstone stood together as the three great ' Italianissimi '
against the Court : Palmerston and the Court were combined against Gladstone on the question of defence.   The
Italianissimi all were eager to support Napoleon, and even
to urge him forward, in so far as his activities in Italy
were concerned ; but all in varying degrees distrusted him,
and wished to hold him in check elsewhere.   The dilemma
which this created for the British ministers was neatly
illustrated in the autumn of 1859 by a new crisis in their
relations with the Chinese government.[79]

The new crisis arose out of the old-fashioned beliefs
of the Son of Heaven that he could maintain the fiction
of being lord of all the earth, and that the rebel barbarians
of the occident could be resisted by guile or even force.
Lord Elgin, in bringing the ' Lorcha *Arrow* ' war to an
end by the Treaty of Tientsin in 1858, had hardly taken
full account of these beliefs.   On the one hand, he had
made such concessions to the feelings of China's Manchu
rulers as had encouraged them in believing that more
concessions still might be obtained by evasion and delay :
on the other, he had followed instructions by insisting
upon terms which the imperial government was determined
to evade at almost any cost.   For the treaty virtually called
for the recognition of the British as equals, by providing
that the exchange of ratifications should be executed at
Peking, and that British envoys should always in future
have the right of residence there.   To the Manchus this
meant disgraceful humiliation for the Emperor, and dangerous disillusionment for his subjects.   Hence, in 1859,
when Elgin's brother, Frederick Bruce, was sent to execute
the exchange of ratifications at the Chinese capital (travelling
by instruction via the Peiho River and Tientsin), he found
every obstacle short of force placed in his way.   And when

at last he set about ascending the Peiho, accompanied by a French envoy, the Chinese ventured to use force ; and did it in the most treacherous manner possible. Claiming that the Peiho had been closed against the Taiping rebels, and that no official on the spot had authority to negotiate its opening (claims of which the falsity was at once suspected and soon proved), they answered the allies' attempts to remove the obstructions placed in the channel by opening fire without warning from the forts. After a brief engagement the English and French found they could do nothing but retire, leaving behind them three gunboats, and taking with them over three hundred dead and wounded men. Such was the news which reached England in September 1859.

No European government would have submitted to treatment of this sort, still less a government which had just succeeded in putting down a mutiny in India, and least of all a government headed by Lord Palmerston. And there was a factor in the situation which made delay in securing redress inadvisable : the progress and the ambitions of the Russians in the Far East. That they had, in the year previous, seized territory on the Amur which included the cradle of the Manchu dynasty ; and that they had just established a mission at Peking, were known facts. That they were aiming at the acquisition of Pacific, ice-free ports, and consequently of strategic and commercial advantages over the nations of the west, was easily deducible from the tone of their official press. That they were aiding the Chinese to resist England and France by the despatch of Russian officers, artillery and small arms, was widely believed.[80] All in all, a new and vigorous British effort in China was unavoidable. Even Gladstone, Russell and Milner Gibson, those three members of the cabinet who had been among the very bitterest of Palmerston's critics in the matter of the ' Lorcha *Arrow* ' war, found it necessary to acquiesce.

But Palmerston, enthusiastically discussing plans, found that the dubious nature of England's relations with the French made planning difficult. In the first place, it would never do to let France take the lead ; and Napoleon, mindful of his own prestige at home and his country's in Cochin China, was even more vehement in promises of punishment for the Peiho outrage than the British government. Moreover, he could easily spare a larger expeditionary force than England, with her small army, her fears of invasion, and her uneasiness about India, cared to send out.[81] The inevitability of a joint expedition also raised troublesome questions of leadership ; for the English leaders, diplomatic and military, had to be chosen with consideration of their ability to ' get on ' with the French. The question of armament was as troublesome. To set against France's rifled guns England had her new Armstrongs ; but was it wise to give the French an opportunity of studying them, when, as the premier pointed out, the old guns would ' do well enough for the Chinese ' ?[82] Even such matters as operations and peace terms might give trouble ; for suspicion deepened from the very first that France would occupy Chinese territory and insist on holding it against the payment of an exorbitant indemnity, thus securing a counterpoise to Hong Kong.[83]

Fortunately, it was unnecessary to solve all of these problems in 1859 ; and such of them as could not be postponed were not so very difficult of solution after all. Thanks to Napoleon's conciliatory attitude, and to his difficulty in finding transportation for his troops, a balance of strength between the British and French contingents was soon arranged. The accommodating and musical Sir Hope Grant was given the military command, as at least a good soldier, and one who would be regardful of French susceptibilities ;[84] while Elgin consented to take the diplomatic end in charge once more. It was even decided to risk allowing the French to obtain some knowledge of the Armstrongs.[85] But to decide on plans for the campaign was difficult, as Palmerston soon found. Of the suggested measures, the commercial blockade of Peking was objected to, as inflicting unnecessary hardship on a population not to be held responsible for its ruler's delinquencies ; and the premier opposed the alternative of an occupation of Chusan as giving the French excuse for taking territory on their own account.[86] But the matter on which he differed

most from his advisers was as to the advisability of sending
the troops eventually to Peking.   Herbert and Elgin both
thought it would involve too great a military risk, and, in
leading to the Chinese emperor's overthrow, would almost
certainly produce political and commercial chaos.   But
Palmerston, willing once more to gamble on his superior
knowledge and insight, scouted these fears.   He was
willing to leave the ultimate decision to the generals and
diplomatic representatives ; but his hope that they would
decide to go to Peking was quite clear :

> The occupation by a barbarian army of a capital into which even
> a barbarian diplomatist is not to be admitted, would go further to
> proclaim our power, and therefore to accomplish our ends, than any
> other military success, and I must own I have no belief whatever in
> the supposition that such an occupation would overthrow the Chinese
> Empire.   Depend upon it, that occupation would bring the Emperor
> to reason.[87]

He had his way in so far as the granting of discretion was
concerned.   In the Far East, as in Italy, he could look
forward with pleasurable excitement to the coming year.

CHAPTER XXX

1860

THE events of 1859, while raising Palmerston to power, had produced a number of issues of which any one might so develop as to bring him down again. His cabinet, it seemed, might easily break up on parliamentary reform, on questions of defence and finance, or even on Victoria's disagreements with her three greatest ministers concerning Italy. And, supposing the cabinet held together, its small and uncertain majority might disappear on either of the great internal issues just referred to, or on any one of a multiplying array of troublesome questions of foreign policy. To observe how these dangers were surmounted, and how most of the real successes which came to Palmerston in his last administration were achieved, is to follow all that is most significant in the story of the two years following. While many questions lay before the ministry at the beginning of these two years, a point of departure is not hard to find. For foreign policy, unlike domestic, waits not on the assembling of parliaments ; and British foreign policy, in the early days of 1860, hinged even more than usual on relations with the French.

A new element in Anglo-French relations, and from all points of view an exceedingly important one, had come into prominence during the closing months of 1859. Lovers of peace and of free trade on both sides of the Channel, headed respectively by Cobden and by the French economist, Michel Chevalier, were attempting to drive the ' bridge of steam ' out of the popular imagination by constructing between the two nations a bridge of friendship, supported on pillars of economic interdependence.[1] The two men, visiting each other's countries in the autumn of 1859, soon made converts as influential as Persigny and Gladstone to the idea of an exchange of English and French goods under lowered customs rates.   Before the end of the year official negotiations were afoot, and ' God's own method of producing an *entente cordiale*,' as Cobden called it,[2] promised excellent results.

To understand, and therefore to do justice to, Palmerston's attitude in the affair, one must note the objections raised by others to Cobden's scheme.   By none were they more clearly stated than by Victoria and her husband. The Queen, writing on Christmas Day, expressed fears that ' if . . . the effect which such a treaty is to have upon the feeling of this Country were to be really what Mr. Cobden anticipated it would be a great national misfortune, arresting as it would our preparations for self-defence.'[3]   The Prince Consort went into particulars :

Strange to say, the treaty will give the Emperor our coals and iron, which he will want if he should come into collision with us ; and by the abolition of the wine duties we shall sustain a loss of two millions in our financial receipts.   And as we have to raise the Income Tax to ninepence in the pound, in order to meet the increased Army and Navy Estimates, and must borrow ten millions for the permanent defences, the Income Tax will have ultimately to be raised to elevenpence, and sober-minded people anticipate that the public will not stand this.[4]

Later on, this ordinarily pacific prince was reported as expressing a conviction that the treaty would be ' perverted into a means of keeping down the warlike spirit of the nation.'[5] Cobden's scheme was, in fact, very widely criticised. Clarendon found that it was ' universally blamed as unsound in principle, doubtful as a political measure, ill contrived as a commercial arrangement and quite indefensible as regards its fiscal consequences.'[6]

That Palmerston should feel the force of such objections to the plan was inevitable ; but that, as Bright stated, ' he did all he dared to make the Treaty miscarry '[7] was, like not a few of Bright's statements concerning him, quite false.   That he was sceptical concerning the political effects of the treaty may be ascribed not only to a breadth of experience which Bright did not begin to share, but to certain secret reports concerning French preparations which Bright did not see.[8] The old statesman who had drilled at Cambridge to resist invasion by the first Napoleon was perhaps excusable in his concern over information from the British attaché at Paris that the third Napoleon was building at this very time a large number of flat-bottomed boats. That a premier who was the nation's greatest advocate of ' preparedness ' disliked the loss of revenue entailed by a reduction of duties was natural.   But as a free-trader and an advocate of good relations with the French as long as good relations seemed to him practicable ; and, again, as the head of a cabinet which included Gladstone, Villiers, and Gibson, and which was saved from dependence on the Conservatives only by ' advanced ' Liberal votes, he neither would nor could oppose Cobden's scheme.   He did insist that the treaty should afford no excuse to Gladstone for opposition to expenditure on armaments ;[9] but that was all.

The worst, indeed, that can fairly be charged against him is indifference toward so beneficent a project, and a too ready acceptance of Cowley's criticism of Cobden's work as negotiator.   Gladstone found the premier ' rather neutral ' when opposition to the treaty developed in the cabinet,[10] and quite forgetful later on of one highly important point which had been discussed.   The reader of the Foreign Office files will look in vain through the papers on the treaty for annotations followed by the familiar ' P.' ; while the searcher of Palmerston's letters to Russell will discover much criticism but no hostility.   He did feel that the ministers had failed to give the treaty proper scrutiny ; and he was guilty of one outburst against Cobden's tendency ' to give all that the other party ask for and get little or nothing . . . in return.'[11]   But, in later years at least, he was ready to give much credit to a man whom he regarded as his bitterest enemy in parliament save Bright and Disraeli.[12] ' Cobden had certainly great merit in the conception of the Treaty, and in working it out,' he wrote Russell privately, in 1863, when offering to propose a pension for his impoverished foe.   And, although political considerations were certainly present in his mind when he

8

446 LORD PALMERSTON

proposed, in February, 1865, to give Cobden a civil service
post, he later recommended the pensioning of Cobden's
widow to the Queen on the basis of the services rendered by
her husband ' to the commercial interests of the kingdom.'
What he failed entirely to appreciate was Cobden's pacifism.

How little account Palmerston took of friendship or
enmity between nations or their rulers is evident when
one turns to pick up again the thread of his Italian policy
at the beginning of 1860. With all his suspicions of
Napoleon and his lukewarmness toward Cobden's great
enterprise, he was now determined to act with France in
promoting the union of *all* the little duchies of central
Italy to Sardinia, and hence in forbidding interference by
Austria. On January 5, he launched a memorandum,
addressed apparently to the cabinet and in support of Russell,
which arrests attention both in the inconsistency of its
language regarding France with that of some of his pronouncements of 1859, and in its haughty and uncompromising tone.[13] Whether a congress met or not, he
argued, but especially if it did not, England's only proper
policy was that of a ' holy alliance ' with France and Sardinia.
Such an alliance would constitute the best means of preserving peace. But if war came with Austria, what
of it ? England's part would be ' chiefly, if not wholly,
naval.' Some might object that Napoleon was sure to
prove an unreliable ally. But Palmerston for his part
could see no ground for ' imputing to Napoleon unsteadi-
ness of purpose in regard to his views about Italy,' nor
remember any occasion on which the Emperor, having
acted in partnership with the English, had thrown them
over and made a separate arrangement without their consent.
If the House of Commons rejected the alliance he would
appeal to the country in perfect confidence : he might
relinquish his office but not his principles.

As Russell stood with the premier, even in threats of
resignation ; as Victoria assumed her customary attitude,
and the cabinet stood as usual for a *via media*, a new crisis
had developed within a week.[14] At its height, and at a time
when the portents indicated defeat for Palmerston, relief
arrived from an unexpected source. News came that

Austria, without giving way on principle, had renounced any intention of using troops in central Italy. The ministers, who had gone into a cabinet meeting looking very tense, came out looking ' foolishly relieved ' ; and perfect agreement between them all was reached within a few days.[15] England was merely to ask both France and Austria not to interfere, and Sardinia to stand aside, until the desire of the duchies to come under the Sardinian crown had been again expressed. ' Talk of humiliation,' wrote Clarendon, '. . . P. and J. R. have their fill of it.'[16] But P., J. R. and Gladstone (for the triumvirate had formed again) saw their wishes for Italy at last realised, and were justified in believing that the realisation was in considerable measure due to their efforts. Fortified by the British proposal, Napoleon lost little time in informing Austria that the terms of the Villafranca agreement could not be carried out. The rulers of Modena and Tuscany would not ' return to their states ' ; and the idea of a confederation was, as Vitzthum wrote, ' buried.' It was Victoria who admitted defeat : ' We could *not prevent* this *proposal* . . . as the rest of the Cabinet thought it could *not* be opposed, and entailed *no* material *support*.'[17] The Court was really powerless for the time being. ' It is amusing,' wrote Granville to the Prince Consort, ' to hear M.P.s declare that the great strength of the Govt. is the conviction that " nobody can keep us out of entanglement in Foreign Affairs but the two old boys." '[18]

Yet the Queen was to find consolation in the extraordinary change both in the language and attitude of her premier and foreign secretary which developed in the three months following, in connection with the French annexation of Savoy and Nice. Napoleon's bargain with Cavour for the acquisition of these semi-French and strategically important border provinces, as the price of French consent to Sardinia's expansion in central Italy, had been known to Palmerston and Russell for some months. But it seems to have been concealed from the British public and the Court ; and even the two ministers were apparently in hopes that it would not be carried out. Napoleon's announcement in February that the annexations would go through was a rude shock to them all. A new wave of indignation and distrust against the French arose; and the British ministers were charged, now with having been made dupes, now with having been bought off through Cobden and his treaty.[19]   Privately, Palmerston found some consolation for the transfer of Savoy and Nice in reflecting that it would unite Germany against Napoleon and make the British people more ready to spend money on defence.[20] But he likened the French emperor to a tiger that had learned the taste of blood ; and he realised full well the impossibility of mere acquiescence on his own and Russell's part. Public disapproval was a political necessity even though it should invite (as it did) complaints from Napoleon's ambassador that the pronouncements of the premier and foreign secretary were distinctly disingenuous.[21]   And had matters stopped there no harm would have been done ; since official objections break no bones, and everyone realised that to prevent the annexation was impossible. But Palmerston and Russell went further.   The latter, late in March, evoked ' frantic cheers ' from both sides of the House by suggesting that Napoleon's unreliability would force England to look elsewhere for friends ;[22] and the two ministers proceeded to give point to the threat by soliciting support from the three eastern Powers for a demand that the districts of Chablais and Faucigny should be separated from Savoy and given to Switzerland.

The idea of making a stand against France's acquisition of Faucigny and Chablais must have been especially attractive to the premier.   The two districts, lying just south of Lake Geneva, had been included in the neutralisation of the Swiss territories in 1815, and held by Sardinia under the obligations which this neutrality imposed.   The Swiss, feeling that their transfer to France would lay bare the other shores of Lake Geneva to French attack, protested. Hence, Palmerston, in coming to the aid of his old Swiss protégés of 1847, would be re-asserting England's leadership in a great international question, curbing Napoleon, protecting the arrangements of 1815, acting as the champion of the weak, and altogether gratifying British public sentiment.   The game seemed a safe one ; for Napoleon had allowed both the British government and the Swiss to understand that he was open to argument.[23]

But as the ensuing negotiations took their course sweet reasonableness soon disappeared. Palmerston seems to have taken up the project without much expectation of success,[24] but to have become so much more optimistic and determined as the weeks went by that he refused a compromise that would have given the Swiss at least a portion of Faucigny bordering on the lake. Apparently it seemed to him quite possible to ' shame ' Napoleon out of taking the district at all.[25] But the Emperor, incensed at violent attacks in the British parliament and press, and by the lack of candour of the British ministers, was quite indifferent to the premier's argument that the ' *bonne opinion de l'Europe* ' was cheaply bought at the price of a '*petit bout de territoire.*'[26] And as Napoleon proved obstinate Palmerston grew bitter. When his old friend Flahaut, journeying to France at the end of March, just after Russell's too frank speech, asked for a message to the French emperor, Palmerston, ' in the most friendly manner,' accused the French government of ' such frequent changes of purpose and of conduct ' as to destroy all ' reliance . . . upon the continuance of the intentions or policy of the moment.'[27] When Flahaut suggested that the growing irritation between the two countries might bring on war and a French descent upon the British coasts, he was reminded of Blenheim and of the fact that steam was as effective for defence as for attack. ' Persigny and his wife are like two wild cats,' wrote Clarendon, ' and Lady Palmerston is not much better.'[28]

The dispute between Downing Street and the Tuileries had indeed gone far beyond the question of Nice and Savoy. There were other grievances on both sides. Clarendon thought his countrymen had well deserved sharp language from Napoleon :

. . . for thwarting the Emperor and . . . taking to ourselves credit for the arrangements agreeable to the Italians without our having made the smallest sacrifice or even being prepared to share with the Emperor the slightest responsibility. . . . We have been on velvet and have stuck more thorns into the Imperial bed which was already not deficient in them.[29]

And this was before Russell's very thorny speech. England, on her side, was full of suspicions, not to say grievances. Napoleon seemed more and more to be courting the Tsar, and there was open talk in Paris and London of a possible French annexation of Belgium.[30] There was similar talk in Brussels, as witness the circulation of ' Napoleon's Lord's Prayer ' :

> Our Father, which art in Fontainebleau,
> Thy name is no longer hallowed in England.
> Thy kingdom is not yet large enough.
>
> .   .   .   .   .   .
>
> But deliver us from friend Jacobin and from
> the domination of thy sabre.[31]

To make matters worse, Napoleon, on March 6, had spoken most improperly to Cowley concerning British Francophobia in the hearing of the Russian ambassador.[32]

By the middle of March, Palmerston, Napoleon's old defender, was giving him credit for the very worst designs :

> There seems good reason for thinking that Napoleon has great schemes in his head for which he is trying to get the concurrence and co-operation of Russia and that the dismemberment of the Turkish Empire is the object he will next aim at, afterwards the Rhine and perhaps Belgium, but all in the most friendly manner and spirit towards England. Do you remember the objection he made at first to the treaty and free trade namely that if these arrangements were to beget a commercial and moneymaking spirit in France he would be hampered when he might want to get the country to support him in a war . . . ? [33]

The Court was more uneasy still. Prince Albert, Clarendon wrote, seemed 'demented' on the subject.[34] More and more bitter grew the quarrel, through sharp speeches in both legislatures, sharp despatches sent out from both Foreign Offices, and sharp words used by statesmen and ambassadors on both sides. Hardly had Flahaut set off for France than Palmerston and Persigny were discussing the probabilities of war, and disputing as to which country would have greater success in finding support on the continent.[35] The upshot was that Persigny, the greatest French friend of the Anglo-French entente, was recalled from the French embassy at London, reputedly by Palmerston's desire.[36] The premier granted Persigny's last request by facilitating the submission to parliament of despatches which operated to relieve the tension in so far as the press and public of the two countries were concerned ; but between the governments suspicion and ill-will remained. Russia chose this moment to circularise the other four great Powers with charges against Turkish administration and the demand for an international inquiry ; while Prince Napoleon chose it to visit the Bosphorus. Vitzthum, writing from London on May 13, reported the results :

> Napoleon is credited with the wildest schemes of adventure. Some talk of a new Byzantine-Frankish Empire for Prince Napoleon, others of a South-Italian one for Prince Murat. . . . The latest Austrian despatches have given rise to very exhaustive interviews, not only with Lord John, but also with Lord Palmerston.[37]

But Russell and Palmerston had been attentive to Austria for some time.

This had been strikingly shown in the proceedings of a cabinet that had met on April 21.[38] Rechberg, the Austrian foreign minister, thinking the time ripe for driving a wedge between the British and the French, had proposed that England should ally herself with the two great German Powers to resist French encroachments or acquisitions, and perhaps to guarantee Venetia to Austria and the Neapolitan kingdom to its Bourbons. Was the idea rejected by the two British ministers who had stood in the cabinet as the two greatest protagonists of France and Italy ? By no means. In January Russell had, on his own responsibility, snubbed the Prussian government for making a similar advance ; but the dispute with Napoleon had caused him to reverse his attitude within two months.[39] Now, like a true British foreign secretary, he explained to Rechberg how impossible it was for England to conclude an alliance covering merely anticipated developments ; but he was quite willing to accept the suggestion of the Court that England should enter into an understanding of the kind that was to become so popular in later times. Hence the cabinet of April 21 produced the curious spectacle of Russell,

backed by Palmerston, urging an agreement by which
Austria, Prussia and England should exchange information
concerning any suspicious moves of the French emperor ;
while the rest of the cabinet, headed by Granville, rejected
the proposal, on the grounds that it would drive France
more than ever into Russia's arms without pledging
Austria and Prussia to anything at all. It is not surprising
that Granville wrote to Prince Albert : ' I am afraid your
Royal Highness will be with Lord Palmerston ' ; that the
Prince found the premier quite convinced that war would
come ; or that Victoria pronounced her most troublesome
servant ' *very stout and right* about our neighbour.'[40]
She had, in fact, been ' *very much* pleased ' with ' the two
old boys ' for several weeks. The ' stoutness ' of Palmerston and Russell was not, perhaps, without some effect ;
for Napoleon consented to respect the neutralisation of
Chablais and Faucigny as Sardinia had done. But he got
little thanks. ' The security thus to be obtained for
Switzerland is much of the same nature as if a gang of
housebreakers offered to do duty at one's door instead of
the police,' wrote Palmerston.[41]

It will be seen that Palmerston's old vivacity in language
at least had not deserted him : and indeed his youthfulness
in all respects was increasingly a matter of remark.[42] He
could still take out a shooting party of young men, bring
home a larger bag than any one of them, and beat them all
at billiards after dinner. Lady St. Helier, meeting him
at a concert at Apsley House, was instructed concerning
the music that was being played, and charmed by the
most boyish laugh that she had ever heard. Even his
unpunctuality seems to have clung to him : Vitzthum,
reaching 94 Piccadilly at eight-thirty, for one of the dinners
which rivalled Rothschild's own, found his host just mounting
for a pre-prandial ride in Rotten Row. But the unpunctuality of host or hostess did not keep guests away from Cambridge House. Never had Lady Palmerston displayed her
charm with more effect : never had her invitations, still
sent out with as much discrimination as profusion, been
more highly prized.[43] Vitzthum regarded her salon as ' the
headquarters of the Liberal party, and the truest barometer

when Parliamentary storms were brewing ' : a morning call
on her ' was often more instructive than studying the newspapers.' It may well have been, if he was right in believing
that she copied such of her husband's papers as were too
confidential to be shown to any secretary.

But there is no testimony of the premier's vitality so
striking as that offered by his daily reports on the debates,
always despatched so as to reach the Queen at breakfast time,
before she read the press accounts. Composed in the early
morning hours, as late sometimes as four o'clock, and after
days of incessant labour that began at nine, they are
written with a sarcasm and a flippancy which suggest
anything but a tired old man.[44] A vote for interior alterations of the National Gallery was objected to by Mr.
Conyngham ' who thinks himself peculiarly privileged
to be wrong and violent on all matters connected with art.'
In a debate on religious enumeration in the census ' Sir
John Trelawney was for the Dissenters as vehemently
as the dullness of his nature enabled him.' A discussion
on Maynooth brought remarks from Mr. Whalley, ' a
Welshman of small stature and capacity, but becoming
by no means a small bore in the opinion of the House.'
One wonders how the royal sense of humour reacted to
such stimulation in the morning hours.

White has left the best testimony concerning Palmerston's ability, at the age of seventy-five, to carry on where
younger men were taxed to the limit of endurance : [45]

The Session of 1860 . . . has been the longest Session which
we have had for many years. It began on Tuesday, January 24 ;
it finished on Tuesday, August 28 : . . . And not only has it been
the longest but the severest of modern Sessions. Indeed, it may be
questioned whether the House of Commons has ever before in one
Session sat so many hours. In the earlier part of the Session—about
the first week or so—the House occasionally rose before twelve ;
but since then, as a rule, it has sat on till two o'clock, often till three,
and in several instances it touched upon four in the morning. The
labour of the Session, therefore, has been exceedingly severe.

If the temperature had not been moderate and the Thames
' unusually inodorous ' the officials of the House and the

members of the ministry, who could not absent themselves,
' would certainly have broken down ' :

> . . . we must except, however, Lord Palmerston, for upon him
> neither labour nor weather seems to make the smallest impression.
> He enters the House soon after it meets ; he stops, as a rule, till it
> closes, and then walks away seemingly as fresh as he was when he
> came.   Some people wonder when he eats and sleeps.   The answer
> is, he eats and sleeps on the premises—eats at the restaurant ; sleeps
> on the benches.   The noble Lord apparently has the power to sleep
> at will.   When a long-winded orator rises he can fold his arms, and
> at once, without effort, enter the land of dreams ; when another gets
> up whom he wishes to hear, he can, with equal facility, shake off his
> sleep. . . . Suddenly he falls asleep when he wishes, and suddenly,
> when required to be so, he is wide awake, attentive, and ready to
> speak, and, what is more remarkable, he seems to lose nothing by his
> sleep ; for in his winding-up speeches, . . . not an argument of any
> weight is left unanswered. . . . It is a wonderful faculty, this, . . .
> but to others who have it not it is disadvantageous, for it makes the
> noble Lord— . . . careless of the prolongation of the sitting of the
> House. . . . It has long been noticed in the House that when
> Lord Palmerston is leader of the Government we always sit
> late, whilst Lord John Russell and Disraeli are averse from long
> sittings. . . .

White's summary of the results of the session is also
worth noting :

> ' Well, it has been a barren Session,' . . . Thus grumble, no
> doubt, nine-tenths of our readers, for thus barks the *Times*, . . . But
> . . . when the historian shall sum up the results of the Session of
> 1860 it will be found to have been a long way from fruitless.   For
> instance, it has accepted and ratified the French Treaty, and passed
> all the measures springing therefrom.   It has voted about £72,000,000
> of money ; it has decided upon fortifying our dockyards, &c. ; it has
> abolished the Indian Army ; it has reformed the naval code of laws ;
> and, altogether, it has passed about 100 public and some 250 private
> Bills.

White, omitting mention of all measures which perished
in the annual ' Massacre of the Innocents,' said nothing of
the ill-starred Reform Bill of this year.[46]   To most of the
Liberals, in fact, the Reform Bill of 1860 was an unwanted
child.   It had been conceived in Willis's rooms in June

1859, through the union of the old party with the advanced wing ; and the latter had unwittingly, during the ensuing months, prejudiced its chances by foretelling that it would prove a very David of democracy. But, wanted or not, preparations for its appearance had to be made ; and during the last two months of 1859, a committee of ten members of the cabinet, including the triumvirate, the three baronets, and the two most advanced members, Milner Gibson and Villiers, drafted a project calling for a £10 occupation franchise in the counties, a £6 franchise in the boroughs, and for some redistribution of constituencies on an equally moderate scale.[47] Quite appropriately the bill saw the light in March ; and, though Lewis had apparently taken the lead in its preparation, Russell, with his taste for ' attaching his name to something,' presented it to the House on the twenty-ninth anniversary of his introduction of its great prototype.[48]

If the bill had been unwanted before its birth, it was if anything less popular afterwards.[49] Too advanced for any group save that of the advanced Liberals, and not advanced enough for them, it involved for all members of the lower House the displeasing prospect of a third dissolution within three years. Russell himself, more and more engrossed by his work at the Foreign Office, and noting the ' profound indifference,' the ' general apathy,' of the House, was soon pointing out that he had promised Bright to bring in the measure, but not to see it through.[50] Gladstone, now swinging distinctly to the left, and no doubt appreciating Bulwer Lytton's prophecy that the prospective new electors would be chary of granting money for defence, showed rather more good will. But Gladstone had another, and to him far more vital, struggle on his hands. Thus the prime minister found himself in a position where encouragement or discouragement on his part might conceivably effect considerable results.

Palmerston's desire was to see Russell's bill modified in a conservative direction if possible, but to see it passed, whether modified or not.[51] He was as opposed as ever to the old Whig theory and the new Liberal conviction in favour of mere majority rule—opposed especially to ' giving

up the representation of the great towns to the trades unions,'
and 'practically disfranchising . . . the wealthy and
intelligent men in those seats of manufacture and trade.' [52]
But whether from desire to please his followers in cabinet,
parliament or country ; whether because he wanted
excuse for an early dissolution that could be expected to
give him a more secure majority ; or whether he desired
to tuck away a question of perennial difficulty, he hoped,
almost to the end, that the bill would become law. He
himself would have preferred much higher qualifications,
both for county and for borough electors.   But the adoption
of compromise figures (£15 for the counties and £8 for the
boroughs), coupled with arrangements for postponing the
dreaded dissolution, would give the measure better chances
of success.   As late as June 6, when almost everyone,
except perhaps Gladstone and Russell, had given up hope,
he was still considering measures for saving the bill.
Parliament might be prorogued till late in the year : but
that might ' continue the session of 1860 into 1861,' thus
creating ' a Long Parliament.' [53]   An act might be asked
from parliament, carrying the bill over into the next session,
instead of allowing it to lapse : but it would be asked in
vain.   No, reform would have to be given up.   So the
cabinet decided on June 9.[54]   On June 11, the fourth
unsuccessful Reform Bill of recent years was buried under
those decent forms which parliament uses for disposing
of offspring that it does not care to raise.

The apathy shown by ministers and members concerning
parliamentary reform was in some part due to the excitement
aroused, from February on, by Gladstone's financial schemes.
Never perhaps was Gladstone greater, as financier or as
orator, than in this spring ; and never perhaps did his
financial proposals involve so many other issues.   What
is more, these other issues were mainly of a sort on which
fundamental disagreement existed between the chancellor
of the Exchequer and the premier.   The increased distrust
of Napoleon which arose from his acquisition of Savoy and
Nice, and from the alleged activities of his agents in
western Germany, the Palatinate, Belgium, Poland and
Ireland,[55] not only made Palmerston more insistent than

ever on large appropriations for defence, but emphasised
his disagreement with Gladstone on foreign policy. The
chancellor, increasingly influenced by Cobden and Bright,[56]
believed that the conclusion of the commercial treaty,
coupled with avoidance of any provocation in the matter
of armaments, constituted the best method of meeting
whatever aggressive tendencies were being harboured by
Napoleon : [57] while the premier held that since the adoption
of free trade was sure to strengthen any Power, and since,
therefore, the Cobden Treaty would add to the national
resources of the French, so England must be more than
ever armed.[58]   And, when it came to the question of economy, Palmerston was ready to argue that preparations for
defence were ' infinitely cheaper ' than the fighting which
they tended to prevent.[59]   Again, the question of democratic evolution in England, a question which was beginning
to divide the two statesmen even at this time, was involved
in the chancellor's plans for altering the rates of customs
and excise.   Gladstone, already noticeably liberal as well
as economical,[60] planned to reduce the cost of paper by
relieving its consumers from the payment of the prevailing
excise.   To abolish this ' tax on knowledge ' was to
sacrifice £1,750,000 of revenue, but to give the 'advanced'
Liberals greatly increased facilities for converting the
English people to their views through the agency of cheap
newspapers.   Palmerston, who disliked radical propaganda,
was therefore asked to favour it by a sacrifice of revenue
which he badly wanted for armaments.   The question, however, which confronts the student of his life is
not that of his acquiescence or resistance, but of his
frequently alleged treachery and flippancy toward a great
colleague.

    At the opening of the year both men were busy with
their plans.   Palmerston had before him the majority
report of the commission on national defence, maintaining
that protection against invasion could be most economically
secured through fortification of the dockyards, and of the
arsenals which lay near the coast.[61]   After long discussions,
in which the premier took an active part, it was decided
that the conclusion of the commercial treaty should not

affect the estimates, and that necessary work on the fortifications would call for an expenditure of something like
£9,000,000.[62]   At the same time, Gladstone was elaborating a great budget, in which provision was made for
increased naval and military appropriations, and for the
losses of revenue entailed by the Cobden Treaty and the
abolition of the paper excise, through increased taxation
elsewhere.   In particular, he planned to increase the
already onerous income tax, quite conscious (as no doubt
was Palmerston) that a heavy income tax is apt to have
a particularly depressant effect on popular enthusiasm for
armaments.[63]   Conflict of opinion between the two great
proponents of the two schemes extended to a variety of
issues, such as the disembodiment of the militia force ;
but it was most notable and most informing on two specific
points.[64]   Palmerston wished at least to postpone the abolition of the paper excise duty, and to meet the extraordinary
expenditure for fortifications by a loan.   Gladstone laid
the utmost emphasis on the immediate abolition of the ' tax
on knowledge ' ; and not only wished to keep down expenditure for fortifications, but to meet it out of current
revenue.

For three months, beginning with the latter part of
January, struggles, by no means concealed from outsiders,
went on within the cabinet.   The two old friends, Gladstone
and Herbert, were completely at loggerheads ; and Palmerston found himself called upon to act both as mediator
between them, and as a second to his secretary at War.
Compromise of some sort was inevitable ; and for a time
it seemed to work out mainly to the advantage of Gladstone.
Palmerston's repeated and not entirely unreasonable appeals
that the abolition of the paper duties might be postponed
for at least one year, were all in vain.[65]   In fact, parliament's
acceptance, before Easter, of an increase in the income
tax convinced him for the time being that the abolition
of the paper duties was inevitable.   On the other hand,
the fortification question was left an open one.   Gladstone
agreed to provide a lump sum which might, according to
later agreement, be used either to defray the expenses
of works immediately undertaken, or to supply the interest

WILLIAM EWART GLADSTONE, M.P.

and sinking fund for a loan which should cover works to be executed during the next four years.[66]

On May 7 the Paper Duties Bill passed its third reading in the lower House : but the prime minister was still dissatisfied. Shortly before the vote was taken he had again tried to persuade the cabinet to withdraw the bill, urging that the ' world situation ' had been altered since he had given his assent, by further revelations of Napoleon's territorial designs and by the mounting expenses of the war in China.[67]   Some of the cabinet had agreed with him, and he seems to have believed that a majority might have done so had any reasonable method of justifying themselves and mollifying Gladstone been available.   He had ' acquiesced ' in the decision of the cabinet, but without changing his opinion that ' no sane man ' would propose to ' throw away ' so large a proportion of the permanent revenue, at the cost of limiting the ' reserve resource ' made available for ' extraordinary efforts ' by the increased income tax.[68]   Even with the paper duties unrepealed, he foresaw a deficit for 1860, and still heavier taxation for 1861.   He was convinced (apparently with some reason) that public opinion was strongly on his side ; [69] and he could point out that the bill had passed the third reading by a very small majority.   In the midst of his dissatisfaction he heard that Lord Monteagle would move the rejection of the bill in the House of Lords.

In the indictment of Palmerston over this affair, the common charge is that he betrayed his own cabinet by encouraging the Lords to support Monteagle's motion. It has even been said that his action was taken according to an understanding with the Conservatives.   Further investigation may substantiate the charges ; but the evidence now accessible seems inconclusive, to say the least.   Bitterly sarcastic have been the comments on his letter to the Queen on May 7, expressing his feeling (which coincided perfectly with hers) that the Lords would ' perform a good public service ' in throwing out the bill.[70]   But if it can be supposed (and the supposition is very difficult) that the Queen thus learned for the first time of his attitude, he was by no means the first premier nor the last to inform

the sovereign of his private disagreement with the cabinet.
Nor, so long as his confidence was respected, could the letter
have affected the issue in any way.   It cannot even be
stated with any certainty that in the end he wished Monteagle's motion to succeed.   Four days before the Lords,
on May 21, rejected the bill by a large majority, he wrote
Lansdowne that he had ' a good deal modified [his] opinion '
regarding the effects of such action on their part :

> My own opinion is that the House of Lords has a perfect right
> to do what Lord Monteagle proposes ; but there are strong opinions
> that the exercise of that right would not be advisable ; and it is
> probable that it would lead to some motion in the House of Commons
> which it would be very embarrassing for the government to know
> how to deal with ; and on the whole I have come to the conclusion
> that for many reasons it is desirable that the motion should not be
> carried.[71]

It is apparently true that Lady Palmerston, sitting in the
gallery of the House of Lords, so audibly expressed her
hopes for the defeat of the bill as to elicit protests even
from the Whigs.[72]   But to what extent can her husband
be held responsible ?   Let those most conversant with the
lady's temperament decide.   As for Palmerston's alleged
understanding with the Conservatives, that not only rests
unproved, but would surely have been quite superfluous.
True, Malmesbury, commissioned by Derby, offered any
support which Palmerston, in a break with Gladstone,
might require.[73]   But the Conservatives, much more
concerned in combating the advanced Liberals than in
upsetting the ministry, made several such offers quite
voluntarily in these years.   Their knowledge of the premier's
attitude can be fully accounted for by Clarendon's con-
fidences to Greville.[74]

Palmerston's fears that ' it would be very embarrassing
for the government ' to deal with the situation created by
the Lords in rejecting a money bill, and one on which
his indispensable chancellor of the Exchequer had set his
heart, were all too soon justified.   ' We certainly must not
lose Gladstone,' he wrote : [75] but keeping Gladstone, and
keeping at the same time within the limits of what the

premier and most of his ministers considered the proper
course of action, was no easy matter. Gladstone was all
for forcing the issue. He would have repassed the Paper
Duties Bill and sent it back to the Lords with the addition
of clauses imposing so heavy an additional duty on spirits
as more than to provide for the loss of revenue which the
repeal of the paper duties entailed. ' It would be,'
Palmerston wrote to the Queen, ' as if a man who would
not easily get through a doorway by himself were to think
he could do it more easily by taking a fatter and larger
man by the arm and endeavouring to force the two abreast
through the doorway too narrow for one.' [76] Scotch
members, Irish members and English distillers would all
contribute to the size of the ' fatter and larger man.'
Palmerston continued to believe in private that the Lords
had every right to reject the Paper Duties Bill ; but,
with the cabinet's support, he took in public a position
that was certainly pacific, and seemingly quite reasonable.[77]
Although it was against recent precedent that the Lords
should reject a money bill, one could not say with certainty
that such procedure had become unconstitutional. Was
it wise then to condemn it outright, and to provoke a conflict
between the two Houses in which the Lords would be supported by public opinion and a strong minority of the Lower
House ? Better, he argued, to search for precedents, to
assert the Commons' rights, and to leave further action for
another year.

There was not, because there could not be, sustained
resistance to this plan. Even Bright and his friends, who
had endeavoured, by placards and public meetings, to
rouse agitation against the upper House, were obliged to
admit that the reference to precedents was a proper thing.[78]
Even Gladstone had to confess that the resolutions asserting
the privileges of the House were worthy of support.[79]
Well he might, for ultimately they represented the combined
wisdom and phraseology of Russell, Graham, Palmerston,
the Speaker, T. E. May (one of the greatest living authorities on the constitution)—and Gladstone himself.[80] For
some time the chancellor tried to insist upon pursuing
his own more aggressive course : his resignations, so the

premier told Delane, had fed the study fire at Broadlands until the chimney was in flames.[81]　But in the end he chose to submit rather than to resign, saving his dignity by reservation of the rather empty right to support a more active vindication of the Commons' privileges when opportunity arrived.　In the judgment of many contemporaries the honours of war rested with Palmerston.　Throughout he had both kept his head and kept intact his cabinet. There was obviously truth in the charge that he had introduced his resolutions in a manner too apologetic to the Lords,[82] and hence gratifying to some at least of the Conservatives : yet one cannot put down to mere partisanship the eulogies which emanated from their side. He had used, wrote Greville, 'consummate tact and discretion' : Derby and Disraeli spoke of his conduct as 'beyond all praise.'[83]

But alas! his 'consummate tact and discretion' were lacking in those little notes to the Queen, which in some inexplicable way (possibly through his own inability to resist repeating his own jokes) obtained a good deal of publicity.　Hardly had the House of Lords rejected the Paper Duties Bill, when Palmerston wrote one of the best known and most blamed of them all, pointing out that 'it would be better to lose Mr. Gladstone than to run the risk of losing Portsmouth or Plymouth.'[84]　For, as the letter also pointed out, the fortifications question had reached a crisis.　Herbert had now definitely asked the cabinet to approve a loan of eight and a half millions to carry out the recommendations of the commission ; and Gladstone (influenced, so the premier feared, by Bright) was showing himself 'sadly deficient in good sense and statesmanlike views.'[85]　The matter hung fire through June and nearly all July. Gladstone, hostile as ever to any endorsement of the commission's comprehensive scheme, seemed immovable, his resignation as much as ever imminent; but he was met with quite equal resolution on the part of the premier and the majority of the cabinet.　The struggle seemingly ended in a sensible compromise.[86]　Only about a quarter of the work (that recommended by the commission for Portsmouth and Plymouth) could in any case be undertaken before the next budget was framed. Gladstone consented that this should be carried out without delay, and paid for by the issue of annuities. But disagreement occurred again when Palmerston announced this to the House.[87] Gladstone and his two main sympathisers, Russell and Gibson, having swallowed the ' camel' of the fortifications scheme, could not get over the ' gnat ' of hearing Palmerston proclaim the fact. When Gladstone learned that the premier, in announcing the commencement of the fortifications, had promised their completion in the succeeding years, he charged that one of the essential undertakings which made up the compromise had been broken. Palmerston, while denying that there had been any breach of faith, remained quite unperturbed. After all, Gladstone had stayed on, possibly for the reason that no member of the cabinet, not even Milner Gibson, had shown the least inclination to retire with him.[88] Palmerston wrote his usual sarcastic little note about it to the Queen :

Mr. Gladstone . . . though acquiescing in the step now taken about the fortifications, . . . kept himself free to take such course as he may think fit upon that subject next year. . . . That course will probably be the same which Mr. Gladstone has taken this year namely ineffectual opposition and ultimate acquiescence.[89]

Granville thought the premier quite right in believing that the only way to deal with Gladstone was ' to bully him a little ' ;[90] but the episode did not bode well for the future.

In the relations between the two men, nothing perhaps is more significant than the condition in which each emerged from this exhausting session, and from their own protracted duel. White did not exaggerate concerning the weariness of parliament. On the day of prorogation the peers were represented by one solitary bishop, and the members of the lower House dispersed in ' general delight.'[91] The cabinet had given greater evidences of exhaustion still. A week before, they had adjourned to Greenwich, to celebrate as usual their own coming release with the annual sacrifice of innumerable whitebait. But so surfeited were they with speech, that ' the real business of the evening ' was performed without even the usual ' bantering toasts.'[92] Even earlier than this Russell had fled to Scotland for his health. And earlier still, Gladstone had complained that never in his life before had he 'had such a sense of mental and moral exhaustion.'[93] But the premier attended both the whitebait dinner and the final session of parliament, wrote amusing accounts of both for the Queen, and was singled out as the one member of the cabinet in the lower House who showed no strain.[94] Gladstone was not only exhausted but querulous : ' He discoursed [to Robert Phillimore, at the time completely outside government circles] without the smallest reserve upon . . . the feebleness of the government, mainly attributable to the absence of any effective head ; Palmerston's weakness in the cabinet and his low standard for all public conduct.'[95] It is curious to read this in face of Greville's praise of the premier, Granville's belief that he was ' decidedly the most powerful man in the country,' and the rather fulsome tribute of Sir Richard Bethell, the attorney general, to the ' great knowledge, great judgment, great temper and forbearance, infinite skill and tact, matchless courtesy, and great oratorical talent ' which he had displayed all through the year.[96]

What makes the premier's freshness all the more remarkable is the fact that he had been as much on the alert during the second as during the first half of the session with regard to foreign affairs, and especially with respect to developments in Italy. There had been need for alertness, in view of the great events which were proceeding in the southern and central portions of the peninsula. In May, Garibaldi with his filibustering redshirts had left Genoa to help the Sicilians rid themselves of Neapolitan rule ; by mid-August he had long since completed this first task, and was crossing to the mainland to assist the Neapolitans in shaking off Bourbon rule ; by early September he was master of all the Neapolitan territories. Before October was out Victor Emmanuel had taken over those territories as a part of his new kingdom of Italy. He had joined up his newest with his earlier acquisitions by seizing all of the Pope's remaining possessions, save Rome and its environs, on his way south.

Palmerston's attitude toward all these heroic episodes

suggests far less a sympathiser with Italian aspirations than a disillusioned and cynical statesman of an older school. When news of Garibaldi's expedition first arrived he seemed little concerned about the fate of southern Italy. Though sharing with Russell a preference for the *status quo* in the Neapolitan kingdom, he had ' no strong objection to the union of all Italy and of the Island of Sicily into one monarchy.'[97] But his suspicions of the French, ' deceivers ever,' were now at their height, and he was almost obsessed with the fear that Napoleon would demand and secure Genoa, or some other territorial ' compensation ' from Victor Emmanuel. This was to be prevented at all costs. So why not demand from Sardinia a treaty binding her to alienate no territory without British consent ? If the treaty were signed England would ' stand aloof from the Sicilian and Neapolitan insurrection ' ; if it were refused :

. . . we should tell the King of Naples that our desire is to maintain his dynasty and the integrity of his dominions, but that we cannot be of any active assistance to him unless he will at once alter his system of government. . . . That if he will do this and immediately we will endeavour by our naval force to prevent all landings of hostile bands in any part of his dominions, and give him moreover our political support.[98]

The plan was a trifle too cold-blooded for Russell, who could not ' stomach defending Bombino.' But Lord John, like the premier, was far more concerned to keep Napoleon from profiting at the expense of Italy than to help the Italians achieve national unity. He was at first most anxious to prevent Victor Emmanuel from annexing Bombino's territories, insular or peninsular ; and he was willing, if necessity arose, to take a line of action in the north which Palmerston could not stomach—that of promising to assist Austria in keeping Venetia.[99] The change of attitude observable in both British ministers when they were persuaded that Victor Emmanuel would give no further *pourboires* to the French showed still more strikingly how great their fears of French aggrandisement had been. Palmerston, working hand in glove with his foreign secretary as usual, was soon rejecting French suggestions for joint action in preventing Garibaldi from crossing to the mainland, on the ground that Garibaldi's enterprise was ' an Italian & domestic action and not a foreign interference that would justify interference by any Power out of Italy.'[100] Later in the year he was showing off Garibaldi's thirteen year old son at an evening party, and backing Russell in sending a despatch so eulogistic of the revolutionists of central and southern Italy as to be, in the eyes of the Russian ambassador at least, pure ' *polissonnerie*.'[101] But he was also considering possible methods of defending Austria in her possession of Dalmatia and of preventing France from stirring up fresh insurrection in Hungary.[102]

Considering Palmerston's comparative indifference to Victor Emmanuel's success or failure in adding Sicily, Naples, and the Papal States to his rapidly expanding kingdom, it is startling at first to discover his eagerness that Venetia and Rome itself should go the way of the rest of Italy. Garibaldi himself was hardly more ready to assist in putting the finishing touches to Italian unification than was the British premier. Facing the realities of the situation, he had regretfully to admit that the political atmosphere of Italy might be ' tainted ' for some time to come by the ' corrupting miasma ' of an uncleansed papal stall in the ' Augean stable ' of the peninsula ;[103] but he bent himself to the task of promoting the sale of Venetia to the Italians without delay.

To say that her [Austria's] honour and her interest forbid the transfer of Venetia for 20 million sterling is all *bosh* : and to say that the fortresses on the Mincio are the outposts and defences of Germany is about as rational as it was to say that Gatton and Old Sarum were the bulwarks of the British constitution.[104]

Here the reason for his impatience is beginning to peep out ; and in two other letters, written at about the same time, it stands fully revealed. Austria should sell the province because Venetia was as much a protection to Germany as ' a steeple is a defence for a church against lightening [*sic*] ' ; Italy should buy it because she could then count upon the protection of a friendly Austria against France,

' always threatening and encroaching.'[105] His liberalism
and humanitarianism were not dead. He still inveighed
against Austria's ' oppressions and cruelties ' in Venetia,
and looked forward to the pleasure of ' every liberal minded
man ' when her ' iron heel ' should be removed.[106] But his
commiseration for the Venetians was overshadowed by his
fears for Europe's equilibrium. The Austrian government,
he wrote, was ' sliding deliberately toward its Ruin ' ; while
Napoleon was ' constantly trying to shape his course not
according to any fixed plan or determined principle of action
but according to the shifting breeze of momentary expediency.'[107] What could Palmerston and Russell do to steady
either one ? Victoria, horrified at the idea that the sale of
Venetia should even be suggested at Vienna, prevented the
matter from being raised officially.[108] Nor would the
suggestion have been of the least avail. Austria was to
retain her ' steeple '; and Napoleon was to keep Europe
unstable and Palmerston anxious to the very end.

His uneasiness was very much accentuated by the naval
situation.[109] Though Gladstone had consented to increased
naval estimates, and the Admiralty, with hearty endorsement
from the public, was enlarging its building programme, the
prospects were that the British navy would for some time
be inferior to the French with respect to armoured ships.
The British Admiralty, slowed up by the changes in
personnel incidental to the change of government in June
1859, had found rapid progress impossible ; and France,
as though resolved to keep her lead, had in this year adopted
a building programme for armoured ships far in advance of
anything that England had even planned. It is hardly
strange, then, if Palmerston not only grew concerned over
the possibilities of French dominance in the Mediterranean
but shared those fears of an invasion of England which he
had scouted the year before. To the French, of course,
he would confess no fear of any kind. When Napoleon
threatened, through Persigny and Borthwick, that his
subjects would force him into war unless he could show
evidence of British friendliness, and that, if war came,
France would destroy Britain's dockyards by using armoured
ships, the prime minister scornfully pointed, not only to

England's coal and iron, but to the ' *quelques dix minutes de ténacité de plus* '[110] possessed by English over French warriors. No doubt he was perfectly sincere ; but no doubt he realised that even tenacity cannot always avail against surprise.

Unfortunately, his anxiety for England's welfare led him into suspicions impossible to justify ; and submerged, though without at all extinguishing, his humanitarian impulses. One sees this in his attitude toward a new crisis which occurred this year in the Near East, a crisis growing out of a bloody contest between the Druses and the Maronites.[111] The two peoples, it will be remembered, though sharing the comparatively small district of the Lebanon in Syria, were almost inevitably fierce enemies. For the Maronites had long professed the Roman Catholic faith ; while the Druses wcre Mohammedans who contrived to reconcile allegiance to the prophet, a streak of paganism, and the toleration of Protestant missions. When the political and religious hatreds endemic in the Lebanon produced a hideous outbreak in the summer of 1860, the Druses, much the more numerous and apparently the more ferocious of the two, perpetrated outrages which horrified the Christian world, and particularly France. For France had looked upon the Maronites as protégés since the time of the crusades. The horror grew when fanatical Mohammedans in Damascus fell upon defenceless Christians there, killing, burning and ravishing without interference from the Sultan's representatives, and with actual co-operation from some of the Sultan's troops. The Mohammedans were even so thoughtless as to sack European consulates. The cry for a punitive expedition from Europe was general; and France, though quite willing to act with and under the mandate of the other Powers, desired to take the lead.

Palmerston's heart but not his policy was with the Maronites. Though he believed, and produced good evidence for believing, that they had been responsible for the original outbreak of hostilities ;[112] though he was irritated at hearing that they had sent a Jesuit to lobby for them in parliament,[113] he gave them his sympathy. Publicly and privately he condemned the brutality of the Druses,

and still more the ' infamous ' and ' abominable ' conduct
of the local Turkish officials and soldiery.[114]   But it seemed
to him that a punitive expedition from Europe, and above
all one executed by the French, would be very undesirable.[115]
Certain alarms of the late spring, caused by Russia's
demand for an international investigation in Turkey, and
by Prince Napoleon's visit there, were still causing him
uneasiness ; and he saw himself again defending Turkey,
in the interests of England, against two rapacious Powers :

> These French proposals look very suspicious, and greatly resemble
> their twin brothers from Russia, for an occupation of the northern
> provinces of Turkey.   With the Russians in Bulgaria and the French
> masters of Syria the Eastern Question as it is called would be pretty
> well settled.[116]

Moreover such a settlement, impossible in itself to contemplate, was not likely to be reached without a general
European war.

But, even leaving aside the possible partition of Turkey
and the terrible consequences it might involve, a French
expedition could hardly be tolerated.   For the French, he
was convinced ' *Partant pour la Syrie* ' meant *restant dans
la Syrie*.   With Northern Africa in mind, he asked how the
French having once entered could be got out again.   They
had only to incite the Maronites to fresh provocation in
order to justify their permanent occupation of the Lebanon.
What, in fact, would rid Syria of them save a war ?   And
what would the House of Commons have to say to a ministry
which had been so negligent in guarding British interests ?

> Depend upon it public opinion will turn against us . . . as soon
> as the disturbances are over and the massacres forgot and it will be
> made a charge and an unanswerable one against us that we agreed
> to this suicidal measure after we knew that the Turkish government
> had taken effectual steps for doing that which would render any
> foreign interference entirely unnecessary.[117]

For the Turkish government was hurrying forces to the
seat of trouble, and promising dire punishment to those
responsible for the massacres.

Palmerston's alarm at the situation and his suspicions
of the French seem to have outlived all reasonable cause.

That he was nervous at the outset is comprehensible enough. The French government, as he understood it, proposed to intervene singly, to remain in occupation of Syria as long as it might choose, and to bill the half bankrupt Turkish government for the large and undetermined expenditure which the expedition would entail.[118]   Small wonder he implored his cabinet to refuse endorsement of Napoleon's project, or that, being overridden, he accused them of 'handing over Syria to France.'[119]   To Russell, who for once stood in clear opposition to his chief, he declared they were in 'one of the greatest scrapes any English government ever got into.'[120]   But, from August on, the situation was radically changed.   The French accepted a convention with the Sultan and the other four great Powers, calling for an international expeditionary force of which Napoleon was to supply only half, and to which the British might easily have contributed.   No corresponding change appeared in the attitude of England's premier.   The French troops were already on the ground ; and Sir Henry Bulwer, who had been sent out to the Porte, was sure that the French emperor had in mind the establishment of 'a quasi-independent sovereignty' which would be actually a protectorate.[121]   Palmerston, impressed as usual by the 'trickiness' of 'the French of all parties and politics,'[122] listened only too readily.   In vain Cowley wrote from Paris that Napoleon would withdraw the expedition as soon as possible.   The prime minister merely bemoaned the fact that Cowley, invaluable at the Tuileries as he was, laboured under 'a moral as well as a physical French influenza.'[123]   When the French foreign minister, Thouvenel, replied to a demand for the evacuation of Syria by stating that Napoleon could not promise to bring home the expeditionary force within a given time, Palmerston pounced on him like a terrier on a rat.   What was this, he wrote Russell, but evidence that Thouvenel was planning to keep the French force on shipboard near the Syrian coast in the hope of 'creating some after pretence for landing it again ? '   And what was Thouvenel but 'a baffled and detected cheat ? '[124]   Not till, in 1861, the expeditionary force was back in France again were Palmerston's suspicions stilled.

Anxiety had dogged Palmerston all the year, but it was to be tempered by good news from China before the year was out. The premier, who had utilised the autumn for a triumphal progress through Yorkshire,[125] ended it in the knowledge that Sir Hope Grant had made a triumphal progress to Peking. For the expedition planned in the preceding autumn had proved an almost unqualified success.[126] The British forces, swelled by the too great zeal of the viceroy of India to a size which neither the British treasury nor the French government had bargained for, had, as Palmerston delightedly recorded, ' throughout had their own way and . . . led the way.'[127] The excellent functioning of the infantry had demonstrated the vast improvements made in equipment and supply since the Crimean war ; and the Armstrong guns had more than answered every test. But it was the occupation of Peking which most delighted Palmerston. His foresight had been doubly justified ; since the occupation had proved virtually inevitable, and had been accomplished without the overthrow of the Manchu dynasty. The Chinese had shown themselves incorrigible, both in refusing the allies' moderate demand for an apology and the full execution of the Treaty of 1858, and in resorting to treachery and cruelty. While peace negotiations were proceeding at a point between Tientsin and the capital, they had seized several British and French officers and correspondents, returning from Chinese headquarters under a flag of truce, and tortured some of them to death. The Emperor had fled from his capital ; but even in his absence nothing short of its occupation had seemed adequate for bringing him to terms. And in view of the tortures inflicted on the captured officers and correspondents, Grant and Elgin, humane men both, had decided upon a more imposing demonstration still. Feeling that condign punishment would be the best deterrent against a repetition of such barbarities, and that it would be most just and most efficacious if inflicted directly on the Emperor, they had burned his famous summer palace to the ground. The day of submission to Chinese cruelty in the interests of British trade had passed, as Elgin wrote, when the modern *civis Romanus* had appeared.[128]

Here, indeed, was a happy ending to a troubled year for Palmerston. It was not only that the affair had justified his foresight, strengthened his hold on country and parliament, and involved the infliction of a much needed ' public humiliation ' on the Chinese emperor and his Tartar myrmidons : it was agreeable to the premier's *Weltanschauung* as well. One can imagine the satisfaction with which he added this paragraph to the letter in which he conveyed the season's greetings to the Queen :

This Autumn and Winter, however, have been productive of events in three of the four quarters of the Globe, which future years are not likely to repeat. The capture of Pekin in Asia by British and French troops ; the Union in Europe of nearly the whole of Italy into one Monarchy ; and the approaching and virtually accomplished Dissolution in America of the great Northern Confederation, are events full of importance for the future, as well as being remarkable in time present.[129]

For the greetings themselves he drew on Pope :

May day improve on day, and year on year,
Without a pain, a trouble or a fear.

Remembering the customary relations between sender and recipient, one realises that Palmerston could be exquisitely Victorian.

CHAPTER XXXI

1861

WE have the evidence of the *Annual Register* that Palmerston was justified in looking forward to developments in the new year with every confidence :

The internal state of the country at the opening of the year 1861 was generally prosperous and tranquil. . . . The state of the agricultural and manufacturing interests . . . was apparently sound. . . . Whatever demand had temporarily existed for constitutional changes appeared to have now completely subsided. . . . In the absence of stirring events at home, attention was chiefly bent upon the progress of affairs abroad, especially upon the gradual development of Italian unity. . . . The successful and honourable termination of the war in China was hailed with cordial satisfaction. On the other side of the Atlantic, the first scene of a revolution of great importance, no less than the disruption of the hitherto United States into two hostile sections, had just begun to excite a warm interest in this country.' [1]

It was no wonder he sent such optimistic greetings to his sovereign. Yet, how events were to darken these fair prospects ! For the Queen, this year was to bring the greatest sorrow of her life : for her first minister it was to prove a time of much anxiety, and at the close, of deep distress. He was to find his own position seriously threatened from the benches of the House ; and he was to believe, at least, that the safety of his country and of the established order in Europe was more menaced than ever from the Tuileries. Pains, troubles and fears were to beset him constantly ; and no small part of them were to find their origin in just those developments in Italy and North America to which he had referred so jauntily.

Belief in ' the approaching and virtually accomplished

T

Dissolution ' in America was an important element in
Palmerston's world outlook during the year 1861 ; but
the satisfaction he found in it must not be exaggerated.
The prospect of the break-up of the Union produced a
certain contentment, that was all.   True, he had no great
liking for the Americans with their republicanism, their
assertiveness, their turbulent Irish journalists, and their, to
him, ill-formed manners.   He had no liking at all for Seward,
whom he too long regarded as a dictator where American
foreign relations were concerned.   This man, whom the
premier remembered as having shown himself quite un-
acceptable to good society in England, and as having
displayed an unfortunate inclination to spend time in
drinking brandy and water with ' some editors of second
rate newspapers,' seemed an inveterate foe, not disinclined
to bring back the difficult relations of five years before.[2]
On the other hand, Palmerston was far too sensible to disapprove of all Americans, or to decline their company.
Stevenson's daughter, for example, married and living in
England, was one of Lady Palmerston's great friends.   And
Palmerston, who hardly ever cherished grudges, apparently
felt none against the American people as a whole.   But it must
have been hard for him to take American institutions very
seriously.   Was he not himself older than the Constitution ?
Could he not remember America in its swaddling-clothes,
when Washington was president for the second time ?
The precocious nation had grown fast enough, but only
to use its strength from time to time in rudely jostling
England, and making her anxious about Canada.   Its
dissolution could hardly have struck the premier as a
calamity in any case ; yet the satisfaction in such a prospect
which his New Year's letter to the Queen reveals may have
been due in some part to the fact that the Americans had of
late been misbehaving again.   They had, indeed, given a
proper reception to the Prince of Wales ; and the prime
minister had suggested that Mr. and Mrs. Dallas should
be invited to Windsor in return.   But American troops
had been landed in the little island of San Juan, lying
between Vancouver and the state of Washington ; and the
premier was even at this moment discussing with Russell the

transfer to Vancouver of some troops which could be spared from the far East.³ This, according to his familiar way of thinking, was the best way of keeping the truculent American secretary of State in bounds. To allow Seward to discover any weak joint in Britain's armour would make Anglo-American relations more difficult.

Quite as obvious is the fact that Palmerston had no intention of offering any provocation to the Federal government. At this juncture it was the southern states which felt aggrieved.⁴ To keep hands off the dispute in the United States, eyes on the defences of Canada, and diplomatic faculties alert for any opportunity of striking at the slave trade : these seem to have been the original, and for some time the dominant, principles of the premier's policy.⁵ It is surprising that he should, so early as the beginning of 1861, have considered the break-up of the Union inevitable: yet one must judge from his private letters that he had no desire to take the risk of furthering it. By rag-tags of doggerel he reiterated his settled conviction that ' nothing could be more unadvisable ' than interference :

' They who in quarrels interpose, will often get a bloody nose,' and
' If you would keep out of strife, step not in 'twixt man and wife.' ⁶

He was, it is true, considering the possibility that England might offer mediation ; but mediation from his point of view involved no unfriendliness to the North. In fact, as he saw the situation, one of the chief obstacles to the initiation of such a step lay in the difficulty of presenting any basis for negotiations possible of acceptance by the South without ' some formal approval of the condition of slavery in the Southern states,' extending even to a fugitive slave law.⁷ Approval would hardly be seemly on the part of Palmerston, the life-long enemy of the slave trade in three continents.

On the other hand, it was the desire to deal a new blow to the slave trade which first tempted him to modify the policy of rigid abstention from all interference on which he, the Court and the cabinet had all agreed. There is no sign of any concern for British commerce, of resentment against the Union government, or of sympathy for the

South in his first tentative suggestion that the Foreign Office might concern itself with the crisis :

> . . . its most interesting bearing will be on the slave trade. The Northern states will be more ready to help us to put it down. There is danger that the Southern states would legalize and encourage it but we might make some engagement against slave trade the condition of acknowledgment.[8]

As the spring advanced, the premier, noting Seward's apparent desire to pick a quarrel,[9] and being ignorant of Lincoln's growing control, showed some uneasiness. But the crusade against the traffic in negroes was apparently still uppermost in his thoughts. He was willing that the government should feel its way towards mediation informally ;[10] but what seemed to concern him more was the development of an idea he had put forward early in the year. England, after granting recognition to the Southern Confederacy, at the price of a treaty for the joint suppression of the slave trade, might invite the co-operation of the Federal government and of Napoleon in asking Mexico to forbid the establishment of slavery in her territories by ' adventurers ' from the southern states ![11] Only with the coming of summer did he reluctantly give up the plan.

There is a decided element of finality about many of Palmerston's activities in this year of 1861. In reviewing them in connection with his life one has the feeling of reading the last acts of several plays. As regards parliamentary reform, the dispute over the paper duties, and the unification of Italy one may write *finis* in so far as one great actor is concerned. Moreover, the beginning of the year saw what was virtually a permanent break in his understanding with the ' advanced ' Liberals : while its close brought to a tragic end his long relationship with the Prince Consort. But the element of finality was little visible to his contemporaries. As regards domestic politics no one could tell how events would turn ; while, to many persons, conditions on the continent portended new developments in old questions which might shake Europe as it had not been shaken for many years. Among the most apprehensive of these persons was the premier himself.

It is not strange that Napoleon and the French constituted as usual the focus of his anxieties. The distrust
of England's neighbours across the Channel, for which he
had so long and so often had excuse, must naturally have
hardened into a fixed idea in his old age. And, according
to Clarendon, his suspicions were constantly being fed
through family influences :

> Shaftesbury's is a house of call for refugees and they are always
> full of 'wars and rumours of wars' and of secret information,
> especially with respect to the Emperor's intentions, that Shaftesbury
> believes as he does his Bible, and hammers into the predisposed Pam
> through Lady Shaftesbury and Lady Palmerston as well as by himself
> and Azeglio, till Palmerston believes that he gets the same information
> from many quarters and that it must therefore be true.[12]

But it is only just to Palmerston to remember that suspicion
of the French emperor was very general. ' The rumour of
the [Franco-Russian] Alliance, like the fabulous sea serpent,'
wrote Vitzthum at this time, ' has been cropping up in all
directions ever since Villafranca.'[13] And few men save
Cowley seem to have doubted that the eyes of Napoleon
and his subjects were fixed greedily upon the Rhine.

Hence the premier was suffering from the same night-
mare that had returned to him incessantly from the time
when, over thirty years before, he had first received the
Foreign Office seals—a general European war accompanied
by a cycle of revolutions, and all set on foot by France.
The essential difference between his earlier and later nightmares was the larger place occupied after 1859 by Italy.
In the spring of 1861 he was very much concerned lest
Sardinia should break her promises and give Napoleon
the island of Sardinia in order to secure Venetia or Rome
or both.[14] But the greatest of his immediate fears was
that the Emperor would join Cavour and even Garibaldi
in attacking Austria—in raiding her Adriatic coast and
stirring revolutions in Hungary and Galicia. Reports
arrived that Garibaldi's legion was reassembling, and would
probably resume its old raiding activities in Dalmatia ;
that arms were being loaded at Genoa for use of the Hungarians ; and that Kossuth was issuing a new Hungarian

currency.[15] And this at a time when Napoleon was keeping in Rome some 20,000 troops, troops available either for a blow at Austria, or for some stroke in northern or southern Italy which might even yet block the unification of the peninsula. Once the mêlée commenced, the main French army, by a mere military parade, would seize all German territory to the Rhine. Nor did it seem certain that France would open the hostilities. In April, Elgin, arriving from Vienna, reported that the Austrian government was convinced of the inevitability of war, and embarrassed by the necessity of keeping its forces on a war footing.

Palmerston and Russell, as usual skirmishing with the Queen, were full of expedients for removing every possible excuse for war. Despite Victoria's objection to the treatment of Garibaldi as a 'Power,' the foreign secretary sent him a letter urging him to leave well enough alone.[16] Palmerston would even have invited him to England, thinking ' he would be much better employed in having dinners given to him ' than in raiding the Dalmatian coast.[17] Both ministers wished to send Clarendon to Vienna to implore the Austrians to sell Venetia, or at least (for the first suggestion had immediately to be dropped) not to ' repeat the error of 1859.'[18] Both longed to carry out an old suggestion, now brought forward by Persigny in somewhat altered form, that Italy should buy Herzegovina from Turkey and trade it for Venetia with Austria.[19] They would both, if they had seen their way to it, have done away immediately with the Pope's temporal power, and consequently with the only possible excuse for the presence of French troops in Italy. Why should a portion of the Italian people, argued Palmerston, be doomed to misery on the theory that the Pope ' would not open the gates of the kingdom of paradise if he had not the power to make some little hell on earth.'[20] But Palmerston showed himself the more cautious of the two. Russell would have placed a time limit on the existence of the temporal power by diplomatic means : Palmerston was for leaving it to die a natural and, as he hoped, a speedy death.[21] Russell would have promised moral support to Austria in the

impending war : Palmerston was for a general warning
that the aggressor, whosoever he might be, would find
England's influence on the other side.[22]

The danger died down temporarily with the advance of
spring ; and June brought the startling news of Cavour's
death. Not a shadow of any former disagreement or
resentment lay across Palmerston's eulogy of a man after
his own heart :

> The tale with which his memory will be associated is one of the
> most extraordinary—I may say the most romantic—recorded in the
> annals of the world. We have seen under his influence and guidance
> a people who were supposed to have become torpid . . . enervated
> . . . and to have had no knowledge or feeling on politics, except
> what may have been derived from the traditions of their history and
> the jealousies of rival States—we have seen that people, under his
> guidance and at his call, rising from the slumber of ages . . . breaking
> that spell by which they had so long been bound, and displaying on
> great occasions the courage of heroes, the sagacity of statesmen, the
> wisdom of philosophers, and obtaining for themselves that unity of
> political existence which for centuries had been denied them.[23]

Palmerston's farewell to Cavour was virtually his farewell
to Italy. His suspicions of Napoleon and his alarm at the
prospect of a general war grew more pronounced again as
the year went on ;[24] but there was nothing he could do.
To the end he kept his old views and plans, and in the last
year of his life was still hoping for 'a pacific solution of the
Venetian difficulty by means of an exchange of territory.'[25]
But he could no more keep Austria from ' sliding ' than he
could keep Napoleon from drifting. It was left for Bismarck to note, like Palmerston, the Venetian ' steeple ' and
Napoleon's habit of yielding to a shifting breeze.

Palmerston had delivered his eulogy of Cavour to a
House of Commons in which the Liberals of the left wing
made no secret of their hostility to the Liberal ministry,
and in which the bulk of the Conservatives seldom offered
more opposition than was demanded by parliamentary
proprieties. The Liberal party had exchanged the
radical and exigent wife which it had taken unto itself in
June 1859 for a rich and good-natured, though not
entirely reliable Conservative mistress. The divorce be-

tween the Liberals of the left and right could almost have
been predicted when their unhappy offspring perished in
the session of 1860. It came when Bright, attending the
opening of parliament on February 5, 1861, not only noted
the omission from the Queen's speech of any mention of
parliamentary reform, but heard Russell himself announce
his approval of the omission ' in a speech of offensive tone
and language.' [26] ' I shall keep no terms with this Government for the future,' he wrote. That even Locke King,
the veteran and inveterate advocate of a broader suffrage,
admitted the absence of any spontaneous demand, could not
reconcile Bright to the cabinet's decision to let private
members' bills on the subject take their chance.[27] But the
grounds for divorce between the two great sections of the
party lay in incompatibility as well as infidelity. There
had been a growing alienation on questions of defence and
finance. Before parliament met, some sixty members of the
advanced wing, inspired apparently by Cobden, had signed
a round robin demanding a reduction in the appropriations
for armaments.[28] At the same time Bright and Cobden
had been making overtures for a distinctly illicit union
with the Conservatives.[29] According to Disraeli's account
they had offered to assist in turning out the government,
and in keeping it out for the two years necessary to bring
into operation a new and ' proper ' measure of parliamentary
reform. News of these overtures and of their rejection,
given immediately to the Court, had at once reached
Palmerston.

The premier had no reason for immediate alarm.
Prince Albert described his position to Stockmar :

> In Parliament Palmerston is entirely master this year. The
> Tories do not want office ; the country does not want a Reform
> Bill, and it does want defences.[30]

In fact, the Conservatives had already indicated their readiness to combat ' intrigues emanating from the Tuileries
and Mr. Cobden ' by renewing the assurances of support
they had given a year before.[31] Disraeli promised Prince
Albert that ' a compact and formidable party ' of ' more than
300 M.P.'s ' would support the cabinet so long as it steered

clear of ' democratic finance ' ; while Malmesbury, acting once more as intermediary, brought the Conservative offers to Palmerston just prior to the opening of parliament. If Gladstone's desire to substitute direct for indirect taxation should lead to his withdrawal from the ministry, Palmerston should have Conservative support for the continuance of his government in power. It was taken for granted that the cabinet would follow ' a bold national policy.' Conventional party warfare would, of course, go on in parliament ; and the opposition might (as it almost did) overturn the government on some matter not covered by its promise. Derby was apparently sincere in stating that his followers as a whole had no wish to upset the ministry.[32] Without such a majority as only a new and fortunate election could give them, the reversal of England's foreign policy, which constituted their chief aim, would obviously be impossible ; and even ordinary business would be extremely difficult. It seemed better to ' *ménager* ' Palmerston, whose policies were certainly very tolerable after all, than to be at the mercy of the radicals. And time seemed on their side. By-elections were beginning to go their way ; and in the House they were able to draw increasingly on the Catholic vote.[33] For many English and Irish Catholics were disgusted with the late developments in Italy ; and preferred a Semitic leader who happened to regard the Pope's enemies as modern Huns, to such bitterly anti-papal Christians as the foreign secretary and prime minister. Cardinal Wiseman promised Disraeli the Catholic vote before the spring was out ; and it was calculated that a new election would throw almost the complete Irish representation to the Conservatives.[34] Disraeli's hopes ran high : but Disraeli did not yet know the country as he was to know it in later years.

A shrewd politician might at this time have seen something very suggestive in a little pen portrait which Granville made of Palmerston : ' I saw him the other night looking very well, but old, and wearing a green shade, which he afterwards concealed. He looked like a retired old *croupier* from Baden.'[35] For, indeed, the old premier was holding the bank, letting others make their stakes, and on the whole deriving distinct profit for the house. There were differences of opinion as to how long he could hold his place ; but most men agreed that the life of the ministry depended largely on its leader's health. His hold on the country seemed to become stronger year by year ; and the time was approaching when, according to the wits, the Liberals could go to the country ' on the cry of " Palmerston and no Politics," or " Palmerston and no Principles." ' Politics and principles were still in some demand in parliament ; but the premier was no less a popular idol than he was a master parliamentarian. He had learned many things since the downfall of his first ministry.

Yet the cabinet came very close to shipwreck more than once in 1861 on the related questions of defence and finance. In some ways these questions were more than ever vital. Military expenditures stood at their peak ; while both Herbert and Cornewall Lewis, who succeeded him at the War Office in July, were determined to see the projected fortifications carried through.[36] And Palmerston, while willing to concede to Gladstone that ' no doubt a full Exchequer ' was ' a good foundation for National Defence,' felt impelled to emphasise the point that ' if the French had the Command of the Sea they would soon find means to make a full Exchequer empty.'[37] Naturally, then, the premier and his chancellor of the Exchequer soon entered on a new series of duels, each having some seconds within the ministry. As before, their opposing sets of views related not only to the current situation in foreign affairs, but to conditions of party politics. The connection becomes clear when one reads a letter written to Palmerston by Prince Albert on January 24—a letter relating to the round robin of the advanced Liberals on the question of expenditure for armaments, and Disraeli's offer of Conservative assistance to the ministry :

It is evident that there exists great fear [on the part of the Conservatives] of the Peace Party and a full knowledge that the Emperor [Napoleon] desires a ' Gladstone-Cobden ' Government to disarm this country, in order to domineer over it, if not to attack it.[38]

Palmerston's apprehensions may not have gone so far as

this ; but a reference in one of his letters to Bright as ' our real budget maker and chancellor of the exchequer '[39] illuminates his attitude towards Gladstone. And among those whom Gladstone regarded as having, in their alarm, gone ' far beyond the bounds of reason '[40] he must certainly have included the prime minister. What wonder then if the two statesmen found it difficult to agree on figures for the military and naval estimates ?

Their views on questions of supply were as difficult to reconcile.[41] They both desired remission of taxation, and especially the reduction or abolition of the still high income tax, and the extra duties imposed on tea and sugar in 1853. But Palmerston saw remissions merely as ' reliefs ' to tax-payers—reliefs which it would be desirable to make as politically serviceable as possible : Gladstone thought of remissions as ' reforms,' and reforms along democratic lines. And should there, after all, be any remission at just this time ? Gladstone, pointing to a surplus approximating £2,000,000, was sure of it : but Palmerston was not. Would it not be wise in such a time of peril, he argued, to budget for a surplus, available in some national emergency ? Or might it not be better to pay off exchequer bonds issued at the time of the Crimean war, in order (if it is fair so to construe his thought) that new ones might be floated to meet some sudden need ? Again, supposing that remissions were desirable, at what specific point should they apply ? Gladstone thought of repealing the paper duties and stopping there. But even this suggestion raised difficulties. Palmerston, foreseeing fresh disputes both in the House and between the two Houses, was hesitant concerning the repeal ; and some of the cabinet did not believe in it at all. The majority were sure at least that the repeal must be accompanied by some remission of the special taxes, that on incomes or, perhaps even preferably, that on tea.

Hence cabinet struggle followed cabinet struggle from the beginning of the year to mid-April, when Gladstone put his final scheme before an expectant and excited House.[42] In January, after ' two long days' hard fighting ' and a threat to resign, the chancellor obtained a small reduction in the naval estimates. In February, after the estimates had been announced, the Admiralty, with the premier's and apparently the cabinet's full support, decided that a much larger sum than had been asked would be required for the construction of iron-plated ships. Gladstone had composed another resignation, most dignified in tone, when the ' project ' to which he especially objected (whatever that may have been) was given up. In March came another crisis, relating this time to the army estimates ; another threat of resignation on Gladstone's part ; and another settlement based on his acceptance of a reduction which he regarded as ' purely nominal.' In this same month, too, he agreed to a special provision of some two millions for iron-plated ships. His sympathisers were a little disappointed ; his adversaries, who had been led and encouraged constantly by Palmerston, pleasantly surprised. Finally, a whole succession of hectic cabinet meetings preceded the presentation of the budget on April 15. Gladstone, much more successful in these than in the earlier meetings, consented that the repeal of the paper duties should be accompanied by a ten per cent. reduction of the income tax. Palmerston, defeated in his general schemes regarding a possible surplus, retreated ' gracefully.' But he gave the chancellor clear notice that he should not regard the defeat of the budget by the House as placing him under any obligation to resign.

Judging from the excellent reception given to Gladstone's statement by the House, this precaution of the premier's seemed at first rather superfluous ; but during the six weeks following it came near to being useful more than once. The Conservatives had, of course, promised only to support the premier in case he could not agree to the financial proposals of the chancellor ; and the fresh offensive against the House of Lords involved in the proposed repeal of the paper duties almost compelled them to resist the government. When it was disclosed that Gladstone intended, not only to make sure of the repeal, but to assert the financial powers of the House of Commons once for all by including the repeal of the paper duties in the budget as a whole, the Conservative opposition became sharply intensified. As among the various proposals, alternative to the repeal of the paper duties, which were laid before the

House, the opposition shrewdly concentrated for a time
on one that was sure to prove especially popular—a
reduction of the tax on tea. Their strength was temporarily
augmented, too, through the indignation of certain Irish
members at the government's cancellation of a contract for
the carriage of mail which had made practicable the operation
of a line of steamers from Galway to America.[43]   And the
opposition was overlooking no chances.   Roebuck complained that one Conservative member had been brought from
a lunatic asylum to record his vote.   His partner in the
constituency insisted that the unfortunate gentleman's
vote was quite valid, since he had entered and left without
restraint.   Palmerston told the Queen that he intended
writing to the lunacy commissioners ; but his interest
in the case apparently expired when the government
proved victorious by a majority of eighteen votes.[44]   The
premier was very much relieved ; for he had made up
his mind that it would be ' a good thing to get the Paper
Duty quarrel into the list of things done and gone.'[45]   But
his anxiety during the debates had not dampened his spirits.
Sir Algernon West records that ' while the debate was proceeding in the House of Commons, Lord Derby wrote a note
to Lord Palmerston, saying, ' Is it to be tea and turn out ? '
Lord Palmerston wrote back, ' No ; paper and stationary.'[46]

But the great test came on a motion to strike from the
budget the clause abolishing the paper duties.   On May 27,
when the debate was in its early stages, and all the Irish
members were ' in a state of great excitement,' the premier
was glad to avoid a division in which he feared defeat,
by an adjournment of the House.[47]   On the same date
he suggested to Granville a private agreement with Derby,
by which the House of Lords should consent to pass all
financial measures sent up to them, on condition that the
repeal of the paper duties was presented separately. ' Putting
the whole into one bill ' seemed to him ' unusual, not
quite in conformity with the different nature of enactment
and repeal.'   And, unless the budget could not be carried
otherwise, it might be ' regarded generally as a small and
petty revenge on the Lords.'[48]   His project seems to have
been still-born ; and three nights later he was rejoicing

in a victory by fifteen votes for Gladstone's scheme. 'This
will probably be the last trial of party strength this session,'
he wrote the Queen.[49]

In general the session was an uneventful one ; but
even the briefest account of Palmerston's parliamentary
activities of this year should include a word concerning his
struggle with the great apostle of neo-Gothic architecture,
Sir Gilbert Scott, over the building of the new Foreign
Office.[50] For those who gaze upon the Foreign Office
building even to this day, and reflect what might have been
put there in its stead, may possibly decide that it constitutes
a monument to Palmerston's good sense and pertinacity,
perhaps even to his good taste. The struggle, which concluded in this summer, had been in progress for five years :
and what a struggle it had been ! As the premier himself
said, 'the battle of the books, the battle of the Big and Little
Endeans, and the battle of the Green Ribbands and the
Blue Ribbands at Constantinople were all as nothing compared with this battle of the Gothic and Palladian styles.'
But consider the champions. Scott, with one eye fixed on
the medieval churches of France and Italy and the other
on his bank account, had been gothicising half of England
(mainly in brick and tile) for a quarter of a century, the
while he was not ' restoring ' England's ancient churches
with a relentless hand. He was not exactly a modest man.
When, in 1856, new homes for the Foreign and War
Offices were decided on, and a competition opened among
English architects, he submitted a set of drawings judged
by himself to be ' perhaps, the best ever sent in to a competition,' [here modesty asserted itself] ' or nearly so.' His
glorious designs, though deriving principally from French
Gothic, ' aimed at . . . a certain squareness and horizon-
tality of outline . . . which people consider Italian . . .
combined with gables, high-pitched roofs and dormers ' ;
and involved the acceptance of ' a few hints from Italy,
such as the pillar-mullion, the use of differently coloured
materials, and of inlaying.' The judges, dreadfully in-
competent, of course, could not even realise that these
drawings were the best sent in ; and Lord Palmerston,
dreadfully arbitrary, flippant and lacking in taste, of course,

passed over all the competitors. But Scott was no more given to surrender than Palmerston. Complaints, a select commission, and the advent of the Derby administration in 1858, brought him the commission for the Foreign Office after all.

Thus, on the return of Palmerston in 1859, was issue joined. For Palmerston, who had no taste for Gothic and not over much for Scott, had quite made up his mind that the ' Palladian ' (*i.e.* pseudo-classical) style was the proper one. It seemed to him that the proponents of Gothic were ' swayed by erroneous views in religion and taste.' Even the consideration that Gothic allowed ' variety of colour and ornament, by means of the introduction of serpentine, Cornish granite, &c.' did not appeal to him. It ' might be suited to monastic buildings or a Jesuits' College,' but it was not suited to the purposes of a government office or to the architecture of other buildings in Whitehall. He did not know the peculiarities of Scott's Lombardo-Gothic, but he supposed ' it combined all the modifications of barbarism.' In particular, it did not admit enough light. Objection had been made that Palladian was not a national style. But if one were to talk of national styles he had ' never heard of the Goths, the Vandals, or the Saracens doing much in this country ' ; and he had ' been told . . . that the Romans were in this country for a considerable number of years.' Indeed, if a national style were desired, why not model the building after Stonehenge or after ' mud huts and wicker wigwams ' ? And he would remind the House that if England could not boast of a distinctive style she could boast of great national architects— Vanbrugh, Sir Christopher Wren and Inigo Jones. And what would these great Englishmen have said to Scott's first designs ?

He had treated parliament and the public to the same sort of appeal that he used when an emperor instead of an architect was his antagonist ; and he treated Scott privately rather as he would have treated a foreign diplomat. He was a little sharp, a little overbearing now and then ; but customarily he was as smooth and easy in his address as he was pertinacious in his resistance. Scott was first told that his original plans (later used for St. Pancras station by their admiring and economical author) would not do, and requested to produce new and Palladian ones. Quite like a continental diplomat, Scott tried a little subterfuge, producing new designs which only in certain details differed much from the old. But who was Sir Gilbert Scott to succeed where even Talleyrand had failed ? Once again he was sent back to his drafting boards. His next sketches were more or less Byzantine ; and the premier became more diplomatic and more impatient. After all, he admitted, it was hardly fair to ask an architect so eminent and so successful in producing Gothic buildings to design one in another style. Surely, then, it would be better to associate with him someone who would experience less pain in adopting the Palladian. The mere suggestion was enough. Scott, thinking of his family of course, decided that it was his duty to comply. After a little badly needed recuperation, he devoted himself to a special study of the style which Palmerston so unaccountably insisted on ; and produced what some people at least regard as the best of his designs. In the session of 1861 Palmerston, marshalling all his arguments, carried the acceptance of the new plans triumphantly through the House.

There is a stanza by a flamboyant but obscure eighteenth century poet which expresses the feeling apparently uppermost in Palmerston during the summer of this year :

> Thine oaks, descending to the main
>   With floating forts shall stem the tide :
> Asserting Britain's liquid reign
>   Where e'er her thundering navies ride.

For the tide of anticipated French aggression still troubled him ; and floating forts were again taking precedence with him over stone ones. If the poet had been sufficiently in advance of his age to suggest that England's iron mines should descend in company with the oaks, the lines would have expressed the premier's feelings admirably. It was the justifiable fear that France was outbuilding England in iron-plated ships which specially troubled him. He had been on the alert all through the year. He had eagerly

" Beggar My Neighbour "

Pam. : " Is not your Majesty tired of this foolish game ? "

Punch, March 23, 1861

absorbed such information as had come to him (a report,
e.g. forwarded by the Prince de Joinville to Prince Albert on
developments in American shipyards) [51] and had written
letters and memoranda on the contest now under way
between the makers of projectiles and the makers of pro-
jectile-resisting plates for ships.   He was versed, or thought
he was, in the resisting power of teakwood and iron at various
thicknesses to shot and shell.   As yet such armament,
although not proof against shot fired at close range, would
resist shell.   But the premier realised the possibility that
' elongated projectiles may be invented which will contain
in their fore part weight and strength enough to pierce
the iron and in their after part explosive matter enough to
burst that part like a shell.' [52]   As carefully did he watch
the development of naval artillery :

> I imagine that with regard to rifled cannon the advantage con-
> sists not merely in accuracy of direction which even at sea must be
> an advantage as taking away one element of uncertainty although
> the other depending on the rolling and pitching of the ship must still
> remain, but the spinning motion of the projectile gives it a greater
> power of penetration than is possessed by a ball from a smooth bore
> cannon, and I have always understood that the shot from the rifled
> gun will ricochet because the merit of Whitworth's blunt ended
> projectile was said to be that it does not ricochet as a sharp pointed
> projectile does.[53]

Before the year was out he was writing excitedly of the
testing of new ' cupola covers for cannon on a ship's deck ' :

> These iron domes from under which heavy guns are to fire have
> been pounded at from short distance by all the heaviest guns we have
> and nothing has made any impression on them.[54]

But his fervent interest in these matters and his careful
study of them—how careful those who have read Mr.
Guedalla's *Gladstone and Palmerston* will recall [55]—persuaded
him that the construction of Great Britain's first ironclads,
the *Warrior* and the others of her class, had been ' sadly
wrong in Principle.'   In order to secure a degree of
buoyancy that would allow the firing even in rough weather
of broadsides from the lowest tiers of guns (still situated in
the hulls) the builders had confined the heavy plating to

the central portions of the ships, leaving bows and sterns
protected only by a thin 'Iron Skin.' It was all
very well to show that the rest of the hulls was enclosed
on all four sides by thick plates of iron, and that watertight
compartments had been constructed in the vulnerable ends.
But how, the premier inquired, was one to manage the 'Mere
Box floating on the Water' (and waterlogged at that)
which would remain when the enemy had 'Shattered away'
the 'Fore and after Part'?

> I have repeatedly and strongly remonstrated with the Duke of
> Somerset [the first lord of the Admiralty] against this Paste Board
> Construction of our so called Iron Ships of War ; and the Iron
> Cased Ships henceforward to be built will be so shaped in their Hulls
> as to have Buoyancy enough to bear being Iron Plated along their
> whole Length from Stem to Stern.[56]

Truly it was not for the Admiralty to slumber or sleep in
1861, with Lord Palmerston as prime minister.

Neither was it for Napoleon, nor yet for Gladstone.
The French were beginning to outbuild the English in iron-
plated ships : ergo, the French must be immediately overhauled, even though the chancellor of the Exchequer might
groan.   There were those who suggested an agreement with
the French on the limitation of naval armaments.   But the
premier would have none of it.[57]   Was England, he asked
the House, willing to allow the measure of her defences to
be set by any foreign Power?   And were she ever so willing,
how could an agreement be practicable in face of the
probability that other naval Powers might combine their
fleets against hers in time of war?   What was more, would
not the incessant spying and suspicion engendered by any
agreement of the sort prove more dangerous than any
competition could be?   No, the only policy was to go
ahead and build as rapidly as possible.   It was noted that
the premier's view was received 'with much approbation'
by the House.[58]

It was not noted that this, approval was shared by the
chancellor of the Exchequer.   When projects for laying
down new ironclads, for plating wooden ships still on the
stocks, and even for plating old wooden ships, cut down

to single deckers, were set on foot, Gladstone (in one case at least without the knowledge of the cabinet) [59] was asked to provide the cost. Resistance to such a premier, whose views were received with such favour by the House, was difficult—too difficult on the whole for the unhappy chancellor. Palmerston got less than he asked for, but enough to go ahead. And the House allowed him to put through a bill authorising the employment of officers of the mercantile marine for the naval reserve.[60]

Nor could Gladstone even comfort himself with the reflection that the money spent for ' floating forts ' could be found by a reduction of expenditure on land fortifications. The premier demanded and received enough to carry on the work projected for this year. For Palmerston's newer plans for thwarting Napoleon's use of Cherbourg as ' a Place D'Armes, for the assembling of a naval & Military Force for our Benefit,' [61] had brought no abandonment of his older ones. So much was he still interested in the fortifications of the south coast that he spent part of his autumn holidays in inspecting them.[62] Incidentally, it was noted that during the inspection he spent eight hours in the saddle in a single day. He was carrying his seventy-five years very lightly in every way :

I assure you that for the last twenty years you have not seen Palmerston look as he does now. The warmer breezes have agreed with him wonderfully, the sea has washed all the dye out of his whiskers and given him a bright colour of his own, he has a new set of teeth, and altogether he looks, and I am sure he feels, as if he did not care one straw for any man or thing on earth.[63]

But he was really caring a good deal for developments at Washington.

So far back as the early summer Palmerston had commenced to readjust his attitude toward the struggle in America. For the time being no bargain with either side concerning the suppression of the slave trade seemed possible ; and it was beginning to be a question whether the cabinet's policy of complete aloofness from the struggle could be maintained. For the Union showed itself increasingly dissatisfied with the procedure which England regarded as

a proper expression of her detachment. The British proclamation of neutrality, issued on May 13, had produced in
the North a popular irritation more threatening in appearance than Seward's personal attitude had been : while the
government at Washington showed no regard whatever for
the British point of view.   Hardly had Victoria's ministers
rejected a request that they should enforce the abolition
of privateering on the South,[64] when Congress gave the
President power to proclaim what amounted to a paper
blockade of the whole coastline of the Southern States.

With all his hopes of dealing an immediate blow at
the slave-trade gone glimmering, Palmerston commenced to
react as he always reacted to what he regarded as high-
handed and provocative action on the part of a foreign
government.   Before the final passage of the bill in Congress,
he recorded his conviction that England 'ought not and
could not submit to such a violation of international rights,'
a conviction based on his familiar dictum that ' we should
only invite aggression by tamely submitting to obvious
wrong.'[65]   The account which he gave to Russell of a
conversation between himself and Flahaut, in the middle
of July, shows that, unofficially at least, he was working
toward an understanding with Napoleon.   Flahaut, he
wrote, had not only agreed that the two countries should
make common cause, but had volunteered the suggestion
that when there arose occasion for taking ' any disagreeable
step towards America . . . France should take the most
prominent part, as the best means of undeceiving the Yanks.'
' I said,' concluded the prime minister, ' I could see no
objection to this division and allotment of parts.'[66]

Not yet, however, did he show any inclination to ' step
. . . in 'twixt man and wife.'   For all his well-known
jibe that the battle of Bull Run should have been called
' Yankee's Run,' he paid full tribute to the bravery of the
Union troops : for all his discovery that the North was
' fighting for an idea chiefly entertained by professional
politicians,' and the South ' for what they consider rightly
or wrongly vital interests,'[67] he seemed as anxious as ever
to maintain peaceful relations with Washington.   This
was apparent when Seward demanded the recall of the

British consul at Charleston, Bunch by name, for acts allegedly unneutral and beyond his competence. It was feared in England that the Union government, on hearing that Bunch's recall had been refused by Russell, would send home Lyons, the British ambassador. Palmerston, refraining from any fulminations, advised that Lyons, instead of returning to England, should betake himself to Canada, pending the time when Seward might come to a better frame of mind.[68]

In the premier's letters of the late summer and early autumn one sees a growing dislike of the proceedings of the Union government, an increasing inclination to hold it to a moderate policy by a show of force, and a dawning realisation of the hardships which its methods of putting pressure on the South would impose upon the English working class.[69] Lincoln and Seward had 'shown themselves so wild that any act of intemperance' might be expected from them. He was disgusted to find that 'these North Americans' were 'following fast the example of the Spanish Americans and of the continental despots,' ruling 'by spies and police and martial law.' How then were they to be held in check ? Motley said that the sending of reinforcements to Canada would have no effect at Washington ; but the prime minister knew better. Moreover, Motley, who though a good diplomatist (!) had 'not quite lost the frankness of a private man,' had denied only that the Americans *spoke*, not that they *thought*, of conquering Canada. Quite probably they were waiting till navigation closed. More troops must go to Canada at once. Something, too, would have to be done about the blockade. Thus to Russell on October 6 :

This cotton question will most certainly assume a serious character by the beginning of next year ; and if the American civil war has not by that time come to an end, I suspect that we shall be obliged either singly or conjointly with France to tell the northerners that we cannot allow some millions of our people to perish to please the Northern States and that the blockade of the South must be so far relaxed as to [allow] cotton loaded ships to come out.[70]

Even yet, be it noted, intervention found no place in his

programme. He was not ready for the action ' on a grand
scale ' suggested by Russell ten days later : that England
and France should, early in the coming year, impose terms
on the Union and Confederacy on pain of probable war.[71]
For, wrote the premier :

> . . . The love of quarrelling and fighting is inherent in man,
> and to prevent its indulgence is to impose restraints on natural liberty.
> A state may so shackle its own subjects ; but it is an infringement on
> national independence to restrain other nations. The only excuse
> would be the danger to the interfering parties if the conflict went on ;
> but in the American case this cannot be pleaded by the Powers of
> Europe. . . . The only thing to do seems to be to lie on our oars and
> to give no pretext to the Washingtonians to quarrel with us, while,
> on the other hand, we maintain our rights and those of our fellow-
> countrymen.[72]

This was his position when Captain Wilkes of the *San
Jacinto*, on his own responsibility, boarded the *Trent* and
took off the Confederate agents, Mason and Slidell.

To work for peace, prepare for war, and promise a
happy outcome in either, was Palmerston's reaction to the
Trent affair. He had feared that such a crisis would arise
through an attempt to seize Mason and Slidell in European
waters. Having prudently consulted the law officers of
the Crown, he had warned and appealed to the American
minister Adams, a fortnight before he heard of the *San
Jacinto's* encounter with the *Trent*.[73] Faced with the situation he had feared, and ignorant that Wilkes' action was
unauthorised, he seems to have agreed with Clarendon in
regarding the seizure of the envoys of the Confederacy
as ' a deliberate and premeditated insult,' and as the outcome
of Seward's determination to ' provoke us into a quarrel.' [74]
But he showed no eagerness to push matters to extremities.
Only after a second conference with the legal advisers of
the Crown, and only with the concurrence of his cabinet
did he decide that the government at Washington should
be required to give satisfaction for a gross outrage and
' violation of international law ' by tendering an apology
and giving up the prisoners.[75] When the Queen and her
dying husband suggested softening the language to be used
in making these demands, Palmerston cordially concurred ;

and apologised for the drafting of the criticised despatch, framed ' by the help of fourteen people . . . each proposing verbal alterations.' The final draft was as gentle as the Court could have desired ; and Lyons was ordered privately to use the greatest tact with Seward.[76]

Yet the premier was very active in pushing the preparations for hostilities. ' It is difficult,' he wrote, ' not to come to the conclusion that the rabid hatred of England which animates the exiled Irishmen who direct almost all the northern newspapers, will so excite the masses as to make it impossible for Lincoln & Seward to grant our demands ; and we must therefore look forward to war as the probable result.' For in his political philosophy public excitement was likely to prove the determinant :

> Nations and especially republican nations or nations in which the masses influence or direct the destinies of the country are swayed much more by passion than by interest and for this plain reason, namely that passion is a single feeling which aims directly at its object, while interest is a calculation of relative good and evil and is liable to hesitation and doubt. Moreover, passion sways the masses but interest acts comparatively on the few.[77]

Hence he urged the sending of reinforcements to Canada, still ' lamentably unprepared ' despite his previous efforts. And he came rapidly to Russell's view that England should at once forbid the export of arms and ' warlike stores ' of every sort, as a measure which would not only diminish the Union's fighting power, but might deter it from risking war at all.[78] Having provided as well as possible against all contingencies, and being greatly reassured by the ' very satisfactory ' attitude of Napoleon, he contemplated the outcome with serenity :

> If the Federal government comply with the demands, it will be honourable for England and humiliating for the United States. If the Federal Govt refuse compliance Great Britain is in a better state than at any former time to inflict a severe blow upon and to read a lesson to the United States which will not soon be forgotten.[79]

But he regarded the peaceable settlement of the dispute as ' indeed a happy event.'[80] One may grant him reason for being satisfied. Competent judges then and since have felt that England's preparedness, as well as her tactfulness, contributed to her success : and in the use of both, Palmerston had had a fitting share. The issue was still in doubt when the year came to its close ; but the old statesman might again have greeted a new year hopefully had it not been for his own illness and for Prince Albert's untimely death on December 14.

There is something very arresting, not to say surprising, about the devouring anxiety and utter consternation produced in Palmerston by the illness and death of the Prince Consort. Even in the last stage of their connection the relations between the two men had been unsatisfactory. When, early in this very year, the editor of *The Times* had taken it upon himself to ' touch up ' the Court on its opposition to the Italian policy of the ministers, the Prince had not only jumped to the conclusion that Palmerston was responsible, but had persisted in his suspicions after they had become almost untenable.[81]   When Victoria, later on, was obliged, in spite of ' desperate resistance,' to accept Layard as under-secretary for foreign affairs, the Prince complained that Palmerston showed neither candour nor consideration in dealing with the Queen, and that his attitude was rendered ' still more offensive to delicate feeling by the uncalled for flattery ' which he employed.[82]   The premier, with all his capacity for seeing the best side of all situations at all times, must have been aware that the bitter complaints and reproaches constantly emanating from the royal pair in former times had been replaced only by a certain weary and resigned acceptance of himself, varied by occasional ' nags.' Yet no one could have shown more concern and distress than Palmerston when the great tragedy of Victoria's life occurred. Happening to be at Windsor when the Prince was first taken ill, he showed alarm when none was felt by the royal physicians.[83]   As the possibility of the event which he found ' too awful to contemplate ' became clearer, he intervened again and again to insist that the Prince should have more expert medical advice and closer supervision.[84]   He was determined that the ' highest interests of the nation ' should not be 'sacrificed to personal and professional jealousies' on the part of highly placed doctors. Apparently he found the task of securing the best possible advice too much for him, contending, as he seems to have been, against the resentment even of the Queen ; but he was successful in insisting that a fresh consultant should be brought in, and that one of the attendant physicians should sleep within call.

The Prince's death seems simply to have staggered him. At the time when it occurred he himself was apparently more ill than he had ever been—so ill that rumours spread through England of his death—so ill as to receive a warning that ' if he did not take more care of himself, he would wake some morning with a paralysed arm and leg.' [85] But the actual malady seems to have been merely an excruciating attack of gout. This would not account for the duke of Cambridge's report that on his announcement of the Prince's death the premier fainted several times, or even for Clarendon's remark that Palmerston was ' more shocked and *overwhelmed*' by the news from Windsor than would have seemed possible. Granville ' never saw him so low.' [86]

No doubt some of his emotion was quite impersonal. Not all of Prince Albert's coldness or open hostility would ever have made Palmerston forget that the Prince's ability, connections and experience had made him a national asset— an asset which it was the duty of the premier to guard, and the loss of which the premier could not but mourn. Moreover, the Prince Consort had apparently acted as a buffer between Palmerston and the Queen ; and both were apprehensive of the increase of direct contact that his death made unavoidable. This is suggested, not only by the fact that the Prince had frequently acted for his wife in what had promised to be unpleasant interviews, but by the appeal now made simultaneously by Queen and premier for the good offices of King Leopold.[87] While Victoria and her especial friends were appealing to the King by letter to make Victoria's way easy in her contacts with Palmerston, the latter was soliciting Leopold's help in a personal interview.

The outcome was a happier one than might have been hoped.[88]   Victoria shrank at first from seeing her premier, allegedly because she needed complete repose, but in reality because she entertained either a feeling of resentment or the fear that she would find Palmerston unsympathetic and ' hard.'   At the urgent solicitation of her friends, however, she commanded his presence for January 27 at Osborne ; and there an unlooked-for reconciliation took place.   If Palmerston really appeared in light clothes, green gloves and blue studs, as Clarendon, his tongue as usual in his cheek, has recorded, the Queen was more observant of his obvious distress, his stammering attempts at condolence, and his eulogies of the Prince.   She found, too, that they had other things in common, especially the feeling that ' *the* difficulty of the moment ' was the Prince of Wales.   They discussed the desirability of his marrying soon ; and the Queen ' would hardly have given Lord Palmerston credit for entering so entirely ' into her ' anxieties.'   He was quite in favour when he left.   What is more, the reconciliation was to hold well enough through the ensuing year.   The Queen continued to be impressed by her prime minister's obvious sympathy and solicitude. Nor was she deceived in regarding them as genuine. Palmerston, as Gladstone later said, had ' a nature incapable of enduring anger or the sentiment of wrath.'   His genuine regret for the Prince and commiseration for the Queen may be noted in letter after letter of the most private sort. There is no reason for doubting the story that when, in the spring of 1863, Victoria sat alone in the gallery of St. George's to watch the marriage of the Prince of Wales, her prime minister was affected by her desolation to the point of actual tears.[89]

If only the reconciliation could have been permanent. But Palmerston, as quick to understand others as to sympathise with them, foresaw one of the main sources of difficulty in his future relations with his sovereign even at the time of her, and his own, deepest distress :

Her determination to conform to what she from time to time may persuade herself would have been at the moment the opinion of the late Prince promises no end of difficulties for those who will

have to advise her.   We must deal with her with the most gentle hand.
I shall however write to King Leopold to give us his assistance.[90]

And he could not have known that the Queen had written
King Leopold four days before :

. . . *his* wishes—*his* plans—about everything, *his* views about
every thing are to be *my law* ! . . . I am *also determined* that *no one*
person, . . . is to lead or guide or dictate *to me*. . . .[91]

CHAPTER XXXII

1862

Arrival at the year 1862 tempts one to stop and consider some of the more general aspects of Palmerston's second premiership. For one thing the year bisects the six years' period. Does it in any sense, then, form a watershed? Possibilities of this appear as one considers the years 1859–1862. According to the measure of the premier's own aims, they had been years of almost uniform success. He had raised himself to unrivalled influence with parliament, the public and the press : he was even on fairly satisfactory terms with Queen Victoria. Postponing the discussion of any possibilities of a decline, it may be well to observe him as he stood.

It was in no way strange that he remained the favourite of John Bull ; for early Victorian Englishmen in the mass must have found him very close to their ideal of a statesman. Aristocrat enough to satisfy the dominant feeling that the highly born should hold high place, man of the world enough to carry his rank and station jauntily, he had been at once a *grand seigneur* and a dispenser of rough merriment, a master at once of the lofty style of rhetoric which impressed the average citizen, and of homely quips and jests which the lowliest could understand. He had always been sound, too, in every sense—so sound that men could overlook some indiscretions here and there, and bear quite patiently with a conservatism regarding government which was old-fashioned. His homely jests clothed homely truths, and gave new life to those stout principles (the early Victorians were unaware of prejudice) on which generations of stout Britons had built their lives. At times he seemed as independent of party leaders and party shibboleths as

of foreign ministers and potentates ; and he was far more
British than the Court. He was a sportsman, and in every
way that mattered publicly, a stalwart Protestant. He had
been a bulwark of the nation against the restless ambitions
of the French, a preserver of its possessions against French
and Russian greed and guile. He had made John Bull
content in knowing that his island was secure, and proud in
seeing it a haven for the refugees from other lands. Even
yet he was Jupiter Anglicanus, prepared to check and
browbeat any other state : he seemed at times the British
lion personified. For all these qualities the British populace still held him in their hearts. Their attitude was very
evident to the speaker of the House, at the festivities
attendant on the opening of the International Exhibition of
1862. Through the Crystal Palace the two men passed
abreast.

As we walked along I could gauge the popularity of Lord
Palmerston. The moment he came in sight, throughout the whole
building, men and women, young and old, at once were struck as
by an electric shock. ' Lord Palmerston ! Here is Lord Palmerston ! Bravo ! Hurrah ! Lord Palmerston for ever ! ' . . .
One voice : ' I wish you may be Minister for the next twenty
years.' [1]

It is the spontaneity which strikes one as significant.
Yet spontaneous cheers may testify to a carefully
nurtured popularity ; and Palmerston's popularity seems
to have been partly of this kind. His speeches, his connection with the press, even his use of ecclesiastical
patronage—all served him to this end. In speaking he was
still ' intensely the Englishman . . . always talking, or
seeming . . . to talk, from the national cue ' ;[2] and his
patriotic utterances were assured of generous space and
favourable comment in most of the leading London newspapers. Indeed, his influence with the editors went further
still. Delane of *The Times*, now one of his firm friends and
frequent visitors, was not above adopting a suggestion
now and then.[3] Borthwick of the *Post*, who once, at least,
arrived at Broadlands as an unofficial envoy of Napoleon's
government,[4] was even more amenable to suggestion, praise

or blame. Hunt of the *Telegraph* had frequent interviews
with Palmerston at Cambridge House. But Hunt, on the
basis, probably, of these interviews, made a comment which
suggested a weak point in the premier's cultivation of
popularity : ' Lord Palmerston knew nothing of human life
below his carriage steps.'[5] Men below all carriage steps,
men who did not read *The Times* or *Post* or *Telegraph*, might
lose the impulse to cheer their premier so heartily, without
his realising why.

The use of ecclesiastical patronage for political advantage
was no simple matter in these years ; for all sections
of the English church were, as against each other, true
members of a church militant. High churchmen were
deeply disturbed at seeing assistance given by certain
broads and lows (*i.e.* evangelicals), to efforts yearly made
by dissenters in parliament to end the compuls ry levy of
church rates. Low churchmen were upset by ritualists,
with their stone altars, sung services and vested choirs ;
and downright scandalised by Puseyites, with their Anglo-
Catholic theology. To cap the climax, lows and highs
and Puseyites were brought together in alarm when, in 1860,
some rationalistic broads set forth their doctrines in *Essays
and Reviews*. Palmerston, who had ' no time ' for ' doc-
trinal points,' but time to listen to that old champion
of the lows, his step-son-in-law, Lord Shaftesbury, seems
to have acted mainly on three principles. The Puseyites,
who were popish, unpopular and few, should be put down ;
theological discussion among the clergy should on principle
be discountenanced ; and satisfaction should be given to
the greatest number of Englishmen (or should one say
voters ?), *viz.* the evangelicals and dissenters. A contributor to the *Quarterly* pointed out how fruitful such
a policy might be :

The Dissenting Radicals are . . . weak in talent . . . strong
in fanaticism and numbers. Even in the House of Commons they
are far the heartiest believers in the votes they give. . . . In every
constituency they furnish the nucleus of a Radical party. . . .[6]

In his opposition to the Puseyites, Palmerston not only
excluded them from all ecclesiastical patronage, but went

POLITICS AND RELIGION 303

the length of urging Russell to protest at Rome against
Cardinal Manning's appointment to the archiepiscopal see
of Westminster. For Manning, he argued, having the
entrée into British society, would not only make converts
among the highly placed, but would be ' hand in glove with
the Bishop of Oxford, the Tractarians and the high church
party.'[7] The quelling of theological discussion he accomplished quite simply by refusing to appoint ' theological '
clergymen to the bishoprics. Disraeli might stigmatise
some of his selections as ' mean and insignificant'; the
Queen might protest that the episcopal bench needed men
who were something more than ' respectable parish priests;'[8]
but Palmerston would not listen.[9] He was glad to appoint
men of ' classical and academical attainments,' but he wanted
no more men of ' theological learning ' like Phillpotts of
Exeter to cause fresh ' mischief' in the church. It was
the function of a bishop to keep clergy and laity, churchmen
and dissenters, on good terms ; and for this work ' practical
knowledge of parochial functions ' was the primary requisite.
Bishop Villiers of Durham, who died in 1861, was classed
in the *Annual Register* as ' a good specimen of the Palmerston
Bishop ' :

The deceased . . . made himself a great name . . . as . . . the
hard-working, much-trudging pastor of a parish that numbered
17,000 souls. He had a genial, easy nature, . . . Mr. Villiers was
the lowest of Low Churchmen, and . . . Like most Low Churchmen, he . . . preached too uniformly to the poor in intellect as
well as to the poor in spirit and the poor in pocket. . . . If he hated
High Church doctrines, if he shrank from the shadow of Roman
Catholic practices, if he told young men to avoid theatres as an
' unmixed evil,' and to look well to their steps in the ballroom—if by
that plainness of preaching . . . he failed to win over men of cultivation, yet on the other hand he worked vigorously with the Dissenters ;
there were Dissenters in his vestry who eagerly supported him ; he
turned the City Mission to account, and with men of every sect and
stamp who belong to the so-called Evangelical order he had the most
ample sympathy . . . throughout the country. . . . Dissenters of
every denomination have combined with Churchmen to offer up
prayers for his recovery.[10]

In such appointments Palmerston persisted, despite objections from Gladstone, Newcastle and the Queen, so long

as they seemed safe politically.[11]   But no longer.   When, towards the end, his favour toward the evangelicals appeared to have been a little overplayed, he redressed the balance on the episcopal bench by the appointment of one broad churchman and a brace of moderate highs.[12]   He was even more careful in weighing churchmanship than in observing ' the old Practice of taking alternately a Cambridge and an Oxford man.'[13]   In matters of legislation he was equally cautious, as in refusing to commit his ministry either to the abolition or to the maintenance of church rates. But in justice it must be remembered, too, that in one instance at least he urged a measure repugnant to the religious inhibitions of John Bull—an act breaking the control of Anglican chaplains in the gaols, and allowing Catholic prisoners to receive the consolations of religion from their own priests.[14]

In explanations of his increasing hold on parliament, there has been a tendency to stress the members' veneration for, and patience with, a distinguished veteran.   So eminent an authority as the speaker of the House, writing in 1862, repudiated this idea specifically :

Lord Palmerston has spoken admirably well this session.   It is not that the House respects a public servant who has done great service ; that they are indulgent to advanced years.   It is that he still can make a better and more effective speech than any other man, taking the House between wind and water with wonderful skill ; that he has more vigour and force about him than the younger men.[15]

The entry was made just after the premier, with his eightieth birthday only two years off, had roused himself ' like a giant ' from a nap, to make a most effective speech, ' fairly smashing Disraeli.'   Russell, according to the same authority, believed that his chief had not come to his full intellectual development until less than ten years before.[16]   And Russell emphasised in another place that parliament placed more value on sincerity, on ' decision and calmness in days of peril ' and on common sense than on ' the most brilliant flights of fancy and the keenest wit.'[17]   Yet, granting that Palmerston profited by the possession of these qualities, by his service record and his still remarkable ability in debate, there is no question that he reinforced his hold by parliamentary tactics at once cautious and conciliatory. He no longer domineered as he had done in his first ministry. The whips discovered that an admonitory touch to his coat-tails would bring him down almost immediately to his seat.[18]   When ministerial appointments were afoot, he was shrewd in strengthening his parliamentary armament. In 1863 he made two proposals simultaneously with this in mind.[19]   Lord Hartington should, as under-secretary, represent the War Office in the House, since 'his personal bearing and his being the son of the Duke of Devonshire' would ' tend to keep in order the Tory colonels & generals.' At the same time the premier planned that a vacant post at the Admiralty should go to someone whose appointment would be regarded by the left wing Liberals as a pledge that due economy should be observed in connection with the fleet.   And well he knew from what quarters his parliamentary armament might be dangerously assailed. ' Beware of that young man,' he said of Lord Robert Cecil, later the great Lord Salisbury, ' he possesses one of the secrets of success, for instead of defending himself and his cause he attacks the other side.'[20]

' There is an old saying,' wrote Sir Henry Drummond Wolff, ' that men reach distinction as much by the heart as by the head, and this was certainly the case with Lord Palmerston.'[21]   The premier's unaffected geniality was in some way preserved against all the impatience and weariness of age.[22]   A rather obscure young member, returning after a short illness to the House, found himself patted on the back.   'Ah! my dear fellow ; . . . had the gout, eh? Slacken the fire, that's the only way . . . glad to see you back.'   Another obscure member, after being snubbed by Graham, found that his opinions concerning matters before the House were solicited by the prime minister.   Seldom could any supporter, or perhaps even any potential one, feel a shadow of neglect.   Lady Palmerston requested the proprietor of the *Morning Post*, in 1864, not to mention the names of her guests for a certain dinner, unless he might ' weave up their names in the evening party. . . . I think it has a bad effect with the House of Commons Members,

and they cavil at my Tory company. . . . It puts them
out of temper.'[23]   When young Mr. Goschen, selected
in the same year to second the address, acquitted himself
to the satisfaction of the ministry, it was no time before
Lady Palmerston arrived to call upon his wife, and invite
the gratified couple to her next party.[24]   When did members
of the House receive consideration more delicate than this ?

How well entrenched, how full of honours, the premier
then seemed.   He had just received an invitation to stand
for the chancellorship of his own university (an invitation
which for some reason he refused), and had just accepted
an Oxford D.C.L.   The Queen was no longer offering
him peerages which, for political reasons, were sure to
be refused ; but she had lately given him the wardenship
of the Cinque Ports, an honourable sinecure, made most
honourable in its long tenure by the younger Pitt and the
great duke of Wellington.   And, what no doubt counted
more than all, his countrymen still exalted him.

But would they continue to exalt him until he died ?
We can see that the answer was becoming a little doubtful
in 1862.   Suppose that England should be checked and
browbeaten in her turn ; suppose that John Bull should
lose some of his confidence in the divine right of jaunty
and old-fashioned aristocrats, some of his appreciation of
merriment, some of his apparent indifference to reform.
What then ?   And just such possibilities were commencing
to appear, as one now sees, while the premier stood on his
eminence of 1862.   Danger, remote as yet, but perhaps
not inaptly to be considered here, was looming ahead, both
in foreign affairs and in domestic politics.

In the arena of foreign politics, where Palmerston, with
a long succession of partners, had fought so long and so
successfully before the eyes of a delighted British audience,
there came something like a pause in this year of 1862.
The situation created by the Civil War in America demanded
careful handling by the British and French cabinets ; and
other issues of great interest to these and other chancelleries
arose out of other developments overseas.   But in Europe
itself there was a lull—a lull, as it proved, of sinister import
for Palmerston.   For as the French menace became dimmer

DRAWING THE STUMPS

bden to Dizzy : " Carries out his bat ?   Of course he does !   Your underhand bowling 'll never get him out !
I'll show you how to do it next innings.

Punch, August 16, 1862

even in his eyes, the last, the greatest, and the most successful of his diplomatic adversaries was taking up the position
from which he was soon to engage England's great champion.
Time and again Palmerston had measured his country's
strength and prestige against those of France and Russia
and Austria.   He had contended with almost every first-
rate European diplomatist of two generations, and had
supported the master of them all, Cavour.   But he had
yet to match his country against a Prussia whose growing
might no one in Europe had so far understood ; and he
had yet to try conclusions with Bismarck.   Now in his
old age, with none too strong a foreign secretary, and with
a sovereign who could believe no ill of the country of her
son-in-law, he was to meet this final test.

He had not seriously encountered Prussia yet ; but
neither his attitude toward the question of German unification nor his latest exchange of compliments with the Prussian
government was calculated to make the coming encounter a
cordial one.   He had never shared the Prince Consort's
deep regret that the German nation cut no figure in the world,
or his earnest hope that the king of Prussia, by agreements
with the minor German princes, would form a new German
Empire to the exclusion of Austria.[25]   And certainly he
could not subscribe to the idea (communicated to him as
early as September 1859, by a young Bethmann-Hollweg)
that friendship between the two rivals would become
possible only when the Prussians had had ' *une bonne
guerre avec l'Autriche.*'[26]   To him it seemed desirable, not
to say necessary, that Austria should enjoy the protection
of the whole German people against the encroachments
of the French.   And what would be the French attitude
toward the Prussian plan ?

As to the idea that France would assist Prussia in placing herself
at the head of United Germany any Prussian Minister who believes
in that will some day or other find the film very disagreeably torn
from his eyes.[27]

It was of the French that the Prussians had to beware :

The Prussian army, though brave, is quite behind the progress
which the French have made in the art of war.   They still attack in

columns which would be blown to pieces by the French rifle artillery long before they could come into contact with their opponents. The French officers who were at the Prussian reviews were delighted with what they saw, and said with radiant countenances, that they should be in Berlin in a fortnight after a declaration of war.[28]

So, thought the premier, it was desirable that the Austrians and Prussians should come to terms. There was not much to choose between them ; for the Prussians were 'selfish and foolish' and the Austrians 'pigheadedly blind to their own interests.'[29] Neither need necessarily predominate :

. . . Perhaps all things considered dualism is the only arrangement possible in Germany. Austria & Prussia are like Caesar & Pompey. Prussia like Caesar will not brook a superior, and Austria like Pompey will not endure an equal. Each might be a centre around which the smaller states might range themselves . . . and there would be two strong bodies who would unite against a foreign foe.[30]

All of these dicta were pronounced for the private edification of the British foreign secretary and the British ambassador to France ; and it is possible that Palmerston's views were known only in general to the Prussian Court. But perhaps one may be allowed to anticipate in so far as to point out that in June 1863, when Bismarck was obviously controlling Prussian policy and defying the Prussian Liberals, the premier delivered himself of a witty little commentary on Prussian government which could hardly with propriety have been communicated by a British prime minister to anyone :

I gave Gudin [?] no message for Bismarck but I told him jokingly that as he is a rapid painter he might present the King with two sketches one representing him sitting on his throne with his crown on his head, the other representing him lying on the ground with his crown on the floor and that he might leave the King to draw his conclusions.[31]

The fact that this piece of humour is recorded in a holograph memorandum, preserved among the Russell papers, suggests that the implied admonition was intended to go further and to be taken seriously. And Palmerston was later to complain of Bismarck's 'impudence' ![32]

The exchange of compliments between Palmerston and the Prussian government, to which reference has been made, arose out of the most trivial incident imaginable.[33] A Captain Macdonald of the Queen's bodyguard, passing through Bonn in September 1860, had engaged in a scuffle with some railroad officials over the eternal question of the right of a traveller to reserve seats by leaving luggage on them. His arrest and punishment (brief imprisonment and a small fine) had been perfectly in accordance with Prussian law ; but the harshness of the whole proceeding, and certain insulting remarks by the Prussian *Staats-Procurator* concerning the boorishness of English travellers, aroused British indignation to a high pitch. *The Times* thundered, and the German press boomed back again. The two foreign offices engaged in an exchange of sharp despatches, featured by one of Russell's under date of February 11, 1861. In this, the Prussian officials were accused of having enforced their law with ' extreme and unnecessary harshness,' and in a manner Englishmen would ordinarily ' ascribe to a malignant spirit, violating the limits of a temperate administration of justice.' What was more serious, Russell found ' the conduct of the Prussian Government . . . to have been in a high degree unfriendly,' and ' too clearly evincing a disregard of international goodwill.' [34]

Two months later the matter came up in parliament.[35] Palmerston, asked by the opposition whether he would warn intending travellers through Germany ' of the brutal and barbarous conditions to which travellers in Prussia must submit,' apparently went out of his way to deepen the exasperation which Russell's despatch had created at Berlin. He did not find any of Russell's expressions ' a bit too strong,' quite agreeing that the proceedings of the Prussian law officers at least were ' of a most unfriendly character, and most unworthy of a Government in alliance with England.'

I must say I am astonished that a Government like that of Prussia, . . . should not at once have said, ' Our officials have not overstepped our law ; . . . but, . . . we entirely condemn the conduct of our officials, and are ready to make every satisfaction which, as between gentleman and gentleman, Captain Macdonald could require.' . . . it is the interest of Prussia to cultivate, not the friendship of the English Government only, but the good opinion and the goodwill of the English nation ; and, therefore, I should say that their conduct in this affair has been . . . a blunder as well as a crime . . . we were told by the law officers of the Crown that, . . . those proceedings appeared to be within the limits of the Prussian law. One regrets, for the sake of the Prussians, that they should have such a law.

Disraeli suspected that this ' coarse outburst ' was directed more at the British Court than at the Prussian cabinet ; while some of Palmerston's friends traced it to his ill-humour over the prospect that Prussian schemes for German unification would ' provoke an interminable civil war and tend to strengthen French influence.'[36] Certainly he disliked Prussian policy as much as Prussian officialdom :

Prussia sets public opinion in England against her by her aggressive policy against Denmark, by her anti-English policy all over the world, and by the rudeness and roughness of all her people employed either by the Govt. or by railroad companies.[37]

But whatever the motive for the outbreak, even pre-Bismarckian Prussia could not accept chastisement of such a sort ; and Schleinitz, the foreign minister, not only sent a sharp protest against the speech, but read it ' with a flourish ' in the Prussian chamber.

After this there was no restraining Palmerston.[38] The affair, he said, had now become personal to himself, and it was his right to draft an official reply to Schleinitz which he would be content to lay before parliament. He would be willing to ' knock under ' to the Queen, as Russell proposed, but not to the Prussian minister. He regarded it as ' absolutely necessary ' that the official despatch should follow closely his own words :

. . . he deems it right to state that what he said on the occasion in question was said advisedly and upon full conviction ; that he deliberately abides by all that he then said ; and that he sees nothing in it either to be retracted or to be explained away ; and he is convinced that the opinions then expressed are entirely shared by the great bulk of his Fellow-countrymen.

And he had his way.[39]   Russell's despatch stated that, since Schleinitz's despatch had contained a personal attack on the premier, the latter had been ' consulted ' as to the reply.   Then followed the premier's statement, word for word as given above.   The despatch was hardly softened by the statement that the premier's ' opinions . . . were confined to the conduct of the Prussian Government and of their subordinate officers.'   He had said nothing to cause legitimate offence to the Prussian ' nation.'   Palmerston had provided a very nice *mise-en-scène* for his coming encounter with the haughtiest as well as the shrewdest of living diplomatists.

At home, as abroad, a so far comparatively disregarded, but very formidable opponent was preparing for onslaughts which the premier would find vexatious and even dangerous. He had broken with the old Tories in the early part of his career, and helped to bring about their fall ; he had forced himself and his policies on the Whig leaders time after time ; he had had very much his way in the Peelite-Whig coalition of Aberdeen, and on its collapse had proved himself independent of the great Peelite triumvirate.   And in this, his last ministry, he had played fast and loose with the left wing Liberals.   But now the ' advanced ' Liberal tide was creeping forward again, creeping more and more into his very cabinet, by taking more and more to itself his indispensable chancellor of the Exchequer.   It would never come to control his policies, this liberalism of a new day.   He would be saved from that by his own inveterate resistance, by the affection and admiration of a people and a parliament, and at last by death.   But it would impose some limitations on his policy, and make gradual inroads on his popularity.   Hence he who reviews these last years of Palmerston's will need to be watchful of tendencies.   He will probably be more watchful than was ever the premier. For questionings and forebodings were never to Palmerston's taste : better, it seemed to him, to think of the task in hand. And the task most in hand in January 1862 seemed to be that of keeping watch jointly on France and the United States.   He was finding the task in some ways complicated and in some ways eased by the febrile activity of the Mexicans.

It will be remembered that at this time the Mexicans were not only fighting as usual among themselves, but had for some months previously been doing everything possible to draw upon them the displeasure of three European Powers.[40] Not content with violating treaties with England, France and Spain, which called for the assignment of a portion of their customs revenues to the payment of foreign bondholders, they had seized by violence money collected to this end, going even so far as to break open a room in the British legation and to carry off property placed under the legation's official seal. Naturally enough the three Powers decided to bring joint pressure by force of arms. The United States entered the picture when Seward authorised negotiations for a treaty by which the United States would have become responsible for interest payments on the foreign debt for a period of five years, and would have secured in return a mortgage on public lands and mineral rights in several of Mexico's provinces. Remembering past days, one might be prepared to read that the British prime minister favoured action of the most violent and independent kind.

Cornewall Lewis, who would have preferred to ' leave the matter in the hands of the Americans,' sneered at England's part in what ensued as a ' Pacifico affair ' ;[41] but the analogy was no more justified as regards Palmerston's attitude than by the circumstances out of which England's action arose. The premier began by advocating isolated action on the part of his own government ' to obtain satisfaction for the claims of other European nations *pari passu* ' with England's own. He ended by advocating strongly the joint action of the three aggrieved European Powers, as calculated to defeat any designs for the acquisition of territory which Napoleon might secretly entertain.[42] For Seward's plan he had nothing but scorn :

But the Washington government inspired by a chivalrous sense of justice, not satisfied with its own enormous expenditure on account of the Civil War, proposes to undertake to pay the interest on the foreign debt of Mexico. . . . This scheme in the [first] place makes no provision for the satisfaction of the money claims of the three European Powers, nor for the punishment of the Mexican murderers of the subjects of the three Powers ; and in the next place it lays the

ground for foreclosure by the new creditor . . . and then further it
tends to continue the present state of anarchy in Mexico ; and indeed
Motley complained that we and France are wanting to organize
a strong government in Mexico to the detriment of the views of the
United States. Perhaps the best answer . . . would be a counter-
proposal to the United States government to join the three Powers
either morally or physically.[43]

Three days later, on September 27, 1861, Russell informed
Victoria that he regarded it as necessary that the three
Powers should invite the United States to become a party
to the intervention, and that the British government should
announce in advance its resolution not to interfere with
Mexico's internal government.[44]   In view of subsequent
developments the adoption of this two-fold policy is worth
noticing.   Seward, as was to be expected, refused to make
the United States a partner to European intervention in
North America ; though the projected treaty between the
Union and Mexico did not go through.   But France and
Spain agreed to pledge themselves as England did.   A
convention, signed in October 1861, bound the intervening
governments not to ' exercise, in the internal affairs of
Mexico, any influence of a nature to prejudice the right of
the Mexican nation to choose and to constitute freely the
form of its Government.'[45]

How soon and how utterly Napoleon commenced to
violate his pledge, by attempting to make Mexico an
empire under Maximilian of Austria, is known to everyone :
how faithful to its undertaking was the British government
is almost equally well known.   But perhaps there is less
appreciation of the fact that England's prime minister was
hardly more true to the spirit of the agreement than was
the French emperor.   Not that he wished, or perhaps
would have allowed, England to violate her pledge.   He
was merely pleased that France, by violating hers, should
draw certain British chestnuts from the fire :

As to the monarchy scheme if it could be carried out it would
be a great blessing for Mexico and a godsend to all countries having
anything to do with Mexico. . . . It would also stop the North
Americans . . . in their absorption of Mexico.   If the North and
South are definitely disunited and if at the same time Mexico could

be turned into a prosperous monarchy I do not know any arrangement that would be more advantageous for us. We cannot with our seven hundred marines take part in such an enterprize, but if France and Spain can manage it and the Arch Duke Max. could become king, I do not see that we need complain.[46]

But of this more anon. It is time to turn immediately, as Palmerston did, to the question of Anglo-American relations in their more direct and dangerous aspect.

In the shaping of Anglo-American relations at this time, Palmerston's hold on the House of Commons seems to have been a factor which, if usually neglected, is not entirely negligible. Considering that the pronounced tendency of many members of parliament to take some sort of action on behalf of the Southern States was being constantly strengthened by the mounting distress of the cotton operatives, and the mounting dissatisfaction of the commercial and shipping interests ; considering the eagerness of the friends of the South on both sides of the English Channel to exploit this tendency, and the sensitiveness of the enemies of the South on the other side of the Atlantic concerning it, one may fairly conclude that a speech or two in the premier's best jingoïstic style might have made relations between London and Washington more critical. Nor should one overlook the fact that such pronouncements would, early in the year at least, have been greatly relished by John Bull.[47] But no such speeches came. In private, Palmerston drove Adams to the last point of exasperation and protest ; but in public he restrained himself, and in restraining himself, did much to restrain parliament.

It seems that this restraint arose from determined adherence to the official policy of rigid abstention from interference of any kind ; for his letters, even in the first half of the year, show extreme irritation and impatience. It is probably true that the settlement of the *Trent* affair, involving what he chose to regard as the ' humiliation ' of Bright's ' favourite North American Republic,'[48] soothed his feelings toward the northerners. So also, no doubt, did the first hanging of an American slave-trader, and Seward's conclusion, in April, of an Anglo-American anti-slave trade treaty, providing for the exercise of a mutual right of search, and the establishment of mixed commission courts.[49]   But any real friendship between England and the North seemed to him unattainable, and the activities of the Union navy a matter for protest.   The best that he could say concerning the prospects of cordial relations was that the Northerners' ' hatred ' of England was ' not likely to be much greater ' than it long had been ; [50] while his attitude toward the exercise of their belligerent rights at sea, if it had been translated into action, would hardly have allowed even this footing to remain undisturbed.[51] In his private letters he protested that England could not be subjected to ' the scandal and inconvenience of having Federal and Confederate squadrons watching and fighting each other ' in the vicinity of her shores : she could not allow her vessels to be overhauled by Federal cruisers ' without rhyme or reason,' and sent to New York for trial. Seward should be admonished and Adams warned : British West Indiamen should be convoyed through home waters, and British ports closed to all American war - ships : offending ' Yankee captains ' should be ' dealt with in a very summary manner.'   The letters stand out in sharp contrast to the very cool and correct official pronouncements which were issuing simultaneously from the Foreign Office and Admiralty ; but it should be noted that at their worst they reveal the jingo, not the interventionist.   Palmerston did indeed confide to Russell the not unnatural feeling that England would be a gainer by the separation of South from North ; and even found it worth while to add that ' the officers of the *Nashville* say the South will never really prosper till it becomes a monarchy.' [52]   But in June he believed as much as ever that to offer mediation ' would be like offering to make it up between Sayers and Heenan after the third round.' [53]

Nor should it be forgotten that his most intemperate pronouncements against war measures on the part of Lincoln's government referred little or not at all to British interests.   The blocking of some of the channels into Charleston harbour by the sinking of boats laden with stone (incorrectly assumed in England to involve the blocking, and perhaps the permanent blocking, of the main entrance) seemed to him a proceeding to 'revolt the feelings of all mankind,' and one which might well be made the basis of an Anglo-French protest.[54]   But his condemnation laid more emphasis on the violence done to humanitarian principles and public policy than on anticipated injury to British commerce. A victorious North, he pointed out, would discover that by blocking the harbours it had injured its own citizens : a vanquished North would find that it had made reconciliation with the Southern States far more difficult :

> The object of war is peace, and the purposes of peace are mutual good-will and advantageous commercial intercourse.[55]

Palmerston's words would have seemed strangely old-fashioned in 1919. But what roused his indignation to its fullest pitch was General Butler's general order at New Orleans, ordering that women who insulted the Northern troops were to be treated as street-walkers. Again he suggested to Russell an official protest on the grounds :

> That construed in its literal sense it authorizes proceedings revolting to every manly feeling and without example in the history of nations, and that taken in its narrowest and most restricted inter-pretation it is an outrage upon the feelings and practices of Christian nations, by rendering ladies and respectable women of every class [liable] to be sent to be imprisoned with the most abandoned and profligate and degraded of their sex, and this upon pretences which it would be within the power of any officer or soldier of the federal occupying force to allege against them and possibly without the slightest real foundation ? [56]

Certainly no British interest was being subserved there.

The Foreign Office as usual kept its head ; but the premier's insistence on a personal expression of his chival-rous indignation had the unfortunate effect of widening the breach between him and the American minister. Palmerston wrote Adams in terms as unrestrained as those he had used to his foreign secretary, adding the quite superfluous reflection that, if the Federal government chose 'to be served by men capable of such revolting outrages, they must submit to abide by the deserved opinion which mankind will form of their conduct.'[57] This was the beginning of an acrimonious correspondence, punctuated by Adams' complaints to Russell, and ending in a grudging half-admission by Palmerston that he had spoken unofficially.[58] The outcome left scars on both sides, scars of which the healing was postponed by less known incidents. The prime minister, for example, accused Adams of entirely mis-reporting a private interview on the searching of British merchant ships, and of putting into his (Palmerston's) mouth the phrase, ' catch them if you can.' Such a discussion, he wrote Russell, ' I shall take care not to have again and pray tell him so from me.'[59]

The premier's testiness concerning the war measures of the Union government may have been in part a reaction to the increased difficulties at home which the American Civil War was helping to bring on him. For the adverse effects of the struggle in America on British commerce tended to diminish the government's income, and to stimulate the demand for economy in defence. In consequence, Gladstone increasingly felt it his duty to oppose, both in private and in public, what he regarded as excessive expenditure for military and naval purposes. The advanced Liberals below the gangway, much encouraged, redoubled their charges of extravagance : while the Conservatives, glad to find a popular issue on which they could embarrass the government, took this part of the radical programme for their own. It was not the first time that Palmerston had had to face the danger of a combination between his ' friends below the gangway ' and ' the gentlemen opposite ' ; it was not the first time he had had to veil (for it was out of the question to conceal) the difference between his views and those of his chancellor. But the danger of a serious outcome now seemed more imminent ; and the attacks on his position were now more vigorous and prolonged. To deal at the same time with Gladstone in the cabinet, and with Disraeli, Bright and Cobden in the House, was rather a large assignment, even for Palmerston. To reach a working agreement with his chancellor was the first necessity of all.

But a working agreement between two men whose views were as divergent as their convictions were deep-rooted, who shared in this matter scarcely a single impulse

save the sense of profound obligation felt by each to make
his own views prevail, was more than difficult. In the
correspondence which ensued they were not discussing issues
of any specific character ; for the budget, thanks to some
concession on each side, seems to have been settled with
unusual ease.   What called forth their frank interchange
of views were Palmerston's criticisms of some public
speeches made by Gladstone, in April, at Manchester, and
Palmerston's demands that Gladstone should veil their
differences when speaking in the House.[60]

What the premier most objected to was Gladstone's
statement that the nation, seized with panic, had forced
parliament and the government to adopt an unnecessarily
high scale of military and naval expenditure :

It is . . . a mistake to say that this Scale of Expenditure has
been forced upon Parliament or upon the Government, and it is a
still greater Mistake to accuse the Nation as Cobden does of having
rushed headlong into Extravagance under the Impulse of Panic.
Panic there has been none, on the Part of any Body.

The ministry, parliament and the nation had operated in
perfect harmony :

But have the Government, or rather have both Liberal and
Conservative Governments—have the Parliament and the Nation
been wrong, and have Bright and Cobden and yourself been right ? [61]

The premier, remembering that mightily armed nation
across the Channel who hated England 'from the Bottom of
their Hearts,' whose passion was ' Glory in Wars,' and whose
sovereign was ' able, active, wary, counsel keeping, but ever
planning,' ventured to think not.[62]   But the most serious
part of the letter here reviewed was still to come.   Save
in the coupling of Gladstone's name with the names of two
men who were not only radicals but notoriously his inveterate political enemies, Palmerston had managed so far to
observe all the amenities.   But at the end came a paragraph
highly provocative, not to say offensive, in its tone :

. . . I cannot but regret that you should by speeches in and out
of Parliament invite an agitation to force the Government of which
you are a Member to retrace steps taken upon full Deliberation and

in Fulfilment of Duties, for the faithful Performance of which it is responsible to the Crown and to the Nation.[63]

Perhaps it was as well that he closed with an apology for his remarks and an assurance of the 'friendly spirit' in which they had been made.

In poise, in skill, in firmness and above all in exquisite courtesy, Gladstone's answer was remarkable. Truly its author was, as Palmerston's near relative and private secretary, Evelyn Ashley (quoting Sir William Harcourt), later said, 'a great gentleman.'[64] Fully admitting his complete responsibility for any expenditure to which he had agreed, and his obligation to use no words which would disclose the objections raised in the cabinet, he still claimed the right to guide public sentiment on matters of general policy according to personal conviction :

. . . if he conceives that public opinion requires in matters bearing upon his department, to be either stimulated or restrained, it is his right and duty, subject to the conditions above laid down to improve as far as he can by any arguments couched in moderate and becoming language, and sufficiently guarded against misapprehension, the state of opinion and feeling which may at the time prevail among the public.[65]

Using this claim as a *point d'appui*, he shrewdly turned the premier's position. If it was proper for one minister to rouse the nation to a realisation of military or naval deficiencies, was it not equally proper for another, and in particular, of course, for the chancellor of the Exchequer, to warn the people of impending danger in the matter of finance ? Was not the chancellor, in fact, making an essential contribution to the country's security in pointing out that the 'system of defence' was 'becoming silently impaired . . . in . . . one of its capital and primary particulars, namely the state of our finances ?' He could not retract what he had said about panic, or agree with the premier's views concerning France : and, apart from the avoidance in future of any violation of his cabinet obligations which the premier might be able to point out, he could not promise to change his course. He believed that 'by the firm hand of an united Government' the national expenditure ' might be and ought to be gradually reduced by some millions.' He recognised the friendly spirit in which Palmerston's letter had been written ; but he had one protest to make ;

> In all good humour, I prefer not being classed with Mr. Bright or even Mr. Cobden, first because I do not know their opinions with any precision, and secondly because as far as I do know or can guess them, they seem to contemplate fundamental changes in taxation which I disapprove in principle, and believe also to be unattainable in practice : and reductions of establishment and expenditure for which I am not prepared to be responsible.

It was a difficult letter to answer convincingly. Even the Palmerstonian quip that a policy which allowed ' some Hundreds of Merchants & Manufacturers ' to acquire ' great Stores of Three per Cents, or large Landed Estates ' would result in ' offering to the Butcher a well fatted Calf instead of a well armed Bulls head,' [66] hardly met the situation. The two men were as far apart as ever when the matters on which their differences were founded came before the House.

Debates on the subject were many ; but for interest none exceeded that of May 8, during which Palmerston engaged in a rough-and-tumble fight with the leader of the opposition in the House over the Customs and Inland Revenue Bill. Disraeli, who had been unusually inactive since the commencement of the session, even with respect to foreign affairs, emerged as a protagonist of economy. In demanding that the ministry should abandon a scale of expenditure on armaments that would inevitably involve a heavier burden in income taxes on the landed class, he took occasion as usual to indict the government as much for its foreign as for its financial policy. England, he complained, was ' managing the affairs of the world, not by a cordial alliance with France, but by a new process, called the exercise of moral power.' [67] Such a policy not only led to war by promoting competition in armaments, but in exhausting England's resources was rendering her less and less fit to meet the test.

> There is no fleet and there is no army which gives England such power and influence in the councils of Europe as the consciousness that the income tax is in a virgin state.

It was a very neat method of bringing together Conservatives and radicals : and Disraeli, in suggesting the union,
did not fail to twit the government on the obvious differences
of opinion respecting Anglo-French relations and appropriations for armaments which divided the premier and
chancellor. The journalistic and perhaps partisan William
White describes the *dénouement* :

> When Disraeli sat down the noble Lord sprang to his feet—yes,
> literally so—with as much agility and briskness as if he had been
> forty years old instead of seventy-eight, as he is. And never did this
> marvellous old man speak with more life, jollity, fun, and energy
> than he did on that Thursday night. And how sagaciously did he
> seize the salient points of his opponent's studied harangue, clear them
> of their rhetorical mist, and turn his guns upon himself ! [68]

But his description of the manner in which Palmerston was
received really demands that the reader should have before
him an example of the premier's style :

> Sir, there is no sight more interesting than to behold a gigantic
> frame which has long been in a state of lethargy suddenly rising into
> vigour and strength, especially when *lethargicus nec fit pugil*, and dis-
> playing all that power which nature and cultivation have combined
> to bestow upon him. . . . When I found the right hon. Gentleman
> dilating on Italian affairs, I was at first disposed to think he was
> perhaps in the condition of the soldier who, having failed to let off
> his musket in the review, discharges it as he goes home, to the alarm of
> all who happen to be near.[69]

It is not difficult to believe White's description of the
reaction of the House :

> Indeed, the speech was a triumph from beginning to end. Cheers
> broke forth at the conclusion of every sentence, and every now and
> then there were bursts of hearty laughter so loud and long-continued
> that the House seemed for a time more like a theatre during the per-
> formance of a broad farce than a hall of legislation. And here let it
> be noted that the Conservatives cheered this speech and joined in the
> laughter as loudly as the Liberals. . . . Some weeks back report
> said that Palmerston was miserably ill ; and when he came to the
> House, and men saw his pale face, they exclaimed, ' Ah ! the old man
> is breaking up ' ; and we ourselves had our misgivings. But lo ! he
> seems now to have renewed his youth, like the eagle. At all events,
> on Thursday night there were no signs of ' breaking up.' [70]

But Palmerston's speech was notable for things other than
jollity.   From the array of hard facts, figures and pointed
arguments which he seems to have marshalled on the spot
against Disraeli's carefully prepared though apparently
unlooked-for assault, selection would be difficult.   In view
of what followed, perhaps the most interesting portion of
the speech was that showing Palmerston's perception and
frank acceptance of the impending attempt to discredit or
overthrow the ministry :

> Sir, I assume from what we have heard that the quietude which
> has hitherto prevailed during the Session is likely soon to be disturbed,
> and that we may expect what is commonly called ' a political crisis.'
> The right hon. Gentleman very dexterously prepared the way for
> that event.   He began by throwing out an alluring bait to the Roman
> Catholic Members ; he held out encouraging expectations to the
> country gentlemen behind him.   He then coquetted with the Re-
> formers and the economists below the gangway on this side . . . the
> right hon. Gentleman . . . evidently is preparing to be Member of
> some new Administration. . . .[71]

From this time on the premier was watching for developments.

He did not have to wait long.   On the very day after
the debate, three radicals, headed by Mr. Stansfeld, member
for Halifax, waited on Gladstone to inform him that they
had decided to take some measures to secure the reduction
of expenditure.   They had no connection with the opposition, and wished to act ' in the manner most friendly to the
Government ' : they would be glad to have him look at
the draft of a resolution which they thought of moving in
the House.[72]   Stansfeld's resolution, as finally formulated,
declared that ' the national expenditure ' was ' capable of
reduction, without compromising the safety, the independence, or the legitimate influence of the country.'
Gladstone, in endorsing it, would have endorsed a condemnation of, as well as a mandate to, the ministry.   But
Gladstone did not even look at it.   Rejecting the bait, he
informed his callers that he could have no dealings with
them, and would at once inform the prime minister of their
plan.   In spite of the rebuff the radicals persevered, and
the moving of the resolution was set for June 3.

But Stansfeld's resolution was not to appear alone. Interest in the subject was intense ; and before June 3 no less than seven amendments to the resolution, or amendments to amendments, were down for the same date.[73] The third of these (that of Horsman) not only negatived Stansfeld's, but declared that all the naval and military expenditures of past years had been quite justified : the fifth (Palmerston's) congratulated the ministry on reductions already made, and expressed confidence that such further economies would be effected ' as the future state of things may warrant.' The sixth (Walpole's) need not be described until some of the events which lay back of the formulation of this array have been summarily described.

If the radicals had failed in enticing Gladstone on May 8, they had at least succeeded in adding to the premier's difficulties : for it soon became apparent that in the matter of dealing with the amendments he and his chancellor of the Exchequer could by no means see eye to eye.[74]   Palmerston, who regarded Stansfeld's resolution and most of the amendments as ' nothing but a Trap for a Government,' an attempt, *i.e.* to compel the ministry in future to sacrifice either the country's security or its own reputation for good faith, at first wished, by moving the previous question, to dispose of the whole lot.   Even Horsman's was to go ; for, though the assertion it contained was one ' which no Member of the present Government could deny ' (this to Gladstone !), its adoption by the ministry might be taken by its ' Friends below the Gangway as a Slap in the Faces, richly deserved indeed, but which it might not be useful in a Party Sense for us to administer.'   But Gladstone objected, urging that ' prospective reduction ' was essential, and that the House was entitled to demand a statement of the government's policy on this point.   For him, the use of the previous question would not only be an infringement of the ' just rights ' of the movers of resolutions and amendments, but ' an unworthy evasion of a difficulty ' by the government.   If he could bring himself to vote for it at all, he would be ' under the necessity of reiterating in the most pointed manner in a speech ' what he had ' heretofore said on the subject of retrenchment.'   When Palmerston suggested that, in case the amendments were voted on, Horsman's could not be officially opposed, Gladstone once more balked. Was he, for example, to endorse the expenditure incurred by ' great mistakes ' such as ' the immense and costly conversion [into iron-plated vessels] of wooden ships of the line,'—he who had in vain objected at the time, and submitted to the ' authority ' of the premier ? His desire was to move a set of resolutions of his own, and to stand aside from the debate. The issue was somewhat clarified by the premier's discovery that the use of the previous question, as he planned it, was forbidden by parliamentary rules ; but Palmerston still had a serious question to face in the attitude of his chancellor. His first step toward meeting it (though the succession of events at this point is not clear) seems to have been in framing his own amendment.

It was at this point that the Tories moved, and that Walpole's amendment was set down with the rest. In a meeting at Lord Derby's house it was decided that some member of the party should move an amendment to Palmerston's, directing the government to effect (with due regard to defence) such reductions as would not only equalise revenue and expenditure, but diminish the burden of ' temporary and exceptional ' taxes.[75] Walpole, who had not appeared at the meeting, was persuaded to undertake the task. The amendment, in offering to the radicals a good second-best, would probably command a vote sufficient to humiliate if not to destroy the ministry. Such an indirect attack would divide, just as a direct attack would probably unite, the liberally-minded in the House. It might even, one would think, have proved decidedly embarrassing for Gladstone.

The outcome, if it is properly attributable to the premier's brains, testified to his powers as a parliamentary strategist : for the concealment of intention, and the seizure of initiative are surely parts of all good strategy.[76] It was only when the great night of June 3 arrived that the ministry's plan was revealed. Before even Stansfeld's resolution could be put, Palmerston transformed the projected moving of the Walpole amendment into a direct attack, by announcing that the government would treat the vote on it as one of confidence. If the House wished for a Tory ministry, it could realise its wishes then and there. To clear the issue he would ask the movers of amendments lying between Stansfeld's resolution and Walpole's amendment to stand aside. It was a shrewd stroke ; but not even he could have foreseen how immediately and completely effective it would prove. For Walpole, taken unaware, completely lost his nerve and withdrew his amendment with the rest. Bernal Osborne reminded the House that ' on the eve of the Derby " favourites " ' were ' sometimes found " bolting," ' and treated it to the couplet :

> ' Back recoils, he knows not why,
> E'en at the sound himself has made.'

It was all over. Stansfeld's resolution was smothered, and the premier's meaningless amendment accepted without even a vote. Disraeli, forced to devour the ' Leek of Humiliation ' which he had prepared for his great foe,[77] vented his feelings on the unfortunate Walpole : Palmerston went home to write Granville : ' Our decision was quite right and was wholly unsuspected by the gentlemen opposite.' [78] To the Queen he reported ' a most triumphant night.' [79]

The same term could hardly be applied to the session as a whole ; yet it was to prove at least satisfactory from the premier's point of view. The government, announcing decreases in the estimates for army and navy which were more apparent than real, received from parliament what it asked : it even obtained permission to issue terminable annuities to cover the cost of proceeding with the fortification of dockyards, ports, and arsenals. Again, it turned back without undue difficulty the more radical proposals for administrative or constitutional reform. The House accepted Palmerston's contention that the purchase of army commissions, if theoretically indefensible, had worked well ; and that its abolition might involve unpleasant consequences in a country with England's democratic government.[80] The usual attempt to secure the adoption of the ballot in parliamentary elections was defeated with the usual ease. On the other hand, the premier may have noted indications that a liberal tide was setting in. He may have marked the increasing restiveness of the House about expenditure, and perhaps also the fact that a fair number of members who still opposed the use of the ballot where parliamentary elections were concerned, now favoured its introduction for the municipalities. The sharp-eyed Vitzthum recorded a 'seemingly irremediable split between Lord Palmerston and the Radicals,' thanks to the government's neglect to pay deference to the radical watchwords, 'Economy, Non-Intervention, and Reform.'[81] Nevertheless, the premier had held his own in the domestic field. Perhaps the same general estimate might be made as to the government's success in foreign policy for the year, if one should judge by developments in connection with the Eastern question and the American Civil War.

Throughout the spring and early summer, Palmerston stood against interference in the American struggle : in the late summer and early autumn he was one of its leading advocates. One might easily suspect that his disgust with the war measures of the Union government, and even, perhaps, his sharp skirmishes with Adams, contributed to bring this change in attitude. And, suspecting this, one might easily go on to conclude that the alteration of his policy reflected a general alteration in his feelings towards the combatants. But these suppositions are not borne out by his letters. All that actually appears is a deepening conviction that the Confederacy's independence was assured,[82] and an increasing desire to put as short a term as possible to the distress occasioned on both sides of the Atlantic by the war. It may be assumed, of course, that he still desired the division of the republic, as a consummation which would offer great advantages for his country. But his available letters for these months contain, as it happens, no references to this desire, much less expressions of that deep hostility to the North with which he and some of his colleagues have been credited. Like other members of the cabinet, he seems to have been drawn slowly from his original determination to avoid risking ' a bloody nose,' by the effects of Southern propaganda in the country and the House, reports

of Southern successes on the battlefield, and evidence, only
too palpable, of the distress to be anticipated by his countrymen if the war went on. Around the middle of July he was
very much engrossed in devising measures of relief for the
sufferers in the cotton-manufacturing areas.[83]   He turned to
the idea of intervention at the beginning of August : two
months later he was returning to his own and the cabinet's
earlier stand.

Gladstone announced the prime minister's change of
heart on July 29 : 'Lord Palmerston . . . has come
exactly to my mind about some early representations of a
friendly kind to America, if we can get France *and* Russia to
join.'[84]   Eight days later Palmerston wrote to the Queen
that October would apparently be the proper time, and
Russell to Palmerston that his own expectations were the
same. The proposal of an armistice was to be the opening
step.[85] By mid-September, news that the Confederates
were advancing to the North brought to Russell a suggestion
from the premier that, in case Baltimore or Washington
should fall, the British and French governments might
recommend 'an arrangement upon the basis of separation'
to both sides. Russell, who had already instructed Cowley
to sound out Napoleon's government, not only agreed, but
was ready to go a step beyond the premier. He was prepared to recognise the independence of the Southern States,
in case attempts at mediation should fall through.[86] Ten
days later, when Europe was still awaiting the news from
Antietam, Palmerston showed that his caution had not yet
deserted him. Unless, he wrote, the Northern armies should
'sustain a great defeat,' it might be better to 'wait awhile.'
And it would be better, too, that England and France, in
proposing mediation, should have Russia for a partner.[87]
Apparently he did not know as yet how anti-interventionist
was Russia's policy, or how Seward was relying on her aid ;[88]
but he must at least have realised that he was playing for
the maximum of safety. Nor was any marked preference
for the South in evidence. The even balance of forces
between the combatants, he wrote, presented 'just the case
for the stepping in of friends. One thing must be admitted
and that is that both sides have fought like bull dogs.'[89]

By the beginning of October the premier was commencing to think that the time for 'the stepping in of friends'
had not as yet arrived : three weeks later he was sure
of it.[90]   Whatever the personal feelings of the interven-
tionists, the proposed mediation was so clearly to the
advantage of the South that the North could hardly be
expected to consider it, save under pressure of severe
defeat : and news of Antietam now disclosed that defeat
had been on the Southern side.   The defence of Canada
had to be considered in connection with any step calculated
to rouse the animosity of the North ; and the season was
fast approaching when the British fleet would be powerless
to help.   Again, the old difficulty concerning slavery was
ever present in the premier's mind.[91]   How could one
find a basis of agreement acceptable to the North, the
South and the British populace ?   So Palmerston was glad
enough to let mediation wait.   His expectations were
unchanged : he still thought the Civil War had ' manifestly
ceased to have any attainable object as far as the Northerners were concerned, except to get rid of some more
thousand troublesome Irish and Germans.'[92]   But he had
' very much come back ' to thinking that the English should
be lookers-on until the war had taken a more decided turn.[93]
Such a development might be hoped for by the spring.   It
it true that when Napoleon, in November, proposed that
England, France and Russia should unite in pressing the
suspension of hostilities for six months, Palmerston supported Russell and Gladstone in urging the cabinet to
concur.   But Lewis, who had an excellent opportunity
to judge, believed that the premier was actuated only by
a desire to support his foreign minister, and Russell only
by reluctance to displease Napoleon.[94]   And even this
project fell through.   The reserved and apparently wise
policy of the ministry and its head in dealing with the American struggle had been barren of any positive results.   And
the same was true of the premier's more personal efforts
to control developments in the Balkan peninsula.
   It seems almost an error that it was not Palmerston
who made the famous analogy between the Eastern question
and the gout : both beset him so frequently, so inoppor-

tunely, and at such varied localities in these, his latter years.
There were crises, such as that in Syria, which came and
passed ; but there were nearly always twinges in the Balkans,
in other words near the heart, twinges which might have
attracted more attention if the premier had not been so
engrossed with Italy.   And indeed it must have required
constant if unconscious mental readjustment on his part
when he happened to deal with the Italian and the Balkan
peninsulas simultaneously ; for, east of the Adriatic and
north of Greece, the rights of peoples to resist ' iron heels,'
the ' romance ' of peoples ' rising from the slumber of
ages,' or even the nobility of peoples emulating the glorious
British revolution of 1688, impressed him not a whit.
Like almost all other statesmen, British or continental,
of whom one can think, he could not look with favour
on Balkan movements which might result in the blocking
of commercial or imperial routes, or in upsetting (in the
wrong direction) the balance of power.   Now ' awakenings '
and constitutional movements in European Turkey would,
as he saw things, have precisely such results.   Turkey,
according to his wishes and expectations, might survive
indefinitely ; but the chances of her survival depended to
some extent on her ability to regenerate herself, and, to
a much greater extent, on her being left intact and undisturbed.   All the more would she survive if England could
pursue that policy of assisting in her regeneration which
the premier, as foreign secretary, had been so eager to
promote.   It had, in fact, become second nature to him to
keep watch on the Danube, both by trying to reinvigorate
the Turks, and by unceasing vigilance with regard to the
manœuvres of the Russian Empire.

Mutual watchfulness had been the predominant note in
the relations between the British and Russian governments
since 1859.   Outwardly their relations had been perfectly
correct.[95]   Gortchakov, the Tsar's foreign minister, assured
the British ambassador of his pleasure in observing how
much fairer England's attitude toward Russia had become ;
declared that his master harboured no resentment toward
any Power save Austria ; and inquired whether England
had any complaints to make of Russian activities in the

Middle East. Palmerston found that he had no complaints
at all ; and suggested that a Russian grand duchess,
known to have much influence with Alexander, should be
invited to Windsor by the Queen. But fair words and
courtesies were only anodynes : there remained always the
provisions of the Treaty of Paris concerning the Black Sea
and Bessarabia—provisions which the Tsar was confessedly
as determined to nullify as Palmerston and his cabinet to
maintain.[96] Moreover, if Russia's expansionist activities
justified no actual complaints, Palmerston could not without
uneasiness watch Russian soldiers taking up positions in
Manchuria and Sakhalin, spreading down through Turkes-
tan, and up through the mountains of Daghestan and
Circassia.   And he was more uneasy still concerning the
entente (he hoped, without being sure, that it was nothing
more) between the courts of Paris and St. Petersburg.   To
him, as to other nineteenth-century British statesmen, the
combination was a bugbear in itself ; and he suspected
Gortchakov of using it to promote his favourite scheme of
encouraging the emerging nations of the Balkan peninsula
to resist their Turkish overlords.   And this at a time when
the British ambassador to the Porte described the Turkish
empire as ' everywhere mined or threatened.' [97]   Palmerston
had no desire to see the ' slumber of ages' further dispelled
by a Romanov and a Bonaparte.

It was above all in Serbia that the curious irony of the
situation now stood out—that a Russian tsar appeared as
a patron, and Palmerston of all men as an opponent, of a
people trying, not merely to rid themselves of alien rule,
but in some degree to fall in line with constitutionally
governed European states.   For the Serbian ruler, Michael
Obrenovič, was not only trying to raise a conscript army
and expel all Turks save those who by treaty provision were
permitted to reside in certain real or so-called fortresses,
but had apparently decided to reorganise his state into
an hereditary monarchy approximating to the British type.
Palmerston was willing enough to keep his hands off the
organisation and division of powers within the Serbian
government ; but he opposed Michael's efforts to liberate
his people from the Turks.   When, in this year, 1862,

rioting and bloodshed in Belgrade brought intervention by the Powers, Palmerston's influence seems to have been thrown entirely on the Turkish side :

> It is for the Turks and not for the Servians to determine what works are necessary for the defence of the citadel. . . . The Turks can have no motive for locking up in Belgrade a larger force than is necessary for defence and they ought to be left to judge for themselves on that matter. . . . [98]

He was simply thinking of the Eastern question in the terms that had become traditional with him. ' The Russian plan about Turkey ' was ' new only in its application to the whole of European Turkey ' ; it was ' the old plan of 1825–1826 . . . *divide et impera.*'[99] And, as he frankly told Brunnow, in November 1862, it was being developed by methods wholly unjustifiable :

> Russian agents are everywhere undermining the Sultan in his provinces and the Russian government is encouraging every rebel who opposes the Sultan's authority. . . . It was Russian encouragement that misled the Montenegro chief . . . it was Russian encourage-ment that made the Servian chief resist all reasonable arrangements, and I had that morning received information that four hundred and fifty carts full of muskets & ammunition had just passed the Danube on the way from Russia to Servia, a quantity so large that it could only have been sent by the Russian government to the Prince of Servia to enable him to make war upon the Sultan.[100]

It was in vain for Brunnow to make denials. The number of waggon-loads had grown to a thousand, in Palmerston's mind at least, within a month.[101] In his apprehension, he could make no allowances for the aspirations or needs of any branch of the South Slavs. What was the use of talking about an outlet for Montenegrin commerce ? How could so poor a country need an outlet ? The demand for it was merely a scheme to ' place the Montenegrins in open and easy communication with French and Russian and Italian intriguers.'[102]

If he was most apprehensive of the results of Russian ' intrigue,' his letters show more bitterness concerning that of the French. No doubt he augured ill from the appoint-ment in Serbia of a reputedly Francophil first minister and a French chief of staff. At any rate he suspected that French intrigue was aimed at securing Turkey's downfall, ' paralysing our arm and preventing us from arresting the downfall or averting it.'[103]   This was all the more disappointing in view of his need for French co-operation in executing the more constructive part of his own programme.[104]   He had hoped that the French might assist him in displacing the Turkish commander-in-chief, Riza Pasha, who, he discovered, was fattening on corruption while the army deteriorated. He had wanted to secure the appointment of an Anglo-French commission to examine Turkish finances, and obtain an undertaking from the Sultan to institute reforms.   Instead, he had to counter French ' intrigue.'   And counter it he would, even by French and Russian methods if required. For of course in British hands such methods would not be intrigue at all.   When Russell cautioned the British ambassador at Constantinople not to be too active in securing the appointment and dismissal of Turkish ministers, Palmerston was displeased.   The French and Russians, he pointed out, would play this game in any case, and would use their influence for evil purposes.   England sought only the appointment of ' good and honest men ' ; and, by playing a straight game, would ' beat French intrigue in the long run.'[105]   He even boasted of ' the success of English policy,' and the mortification that must have come to the Russians and the French from ' the signal failure of their anti-Turkish intrigues in Servia, Montenegro and in the Herzegovina.'[106]   But in considering the protocol which brought temporary peace to Serbia [107] it is hard to see how the prime minister's policy could be credited with much success.   Here again he was encountering a force which was too strong for him ; here again he was displaying his failure to grasp the power of liberal nationalism.   This came out as clearly where the Roumanians were concerned. To the end he did not give up hope that Austria's retirement from Italy might be secured through her purchase of the Roumanian principalities, though he did admit that ' such a scheme would . . . no doubt be much opposed by Russia and probably objected to by the Moldo Wallachians ' ![108]

If it is somewhat sad to observe how Palmerston's sym-

pathy for struggling peoples wilted and died in passage
eastward across the Adriatic Sea, one may at least be comforted in noting how this sympathy revived again in the
more southerly air of Greece. There was fresh evidence of
this in the winter of 1862–1863, when the Greeks, after at
last sending King Otto back to Bavaria, set about providing
themselves with a new sovereign. In this far from easy task
they found the three ' protecting ' Powers quite prodigal of
assistance and advice. For, while all three paid more or
less lip service to the old rule, excluding members of their
own ruling families from the vacant throne, it was not for
some time that their adherence to the rule was definitely
announced. In the interval, the three governments
manœuvred and plotted as had been their habit when Otto
was first king. There was really some excuse ; for the
limits of proper self-denial were difficult to trace. Who
could decide the exact degree of consanguinity to Victoria,
Napoleon or Alexander which would properly disqualify a
candidate ; who could forget that wives (as so notably in
Otto's case) often influenced their husband's policies ; and
who could ignore the fact that partisanship in international
affairs is not necessarily a question of relationship to
sovereigns at all ?

If one may judge by the length and frequency of
his letters, Palmerston gave to this subject an inordinate
amount of time and thought. Perhaps, as he once suggested, his responsibility for Otto's choice, and failure to
' make a silk purse ' out of him still weighed upon his
mind ;[109] perhaps he was moved by the desire to settle for
all time a question which for so long had troubled him ; perhaps the mere fact that he was contending against the forces
of unrighteousness, against the wiles of the two courts
which he and England principally feared, was in itself
enough. At any rate, he took the question up with might
and main, opposing Russell's policies, correcting his
despatches, drafting despatches of his own, and apparently,
in part at least, having his own way. Whatever may have
been the secret intentions of the other two great courts, he intended to play the game honestly enough, reaping, of course,
what benefits he could, but not attempting to secure the

throne for any member of Victoria's family.[110] But age had not impaired his resolution that the Greeks should have a constitutional sovereign, and one who should, to the greatest possible degree, be Anglophil. Granted the right man was chosen, Palmerston stood prepared to smooth his path by gratifying the expansionist longings of his turbulent subjects. The British government would relinquish the Ionian Islands, even to Corfu. He decided to part with Corfu reluctantly, at first believing that England could not afford to give up so strong a base. But other arguments prevailed. After all, the islands had merely been committed by the Powers to England's care ; after all, neither Greeks nor Corfiotes would be content to see the island separated from the rest ; and, after all, it was pleasant to hold so rich a bribe in a contest with Gallic and Muscovite ' intrigue.' [111]

A detailed description of the negotiations which ended in the choice of Prince William of Glücksburg (re-christened, for the occasion, George) should make rare material for some satirist. Europe proved to be simply overflowing with princes of all ages, all degrees of princeliness, and of almost all established religions and nationalities, each of whom, if not precisely fitted to rule a turbulent, half-bankrupt, Greek Catholic state, might at least ' do.' Russia and France favoured, above all, the duke of Leuchtenberg, bonapartist through his father, Eugène de Beauharnais, and Russian through his marriage with a daughter of Nicholas I. The Greeks, perhaps actuated mainly by the prospect of rewards, declared their preference for an Englishman, at best Prince Alfred, the Queen's second son, at worst Lord Stanley, Derby's heir. ' Demosthenes *with* his pebbles,' scoffed Palmerston.[112]

He could afford to take the affair jauntily, holding so strong a hand. When Russia and France held back from promising the refusal of the throne by all members of their reigning families, he was eager that Prince Alfred should accept, and deeply grieved when Victoria declared that ' upon ·no earthly account and under no circumstances ' would she consent.[113] But he still had means of achieving some success.[114] At least he could conceal the Queen's decision, and use the choice of Prince Alfred as a means of persuading Russia to withdraw support from Leuchtenberg. He could still put forward a succession of more or less Anglophil candidates (including two Coburgs) ; and suggest a delicate inquiry to the Sultan as to whether the Epirus and Thessaly might not be handed over to the Greeks, on the condition of their choosing some prince ' pointed out by England and whose policy would be safe and peaceful.' Gradually he forgot that he had talked of allowing the Greeks to follow their own choice. ' We ought to name a candidate and make his election the condition of the gift of the Ionian Islands,' he wrote Russell, on December 21.[115] Four days later he made what may have been the first suggestion that the throne should go to Prince William.[116]

This was the beginning of the end. It was some time before the Powers agreed to accept this son of the heir apparent. to the Danish throne, this future brother-in-law of the Prince of Wales and of the Tsarevitch ; it was some time even before he became Palmerston's favourite candidate. But, when his other choices failed one by one to come to an understanding with the Greeks, the premier accepted Prince William as a young man ' of a good race connected with the English Crown,' and one on whom the French and Russians would have no influence.[117] Here, then, he could claim some measure of success for his country and himself. How well deserved it was by his country he had explained beforehand to the Russian ambassador :

I said [to the ambassador] that this is a sample of the difference between the position held by England and that held by Russia arising from the difference between the foreign policy of the two. We are generally liked and trusted. Russia is generally feared and disliked. Portugal looks upon us as her old and faithful ally. The Spaniards give us confidence and friendship. The Italians adore us. The Greeks are all for an English prince. The Turks lean upon us as their surest friends. The Austrians court our alliance, the Prussians in spite of the Macdonald affair look to us for support. Denmark sends us her loveliest princess and Sweden is proud of our friendship. The only Powers whose people may not be so fond of us are those whose ambitions and aggressive schemes we may be thought to oppose and these are France and Russia, though we are on good terms with the governments of both.[118]

On such an eminence did Palmerston behold the nation which he served and ruled. And there were those who believed his own position to be equally secure and glorious :

So long as ' old Pam ' is at the helm we need have no care about the honour and interests of England—such is the leading thought of the public since the settlement of the difference with North America. This thought consoles the starving cotton-spinners of Lancashire no less than the rich. . . .[119]

Neither John Bull nor Palmerston could realise that the peak of glory had been already passed.

CHAPTER XXXIII

1863

IN 1862 Palmerston had held his own : 1863 was to see him still bestriding his political world, unconscious of the fact that the foundations on which it rested were commencing to weaken under him. But there were sharp-eyed critics, both abroad and in England, who were quick to note the change ; and who, with the touch of exaggeration which animosity so readily supplies, were as quick to point it out. Prosper Mérimée, for example, criticized British foreign policy for its lack of that vigour and assertiveness which had been so essentially Palmerstonian :

That England will become a second-rate Power is a foregone conclusion, at all events so long as she invariably backs out whenever she is called upon to take action as a first-rate Power.[1]

Exaggerated though his language was, Mérimée had sensed a fundamental change. A situation, already evolving for some time, was now beginning to be manifest : the day of success for Palmerstonian policy had virtually passed. No longer would haughty words, orders to the fleet, and patronage of the smaller continental states give England a pivotal position in international affairs. Developments on the continent and among her own people were co-operating to diminish her influence. Already in this year, Bismarck's emergence was commencing to show effects. Russia was beginning to exhibit a stiffer front, Austria to yield to Prussian leadership, and France, so often England's useful and even complaisant partner, to find herself checkmated by Prussian diplomacy. Possibly an England heavily armed and ready to take risks, might, through astute diplomacy, have continued for a little longer to hold her place. But England, every year more businesslike, was yielding to the persuasion of her Cobdens and her Brights that it was better to economize on armaments, and to avoid so much as risking her blood and treasure for issues in which her own interests were not obviously concerned. A change was noticeable, too, in the conduct of British diplomacy. Palmerston's astuteness, his adventuring spirit, even his desire to take an active part, seemed gradually to be deserting him ; and Russell could do little to supply the loss. The Queen, as she showed both earlier and later, would have been quite capable of supporting British prestige on her own account ; but at this time she was more concerned to oppose than to support her premier. His letters show that the old antagonism had fully come to life again :

I fear we shall have to request her to remember that she is Queen of England and not a German sovereign. The feelings & opinions & German leanings of the Prince Consort which he had sagacity enough to keep tolerably in the back ground are breaking out in her & she thinks it a duty to his memory to put forward strongly everything which she knew him to think and feel.[2]

Victoria, writing to King Leopold, was more emphatic still :

I *miserable*, wretched, almost frantic without my Angel to stand by me, and *put* the *others* down, and in their right place ! No respect is paid to *my* opinion *now*, and this helplessness almost drives me *wild* ![3]

No wonder continental statesmen, who must have been more or less cognizant of all these things, paid less attention than in former times to the premier's speeches at public gatherings or even in the House.

At home a critic more hostile than Mérimée pointed out, in terms as suggestive as they were at times far-fetched, the existence of a situation which might well have caused Palmerston some concern. In the early summer of 1863, the 'dangerous' young Lord Robert Cecil attacked the ministry through the columns of the *Quarterly Review*.[4] Convincing and utterly unfair by turns, lighted by wit and sarcasm all through, his article left few of the major

activities of the cabinet unassailed.   But its gravamen was the
premier's use of ' a new system of corruption, less disgraceful
than that of Sir Robert Walpole, because more veiled ;
but on that very account more dangerous,'—a system of
bribery by ' the expressions of opinions that are not really
held, and empty pledges which are carelessly uttered and
recklessly flung aside.'   Cecil, like Clarendon, seemed to
see in Palmerston something of the croupier :

> The triumph of his dexterity was that he contrived to make the
> Radicals, out of hatred to himself, and the Conservatives, out of dis-
> trust of Mr. Gladstone, each give their support at critical moments
> to the Government to which both Ministers belonged.

Though Lord Robert was happy that ' the great Reform
delusion ' had passed away, he professed himself deeply
shocked at the bribing of the radicals.   To the religious
radicals the Church, that ' constant resource of Liberal
Ministers who are in want of a policy, and Liberal Members
who are at a loss for a pledge,' had been offered up : to the
sentimental radicals had been granted the policy of interference in Italy.   As for the commercial radicals, the Bright
and Cobden group, theirs had been the richest bribes of all :
the appointment of two of their members to the cabinet,
and the recasting of the system of taxation ' in the moulds
of their narrow philosophy and adjusted to favour their
commercial undertakings.'   But, as Lord Robert noted
with gloomy satisfaction, they were still unappeased.
Cheated of parliamentary reform, they were now blackmail-
ing the prime minister by ' demanding to have the expenditure as well as the taxation remodelled according to their
own ideal.'   The premier must know that the day was not
far off when ' his pitiless creditors ' would ' foreclose.'

Was Palmerston to be brought low by Bismarck or
by Bright ?   Looking back, one can see that the question
had some pertinence in 1863.   Unconditional defiance or
unconditional surrender to either of the two might have
damaged him irretrievably in the eyes 'of his fellow-countrymen.   But neither unconditional defiance nor unconditional
surrender was to be expected from him at this time.   He
had nearly always been ready to make some concession to

public opinion ; and age had brought him even closer to his heraldic motto, *flecti non frangi.* On the other hand, his courage and optimism were with him still. Perhaps he had his moments of despondency when, as in this year, old friends or political associates, Elgin, Ellice, Lansdowne, Lyndhurst, Normanby, and, above all, Lewis, were carried to their graves. Perhaps there were times when it seemed hard to be assailed at once by age and gout and Queen Victoria. But if he had his moments of depression they were not for his political associates or even for readers of his letters to see.

Certainly there was no sign of depression when he appeared, in early February, at the opening of the House :

> Cheers burst forth from his supporters when they saw that he walked as firmly as ever. . . . Nor is it wonderful that we should be anxious about this old man's health, for . . . upon his shoulders rests . . . the whole framework of our party arrangements. Like Atlas, he alone holds up the structure ; and when he shall fail all will collapse and sink into temporary ruin. . . . Fail ! Why, the noble Lord has no thought of failing, for it was only the other day that he appeared in the hunting-field with a new scarlet coat.[5]

And the *Star* (not unnaturally regarded by Clarendon as ' Bright's paper ')[6] apparently took the lead in offering the British public what may have been regarded as another piece of testimony to the youthfulness of John Bull's favourite. Suit was entered against him for £20,000 by the allegedly aggrieved husband of a young woman who in some capacity had visited Cambridge House. It seems never to have come to trial.[7]

He had approached the session with perfect confidence, as a letter to Clarendon of the preceding October shows :

> As to Derby's intentions for next session . . . he will be unable to resist the pressure of Disraeli and the most impatient of his followers, aided by the blandishments of Cobden, Bright and Co. But a House of Commons defeat will not kill us, and we shall still have in reserve an appeal to the country, which I think would be in our favour. . . [8]

Now he found this confidence more than justified. Save for the distress in Lancashire, the country abounded in prosperity ; and the taxes yielded excellent returns. Thanks to this, and to considerable reductions in the army

THE STAIRCASE AT CAMBRIDGE HOUSE

(Now the Naval and Military Club).   The bust is of Lord Palmerston

and the navy estimates, Gladstone was able to lower the tax on tea, and restore the income tax to the old pre-war figure set by Peel. With prosperity came, as usual, contentment and general quiescence regarding projects of reform. Even Russell's uneasy spirit seemed at rest. Witness his speech to his neighbours at Abergeldie :

With regard to domestic policy I think we are all very much agreed, because the feeling of the country, and of those who have conducted great reforms, is very much like that of the man who, having made a road in your own highlands, put a stone on the top of the mountain with an inscription ' Rest and be thankful.' [9]

It was in vain that Disraeli fretted, or that ' Cobden, Bright and Co.' longed to ' foreclose.' Derby had announced beforehand that there would be ' no serious fighting ' ; [10] and the Conservative rank and file proved so far from anxious to displace the ministry that the premier did not even have to put forth his strength. Hence the session, as men reviewed it afterwards, was remarked as notable for two things : that the speech from the throne with which it opened suggested not a single specific measure of internal reform, and that throughout its course there was not one division on strictly party lines.[11] ' It seemed,' said the *Annual Register*, ' as if the long and warm contentions, which had resulted in the great reforms of the preceding thirty years, had been succeeded by a season of reaction and repose . . . an indefinite portion of professed Conservatives in Parliament . . . felt that the veteran statesman, with his great tact and knowledge of the world, his large experience and skilful management of affairs and men, was, of all whom the times afforded, the person best adapted for the situation which he filled . . . no Minister of late years has possessed so great an ascendancy in the House of Commons.' [12] No wonder the prime minister was lulled into false security.

Relieved of any anxiety concerning developments at Westminster, he had been able to cultivate the favours of the public with what seems to have been even unwonted assiduity.[13] On a March day he was installed as Rector of Glasgow University, exhorting a cheering throng to

strive after scholarly excellence.   Next morning he sailed
down the Clyde, was fêted at Greenock, and returned to
Glasgow to address a great meeting composed mainly of
working men.   Edinburgh came next.   In the course of
one day he appeared as the principal figure and speaker in
three separate festivities.   In receiving the freedom of the
city he spoke as a former resident ; in accepting an LL.D.
from the University of Edinburgh he was the old student of
Stewart and Playfair ; but at the banquet which followed
in the evening the citizens heard the familiar tones of
England's proud leader :

> His lordship dwelt long and eloquently upon the moral influence
> of Great Britain on other nations.   There was hardly a single
> country in Europe, he said, that had not in some shape or other,
> with some modification or other, institutions formed after the pattern,
> or at least upon the principles, of her Constitution ; and he was
> proud to say that some of those nations were greatly indebted for the
> benefits they enjoy to the assistance and countenance which they
> received from the Government of England.

Even those who best knew the old statesman were aghast
at the strain he was putting on his energies.   ' Few of the
great acrobats die a natural death and I expect that Palmerston one of these days will finish himself off by doing
something more than any other man ever attempted,' wrote
Clarendon. [14]

But the aged acrobat gave no sign of exhaustion in his
public appearances of the following month.   When the
Prince of Wales passed through the streets of London with
his bride, he was greeted from Cambridge House by a
smiling premier, who had written only two months before
of the difficulties of knowing ' what to do with Royal
Princes so as to make them respectable and to keep them out
of mischief.' [15]   And, before the decorations used at the
Guildhall for the ball to the Prince and Princess had been
taken down, they served as a setting for Palmerston's
entertainment by the mayor on Lord Mayor's Day.[16]   The
mayor, introducing his guest as the most popular premier
since the great Earl Grey, referred approvingly to the
English public's ' habit of criticizing boldly and fearlessly
the acts of all Sovereigns and of all nations, and showing its

sympathy with countries struggling for independence and liberty.' The guest did not disappoint his audience. His hearers were invited to approve the government's restraint in resisting ' blandishments on the one side and threats on the other ' which had been employed to draw England into the conflict in America. What is more, they were asked to admire the remonstrances made to the Russian government against the ' barbarous system of deliberate extermination ' being carried on in Poland. This was language as reminiscent of a younger Palmerston as was the scarlet hunting coat or even the action for damages. But as men knew that the coat clothed an aged and enfeebled frame, so were they soon to learn that the valorous words levelled at the Tsar covered an outworn and impotent policy.

The Polish question, simple enough in itself, soon became the focus for some highly intricate diplomacy.[17] It will be remembered that the bulk of Russia's Polish subjects, encouraged by the success of the Italians against Austria, had for some time been demanding autonomous government. The Tsar's attempts to calm their passionate agitation by slight concessions as to local self-government were scornfully repudiated until the Tsar's patience, not too robust at any time, gave out. In January 1863, he took the drastic step of forcibly enlisting in his army great numbers of young Polish revolutionaries. When this harshness provoked a widespread but pathetically ill-organized revolt, and when the revolt gave rise to a struggle prosecuted with atrocious cruelty, the governments of three great Powers found the situation perplexing and not a little dangerous. The Austrian government, while happy enough to see Austria's vengeful Slavic neighbour in difficulties that would tie her hands elsewhere, had to consider the effects of possible Polish success on Francis Joseph's own Polish subjects, and on the other dissatisfied nationalities of his ill-compacted empire. It did not take long for the Austrian ministers to decide that caution should be the keynote of their policy ; but they allowed their intentions to seem doubtful for some little time. The French government found the affair much more troublesome than did the Austrian ; since Napoleon could neither forget the value of his entente with the Tsar, nor overlook the danger of showing indifference to the overwhelming sympathy of all sections of his subjects for the Poles. His first decision was to keep on good terms with the Russian government as long as possible.

The British cabinet, unhampered by any understanding with St. Petersburg, found its position less embarrassing. But its perplexities were great enough. In England also pro-Polish sentiment was a considerable factor. Up to the early summer, *The Times* was unmeasured in its condemnation of Russian ' iniquity ' ; while the *Morning Post* and others of the more nationalistic journals spoke of intervention, of the suspension of diplomatic relations, and even of war.[18] And how could public sentiment be satisfied ? Not only was effective action on the Poles' behalf almost impossible ; but, at a time when British relations with the United States were on a precarious footing, the Foreign Office could not be unmindful of the fact that Seward was lined up flatly with the Tsar.[19] And then there was the Queen. For Victoria, who had never ceased to supervise her ministers' activities in foreign policy, threw herself into this question as she had thrown herself into nothing since the Prince Consort's death. Piously bent on carrying out to the last detail what she believed to have been her husband's views, remembering that the Prince had foreseen a Polish revolution and had warned her of the danger it would bring, and reinforced in her convictions by King Leopold, she resisted all suggestions that England should interfere in any way.[20] But what, perhaps, hardened her determination more than all, was Bismarck's first master stroke of diplomacy. The Prussian minister, seeing a godsent opportunity to establish a claim on Russia's gratitude in the future, and to weaken or break a Franco-Russian entente which threatened all his plans, hastened to put forward Prussia as Russia's one true friend. Russian troops were offered liberty to pursue Polish refugees across the Prussian frontier. Naturally, then, Victoria feared that any British action in favour of the Poles would create hostility between her country and her eldest daughter's adopted one ; and that British encouragement of French action might clear the way for a French attack on Prussia's Rhenish provinces. This last fear her prime minister quite shared with her.

That this fear was genuine and by no means unjustified is well worth remembering. For, taken in conjunction with the other difficulties encountered by Palmerston and Russell, it partially explains what would otherwise appear as mere diplomatic ineptitude. It is easy to point out that in handling this affair the Foreign Office helped to prepare the way for German dominance ; but it is also easy to forget the handicaps under which the Foreign Office worked. They were quite evident at the time to that shrewd and well-informed diplomatist, Count Vitzthum :

. . . fear of Bonapartist ambition, the growing infirmity of Palmerston, the naive inexperience of Lord Russell in the region of high policy, the credulity of the public, and, lastly, the inflammatory language of the superficial daily press—all this explains the errors and inconsistencies of a Government which was hovering between war and peace. . . . The British Ministers did not wish for war ; on the contrary, their wish was to prevent Napoleon from possibly picking a quarrel. But, on the other hand, they were anxious not to be outflanked by the French, and thus they found themselves in a vortex of embarrassments. . . .[21]

And Vitzthum forebore all mention of the Queen. It is noticeable, too, that he began and ended by referring to England's embarrassment and dread concerning France. The dread was natural. Whatever the personal intentions of Napoleon may have been, some of his servants played with the idea of going to war with Austria for an ally ; while the Ballplatz, before exhibiting its settled policy, at least pretended to dally with the plan. But to justify the fears of Palmerston is not to deny the evidences of his ' growing infirmity.'

One is tempted at least to see some evidence in his failure to formulate any line of policy which could be related to any possible line of action. He sketched, indeed, two policies ; but how to carry out either of them he could not see. One was a sort of ideal which might be realized if things went very badly for Russia, or if France became

sufficiently ' warlikely.' [22] The result of his ' meditations '
during the early spring was a plan for the creation of an
independent Poland, corresponding generally in boundaries
with the Russian Poland which the treaties of 1815 had set
up, but perhaps acquiring Cracow from Austria, and
receiving an Austrian archduke for its sovereign. ' Such
a scheme,' he wrote, ' would be a security to Germany by
removing Russia from her advanced wedge on the Vistula
without putting France there in the place of Russia.'
There would, of course, be objections from the Poles and
from some of the Great Powers, but these could be adjusted
later on ! The project, as he saw it, would be perfectly
realizable—if France and England chose to fight. But as
the English, himself included, chose to do nothing of the
sort : and as they were especially anxious to keep France
from launching into hostilities by herself, this ' policy '
was nothing save provision for an unexpected and even
undesired eventuality. But, so perfectly did it accord with
all his principles of foreign policy, that Palmerston reverted
to it longingly throughout the year.

His less ambitious policy, the policy of Russell, of the
cabinet, and at times of France and Austria, was really not
much more realizable. Generally speaking, it called for
the suspension of all hostilities for the period of a year, and
the restoration to Poland of the constitutional status
enjoyed during the fifteen years which followed the conclusion of the Vienna settlement.[23] Just how the suspension
of hostilities was to be arranged between the enraged
Russian government and the headless mass of Polish
insurgents now fighting in some of Russia's only partially
Polish provinces ; or how the Tsar was to be persuaded to
revive an experiment which had failed so signally, Palmerston was unable to point out. Yet in persevering with this
plan he sacrificed a possible opportunity of bringing the
struggle in Poland to an early close, and securing some
amelioration of the ' poor Poles' ' lot.[24] His old sense for
the realities appears to have been deserting him.

Had the aged and embarrassed premier stopped at the
formulation of impracticable policies, no harm would have
been done. But, as Russell wrote the Queen, the ministers,

while innocent of any ' wish or intention to go to war for
Poland,' believed that a statement to this effect might
' give a license to the violence and murdering habits of the
Russian soldiery.' [25]   And the Palmerston of earlier days,
who still emerged at times, the Palmerston so full of sympathy for the underdog, of belief in England's mission, and
of the taste for popular applause, could not refrain from
expressing himself in the old way.   Hence the Guildhall
audience was called upon to witness Russian brutality ; the
Russian ambassador informed that his master should regard
the rebellion as an act of God, a direct punishment for
attempts to sow revolution in Turkey's north-eastern
provinces ;   and Victoria kept busy censoring drafts
designed to call the attention of the Russian government to
its obligations under the Vienna treaty of 1815, to its mis-
treatment of innocent Polish subjects, and to the British
government's ' indisputable right to interfere ' in any
manner which it might think proper.[26]   The Queen,
greatly alarmed, and as faithful to her dead husband's
methods as to his policies, attempted to undermine the
authority of the premier and foreign secretary within the
cabinet.[27]   But Gortchakov, apparently too well informed
to be disturbed, was content to repay the Foreign Office in
its own coin.   The only possible sufferers from the premier's
outbursts were the French emperor and the Poles, encouraged against their better judgment to hope for support
which no British minister had any thought of giving them.
    To review here all Palmerston's contributions to the
negotiations of 1863 concerning Poland would be impossible : but a good deal that is typical, both of his attitude
and of his difficulties, can be noted in one or two of the
earliest and latest episodes.   At the end of the third week
in February, the cabinet had to act upon a proposal of
Napoleon's that the French, Austrian, and British governments should protest jointly against Prussia's offer of
assistance to the Tsar through the medium of an identic
note.   The premier in talking to the Queen must have
adopted much the same tone he was to use at the Guildhall
later on ; for Victoria immediately complained of him to
Granville in the old manner ; and implored Granville's

help in securing the cabinet's rejection of the French
démarche. She had ' never been more alarmed about anything since God took her whole life and happiness ' ; for if
the plan were followed up there would be a ' French Army
on the Rhine before we could turn round.' [28] She might
have spared her fears. Palmerston, though ready to egg
on Napoleon to make such protests at St. Petersburg as
would break up his understanding with the Tsar, was as
anxious as the Queen herself to keep the French in leash
where Prussia was concerned. Believing that the French
policy was ' dictated by a desire to conciliate Catholic
support, and probably by ulterior plans of aggrandisement,'
he had twice shown himself (as Granville and Wood
assured their frightened sovereign) more cautious than
Russell about supporting French action at Berlin.[29] And
this was his comment to Russell on the cabinet's refusal to
adopt Napoleon's plan :

The French government are evidently much disappointed that
we have not fallen into the trap laid for us, and that we have not
joined them in laying the ground for an attack by France on the
Prussian Rhenish provinces.[30]

The words might easily have been Victoria's.

That Palmerston was as anxious to egg on Napoleon
at St. Petersburg as he was to restrain him at Berlin, seems
evident from other letters which he wrote early in the year.
On first news of the rising in Poland he found ' much to be
said ' against any ' formal representation to Russia,' feeling
that only through ' friendly and informal ' communication
could the lives and houses of the ' poor Poles ' be saved.[31]
That his policy changed, before the end of February, into
one of sharp and persistent official protests at St. Petersburg
is perhaps attributable mainly to his discovery that the House
of Commons was ' unanimously Polish,' and that in face of
public sentiment the ministry would not ' stand well ' if it
did not ' do something.' [32] But even in helping Russell
to exchange thrusts with Gortchakov he did not forget how
desirable it was to involve the French :

But we ought to play their [the French] game [of protesting at
Berlin] back upon them and urge them . . . to join us in making
a representation about Poland to the government of Russia.[33]

Unfortunately for his prospects of success, the French knew their own mind. When Russell, on March 2, sent to St. Petersburg a dry and almost intolerably didactic note, suggesting the revival of the ' congress ' Poland of 1815, Napoleon's ministers refused to have ' their game ' played ' back upon them.' In vain the Foreign Office urged them to co-operate.

As was the beginning, so in substance were the development and the end of Palmerston's connection with the Polish revolt. During the spring and summer, the British, French and Austrian governments, brought by divers reasons to a common policy, became insistent that Russia should grant an armistice and autonomy to the Poles, and consent to a consideration of the whole matter by the signatories of the Vienna settlement. All three sent notes in April, in June, and in August—but never conjointly. The French and British rôles became reversed. Napoleon grew as anxious for the sending of an identic note by the three Powers to the Tsar as he had been that they should send one to the Prussian king. But Palmerston, like his cabinet, would not hear of it.[34] Pressure so concerted and so threatening might lead to war. And, if French public opinion compelled Napoleon to send sharp notes, why should a British cabinet help to shelter him by sharing the impact of Alexander's wrath ? This policy may have made things harder for the French ministers ; but it did not make them easier for the British. They shared the snub administered by Gortchakov in declining to discuss the Polish question with any states other than Prussia and Austria ; and they were more affected than the French by the despatch of Russian warships to San Francisco and New York.[35] Moreover, it was for the two old ministers in Downing Street that Gortchakov reserved his sharpest thrusts. It was not pleasant for Palmerston to be told, even through Russell, that it would have been better to read the terms of the Vienna settlement before making them a basis for protest.

Yet the premier's attitude remained unchanged. Insults and snubs availed no more than had the sufferings of the Poles to move him from his settled determination to keep the peace. In the autumn, when Napoleon again urged action, and tension again became acute, he wrote Russell that England could not follow the French in another 'Moscow campaign.'[36] If war were near, as some have thought, it could have come only when the British public and their parliament had urged it upon their provocative but pacific premier. If Mérimée was justified in accusing the ministers of backing down, or Vitzthum in charging that they did not 'know their own minds,'[37] their chief was to no small extent responsible. And perhaps no one felt it more than the French emperor. For Napoleon, his entente with Russia gone, his government now urged ahead and now held back from Downing Street, his personal standing with the French impaired by his forced acceptance of rebuffs from Alexander and from Gortchakov, had lost nearly all his confidence in Palmerstonian diplomacy.

The last phase of Anglo-French negotiations regarding the Polish revolt of 1863 produced the gravest effects of all. Both governments were apparently to blame, the French for indiscretion, the British for brusquerie. At the beginning of November, the French emperor made two rash moves. To commence with, he sent out letters to the principal sovereigns of Europe, inviting their participation in a congress to be held at Paris for a general regulation of international affairs. If his proposal was startling, the language in which he justified it was still more so : ' the treaties of Vienna upon almost all points are destroyed, modified, misunderstood, menaced.'[38] His second step was similar but more spectacular. In the speech with which he opened the legislative session on November 5, he restated—this time for all the world to hear—his conviction that the settlement of 1815 was no longer in effect. And in one respect the speech grated especially on English ears ; for it stressed Napoleon's regret that the Polish question, in affecting his formerly cordial relations with the Tsar, had compromised '*l'une des premières alliances du Continent.*'[39] The Emperor's primary object was no doubt to reinstate himself at home.[40] His diplomatic move gave him the appearance of taking leadership in European politics, and might even gratify his subjects' insatiable longing for a rectification of French frontiers. But its repercussion in other countries was widespread and immediate. There was a panic on the

Vienna exchange, and Austrian securities fell alarmingly.[41] The sovereigns and statesmen of all the principal European governments save one concocted most gentle refusals of Napoleon's invitation to the congress.[42] The one and only government which seemed indifferent about offending the French emperor was that of Great Britain.

What makes this fact more striking is that Palmerston, as his private letters show,[43] was personally much in sympathy with Napoleon's project :

If there was any chance that a congress would give Moldo Wallachia to Austria and Venice and Rome to Italy, and incorporate Sleswig with Denmark, and separate the Poland of 1815 from Russia & make it an independent state not touching the question of the Rhine as a French frontier nor the relieving Russia of what was imposed on her by the Treaty of Paris such a congress would be a well-doer by Europe. . . .

But no such useful accomplishments could be expected ; for

. . . there would be France and Russia on one side, England and Austria on the other and the other states voting according to their views. . . .

With thirteen or fourteen participants in the congress, he doubted whether England could even ' get Spain to give up her slave trade or France to abide [by] & faithfully to execute her abandonment of that crime.' The only probable result would be that of ' recording, and making more irreconcilable, fundamental differences of interests and opinions.'

If Russell's official answer, despatched after two weeks' deliberation, had reflected only this spirit, there need have been no unfortunate results. But it reflected instead the premier's feeling that the French were ' always repudiating, and upon every occasion trying to get rid of ' the Treaty of Vienna, which was England's ' main security against encroachments by France.'[44] And it was couched in terms so abrupt as to constitute a savage snub :

It is the conviction of Her Majesty's Government that the main provisions of the treaty of 1815 are in full force . . . and that on those foundations rests the balance of power in Europe. . . . Her Majesty's

Government would feel more apprehension than confidence from
the Meeting of a Congress of Sovereigns and Ministers without fixed
objects, ranging over the map of Europe, and exciting hopes and
aspirations which they might find themselves unable either to gratify
or to quiet.[45]

'There will be no more talk now of the beneficent
Anglo-French alliance,' remarked one of the cabinet to
Vitzthum. That 'foolish catchword,' he decided com-
placently, was 'now put by in the lumber-room.'[46] And
this at a moment when England, coming more and more to
grips with Bismarck, stood in need of French support as
she had seldom done before.

Through all the anxious months of negotiations about
Poland, Palmerston had continued to find great satisfaction
in the part the French were playing in the affairs of Mexico.
The more Napoleon became involved there, the less likely
was he to make any warlike move near home. England's
best policy, then, according to her premier, was to reproach
him gently for the violation of the convention of October
1861, and at the same time to encourage him to carry the
violation to as successful a conclusion as possible. Such is
the clear meaning of the advice tendered the foreign secretary
on various occasions by his chief. Indeed, Palmerston
wrote Russell frankly that the French could go to any length,
for all he cared, provided that Mexico did not become a
French colony, and that England was in no way involved.[47]
He was gentle in turning aside the requests of Maximilian
for advice, and the suggestions of Maximilian's agents that
England should acknowledge the projected monarchy in
advance ;[48] but he dissented sharply when Russell proposed
to send a despatch to Austria, hinting that Maximilian
would be wiser to stay at home, and that Napoleon's proceedings were unjustifiable.[49] It was not only that a
Mexican monarchy 'would be a great advantage to all
European nations having commercial intercourse with
Mexico' :

> For my part though systematically and on national principle
jealous of the ambitious policy of France I feel no jealousy as to the
proceedings of France in Mexico. What she is doing there . . .

will have a tendency to fetter her action in Europe . . . for some years to come.[50]

And again :

. . . we think and have implied by our withdrawing that the Emperor has acted at variance with the principles . . . upon which the original expedition to Mexico by the three Powers was founded, but it would surely be an uncivil and an unfriendly act towards the Emperor to send to a third party without any particular reason and so late in the transaction this formal act of accusation.

He grew even more emphatic as his pen went on. What Russell was proposing was to give Napoleon not ' a slap in the face ' but ' a kick on the tender parts.'

Cautious as he was in dealing with the affairs of Poland and Mexico, the premier was no less discreet in his attitude toward the United States. To judge from his letters, Anglo-American relations had, indeed, ceased to mean very much to him. Perhaps this was in part because the question of mediation, which might have given England a chance to play a leading part in a settlement of worldwide significance, had practically disappeared, and minor issues concerning the observance of her neutrality had supervened. He seems to have accepted the change rather regretfully. Even after the Conservative leader, in the debate on the Address, had endorsed the government's non-intervention policy, Palmerston inquired of Russell whether it would be worth while suggesting that Switzerland, as ' a European Federal Republic,' should ' recommend to the North American contending republican states communication with each other with a view to pacification.'[51] But the project was still-born ; and the question of the year, in so far as the relations of England with ' the North American contending republican states ' was concerned, was as to whether the southerners should continue to secure war vessels from British shipyards. The *Alabama* and other southern commerce destroyers of British build had for some time been working havoc on northern shipping ; and Seward was determined that British shipbuilders should make no further contributions of any sort to the Confederacy's sea power. It was here that Palmerston's discretion was put to the test.

The test was a real one ; for his irritation with the Union government, the delicacy of the issues which it raised, and the attitude assumed by Seward, all tempted him to act brusquely.   He was as certain as ever that the North was merely waiting for victory before indulging its rancour towards the British government by an attack on Canada ; and he was exposed to the additional irritation of noting that Bright's group of radicals associated the support of the Union with the advocacy of more democratic institutions for the United Kingdom.   It was probably this irritation which drew from him his greatest lapse from discretion in this year where America was concerned—a statement in the House, on March 27, that the practice of American political parties in raising anti-British cries ' as a means of creating what in American language is called political " capital " ' had ' a great tendency to endanger friendly relations between the two countries.' [52]   In this irritated frame of mind he had to face the American demands : demands that the British government should resort to stricter enforcement, as against its own subjects, of a purely domestic statute, the Foreign Enlistment Act.   In fact, Seward was demanding that the act should be interpreted and enforced in a manner which the legal advisers of the Crown deemed unjustifiable.   Nor did he abstain from using what could be taken as veiled threats, such as the suggestion of commissioning privateers.

With all the exchanges between Seward and Lyons, and Adams and Russell, Palmerston had apparently little to do ; but he wrote and spoke at sufficient length to make his position clear.[53]   From beginning to end he gave his foreign secretary full support in preventing the South from securing the ironclad ' rams ' that were being built at Birkenhead.   No one stated more firmly than he the British case ; no one appreciated better the difficulty of meeting Seward's demands under the provisions of a law which gave the government no legal authority to act without proof of distinct intent to place vessels at the disposal of the Southern Confederacy.   But no one, perhaps, had a more thorough appreciation of two other elements in the case.   He pointed out with every emphasis that, in view of the damage which

American built cruisers might inflict on British commerce during the next war in which England became involved, the government, by allowing the Southerners to secure ironclads from British yards, had been playing ' a suicidal game.' And a ' far graver question ' was the virtual certainty that a continuation of this game would mean immediate war. He was anxious to avoid even ' a diplomatic wrangle with the Federals.' [54]   Hence he seized on every means for preventing the escape of any more *Alabamas* from English ports. He was quick to endorse the detention of the rams ; and, on reading the preliminary report of the law officers to the effect that the government had no lawful ground for doing this, equally quick to suggest that the vessels should be purchased for the Admiralty.   He caught at the reported arrival of Confederate sailors at Liverpool as evidence of intent that the rams were destined for the Confederacy. It is perhaps still more significant that, on September 5, he readily agreed to inform Seward confidentially ' that we are going to detain the ironclads at our own risk although there is some reason to suppose that they have been built upon an order not proceeding from and not connected with the Confederates.' [55]   He comforted himself somewhat with the reflection that England was behindhand in ironclads, and that the rams ' would be greatly useful for Channel service in the event of war, and would therefore tend to be peace keepers.' [56]   Yet such compliance went sadly against the grain.   How much so can be seen from a letter to Russell on September 22 :

I suggest an addition to the answer to Adams.   It seems to me that we cannot allow to remain unnoticed his repeated and I must say somewhat insolent threats of war.   We ought I think to say to him in civil terms ' You be damned ' and I endeavoured to express that sentiment to him in measured terms.[57]

Surely this irritated but cautious statesman was a new Palmerston.
    More of the old Palmerston was in evidence when the Foreign Office was dealing with old questions which related to England's direct and vital interests, such as that of the Suez Canal.   To the canal project he had always been

opposed ; and, since his return to office in 1859, the increasing probability that the French company, supported by
the French government, would succeed in carrying out
de Lesseps' scheme made him increasingly hostile. But
it was the growing tendency of some of his own compatriots
to favour the building of the canal which drew from him
the most definite and reasoned statement of his position
which is on record. *The Times*, in December 1859, had
approved the construction of the canal on the ground that
it would be essentially British, ' traversed by British ships,
devoted to British traffic, and maintained by British tolls.' [58]
The premier, marshalling his arguments in impressive
array, made them the basis for a reproachful letter to
Delane.[59] And it is notable that these same arguments
formed the substance of a Foreign Office memorandum,
undated and unsigned, but apparently composed about this
time, which set forth the ' *Insuperable Objections of Her
Majesty's Government to the Projected Suez Canal.*' [60] Clear
and specific as were the reasons for his attitude which
Palmerston gave Delane, the main point of his charge, the
point which he repeated for the sake of greater emphasis,
was a flat assertion that the French had conceived the whole
project 'in hostility to the interests and policy of England.'
The only ' authority ' which he could cite was a statement
from Émile Girardin, the most irresponsible of French
journalists ; but his conviction, conforming as it did to his
declared principle of being ' systematically and on national
principle jealous of the ambitious policy of France,' [61] was
undoubtedly sincere. Believing this, it was disturbing to
hear from his ambassador at Constantinople that the
Khedive was ' placing Egypt in the hands of France.' [62]
And then, of course, there was India to be thought of.

As regards Egypt, the arguments he gave Delane were
logical and even cogent, provided one could accept his
interpretation of certain essential facts. It was vitally
important for England to keep the French from establishing
a dominant influence on the Nile ; and this end could most
easily be attained if Egypt were to continue under Turkish
suzerainty. But the building of a canal which the French
could partially control would be the final step in opening

the way for Egypt's independence of Turkey and subjection to the French government. Already the great fortifications at Alexandria and other coastal points, fortifications constructed and to a large extent financed by Louis Napoleon's subjects, had made it difficult for Turks or non-French Christians to effect a landing on the north ; while ' a military work erected under the modest name of "a barrage for agricultural purposes " ' could be used to block an advance on Cairo from the Red Sea. And now de Lesseps' ' trench . . . three hundred feet wide and thirty feet deep . . . would be an impassable barrier to a Turkish force ' advancing on Egypt *via* Syria. Hence :

. . . the Pasha of Egypt for the time being would only have to choose his own time for throwing off all connection with the Sultan.

He was quite as emphatic with respect to India :

But if the canal could be made, it would open to the French in the event of war a short cut to India, while we should be obliged to go round the Cape. The first thing the French would do would be to send a force from Toulon or Algeria to seize the canal. An expedition, naval and military, would steam away through the canal to India, sweep our commerce, take our colonies, and perhaps seize and materially injure some of our Indian seaports, long before our reinforcements, naval and military, could arrive by long sea voyage ; and we might suffer in this way immense loss and damage.

His basic assumption that French fleets from Toulon or Algiers could seize the canal in time of war is not so difficult to understand when one remembers that this was the year 1860, a year when French naval armaments were giving England great uneasiness. And if his general suspicions of the French must be judged unjustifiable, surely French journalists who spoke of the piercing of the Isthmus of Suez as ' the defect in the British cuirass ' [63] were to some extent responsible. But his opposition was at this time based, not merely on the effects which the construction of the canal by a French company might be expected to produce, but upon a French demand for territorial concessions in the region where the canal was to be built :

Then comes in French influence. Part of the scheme is an extensive grant of land in Egypt for Mr. Lesseps's company, a wide

district on each side of the canal and a large district at right angles
to the canal from the canal to the Nile—a French colony in the heart
of Egypt.   It requires no great sagacity to see how in many ways
this would lead to constant interference by the French Government.

What Palmerston had combated from the first was not
the building of a Suez Canal, but of a French Suez Canal ;
and he was genuinely afraid that the building of the French
Suez Canal would lead to the creation of a French dependency
on the Nile.[64]   The fear of seeing the Mediterranean made
into a French lake was very common to English statesmen
of the earlier nineteenth century.

Palmerston's letter to Delane went on to pile up arguments : that ' the commercial advantage of the canal . . .
would be next to nothing ' ; that railways would make it
quite superfluous ; and that navigation in the Red Sea was
so difficult that vessels would incur no more expense in
going round the Cape.   Fantastic as they seem, the same
misstatements and the same *ad hoc* reasoning are to be found
in the letters of men who enjoyed much better opportunities
than the premier to know the truth.   Colquhoun, the
British consul at Alexandria, wrote in 1861 that the Egyptian
viceroy did not expect to see the canal completed within
the lifetime of any living individual ; that most Egyptians
disliked the project as the source of their government's
financial embarrassments ; and that nine-tenths of the better
informed among them saw ' that as a commercial undertaking
its value is nil.' [65]   From the British embassy at Paris came
news that Cowley, having interviewed Thouvenel, Napoleon's
foreign minister, believed him to be ' aware that . . . it
could never become what is vulgarly called a paying concern.' [66]   Bulwer, the British ambassador at Constantinople,
reporting early in 1863 on a tour of inspection which he
had made in the previous year, agreed with Palmerston that
the development of railroads had deprived all canals of any
great importance, and that the French would use de Lesseps'
project for political ends.[67]   Assured that he was following
a traditional policy which had brought him brilliant success
in 1840–1841, consumed by fears that his country would
suffer from Napoleon's ambitions and intrigues, and fortified with the misstatements and misjudgments of his agents,

the premier had, by 1863, been carrying on a continuous offensive against the canal project for four years.

As the offensive was conducted at London, Paris, Constantinople and Cairo, and sometimes simultaneously at all four,[68] it is impossible to do much more than indicate its general nature here. What Palmerston especially hoped, was to persuade the French to co-operate with England in seeing that the Sultan's rights in Egypt were upheld, and to withdraw all government support from the *Compagnie du canal de Suez*. Mere official disclaimers of political ambitions in Egypt would not suffice, since French subjects had ' by a great variety of complicated transactions so involved the Pasha in pecuniary difficulties and obligations ' as to raise ' grave doubts ' as to whether these transactions were not undertaken for political ends.[69] ' I should say . . .,' he wrote Russell, in December 1861, ' on the whole that it would be best . . . to leave this scheme as a commercial and engineering question to be settled by the result of experience in the money markets of Europe . . . all that we ask of the French government is not to interfere.' [70] But, considering the state of French public opinion and the amount of French money invested in the company, this was asking a good deal. Thouvenel countered by suggesting that the question of the canal's utility be passed on by a European commission ; and that, if its construction were approved, it should be closed by European guarantee to all warships. Palmerston was merely amused. France would almost certainly contrive that England should be outvoted in the commission, and as for the guarantee :

Thouvenel proposes indeed that the passage of ships of war should be forbidden as at the Dardanelles, but I presume he only expects us to receive such a proposal except [*sic*] with a decently suppressed smile. Of course the first week of a war between England and France would see 15 or 20,000 Frenchmen in possession of the canal. . . .[71]

There was nothing for it but to make his opposition effective at other points.

At Constantinople, Cairo and London he was not especially particular as to his choice of means. He allowed, if he did not instigate Russell, both to threaten the Sultan with the loss of British friendship if the canal project was carried through, and to suggest that the pasha of Egypt, having disposed of Egyptian funds without the authorization of his suzerain, might be deposed. The Sultan agreed at least to remonstrate ; but the Khedive, instead of yielding, promised another large subvention to the Suez Company. In 1862 he set out for a visit to the French and British capitals. At London he found the premier all friendliness. Not only did Palmerston suggest to the Queen that the Egyptian ruler should be invested with the Grand Cross of the Bath as a means of preventing him from becoming ' the instrument of French intrigue,' but that it should be sent to him at Cairo after he had returned there. For if conferred in England it might occasion him some embarrassment on his journey home through France, and might seem to have been bestowed ' merely as a compliment to a visitor.' [72] But to the great promoter of the canal Palmerston showed nothing but hostility. How bitter was his animosity, and how far he went in satisfying it, appears in a letter written to Borthwick of the *Morning Post* in 1860 :

> It is said that at a late meeting of the shareholders of the Suez Canal Company at Paris accounts of the Company were produced by which it appeared that a million of francs have been expended in the cost of the direction ; that of this sum 500,000 francs had been charged for the journeys of M. Lesseps, a further sum for furnishing his apartment at Paris, and 400,000 francs for the salaries of the members of the direction, consisting of M. Lesseps and one or two associates. There would be no harm in letting this be known.[73]

But, in spite of all, the canal project was flourishing at the beginning of 1863.

Then a gleam of hope came to the premier, when a new khedive, less ready than the old to make liberal concessions to the Suez Company, and more ready to submit to the direction of the Porte, succeeded to the Egyptian throne. Bulwer was prodigal of suggestions for drawing advantage from this happy change.[74] The Khedive might be persuaded to buy out the Company with money furnished by the Porte ; or, better still, the Porte might be led to insist that the Company should operate under restrictions fatal to its success. Russell gladly made some of these suggestions the basis for diplomatic action ; and the premier warmly sustained his ambassador and foreign minister.[75] Even in this year, when caution seemed the keynote of his policy, he appeared like his old self where Egypt was concerned :

> This is not a struggle for influence at Constantinople between the English and French ambassadors. It is a breaking out of that struggle which for more than half a century has been going on between England and France about Egypt. . . . We fought one round of this battle very successfully in 1840 & 1841.[76]

With the French ' much engaged in other quarters,' and dependent on British support, the time was ripe for contesting ' their scheme of getting hold of all the southern shore of the Mediterranean in order to make it practically a French lake and to shut us out of it.' [77] One thing was sure : England could not give way. But the days when he had triumphed by merely ' standing fast ' were gone. The French government was not really dependent on England ; nor had the Porte finished with its old policy of procrastination and of compromise. The sequel may be read sufficiently in Palmerston's words to Russell when Bulwer, a year later, asked for a peerage as reward for having solved the Egyptian question : " But alas, that question, that is to say its solution, recedes as we advance like the mirage in the desert.' [78] If de Lesseps by his excavations had unearthed the old Palmerston, the old seemed no more successful in Egypt than the new in Poland. Was his diplomatic career, then, to end in failure—that career which had so long seemed one of almost unbroken success ? The answer was to depend on the outcome of another great diplomatic question in which he had formerly won success, the question of Schleswig-Holstein.[79]

The re-emergence of this issue as a dangerous factor in European politics had been threatened for ten years. Ever since the Treaty of London and the other agreements of 1851–1852 had provided that the next king of Denmark should rule the duchies of Schleswig and Holstein

(Augustenburg having been persuaded to sell out his claims), and that their relations to one another and to the Danish monarchy should remain undisturbed, trouble had always been in the offing. For matters had in many respects gone on as though those arrangements had never seen the light. Denmark had not ceased to plan the separation of the duchies from one another, and the incorporation of Schleswig ; the duchies had not ceased to look for help from the German Confederation at Frankfort ; the Confederation had continued to threaten federal execution on the duchies' behalf, and the Prussians to contemplate action of their own. Since 1860, Russell had been attempting to prevent trouble, coached occasionally at least by the prime minister. But Palmerston, who had joked about the three masters of the question, one dead, one insane, and one who had forgotten it, now qualified only too well for the third. By 1860 he did not ' rightly know ' why federal execution impended, though he trusted, the Foreign Office did. The whole affair seemed to him ' more intricate than any sphynx's riddle, and more difficult to unravel than any Gordian knot.' [80] Bismarck, who called upon both him and Russell in the summer of 1862, is said to have found him so ignorant of essential facts regarding it that discussion was not worth while.[81]

At the end of March 1863 (it seems suggestive that this was the month of the marriage of Princess Alexandra of Glücksburg to the Prince of Wales), serious trouble, already barely averted more than once, became imminent again. The Danish government issued an ordinance, the ' March Patent,' which was obviously intended to pave the way for the separation of Schleswig from Holstein and its incorporation with Denmark. The Powers, deeply engrossed in the Polish question and in various difficulties of their own, were contented for the time being to reserve their rights. But, early in July, the German Diet denounced the March Patent as a violation of Denmark's promises, and threatened federal execution if Denmark did not take satisfactory action within six weeks. The stage was nicely set for the appearance of the old time Palmerston.

For what immediately ensued Palmerston was unques-

tionably, in some part at least, to blame. With all his old
time impulsiveness he charged into the affair. 'Both parties,'
he had admitted, early in the preceding year, appeared
to be 'somewhat in the wrong.'[82] But now the Danes,
whom he had once befriended, who had lately given a
princess to England and a king to Greece, and who had
set an example to greater Powers by protesting to Russia
against her treatment of the Poles, the Danes were being
bullied ; and who better than he, Palmerston, knew how to
bolster their courage ? A fortnight after the German Diet
had released its threat Palmerston answered it from his
place in parliament :

> I am satisfied with all reasonable men in Europe, including those
> in France and Russia, in desiring that the independence, the integrity,
> and the rights of Denmark may be maintained. We are convinced
> —I am convinced at least—that if any violent attempt were made to
> overthrow those rights and interfere with that independence those
> who made the attempt would find in the result that it would not be
> Denmark alone with which they would have to contend.[83]

The Danes, delighted with the speech, and with the receipt
of promises of support from Sweden and encouragement
from France, observed that the international situation
seemed to favour them. They saw that England was
linked with France and Austria, that Austria and Prussia
were very much at odds, and that the situation in Poland
was keeping all the great Powers much occupied. They
decided, then, that prudence could wait on opportunity.
Before August was out they had flatly refused the Diet's
demand. Early in October they received the ominous
news that federal execution had been voted by the Diet
and assigned to Hanover and Saxony ; but still they would
not pause. Confident of strong outside support, they drove
the Powers to action by framing a constitution which, by
virtually incorporating Schleswig, clearly violated the
settlement of 1852. By November this constitution lacked
only the royal signature.

Just at this time, when the status of the duchies had
once more become a matter of great international significance, fate decreed, most unfortunately for the Danes, that

the question of the succession to the duchies should arise as
well.   On November 15 the new constitution lay before
a new Danish king, Christian IX (the father of the Princess
of Wales), who had succeeded Frederick VII under the
treaty of 1852.   Christian of Augustenburg at once proceeded to renounce his claim to the succession in Schleswig-
Holstein in favour of his eldest son, Frederick.   His
promise that neither he nor his family would do anything to
disturb the succession of Christian IX in the duchies could
not apply to Frederick, he claimed, since Frederick had
been a minor when the promise was made !   The smaller
German states, snatching even at this excuse to detach
Schleswig-Holstein from the Danish monarchy, hailed
Frederick as ruler of the combined duchies.   When
Christian IX of Denmark signed the new constitution, all
the manifold issues of the Schleswig-Holstein question were
opened up again.   So were the domestic difficulties which
had confronted Palmerston a dozen years or so before.
While the English people, entranced by the beauty and
graciousness of the Princess of Wales, were more than ever
pro-Danish, the Queen, both from her habit of placing
exaggerated emphasis on the Prince Consort's views, and from
her attachment to her eldest daughter at Berlin, was more
militantly German than she had ever been.   With great
solemnity she submitted to the cabinet an ingenious but
unconvincing piece of reasoning by Baron Ernst Stockmar
to show that King Christian's claim to Holstein need not
be acknowledged by the Powers.[84]   And as solemnly she,
who had wished to see the Italians compelled by Austrian
troops to take back their old rulers, complained that ' *an
attempt to coerce the people of Holstein* to accept a Sovereign
imposed upon them by a Treaty, to which they were no
parties . . . would be too much like the principle on
which the old Holy Alliance acted.'   Was England ' to
dispose of people without their own consent ' ?[85]

It was under these conditions that Palmerston, old,
forgetful, cautious and rash by turns, advanced, arm-in-
arm with Russell, to his principal encounter with Bismarck.
Bismarck, too, was advancing, though by slow and careful
steps, and with his aims and methods carefully veiled.

From the first he saw the Schleswig-Holstein question as a field for exploitation ; and, with that opportunism which was one of the greatest of his gifts, altered his methods and enlarged his aims as opportunity arose. Of England, that country, as he wrote, which now always ran away from war and profited by having others pull her chestnuts from the fire, he had no fear. Its premier was an old and tooth-less lion, whose ' snarls and grimaces ' were scarce worthy of a thought. But England, if supported by allies, was not yet to be despised ; so England must be isolated in so far as possible. Fortune was kind to him. Early in November came Napoleon's spectacular pronouncement that the treaties of 1815 had lost all force, and inviting Europe to inaugurate at Paris a new order of things. Austria, growing panicky over the possible loss of Venetia, Galicia, or even Hungary ; fearful, too, of sacrificing her prestige in Germany if she allowed the Prussians to handle the question of Schleswig-Holstein alone, consented to become Prussia's partner in Prussia's dealings with the Danes. As for France, it needed only Russell's offensive answer to Napoleon's invitation to the international con-ference to bring the Emperor's disgust with England to a climax, and turn his thoughts from London and Vienna to Berlin and St. Petersburg. Two months before, he had refused to co-operate diplomatically with the British govern-ment, pointing out that, having through England's timidity received a rebuff from the Tsar about Poland, he could not afford to invite another from the Prussian king. Now he was more inclined to co-operate on the Prussian side. When Bismarck hinted at some possible satisfaction of France's eternal longing for territorial acquisitions to the east, the Emperor seemed ready to bargain away not merely Schleswig-Holstein but other territories adjacent to Prussia. Bismarck did not allow the discussions to become too definite : it was enough to keep France in play and isolate England.

Slowly and secretly, without taking even King William into his confidence, Bismarck developed his amazing strategy. He had need to proceed carefully. The king and crown prince of Prussia were all for the repudiation of

the treaty of 1852 and the acknowledgment of Augustenburg ; while Austria stood for adhesion to the arrangements of 1851–1852, and consequently for Christian IX's
succession in Schleswig-Holstein. But Bismarck, who was
commencing to see the possibility of securing the two
duchies for Prussia, found a way to manipulate the whole
question. The Diet could safely be supported in carrying
out the 'execution' in Holstein, since the duke of Holstein
was one of its members ; but its invasion of Schleswig
would be a violation of an international treaty, and would
invite intervention from the other Powers. Hence Bismarck decided to push the Austrian and Prussian troops
through the Diet's army of occupation in Holstein, and so
into Schleswig ; and he would do this on the pretext
that the Diet and Denmark must both be forced to recog-
nize the validity of the arrangements of 1851–1852. But
at the same time he would make Prussia's ultimate fidelity
to those arrangements conditional upon Denmark's giving
satisfaction to Prussia's own demands. Then, by presenting demands with which the Danes would not or could not
comply, he would free the Prussian government from her
treaty obligations of 1852 to Denmark and to all the other
signatories. With the London treaty thus torn up, and
Denmark crushed (and what could save Denmark, if the
intervention of France and England were held off ?) the
ultimate disposition of the duchies could be arranged
with reference to Prussian interests. Thus were his plans
developing when, at the year's end, the troops of the Confederation had just completed the occupation of Holstein.
He was immensely aided by the rash obstinacy of the Danes,
an obstinacy for which Palmerston was in part responsible.

Against the consummate craft and extraordinary good
luck of the great Prussian diplomat, Palmerston and Russell
were now pitting themselves. The old premier possessed
no conception of what the task involved. If he had ceased
to understand the situation which Bismarck was exploiting
so skilfully, he had not begun to understand Bismarck :

Bismarck is a man with whom one knows not how to deal
because his mind is inaccessible to those arguments & motives. which
ought to sway a man in his position. To tell him that if Prussia

goes to war with Denmark, France may probably side with Denmark and take the Rhenish provinces of Prussia would have no effect upon him ; because he said at Paris last year that France will and must have those Rhenish Provinces ; but that consideration might be usefully pressed upon the King of Prussia.[86]

It never occurred to him that Bismarck might exploit the territorial ambitions of the French for his own purposes. In his ignorance of the Prussian minister's activities, Palmerston believed that the British government could pursue a simple and straightforward policy.[87] What he worked for was peace, a literal enforcement of the treaty of 1852, and the fulfilment by Denmark of her promises, through the establishment of a ' parliamentary constitution of the three parts of the Danish monarchy.'[88] The main point for England was Danish integrity : for Denmark, like Turkey, commanded the entrance to a great inland sea :

. . . we have an interest in maintaining and keeping together the little monarchy which holds the keys of the Baltic and which is already weak enough.[89]

If Denmark, after every persuasion, should refuse to meet her obligations to Schleswig-Holstein, England would permit the Germans to inflict some chastisement ; but, as he saw it, the king of Denmark's possession of the duchies rested on an international treaty, which neither Danish bad faith nor even a Danish-German war could abrogate. To defend this treaty was England's right (though not her obligation) ; and to defend it was also to England's interest. Kiel, with its great strategic possibilities, should be ruled from Copenhagen, not from Frankfort or Berlin. But especially not from Frankfort. Palmerston's contempt for the minor German states, his disgust at their presumption in claiming to decide who should be sovereign of the duchies, knew no bounds—no bounds in expression certainly :

. . . but really it is the Duke of Devonshire's servants' hall assuming to decide who shall be the owner of a Derbyshire country gentleman's estate.[90]

To German nationalism as a force in European politics he still seemed blind.

Thus Palmerston, now leading, now following his foreign minister, resolved to set a limit to German action, whether of the Confederation or the two great German Powers. ' Interest' required it ; so too, he claimed, did ' honour,' since treaties both ancient and recent were involved. And other considerations were present in his mind : the prestige of England in having her say in all major developments on the continent, a manly preference for the underdog, and the need for response to John Bull's strong pro-Danish sentiment. Yet he hoped and expected to set limits to German action without war. His strongest card was, as he thought, France. He had feared for years that the French would use the Schleswig-Holstein imbroglio to keep the Germans occupied while France helped herself to the Rhine provinces.[91] Surely suspicion of this might check Bismarck :

> The Prussians ought not to be lulled into security by the grim repose of France on this question—she is only waiting to see Prussia fairly committed beyond the power of retreat, and then she will fall foul of Prussia with the approval of all honourable men.[92]

Little did he suspect the true import of France's ' grim repose.' Yet in some respects he saw clearly. Misapprehending many things, he perceived that Austria was the tool of Prussia, that her alliance with the Prussians would work to her undoing, and that her soundest course would lie in reconciliation with the Hungarians. He saw, apparently without understanding, the tendency toward the new grouping of the Powers. It was the immediate situation which baffled and eluded him. Through 1863 his suspicions were only half awake ; while his habitual self-confidence and optimism enabled him to place the best construction upon appearances. For all that, the close of the year found him sick, uneasy and irritated. It does not seem to have been mere love of banter that made him turn off Russell's New Year's wishes of happy returns by begging to be excused from the fulfilment of these courteous hopes. He pointed out that Christmas had brought him a bad cold, and New Year's day a severe attack of gout.   But these merely aggravated the discomfort he was commencing to suffer from the reports that German troops would probably invade Holstein, and his conviction that in such case Denmark would be entitled to England's 'active military and naval support.' [93]   And he had reason to be equally convinced that his sovereign and his cabinet did not agree with him.[94]

CHAPTER XXXIV

1864

THE first Lord Goschen, writing forty years after the event, has left a lively account of an interview with Palmerston, just before the opening of parliament in February 1864. Selected, as has been noted, to second the address, Goschen was summoned to receive instructions from the premier.

The old man's manner to me was one of extraordinary cordiality, and full of life. Instructing me as to the topics to be dealt with in the speech, he ran through the various points of foreign policy that required to be touched. . . . When he came to a stop as if he had finished his instructions, I asked him with becoming diffidence, ' What is to be said about domestic affairs and legislation ? ' ' Oh,' he gaily replied, rubbing his hands with an air of comfortable satisfaction, ' there is really nothing to be done. We cannot go on adding to the Statute Book *ad infinitum*. Perhaps we may have a little law reform, or bankruptcy reform ; but we cannot go on legislating for ever.' [1]

Quite consistent this, one feels at first, with the accepted picture of the rôle played by Palmerston as prime minister. Yet on second thoughts one sees that this disclaimer of interest in domestic matters was too complete and nonchalant to be genuine ; and wonders why Palmerston adopted such an attitude. To ascribe it to mere conservatism on his part is not enough. Few were the English statesmen of the Victorian period so conservative as to lack impulse to better the living and working conditions of the masses ; and who, remembering Palmerston's superabundant kindliness, and knowing anything of his brief activities at the Home Office, would rank him as one of them ? Perhaps a better explanation of his attitude can be deduced from his personality. Intense in all respects, he had engrossed himself during

most of his career in the work of the particular department
in his charge at the time. He had seemed to think
of little but army affairs, until diplomacy became his
opportunity, his passion, almost his very life. And then
he had set himself to the accomplishment of a multiplicity
of tasks, bound up in almost every case with the idea of
giving England prestige and power. Towards the end, he
had begun to be concerned regarding her security. Since
1855, when he became prime minister, the whole field of
government had been his. But in the supervening years
prosperity had made it very easy to go slowly with reform ;
while incessant developments on the continent and overseas
had kept the premier on the alert, lest England's glory or
her safety should suffer. A still greater man might perhaps
have done all he did, and have found impulse and energy
for reform besides : a younger man might have shown
greater diversity of interests. But in 1855 Palmerston was
already old, and therefore fixed in his preoccupations and
his views. Yet, with all this, one still suspects him of acting
a little when he talked to Goschen in February 1864. He
was old and frequently unwell ; but he was not deaf or
blind where public sentiment was concerned. The dinner
which he gave for Garibaldi in April seems evidence of
that.² He was certainly not deaf or blind enough to overlook the fact that domestic issues of the most vital sort, long
present in English politics but latterly obscured, were
coming rapidly to the front. It would seem that in this
very year he began to feel that parliamentary reform should
not much longer be postponed.³ But domestic issues did
not appear to him urgent, not nearly so urgent as the guarding of England's prestige and security. When parliament
assembled for the session of 1864, he was making a last
tragic effort to uphold England's prestige in connection
with the Schleswig-Holstein affair.

He had been in a state of great anxiety and irritation
concerning Schleswig-Holstein since New Year's day—
all the more, perhaps, because he had been confined to
Broadlands for almost a fortnight afterwards by a severe
attack of gout. Granville went down to consult him (and
of course to report the interview confidentially to the

Queen) ;[4] but that could not console him much for having to let the cabinet meet without him at such a time.   For now developments were crowding fast.   Prussia and Austria were demanding the revocation of the November constitution, and threatening an invasion of Holstein.   On January 16, Bismarck was to lay upon Denmark a condition impossible for her to meet, by demanding the abrogation of the constitution within forty-eight hours.   A dawning comprehension of the true situation was adding to Palmerston's distress of mind.   One can see from the letters and memoranda which he poured out during his days of helplessness that even while he was trying to persuade himself and others that Prussia and Austria were acting in good faith, dire suspicions and forebodings were assailing him.   The confusion of mind, the inconsistency of action, to which this internal conflict led him seem almost incredible.   On the one hand, he kept reiterating his belief that the whole matter had now ' become very simple if practically handled.'[5] All that seemed necessary was that Denmark should withdraw the November constitution, and that the troops of the German Confederation should restore Holstein to its rightful sovereign, Christian IX.   And doubtless Russell would be able to draw the signatories of 1852 together on this basis of settlement ; since Austria and Prussia would be only too glad to have support against the small German states.   The annals of diplomacy can scarcely furnish a more astonishing example of naïveté than is afforded in a letter sent by the premier to Russell on January 7 :

> Rechberg [the Austrian foreign minister] and Bismarck are both struggling in the torrent and crying out for help from some friendly hand.   Let us give it them.[6]

Yet, on the very next day, he was expressing himself in almost the opposite sense to Queen Victoria.[7]   Not content with denouncing as usual the ' violent ambition and restless bad faith ' of the smaller German states, he declared that Prussia had, in previously demanding the repeal of the November constitution by New Year's day, demanded what was impossible, thus ' setting up a mockery as an apology for an outrage.'   Moreover Prussia's motives were open to doubt. It was clear that if her troops seized Schleswig, as 'a material guarantee,' the resentment of the Danish people would make it difficult for the Danish government to meet Prussian demands :

> It is possible that the Germans see this and that it is with them a motive for action, as they evidently seek, not a settlement, but a quarrel. But, Schleswig once occupied by German troops, new and unjust demands would be made upon Denmark . . . and revolutionary movements would have been excited . . . under the shelter of the German troops.
>
> The Germans, that is to say the Prussians, would then be summoned to go out of Schleswig, the Constitution having been legally and constitutionally repealed and the original pretence for invasion having ceased. Prussia would refuse. . . .

For the moment he had apparently come near to penetrating Bismarck's scheme, nearer perhaps than did the Austrians. But his growing understanding of the situation was still obscured by Bismarck's cleverness in pretending to be a champion of the treaty. A few days later still, the premier wrote that Prussia and Austria had placed themselves on ' a dignified moral and political eminence ' by announcing, on January 14, the intention to occupy Schleswig as a material pledge that the arrangements of 1851–1852 would be upheld ![8] And even when he decided, within the next ten days, that Prussia was ' going into Sleswig in bad faith ' to get rid of treaties, and that Austria was being ' made a fool of ' by Bismarck,[9] there was nothing that he could do. This fact was perfectly well understood abroad, as a report of Apponyi, the Austrian ambassador, to his government shows :

> The key to the Premier's irritation is his impotence. He senses the fact that the direction of general policy is escaping him and that, in the isolation in which he finds himself, unable to count on any of the Great Powers and not even supported by the Queen and the majority of his colleagues, he can undertake nothing. . . .[10]

To say that he was ' not supported by the Queen ' was to understate the case in a manner almost ludicrous. Victoria was willing to admit that the actions of both the greater and the lesser German governments were open to much criticism ; but she was straining every nerve to prevent her government from giving assistance or encouragement of any description to the Danes. She was ready to ' make a stand,' to test the constitution itself, before she allowed her cabinet to take action that would endanger good relations with Prussia or even Austria. She could always find justification in pointing out that no English interests were concerned. Her determination created a very serious problem for those of her ministers who disagreed with her. It was hard to drive a cabinet against a widowed and nerve-wracked ' female Sovereign,' who dramatised herself into a person undergoing terrible tortures for the sake of righteousness ; and who demanded conformity to her policy in the name of chivalry as well as loyalty.[11]   To convert her was utterly impossible ; for her policy had become unalterably fixed along lines set by certain formulated beliefs and principles.   Her pathetic but somewhat morbid grief, and the encouragement offered by such confidants as Granville and General Grey, fed her determination to hold her ministers to the precepts contained in the great mass of political memoranda which Prince Albert had left behind.[12]   And enshrined in these was one article of faith, which the Queen placed before her daughter, the Crown Princess of Prussia, in this year :

> You and I have but one common object, which was beloved Papa's, viz. the prospering of our two countries, and a good and friendly understanding between them.   Let us therefore spare no pains to try and bring this about.[13]

And, at another time, she revealed herself more clearly still :

> With regard to this sad S. Holstein question, I can really speak with more thorough impartiality than anyone . . . my heart and sympathies are all German.   I condemn the Treaty of '52 completely, but once signed we cannot upset it without first trying (*not* by war) to maintain it, and this adored Papa would have felt and did feel, for all his efforts were directed only to the carrying out by the Danes of the promises made to Germany in '51 and '52.[14]

This was ' thorough impartiality' indeed !   Moreover, the conscientious Prince had died with two other obligations

THE QUEEN
1864

———— " May all love,
His love, unseen but felt, o'ershadow Thee."—*Tennyson.*

especially present in his mind : one calling for the control
and defeat of the aggressive designs of the French emperor,
and the other for the furtherance of German national unity
on the liberal principles of 1848. It is one of the many
ironies of the whole affair that the Queen believed herself
to be contributing as much to the fulfilment of the second
as to that of the first of these in giving Prussia support.
Slow as Palmerston was in discerning the real drift of
Bismarck's policy, he was not nearly so long nor so utterly
deceived as was his sovereign.[15]   That treachery should be
associated with the policy of a country ruled by honest
King William was to her unthinkable.   Her confidence
and her affection extended to Austria, and, in some respects
even more, to the smaller German states.   No one of the
minor German princes was more inveterately or actively
anti-Danish than her ' brother,' the duke of Coburg.
Hence, when her premier wrote sarcastically that ' the
Minor States of Germany ' possessed ' no exclusive privilege
of violence, injustice, perfidy, and wrong ' ; when he took
it upon himself to remind her that she was ' Sovereign of
Great Britain,'[16] he merely increased her determination to
fight the battle of the German princes.   And she had a
particular interest in the young Augustenburg as her near
relative by marriage and the dear friend of her Prussian
son-in-law.   Passionately desirous, then, of German success,
and seeing that this was certain if outside interference
could be warded off, the Queen set the limits of immediate
British action at efforts to induce the Danes to live up to
their obligations, and thus, as she thought, remove all
cause for war.   To make sure of carrying the cabinet with
her in this policy she contrived a sort of strait-jacket for
the Danes' two great defenders among her ministers,
Russell and Palmerston.

The strait-jacket was cut on quite familiar lines.
Victoria simply continued the practice of carrying on secret
intercourse with certain members of the cabinet, informing
herself of the views of individual ministers, and encouraging
resistance among them to their chief.[17]   ' Puss ' Granville,
actuated no doubt by what he considered the worthiest
motives, served her constantly in this ; and Wood lent

aid whenever it was required. It is impossible to say how much effect the Queen's tactics produced ; but since the cabinet was about equally divided during at least one major crisis,[18] she may have had a leading part in determining the final outcome. Certainly she was showered with congratulations and with thanks for her real or supposed success against her two principal advisers on diplomacy. And certainly there was a strange departure from the accepted practices of cabinet government in a letter she sent to Granville when these thanks were reaching her. Enclosing to Granville her correspondence with the duke of Coburg—correspondence which, under recognised practice, the premier and foreign secretary would have been the first or even the only members of the cabinet to see—she authorised Granville to mention its contents to ' any of his colleagues (excepting Lord Palmerston and Lord Russell) whom he thinks it useful to communicate them to ' ! [19]

Nor was Victoria content to limit the use of her royal influence to the cabinet. Realising that the Conservatives were more pro-Danish than the Liberals, she summoned Derby to confer with her just before parliament convened.[20] While she entreated his support for what was officially the cabinet's policy, she was in effect asking his help against Palmerston and Russell. To what degree Derby was influenced one can do no more than guess ; but Count Vitzthum, who had been appealing to the Conservative leader on his own account, has left a suggestive description of Derby's first speech on Schleswig-Holstein in the session of 1864 :

> Every one was awaiting with the keenest anxiety the debate on the Address, and the House of Lords was crowded when Lord Derby (Feb. 4) rose to make his three hours' speech. I stood on the steps of the throne, close by the front railing. It so chanced that Lord Palmerston, who had been fetched by the Duke of Argyll, was standing next to me, and thus I was able to watch the impression produced on the Prime Minister by the eloquence of his opponent. The House listened with breathless silence to Lord Derby's solemn admonitions on behalf of peace, in which he enlarged with statesmanlike tact and rare skill on the proposition that a war with Germany would be the gravest calamity to England. A perfect storm of applause

was the orator's reward.   Lord Palmerston left the House in evident
uneasiness.   His game was up.[21]

Moreover, in a third respect, and perhaps an even more
important one, the Queen fettered her prime minister.
The probable decision of the British government as to helping Denmark was a factor of the first importance in the
deliberations that were going on, and the decisions that
were being reached, in all the great continental capitals.
And to Bismarck, developing his game move by move as
he saw opportunity, confidential information concerning
Palmerston's and Russell's ability to have their way was an
asset of great worth.   Victoria, while protesting that she
had kept her views and her resolutions to herself, had,
as Palmerston complained, succeeded in ' spreading over
Germany the belief that she never would consent to be a
party to active measures in favour of Denmark.'[22]   It may
be that the indiscretions of some of her confidants were
greater than her own ;[23] but indirectly she herself gave
Bismarck, her ministers' great antagonist, an opportunity
to estimate and take advantage of Palmerston's and Russell's
helplessness.   Not only was her attitude a matter of common
knowledge, but it was evidently apparent in the letters
which she wrote to her outspoken daughter at Berlin.[24]

And of course there were other people in England who
had interest in restraining Palmerston.   Count Vitzthum,
for example, as minister from Saxony, did not confine his
attentions to Derby.   Making all proper deduction for
pride of authorship, the Count's activities as related by
himself were not only varied but probably fruitful.[25]   Like
Victoria, he divided his activities between the cabinet and the
Conservatives.   Selecting Villiers as the leader of the peace
party in the ministry, he not only plied him with arguments,
but supplied him with ammunition for use against the
premier.   He employed his persuasions on Disraeli as well
as on Derby (in his own judgment converting both of them) ;
and induced another member of the party to help him in
answering the very pro-Danish letters which Lord Robert
Cecil was sending to *The Times*.

That Palmerston was so aged, bewildered and hemmed
in, accounts in part for the sorry figure that he cut in

diplomatic circles during the late winter and the spring: but had he been at the height of all his powers, his position would have been difficult. He had no desire for war, knowing that England could not undertake to face the whole Germanic group of states alone, and that the only price at which French co-operation might be procurable ('compensation' on France's eastern frontier, and the danger of revolution in various regions of the continent) was far too high. Yet he and the government were committed, or at least believed to be, to some defence of the Treaty of London and of Danish integrity. To stand inactive would not only be to weaken further England's diminishing prestige, but to run counter to British public sentiment. Yet he could not assume that public sentiment would support him in a war. Sympathy with the Danes was strong ; so strong that the pacifists in parliament dared not upset the ministry ; so strong at certain moments of excitement as to arouse an actual desire for war. But it was far from certain, as the premier no doubt felt, that the English people would on deliberation care to spend money and lives where English interests were so remote. Clarendon was convinced that John Bull, though ' humiliated at seeing his little Danish friend mauled by the two big bullies ' would not ' risk a man or shilling for his defence.' [26] Torn constantly this way and that, alternately suspicious and credulous, bewildered and baffled at all times, Palmerston tried to satisfy himself, his public, and the Danes in the manner that had once been so effective and had become so obsolete. High words might still produce effects if they were backed by orders to the fleet. Hence, in the advances which he made toward definitive action (advances invariably defeated, and usually succeeded by recoils), the possible employment of the fleet was almost always a factor. His futile struggle may be observed at closer range in two or three specific episodes.

One of the first important episodes of this sort occurred around the middle of February, when the Prussians and Austrians, having made demands upon Denmark which it was impossible for her to satisfy, were overrunning Schleswig. Palmerston, while still insisting both in casual conversation and in public speeches that he had confidence in Prussia's honesty,[27] was virtually certain that his suspicions of Bismarck were justified. As he was pondering the various means by which some assistance might be given to the Danes, Russell put forward a proposal that England and France should offer mediation on the basis of the arrangements of 1852 ; and that refusal of this mediation by Prussia and Austria should be followed by the sending of a British squadron to the Baltic, and of a French army corps to the frontier of the Prussian Rhineland.[28] Victoria, on learning of this, wrote in an almost frenzied manner to Granville, suggesting that he might use her name to prevent her premier and foreign secretary from securing the cabinet's endorsement of so dangerous a step :

> Though the Queen said she would *not* declare her determination to prevent her subjects from being involved in war—recklessly and uselessly—Lord Granville is quite at liberty to make use of her opinion on this subject . . . when speaking to his colleagues.[29]

She further informed Granville that she would refuse to sanction Russell's proposal, even if his resignation should result.   But she had in point of fact no reason to be alarmed ; for Palmerston had immediately rejected Russell's plan.[30] He could not believe it to be ' at the present moment ' expedient ; for the appearance of England's fleet in the Baltic would make no impression on the Germans unless it was known to be a prelude to ' something more ' ; and he doubted whether active interference would yet be sanctioned by the country or by parliament.   Neither could he think it prudent to suggest to France an attack on Prussia's Rhenish provinces.   Granville, after seeing the two men, assured the Queen that while Russell did not want England to make war alone, Palmerston apparently had ' no wish to go to war at all.'   Wood gave her the same assurance, if anything more emphatically.[31]

But if Palmerston shrank from war, he was ready enough at times to risk using the fleet to save the Danes from utter humiliation and subjugation by their enemies. Rumours that had previously been current of the despatch of an Austrian squadron to the Baltic again became active at this time. The prime minister's views were set forth, on February 22, in a long letter to the Queen. It had seemed to Russell and to him, he wrote, that it would be disgraceful to allow an Austrian attack on Copenhagen or the island of Zealand, on which Copenhagen stood :

> . . . that England, the first and greatest Naval Power, should allow an Austrian fleet to sail by our shores, and go and conquer and occupy the island capital of a friendly Power, towards which we are bound by national interests and Treaty engagements, would be a national disgrace to which Viscount Palmerston, at least, never would stoop to be a party. It makes one's blood boil even to think of it ; and such an affront England, whether acting alone or with Allies, ought never to permit.[32]

There were practical reasons, too :

> If Denmark was to be dismembered, and part were to go to Germany and part to form a Scandinavian Kingdom, all Treaties might be thrown into the fire as waste paper, or used to wrap up cartridges, and English interests would be endangered by the keys of the Baltic being in the hands of one single Power and that Power [Sweden] ruled by a Sovereign by race and descent a Frenchman.

But even at the time when he was writing this letter, the immediate danger was over. Two days before, he had suggested to Russell that inquiry should be made from Austria as to whether the fleet or any part of it was being sent to northern Europe, and specifically whether it was to co-operate with the Austrian and Prussian armies there. On the same night Russell had telegraphed these questions to the Austrian government ; and the Austrians had hastened to reply that they had no intention of attacking Copenhagen or the island.[33] Incidentally, however, the episode had caused a fresh clash between Russell and the Queen. For Russell, before the Austrian disclaimers were received, and without authorization from the Queen or from the cabinet, had telegraphed to Paris and to St. Petersburg that England would send her fleet to the Danish capital, and hoped for the co-operation of the French and Russian governments. The fact that the cabinet, on the Queen's protest, condemned Russell's action as beyond his power, and as a step calculated to involve England in the war, did not improve the relations between Windsor and Downing Street.

But the most enlightening of the various episodes centred around Palmerston's well-known interview with Apponyi, the Austrian ambassador, on May 1.[34] At the end of April the representatives of all the states concerned were negotiating at London for a settlement of the whole dispute ; but an armistice had not yet been arranged, and an Austrian naval attack in the Baltic was still to be feared. On April 29, Russell had tried in vain to persuade the cabinet that a British squadron should go to the Baltic with orders to prevent any Austrian ships from entering, or that the Foreign Office might at least be allowed to demand assurances from the Austrian government. Palmerston, highly disgusted with the ' timidity and weakness ' of his colleagues, decided to ' make a notch off his own bat.' Confined though he was to a *chaise longue* by his old enemy the gout, he would show an example to his timorous colleagues.

The accounts given officially by the two statesmen of this interview reveal some interesting differences, but correspond well enough in general. They both relate that Palmerston, after laying stress on Austria's sins against Denmark, and on the great forbearance the British government had shown, went on to say that Austria must beware of sending ships into the Baltic to attack the Danes. Were England to tolerate such an insult, he, Palmerston, could not continue in office ; and, were he in or out, Austria by such action would risk war. Apponyi replied that none of this was new to him, and that, since his government quite realized that any Austrian vessels which entered the Baltic would probably be burned or expelled by an English fleet, the British ministers might rely upon Austria's common sense, as well as upon the assurances she had more than once given. So far the accounts agree. But, according to Apponyi, Palmerston proceeded to point out that Austria's assurances were good only for the time, and to ask what she would say to a request for a guarantee in writing to cover the period of the war. Apponyi, who had apparently been patience and suavity personified throughout the interview,

could not resist the opening thus offered him. Speaking
unofficially, of course, he suggested that his government's
reply would partially depend on the phrasing of the British
note, '*ces sortes de documens étant en général secs, impérieux et
peu faits pour provoquer une réponse amicale.*'

The interview, unofficial and without definite results,
had in itself no great political significance ; but Russell,
backed if not instigated by the prime minister, decided to
make use of it officially.[35]   The cabinet of April 29 had
compelled him to alter a despatch he was preparing for the
Austrian government, by leaving out a request for assurances
concerning the use of Austrian ships in the Baltic.   The
same thing happened on May 1, just after the Palmerston-
Apponyi interview, when the foreign secretary presented a
fresh draft.   But at this later cabinet the ministers had
listened to Palmerston's account of the interview without
protest ; and there had even been an expression of approval
from Clarendon.   Catching at this, Russell, through self-
deception or pure obstinacy, decided to send a second and
' most confidential ' despatch, describing the interview,
stating that Palmerston's position had been endorsed by
the cabinet, and giving instructions that written assurances
should be requested from the Austrian government.   But in
sending the drafts of the two despatches to the Queen, he
made the sad mistake of forgetting to put even ' confidential '
on the second one.   He had given Victoria a most welcome
opportunity.   But she had to proceed carefully.   She could
rely on Granville to bring the majority of the cabinet to
her aid ; but it was possible that victory would cost her
dear.   Popular sympathy with the Danes was at this moment
running high ; and the Queen was blamed for holding back
her ministers.   Should Palmerston resign on finding his
policy blocked again, the incoming government might be
more difficult to handle than the old.   But again Granville
proved his worth.   His certainty that Palmerston would
not resign encouraged the Queen to hold her course ; and
under his leadership the opposition section of the cabinet
soon called Russell to account.

Hence victory in this symptomatic though otherwise
quite trivial dispute lay as usual with Victoria.   In vain

Russell called on his fellow ministers to support or repudiate their chief, and threatened that repudiation would break up the government : in vain Palmerston suggested that Apponyi might straighten matters out by formal communication of the verbal assurances he had given in the famous interview. The ' two dreadful old men,' as Victoria called her two most internationally respected ministers, had been caught in what looked like an attempt to override the cabinet. And the cabinet, while allowing the despatch about the interview to be sent, deleted every phrase which lent it an official character, or carried the suggestion of a threat to Austria. Palmerston seems to have vented his outraged feelings on his sovereign. He wrote immediately to inform her of a growing impression that she had ' expressed personal opinions on the affairs of Denmark and Germany ' which had ' embarrassed the course of the Government.' With proper regard for the proprieties, he assured her of his personal belief that the impression was erroneous ; but he did not find it necessary to exculpate the persons who made up her entourage.[36] 'Pilgerstein,' the Queen wrote airily to King Leopold, was 'gouty, and extremely impertinent.'[37]

She could afford to take this tone ; for Palmerston and Russell, after months of effort in the face of every obstacle to use English sea power for Denmark's defence, saw the Danes go to their ruin. A conference at London decided that Christian IX, while giving up the rest of the duchies, should keep the northern and Danish portion of Schleswig. But the Danes proved obstinate about the fixing of their new southern frontier. There were fresh negotiations, and fresh struggles between the Queen and the ' two dreadful old men.' But Palmerston and Russell, successfully hemmed in, and more nervous than ever about Napoleon, were defeated on every proposal of action which they made. In the end, Prussia and Austria extinguished the last attempts at Danish resistance and dictated peace. But long before this happened, Victoria's day of triumph had come. Congratulations had flowed in on her from her English confidants, from King Leopold, and, more than all, from the German courts and German newspapers.[38] 'The King never misses an opportunity of saying how much he owes you,' wrote the Crown Princess of Prussia : ' Germany knows very well what it owes to your mild views and your firm will,' was the message of the duke of Coburg. Granville felt that the Queen had ' saved the country,' and General Grey that she could claim ' a principal share in the maintenance of peace.' She herself, while protesting that Prince Albert would never have allowed her policy and actions to be spoken of as separable from those of her ministers, admitted to her intimates her intense happiness in feeling that she had wrought good both for England and for Germany, and had carried out the Prince's wishes. Little did she foresee the time when she would complain that Granville, as her foreign minister, was ' weak ' and behaving ' miserably ' ; and when she would remind him that ' Lord Palmerston . . . with all his many faults, had the honour and power of his country strongly at heart.' [39] And little did she care that her old premier was drinking a cup of humiliation more bitter, one must think, than he had ever known. It was hard enough that all England and all Europe should know that he had had to eat his words ; but surely it was harder still that a majority of the Lords and nearly half the Commons should record by vote that England's position in Europe had been lowered through the policy of his government.

For, in early July, the opposition attempted to overthrow his government on these grounds, as expressed by identical resolutions in the two houses of parliament.[40] During the ten days which elapsed between Disraeli's announcement of the pending attack and the decisive vote, defeat seemed very possible, and a majority of four about the best that could be hoped. It was realised that the premier's ' known propensity to stand up for the honour of the country ' might still save him ; but every possible precaution had to be taken to avoid defeat. Hence, when it came to the debate, he was driven to defend his government on lines very different from those he would presumably have preferred. He stressed commercial and financial achievements which he had done little to further, and at times something to block : he even emphasised Denmark's faults, and the isolation in which England stood.

He was glad to avail himself of Gladstone's defence of his own incautious speech which had so encouraged the Danes a year before ; though only five months previously he had written bitterly of the chancellor's bad habit of forgetting his colleagues and ' following up his own views and opinions behind their backs,' in order that parliament might reduce the income tax and sugar duties at the cost of Denmark and of British influence.[41] At the end he was forced to rest the salvation of his government on the passage of a substitute resolution offered by Kinglake, a resolution expressing the satisfaction of the House in knowing that the Queen had ' been advised to abstain from armed interference in the War now going on. . . .'[42] No wonder Bernal Osborne jibed at him as ' about to achieve the most wonderful feat of his life,' since he was ' to go to the country as the apostle and minister of peace . . . supported by . . . the Member for Birmingham ' (Bright). But at least the ministry was sustained by a respectable majority. The Lords, indeed, condemned it by a majority of nine. But in the Commons some Conservatives, impressed, perhaps, by Gladstone's indignant complaint that the House was ' called upon to record, for the sake of displacing a Government, the degradation of the country,'[43] stayed away or voted with the Liberals. Hence, despite the fact that all the Irish voted with the Conservatives, Kinglake's resolution was carried by a majority of eighteen. However much Palmerston may have felt his humiliation, he seemed overjoyed at this outcome.[44] Though the division came at three in the morning, he forgot his gout, forgot he was almost eighty, and ' scrambled up a wearying staircase to the ladies' gallery ' to receive Lady Palmerston's congratulations and embrace. He was even reported as asking congratulations from some ladies in the lobby who had no idea of what was going on. After all, victory was victory ; and defeat at his age would have been irretrievable.

It was as well for Palmerston that the contest over the Disraeli and Kinglake resolutions constituted the one great parliamentary struggle of the year ; for he was at last failing quite perceptibly. The Queen had begged him to give up a projected visit to Osborne before the opening of the session,

lest colds and gout should handicap him in the management
of parliament ; and the Speaker's diary shows that there
were times when his gifts as a parliamentarian deserted
him :

> Within the last fortnight he has shown symptoms of failure.   He
> does not catch the point of questions, and when a question refers to
> two or three particulars, he does not keep them in his memory.   These
> failings are quite new to him.[45]

But his courage did not fail ; and, as the Speaker saw
soon afterwards, he could rally his faculties when sufficiently
aroused :

> Lord Palmerston laid on the Table papers relating to the con-
> ference, and to the affairs of Denmark and the Duchies.   He seemed
> quite strung up to the occasion ; there was no appearance of age or
> failure of any kind.   His voice was strong and clear.   The statement
> was excellent ; a better narrative of events could not have been
> given.   It was distinct and forcible : enough was said and not too
> much. . . . I was much struck with it, as a remarkable parliamentary
> performance.[46]

Worsted and humiliated as he had been, head of a
government which Clarendon referred to as 'a sinking
boat,'[47] he was ready to take up any challenge which the
Conservatives, or even the advanced Liberals, might offer.
    The leaders of this latter group had been decidedly
active during the late winter and early spring.   While
Palmerston was attempting to persuade not only Goschen
but the House that the statute book needed no additions
for the time, the apostles of the new liberalism were planning
what they would do when the Liberal party was, as Bright
put it, 'restored to life.'   They must have realised, of
course, that much of their programme would have to await
fulfilment until the reanimated party should rise, as a sort
of phœnix, from the old premier's and the old party's
funeral pyre ; but they were not willing to suspend all
operations in the meantime.   Great changes could not be
made of a sudden ; and while Palmerston persisted in out-
living his age, the prophets of the new day might, at any
rate, prepare the ground.   In the matter of finance, they
had already made decided gains and might hope for more

immediately. In 1863 Cecil had pictured them quite correctly as ' demanding to have the expenditure as well as the taxation remodelled according to their own ideal ' : in 1864 they were expanding their plans for attacks on the existing parliamentary system, on Irish land tenure, and even on the Irish church. A number of entries in Bright's diaries show how increasingly he and Cobden were establishing connections with Gladstone.[48]   Through February, March and April, one reads of private interviews between the three, interviews in which they planned fresh economies, the abolition of the income tax (as ' injurious in promoting extravagance ' because money was ' so easily raised by it '), and the substitution of house taxes and taxes on bequests. Moreover, the diaries represent Gladstone admitting that the government, and Palmerston in particular, had treated the people badly in throwing over parliamentary reform ; and agreeing that this issue, as well as the regulation of Irish land tenure and the Irish church, must soon be faced. But an entry of Bright's which makes no reference to any particular issue seems, in some respects, the most significant of all. For March 3 :

> Received this morning invitation from Lord Russell to dinner for the 12th. Since his abandonment of cause of Reform, have not had any intercourse with him, and since his acceptance of a peerage have not even seen him except once or twice in the House of Lords.

One cannot, of course, do more than speculate ; but there is a strong suggestion that Russell feared to ' rest and be thankful ' over long, lest he should find himself resting on the funeral pyre. Whether Palmerston knew of the invitation history does not seem ready to disclose.

For all Bright's and Cobden's private discussions with Gladstone on the subject of finance, no especial effort to realise the advanced Liberals' plans concerning it was made in connection with the budget voted in 1864. The chancellor seems to have adopted a Fabian policy, preferring to postpone his attack until arrangements for the budget of 1865 were taken up. For a general election in the summer of 1865 would be unavoidable ; and its imminence might be expected to wring from the premier some valuable concessions to advanced Liberal sentiment. During the late autumn and the winter of 1863–64 premier and chancellor skirmished as usual over the necessity for the existing scale of expenditure, and compromised as usual on reductions which produced a favourable impression on the House but were, in fact, nominal. The whole matter might have been disposed of with perfect good feeling and tranquillity if Palmerston had not shown his persisting suspicion that the seemingly complaisant chancellor was given to inciting both the House of Commons and the public to resist the official policy of the government. In June he admonished Gladstone in familiar terms : it was ' undesirable that a Member of the Government should advise the House of Commons to object to, or try to reduce ' estimates which the government had proposed, or that he should ' Endeavour to excite Agitation out of Doors ' in order to bring pressure to bear on both government and parliament. Gladstone pointed out in gentlest terms that he had contented himself ' with pointing to future retrenchment ' ; but he frankly warned the premier that he could ' give no pledge of indefinitely prolonged acquiescence in the present scale of expenditure.' [49] The little encounter, almost meaningless in itself, had not been forgotten by the chancellor, at least, when real hostilities concerning finances were opened in the fall.

But even before this the great champions of the two extremes of Liberalism had clashed sharply on quite other grounds. For, on May 11, Gladstone accidentally ' set the Thames on fire ' by making what was interpreted as a declaration in favour of manhood suffrage. It was a very surprising affair all through ; for Gladstone's confession of faith went far beyond anything expected by Palmerston, and its effect far beyond anything anticipated by Gladstone himself. And yet Palmerston had had his fears before the event. The date was that set for the second reading of an independent bill to give the franchise to all £6 occupiers in the boroughs ; and the premier was so far doubtful of the chancellor's discretion as to request him beforehand not to give pledges concerning any future alteration in the suffrage. [50] He took the opportunity to re-state some of his own views. He was quite ready to admit that many of the working men were as fit to vote as many of the enfranchised ' Ten Pounders ' ; but to ' open the Door to the Class ' was to risk allowing the workmen to ' swamp the Classes above them.' The extent to which they were coming under the control of the trades unions, ' directed by a small Number of directing Agitators ' accentuated the risk.

Judging from Gladstone's speech in its totality,[51] his views concerning the practical aspects of the question were not so different from his chief's as one might have supposed. Though he announced his conviction that the workmen would not act as a class in politics, he declared himself opposed for the time being at least to any ' sudden and sweeping measure ' :

. . . if, for example, instead of adopting a measure which would raise the proportion of working men in the town constituencies to one-third, you gave the franchise to two-thirds, . . . there might then be some temptation to set up class interests . . . to grasp at a monopoly of power. . . .

On the whole, he was ready to take his stand on the provisions of the bill which parliament had allowed to die four years before. Concerning statements such as these the premier had little occasion for complaint : but there were two parts of the chancellor's speech against which he protested vigorously. In one, Gladstone described an interview which he had had with a delegation of London working men, who complained of parliament's apathy regarding the extension of the franchise. He had told them that this apathy was ' connected in no small degree with the apparent inaction, and alleged indifference, of the working classes themselves.' To use such language to the working men, wrote Palmerston, was ' to exhort them to set on Foot an Agitation for Parliamentary Reform.' [52] But what roused the premier and all England most was Gladstone's enunciation of a principle :

I venture to say that every man who is not presumably incapacitated by some consideration of personal unfitness or of political danger is morally entitled to come within the pale of the Constitution.

By an outraged Palmerston, by a shocked Disraeli and by an enchanted group of radicals alike, these words were naturally taken as a confession of belief in manhood suffrage. In vain Gladstone protested that his speech was bringing him undeserved praise and blame, and that it should be judged only as a whole. His chief bluntly informed him that it was ' more like the Sort of Speech with which Bright would have introduced the Reform Bill which he would like to propose than the Sort of Speech which might have been expected from the Treasury Bench in the present State of Things.' [53] But Gladstone, if self-exculpatory, was not penitent ; and he warned the premier that he favoured not only parliamentary reform but propaganda in its behalf.[54] He had ' no desire to force the question forward ' ; but,

such influence as argument and statement without profession of political intentions can exercise upon the public mind, I heartily desire to see exercised in favour of an extension of the franchise. . . .

Palmerston, before the year was out, was to find to his cost that argument and statement had already produced a very decided ' influence . . . upon the public mind.'

The realisation came to him in the course of a long series of public appearances at festivities of various sorts (acrobatic performances Clarendon would doubtless have called many of them) which he made during the summer and the early autumn months. At first these were scattered, and of a sort to have occasioned no remark had they been made by a younger and healthier prime minister. It was natural to find him in June at Cambridge, as one of the notables who attended commemoration in the train of the Prince and Princess of Wales, receiving an honorary degree and an ovation from the undergraduates. It was natural to find him attending the speech day exercises at Harrow ; but only of an octogenarian possessing extraordinary vitality could it be told that he had ridden within an hour the twelve miles between his town house and the school. And, with the rising of parliament on July 29 he embarked on a whole series of appearances, undertaken, as he blandly told the Queen, for political purposes. It was possibly

a realisation of how sorry a figure he had cut in connection
with Schleswig-Holstein which drove him to exertions for
which he could so ill afford the strength ; but his main
desire may easily have been to fortify himself and the
institutions for which he stood against the growing activity
of the advanced Liberals.   One of his appearances, as will
be seen, bore the appearance of a challenge to ' Cobden,
Bright and Co.'

The first of these later appearances offered no challenge
to anyone, and was undertaken without delay.   Hardly
had parliament been prorogued when the premier set out
from Euston in a special train for Towcester in North-
amptonshire, to support Lady Palmerston in turning the
first sod for a new railroad line.   His lady acquitted herself
with silver spade and silver-mounted wheelbarrow to the
great satisfaction of the crowd ; but it lay with the premier
to make the principal address.[55]   He had a little to say
concerning the functions of fleet and army in producing
that condition of security within which railroads could be
profitably run ; but he talked principally as a practical
economist, discussing wages, prices, and the happy effects
of better transportation facilities.   The familiar homeliness
and kindliness appeared as he reminded his audience of the
days of ' the old broad-wheeled waggon with its six horses,
all with docked tails, wincing in agony at the bite of the
flies, and in vain seeking relief from the little bit of net that
covered them.'   And he was very witty in pointing out the
connection between the proximity of railroads to large
country houses and the frequency with which invitations
to these houses were accepted or refused.   Everything,
in fact, went happily.

But it was different when, a week later, he went to
Bradford, to lay the cornerstone for a new exchange.   For
Bradford lay in the bustling industrial and commercial
district of the west riding of Yorkshire, in a district, therefore,
where the names of Bright and Cobden were household
words.   Moreover, before his visit, a disagreement concerning it had broken out between the enfranchised employers
and the generally disfranchised employees.   At a working
men's meeting, objection was raised to Palmerston's being

honoured by the town, on the double ground that he had
done nothing for commerce, and had played false to his
undertakings of 1859 in the matter of parliamentary reform.
It was decided that the working men should receive him in
stony silence, and that he should be presented with an
address, stigmatising him as 'the greatest obstruction to
every measure of Reform,' and the promoter of 'extravagance
at home and jealousies abroad.'[56]   When the authorities,
despite some toning down of the address, still refused its
authors any opportunity of presenting it, fresh bitterness
ensued.   As George Holyoake (the 'Agitator'), then editor
of a working men's paper at Bradford and a strong supporter
of the address, pointed out, the authorities had done the
worst possible service to Palmerston :

> Nothing would have pleased him better than to have met a working-
> class deputation.   His personal heartiness, his invincible temper, his
> humour and ready wit would have captivated the working men,
> and sent them away enthusiastic, although without anything to be
> enthusiastic about.[57]

As it was, their hostility was public property.   Unless
Palmerston was singularly out of touch even with the London
press, it must have required a good deal of resolution on his
part to meet the engagement.   It was noted that even on
his arrival he seemed fatigued.

   Whatever one's feelings may be about the grievances
of the working men, it is impossible not to feel a good deal
of sympathy with England's now failing and rather damaged
favourite in connection with what ensued.   After all he
believed, and in many respects had every reason to believe,
that he had deserved well of his countrymen.   At the
beginning things went well enough.   The appropriate flags
and mottoes were all in place ; the appropriate homage of
magnates, territorial and industrial, was duly paid.   And,
though Holyoake claims to have been informed by W. E.
Forster, the Quaker M.P. for Bradford, that Palmerston
was ' " touched and pained " at standing as it were alone
in that vast and voiceless crowd ' which filled the streets,[58]
there is evidence for believing that the working men found
the premier rather irresistible after all.   But when one reads

the accounts of the speech-making which followed the parade, one is a little reminded of those humiliating July days which Palmerston had endured in the House. Even the official address expressed thanks to him, not for those achievements of which he was so proud, but for the Cobden treaty and the connection of the English with the French. Bending, as he had now learned to do, he accepted these rather doubtful compliments and almost pleaded for applause :

> I know that I am welcome here (cheers) and I know how warm-hearted the hearts of Yorkshiremen are,—how kind they are to those whom they have invited, and how disposed they are to show the warmth of their feelings by the strong outward demonstration of their voices (cheers).[59]

This reception, he assured them (perhaps trying to assure himself), was the warmest that the county had ever given him. For the rest, he took as his text the official address. Of Jupiter Anglicanus there seemed to be no trace.

But the worst, by far the worst, came at the ensuing banquet, where Palmerston, Forster and Sir F. Crossley, a county M.P., addressed a gathering of four thousand, drawn from Bradford and the surrounding towns.[60] On this occasion the premier ventured to boast a little of the security he had given England ; but he was careful to claim approbation for the ministry on the ground of its having kept the peace, and to remind his hearers of his own devotion to free trade :

> Every class which is protected puts on its nightcap and goes to sleep (cheers and laughter) and it requires that which the schoolboys call ' the cold pig,' the application of competition, to stimulate the energies of the man and make him bestir himself.

On the other hand, he did not mention parliamentary reform. When Forster rose the omission was soon supplied :

> The people of Bradford had extreme opinions ; . . . the noble lord must conclude from their conduct and from the reception he had met with that the people of Bradford had abandoned those opinions . . . their forbearance must be taken as a proof not that they did not desire their political privileges, not that they were not worthy of them (cheers).

His constituents, he went on, were grateful that the
ministry had kept England at peace ; for England's honour
and interests had not been involved ; and

this result, he trusted, would be a lesson to the noble lord and the world
at large that we must interfere less in foreign affairs and mind our
business for the future.

Crossley was more offensive still.   He had often heard
the premier speak, but on some occasions with great pain :

. . . he meant on those occasions when the noble lord had given the
cold shoulder to political and ecclesiastical reforms.   (Loud cheers,
with some hisses.)   He mentioned this because meetings had been
held in the borough of the unenfranchised classes to consider in what
manner they ought to receive the noble lord and the decision which
some wished to come to was to receive him with profound silence (cheers
and laughter).   The noble lord would not misconstrue the cheers
with which he had been received, for those who were to have kept
silence were the loudest in their hurrahs. . . . The noble lord had
now seen the working men of Bradford face to face . . . he (Sir F.
Crossley) trusted that when he returned to London he would go to
his right hon. colleague, Mr. Gladstone, and tell him that he had not
made so great a mistake as he thought he had when he made his
Reform speech (loud cheers).

Had Forster and Crossley forgotten that they were
speaking, not in the House, but at a festival ; that they
were publicly humiliating, not only their supposed leader,
but a very aged and distinguished guest ?   Their speeches
constituted a peculiarly distressing example of the kind of
taste not infrequently exhibited by some of the reformers of
those days.   But, apart from considerations of manners,
the whole affair at Bradford seemed a portent that the day
of jaunty, sporting aristocrats as political leaders was passing
or had passed.

One wonders whether this experience at Bradford had
any connection with Palmerston's announcement that he
would attend the races at Tiverton a fortnight afterwards.
He had not been there for several years, and the experience
was bound to be rather an exhausting one.   For of course
a banquet was at once arranged, and some speaking was
inevitable.   But at Tiverton he was sure of a relatively

sympathetic audience.   Perhaps that was why he appeared
to be in excellent health and spirits when he arrived.   Once
again an enthusiastic crowd cheered the familiar figure in
the window of the ' Three Tuns,' though it was a figure
very different from that to which they had been accustomed
in early days :

> . . . an old man with a genial cheery smile playing over his
> furrowed features.   His dress was very plain and peculiar, consisting
> of a somewhat rusty green ' swallow tail ' coat ; a check neckerchief
> tied stiffly and in ample folds round his neck ; coarse striped trousers
> and a white hat very much the worse for wear—all that was left of
> the once ' gay Pam.'   Few and pleasant were the words which he
> addressed to his eager audience. . . .[61]

But the attention of the country centred on his speech
to the select company assembled at the banquet.   The preliminaries were encouraging.   For while at Bradford some
of the dissenters had joined the agitation against him on
account of his attitude on such matters as church rates, his
dissenting constituents at Tiverton came forward to thank
him, in the name of all denominations, for the church
appointments he had made.   Thus heartened, he seemed
almost himself again.   True, he laid great emphasis on his
success in preserving peace ; but he made no secret of
his sympathy for the Poles and his regret at having been
powerless to assist the Danes :

> I am sure every Englishman who has a heart in his breast and
> a feeling of justice in his mind sympathises with those unfortunate
> Danes (cheers) and wishes that this country could have been able to
> draw the sword successfully in their defence (continued cheers).[62]

With some references to the advantages of economic
liberalism (for Tiverton had its industrial and commercial
interests, too) the speech came to rather a tame end.   But
not the visit.   Next day Palmerston was on the race-course,
' watching the races with the keenness and zest of youth ' ;
and the race dinner found him in delightful form.   His
hearers were treated to a comparison between the House of
Commons and a race-course :

> Our rules are somewhat similar to those which guide the turf
> because there is that good feeling in the House of Commons which
> gives weight for age.[63]

Even during a parliamentary recess he did not forget
to be a skilful parliamentarian.

The premier's ' acrobatics ' stretched on into September.
Toward the beginning he went to Herefordshire to speak
at the dedication of a monument to Cornewall Lewis, to
pronounce, as *The Times* put it, ' a panegyric over the ashes
of his best and most valued friend.' [64]   Before the month
was out he visited Wilton Park, the earl of Pembroke's seat
and Sidney Herbert's old home, to preside at the annual
meeting of the Wilts Volunteers.   This gave him an
opportunity for making a speech after his own heart—for
pointing out that no nation had ever witnessed ' a nobler
display of national feeling, of sagacious patriotism, and of
persevering courage ' than that offered to England by her
volunteers.

Before parliament would meet again there remained
four months—months which he might have used to obtain
some rest : instead, he employed no small portion of them in
seeking to provide for his country's security.   He celebrated his eightieth birthday by leaving Broadlands in the
morning at half-past eight, proceeding by train to the south
coast, and inspecting coast fortifications on horseback and
on foot till late in the afternoon.   But his main exertions
in rendering England safe were made in carrying on an
epistolary duel with Gladstone.   And the word ' exertions '
is not lightly used.   Letters of such length, such vigour
and such clarity as those in which he carried on the fight
would have made demands upon the energy of a young and
vigorous man.   There is no question that they made demands upon the energy of the recipient.   ' This *sort* of
controversy keeps the nerves too highly strung,' wrote
Gladstone to his wife.   ' I am more afraid of running away
than of holding my ground.' [65]

The chancellor, who, as it will be remembered, had
avoided any conflict in the preceding spring, opened the
contest early in October by suggesting immediate consideration of the general bases on which he should frame his
estimates for the coming financial year.[66]   In his view
' public opinion, especially the inclination of the public
mind with respect to foreign policy . . . the general

interests of the nation, and the narrower but equally clear interests of the Government and its party ' all required a diminution of military and naval expenditure. Moreover, he, as the minister sharing with the premier the main responsibility in all matters of finance, could not feel that the existing annual rate of expenditure (amounting to some £26,000,000) was justified. In the first place, it was higher than the amount voted by the Conservatives for 1858. Nor could he forget that after the House had passed a measure favouring retrenchment in 1862, and ' ostensible ' reductions to the extent of two millions had been made, the premier had himself ' indicated a course of gradual retrenchment as the interests and circumstances of the country might permit.' But the figures since that time had been practically stationary. In view especially of the general election to be held in 1865, he regarded further reduction as a ' necessity.'

After an interval of two weeks ' a pamphlet letter ' from the premier reached Hawarden.[67] It remains among the most Palmerstonian of surviving documents. After paying his compliments to the ' Clap Trap Motions ' in favour of economy likely to be made in parliament by men who would ' imagine by such means to serve their personal Interests with the Constituents they represent,' the premier turned to deal with Gladstone's objection to expenditure greater than that of 1858. Just how would the chancellor show that ' the Establishments of that year were fully sufficient for all the Risks and Chances of that Time,' or that existing circumstances were identical with those of that year ?

Such a Mode of arguing, if argument it can be called, has no Limit in its application. Why stop at 1858–1859 ? Why not go back to 1835 ? or as old Joseph Hume used to do to 1792 ? The only rational, and statesmanlike way of dealing with these Matters, is to look carefully at the Posture of affairs in the World at the present Time. . . .

As for Gladstone's assumption that the existing figure was intrinsically too large, he would like to know what was ' the necessary and inherent Connexion between any arithmetical Sum, and the wants of the various Services of a great Nation ? ' Gladstone was returning to Hume's ' Fallacy,' that a nation like an individual should fit expenditure to income, instead of realising that adjustment should be the other way. No, he, Palmerston, could not consider reduction possible. With the improvements in armaments effected through scientific discovery, with the advances in comfort and sanitation which England's soldiers and sailors should share with all classes of civilians, it would be natural that the army and navy should cost more year by year. Had not the cost of battleships more than doubled through the use of steam and of armour plate ? Did not an Enfield or Whitworth rifle cost more than a Brown Bess ? With regard to personnel, some reduction in that of the army might prove possible ; but was it prudent to weaken the navy in the existing state of international affairs ? As for public sentiment, what he observed was 'a steady Determination that the Country shall be placed and kept in an efficient Condition of Defence.' How else account for 'the zealous and persevering Devotion of Time and Money' on the part of 170,000 volunteers ? 'It seems to me that this Conclusion is as demonstrable as any Proposition in Euclid.'

In spite of the pamphlet letter, or possibly a little because of it, the chancellor hardened his heart, and answered 'in a rather decisive tone.'[68] He could agree with the premier neither as to existing dangers nor as to public apprehensions concerning non-existing ones. He believed that a high rate of expenditure was maintained, not in response to public sentiment, but on account of Palmerston's personal popularity. Reverting to the subject of their correspondence in the preceding spring (to which Palmerston had made no reference at all), he felt it necessary to point out that he had been able to retain office only on condition of being able to refer 'to the hope and the possibility of prospective reduction' in the estimates. In fact, the question with him had not been that of saying what he had said or saying less, but 'between saying it and saying, or doing, more.' The premier had proposed a cabinet meeting to discuss the various heads of estimates. But his (Gladstone's) aim could not be achieved by the whittling of estimates. He demanded that retrenchment should be agreed upon in advance.

It was when this 'rather decisive' letter had been digested at Broadlands that the storm really broke. The premier's answer must be read to be appreciated, but two passages will give at least the flavour of the whole :

. . . if I rightly understand the Drift and Statements of your Letter, you are disposed to propound a Theory which would hardly be consistent with the Position of the Constitution ; that is to say that a Chancellor of the Exchequer . . . is . . . to be entitled . . . to come to an arbitrary Conclusion as to the proper amount of our Naval and Military Establishments : and to impose his Will upon the Government of which he is a Member, upon the Plea that his Honour requires that his opinions whatever they may be, should be blindly adopted, under Pain of those Consequences which his Colleagues . . . would be very sorry to be compelled to accept. To justify such a Theory the Chancellor of the Exchequer ought to add to a Supreme Control at Home a Command over all those Transactions and Schemes of Policy of the other Nations and Governments of the World upon which our Course must from Time to Time necessarily depend.[69]

At the end came a sort of peroration of unusual magnificence :

You say that you think that it has been my personal Popularity, and not the Conviction or Desire of the Nation that has kept up the Estimates at their present Amount. In this it appears to me that you misplace Cause and Effect. This British Nation is not one that would be disposed to bear unnecessary Burthens out of Regard for any individual Man ; and if I have in any Degree been fortunate enough to have obtained some Share of the Good will and Confidence of my Fellow-Countrymen, it has been because I have rightly understood the Feelings and Opinions of the Nation, and because they think that I have, as far as any Scope of Action of Mine was concerned, endeavoured to maintain the Dignity and to uphold the Interests of the Country abroad, and to provide for its security at Home. You may depend upon it that any Degree of Popularity that is worth having can be obtained only by such means and of that Popularity I sincerely wish you the most ample share.

This letter seems to have been written from Palmerston's very soul. For all his great appreciation of the value to the government of Gladstone and his speeches,[70] for all the fact that a break between them would almost indubitably mean that his own last days would be days of defeat and obscurity,

he still judged it better to risk losing Gladstone than to risk
England's security.   And his conclusion, for all its grandi-
osity, contains what his life had shown to be a real confession
of faith.   Perhaps it was a realisation of this, as well as an
appreciation of the premier's condition and of the fact that
a change in the leadership of the party could not be far off,
which made Gladstone accept the letter so quietly.   In
dignified but gentle terms he suggested that the premier
should take the opinion of the cabinet by circulating the
whole correspondence.   Palmerston, well satisfied, received
the ' cordial unqualified approval ' of his sovereign on ' every
word ' he had written to his chancellor of the Exchequer; [71]
and girded himself for the battle which was sure to come
in 1865.

CHAPTER XXXV

1865

IT seems fitting that the opening of Palmerston's last year found him engaged in a struggle for England's security, even though his opponent was so great an Englishman as Gladstone. The two men, seeing alike on so few things, were at least agreed as to the rigour of the conflict. Thus, Gladstone's diary for January 19 :

> The cabinet has been to-day almost as rough as any of the roughest times. In regard to the navy estimates, I have had no effective or broad support ; platoon-firing more or less in my sense from Argyll and Gibson, four or five were silent, the rest hostile. Probably they will appoint a committee of cabinet, and we may work through, but on the other hand we may not. My *opinion* is manifestly in a minority ; but there is an unwillingness to have a row.[1]

And Palmerston to the Queen on the day following :

> The Cabinet have yesterday and to-day been considering the plan for fortifying Quebec, and the amount to be proposed for the Army and Navy services for the ensuing financial year.
>
> Mr. Gladstone has been as troublesome and wrong-headed as he often is upon subjects discussed in Cabinet. He objected strongly to fortifying Quebec, and insisted upon a considerable reduction in the number of men for the Navy. The whole Cabinet, however, was against him, with the exception of Mr. Milner Gibson, who feebly supported him, and the Duke of Argyll, who put in a word or two in his favour. It has been, however, pretty well decided that a sum of fifty thousand pounds shall be put into the Army estimates, for the purpose of making a beginning of the fortifications of Quebec. . . .
>
> Mr. Gladstone at great length urged a reduction of five thousand men in the Navy, but . . . it is felt by the majority of the Cabinet that the best security against a conflict with the United States will

2 D

be found in an adequate defensive force.   Mr. Gladstone seems disposed to yield . . . and as a way to let him down easy . . . a Committee of the Cabinet is to meet . . . to see if any reduction can safely
be made in any of the other heads of the Naval service.[2]

And Gladstone once more gave in.   Only a week later he
admitted that the feeling of his fellow ministers on the navy
estimates was ' generally ' against him ; and professed himself ' sincerely thankful ' that some concessions had been
made.[3]   Perhaps another concession was represented by the
fact that only £50,000 was appropriated for the defences
of Quebec.   J. A. Macdonald, the Scotch-Canadian
statesman, was horrified to the point of incredulity.[4]

Palmerston's pleasure in his success apparently inspired
him to betake himself to verse, whether of his own or of
another's composition it seems impossible to say :

> When Gladstone gleans from each Man's Yearly Hoard
> How much more free the workman than the Lord
> Safe Skulk the Poor beneath the taxing Power
> And leave the wealthier Grumbler to look sour.[5]

And if the lines would hardly find a place in an anthology,
they are notable for something besides the evidence they
give of the octogenarian's persisting jauntiness.   For they
mark the fact that the premier was challenging financial
proposals that his chancellor of the Exchequer was resolved
to carry through, and challenging them on the ground that
they afforded insufficient relief from taxation to the poor.
This new conflict arose in connection with proposals for the
further reduction of the income tax, already reduced to a
sixpenny rate.   Although it was levied only on the wealthy
and well-to-do, Gladstone had confided to Bright, almost
a year before, that he was anxious to abolish it.   For he
felt that any tax by which money could be so easily raised
was conducive to extravagance.[6]   But he stated no such
argument to the premier.   Pleading that he was committed
by earlier pronouncements to work toward an eventual
abolition of the tax, he proposed an immediate cut to a
fourpenny rate.   This, he claimed, would not only be
welcome to the taxpayers, but would make it practicable
for the next parliament either to abolish or retain the tax.[7]

Remembering the allegedly depressant effect of income taxes on parliamentary enthusiasm for armaments ; and remembering, too, Palmerston's reputed bias in favour of the wealthy and well-to-do, it seems surprising that he opposed a cut of more than one penny. One of his objections, to wit, that a larger reduction would make abolition almost sure, suggests the possibility that he was anxious to retain the tax for just the reason which Gladstone had given Bright for wanting to do away with it. And, of course, there was the coming election to think of. But the main argument which he put forward to the chancellor, in a letter that was confidential and presumably sincere, was one which the most advanced of Liberals might well have used :

It is said that the Income Tax is unequal in its Bearing ; but quite as much so, if not more, are the Taxes on the Consumption of articles in general use. The Taxes on Tea, Sugar, Coffee, Beer & Spirits take away a far larger Proportion of the Spendable Means of the Poorer Classes than of the richer Classes, and in this Point of view they may be said to bear unequally on those who contribute to pay them. The Income Tax bears exclusively upon the upper and middle Classes . . . and the labouring Classes, the most numerous Part of the Nation are intirely exempt from its operation.[8]

In the end the chancellor had his way ; and the people of England presumably never knew that the premier, for whatever reasons, would have preferred to give them more relief. Gladstone had other successes, too, in so far as taxation was concerned ;[9] but Palmerston was no doubt satisfied. Appropriations for defence were what he cared chiefly about ; and the House of Commons, though objecting to the budget here and there, accepted almost nominal reductions in the naval and military estimates with passivity.

Passivity was indeed the keynote of this, the premier's last session. ' It is remarkable,' he wrote the Queen, early in March, ' that although parliament has been sitting a month, and some questions of importance have been discussed, such as the state of Ireland and the malt duty, the leader of the opposition has not yet opened his mouth.'[10] It is hard to believe that he did not understand why the session was passing so quietly. Some of the reasons were obvious:

the approach of the general election, and the continuance of prosperity. But there was another which emerges clearly enough from a letter written by Clarendon to Henry Reeve :

Palmerston had the gout all last week. . . . The uneasiness on one side and excitement on the other, whenever he is ailing, are curious to observe ; for it is pretty generally understood that until he dies there will be no real shuffle of cards.[11]

The old statesman himself may not have connected his failing health with the apathy of the House ; but he well knew what his death would mean. ' Gladstone will soon have it all his own way,' he said once to Shaftesbury, ' and, whenever he gets my place, we shall have strange doings.'[12] In the meantime the left wing should wait. But if the reformers could not yet act, they could at least talk ; and they insisted, even during this period of calm, in pushing the questions of the Irish Church and Irish land tenure to the fore. From the debates on the church question the premier stood aside, after making a vain effort to prevent Gladstone from committing himself ;[13] but on the land question he was quite ready to explain his attitude, as he had been doing at intervals for some years.[14]

It seems necessary to follow his explanation rather carefully ; for one meets the statement constantly that he dismissed the whole matter with an epigram. It is of course the penalty for making a striking epigram that later generations may not only interpret it in its most literal sense, but may regard the maker as a very personification of the point of view which it suggests to them. Hence it has been customary to take Palmerston's *jeu de mots*, ' Tenant right is landlord wrong,' as the flippant expression of a superficial, heartless and obscurantist outlook. Whether it may not have been based on some kind of reasoned conviction as well as on instinctive conservatism ; whether, in the interpretation which its author gave it, it may not have represented some degree of sober sense as well as insensitiveness to realities, Palmerston's critics have not always troubled to inquire.

So much of the Irish land question is suggested by the two words, ' tenant right.' They recall the Irish peasants' feeling that their proprietary interest in the soil had never been extinguished through the grants made by British governments to landlords of British origin. They recall, again, the failure of those landlords, often absentees, often burdened with mortgages, and nearly always limited by entail in the control of their estates, to make those ' improvements ' in building, fencing and draining which English landlords made, and without which proper cultivation was impossible. Yet the peasant, making these improvements for himself, found that the law allowed the landlord to rob him of the fruits. Just because he had made the improvements his rent was often raised ; and, should he be evicted or voluntarily give up his lease, no compensation would be due him unless he lived in Ulster, where ' tenant right ' prevailed. As the population had increased and the subdivision of small holdings had gone on, the situation had become agonising. One saw peasants, forced to find land or starve, scrambling for tiny holdings on almost any terms, securing them at rents that made subsistence almost impossible and on short term leases that permitted eviction at almost any time. After eviction they had the happy choice of finding other holdings (if they were fortunate) where they could begin the struggle once again, of emigrating if they could find the means, or of simply starving where they were. Since the famine of 1846 and the time of appalling want which had followed it, eviction and emigration had both been in full swing. Though the population of some sections had been tragically reduced, the situation of the peasants was in some respects more hopeless than before. Much land had come into the hands of new and more profit-seeking landlords. Landlords old and new, and the more business-like agents whom many of them now employed, were consolidating little holdings and turning cultivated into grazing lands. Houses, even at times whole hamlets, were burned over the heads of families who had little or no hope of finding other homes. Outwardly, Ireland seemed more tranquil and more prosperous : but underneath the surface bitter resentment, fed by the sense of injustice as well as by pure misery, burned.

How could Palmerston the humanitarian, the model

Irish landlord, the friend of oppressed peoples, dismiss such misery with an epigram ? His letters and speeches, if looked at carefully enough, show that he did nothing of the sort. If he lacked the understanding, sympathy and fine courage with which Gladstone was to attack the problem a few years afterwards, he tried at least to understand and deal with it. He saw the misery ; he even saw what proved the ultimate remedy. But in his old age he could not reconcile himself to the weakening of the British ' establishment,' to the sapping of some of those institutions he had defended for so long :

> The fact is that the Catholic priests see that their fees and endowments are dwindling with the decrease of the population, and they set up their members in the House of Commons to decry it. . . . Mr. Monsell [M.P. for Limerick county] is an organ of the Catholic party, and their object is, by Tenant Right or by sale and purchase, to transfer the lands in Ireland from Protestant landlords to Catholic middle-class men, and thus to lay the ground-work for abolishing the Protestant Church and setting up the Catholic Church in its stead.[15]

And, although his personal feelings as an absentee landlord quite clearly entered in, he could ground his objection to the extension of tenant right from Ulster to the other Irish provinces on a doctrine sacred to Englishmen for long centuries, and on the economic teachings of his youth. In regard for the sanctity of property he yielded to no Whig, or for that matter Tory, of his time : in his acceptance of inflexible economic law, controlling such matters as rent, population and cultivation of the land, he was still a child of the early nineteenth century. Now ' tenant right,' as he saw it, was virtually the confiscation of property. How else, he asked, could one regard the placing on a landlord of an obligation to pay for improvements which he had neither desired not authorised ?

> The object of a Government ought to be . . . to give security to life and property, to leave the buyer and seller, the hirer and letter, to settle their own bargains, unshackled by law . . . no change . . . can be advantageous, if it is founded upon a violation of the natural rights of property. Gentlemen talk in the easiest way possible of the manner in which owners of land should be compelled to make such and such arrangements with their tenants, and should receive

only such rent as other people adjudge them entitled to.   I say these
doctrines are Communistic doctrines. . . .[16]

The determination of rental values by outside authority
appeared to him, not only as an attack on property, but
as a defiance of economic law as well.   And economic law
would do much to ameliorate conditions if given time.   Irish
peasants obeyed it when they found themselves compelled to
emigrate.   And were they not the better for the larger
wages earned in Great Britain or America ?   Was not
Ireland the better, both for the consolidation of small
holdings that their departure made possible, and for the
money that they sent home ?   Was England to blame for
bad harvests, or lack of minerals, or an unnecessarily
high birth rate ?   Those who treated the Irish cottier hardly
had much to answer for ; but why attempt to keep him in
a country where his living came so hard ?
But Palmerston did not rely wholly on *laisser faire.*   In
1860, he had gone as far in the direction of extending
tenant right as his convictions permitted him to do, by
favouring the passage of a bill giving compensation to
tenants for improvements which they and the landlords
had previously agreed upon.   The act had naturally proved
ineffectual ; but why this was he could not or would not
understand.   Nor would he even now, in 1865, meet the
demand of the Irish and the left wing Liberal members
that compensation should be given for improvements to
which the landlord had not given consent.   To concede
this, he argued (and he was still good at *ad hoc* reasoning),
would be, not only to infringe the rights of property, but
to defeat his plan for making the Irish busy and prosperous.
What they needed was the introduction of more manufacturing ; but security of property was a condition necessarily
precedent to the influx of industrial capital.   One might
suppose, then, that it was in a spirit of determined resistance
to any further change that Palmerston took leave of the
Irish land question.   But this was not the case.   What
the Irish were demanding at the time was a committee of
inquiry ; and the premier readily granted a select committee
to inquire into the reasons for the failure of the act passed

five years before. The committee, predominantly Irish and advanced Liberal, had not reported when he died.[17]

After Palmerston's death *The Times* referred sympathetically to the difficulty of his position in his last years :

. . . it had been the purgatory of his old age to have to do what he did not care about ; to see what he cared for ill done ; to hold things together for an inadequate purpose ; and to prepare a seat for the Minister with whom he had oftenest been at variance. Well, when we call a man a patriot we remember that he has had struggles, and that he has to make sacrifices. When we call a man an English gentleman we suppose him patient and forbearing, and with something to swallow now and then.[18]

The idea was, of course, by no means fanciful ; but, even in 1865, when the depths of his ' purgatory ' had been reached, he had not so very much to swallow regarding domestic matters after all. No fundamental changes in British or Irish institutions had been carried through ; nor had even the system of taxation been radically altered. And with respect to two matters which lay closest to his heart he had achieved success. He was leaving his country armed against any conceivable emergency ; and he was about to see the virtual extinction of the international slave trade.

For the international slave trade virtually died at the same time as its most famous enemy. It died slowly and died hard, succumbing to blows of which the old premier's were still the most persistent and the most vigorous.[19] Opportunist as he was in much of his foreign policy, he never shifted his position with regard to that ' abominable crime.' Giving ground in his last years to opposition domestic and international, he yielded not an inch to fellow-countrymen or foreign governments desiring to stay his hand where this matter was concerned. Rather, he pressed on to destroy the enemy utterly, still devoting, as his letters show, as much thought and energy to this crusade as to any question of high European politics.[20] Yet there were no bright laurels of popular favour to be gathered here, no great diplomatic risks and adventures to enjoy.

He had faced a discouraging prospect when he took up the old struggle in 1859 ; for the slave trade was showing signs of renewed vitality ; and Malmesbury, in 1858, had weakened the hands of the British government. France was buying negroes both on the east and on the west coast of Africa, for introduction as ' free labourers ' into certain of her colonies.[21] Whatever the status of the immigrants on French soil, the method of their recruitment at the source involved all the cruelty and loss of life that had ever been attendant on the procurement of ordinary slaves. Portugal, from whose colonies most of these unfortunates were torn, was powerless to interfere. But a heavier burden of guilt rested on the United States and Spain, through the success of American, or professedly American, traders in supplying slaves to that ' plague spot,' that ' centre of abominations,' as Palmerston called it, the island of Cuba. American slave ships, condescending to some camouflage, still operated extensively, even from New York ; while slave vessels of various national origins still hoisted the flag of the United States and carried forged American papers. The American government would neither take vigorous measures for the suppression of the trade nor allow the British to do so.[22] Sadly lax in using its navy to apprehend offenders who were its citizens, it enjoyed no power under American law to take punitive measures against traders who could claim other nationality. Yet, until 1862, it refused to make any agreement with Great Britain for the exercise of mutual rights of visit and search. And Malmesbury, in 1858, had continued Aberdeen's tradition by accepting the American contention that the right of visit to a suspected ship for the inspection of her papers and verification of her nationality, was legally indistinguishable from the right of search. How then was the trade to be put down ? The captain of a slave ship had only to exhibit apparent evidence of American nationality to make interference by a British vessel highly dangerous ; and had only to obliterate all such evidence in order to make apprehension by an American vessel impossible.

As if all this were not sufficiently discouraging, Palmerston had to deal with opposition in parliament, and luke-warmness or worse at the Admiralty. There were members of parliament who could not believe that the annual expenditure of several hundred thousand pounds for this humanitarian crusade was justified ; and Lord Stanley was probably by no means the only one who felt that the life of a single British naval officer might be ' worth more than the merely animal existence of a whole African tribe.'[23]   But the most serious opposition still came from men like Bright, who, in the interests of commerce and international comity, wished to reduce coercion to a minimum.   Their efforts were centred on securing the repeal of the so-called Aberdeen Act of 1845, an act passed in consequence of the Brazilian government's failure to provide for the proper trial and punishment of Brazilian slave traders, and subjecting these offenders to the jurisdiction of British admiralty courts.   It was hard for the premier to believe that the anti-coercionists had the suppression of the trade at heart :

> Moral conviction of the iniquity of the slave trade exists strongly in England with the exception of the ' *atrocem   animum* ' not ' *Catonis* ' but of Bright and Cobden.[24]

But he was almost as indignant with the naval lords of the Board of Admiralty, who had 'never cared a farthing about the suppression of the slave trade,' and who, considering it ' a sort of penal duty ' had ' sent to it all the old tubs that were fit in their opinion for nothing else.'[25]   In face of all these handicaps surely a very old and weary and gout-ridden statesman might have been willing to leave to his foreign secretary, or even to succeeding ministers, the completion of his task.

Instead, he developed the attack in every manner possible, spurring on Russell, bargaining with France, insisting on the continued coercion of the Portuguese, and using every manner of persuasion with the United States and Spain.[26]   Russell was highly praised for his own programme, reminded that concessions regarding the traffic would go ill with the principles on which he had built his political career, promised ' great glory ' in case he could ' exterminate that hydra,' and all the while overwhelmed with suggestions and advice.[27]   In one direction success proved easily attainable.   France, in 1861, agreed to give up ' free '

immigration under the ' Regis contract,' in return for permission to recruit coolie labour in India. But the retention
of the Aberdeen Act, and still more the suppression of the
Cuban slave trade, gave the premier much trouble.

There were sound enough arguments in favour of
milder measures with relation to Brazil. The Brazilian
government was ready to make a suppression treaty of the
most inclusive sort ; the pride of the best Brazilians was
seriously touched ; and Brazilian trade with the United
Kingdom was certainly worth considering. Year after year,
disputes, reprisals and demands for damages made diplomatic relations between the two countries difficult, and at
times even impossible. Russell was inclined to make
concessions to Brazil's feelings ; and many Englishmen,
including Milner Gibson, Palmerston's own president of
the Board of Trade, thought that a treaty might well be
substituted for the offensive act of 1845.[28] But the premier
was determined to ' resist with . . . might and main.' [29]
Privately, he rested much of his opposition on the character
of Brazilians generally :

> The plain truth is that the Portuguese are of all European nations
> the lowest in the moral scale, and the Brazilians ..re degenerate
> Portuguese, demoralized by slavery and slave trade.[30]

It was ' as unreasonable to expect honesty in a Portuguese
or a Frenchman, at all events about the slave trade, as . . .
to look for courage in a Neapolitan.' [31] Theoretically, the
anti-coercionist case might be strong ; but he found it
better to go upon experience :

> When the Brazilians ask us to repeal the Aberdeen Act which
> produced in 1851 & 1852 the miraculous conversion from slave
> trade of a nation which up to that time had committed that crime
> to the greatest extent of any nation, and in spite of the strongest
> remonstrances which the English language could convey, and when
> they tell us to accept a slave trade treaty as a sufficient substitute for
> our Act, it is impossible not to reflect that the slave trade treaty with
> Spain does not prevent some 15 or 20,000 negroes & perhaps more
> from being every year imported into Cuba ; that our slave trade
> treaty with Portugal does not prevent an extensive exportation of
> slaves from the Portuguese possessions in Africa, east and west, and

that the abolition of slave trade and of slavery itself by France has
not prevented the Regis contract which was real slave trade, &
that even the abolition of that contract does not prevent a considerable export of slaves from the east coast of Africa to the Island of
Réunion.   If we were to repeal the Aberdeen Act the slave deluge
would again inundate Brazil.[32]

Commerce and comity, concomitants of supreme importance
to the anti-coercionists, were of less importance than
humanitarianism to Palmerston.   In the end the Aberdeen
Act was saved.   For even the gentler language which the
premier was forced to use in public carried conviction with
the House.

> I do not dispute that the measure we adopted [the Aberdeen Act]
> was a violent one, but . . . I am convinced . . . if the Act were
> repealed the Brazilian slave trade would be revived.   It may be said
> that the opinion of the people of Brazil is altered. . . . But it is not
> by respectable men that the trade is conducted.   It is carried on by
> the scum of the earth in every country, and the profits are so large
> that they can afford to bribe the subordinate officers whose duty it is
> to detect and punish crime.[33]

If only parliament could have settled the other great part
of the problem, the killing of the trade at that 'centre of
abominations,' Cuba.
     In trying to deal with the Cuban slave trade through
his foreign minister, Palmerston ran the gamut between the
employment of the gentlest persuasion and the use of the
most relentless force.   There was no gentleness in his
suggestions for stopping up the 'bung-holes' of the king of
Dahomey's territories, where American slavers loaded their
human freight ;[34] and not too much in his proposals for
inducing the Spanish government to see that the Cuban
market for this freight was closed.[35]   But he was ready to
approach Washington quite tenderly.   In March 1860, he
suggested that Russell might inquire whether the American
and British governments, united in good intentions, might
not unite in action, both in Cuba and in the waters round
about.[36]   The British consul general was in the way of
securing much private information about the arrival and
disposal of slaves, and, in case an Anglo-American agree-

ment should be reached, would be furnished with the pecuniary means of getting more :

> . . . as it is by bribery that the slave trade flourishes in Cuba it would be but fair to fight the slave traders with their own weapons and to kill their trade with those ' silver lances ' which the great poet says ' will conquer all things.'

With England supplying information, the United States might take action against traders who were its citizens. But this, of course, would not be enough. To prevent offenders from escaping by alternately displaying and concealing evidences of American nationality, it would be necessary that American and British ships, commissioned for the suppression of the trade, should cruise in pairs. The suggestion was inoffensive and quite practical ; but, as Palmerston bitterly told the House of Commons in the following year, it ' seemed too well calculated to accomplish its purpose to be accepted by the American Government.'[37] President Buchanan was decidedly tender of Southern susceptibilities. Indeed, at one time, British vessels assigned to the pursuit and apprehension of slave traders had to be withdrawn from Cuban waters in deference to American complaints. It was Lincoln and the American Civil War which at last placed Palmerston within reach of his goal. Once more he urged Russell to plead for the right of visit and search, suggesting that, should it be conceded for vessels which flew the Stars and Stripes, England might 'take without leave the same liberty with any under the Confederate flag.'[38] The Anglo-American treaty of 1862 sounded the death knell of the Cuban slave trade. Achievement of perfect co-operation was delayed by the fact that England's neutrality forbade the admission of American ships of war into British ports on the coast of Africa ; but by 1865 this last obstacle had disappeared.[39]

Thus it was that the international slave trade, in so far as participation by civilized countries was concerned, died at the same time as Palmerston. Here and there some trader was still willing to take the risk ; but the risk at last outweighed the possible profits. Lincoln, in 1862, made the first use of a power that had lain in the hands of the government at Washington for forty years, by hanging an American trader for piracy. Spain decided on similar action in the very month of the prime minister's death.

When parliament was dissolved, on July 7, it may have seemed to most of the members that they had been listening to the same old Palmerston. Intimates knew better.[40] The pious Shaftesbury, too close to him to be deceived by his ' pitiful ' efforts to conceal his increasing infirmities, dared not pray that he would see another session, since this would be to pray for a miracle. Lady Palmerston was alarmed at his condition, and was begging him to give up politics. Russell must have been shocked to learn that he did not remember whether France had been a signatory to the Belgian treaty of 1831. But in public he still treated age and illness as enemies to which no unnecessary concession should be made, still made amazing demands upon the ' iron frame.'[41] Generally abstemious with respect to food and drink, he could still sit down to a banquet ' with the zest of an Eton boy.' The Speaker took note of what he con- sumed at a public dinner in February of this year : soup, fish, three *entrées*, two roasts, game, pudding, jelly and a fruit dessert ! Later in the same evening he assisted Lady Palmerston in receiving the great world. If nowadays he sometimes used a cab in returning to Cambridge House late at night (finding that he could ' get nearly as much fresh air ' as if he walked), men marvelled at the agility he showed in dodging other cabs in Palace Yard. His absences from the House were apt to be more frequent and prolonged ; but this was curiously accounted for by the statement that gout made it impossible for him so shave himself. When he rose to speak it was sometimes observ- able that his memory was at fault ; but he could still dispense with glasses in reading from manuscript, and still acquit himself very creditably on his feet. All these evidences of vigour seem to have been hailed with pleasure by the bulk of his public and his party. Outsiders might ask whether he would not ' get up from the table too late,' and whether his followers in retaining him, were not, like Antar's warriors, tying their leader's corpse on his horse's back in order to frighten their enemies.[42] But neither

England nor the Liberals were done with him yet.   Nor
was he by any means done with them.

This surviving mutual devotion became very evident
as the general election approached.   The contest promised
to be anything but exciting ;   for no specific issue was
involved, and little expectation was entertained that the new
House would be very different from the old.   But there
is always an element of uncertainty in general elections ;
and the outcome of this one was of vital importance to
Palmerston.   It could hardly fail to decide whether his
last days were to be ones of continuing success and fame,
or ones of ultimate failure and relative obscurity.   A
Liberal victory would mean, not only that he might still
remain in power a little while, but that his countrymen
still loved and trusted him—that the demonstrations of
Bradford agitators were of small account as against the
affection and confidence that he had won through half
a century.   But a Liberal defeat would likely mean that
power, even within the party, would have to be relinquished
into other, and as it seemed to him dangerous, hands.
A Palmerston still so popular as to carry the country, in
spite of diplomatic reverses and the notorious disaffection
of the Liberal left wing, would be an asset with which the
party would not, and could not dispense.   But an aged and
failing and repudiated Palmerston—could he expect to hold
the leadership of a party fighting to regain its place on
a programme of which he was known to disapprove ?   The
election was personal to him in more than one respect.
So important was he to the party and the public that his
advisers urged him to make a public canvass at Tiverton :
so important was the public to him that, in spite of
sickness, exhaustion and the protests of his friends, he did
not hesitate to go.

Once more he smiled on Tiverton and Tiverton on
him : once more he knew just how to make the most telling
appeal :

The old Romans had a fable about one of their heroes, a great
wrestler, who when they threw him upon the ground his mother
earth gave him additional vigour, and he got up stronger than when
he fell down.   Now I trust I shall receive renewed vigour by coming

back to the good mother earth of Tiverton, and I hope mother earth
will send me back stronger than when I came here (Cheers).[43]

Rowcliffe, the Chartist butcher, was again the most prominent figure in the crowd. ' "Then you did not vote for me
friend Rowcliffe—you preferred voting for a Tory." " I
did not vote for you, my lord," replied Mr. Rowcliffe, " for
if I had, I should have voted for a Tory." ' [44] And not only
Tiverton smiled on him, but the country, too. Asked to
endorse or repudiate him—for that was really *the* issue [45]—
it gave him an increased majority. It was still the ' average '
Englishman who supported him, even in these more
businesslike and less heroic days. Such, at least, was the
opinion of Bagehot :

> Lord Palmerston . . . had an influence . . . over the common,
> sensible, uncommitted mass of the nation . . . fair, calm, sensible
> persons, who have something to lose, who have no intention of losing
> it, who hate change, who love improvement, who *will* be ruled in
> a manner they understand. . . . These are the men who really rule
> in all localities, in all undertakings, in all combinations ; and it was
> over these that Lord Palmerston possessed unequalled and marvellous
> influence.[46]

And Russell, at the Guildhall, went into the reasons why
these ' fair, calm, sensible persons ' would not repudiate
their failing premier :

> He had the resolution, the resource, the promptitude, the vigour
> which befitted war ; and, when peace arrived, he showed that he
> could maintain internal tranquillity, and, by extending our commercial
> relations, could give to the country the fruits of the blessings of peace.
> The reason why he was able to do this is plain . . . his heart always
> beat for the honour of England.[47]

True, a good many of the successes of his ten years as
premier had been attributable to others ; but in holding
together a group of ministers who could give the country
varied benefits—' a great bundle of sticks,' as Clarendon
put it [48]—he had given England what the average Englishman wanted. Thus, in the last pictures his countrymen
had of him, he was gaily chaffing Rowcliffe, and (though here
of course the picture was imaginary) triumphantly counting
the returns. ' *Felix opportunitate mortis,*' as Russell wrote

Libberals 368
Torys 290
makes
tory
majority 25

Mr BULL

DIZZY'S ARITHMETIC

PAM : " Now, then, youngster, you've no call to be a chalking that wall ;
and if you *must* do a sum, you might as well do it right ! "

Punch, August 12, 1865

afterwards. Happy indeed ! Gladstone, defeated at Oxford, had come in for Lancashire and was 'unmuzzled' at last : Russell had twice again invited Bright to dine with him.

Palmerston's weeks were numbered now. Riding too rough a horse during the spring had brought on new complaints to sap his failing strength. From Tiverton he was taken to Brocket Hall in Hertfordshire, which Lady Palmerston had inherited from the last Lord Melbourne, to rest and recuperate. But the recuperation did not come. Perhaps rest and treatment had been too long deferred : perhaps in his hatred of giving in, he resisted them too much.[49] He would not take his medicines, he would get out of bed, he would be driven out, and he would go out on the terrace without his hat. 'Oh ! it's only what the bathers call taking a "header," ' he answered gaily to his physician's protest. For weeks his recovery seemed possible ; but a chill brought on inflammation, and relapse followed relapse. And yet he held on amazingly. He did not seem to be afraid of death ; but he was determined to measure himself against it as he had done against all his other enemies. Only two weeks before it came, he was seen to go out and climb some high railings twice, in order to find out just how much ground he had lost.

In spite of pain, weariness and, no doubt, impatience with his physical self (Palmerston with sago and brandy for sustenance, and carriage drives for exercise !) his thoughtfulness and even his joviality did not fail. During the early stages of his illness he was urging upon Gladstone the immediate institution of Saturday half-holidays for civil service clerks. He was impatient of the suggestion that the change would necessarily involve an increased demand upon the Treasury :

This was the Line taken by Master Manufacturers against the Ten Hours Bill. If men were mere Machines which would regularly do a given Quantity of Work in a given Time like a Steam Engine such Calculations would be unanswerably decisive, but in considering such Matters we ought to bear in Mind that men are moral and intellectual agents, and that the work performed by them in a given Time, depends much on the cheerfulness & good will with which it is done, and that both Cheerfulness & Goodwill very much depend upon the Belief that those who superintend and direct have some Sympathy for the Employed. . . .[50]

Only a fortnight before his death he learned that Sir Arthur Helps, the clerk of the Privy Council, and Helps' principal assistant were both ' knocked down by excessive work.' At once two letters went out ; one authorizing Helps to cut all red tape in securing what assistance he needed without delay, and the other to the under secretary of the Home Office, directing that someone should be sent to Balmoral to take Helps' place at a council which the Queen had called.[51] Almost at the same time he was arranging that the presents of game which he had always distributed from Broadlands to friends and tenants at Christmastide should be despatched at once. For his joviality, let one letter written to the Queen three weeks before his death suffice :

> Viscount Palmerston begs to thank Your Majesty for your kind and considerate message sent him by Lord Granville, whose head and time being full of the cattle disease and matrimonial arrangements and preparations, the message was not delivered quite as soon as it might have been.[52]

' I wish,' wrote Bright, when news of Palmerston's death arrived, ' there were more to be said in his praise.'[53] Great numbers of persons in England and on the continent would gladly have assisted Bright in finding it.

As inveterate was the dying premier's habit of industry. There was not much, of course, that he could do, save plan for the next cabinet,[54] and correspond with his ministers. And especially with Russell. For he would not lose touch with foreign affairs, or cease to do sentry duty, while breath remained. In September, French and British squadrons fraternized at Cherbourg, Brest and Portsmouth ; and news came to Brocket that the French had been much impressed with British cordiality. The old statesman showed at once that illness had, if anything, heightened his sensitiveness and stiffened his pride. Cowley was enjoined by letter to relieve Napoleon's ministers of any misapprehension concerning England's feelings toward the French nation and its government.[55] The nation she regarded in terms of the utmost cordiality ; but she was precluded from entertaining the same sentiments toward the government by its insistence in acting in a manner detrimental to British interests. The prime minister hoped that neither would the French nation be misled by Britain's ' occasional opposition to the schemes of their Government,' nor would the government be deceived by evidences of British friendliness into thinking that England was ready to sacrifice any of her interests. At the same time Palmerston explained to Victoria the significance which he himself attached to the fraternization of the fleets.[56] It would make for peace both in Europe and in North America, by dispelling the French belief that the English entertained ' a settled hatred of France and Frenchmen,' and by presenting to the North Americans the appearance of ' a sort of preliminary defensive alliance ' between Great Britain and France which they would be indisposed to challenge. Here it was the aged and more pacific Palmerston who spoke ; but there was another passage in the letter which might have been written by the young secretary at War, viewing the French troops in 1818. The French navy, he pointed out, had always been more friendly to the English than the French army, because

The French Army feel that the British Army has stripped from the French brow laurels gathered in every field of European warfare, and that, having beaten in every battle those French troops who had beaten everybody else, the English Army ended by defeating the Emperor Napoleon himself, and sending him prisoner to St. Helena.

In his bed at Brocket he found it pleasant to reflect upon these things. When the end came, on October 18, his mind was still dwelling on foreign affairs. Persons who appreciated characteristic death-bed scenes must have been gratified when one of his physicians vouched for ' Protocol ' Palmerston's last words : ' That's Article ninety-eight ; now go on to the next.' [57]   And there were some who did not fail to note that his passing was followed by a great display of Northern Lights,[58] and to ponder the familiar lines:

All night long the northern streamers
Shot across the trembling sky,
Fearful lights that never beckon
Save when kings or heroes die.

For he had died a hero to the mass of his fellow-countrymen ; and certain of them whose opinions were not lightly to be set aside gave him place then and there with the greatest of England's dead. The matter was argued at some length, especially in *The Times*.[59] Admitted that he had lacked the 'daring spirit' and 'oratorical genius' of Chatham, the governing capacity and 'lofty magnanimity' of Pitt, the fervour of Fox, the vision and 'polished eloquence' of Canning, and the 'constructive ability' of Peel, which one of these, on the other hand, had combined all Palmerston's gifts ? Which of them had met the tests of office so long and in so many capacities ? Which of them could have boasted of possessing at once the dead premier's practical acquaintance with the working of the various departments of English government, his almost unexampled skill in the management of discontented parliaments, his extraordinary mastery of the minutiae of European politics and his gift for making British influence felt everywhere ? *The Times* grew lyrical in describing what John Bull thought of him :

Palmerston, it was imagined, would move the whole force of the British Empire in order that . . . Brown—*Civis Romanus*—might not be defrauded of his Worcester sauce amid the ice of Siberia, or of his pale ale on the Mountains of the Moon. He could do anything and he would do everything. . . . He was supposed to have his pocket full of constitutions, to have a voice in half the Cabinets of Europe, to have monarchs past reckoning under his thumb. He humbled the Shah, he patronized the Sultan, he abolished the Mogul, he conquered the Brother of the Sun, he opened to the world the empire which had been walled round for centuries by impregnable barriers, he defied the Czar. . . .

But it wrote in sober vein enough in paying its own tribute :

In the art of distinguishing the prevailing current of public opinion, in readiness of tact, in versatility of mind and humour, in the masterly ease with which he handled the reins of government, and in the general felicity of his political temperament he had no rival in his own generation.

Nor did it forget the lifetime of toil he had given to his country, his patience and pertinacity in striving to achieve set aims, his fidelity to principles rather than to party,

his far-reaching tolerance, his indifference to personal
affronts and his 'proverbial' fidelity to colleagues and
subordinates.

Save for the Queen (who regretted him as a useful
prime minister and a link with happier times, but could not
forget that she '*never* liked him, or could ever the least
respect him '[60]), the more eminent of his critics for the most
part observed the old Roman rule.   But Delane and his
associates proceeded to meet the criticism of the past.
They were free to admit that on the face of things at least
it had seemed justified.   Palmerston had been ' not unfairly
taunted by advanced Reformers with having " no policy." '
He had seen little in his country which he desired to change ;
and had even lacked faith in what was known as ' world-
bettering.'   ' World-bettering ' was, in fact, difficult to a man
of his temperament :   ' he was too much engrossed with
the task of meeting present exigencies and too distrustful
of human foresight to anticipate the problems of a coming
generation.'   But had he no claims to be regarded as a
liberal ?   Were men to forget that he had backed Catholic
emancipation against his party, that he had been a free
trader before Peel, and that he had fought a sustained and
bitter fight against continental despotism and the slave
trade ?   Perhaps he had been too much ruled by expediency
in forming his last ministry almost exclusively of conserva-
tively minded Whigs and Peelites ;   but had not the
country endorsed his judgment ?   Had it not acquiesced
without sensible protest in the abandonment of all measures
for parliamentary reform ?   Once committed to a Whig-
Peelite ministry, and with its policy accepted by the public,
could he, even had he so wished, have replaced his tried
colleagues with younger men of more liberal views ?   And
was it not arguable that he had been, after all, a very suitable
premier for his time ?   Were not the years of his premiership years when public opinion was in a state of flux, when
' the broadest possible policy was the best,' and when
England's need was that of a premier who ' commanded so
much confidence, so large a belief in his patriotism, his
disinterestedness, his good sense, his experience, and his
personal powers ' ?   Rather surprisingly this last question

was answered by the *Indépendance Belge,* which saw in Palmerston

. . . the keystone of the arch which maintained the balance of parties in that period of transformation through which England, and all Europe with her, are at present passing.[61]

For the press of western and central Europe was on the whole kind to him ; and even that of the three ' Holy Alliance ' Powers paid tribute at least to his burning patriotism. Thus the world spoke of him as arrangements went forward for his funeral.

Perhaps the crushing effect produced by the prime minister's death, on Court and cabinet alike, may account for some thoughtlessness on the part of those whose place it was to do him honour in his burial. At any rate, it was left to Gladstone, that ' great gentleman,' to see that he was buried in a manner befitting his services.[62] He had left directions in his will for burial in the family vault at Romsey ; and the family could of course do nothing but observe his wish. Only three days before the date on which the funeral was to have taken place, Gladstone protested to Russell ; and the two telegraphed the Queen, asking that his burial should be at Westminster. Hence England learned that, by Her Majesty's express desire, his interment in the Abbey, on October 27, had been arranged.

There were certain diarists who found his funeral unimpressive and the people of London unimpressed.[63] Yet those who loved him and admired him seem to have been well satisfied.[64] If royal carriages gave the only note of splendour to an otherwise dull cortège, the fact was not wholly overlooked that the simplicity of his obsequies corresponded to the dislike of ostentation which he had shown all through his life.[65] More to his taste no doubt than any grandeur which might have surrounded him, were the trainful of servants and tenants from Romsey ; the guard of sailors from Trinity House, so suggestive of his trust in England's great fighting arm ; the detachment of those national volunteers whose patriotism he had so fostered and admired ; and more than all, perhaps, the quiet crowds, ' by far the larger portion . . . in mourning,' which packed the route from Cambridge House to the Abbey. It was a crowd, men said, such as had been seen at no funeral save that of the duke of Wellington. Perhaps he would have been touched, too, had he known that Bradford was one of the far distant corporations which had sent a delegation to do him honour, and that all business there was suspended during the time covered by his obsequies. A radical leader suggested sneeringly that the Carlton Club might have joined the Reform Club in paying homage as the procession went down Pall Mall.[66] But the dead statesman would not have minded such a jibe. He had had affiliations with all parties, without ever giving himself wholly to any one of them ; and he was on his way to a spot where the remembrance of party divisions was almost blotted out by records of service to the nation. He was to lie near Chatham, to whom parties were as nothing beside the glory of his country ; near Chatham's great son, to whom England's security had been a first article of faith ; near Castlereagh, who had upheld the balance of power and placed a check on France ; near Canning, who had given him the inspiration for his own policy ; and, finally, near Wilberforce, whose richly fruitful efforts to extinguish slavery had provided a glorious prelude to his own.

' The mighty chiefs sleep side by side.'

A SUGGESTED INTERPRETATION
OF PALMERSTON

' His heart always beat for the honour of England.' —
EARL RUSSELL, 1865.

' Lord Palmerston . . . had the honour and power of his country strongly at heart.' —QUEEN VICTORIA, 1883.

PALMERSTON can best be understood, perhaps, as an exponent of early and mid-nineteenth century nationalism. No formula can explain in their totality the principles and actions of any man, much less of one with a career so long and varied, and a temperament so passionate. But, on the other hand, his displays of deep anger could almost invariably be linked up with the intensity of his nationalism. In fervour for his country's eminence, as he conceived it, and in that alone, he showed the lack of moderation of a bigot. It is very noticeable that, for all his love of place and power, he could accept personal or party reverses with good-natured equanimity or the ' tit for tat ' of sportsmanship ; while opposition to what he regarded as an important national policy seldom failed to arouse his bitter and lasting antagonism. Compare his inveterate dislike of Louis Philippe, who was able at times to block his policies but never his personal career, with his constant readiness for reconciliation with Russell, who several times imperilled his career but nearly always supported his policies. Or compare again his easy tolerance of the worst that was in Russell with his intolerance of what many will regard as some of the best that was in Gladstone. Russell, who dismissed Palmerston from his cabinet, and explained the dismissal to the public in the most damaging manner possible ; who proved unstable and unreliable at important crises, and was difficult at the best of times ; whose jealous desire to regain the premiership from 1853 to 1859 was unconcealed and dangerous, was forgiven repeatedly and, in all instances save one, quite readily.   But Gladstone, for all the strength and lustre he contributed to the government, for all his scrupulous observance of amenities, was never pardoned for wishing to reduce what he regarded as unnecessary expenditure for national defence.   No doubt it was easier to forgive ' a foolish fellow ' like Russell than one who had the power to be so ' troublesome ' as the great financier ; and certainly Russell's co-operation was a political asset over a much longer period.   But Palmerston's attitude toward the two greatest colleagues of his later years seems to have been determined far more by coincidence or conflict of policies involving the international position of England than by personal considerations or political values.

During the last century nationalism has been so diffused, and has appeared in such a variety of forms, that it is difficult to suggest the distinguishing characteristics of a particularly nationalistic statesman at a specific period. But one can at least imagine what combination of aims and policies a nationalistic British statesman of a century ago might be expected to display.   For one has the advantage of being able to assume that he would be a member of the governing class, and would have a lively consciousness of all that had transpired during the revolutionary and Napoleonic era.   Hence, he would not only feel profound respect for the traditions and institutions of England, but an intense pride in them.   And he would be deeply imbued with a sense of England's great position in international affairs.   In general, then, he would probably wish to follow every policy that would give his country stable and efficient government within the traditional framework ; that would enable her at all times to defend herself, and when necessary to take the offensive, against rivals ; that would make her influence significant, and if possible dominant, in all international crises, and in as large a geographical area as possible.   His political philosophy might be one of several ; but he would almost certainly be conscious of the importance of communicating to the British people as much as possible of his own pride and confidence. He might or might not be a demagogue ; but he would find it difficult to resist the temptation to use press and platform for the inculcation of a type of patriotism that would pass easily into chauvinism. Moreover, it would be natural for him to believe and teach that the institutions with which England was blessed should be extended to the other nations of the earth. He would not necessarily be an expansionist, since he might believe that expansion would make a weaker rather than a stronger state ; but he would be anxious that no other nation should make such gains as to detract from the strength or glory of his own. He might or might not seek international understandings or alliances ; but he would probably desire to form some which England could dominate. And it would almost certainly please him to have satellites among the smaller states. One who has followed Palmerston's career can easily decide in how far he answered to these and other tests.

But Palmerston's nationalism was of a particular type : the pre-eminence he coveted for his country was not only material, but even more, perhaps, moral. England should cast the bread of her public opinion upon continental waters, and reap reward in the respect and affection of those peoples whom it might sustain. It has been said of him that he found the force of public opinion a great fact and made it a great doctrine : that public opinions were to him not so much facts as deeds—or title-deeds. Be this as it may, there is no question as to his belief that public opinion properly mobilized, directed and sustained, would ultimately triumph over physical force. And, looking at the continent, he saw, or thought he saw, the ' fleshly arm ' of despotism holding in thrall peoples who struggled to possess themselves of the national and constitutional liberties with which England, first and most abundantly of all nations, had been endowed. Here, then, was his chance to give England moral pre-eminence. It was not for him to spend British lives or British treasure where British honour or British interests were not obviously concerned. But he could lavishly dispense a type of assistance in the end still more effectual, by making himself at once the

guide and the mouthpiece of public opinion in England.
He would teach the English to sympathise with oppressed
brethren on the continent, and hearten the oppressed
brethren with the cordial of English sympathy. He would
preach to the despots better ways, shaming them if that
were possible, but at least warning them of the dangers
that they ran. In all these ways he would place his country
on an eminence. It was easy, of course, for a Peel or a
Disraeli or a Bright to attack this policy : to point out its
cost in friendly relations with the Powers, in resultant loss
of commercial profits, and in resultant expenditure on
armaments. Palmerston considered it worth the price.
It was easy for the same critics to find fault with his
methods : to call attention to instances in which he bullied
smaller states and left struggling peoples to struggle on
alone. Palmerston's answer was that, as steward of
England's prestige and interests, he had always to give them
precedence. If he bullied Greece and ' turned . . . a
molehill into a volcano ' for the benefit of that ' Jewish
pimp,' Pacifico, it was because he had persuaded himself,
in his nationalistic bigotry, that England's prestige required
her dictation of a settlement. If he left the Poles and
Hungarians to their fate, it was because he had no possible
means of saving them without exposing England and
Europe to the incalculable risks of a general and especially
bitter war. And he had never given either Poles or Hungarians the least encouragement to revolt. When had he
been deaf to the appeals of minor peoples struggling for
liberty or constitutional government, provided help could
be given without placing England's own interests in jeo-
pardy ? And which group of his countrymen, powerful
enough to prevail with Court, cabinet and parliament, would
have supported him in any liberal crusade ? And would
England have possessed so great a moral leadership had
she then lived, as Bright and Cobden would have had her
live, entirely to herself, entirely for her own budget, her own
trade balances, and the development of her own democracy ?
And if these ' Manchester ' critics of Palmerston were right ;
if his ' moral leadership ' was not merely a sham but an
obstacle to the development of continental liberalism, how

was it that he received the thanks of liberal leaders from all
over the continent, including those of the Poles and the
Hungarians ?   His intentions and his achievements in
these matters may still, perhaps, be considered as debatable ;
but in one respect at least the reality of his ' moral
nationalism,' if one may use the term, seems impossible to
deny.   No country in the nineteenth century was endowed
by any of its statesmen with a finer achievement in national
altruism than Palmerston's struggle to extinguish the
international slave trade.   In desire to stamp it out there
were doubtless other Englishmen who quite equalled him ;
but the work was mainly his, and was performed *ad majorem
Britanniae gloriam.*

It is at least possible to feel that his nationalism infused
even his parliamentary career.   There is a strong suggestion
of the nationalist in his comparative detachment from
parties, and perhaps as much in his attitude toward the
three or four great questions that wove in and out of so
many political crises during his time.   Is there not ground
for thinking that it was not so much pride and selfishness
of the Whig type, as scepticism regarding the political
capacity of the masses to play their part in the intelligent
and efficient direction of a powerful state, that made him
so insistent that the franchise should be confined to those of
' property and intelligence ' ?   Might not his almost
Prussian reverence for the state, conflicting with his understanding of political economy, have produced his seeming
inconsistencies about free trade ?   Is it not perfectly consistent with a nationalistic attitude that this man, to whom
the Christian faith was a matter of indifference, fought for
the established church as the solder of the state ?   Is it not
possible to suppose that partly from the same source, at
least, came the unwillingness to do anything important for
Ireland, on the part of one so obviously humanitarian, and
so sympathetic with the Irish peasantry ?   No ideas of
abstract justice to Ireland, of righting wrongs by changes
in the ' establishment,' found favour with him at any time.
But, provided the continuance of British control afforded
a continuing guarantee that Ireland would serve the power
and the glory of the British state, he would do what he

could to give contentment and prosperity to her people. His attitude toward the English Catholics was much the same : Catholic emancipation, yes ; friendly relations with the Vatican, yes : but the restoration of the ' popish ' hierarchy,—of a foreign ' dominion ' which might detract from the allegiance of British subjects to the state—no, a thousand times. Desire for colonial acquisitions he had little, vision of a great world commonwealth none at all ; but the checking of Russian and French expansion, the retention to the last square mile of all to which England could lay claim,—these policies were essential for the maintenance of British prestige and British influence.

If Englishmen of his own day stood too close to him for detached analysis ; if their sons, dazzled by Gladstone's and Disraeli's great exploits and conflicts, allowed his image to grow blurred, there were persons on the continent, such as the editor of the Vienna *Debatte*, who saw him in his own time as a great nationalist :

In the clash of principles and convictions he recognized only one— the interest of England—and this he served with sacrificing devotion. Whatever could advance England's power and greatness was law, in following up which he left all other considerations out of sight. . . . He has raised the influence of England to the highest pitch. . . .

And the *Nazione* of Florence, while agreeing that ' Lord Palmerston gave himself up wholly to his country,' added:

. . . every banner under which the defenders of liberty, progress and civilization are grouped will be veiled with crape. . . .

NOTES *

CHAPTER XX

[1] P. 1. Argyll, I, 332–3.
[2] P. 2. Palmerston's memoranda, Sept. 8, 1846, Sept. 16, 1847 ; Palmerston to Bunsen, June 14, 1847 (copy), *Windsor MSS*. I. 1.
[3] P. 3. Martin, *Prince Consort*, I, 364.
[4] P. 3. *Inter alia*, Palmerston to Russell, July 6, 10, 1848, P.R.O., G. and D. 22 : 7.
[5] P. 3. Palmerston to Bloomfield, Aug. 18, 1848, P.R.O., F.O., 356 : 29.
[6] P. 3. Bunsen, II, 149.
[7] P. 4. Palmerston to Prince Albert, May 8, 1849, *Windsor MSS*. I. 13. See also same to same, June 18, 1849, *Windsor MSS*. I. 15.
[8] P. 4. Q.V.L., 1st Ser., II, 328–30.
[9] P. 4. Martin, *Prince Consort*, I, 346–7, 356–64 ; Stockmar, II, 230–48, 254–9, 382 ; Bunsen, II, 148–9 ; C. Greville, *Mem*., VI, 297–8 ; Beust, I, 40, 50 ; Corti, *Leopold*, 171–6 ; Q.V.L., 1st Ser., II, 228–9, 256.
[10] P. 5. Palmerston to Russell, no date (probably Feb. 1851), P.R.O., G. and D., 22 : 9.
[11] P. 5. B. and A., III, 340.
[12] P. 5. *Ibid.*, 159–62.
[13] P. 5. Drafts to Westmorland, June 21, July 8, 1847, Feb. 17, 1848, P.R.O., F.O., 96 : 21, 22.
[14] P. 6. Steefel, chap. I ; C.H.B.F.P., II, 522–41.
[15] P. 7. Palmerston to Victoria, Oct. 23, 1850, *Windsor MSS*. I. 22.
[16] P. 8. Palmerston to Bloomfield, May 19, 1848, P.R.O., F.O., 356 : 29.
[17] P. 8. Palmerston to Victoria, Apr. 18, 1848, *Windsor MSS*. I. 3.
[18] P. 8. Same to same, June 20, 1849, *Windsor MSS*. I. 15. See also Palmerston to Prince Albert, Apr. 30, 1850, *Windsor MSS*. I. 19.
[19] P. 8. Reeve, I, 198 ; Stockmar, II, 407.
[20] P. 9. Drafts to Bunsen and to the British representatives at Berlin, Frankfort and Copenhagen, P.R.O., F.O., 96 : 22 ; Palmerston to Russell, July 5, 1849, P.R.O., G. and D., 22 : 8.
[21] P. 9. Malmesbury (3rd Earl), *Mem.*, I, 246–7.
[22] P. 9. *Supra*, note 16.
[23] P. 9. Palmerston to Victoria, June 20, 1849, *Windsor MSS*. I. 15.
[24] P. 9. *Ibid.*
[25] P. 10. Palmerston to Bloomfield, May 28, 1848, P.R.O., F.O., 356 : 29.
[26] P. 10. Aberdeen, *Corr.*, 1850–2, pp. 23–4, 33–4.
[27] P. 10. *Ibid.*, 24–5.
[28] P. 11. Q.V.L., 1st Ser., II, 264–5.
[29] P. 11. *E.g.* Prince Albert's and Palmerston's memoranda, Aug. 21 ; Victoria to Palmerston, Aug. 24, 1850, *Windsor MSS*. I. 21.
[30] P. 11. Q.V.L., 1st Ser., II, 295–6.
[31] P. 11. *Ibid.*, 296–7.

* See *Guide to Citations* in vol. I, pp. 448–456.

[32] P. 11. Sproxton, *passim.*
[33] P. 13. *Ibid.,* 46.
[34] P. 13. *Ibid.,* 61.
[35] P. 13. *Ibid.,* 78.
[36] P. 13. B. and A., IV, 137.
[37] P. 13. Palmerston to Russell, Sept. 14, 1849 (copy), *Windsor MSS.* J. 103.
[38] P. 14. Greville-Reeve, *Letters,* 189–90.
[39] P. 14. Sproxton, 20.
[40] P. 14. *Hansard,* 3rd Ser., CVII, 809.
[41] P. 15. Palmerston to Ponsonby, Aug. 1, 1849 (no. 102), P.R.O., F.O., 7 : 364.
[42] P. 15. Palmerston to Russell, Aug. 22, 1849, P.R.O., G. and D., 22 : 8.
[43] P. 15. *Hansard,* 3rd Ser., CVII, 811.
[44] P. 15. B. and A., IV, 137–8.
[45] P. 16. *Ibid.,* 139–41.
[46] P. 16. Lane-Poole, II, 191–2.
[47] P. 17. Lucas, *Glenesk,* 132.
[48] P. 17. B. and A., IV, 142–3.
[49] P. 17. Lane-Poole, II, 194–7, 194 n.
[50] P. 18. *Ibid.,* 197–9 ; Sproxton, 122–7 ; Palmerston to Bloomfield, Oct. 6, 1849 (no. 1), P.R.O., F.O., 65 : 362 ; same to same, same date, private, F.O., 356 : 29 ; Bloomfield to Palmerston, Oct. 22, 1849 (no. 15), F.O., 65 : 367 ; B. and A., IV, 144–67.
[51] P. 18. *Ibid.,* 154–5.
[52] P. 18. *Ibid.,* 150–3.
[53] P. 18. Bloomfield to Palmerston, Oct. 16, 19, 22, 1849 (nos. 6, 12, 15), P.R.O., F.O., 65 : 367.
[54] P. 19. Sproxton, 133.
[55] P. 19. Nesselrode, X, 72.
[56] P. 19. B. and A., IV, 167–75 ; Lane-Poole, II, 202–5.
[57] P. 19. *Ibid.,* 201.
[58] P. 19. *Ibid.,* 202.
[59] P. 20. Victoria to Russell, Sept. 12, 1849, *Windsor MSS.* J. 103.
[60] P. 20. Palmerston to Russell, Sept. 14, 1849, *Windsor MSS.* J. 103.
[61] P. 20. Q.V.L., 1st Ser., II, 331.
[62] P. 20. Prince Albert to Russell, no date (copy), *Windsor MSS.* C. 17.
[63] P. 21. C. Greville, *Mem.,* VI, 316–20.
[64] P. 21. Q.V.L., 1st Ser., II, 279–82, 288–90 ; Russell to Palmerston, May 22, 1850, P.R.O., G. and D., 22 : 8 ; Prince Albert to Russell, no date (copy), *Windsor MSS.* C. 17 ; C. Greville, *Mem.,* VI, 335–7.
[65] P. 21. Prince Albert to Russell, no date (copy), *Windsor MSS.* C. 17.
[66] P. 21. Prince Albert to Russell, no date (copy), *Windsor MSS.* C. 17 ; Wilson, *Greville,* II, 88.
[67] P. 22. C.H.B.F.P., II, 589–99 ; Martin, *Prince Consort,* II, 222–9.
[68] P. 22. Martineau, *Newcastle,* 95.
[69] P. 22. Palmerston to Bloomfield, March 11, 27, 1850, P.R.O., F.O., 356 : 29.
[70] P. 23. *Cf.* Reeve, I, 223.
[71] P. 23. Maxwell, *Clarendon,* I, 310.
[72] P. 23. Reeve, I, 225.
[73] P. 23. Martin, *Prince Consort,* II, 226–8 ; Palmerston to Russell, May 26, 1850, P.R.O., G. and D. 22 : 8 (partly printed in Lord J. Russell, *Later Corr.,* II, 75–6).

[74] P. 23. C. Greville, *Mem.*, VI, 330–4 ; *Hansard*, 3rd Ser., CXI, 105 ; Palmerston to Bloomfield, May 17, 1850, P.R.O., F.O., 356 : 29.

[75] P. 24. Parker, *Peel*, III, 534–40 ; Parker, *Graham*, II, 103–4.

[76] P. 24. Trevelyan, *Bright*, 192.

[77] P. 24. C. Greville, *Mem.*, VI, 336.

[78] P. 24. Monypenny and Buckle, III, 256–9.

[79] P. 24. *Hansard*, 3rd Ser., CXI, 1378.

[80] P. 24. B. and A., IV, 225. See also Palmerston to Bloomfield, May 24, 1850, P.R.O., F.O., 356 : 29 ; Q.V.L., 1st Ser., II, 314.

[81] P. 25. Parker, *Peel*, III, 535 ; Reeve, I, 221, 226.

[82] P. 25. *Hansard*, 3rd Ser., CXI, 1293–1332.

[83] P. 25. Vitzthum, *Berlin und Wien*, 280.

[84] P. 25. *Hansard*, 3rd Ser., CXII, 102–6.

[85] P. 25. Broughton, VI, 256.

[86] P. 25. Leader, 240–1.

[87] P. 25. *Ibid.* ; C. Greville, *Mem.*, VI, 342–4.

[88] P. 26. Stanmore, *Herbert*, I, 125.

[89] P. 26. *Hansard*, 3rd Ser., CXII, 315, 687–8.

[90] P. 26. Hertslet, *Recollections*, 72.

[91] P. 26. Wolff, *Rambling Recollections*, I, 118.

[92] P. 26. *Hansard*, 3rd Ser., CXII, 380–444 ; Leader, 241–2 ; Broughton, VI, 257–8 ; Martin, *Prince Consort*, II, 232–6 ; Morley, *Gladstone*, I, 369 ; Argyll, I, 323 ; C. Greville, *Mem.*, VI, 346. *Cf.* Trevelyan, *Bright*, 190.

[93] P. 27. Broughton, VI, 257.

[94] P. 27. Lady Palmerston to Clarendon, July 1, 1850, *Clarendon MSS.*

[95] P. 27. Maxwell, *Clarendon*, I, 311–12.

[96] P. 27. Reeve, I, 228.

[97] P. 28. C. Greville, *Mem.*, VI, 347.

[98] P. 28. *Ibid.*

[99] P. 28. *Ibid.*, 344, 347.

[100] P. 28. B. and A., IV, 225.

[101] P. 28. Quoted by P. de Barante, 'Les Procédés Diplomatiques de Palmerston' in *Rev. d'Hist. Dipl.*, vol. 45, Oct.–Dec., 1931, p. 414.

[102] P. 28. Sproxton, 96.

CHAPTER XXI

[1] P. 29. Prince Consort, *Letters*, 117.

[2] P. 29. Wilson, *Greville*, II, 368–9 ; Q.V.L., 1st Ser., II, 305–6, 309–14.

[3] P. 29. *Ibid.*, 314.

[4] P. 29. Broughton, VI, 291.

[5] P. 30. Martin, *Prince Consort*, II, 442–5, 451.

[6] P. 30. *Ibid.*, III, 101.

[7] P. 30. *Ann. Reg.* for 1850, *Chron.*, 80–1 ; Lucas, *Glenesk*, 133 ; Fagan, *Reform Club*, 83.

[8] P. 30. *Ibid.*, 83–91.

[9] P. 30. C. Greville, *Mem.*, VI, 362.

[10] P. 31. Prince Albert's memorandum, Feb. 24, 1851, *Windsor MSS.* C. 46.

[11] P. 31. *The Times*, Aug. 2, 1847 ; Snell, 77–87 ; the duke of Bedford to Russell, Aug. (?), 1847 ; Palmerston to Russell, July 25, 1847, P.R.O., G. and D. 22 : 6.

[12] P. 32. Grant, *Newspaper Press*, III, 206.

[13] P. 32. Prince Albert's comments on the principal newspapers, 1851, *Windsor MSS*. C. 46.

[14] P. 32. Bowman, 156–69, 182–9.

[15] P. 32. Reeve, I, 338–9.

[16] P. 32. Aberdeen to the Princess Lieven and to Schwarzenberg, March 19, May 2, 1851 ; Aberdeen, *Corr.*, 1850–1852.

[17] P. 33. Bowman, 182–9 ; C. Greville, *Mem.*, V, 406, VI, 39, 260, 365–6 ; Lucas, *Glenesk*, 133.

[18] P. 33. Edward Ellice to Russell, Dec. 22, 1847, P.R.O., G. and D., 22 : 6 ; Dasent, *Delane*, I, 60 n. ; C. Greville, *Mem.*, VI, 127–8, 128 n.

[19] P. 33. Stockmar, II, 349.

[20] P. 33. Grant, *Newspaper Press*, III, 72–3 ; Parker, *Peel*, III, 535 ; Palmerston to Russell, Dec. 23, 1851, *Windsor MSS*. A. 80.

[21] P. 33. Lucas, *Glenesk*, 68.

[22] P. 33. Palmerston to Clarendon, Jan. 24, 1850, *Clarendon MSS*.

[23] P. 33. Reeve, I, 222.

[24] P. 33. Lucas, *Glenesk*, 54–5, 62.

[25] P. 34. *Ibid.*, 72–3.

[26] P. 34. *Ibid.*, 73.

[27] P. 34. Gardiner, I, 62–3.

[28] P. 34. Walpole, *Russell*, II, 65 ; Lord J. Russell, *Later Corr.*, I, 222–7 ; Palmerston to Clarendon, Apr. 11, 18, July 28, 1848.

[29] P. 34. *Hansard*, 3rd Ser., CXXIII, 454.

[30] P. 34. *Ann. Reg.* for 1850 and 1851.

[31] P. 35. *E.g. Hansard*, 3rd Ser., CXIV, 35–6.

[32] P. 35. *Ibid.*, 4.

[33] P. 35. *Ibid,*, CXV, 93.

[34] P. 35. Russell's memorandum, Oct. 27, 1848 ; Palmerston to Russell, same date, P.R.O., G. and D., 22 : 7 ; Lord J. Russell, *Later Corr.*, I, 223–33. See also Palmerston to Clarendon, Oct. 11, 1848, *Clarendon MSS*.

[35] P. 35. *Hansard*, 3rd Ser., CXXI, 580.

[36] P. 36. *Ibid.*, CXV, 183.

[37] P. 36. Palmerston to Russell, Jan. 18, and to Normanby, Jan. 20, 1851 (copy), P.R.O., G. and D., 22 : 9.

[38] P. 36. 16 Ric. II, c. 5 ; Palmerston to Russell, Dec. 9, 1850, G. and D., 22 : 8.

[39] P. 37. Lucas, *Glenesk*, 134.

[40] P. 37. *Ann. Reg.* for 1850, pp. 198–9.

[41] P. 37. For general account, H. C. Bell, ' Palmerston and Parliamentary Representation,' in *Journ. Mod. His.*, vol. IV, no. 2 (June 1932).

[42] P. 37. *Hansard*, 3rd Ser., CXIX, 252 ; Walpole, *Russell*, II, 102, 123.

[43] P. 37. C. Greville, *Mem.*, VI, 414 ; Broughton, VI, 294.

[44] P. 38. Palmerston to Russell, Sept. 21, 1851, P.R.O., G. and D., 22 : 9 ; Lord J. Russell, *Later Corr.*, I, 214–16 ; Walpole, *Russell*, II, 129–30.

[45] P. 38. Lord J. Russell, *Later Corr.*, I, 216.

[46] P. 38. Palmerston to Lansdowne, Oct. 4, 1852, *Bowood MSS*. ; Airlie, II, 141.

[47] P. 38. *Ann. Reg.* for 1852, 21 ; *The Times* for Feb. 10, 11, 13, 14, 1852.

[48] P. 39. Note 2, *supra*.

[49] P. 39. Q.V.L., 1st Ser., II, 315 ; Martin, *Prince Consort*, II, 249–55.

[50] P. 39. *Ibid.*, 282.

[51] P. 39. Broughton, VI, 292.

[52] P. 39. Martin, *Prince Consort*, II, 253–5 ; Q.V.L., 1st Ser., II, 315–16.
[53] P. 40. Palmerston to Lansdowne, Oct. 4, 1852, *Bowood MSS.* ; Broughton, VI, 291–2.
[54] P. 40. *Ann. Reg.* for 1850, *Chronicle*, 110–11 ; Martin, *Prince Consort*, II, 266–7.
[55] P. 40. *Ibid.*, 267–8.
[56] P. 40. Aberdeen, *Corr.*, 1850–2, pp. 73–4 ; Walpole, *Russell*, II, 122–8 ; Q.V.L., 1st Ser., II, 345–52.
[57] P. 41. *Ibid.*, 350.
[58] P. 41. *Ibid.*, 354–5.
[59] P. 41. Prince Albert's memorandum, Feb. 24, 1851, *Windsor MSS.* C. 46.
[60] P. 42. *Ibid.* ; Q.V.L., 1st Ser., II, 358–9.
[61] P. 42. *Ibid.*
[62] P. 42. *Ibid.*, 362 ; Aberdeen, *Corr.*, 1850–2, pp. 74–6, 81–2.
[63] P. 42. Q.V.L., 1st Ser., II, 363.
[64] P. 43. *Ibid.*, 365–6.
[65] P. 43. Martin, *Prince Consort*, II, 287–9.
[66] P. 43. Q.V.L., 1st Ser., II, 377.
[67] P. 43. *Ibid.*, 381.
[68] P. 43. Aberdeen, *Corr.*, 1850–2, pp. 85, 93–4.
[69] P. 44. Stockmar, II, 458–9.
[70] P. 44. Q.V.L., 1st Ser., II, 418.
[71] P. 44. C. Greville, *Mem.*, VI, 413–14.
[72] P. 44. Walpole, *Russell*, II, 133.
[73] P. 44. *Ibid.*
[74] P. 44. Charles Grey to Lord Grey, Nov. 26, 1851, *Howick MSS.*
[75] P. 45. Broughton, VI, 286–8 ; Walpole, *Russell*, II, 134–6.
[76] P. 45. Charles Grey to Lord Grey, Nov. 26, 1851, *Howick MSS.*
[77] P. 45. *Ibid.* ; Martin, *Prince Consort*, II, 333–4 ; Walpole, *Russell*, II, 136–8 ; C. Greville, *Mem.*, VI, 415–16.
[78] P. 46. Malmesbury (3rd earl), *Mem.*, I, 297.
[79] P. 46. Broughton, VI, 289–90.
[80] P. 46. Vitzthum, *Berlin und Wien*, 318 ; H. Greville, *Diary*, I, 405.
[81] P. 46. Nesselrode, X, 77–8.
[82] P. 46. Prince Consort, *Letters*, 125–6.
[83] P. 46. Palmerston to Lansdowne, Oct. 4, 1852, *Bowood MSS.* ; Argyll, I, 348.
[84] P. 47. B. and A., IV, 300–6, 311–12.
[85] P. 47. *Ibid.*, 291.
[86] P. 47. Kerry and Guedalla, 18–19 ; Martin, *Prince Consort*, II, 337 ; B. and A., IV, 287–90.
[87] P. 47. C. Greville, *Mem.*, VI, 68.
[88] P. 47. Lucas, *Glenesk*, 93 ; Malmesbury (3rd earl), *Mem.*, I, 258–60.
[89] P. 47. Palmerston's memorandum, May (?) 30, 1856, *Clarendon MSS.* ; B. and A., IV, 292–4.
[90] P. 48. *E.g.* Q.V.L., 1st Ser., II, 406–12 ; Lady Normanby to Col. Phipps, Dec. 14, 1851, *Windsor MSS.* A. 79.
[91] P. 48. Prince Albert's memorandum, Jan. 21, 1852, *Windsor MSS.* A. 80. *Cf.* Malmesbury (3rd earl), *Mem.*, I, 303 n. ; Martin, *Prince Consort*, II, 339–40.
[92] P. 48. B. and A., IV, 316 ; Palmerston to Lansdowne, Oct. 4, 1852, *Bowood MSS.* (partly printed in B. and A., IV, 325–30) ; Kerry and Guedella, 137.
[93] P. 49. B. and A., IV, 294–5.
[94] P. 49. *Ibid.*, 295–7.

95 P. 49. *Ibid.*, 297–9 ; Martin, *Prince Consort*, II, 340.
96 P. 50. Maxwell, *Clarendon*, I, 337–8.
97 P. 50. *E.g.* C. Greville, *Mem.*, VI, 426–7 ; Parker, *Graham*, II, 146 ; Fawcett, 298 ; Airlie, II, 139.
98 P. 50. Lord J. Russell, *Recollections*, 257–8.
99 P. 50. Martin, *Prince Consort*, II, 341.
100 P. 50. Monypenny and Buckle, III, 339.
101 P. 50. Aberdeen, *Corr.*, 1850–2, p. 233.
102 P. 50. Parker, *Graham*, II, 142 ; Broughton, VI, 290.
103 P. 50. *E.g.* Palmerston to Lansdowne, Dec. 29, 1851, *Bowood MSS.* ; B. and A., IV, 310–11.
104 P. 50. Argyll, I, 348 ; Kerry and Guedalla, 160.
105 P. 51. Maxwell, *Clarendon*, I, 338–9.
106 P. 51. Oldfield, 149.
107 P. 51. Q.V.L., 1st Ser., II, 415–20.
108 P. 51. Maxwell, *Clarendon*, I, 339 ; C. Greville, *Mem.*, VI, 428, 431 ; Parker, *Graham*, II, 142 ; Kerry and Guedalla, 152–4, 154 n.
109 P. 51. *Ibid.* ; Maxwell, *Clarendon*, I, 334–9. *Cf.* Parker, *Graham*, II, 147.
110 P. 51. *Ibid.* ; Q.V.L., 1st Ser., II, 419 ; Kerry and Guedalla, 153–4, 154 n.
111 P. 51. Maxwell, *Clarendon*, I, 341.
112 P. 52. Q.V.L., 1st Ser., II, 423.
113 P. 52. Prince Consort, *Letters*, 125–6.
114 P. 52. Q.V.L., 1st Ser., II, 425–8 ; Fitzmaurice, I, 47–52 ; Granville to Russell, Jan. 12, 1852, P.R.O., G. and D., 29 : 18.
115 P. 52. Fitzmaurice, I, 52.
116 P. 53. B. and A., IV, 316–17.
117 P. 53. Lucas, *Glenesk*, 136 ; Martin, *Prince Consort*, II, 343 ; the *Morning Post*, Dec. 26, 27, 29, 30, 31, 1851, and Jan. 1, 1852.
118 P. 53. C. Greville, *Mem.*, VI, 433 ; Greville-Reeve, *Letters*, 210.
119 P. 53. Lady Palmerston to Mrs. Huskisson, Jan. 9, 1852, Br. Mus., *Add. MSS.* 39949, ff. 266–70.
120 P. 53. Reeve, I, 247.
121 P. 53. *The Times*, Dec. 26, 1851.
122 P. 53. Trevelyan, *Bright*, 197–8.
123 P. 54. Dasent, *Delane*, I, 128–9.
124 P. 54. Parker, *Graham*, II, 149.
125 P. 54. Malmesbury (3rd earl), *Mem.*, I, 293–4. For Palmerston's view, see Lady Palmerston to Mrs. Huskisson, Jan. 9, 1852, Br. Mus., *Add. MSS.* 39949, ff. 266–70.
126 P. 54. Reeve, I, 242.
127 P. 54. Broughton, VI, 293.
128 P. 54. *Hansard*, 3rd Ser., CXIX, 84–156 ; Broughton, VI, 292 ; Lyall, I, 67–8 ; H. Greville, *Diary*, I, 411 ; Malmesbury (3rd earl), *Mem.*, I, 301 ; Martin, *Prince Consort*, II, 345–7, 346 n. ; Monypenny and Buckle, III, 340 ; Q.V.L., 1st Ser., II, 438–41.
129 P. 55. *Hansard*, 3rd Ser., CXIX, 104–116.
130 P. 55. *Ibid.*, 118.
131 P. 56. Monypenny and Buckle, III, 340.
132 P. 56. Stockmar, II, 463–5.

CHAPTER XXII

[1] P. 57. Lyall, I, 68.
[2] P. 57. Q.V.L., 1st Ser., II, 438.
[3] P. 58. Aberdeen, *Corr.*, 1850–2, pp. 219–20.
[4] P. 58. Wolff, I, 141.
[5] P. 58. Prince Consort, *Letters*, 132. See also Airlie, II, 149.
[6] P. 58. Palmerston to Clarendon, Feb. 23, 1852, *Clarendon MSS.*
[7] P. 59. H. Greville, *Diary*, I, 414 ; Broughton, VI, 299.
[8] P. 59. Hodder, II, 378.
[9] P. 59. Malmesbury (3rd earl), *Mem.*, I, 304.
[10] P. 60. Gardiner, *Harcourt*, I, 67.
[11] P. 60. Argyll, I, 360–1.
[12] P. 60. H. Greville, *Diary*, I, 415–17.
[13] P. 60. Q.V.L., 1st Ser., II, 447–8.
[14] P. 60. Monypenny and Buckle, III, 278, 342–4.
[15] P. 61. Malmesbury, I, 305.
[16] P. 61. *Ibid.*
[17] P. 61. Q.V.L., 1st Ser., II, 448 ; Monypenny and Buckle, III, 343–4.
[18] P. 61. Lucas, *Glenesk*, 108–9.
[19] P. 61. Malmesbury, I, 316–18.
[20] P. 61. *Ibid.*, 320 ; Q.V.L., 1st Ser., II, 451.
[21] P. 61. Malmesbury, I, 318–19.
[22] P. 62. Palmerston to Lansdowne, Oct. 14, 1852, *Bowood MSS.*
[23] P. 62. Q.V.L., 1st Ser., II, 458 ; H. Greville, *Diary*, I, 418.
[24] P. 62. Maxwell, *Clarendon*, I, 345.
[25] P. 62. Lucas, *Glenesk*, 139.
[26] P. 63. Q.V.L., 1st Ser., II, 470. See also Burghclere, 256–7.
[27] P. 63. Stanmore, *Herbert*, I, 155.
[28] P. 63. Lyall, I, 71.
[29] P. 63. H. Greville, *Diary*, I, 422.
[30] P. 63. Aberdeen, *Corr.*, 1850–2, p. 354.
[31] P. 63. Airlie, II, 152.
[32] P. 63. *Hansard*, 3rd Ser., CXX, 514 ; CXXII, 1383.
[33] P. 63. Q.V.L., 1st Ser., II, 462–3 ; *Hansard*, 3rd Ser., CXIX, 1111–13.
[34] P. 64. Aberdeen, *Corr.*, 1850–2, p. 307.
[35] P. 64. Dasent, *Delane*, I, 151.
[36] P. 64. Monypenny and Buckle, III, 377.
[37] P. 64. Stanmore, *Herbert*, I, 163.
[38] P. 64. Aberdeen, *Corr.*, 1850–2, pp. 328–9, 334–6, 352–3, 357 ; Parker, *Graham*, II, 173 ; Stanmore, *Herbert*, I, 162–3.
[39] P. 65. Palmerston to Lansdowne, Oct. 14, 1852. See also Lansdowne to Palmerston, Oct. (?), 1852, *Bowood MSS.*
[40] P. 65. Stanmore, *Herbert*, I, 162–3.
[41] P. 65. Lansdowne to Palmerston, Oct. 22, 1852, *Bowood MSS.* See also Parker, *Graham*, II, 175.
[42] P. 65. Palmerston to Lansdowne, Oct. 24, 1852, *Bowood MSS.*
[43] P. 65. Stanmore, *Herbert*, I, 163.
[44] P. 65. Maxwell, *Clarendon*, I, 350 ; Parker, *Graham*, II, 175–6.
[45] P. 66. Aberdeen, *Corr.*, 1850–2, pp. 350–2.
[46] P. 66. *Ibid.*, 315–21, 365–7.

47 P. 67. Stanmore, *Aberdeen*, 207–13.

48 P. 67. Aberdeen, *Corr.*, 1850–2, pp. 301–5 ; Parker, *Graham*, II, 174.

49 P. 67. Stanmore, *Aberdeen*, 207 ; *Hansard*, 3rd Ser., CXXII, 1386 ; Aberdeen, *Corr.*, 1850–2, pp. 297–8.

50 P. 67. Aberdeen, *Corr.*, 1850–2, 365–7.

51 P. 67. Airlie, II, 146–7.

52 P. 67. Parker, *Graham*, II, 176.

53 P. 68. Monypenny and Buckle, III, 407–21 ; Parker, *Graham*, II, 177–87 ; H. Greville, *Diary*, II, 10–11, 17–18 ; Stanmore, *Herbert*, I, 165–6 ; Whitty, 55–62 ; Q.V.L., 1st Ser., II, 488–92 ; Prince Albert's memorandum, Nov. 25, 1852 ; *Hansard*, 3rd Ser., CXXIII, 351–705.

54 P. 68. Airlie, II, 152.

55 P. 68. Guedalla, *Gladstone and Palmerston*, 86–8 ; Morley, *Gladstone*, I, 433 ; Parker, *Graham*, II, 187 ; Monypenny and Buckle, III, 411–12.

56 P. 69. *Hansard*, 3rd Ser., CXXIII, 454.

57 P. 69. Prince Albert to Derby, Nov. 26, 1852 (copy), *Windsor MSS.* C. 28.

58 P. 69. Stockmar's memorandum, Nov. 27, 1852, *Windsor MSS.* C. 28.

59 P. 69. Monypenny and Buckle, III, 423–4 ; Prince Albert's memorandum, Nov. 25, 1852, *Windsor MSS.* C. 28.

60 P. 69. Stockmar's memorandum, Dec. 10, 1852, *Windsor MSS.* C. 28.

61 P. 70. Prince Albert's memorandum, Nov. 25, 1852, *Windsor MSS.* C. 28 ; Q.V.L., 1st Ser., II, 488–92.

62 P. 70. *Ibid.* ; Monypenny and Buckle, III, 423.

63 P. 70. B. and A., IV, 377–9.

64 P. 70. Stockmar's memorandum, Nov. 27, 1852, *Windsor MSS.* C. 28.

65 P. 70. Monypenny and Buckle, III, 437–8.

66 P. 70. Q.V.L., 1st Ser., II, 516.

67 P. 70. *Ibid.*, 501–3 ; Reeve, I, 267.

68 P. 71. H. Greville, *Diary*, II, 20–1.

69 P. 71. Whitty, 75.

70 P. 71. Q.V.L., 1st Ser., II, 504.

71 P. 71. *Ibid.*, 517.

72 P. 71. *Ibid.*, 500–16 ; Stanmore, *Aberdeen*, 213–15 ; Parker, *Graham*, II, 193–5 ; Cook, *Delane*, 64–5 ; Walpole, *Russell*, II, 161–71.

73 P. 71. Q.V.L., 1st Ser., II, 503.

74 P. 72. *Ibid.*, 504 ; Parker, *Graham*, II, 191–2.

75 P. 72. Aberdeen, *Corr.*, 1850–2, p. 429.

76 P. 72. *Ibid.*, 1854–5, pp. 338–41 ; Airlie, II, 151 ; H. Greville, *Diary*, II, 23–4 ; Reeve, I, 268–9.

77 P. 72. *Ibid.* ; Parker, *Graham*, II, 195.

78 P. 72. Q.V.L., 1st Ser., II, 511.

79 P. 72. Prince Consort, *Letters*, 135.

80 P. 73. Q.V.L., 1st Ser., II, 520, 523.

81 P. 73. Hodder, II, 408.

82 P. 73. Q.V.L., 1st Ser., II, 503.

83 P. 73. Reeve, I, 269.

84 P. 73. Airlie, II, 151–3.

85 P. 74. Cook, *Delane*, 63.

86 P. 75. Hodder, II, 444.

87 P. 75. Fagan, *Panizzi*, I, 331–2 ; Lord Grey to Gen. Grey, May 30, 1853, *Howick MSS.* ; Dalhousie, *Letters*, 318, 324.

88 P. 75. Reeve, I, 271.

89 P. 76. *Hansard*, 3rd Ser., CXXIV, 872.

90 P. 76. Hodder, II, 456. See also Palmerston to Aberdeen, Sept. 20, 1853, Br. Mus., *Aberdeen MSS.*

91 P. 76 . Same to same, Aug. 28, and Aberdeen to Palmerston, Aug. 30, 1853, *Aberdeen MSS.*

92 P. 76. *Hansard*, 3rd Ser., CXXIX, 1563–9. See also *ibid.*, CXXXIII, 1395–7.

93 P. 76. *Ibid.*, CXXIV, 38 ; CXXV, 449 ; Palmerston to Granville, Aug. 10, 1853, P.R.O., G. and D., 29 : 18.

94 P. 77. Guedalla, *Gladstone and Palmerston*, 95–6.

95 P. 77. *Hansard*, CXXV, 646–7 ; CXXVI, 1117–25 ; CXXVII, 1017 ; CXXVIII, 1251–68 ; CXXIX, 1322 ; Fitzmaurice, I, 418.

96 P. 77. 6 Geo. IV, c. 129 ; *Hansard*, CXXV, 646.

97 P. 78. *Ibid.*, CXXVII, 1017.

98 P. 78. Palmerston to Granville, June 30, 1853, P.R.O., G. and D., 29 : 23.

99 P. 78. *Hansard*, CXXV, 680 ; CXXIX, 1105, 1535, 1685.

100 P. 78. Hodder, II, 431–2.

101 P. 79. *Hansard*, CXXIX, 1535–60 ; Palmerston to Aberdeen, May 20, and Aberdeen to Palmerston, May 22, 1853, Br. Mus., *Aberdeen MSS.*

102 P. 79. Palmerston to Russell, Dec. 1, 1853, P.R.O., G. and D., 22 : 11 ; Hodder, II, 445 ; *Hansard*, CXXXV, 234.

103 P. 79. Palmerston to Russell, Apr. 3, 1853, P.R.O., G. and D., 22 : 11.

104 P. 79. Aberdeen, *Corr.*, 1853–54, *passim.*

105 P. 80. *Hansard*, CXXV, 1209 ; CXXVI, 797–803, 1142–59.

106 P. 80. Aberdeen, *Corr.*, 1853–4, p. 96.

107 P. 80. Reeve, I, 300.

108 P. 80. Whitty, 151, 302–3.

109 P. 80. H. Greville, *Diary*, II, 66.

CHAPTER XXIII

1 P. 81. For most detailed treatment, Puryear, *passim.* See especially Malmesbury (3rd earl), *Mem.*, I, 402–3.

2 P. 82. Beust, I, 255 ; H. E. Howard, 'Lord Cowley on Napoleon III in 1853 ' in *Eng. His. Rev.*, XLIX (1934), 502–3.

3 P. 82. For the best review and excellent bibliography, B. E. Schmitt, 'Diplomatic Preliminaries of the Crimean War,' in *Am. His. Rev.*, vol. XXV, no. 1 (Oct. 1919). See also Harold Temperley, ' Stratford de Redcliffe and the Origins of the Crimean War,' and ' The Alleged Violations of the Straits Convention by Stratford de Redcliffe between June and September, 1853 ' in *Eng. His. Rev.*, XLVIII (1933), pp. 601–21, and XLIX (1934), pp. 265–98, 657–72. Also, C.H.B.F.P., II, 340–76 ; *Journ. Mod. His.*, vol. IV, no. 4, pp. 635–7.

4 P. 83. B. and A., V, 25–6.

5 P. 83. *Ibid.*, 37. See also *Hansard*, 3rd Ser., CXXIX, 1808–10.

6 P. 83. Aberdeen, *Corr.*, 1853–4, p. 119 ; B. and A., V, 43–9.

7 P. 84. *Ibid.*

8 P. 84. Aberdeen, *Corr.*, 1853–4, pp. 348–9, 351.

9 P. 84. *Hansard*, 3rd Ser., CXXX, 1035–6.

10 P. 85. Aberdeen, *Corr.*, 1853–4, pp. 331–2.

11 P. 85. *Ibid.*, pp. 217–18 ; Monypenny and Buckle, III, 524.

12 P. 85. Maxwell, *Clarendon*, II, 3 ; C. Greville, *Mem.*, VII, 55 ; Reeve, I, 294–5.

[13] P. 85.   Parker, *Graham*, II, 219 ; Aberdeen, *Corr.*, 1853–4, p. 119.

[14] P. 86.   *Ibid.*, 128 ; Stanmore, *Aberdeen*, 222–3.

[15] P. 86.   Parker, *Graham*, II, 219 ; Monypenny and Buckle, III, 521.

[16] P. 86.   Stanmore, *Aberdeen*, 224 ; Temperley, 'Stratford . . . and the Origins,' *loc. cit.*, 618 ; B. and A., V, 30.

[17] P. 86.   *Ibid.*, 31.

[18] P. 86.   *Ibid.*, 26–31.

[19] P. 86.   *Ibid.*, 34–6 ; Stanmore, *Aberdeen*, 225–7 ; Aberdeen's memorandum, July 13, Palmerston to Aberdeen, and Aberdeen to Palmerston, July 15, 1853 (copies), *Windsor MSS.* G. 4 ; Aberdeen, *Corr.*, 1853–54, pp. 169–70.

[20] P. 87.   B. and A., V, 32–3.

[21] P. 87.   Q.V.L., 1st Ser., ; II,   549–50 ; Temperley, 'Stratford . . . and the Origins,', *loc. cit.*, 275–77 Aberdeen, *Corr.*, 1853–4, pp. 243–5.

[22] P. 87.   *Ibid.*, pp. 331–2.   See also *ibid.*, 223.

[23] P. 87.   Palmerston to Aberdeen, July 15, 1853, *Windsor MSS.* G. 4.

[24] P. 88.   Aberdeen, *Corr.*, 1853–4, p. 228 (partly printed in Stanmore, *Aberdeen*, 269–70).

[25] P. 88.   Aberdeen, *Corr.*, 1853–4, pp. 240–1 ; Stanmore, *Aberdeen*, 270–1.

[26] P. 88.   Maxwell, *Clarendon*, II, 22 ; Stanmore, *Aberdeen*, 269–71 ; Argyll, I, 463.

[27] P. 88.   Aberdeen, *Corr.*, 1853–4, p. 205.

[28] P. 88.   *Ibid.*, 348–50, 363.

[29] P. 88.   *Ibid.*, 263–4.

[30] P. 88.   *Ibid.*, 268–71 ; Stanmore, *Aberdeen*, 272.

[31] P. 89.   B. and A., V, 41–2 ; Martin, *Prince Consort*, II, 427–8 ; Aberdeen, *Corr.*, 1853–4, p. 301.

[32] P. 89.   *Ibid.*, p. 261.

[33] P. 89.   *Ibid.*, pp. 281–4 ; Stanmore, *Herbert*, I, 203–4 ; Morley, *Gladstone*, I, 482 ; Maxwell, *Clarendon*, II, 26.

[34] P. 89.   Q.V.L., 1st Ser., II, 551–2, 552 n.

[35] P. 89.   Palmerston to Russell, Oct. 24, 1853, P.R.O., G. and D., 22 : 11. (Incorrectly quoted in B. and A., V, 51.)

[36] P. 89.   Q.V.L., 1st Ser., II, 555–8 ; Stanmore, *Herbert*, I, 209–15 ; Aberdeen, *Corr.*, 1853–4, pp. 308 *et seq.*

[37] P. 89.   Palmerston to Russell, Oct. 24, 1853, P.R.O., G. and D., 22 : 11 (incorrectly quoted in B. and A., V, 49–51) ; C. Greville, *Mem.*, VII, 100–2 ; Palmerston to Aberdeen, Nov. 1, and Aberdeen to Palmerston, Nov. 4, 1853 (copies), *Windsor MSS.* G. 6.

[38] P. 90.   Trevelyan, *Bright*, 252.

[39] P. 90.   Argyll, I, 455–8.   See also *ibid.*, 387 ; Morley, *Gladstone*, I, 450.

[40] P. 91.   Aberdeen, *Corr.*, 1853–4, p. 205 ; Stanmore, *Herbert*, I, 204.

[41] P. 91.   Stanmore, *Aberdeen*, 303.

[42] P. 91.   Morley, *Gladstone*, I, 544–5.

[43] P. 91.   C. Greville, *Mem.*, VII., 91, 94.

[44] P. 91.   B. K. Martin, *Triumph*, 85–102.

[45] P. 92.   Airlie, II, 158.

[46] P. 92.   Argyll, I, 389.

[47] P. 92.   Martin, *Prince Consort*, II, 425.

[48] P. 92.   Malmesbury (3rd earl), *Mem.*, I, 401.

[49] P. 92.   Stanmore, *Herbert*, I, 172.

[50] P. 92.   Lord Grey to General Grey, Dec. 16, 1853, *Howick MSS.* ; Maxwell, *Clarendon*, I, 363 ; II, 16, 18, 35–6.

[51] P. 93.   Whitty, 78, 271.

⁵² P. 93 Layard, II, 247 ; Barante, VIII, 51 ; Monypenny and Buckle, III, 527.

⁵³ P. 93. B. and A., IV, 336–41.

⁵⁴ P. 93. Aberdeen, *Corr.*, 1853–4, pp. 204–5, 219, 233 ; Q.V.L., 1st Ser., II, 548–9 ; Maxwell, *Clarendon*, II, 21–2 ; Wilson, *Greville*, II, 88–9.

⁵⁵ P. 93. Prince Albert's memoranda, Nov. 4, 16 ; Palmerston to Aberdeen, Nov. 5 ; Aberdeen to Victoria, Nov. 7, 8 ; Victoria to Aberdeen, Nov. 7, 1853, *Windsor MSS.* A. 81 ; Corti, *Leopold*, 240 ; C. Greville, *Mem.*, VII, 133.

⁵⁶ P. 93. Aberdeen to Victoria, Nov. 8, 1853, *Windsor MSS.* A. 81.

⁵⁷ P. 93. *Ibid.*

⁵⁸ P. 94. Argyll, I, 471–2.

⁵⁹ P. 94. Prince Albert's memorandum, Nov. 16 ; Russell to Victoria, Nov. 19, 22, 1853, *Windsor MSS.* ; Aberdeen, *Corr.*, 1853–4, pp. 348–9, 355–6.

⁶⁰ P. 94. Palmerston to Russell, Nov. 14, 1853, P.R.O., G. and D., 22 : 11 ; Prince Albert's memorandum, Nov. 26, 1853, *Windsor MSS.* ; Parker, *Graham*, II, 206–8 ; Argyll, I, 472 ; Q.V.L., 1st Ser., II, 569.

⁶¹ P. 95. Palmerston to Russell, Jan. 22, 1854, P.R.O., G. and D., 22 : 11.

⁶² P. 95. Palmerston to Lansdowne, Dec. 8, 1853, *Bowood MSS.* (printed in Aberdeen, *Corr.*, 1853–4, pp. 389–91).

⁶³ P. 96. C. Greville, *Mem.*, VI, 414 ; Broughton, VI, 294.

⁶⁴ P. 96. *E.g.* Palmerston to Lansdowne, Dec. 13, 1853, *Bowood MSS.*

⁶⁵ P. 96. Palmerston to Aberdeen, Dec. 10, 1853 (copy), *Windsor MSS.* G. 7 (partly printed in B. and A., V, 52–4).

⁶⁶ P. 97. Argyll, I, 458.

⁶⁷ P. 97. Aberdeen, *Corr.*, 1853–4, p. 393.

⁶⁸ P. 97. *Ibid.*, p. 364 ; Argyll, I, 472.

⁶⁹ P. 97. Victoria to Aberdeen, Dec. 21, 1853 (draft), *Windsor MSS.* G. 8 ; Lord Grey to Gen. Grey, Dec. 24, 1853, *Howick MSS.* ; Martin, *Prince Consort*, II, 433.

⁷⁰ P. 97. Q.V.L., 1st Ser., II, 567–8.

⁷¹ P. 98. *Ibid.*, 568–9 ; Aberdeen, *Corr.*, 1853–4, p. 384.

⁷² P. 98. *Ibid.*, pp. 393–4.

⁷³ P. 98. *Ibid.*, 397–8.

⁷⁴ P. 98. *Ibid.*, 402–5 ; Prince Albert's memorandum, Dec. 16, 1853, *Windsor MSS.* G. 7 ; H. Greville, *Diary*, II, 75–6.

⁷⁵ P. 98. Aberdeen, *Corr.*, 1853–4, p. 404.

⁷⁶ P. 98. *Ibid.*, 404–5.

⁷⁷ P. 98. Maxwell, *Clarendon*, II, 36.

⁷⁸ P. 98. Aberdeen, *Corr.*, 1853–4, p. 404.

⁷⁹ P. 99. *Ibid.*, 399 ; Palmerston to Lansdowne, Dec. 13, 1853, *Bowood MSS.*

⁸⁰ P. 99. Palmerston to Lansdowne, Dec. 14, 1853, *Bowood MSS.* ; Maxwell, *Clarendon*, II, 35.

⁸¹ P. 99. *Ibid.* ; Malmesbury (3rd earl), *Mem.*, I, 420 ; H. Greville, *Diary*, II, 74.

⁸² P. 99. Reeve, II, 352–6, 356 n. See also Stanmore, *Aberdeen*, 273 ; Maxwell, *Clarendon*, II, 36.

⁸³ P. 99. Lane-Poole, *Stratford Canning*, II, 231 ; Maxwell, *Clarendon*, II, 28.

⁸⁴ P. 99. C. Greville, *Mem.*, VII, 110.

⁸⁵ P. 99. Note 74, *supra.*

⁸⁶ P. 100. Aberdeen to Victoria, Dec. 17, 1853 (copy), *Windsor MSS.* G. 7.

⁸⁷ P. 100. Q.V.L., 1st Ser., II, 568 ; Aberdeen, *Corr.*, 1853–4, p. 385.

[88] P. 100. *The Times,* Dec. 16, 1853.

[89] P. 100. B. K. Martin, *Triumph,* 198–9.

[90] P. 100. Lucas, *Glenesk,* 140.

[91] P. 100. Malmesbury (3rd earl), *Mem.,* I, 416.

[92] P. 100. Lord Grey to Gen. Grey, Dec. 24, 1853, *Howick MSS.*

[93] P. 101. Aberdeen to Victoria, *Dec.* 17, 1853, *Windsor MSS.* G. 7 ; Maxwell, *Clarendon,* II, 31.

[94] P. 101. Argyll, I, 472 ; H. Greville, *Diary,* II, 75–6.

[95] P. 101. Malmesbury (3rd earl), I, 420 ; Q.V.L., 1st Ser., II, 573–4.

[96] P. 101. *Ibid.*

[97] P. 101. Victoria to Aberdeen, Dec. 21, 1853 (draft), *Windsor MSS.* G. 8.

[98] P. 101. Q.V.L., 1st Ser., II, 573–4 ; Lord Grey to Gen. Grey, Dec. 24. 1853, *Howick MSS.*

[99] P. 101. Maxwell, *Clarendon,* II, 31–2 ; Aberdeen to Victoria, Dec. 22, 1853, *Windsor MSS.* G. 8.

[100] P. 101. Aberdeen to Victoria, Dec. 21 ; Palmerston to Aberdeen, Dec. 23 ; Aberdeen to Palmerston, Dec. 24, 1853, *Windsor MSS.* G. 8 ; Palmerston to Lansdowne, Dec. 24, 1853, *Bowood MSS.*

[101] P. 101. Martin, *Prince Consort,* II, 434.

[102] P. 102. Palmerston to Aberdeen, Dec. 23, 1853, *Windsor MSS.* G. 8.

[103] P. 102. *The Times,* Dec 26, 1853. See also H. Greville, *Diary,* II, 77.

[104] P. 102. Palmerston to Lansdowne, Dec. 24, 1853, *Bowood MSS.*

[105] P. 102. Palmerston to Russell, Jan. 22, 1854, P.R.O., G. and D., 22 : 11 ; C. Greville, *Mem.,* VII, 125.

[106] P. 102. Maxwell, *Clarendon,* II, 40 ; H. Greville, *Diary,* II, 84–5, 89 ; *Ann. Reg.* for 1854, p. 110.

[107] P. 102. *Ibid.,* 122.

[108] P. 103. Aberdeen, *Corr.,* 1854–5, p. 96.

[109] P. 103. *The Times,* Apr. 12, 1854.

[110] P. 103. Q.V.L., 1st Ser., III, 18–30 ; Maxwell, *Clarendon,* II, 42-3.

[111] P. 103. Martin, *Prince Consort,* III, 56–7.

[112] P. 103. B. and A., V, 56–9 ; Fagan, *Reform Club,* 93–103.

[113] P. 103. *Hansard,* 3rd Ser., CXXXI, 675–80.

[114] P. 103. *Ibid.,* 680–1.

[115] P. 104. *Ibid.,* CXXXII, 279.

[116] P. 104. *Ibid.,* CXXXV, 524, 772.

[117] P. 104. Martin, *Prince Consort,* III, 58.

[118] P. 104. Prince Consort, *Letters,* 141–4.

[119] P. 104. Martin, *Prince Consort,* III, 93.

[120] P. 104. Martin, *Prince Consort,* III, 49–50 ; Q.V.L., 1st Ser., III, 43–4.

[121] P. 104. Aberdeen, *Corr.,* 1853-4, p. 242.

[122] P. 104. Czartoryski, II, 353–4.

[123] P. 105. Palmerston to Russell, May 26, 1854, P.R.O., G. and D. 22 : 11.

[124] P. 105. *Ibid.,* B. and A., V, 60–5.

[125] P. 105. *Ibid.,* 68 ; Guedalla, *Gladstone and Palmerston,* 99–100.

CHAPTER XXIV

[1] P. 106. Vitzthum, *St. Petersburg and London,* I, 140–4.

[2] P. 107. Tocqueville, II, 90–1.

[3] P. 108. Aberdeen, *Corr.,* 1854–5, p. 378 ; 1855–60, pp. 1–3 ; Walpole,

Russell, II, 237–40 ; C. Greville, *Mem.*, VII, 229–34 ; Stanmore, *Herbert*, I, 245–6 ; Q.V.L., 1st Ser., III, 90–4.

[4] P. 108. *Ibid.*, 92–3 ; Argyll, I, 517–18 ; Martin, *Prince Consort*, III, 169–70.

[5] P. 109. Aberdeen, *Corr.*, 1855–60, pp. 8–9 ; Q.V.L., 1st Ser., III, 99–100.

[6] P. 109. B. and A., V, 70–1 ; Guedalla, *Gladstone and Palmerston*, 100–1.

[7] P. 109. *Ibid.* ; Croker, II, 507 ; Morley, *Gladstone*, I, 523 ; *Hansard*, 3rd Ser., CXXXVI, 975–7 ; Q.V.L., 1st Ser., III, 97–8.

[8] P. 109. *Ibid.*, 92 ; Aberdeen, *Corr.*, 1855–60, p. 4.

[9] P. 110. C. Greville, *Mem.*, VII, 236 ; Argyll, I, 527 ; *Hansard*, 3rd Ser., CXXXVI, 1339 ; Q.V.L., 1st Ser., III, 102, 117, 120. He had also the support of *The Times* (Cook, 95 n.).

[10] P. 110. Aberdeen, *Corr.*, 1855–60, pp. 12–13 ; Prince Albert's memorandum, Feb. 2, and Col. Phipps' two memoranda, Feb. 3, 1855, *Windsor MSS.* G. 23 ; Maxwell, *Clarendon*, II, 58–9.

[11] P. 110. Aberdeen, *Corr.*, 1855–60, pp. 12, 15–17 ; Prince Albert's memorandum, Feb. 2, 1855, and Gen. Grey's memorandum, same date, *Windsor MSS.* G. 23 ; Argyll, I, 526.

[12] P. 110. Victoria's memorandum, Feb. 1, 1885, *Windsor MSS.* G. 23.

[13] P. 111. Aberdeen, *Corr.*, 1855–60, p. 10 ; Monypenny and Buckle, III, 559–60 ; Q.V.L., 1st Ser., III, 103.

[14] P. 111. *Ibid.*, 102 ; Croker, II, 507–8 ; Monypenny and Buckle, III, 559–60. See also Barante, VIII, 95.

[15] P. 111. Prince Albert to Aberdeen, Jan. 31, 1855 (2 letters), and Palmerston to Russell, Feb. 3, 1855, *Windsor MSS.* G. 23 ; Maxwell, *Clarendon*, II, 57, 61 ; C. Greville, *Mem.*, VIII, 64 ; Monypenny and Buckle, III, 562 ; Hodder, II, 489 ; *Hansard*, 3rd Ser., CXXXVI, 1339–54, 1421–32, 1820–2 (Gladstone's explanation) ; Q.V.L., 1st Ser., III, 104.

[16] P. 111. Morley, *Gladstone*, I, 525–7.

[17] P. 111. Maxwell, *Clarendon*, II, 57 ; C. Greville, *Mem.*, VIII, 64.

[18] P. 111. *Hansard*, 3rd Ser., CXXXVI, 1422 ; Q.V.L., 1st Ser., III, 109.

[19] P. 112. C. Greville, *Mem.*, VII, 235. For opinion in Paris, Martin, *Prince Consort*, III, 176.

[20] P. 112. Victoria's memorandum, Feb. 1, and Prince Albert's memorandum, Feb. 2, 1855, *Windsor MSS.* G. 23 ; Aberdeen, *Corr.*, 1855–60, p. 12 ; Morley, *Gladstone*, I, 528–9 ; Stanmore, *Herbert*, I, 253 ; Q.V.L., 1st Ser., III, 108–10. *Cf.* Maxwell, *Clarendon*, II, 57–8.

[21] P. 112. *Ibid.*, 58–60 ; Aberdeen, *Corr.*, 1855–60, pp. 12, 15 ; Prince Albert's memorandum, Feb. 2, 1855 ; Gen. Grey's memorandum, same date, and Col. Phipps' two memoranda, Feb. 3, 1855, *Windsor MSS.* G. 23 ; Morley, *Gladstone*, I, 530–1 ; *The Times*, Feb. 5, 1855 ; Q.V.L., 1st Ser., III, 114–22.

[22] P. 112. *Ibid.*, 116 ; Morley, *Gladstone*, I, 530–1 ; Maxwell, *Clarendon*, II, 61 ; Palmerston to Russell, Feb. 3, 1855, *Windsor MSS.* G. 23 ; Aberdeen, *Corr.*, 1855–60, p. 12.

[23] P. 112. *Ibid.*, p. 15.

[24] P. 113. Col. Phipps' two memoranda, Feb. 3, 1855, *Windsor MSS.* G. 23 ; Stanmore, *Herbert*, I, 253–4.

[25] P. 113. Aberdeen, *Corr.*, 1855–60, pp. 15–17, 23–4 ; Stanmore, *Aberdeen*, 289–90 ; Prince Albert to Aberdeen (two letters) and Aberdeen to Prince Albert, Feb. 6, 1855, *Windsor MSS.* G. 23 ; Maxwell, *Clarendon*, II, 62 ; Palmerston to Aberdeen, Feb. 12, 1855, *Aberdeen MSS.*

[26] P. 113. Hodder, II, 493.

[27] P. 113. Guedalla, *Gladstone and Palmerston*, 101–6 ; Morley, *Gladstone*,

I, 531-5 ; Aberdeen, *Corr.*, 1855-60, pp. 15-17, 19 ; Argyll to Palmerston, and Gladstone to Palmerston, Feb. 5, 1855, *Windsor MSS.* ; Q.V.L., 1st Ser., III, 123-4 ; C. Greville, *Mem.*, VII, 237-8 ; Argyll, I, 526-30.

²⁸ P. 113. *Ibid.* ; Stanmore, *Herbert*, I, 251-62 ; Aberdeen, *Corr.*, 1855-60, pp. 15-17, 21, 25 ; Morley, *Gladstone*, I, 535-6 ; Stanmore, *Aberdeen*, 289 ; Q.V.L., 1st Ser., III, 124-8, 126 n. ; Parker, *Graham*, II, 263-5 ; C. Greville, *Mem.*, VII, 238-41 ; B. and A., V, 80.

²⁹ P. 114. Stanmore, *Herbert*, I, 260.

³⁰ P. 114. Guedalla, *Gladstone and Palmerston*, 105.

³¹ P. 114. B. and A., V, 77.

³² P. 114. Q.V.L., 1st Ser., III, 137.

³³ P. 115. Hodder, II, 493-4.

³⁴ P. 115. Morley, *Gladstone*, I, 537.

³⁵ P. 115. Argyll, I, 536-7, 539-40 ; *Hansard*, 3rd Ser., CXXXVI, 1223-5, 1424-5, 1743-4 (Graham's explanation), 1820-6, 1843-8, 1851-4, 1860-2 ; Guedalla, *Gladstone and Palmerston*, 108-9 ; Dasent, *Delane*, I, 205 ; Q.V.L., 1st Ser., III, 134-9 ; Morley, *Gladstone*, I, 537-43 ; Palmerston to Victoria, May 24, 1855, *Windsor MSS.* G. 31 ; Parker, *Graham*, II, 266-76 ; Stanmore, *Herbert*, I, 262-9 ; C. Greville, *Mem.*, VII, 245-7.

³⁶ P. 116. *Ibid.*, 241 ; *Hansard*, 3rd Ser., CXXXVI, 1429-30 ; Argyll, I, 539 ; Q.V.L., 1st Ser., III, 132-3 ; Maxwell, *Clarendon*, II, 62-3 ; Russell, *Later Corr.*, II, 188.

³⁷ P. 116. Lyall, I, 85.

³⁸ P. 116. Palmerston to Russell, Feb. 24, 1855, P.R.O., G. and D., 22 : 12.

³⁹ P. 116. Hodder, II, 503-4. See also *ibid.*, 490-4 ; Palmerston to Lansdowne, Feb. 7, 1855, *Bowood MSS.* ; Argyll, I, 540-1.

⁴⁰ P. 117. *Ibid.*, 537 ; Morison, 192-3.

⁴¹ P. 117. Monypenny and Buckle, III, 566-7.

⁴² P. 117. Atkins, I, 261-2.

⁴³ P. 117. Dasent, *Piccadilly*, 100 ; Palmerston to Clarendon, March 4, 1856, *Clarendon MSS.*

⁴⁴ P. 118. White, I, 1-2.

⁴⁵ P. 118. Lady Palmerston to Mrs. Huskisson, Br. Mus., *Add. MSS.* 39949, ff. 287-90 ; Palmerston to Granville, Apr. 15, 1855, P.R.O., G. and D., 29 : 18 ; B. and A., V, 88.

⁴⁶ P. 119. *Hansard*, 3rd Ser., CXL, 247-52.

⁴⁷ P. 119. *Ibid.*, CXXXVI, 1649.

⁴⁸ P. 119. *Ibid.*, 1758-9.

⁴⁹ P. 119. Morley, *Cobden*, 146. See also Trevelyan, *Bright*, 241 ; Argyll, I, 558-9.

⁵⁰ P. 120. Maxwell, *Smith*, II, 154. See also Christie, 144-5.

⁵¹ P. 120. Monypenny and Buckle, III, 571-2 ; Layard, II, 266 ; Palmerston to Russell, Feb. 26, 1855, P.R.O., G. and D., 22 : 12 ; Guedalla, *Gladstone and Palmerston*, 107 ; Fitzmaurice, I, 101 ; *Hansard*, 3rd Ser., CXXXVIII, 2209.

⁵² P. 120. Croker, II, 509. See also C. Greville, *Mem.*, VII, 243-4.

⁵³ P. 121. Fitzmaurice, I, 105.

⁵⁴ P. 121. Argyll, I, 532-3 ; Martin, *Prince Consort*, III, 182-8.

⁵⁵ P. 121. *Ibid.*, 151-63 ; Martineau, *Newcastle*, 224-7 ; Argyll, I, 506, 514-16, 542-4 ; Maxwell, *Clarendon*, II, 55, 64 ; Napoleon III to Palmerston, June 3, 1855, *Windsor MSS.* G. 32 ; C. Greville, *Mem.*, VII, 244-5 ; Lane-Poole, *Stratford Canning*, II, 400, 406 ; Panmure, I, 259-60 ; Atkins, I, 216-17 ; Reeve, I, 329.

[56] P. 121. Panmure, I, 286.

[57] P. 122. C. Greville, *Mem.*, VII, 283.

[58] P. 122. Atkins, I, 238–9.

[59] P. 122. Fitzmaurice, I, 102, 114.

[60] P. 122. Correspondence between Palmerston, Victoria, Panmure and Wood, June–July, 1855, *Windsor MSS.* G. 34.

[61] P. 122. Palmerston to Lansdowne, Feb. 7, 1855, *Bowood MSS.* ; Argyll, I, 533–4 ; Q.V.L., 1st Ser., III, 115.

[62] P. 122. For general description, *Hansard*, 3rd Ser., CXXXVI, 1425–8 ; B. and A., V, 81 ; Panmure, I, 98 ; Clode, II, 197, 251, 254, 273, 326, 739–45, 769–76.

[63] P. 123. Panmure, I, 350–1.

[64] P. 123. *Ibid.*, 53–4.

[65] P. 123. Hodder, II, 495–501.

[66] P. 123. *Ibid.* ; Panmure, I, 63, 66–8, 132, 136, 209–10, 225–6, 230–3, 273, 303, 308, 350–1 ; *Hansard*, 3rd Ser., CXXXVI, 479, 486 ; CXXXVII, 849 ; CXXXVIII, 423–8 ; B. and A., V, 81–2.

[67] P. 124. Stanmore, *Herbert*, 27–33 ; Argyll, I, 543–5 ; Martineau, *Newcastle*, 224–7 ; Panmure, I, 124, 149–50, 152, 180, 190–1, 217, 222, 232, 292–3, 360–1, 390–4 ; Parker, *Graham*, II, 258–9 ; Maxwell, *Clarendon*, II, 94–5 ; Mrs. F. S. Macalister, *Memoir of the Right Hon. Sir John McNeill* (London, 1910), chs. xxii–xxv ; Martin, *Prince Consort*, III, 158–63.

[68] P. 125. *Hansard*, 3rd Ser., CXXXVI, 241.

[69] P. 125. *Ibid.*, 1735.

[70] P. 125. Palmerston to Victoria, March 18, Apr. 9, 1855, *Windsor MSS.* G. 26, 28.

[71] P. 125. Panmure, I, 232. See also *ibid.*, 292, 351, 359–60.

[72] P. 127. Maxwell, *Clarendon*, II, 48–9.

[73] P. 127. *Ibid.*

[74] P. 127. Russell, *Later Corr.*, II, 199–200.

[75] P. 127. Maxwell, *Clarendon*, II, 63.

[76] P. 127. *Ibid.* See also Argyll, I, 549.

[77] P. 127. Russell, *Later Corr.*, II, 198.

[78] P. 128. For Russell's side, Walpole, *Russell*, II, 248–69 ; Lord J. Russell, *Later Corr.*, II, ch. xxiii ; Fitzmaurice, I, 106–8.

[79] P. 128. Br. Mus., *Add. MSS.* 39949 ; Palmerston to Russell, Apr. 4, 1855, P.R.O., G. and D., 22 : 12.

[80] P. 128. Fitzmaurice, I, 101.

[81] P. 128. *Hansard*, 3rd Ser., CXXXVII, 882.

[82] P. 129. Memorandum by Drouyn, Walewski, Lansdowne, Clarendon, and Palmerston, March 30, 1855, *Windsor MSS.* G. 27 ; C. Greville, *Mem.*, VII, 253–4 ; B. and A., V, 84–8 ; Lord J. Russell, *Later Corr.*, II, 202.

[83] P. 129. *Ibid.*

[84] P. 129. Q.V.L., 1st Ser., III, 152–3 ; Walpole, Russell, II, 258–9.

[85] P. 129. Br. Mus., *Add. MSS.* 39949.

[86] P. 130. Details in Palmerston to Victoria, Apr. 14, 15 and 17 ; Victoria to Palmerston, Apr. 15 ; Prince Albert's and Gen. Bourgoyne's memoranda, Apr. 19 ; Palmerston to Clarendon and Palmerston to Prince Albert, Apr. 20 ; Prince Albert's memorandum, Apr. 21, 1855, *Windsor MSS.* G. 28 ; Lord J. Russell, *Later Corr.*, II, 206–7 ; Martin, *Prince Consort*, III, ch. lxii ; Q.V.L. 1st Ser., III, 148–51 ; Simpson, *Louis Napoleon and the Recovery of France*, 289–96.

[87] P. 130. Walpole, *Russell*, II, 260.

[88] P. 130. *Ibid.*, 263 ; Palmerston to Victoria, May 7, 1855, *Windsor MSS.*
G. 30.
[89] P. 130. *E.g.* B. and A., V, 92–4 ; Greville-Reeve, *Letters*, 234–6.
[90] P. 131. *Hansard*, 3rd Ser., CXXXVIII, 1755.
[91] P. 131. Palmerston to Russell, July 13, 1855, P.R.O., G. and D., 22 : 12 ;
Russell, *Later Corr.*, II, 209 ; Maxwell, *Clarendon*, II, 85–8 ; Norman Macdonald
to Col. Phipps, July 13, 1855, *Windsor MSS.* G. 34.

CHAPTER XXV

[1] P. 133. Cowley, *Secrets*, 78.
[2] P. 133. Hodder, II, 505.
[3] P. 133. *Hansard*, 3rd Ser., CXXXVIII, 687–8.
[4] P. 133. *Ibid.*, CXXXVII, 1238–41.
[5] P. 133. Palmerston to Victoria, March 15, 1855, *Windsor MSS.* A. 24.
[6] P. 134. *Hansard*, 3rd Ser., CXXXVIII, 944–5.
[7] P. 134. *Ibid.*, CXXXVIII, 687–8.
[8] P. 134. Hodder, III, 196–7.
[9] P. 134. Palmerston to Victoria, March 13, 1855, *Windsor MSS.* A. 24 ;
Hansard, 3rd Ser., CXXXVII, 486, 514.
[10] P. 134. *Ibid.*, CXXXVI, 2161–70 ; CXXXVII, 1238.
[11] P. 134. *Ibid.*, CXXXVIII, 914, 2213 ; CXXXIX, 543–4.
[12] P. 135. *Ibid.*, CXXXIX, 1389–90, 1455.
[13] P. 135. *E.g. ibid.*, CXXXVIII, 420–8.
[14] P. 135. Vitzthum, *St. Petersburg and London*, I, 168–9.
[15] P. 135. Monypenny and Buckle, IV, 15.
[16] P. 135. *Ibid.*
[17] P. 135. Palmerston to Victoria, May 23, 24, 1855, *Windsor MSS.* G. 31.
[18] P. 135. Same to same, June 7, 1855, *Windsor MSS.* G. 32.
[19] P. 135. Same to same, July 19, 1855, *Windsor MSS.* G. 35.
[20] P. 136. Argyll, I, 560–1 ; *Hansard*, 3rd Ser., CXXXVIII, 973–4, 1271–6,
1281–3 ; Palmerston to Victoria, May 25, June 4, 1855, *Windsor MSS.* G. 31, 32.
[21] P. 136. Maxwell, *Clarendon*, II, 92–3.
[22] P. 136. Q.V.L., 1st Ser., III, 172–9 ; Martin, *Prince Consort*, III, 265–89.
[23] P. 137. Panmure, I, 402–11.
[24] P. 137. *Ibid.*, 282–4, 308–9, 394 ; Maxwell, *Clarendon*, II, 92 ; Atkins,
I, 236.
[25] P. 137. Palmerston to Victoria, Feb. 25, 1856, *Windsor MSS.* G. 45 ;
Beust, I, 142–3 ; Maxwell, *Clarendon*, II, 108.
[26] P. 137. *Ibid.*, 93 ; Fitzmaurice, I, 121.
[27] P. 137. Argyll, I, 593–7 ; Q.V.L., 1st Ser., III, 211.
[28] P. 138. Hertslet, *Map*, II, 1241–2 ; Argyll, I, 591–2.
[29] P. 138. Palmerston to Clarendon, Sept. 25, 1855, *Clarendon MSS.*
[30] P. 138. Maxwell, *Clarendon*, II, 108–9 ; Fitzmaurice, I, 124 ; Cowley to
Clarendon, Nov. 30, 1855 (copy), and Clarendon to Palmerston, March 18, 19,
1856, *Windsor MSS.* G. 41, 46 ; Cowley, *Secrets*, 83.
[31] P. 139. For Napoleon's explanation, Clarendon to Palmerston, Feb. 18,
1856, *Windsor MSS.* G. 44 ; for Walewski's, Cowley to Clarendon, Nov. 30,
1855 (copy), *Windsor MSS.* G. 41.
[32] P. 139. Martin, *Prince Consort*, III, 326–30.
[33] P. 139. B. and A., V, 103–4 ; Cowley, *Secrets*, 90–1 ; Maxwell,
Clarendon, II, 119.

[34] P. 139. *Ibid.*, 103–4.
[35] P. 139. Cowley to Clarendon, Nov. 30, 1855 (copy), *Windsor MSS.* G. 41.
[36] P. 139. Palmerston to Clarendon, Dec. 1, 1855, *Windsor MSS.* G. 41.
[37] P. 139. Maxwell, *Clarendon*, II, 107.
[38] P. 140. Fitzmaurice, I, 130.
[39] P. 140. Palmerston to Clarendon, Jan. 6, 1856, *Clarendon MSS.*
[40] P. 140. Same to same, Jan. 7. See also same to same, Jan. 9 and 14.
[41] P. 140. Reeve, *Memoirs*, I, 345.
[42] P. 140. Martin, *Prince Consort*, III, 350 ; Palmerston to Granville, Jan. 17, 1856, P.R.O., G. and D., 29 : 19 ; Q.V.L., 1st Ser., III, 210.
[43] P. 142. U.S., *Senate Docs.*, 2nd Sess., 48th Congress, vol. I, pt. ii, 836–9.
[44] P. 142. Palmerston to Clarendon, Jan. 7, May 27, 1856, *Clarendon MSS.*
[45] P. 142. Same to same, Jan. 26.
[46] P. 143. Same to same, Jan. 9, 18, 29.
[47] P. 143. *Hansard*, 3rd Ser., CXL, 468–70.
[48] P. 144. *Ibid.*, 838–51.
[49] P. 144. J. B. Moore, *The Works of James Buchanan* (Philadelphia, 1910), X, 43.
[50] P. 144. *The Education of Henry Adams* (Boston, 1927), 133.
[51] P. 145. Palmerston to Clarendon, March 18, 1856, *Clarendon MSS.*
[52] P. 145. Dallas, I, 3.
[53] P. 145. Palmerston to Clarendon, Jan. 29, 1856, *Clarendon MSS.* ; Panmure. II, 172–3, 175, 179, 187, 220 ; Palmerston to Victoria, March 31, 1856, *Windsor MSS.* G. 46.
[54] P. 145. Dallas, I, 24.
[55] P. 145. Palmerston to Granville, Jan. 17, 1856, P.R.O., G. and D., 29 : 19 ; same to Victoria, Jan. 18, 1856, *Windsor MSS.* G. 43 ; same to Clarendon, Jan. 17, and Palmerston's memorandum, Jan. 25, 1856, *Clarendon MSS.*
[56] P. 145. Palmerston to Clarendon, Jan. 23, 1856, *Clarendon MSS.*
[57] P. 145. Clarendon to Victoria, Jan. 25, 1856, *Windsor MSS.* G. 43.
[58] P. 145. Palmerston to Clarendon, Jan. 23, 1856, *Clarendon MSS.*
[59] P. 146. B. and A., V, 106.
[60] P. 146. Prince Albert's memorandum, Jan. 25, 1856, *Windsor MSS.* G. 43.
[61] P. 146. Clarendon to Victoria, Jan. 25, 1856, *Windsor MSS.* G. 43.
[62] P. 146. Lord J. Russell, *Later Corr.*, II, 217 ; Martin, *Prince Consort*, III, 355.
[63] P. 146. Maxwell, *Clarendon*, II, 114 ; Eardley-Wilmot, 415–18 ; Fitzmaurice, I, 144 ; Palmerston to Clarendon, Jan. 17, 1856, *Clarendon MSS.*
[64] P. 146. Maxwell, *Clarendon*, II, 118–19, 121 ; Fitzmaurice, I, 168–9. Especially Palmerston to Clarendon, March 5, 1856, *Clarendon MSS.* ; and Clarendon to Palmerston, March 9 and Apr. 9, 1856, *Windsor MSS.* G. 46, 47. See also Wolff, I, 233 ; Victoria to Palmerston and Palmerston to Victoria, Mar. 5, 11, 13, 15, 18, 1856, *Windsor MSS.* G. 45, 46.
[65] P. 147. Clarendon to Palmerston, March 19, 1856, *Windsor MSS.* G. 46.
[66] P. 147. C. Greville, *Mem.*, VIII, 19.
[67] P. 147. Palmerston to Victoria, Feb. 25, 1856, *Windsor MSS.* G. 45.
[68] P. 147. Palmerston to Clarendon, Feb. 25, March 13, 1856, *Clarendon MSS.*
[69] P. 148. Palmerston to Clarendon, Jan. 21, Feb. 19, 25, 29, March 1, 2, 3, 4, 5 (2 letters), 1856, *Clarendon MSS.* ; Palmerston to Victoria, Feb. 25 (2 letters), Feb. 29, March 1, Victoria to Palmerston, Feb. 28, Clarendon to Palmerston, March 2, 7, 1856, *Windsor MSS.* G. 45 ; Q.V.L., 1st Ser., III, 226–34.
[70] P. 148. *Ibid.*, 226–7.

NOTES

447

71 P. 148. Maxwell, *Clarendon*, II, 116–20 ; Nesselrode, XI, 112–16 ; Fitzmaurice, I, 170 ; Clarendon to Palmerston, Feb. 20, 1856, *Windsor MSS.* G. 45.

72 P. 148. Palmerston to Clarendon, March 16, 1856, *Clarendon MSS.*

73 P. 149. Same to same, Feb. 10.

74 P. 149. Same to same, Feb. 25, March 7, 11. *Cf.* Maxwell, *Clarendon*, II, 121.

75 P. 149. Dallas, I, 25.

76 P. 149. Fitzmaurice, I, 178. See also Wolff, I, 233.

77 P. 150. Palmerston to Clarendon, and Palmerston's memorandum, Feb. 3, 1856, *Clarendon MSS.* ; Clarendon to Palmerston, Feb. 18, 22, 1856, *Windsor MSS.* G. 44, 45.

78 P. 150. Fitzmaurice, I, 163 ; Palmerston to Victoria, Feb. 13, 1856, *Windsor MSS.* G. 44.

79 P. 150. Palmerston to Clarendon, March 7, 1856, *Clarendon MSS.*

80 P. 151. Same to same, March 1, 8.

81 P. 151. Same to same, March 7.

82 P. 151. Same to same, March 30.

83 P. 151. Clarendon to Palmerston, March 31, 1856, *Windsor MSS.* G. 46.

84 P. 151. Same to same, Apr. 7, 1856, *Windsor MSS.* G. 47.

85 P. 152. Palmerston to Clarendon, June 29, 1856, *Clarendon MSS.*

86 P. 152. Palmerston's memorandum, May 30, 1856, *Clarendon MSS.*

87 P. 152. Palmerston to Clarendon, May 27, 1856, *Clarendon MSS.*

88 P. 153. Palmerston's memorandum, Apr. 30, 1856, *Clarendon MSS.*

CHAPTER XXVI

1 P. 154. Dallas, I, 11.

2 P. 154. *Ibid.*, 21.

3 P. 155. *Ibid.*, 19.

4 P. 155. Palmerston to Clarendon, June 1, 2, 1856, *Clarendon MSS.*

5 P. 155. Same to same, May 27, 1856.

6 P. 155. Same to same, June 1, 1856.

7 P. 155. *Ibid.* ; Palmerston to Victoria, Apr. 23, 1856, *Windsor MSS.* G. 47 ; Dallas, I, 27, 29.

8 P. 155. *Ibid.*

9 P. 155. *Ibid.*, 44.

10 P. 156. Palmerston to Clarendon, May 7, 1856, *Clarendon MSS.*

11 P. 156. Same to same, June 6, 1856.

12 P. 156. Same to same, June 11.

13 P. 156. *Ibid.*

14 P. 156. Dallas, I, 58.

15 P. 156. *Ibid.*, 61, 66–7.

16 P. 156. Argyll, II, 47–8 ; Palmerston to Clarendon, June 9, 11, 16, 1856, *Clarendon MSS.*

17 P. 156. *Hansard*, 3rd Ser., CXLII, 1508.

18 P. 156. Stanmore, *Herbert*, II, 46.

19 P. 157. *Ibid.*, 48.

20 P. 157. Hodder, III, 36.

21 P. 157. Q.V.L., 1st Ser., III, 276 n. ; Palmerston to Victoria, Nov. 22, 1856, *Windsor MSS.* A. 25. See also Hodder, III, 191–200.

22 P. 157. *Hansard*, 3rd Ser., CXLII, 221.

23 P. 157. Snell, 97–8.

[24] P. 158. Palmerston to Victoria, July 6, 1856, *Windsor MSS.* A. 25.

[25] P. 158. Same to same, Sept. 10, 1857.

[26] P. 158. Same to same, July 8, 1856 ; ' Votes of Members in Office— Session 1856,' *Windsor MSS.* A. 25.

[27] P. 158. Walpole, *Russell*, II, 283-4.

[28] P. 158. Palmerston to Clarendon, Feb. 19, 1856, *Clarendon MSS.* ; Argyll, II, 10-20.

[29] P. 158. Dallas, II, 47 ; Argyll, II, 49 ; *Hansard*, 3rd Ser., CXLI, 1924–5 ; CXLII, 326 ; Hodder, III, 30–2 ; Q.V.L., 1st Ser., III, 171–2, 247, 247 n.

[30] P. 158. *Hansard*, 3rd Ser., CXL, 1114.

[31] P 158. *Ibid.*, CXL, 1846.

[32] P. 159. *Ibid.*, CXLI, 527, 537. See also *ibid.*, CXL, 2010.

[33] P. 159. Dallas, I, 82.

[34] P. 159. Argyll, II, 50.

[35] P. 159. *The Times* ed., Oct. 21, 1865.

[36] P. 160. Argyll, II, 51.

[37] P. 160. For Palmerston's view, B. and A., V, 111–17 ; Malmesbury (3rd earl), *Mem.*, II, 49–50. For Russia's, Nesselrode, XI, 116–31.

[38] P. 160. Fitzmaurice, I, 186 ; Palmerston to Clarendon, July 27, Aug. 4, 15, 23, 1856 *et al.*, *Clarendon MSS.* ; Malmesbury (3rd earl), *Mem.*, II, 49 ; B. and A., V, 113.

[39] P. 160. For best account, Riker, chs. i and ii.

[40] P. 161. Palmerston to Clarendon, Aug. 4, 1856, *Clarendon MSS.*

[41] P. 161. Same to same, July 20, 1856, *Clarendon MSS.*

[42] P. 161. Same to same, July 21, 1856.

[43] P. 161. Same to same, March 9, 1856.

[44] P. 161. Same to same, July 8, Aug. 8, 15, 1856.

[45] P. 162. For the rapprochement and the treaty to which it led, B. H. Sumner, ' The Secret Franco-Russian Treaty of 3 March, 1859,' in *Eng. His. Rev.*, XLVIII (1933), 65–83.

[46] P. 162. Palmerston to Clarendon, Aug. 4, 1856, *Clarendon MSS.*

[47] P. 162. Same to same, Aug. 25, 1856.

[48] P. 162. Same to same, Aug. 7, 20, 1856.

[49] P. 162. Same to same, Aug. 15, 1856.

[50] P. 162. Malmesbury (3rd earl), *Mem.*, II, 50.

[51] P. 162. Palmerston to Clarendon, July 24, 1856, *Clarendon MSS.*

[52] P. 163. October, 1856. They were almost as numerous in other months, *Clarendon MSS.* for 1856, *passim.*

[53] P. 163. *E.g.* Palmerston to Waleswki (copy), enclosed in Palmerston to Clarendon, Sept. 16, 1856, *Clarendon MSS.*

[54] P. 163. Palmerston to Clarendon, Oct. 14, 1856, *Clarendon MSS.*

[55] P. 163. Same to same, Sept. 9, 1856 (two letters).

[56] P. 163. Same to same, Sept. 1, Oct. 25, Nov. 7, 10, 1856 ; C. Greville, *Mem.*, VIII, 62.

[57] P. 163. Palmerston to Clarendon, Sept. 12, 14, 1856, *Clarendon MSS.*

[58] P 164. Same to same, Sept. 13, 22, 25, 1856, *Clarendon MSS.* ; Maxwell, *Clarendon*, II, 124–5.

[59] P. 164. *Ibid.*, 131–2.

[60] P. 164. *Ibid.*, 133.

[61] P. 164. Palmerston to Clarendon, Oct. 27, 1856, *Clarendon MSS.*

[62] P. 164. Malmesbury (3rd earl), *Mem.*, II, 53.

[63] P. 165. Palmerston to Clarendon, Oct. 10, 1856, *Clarendon MSS.*

[64] P. 165. Same to same, Oct. 17, 1856.

65 P. 165. Same to same, Oct. 25, 1856.
66 P. 165. Same to same, Oct. 18, 1856.
67 P. 165. Same to same, Oct. 21, 1856.
68 P. 165. Maxwell, *Clarendon*, II, 103–5.
69 P. 165. Palmerston to Clarendon, Nov. 15, 1856, *Clarendon MSS.*
70 P. 166. Palmerston to Clarendon, Nov. 26, 1856, *Clarendon MSS.*
71 P. 166. Malmesbury (3rd earl), *Mem.*, II, 53 ; C. Greville, *Mem.*, VIII, 67–8 ; Palmerston to Clarendon, Oct. 6, Nov. 29, Dec. 1, 1856, *Clarendon MSS.*
72 P. 166. Palmerston to Clarendon, Nov. 27, Dec. 14, 1856, *Clarendon MSS.* ; Palmerston to Lansdowne, Jan. 9, 1857, *Bowood MSS.* ; Maxwell, *Clarendon*, II, 135.
73 P. 166. *Ibid.*, 138.
74 P. 166. Maxwell, *Clarendon*, II, 123–5 ; Dasent, *Delane*, I, 291–2 ; Lord J. Russell, *Later Corr.*, II, 219 ; Palmerston-Clarendon correspondence, 1856, *Clarendon MSS.*
75 P. 166. *Ibid.*
76 P. 166. Palmerston's memorandum, Oct. 9, 1856, *Clarendon MSS.*
77 P. 167. Morse, ch. XVI.
78 P. 167. Palmerston to Clarendon, Oct. 28, 1856, *Clarendon MSS.*
79 P. 167. Morison, 203–4.
80 P. 167. Q.V.L., 1st Ser., III, 286.
81 P. 168. Cowley, *Secrets*, 106.
82 P. 168. *Hansard*, 3rd Ser., CXLIV, 1393, 1410–21.
83 P. 168. Argyll, II, 67–9.
84 P. 168. Q.V.L., 1st Ser., III, 288–9.
85 P. 169. Stanmore, *Herbert*, II, 68.
86 P. 169. Maxwell, *Clarendon*, II, 139 ; Leader, 264–5 ; Morley, *Gladstone*, I, 558–63.
87 P. 169. *Hansard*, 3rd Ser., CXLIV, 1809–34.
88 P. 169. Dallas, I, 223.
89 P. 169. Q.V.L., 1st Ser., III, 290.
90 P. 169. Wolf, *Ripon*, I, 130–1.
91 P. 169. Dallas, I, 219.
92 P. 169. Fitzmaurice, I, 227 ; Stanmore, *Herbert*, II, 80 ; Morley, *Gladstone*, I, 564–5 ; Hodder, III, 43 ; Martin, *Prince Consort*, IV, 29–30.
93 P. 170. Argyll, II, 74.
94 P. 170. Martin, *Prince Consort*, IV, 30 ; Q.V.L., 1st Ser., III, 287.
95 P. 170. Stanmore, *Herbert*, II, 56.
96 P. 170. Palmerston to Granville, March 25, 1857, P.R.O., G. and D., 29 : 19.
97 P. 170. Same to same, March 26, 1857.
98 P. 170. Palmerston to Victoria, March 31, 1857, *Windsor MSS.* A. 25.
99 P. 170. *Ibid.* ; Dallas, I, 230, 251.
100 P. 170. Stanmore, *Herbert*, II, 69. See also Monypenny and Buckle, IV, 80–2.
101 P. 170. Dallas, I, 257–8.
102 P. 171. *Hansard*, 3rd Ser., CXLIV, 843–5.
103 P. 171. Palmerston to Victoria, May 6, 1857, *Windsor MSS.* A. 25 ; *Hansard*, 3rd Ser., CXLV, 319–20.
104 P. 171. Palmerston to Victoria, June 8, July 14, 1857, *Windsor MSS.* A. 25.
105 P. 171. Same to same, June 26, 1857.
106 P. 171. *Hansard*, 3rd Ser., CXLVII, 1858.

II. 2 G

[107] P. 172. *Ibid.*, CXLVII, 413.
[108] P. 172. *Ibid.*, CXLVII, 1073. See also Palmerston to Victoria, July 6, Aug. 13, 1857, *Windsor MSS.* A. 25.
[109] P. 172. T. W. Riker, 'The Pact of Osborne,' in *Am. His. Rev.*, vol. XXXIV, no. 2 (Jan. 1929).
[110] P. 172. Fitzmaurice, I, 281.
[111] P. 172. Palmerston to Victoria, Oct. 30, 1857, *Windsor MSS.* N. 5.
[112] P. 173. Panmure, chs. XXX–XXXIV.
[113] P. 173. *Ibid.*, vol. II, 406, 428–9, 432–3, 436 ; Maxwell, *Clarendon*, II, 153 ; Victoria to Palmerston, Sept. 18, 1857, *Windsor MSS.* N. 4.
[114] P. 173. Cowley, *Secrets*, 131–2 ; B. and A., V, 140–1 ; Panmure, II, 392, 446 ; Maxwell, *Clarendon*, II, 152–3.
[115] P. 173. Panmure, II, 399 ; Q.V.L., 1st Ser., III, 297–8.
[116] P. 173. Cowley, *Secrets*, 122–3 ; Martin, *Prince Consort*, IV, 82–3, 110 ; Q.V.L., 1st Ser., III, 306–10 ; Panmure, II, 411–23.
[117] P. 174. *Ibid.*, 421–2.
[118] P. 174. Q.V.L., 1st Ser., III, 306–10 ; Palmerston to Victoria, July 15, 1857, *Windsor MSS.* N. 4.
[119] P. 174. Q.V.L., 1st Ser., III, 310–12.
[120] P. 174. Fitzmaurice, I, 259.
[121] P. 174. Lord Grey to Gen. Grey, Sept. 20, 1857, *Howick MSS.* ; Stanmore, *Herbert*, II, 104–5 ; Walpole, *Russell*, II, 293 ; Maxwell, *Clarendon*, II, 149, 153 ; Vitzthum, *St. Petersburg and London*, I, 265–6 ; Monypenny and Buckle, IV, 85–6. *Cf.* Fitzmaurice, I, 255 ; C. Greville, *Mem.*, VIII, 119.
[122] P. 174. Cowley, *Secrets*, 133–4.
[123] P. 174. Palmerston to Granville, Dec. 2, 1857, P.R.O., G. and D., 29 : 19.
[124] P. 174. Fitzmaurice, I, 251–2.
[125] P. 174. *Ibid,*, 263 ; Maxwell, *Clarendon*, II, 155.
[126] P. 174. Fitzmaurice, I, 276.
[127] P. 174. Maxwell, *Clarendon*, II, 154–5 ; Clarendon to Victoria, Nov. 7, 1857, *Windsor MSS.* N. 5 ; C. Greville, *Mem.*, VIII, 127–8.
[128] P. 175. Fitzmaurice, I, 264–5, 283–6, 303 ; C. Greville, *Mem.*, VIII, 128–9, 142 ; B. and A., V, 138–41.
[129] P. 175. *Hansard*, 3rd Ser., CXLVIII, 873–4.
[130] P. 175. Cowley, *Secrets*, 138–9.
[131] P. 175. B. and A., V, 140.

CHAPTER XXVII

[1] P. 177. Maxwell, *Clarendon*, II, 299.
[2] P. 178. White, I, 45 ; B. and A., V, 146–7.
[3] P. 178. Stanmore, *Herbert*, II, 105. See also Monypenny and Buckle, IV, 111 ; Dasent, *Delane*, 273–4 ; C. Greville, *Mem.*, VIII, 157.
[4] P. 178. Barrington, *The Servant of All*, II, 96–9 (also excellent for general situation).
[5] P. 178. Maxwell, *Clarendon*, II, 158. See also Parker, *Graham*, II, 324.
[6] P. 178. *Hansard*, 3rd Ser., CXLVIII, 130.
[7] P. 178. Palmerston to Victoria, Oct. 18, 1857, *Windsor MSS.* B. 69.
[8] P. 180. Vitzthum, *St. Petersburg and London*, I, 230–1. See also C. Greville, *Mem.*, VIII, 156, 163.
[9] P. 180. Q.V.L., 1st Ser., III, 339.

[10] P. 180. *Ibid.*, 338, 340 ; Bright, *Diaries*, 233 ; Martin, *Prince Consort*, IV, 164–5.

[11] P. 180. De la Gorce, *Second Empire*, II, livre xiii.

[12] P. 180. Cowley, *Secrets*, 153 ; Martin, *Prince Consort*, IV, 160–1 ; de la Gorce, II, 226, 242.

[13] P. 181. Cowley, *Secrets*, 153.

[14] P. 181. Hansard, 3rd Ser., CXLVIII, 933–8, 1069–77, 1741–5.

[15] P. 181. *Ibid.*, 130, 1470–1.

[16] P. 181. Cowley, *Secrets*, 148.

[17] P. 181. Lord J. Russell, *Later Corr.*, II, 226 ; MacCarthy and Russell, 173 ; Elliot, *Mill*, I, 202–3 ; Parker, *Graham*, II, 336.

[18] P. 182. *Ibid.*

[19] P. 182. Cowley, *Secrets*, 156. See also Q.V.L., 1st Ser., III, 335.

[20] P. 182. Hansard, 3rd Ser., CXLIX, 65–6.

[21] P. 182. C. Greville, *Mem.*, VIII, 164–5 ; White, I, 44 ; Vitzthum, *St. Petersburg and London*, I, 271–7 ; Q.V.L., 1st Ser., III, 335–8.

[22] P. 182. White, I, 46.

[23] P. 183. *Ibid.*, 45.

[24] P. 183. Memorandum on the state of foreign relations at the close of Lord Palmerston's administration, *Windsor MSS.* J. 78.

[25] P. 184. Vitzthum, *St. Petersburg and London*, I, 275–6 ; Q.V.L., 1st Ser., III, 339 ; White, I, 48.

[26] P. 184. Q.V.L., 1st Ser., III, 340 ; Airlie, II, 169–70 ; Barrington, *The Servant of All*, II, 73 ; C. Greville, *Mem.*, VIII, 169.

[27] P. 184. Wolff, I, 207 ; Martin, *Prince Consort*, IV, 167.

[28] P. 184. Dallas, II, 26.

[29] P. 185. White, I, 50.

[30] P. 185. Q.V.L., 1st Ser., III, 381.

[31] P. 185. C. Greville, *Mem.*, VIII, 199.

[32] P. 185. Fitzmaurice, I, 294, 310.

[33] P. 185. White, I, 47–8 ; C. Greville, *Mem.*, VIII, 181.

[34] P. 185. Fitzmaurice, I, 294.

[35] P. 185. C. Greville, *Mem.*, VIII, 176 ; Fitzmaurice, I, 305 ; Dallas, II, 52.

[36] P. 186. Hansard, 3rd Ser., CXLIX, 1675. See also C. Greville, *Mem.* VIII, 182.

[37] P. 186. *Ibid.*, 183–4 ; Fitzmaurice, I, 299–300 ; Argyll, II, 112–14.

[38] P. 186. Fitzmaurice, I, 300.

[39] P. 186. Martin, *Prince Consort*, IV, 175–9, 184–5 ; C. Greville, *Mem.*, VIII, 185–6 ; Q.V.L., 1st Ser., III, 354–5.

[40] P. 187. Hansard, 3rd Ser., CXLIX, 863.

[41] P. 187. *Ibid.*, 1674.

[42] P. 187. C. Greville, *Mem.*, VIII, 197.

[43] P. 187. Q.V.L., 1st Ser., III, 356–71 ; Fitzmaurice, I, 306 ; Martin, *Prince Consort*, IV, 192–6 ; White, I, 60–75 ; Monypenny and Buckle, IV, 143–6 ; C. Greville, *Mem.*, VIII, 194–8, 194 n.

[44] P. 188. Fitzmaurice, I, 307.

[45] P. 188. *Ibid.*

[46] P. 189. Monypenny and Buckle, IV, 145–6.

[47] P. 189. Q.V.L., 1st Ser., III, 359, 364–5, 367, 369–70 ; Parker, *Graham*, II, 342–3 ; Monypenny and Buckle, IV, 143–5.

[48] P. 189. Fitzmaurice, I, 309 ; Parker, *Graham*, II, 342–3.

[49] P. 189. Hansard, 3rd Ser., CL, 959.

[50] P. 190. Martin, *Prince Consort*, IV, 196–7.

[51] P. 190.   Fitzmaurice, I, 308–9.
[52] P. 190.   Q.V.L., 1st Ser., III, 366.
[53] P. 190.   C. Greville, *Mem.*, VIII, 198.
[54] P. 190.   Parker, *Graham*, II, 344ff.
[55] P. 190.   Fitzmaurice, I, 310.
[56] P. 191.   Motley, I, 262.
[57] P. 191.   Fitzmaurice, I, 320.
[58] P. 191.   Prince Consort, *Letters*, 187.
[59] P. 191.   Palmerston to Granville, Aug. 30, 1858, P.R.O., G. and D., 29 : 18.
[60] P. 192.   Maxwell, *Clarendon*, II, 164.
[61] P. 192.   C. Greville, *Mem.*, VIII, 189–91, 193–4, 213–14.
[62] P. 192.   *Ibid.*, 188.
[63] P. 192.   *Ibid.*, 194.
[64] P. 192.   Especially *Hansard*, 3rd Ser., CL, 1204–16.
[65] P. 192.   Q.V.L., 1st Ser., III, 382.
[66] P. 192.   Motley, I, 254.
[67] P. 193.   Dallas, II, 113.
[68] P. 193.   Q.V.L., 1st Ser., III, 382 ; Palmerston to Granville, Sept. 30, 1858, P.R.O., G. and D., 29 : 18.
[69] P. 193.   Dallas, II, 46.
[70] P. 194.   Vitzthum, *St. Petersburg and London*, I, 243 ; Dallas, II, 102–3 ; Martin, *Prince Consort*, IV, 222–34 ; Maxwell, *Clarendon*, II, 164.
[71] P. 194.   Dallas, II, 103.
[72] P. 194.   Malmesbury (3rd earl), *Mem.*, II, 141.
[73] P. 195.   Dallas, II, 124.
[74] P. 196.   Vitzthum, *St. Petersburg and London*, I, 235, 297 ; Malmesbury (3rd earl), *Mem.*, II, 150–2.
[75] P. 197.   C. Greville, *Mem.*, VIII, 302.
[76] P. 197.   Dasent, *Delane*, I, 302–3.
[77] P. 197.   Dallas, II, 114, 120, 126. See also Barrington, *The Servant of All*, II, 99.
[78] P. 198.   Maxwell, *Clarendon*, II, 163. See also Dasent, *Delane*, I, 302–3.
[79] P. 198.   Vitzthum, *St. Petersburg and London*, I, 239.
[80] P. 198.   Maxwell, *Clarendon*, II, 168 ; Malmesbury (3rd earl), *Mem.*, II, 144.
[81] P. 198.   C. Greville, *Mem.*, VIII, 215 ; Vitzthum, *St. Petersburg and London*, I, 297.
[82] P. 198.   *Ibid.*
[83] P. 198.   Dasent, *Delane*, I, 305–6.
[84] P. 198.   Barante, VIII, 199 ; Vitzthum, *St. Petersburg and London*, I, 297.
[85] P. 198.   Dallas, II, 131 ; Parker, *Graham*, II, 374 ; Barrington, *The Servant of All*, II, 99–100.
[86] P. 198.   Maxwell, *Clarendon*, II, 165, 167 ; C. Greville, *Mem.*, VIII, 214 ; Dallas, II, 139.
[87] P. 199.   Palmerston to Lansdowne, Oct. 19, 1858, *Bowood MSS*.
[88] P. 200.   Trevelyan, *Bright*, 268–78 ; Bright, *Diaries*, 234.
[89] P. 200.   C. Greville, *Mem.*, VIII, 213.
[90] P. 200.   Maxwell, *Clarendon*, II, 174.
[91] P. 200.   *Ibid.*
[92] P. 200.   *Ibid.*
[93] P. 200.   Parker, *Graham*, II, 365. See also Fitzmaurice, I, 320.

NOTES

453

94 P. 200. Maxwell, *Clarendon*, II, 173. See also C. Greville, *Mem.*, VIII, 200.
95 P. 200. *Ibid.*, 209 ; Dallas, II, 122–3.
96 P. 200. Maxwell, *Clarendon*, II, 170.
97 P. 201. *Ibid.*, 171–2 ; C. Greville, *Mem.*, VIII, 190.
98 P. 201. Palmerston to Lansdowne, Dec. 4, 1858, *Bowood MSS.*

CHAPTER XXVIII

1 P. 202. Baxter, ch. VII.
2 P. 202. Quoted from Baxter, 138.
3 P. 203. Cowley, *Secrets*, 175.
4 P. 203. *Ibid.*, 175.
5 P. 203. *Ibid.*, 177.
6 P. 203. Parker, *Graham*, II, 374.
7 P. 203. C. Greville, *Mem.*, VIII, 218–19 ; Maxwell, *Clarendon*, II, 188 ; Fitzmaurice, I, 337–8.
8 P. 203. Q.V.L., 1st Ser., III, 401.
9 P. 203. C. Greville, *Mem.*, VIII, 219.
10 P. 203. *Ibid.*
11 P. 203. *Ibid.*, 220–1.
12 P. 204. Cowley, *Secrets*, 173.
13 P. 204. *Ibid.*, 173–4.
14 P. 204. Fitzmaurice, I, 325–6 ; Maxwell, *Clarendon*, II, 181–4 ; Cowley, *Secrets*, 174–5.
15 P. 205. *Ibid.*, 179.
16 P. 205. Parker, *Graham*, II, 363–6 ; Stanmore, *Herbert*, II, 164–6 ; Fitzmaurice, I, 325–7 ; C. Greville, *Mem.*, VIII, 227.
17 P. 205. *Ibid.*, 218.
18 P. 205. Derby to Victoria, Feb. 3, 1859, *Windsor MSS.* J. 15.
19 P. 205. Q.V.L., 1st Ser., III, 405.
20 P. 205. Monypenny and Buckle, IV, 243–4.
21 P. 205. C. Greville, *Mem.*, VIII, 221.
22 P. 205. *Hansard*, 3rd Ser., CLIII, append.
23 P. 206. Dallas, II, 174.
24 P. 206. Bright, *Diaries*, 235–6.
25 P. 206. Dallas, II, 174 ; C. Greville, *Mem.*, VIII, 226.
26 P. 206. *Ibid.*, 228–9, 230–1 ; Dallas, II, 182.
27 P. 206. *Hansard*, 3rd Ser., CLII, 1618.
28 P. 206. Fitzmaurice, I, 317.
29 P. 206. C. Greville, *Mem.*, VIII, 237.
30 P. 207. White, I, 100.
31 P. 207. Denison, 31–2.
32 P. 207. *Hansard*, 3rd Ser., CLIII, 1899 ; Q.V.L., 1st Ser., III, 424 ; Maxwell, *Clarendon*, II, 184–5.
33 P. 207. C. Greville, *Mem.*, VIII, 236. See also Monypenny and Buckle, IV, 204–5.
34 P. 207. *Hansard*, 3rd Ser., CLIII, 880. For Russell's view, *ibid.*, 390–405.
35 P. 207. Argyll, II, 134. See also Dallas, II, 177–8.
36 P. 208. Parker, *Graham*, II, 377 ; C. Greville, *Mem.*, VIII, 241.
37 P. 208. *Inter al.*, C.H.B.F.P., II, 430–8 ; Cowley, *Secrets*, 170–81 ;

Malmesbury (3rd earl), *Mem.*, II, 148–75 ; Q.V.L., 1st Ser., III, 395–420 ;
Windsor MSS. J. 15 ; P.R.O., F.O., 27 : 1280.

[38] P. 209. Cowley, *Secrets*, 180.

[39] P. 209. Palmerston to Granville, Apr. 22, 1859, P.R.O., G. and D.,
29 : 19.

[40] P. 209. Maxwell, *Clarendon*, II, 184.

[41] P. 209. Beust, I, 175–80 ; Prince Consort, *Letters*, 195–6.

[42] P. 209. C. Greville, *Mem.*, VIII, 236.

[43] P. 209. Dallas, II, 186.

[44] P. 209. Q.V.L., 1st Ser., III, 419. See also C. Greville, *Mem.*, VIII, 244.

[45] P. 210. Lucas, *Glenesk*, 181–2.

[46] P. 210. *The Times*, Apr. 30, 1859.

[47] P. 210. *Ibid.*, Apr. 26, 1859 (partly printed in Walpole, *Russell*, II, 304).

[48] P. 211. *The Times*, Apr. 30, 1859.

[49] P. 211. Parker, *Graham*, II, 388.

[50] P. 211. Stanmore, *Herbert*, II, 197.

[51] P. 211. Barrington, *The Servant of All*, II, 156.

[52] P. 211. *Ibid.*, 152–7 ; Monypenny and Buckle, *IV*, 238–40 ; Sir George
Grey to Granville, May 12, 1859, P.R.O., G. and D., 29 : 18 ; C. Greville, *Mem.*,
VIII, 245 ; Stanmore, *Herbert*, II, 181–7 ; Parker, *Graham*, II, 383–5 ; Walpole,
Russell, II, 304–6 ; Morley, *Gladstone*, I, 623 ; Palmerston to Russell, May 19,
1859, P.R.O., G. and D., 22 : 13 ; Reeve, II, 26–7.

[53] P. 211. Monypenny and Buckle, IV, 235.

[54] P. 212. *Ibid.*, 235–6.

[55] P. 212. *Ibid.*, 237.

[56] P. 212. *Ibid.*, 238.

[57] P. 212. Fitzmaurice, I, 329–30 ; Stanmore, *Herbert*, II, 181–91 ;
Palmerston to Russell, May 19, 1859, P.R.O., G. and D., 22 : 13 ; Parker,
Graham, II, 387–8 ; C. Greville, *Mem.*, VIII, 247–8. For the accuracy of
Disraeli's information, Monypenny and Buckle, IV, 244.

[58] P. 212. Fitzmaurice, I, 327.

[59] P. 213. *Ibid.*, 328 ; Stanmore, *Herbert*, II, 193.

[60] P. 213. Fitzmaurice, 327–9 ; Stanmore, *Herbert*, II, 195.

[61] P. 213. Walpole, *Russell*, II, 305–6 ; C. Greville, *Mem.*, VIII, 248–9 ;
Fitzmaurice, I, 331.

[62] P. 213. Bright, *Diaries*, 236.

[63] P. 213. Parker, *Graham*, II, 383–4.

[64] P. 213. Bright, *Diaries*, 240.

[65] P. 213. Fitzmaurice, I, 329–30.

[66] P. 213. Bright, *Diaries*, 237–8.

[67] P. 214. *Ibid.*, 239.

[68] P. 214. Stanmore, *Herbert*, II, 198–9.

[69] P. 215. Wilson, *Carlyle*, 344.

[70] P. 215. Malmesbury (3rd earl), *Mem.*, II, 190 ; Cook, 120.

[71] P. 215. Q.V.L., 1st Ser., III, 438–40.

[72] P. 215. Fitzmaurice, I, 333–41 ; Q.V.L., 1st Ser., III, 440–1.

[73] P. 216. *Ibid.*, B. and A., V, 155–7.

[74] P. 216. Fitzmaurice, I, 337.

[75] P. 216. C. Greville, *Mem.*, VIII, 252–3.

[76] P. 216. Sir George Grey to Granville, June 12, 1859, P.R.O., G. and D.,
29 : 18.

[77] P. 216. Q.V.L., 1st Ser., III, 442–3 ; Palmerston to Russell, June 12,
1859, P.R.O., G. and D., 22 : 13 ; Reeve, II, 32 ; Maxwell, *Clarendon*, II, 185–7.

[78] P. 216.   Ibid.; Stanmore, Herbert, II, 200.
[79] P. 216.   Dallas, II, 232.
[80] P. 216.   Ibid.
[81] P. 217.   Trevelyan, Bright, 282–3 ; Q.V.L., 1st Ser., III, 444–5.
[82] P. 217.   Ibid., 446 ; Holyoake, Sixty Years, I, 228 ; Trevelyan, Bright,
282–3.
[83] P. 217.   Ibid., 282–3, 282 n. ; Morley, Gladstone, I, 626 n.
[84] P. 217.   Lord J. Russell, Later Corr., II, 233.
[85] P. 217.   Bright, Diaries, 242.
[86] P. 217.   Ibid.
[87] P. 217.   Parker, Graham, II, 391.
[88] P. 218.   Sir Benjamin Hall to Sir Charles Phipps, June 15, 1859, Windsor
MSS. C. 30.   See also Fitzmaurice, I, 344 ; C. Greville, Mem., VIII, 254.
[89] P. 218.   Dallas, II, 232.
[90] P. 218.   Morley, Gladstone, I, 628.
[91] P. 218.   Lady Frederick Cavendish, I, 92–3.
[92] P. 218.   Fitzmaurice, I, 345.
[93] P. 218.   Martineau, Newcastle, 285–6.
[94] P. 218.   Fitzmaurice, I, 345.
[95] P. 219.   Hodder, III, 88.
[96] P. 219.   C. Greville, Mem., VIII, 263.
[97] P. 219.   Quar. Rev., vol. CXIII (1863), 256.

CHAPTER XXIX

[1] P. 221.   Aberdeen to Prince Albert, July 18, 1859, Windsor MSS. J. 21 ;
Cowley, Secrets, 185.
[2] P. 221.   Stanmore, Herbert, I, 160 ; Lord J. Russell, Later Corr., II, 235.
[3] P. 221.   Vitzthum, St. Petersburg and London, I, 358–9.
[4] P. 221.   Cowley, Secrets, 184 ; Maxwell, Clarendon, II, 187–8.
[5] P. 221.   Palmerston's memorandum, June 28, 1859, P.R.O., G. and D.,
22 : 27.
[6] P. 221.   Lord J. Russell, Later Corr., II, 235.
[7] P. 222.   Palmerston to Russell, June 26, 1859, P.R.O., G. and D., 22 : 13.
[8] P. 222.   Vitzthum, op. cit., I, 360–1.
[9] P. 222.   Palmerston to Russell, June 26, 1859, P.R.O., G. and D., 22 : 13.
[10] P. 222.   Q.V.L., 1st Ser., III, 461–3.
[11] P. 222.   E.g. Fitzmaurice, I, 350–2. For Granville's private correspondence with Prince Albert, see especially Windsor MSS. J. 22 ; Q.V.L.,1st Ser.,
III, ch. XXVIII.
[12] P. 223.   Infra, passim.
[13] P. 223.   Fitzmaurice, I, 351.
[14] P. 223.   De la Gorce, Second Empire, III, 107 ; B. and A., V, 158–60.
[15] P. 224.   Ibid.
[16] P. 224.   Vitzthum, op. cit., I, 367.
[17] P. 224.   Q.V.L., 1st Ser., III, 450 ; note 20, infra.
[18] P. 224.   Q.V.L., 1st Ser., III, 450–1.
[19] P. 225.   Ibid., 451–2 ; Lord J. Russell, Later Corr., II, 237 ; Fitzmaurice,
I, 350–2 ; Vitzthum, op. cit., I, 373–4. Cf. Hansard, 3rd Ser., CLV, 1220–2.
[20] P. 225.   Q.V.L., 1st Ser., III, 476 ; Vitzthum, op. cit., I, 306–7.
[21] P. 225   Cavour-Nigra, Carteggio, 1st Ser., II, 237–52 ; Hertslet, Map,
II, 1375.

[22] P. 226. Q.V.L., 1st Ser., III, 452–3 ; Russell to Victoria, July 14, 1859, *Windsor MSS*. J. 21.

[23] P. 226. Fitzmaurice, I, 351.

[24] P. 226. B. and A., V, 162.

[25] P. 226. Lavisse, VII, 114–15 ; Martin, *Prince Consort*, IV, 390–2.

[26] P. 226. Lavisse, VII, 114.

[27] P. 226. Cavour-Nigra, *Carteggio*, 1st Ser., II, 245–7.

[28] P. 226. Walpole, *Russell*, II, 310–11, 321–2.

[29] P. 226. Q.V.L., 1st Ser., III, 464.

[30] P. 227. Fitzmaurice, I, 354.

[31] P. 227. Q.V.L., 1st Ser., III, 463.

[32] P. 227. Walpole, *Russell*, II, 312 ; Lord J. Russell, *Later Corr.*, II, 238.

[33] P. 227. Victoria to Russell, July 20, 22, and Russell to Victoria, July 21, 23, 1859, *Windsor MSS*. C. 11, J. 21 ; Memorandum of Conversation between Sir C. Wood and Lord Palmerston, Aug. 25, 1859, *Windsor MSS*. J. 22.

[34] P. 227. Granville to Prince Albert, Aug. 10, 15, Russell to Victoria, Aug. 22, Victoria to Russell, Aug. 23, 1859, *Windsor MSS*. J. 22 ; Palmerston to Russell, Aug. 22, 1859 [misdated 1858], P.R.O., G. and D., 22 : 13 ; Walpole, *Russell*, II, 312 ; Q.V.L., 1st Ser., III, 462–8 ; Lord J. Russell, *Later Corr.*, II, 241.

[35] P. 228. Fitzmaurice, I, 354 ; Q.V.L., 1st Ser., III, ch. XXVIII ; *Windsor MSS*. J. 22 and C. 11, *passim*.

[36] P. 228. Victoria to Russell, July 20, Aug. 15, 1859, *Windsor MSS*. C. 11 ; Q.V.L., 1st Ser., III, 464–5.

[37] P. 228. Fitzmaurice, I, 355.

[38] P. 228. Russell to Victoria, July 23, 1859, *Windsor MSS*. J. 21 ; Vitzthum, *op. cit.*, I, 358–9, 371, 373–4.

[39] P. 228. Victoria to Russell, July 6, 1859, *Windsor MSS*. C. 11.

[40] P. 229. Q.V.L., 1st Ser., III, 461 ; Palmerston to Russell, Aug. 22, 1859, P.R.O., G. and D., 22 : 13 ; Fitzmaurice, I, 353–7 ; Argyll, II, 142.

[41] P. 229. Palmerston to Russell, Sept. 4, and Granville to Sir G. Grey, Sept. 9, 1859 (copies), *Windsor MSS*. J. 23.

[42] P. 229. Q.V.L., 1st Ser., III, 467 ; Fitzmaurice, I, 357 ; Argyll, II, 144.

[43] P. 229. Q.V.L., 1st Ser., III, 469–70, 473–6.

[44] P. 229. Palmerston to Russell, Sept. 4, 1859 (copy), *Windsor MSS*. J. 23 ; Fitzmaurice, I, 361 ; Lord J. Russell, *Later Corr.*, II, 240.

[45] P. 229. Q.V.L., 1st Ser., III, 470, 473–5 ; Victoria to Russell, Sept. 8, 1859, *Windsor MSS*. C. 11.

[46] P. 229. Minute of Conversation between Sir C. Wood and Lord Palmerston, Aug. 25, 1859, *Windsor MSS*. J. 22.

[47] P. 229. C. Greville, *Mem.*, VIII, 267 ; Fitzmaurice, I, 360.

[48] P. 230. *Ibid.*, 352 ; Sir G. Grey to Granville, Sept. 6, 1859, P.R.O., G. and D., 29 : 18 (partly printed in Fitzmaurice, I, 361).

[49] P. 230. Fitzmaurice, I, 357 ; Maxwell, *Clarendon*, II, 192.

[50] P. 230. *Ibid.*, 197. See also Q.V.L., 1st Ser., III, 468.

[51] P. 230. Prince Albert's memorandum, Dec. 31, 1859, *Windsor MSS*. A. 31.

[52] P. 231. Prince Albert's memorandum, Nov. 24, 1859, *Windsor MSS*. J. 23.

[53] P. 231. Victoria to Russell, and Russell to Victoria, Oct. 30, 1859, *Windsor MSS*. J. 23 ; Argyll, II, 145.

[54] P. 231. Q.V.L., 1st Ser., III, 477–82 ; Lord J. Russell, *Later Corr.*, II, 250 ; Russell to Victoria, Dec. 3, 1859 ; Sir Chas. Wood to Gen. Grey, undated ; Prince Albert's memorandum, Dec. 20, 1859, *Windsor MSS*. J. 24.

[55] P. 232. Cowley, *Secrets*, 191.

[56] P. 232. Fitzmaurice, I, 360.

[57] P. 232.   C. Greville, *Mem.*, VIII, 269–70 ; Maxwell, *Clarendon*, II, 206. See also Greville-Reeve, *Letters*, 277.

[58] P. 233.   *E.g.* Walpole, *Russell*, II, 318.

[59] P. 233.   Palmerston to Russell, Dec. 31, 1862, P.R.O., G. and D., 22 : 14. See also same to same, Sept. 13, 1863, G. and D., 22 : 22 ; Lord J. Russell, *Later Corr.*, II, 324.

[60] P. 233.   *E.g.* Russell to Granville, Nov. 8, 1862, P.R.O., G. and D., 29 : 18.

[61] P. 233.   Beust, I, 252.

[62] P. 233.   Palmerston to Clarendon, Jan., 1859 (copy), *Windsor MSS.* A. 31.

[63] P. 233.   Hodder, III, 187.

[64] P. 234.   Burghclere, 33.

[65] P. 235.   Stanmore, *Herbert*, II, 212.

[66] P. 236.   Cowley, *Secrets*, 188–9.

[67] P. 236.   *Ibid.* ; ' Memorandum of the State of Foreign Relations at the close of Lord Derby's Administration,' June 14, 1859, signed by E. H. H[ammond], *Windsor MSS.* C. 30.

[68] P. 236.   *E.g.* Stanmore, *Herbert*, II, 168–9, 208 ; Vitzthum, *op. cit.* I, 331 ; Morley, *Gladstone*, II, 43.

[69] P. 237.   Baxter, chaps. I to X.

[70] P. 237.   *E.g. Hansard*, 3rd Ser., CLV, 704–23.

[71] P. 237.   Lord J. Russell, *Later Corr.*, II, 241–2 ; B. and A., V, 168–72.

[72] P. 238.   *Hansard*, 3rd Ser., CLIV, 511–16, 534–6, 947–9.

[73] P. 238.   Stanmore, *Herbert*, II, 209.

[74] P. 238.   Guedalla, *Gladstone and Palmerston*, 113–14.

[75] P. 238.   *Ibid.* ; Palmerston to Prince Albert, Nov. 16, 1859, *Windsor MSS.* E. 48 ; *Hansard*, 3rd Ser., CLV, 725–8.

[76] P. 238.   *Ibid.*, 399–416.

[77] P. 238.   Palmerston to Prince Albert, Nov. 16, 1859, *Windsor MSS.* E. 48.

[78] P. 239.   *Ibid.*

[79] P. 239.   *Inter al.*, Stanmore, *Herbert*, II, chap. VII ; H. B. Loch, *Personal Narrative of Occurrences during Lord Elgin's Second Embassy to China* (London, 1900) ; S. Lane-Poole, *Life of Sir Harry Parkes* (London, 1894) ; Laurence Oliphant, *Narrative of the Earl of Elgin's Mission to China and Japan* (New York, 1860) ; Walrond, *Elgin* ; G. J. (Viscount) Wolseley, *Story of a Soldier's Life* (London, 1903) ; Morse, I, chaps. XXV, XXVI.

[80] P. 240.   Extract from the *Journal de St. Pétersbourg*, Sept. 8/20, 1859. Enclosed in Crampton to Russell, Oct. 7, 1859 (no. 47), F.O. 65 : 537 ; W. A. White (acting consul-general at Warsaw) to Russell, Sept. 20, 1859 (no. 36), F.O., 65 : 538 ; Russell to Crampton, Sept. 24, 1859 (no. 58), F.O., 65 : 533 ; Crampton to Russell, Nov. 18, 1860 (no. 35), F.O., 65 : 555.

[81] P. 241.   Stanmore, *Herbert*, II, 298–9.

[82] P. 241.   *Ibid.*, 299–300.

[83] P. 241.   Note by Russell, Dec. 21, 1859, on Cowley to Russell, Dec. 9, 1859 (no. 850), with comments added by members of cabinet, F.O., 27 : 1305.

[84] P. 241.   Stanmore, *Herbert*, II, 310–11.

[85] P. 241.   Loch, *op. cit.*, 19.

[86] P. 241.   Stanmore, *Herbert*, II, 296.

[87] P. 242.   *Ibid.*, 314–15.

CHAPTER XXX

[1] P. 243. Dunham, *passim*.

[2] P. 244. A. L. Dunham, 'The Origins of the Anglo-French Treaty of 1860,' in *Nineteenth Century*, vol. XCII (Nov. 1922), p. 792.

[3] P. 244. Victoria to Russell, Dec. 25, 1859, *Windsor MSS.* C. 11.

[4] P. 244. Martin, *Prince Consort*, V, 23.

[5] P. 244. Vitzthum, *St. Petersburg and London*, II, 65.

[6] P. 244. Cowley, *Secrets*, 195–6. See also Malmesbury (3rd earl), *Mem.*, II, 216.

[7] P. 244. Bright, *Diaries*, 264.

[8] P. 245. Cowley to Russell, Dec. 9, 1859 (no. 847) ; Col. Claremont to Cowley, Dec. 16, 1859, P.R.O., F.O., 27 : 1305.

[9] P. 245. Notes 58 and 62, *infra*.

[10] P. 245. Morley, *Gladstone*, II, 22.

[11] P. 245. Russell to Palmerston, Oct. 6, 1860, P.R.O., G. and D., 22 : 21.

[12] P. 245. Guedalla, *Gladstone and Palmerston*, 276–7 ; Palmerston to Victoria, Feb. 7, May 18, 1865, *Windsor MSS.* A. 33 ; Morley, *Cobden*, II, 470–2.

[13] P. 246. B. and A., V, 174–80. See also Maxwell, *Clarendon*, II, 199–200 ; Palmerston to Russell, Jan. 5, 1860, P.R.O., G. and D., 22 : 21.

[14] P. 246. Guedalla, *Gladstone and Palmerston*, 119–21 ; Fitzmaurice, I, 367–8 ; Granville to Prince Albert, Jan. 3, 1860, *Windsor MSS.* J. 24 ; Martin, *Prince Consort*, V, 16–20 ; Maxwell, *Clarendon*, II, 202, 206–7 ; Palmerston to Russell, Jan. 8, 9, 1860, P.R.O., G. and D., 22 : 21 ; Victoria to Russell, Jan. 9, 1860, *Windsor MSS.* C. 11. *Cf.* Malmesbury (3rd earl), *Mem.*, II, 213.

[15] P. 247. Granville to Prince Albert, Jan. 10, 13, 1860, *Windsor MSS.* J. 25 ; Q.V.L., 1st Ser., III, 488–9 ; Lord J. Russell, *Later Corr.*, II, 255–6 ; Victoria to Russell (with memorandum enclosed), Jan. 13, 1860, *Windsor MSS.* C. 11; Fitzmaurice, I, 369.

[16] P. 247. Maxwell, *Clarendon*, II, 204.

[17] P. 247. Q.V.L., 1st Ser., III, 490.

[18] P. 247. Granville to Prince Albert, Feb. 10, 1860, *Windsor MSS.* J. 26.

[19] P. 248. Martin, *Prince Consort*, V, 34–5 ; C. Greville, *Mem.*, VIII, 295 ; Vitzthum, *op. cit.*, II, 49 ; Victoria to Russell, March 10, 1860, *Windsor MSS.* C. 12 (partly printed in Q.V.L., 1st Ser., III, 501).

[20] P. 248. Palmerston to Russell, Feb. 7, 1860, P.R.O., G. and D., 22 : 21 ; B. and A., V, 182.

[21] P. 248. Maxwell, *Clarendon*, II, 212.

[22] P. 248. Cowley, *Secrets*, 202 ; *Hansard*, 3rd Ser., CLVII, 1252–8.

[23] P. 249. Malmesbury (third earl), *Mem.*, II, 224 ; Palmerston to Russell, March 27, 28, and Russell to Palmerston, March 28, 1860, P.R.O., G. and D., 22 : 21. See also Cavour-Nigra, 1st Ser., IV, *passim*.

[24] P. 249. Palmerston to Russell, March 6, 1860, P.R.O., G. and D., 22 : 21 ; Palmerston's cabinet memorandum, March 25, 1860, P.R.O., G. and D., 22 : 27.

[25] P. 249. Reeve, II, 43–4 ; C. Greville, *Mem.*, VIII, 296 n.

[26] P. 249. Palmerston to Persigny, Apr. 17, 1860 (copy), P.R.O., G. and D., 22 : 21.

[27] P. 249. Martin, *Prince Consort*, V, 70–1 ; B. and A., V, 190–2.

[28] P. 249. Cowley, *Secrets*, 202.

[29] P. 249. *Ibid.*, 199.

[30] P. 250. Vitzthum, *op. cit.*, II, 65, 83.

[31] P. 250. Corti, *Leopold*, 273, 273 n.

[32] P. 250. Q.V.L., 1st Ser., III, 497–501.

[33] P. 250. Palmerston to Russell, March 15, 1860, P.R.O., G. and D., 22 : 21. See also Vitzthum, *op. cit.*, II, 72–3.

[34] P. 250. Cowley, *Secrets*, 207.

[35] P. 250. Palmerston to Russell, Apr. 1, 1860, P.R.O., G. and D., 22 : 21.

[36] P. 251. Malmesbury (3rd earl), *Mem.*, II, 224–6, 240–1 ; Vitzthum, *op. cit.*, II, 8.

[37] P. 251. *Ibid.*, II, 73.

[38] P. 251. *Ibid.*, 6 ; Granville to Prince Albert, Apr. 21, 1860, *Windsor MSS.* J. 28 ; Palmerston to Russell, May 14, 1860, P.R.O., G. and D., 22 : 21 ; Lavisse, VII, 131.

[39] P. 251. Victoria to Russell, Jan. 21 and 22, March 13, 1860, *Windsor MSS.* C. 11, 12 ; Sir Charles Wood to Prince Albert, Jan. 23, 1860, *Windsor MSS.* J. 25.

[40] P. 252. Granville to Prince Albert, Apr. 21, 1860, *Windsor MSS.* J. 28 ; Q.V.L., 1st Ser., III, 509 ; Victoria to Russell, March 21, 1860, *Windsor MSS.* C. 12 ; B. and A., V, ch. VII.

[41] P. 252. Palmerston's (cabinet) memorandum, March 25, 1860, P.R.O., G. and D., 22 : 27.

[42] P. 252. Meath, 76 ; St. Helier, 81–2 ; Vitzthum, *op. cit.*, I, 228–30.

[43] P. 252. *Ibid.* ; Meath, 75–6 ; St. Helier, 80, 180.

[44] P. 253. Palmerston to Victoria, July 11, 20, Aug. 18, 1860, *Windsor MSS.* A. 28.

[45] P. 253. White, I, 152–5.

[46] P. 254. H. C. Bell, ' Palmerston and Parliamentary Representation ' in *Journ. Mod. His.*, IV, no. 2 (June 1932), 186–213.

[47] P. 255. Palmerston to Victoria, Nov. 24, 1859 ; *Memorandum on Parliamentary Reform*, signed by G. C. Lewis, Dec. 22, 1859 (copy), *Windsor MSS.* B. 70.

[48] P. 255. *Ibid.* ; C. Greville, *Mem.*, VIII, 276–7, 294 ; Argyll, II, 152.

[49] P. 255. C. Greville, *Mem.*, VIII, 297 ; Bright, *Diaries*, 248 ; Palmerston to Russell, Apr. 16, June 1, 6, 1860, P.R.O., G. and D., 22 : 21 ; Martin, *Prince Consort*, V, 54–8. *Cf.* Reeve, II, 42 ; Russell to Palmerston, Nov. 16, 1860 (copy), *Windsor MSS.* B. 70 ; Stanmore, *Herbert*, II, 268.

[50] P. 255. C. Greville, *Mem.*, VIII, 294, 298, 304 ; Vitzthum, *op. cit.*, II, 5 ; Reeve, II, 42.

[51] P. 255. Palmerston to Victoria, May 24, June 9, 1860, *Windsor MSS.* B. 70 ; Guedalla, *Gladstone and Palmerston*, 133–4 ; Palmerston to Russell, Apr. 16, June 1, 6, Nov. 16, 1860, P.R.O., G. and D., 22 : 21. *Cf.* C. Greville, *Mem.*, VIII, 306 ; Monypenny and Buckle, IV, 273.

[52] P. 256. Palmerston to Granville, Dec. 26, 1859, P.R.O., G. and D., 29 : 18.

[53] P. 256. Palmerston to Russell, June 6, 1860, P.R.O., G. and D., 22 : 21.

[54] P. 256. Palmerston to Victoria, June 9, 1860, *Windsor MSS.* B. 70.

[55] P. 256. Russell to Cowley, Aug. 4, 1860 (no. 770), P.R.O., F.O., 27 : 1327; Martin, *Prince Consort*, V, 61.

[56] P. 257. Williams, *Gladstone*, chs. III and IV ; Bright, *Diaries*, 244–6.

[57] P. 257. Stanmore, *Herbert*, II, 222–3.

[58] P. 257. Palmerston to Russell, Feb. 5, 1860, P.R.O., G. and D., 22 : 21.

[59] P. 257. B. and A., V, 221. See also Guedalla, *Gladstone and Palmerston*, 143.

[60] P. 257. C. Greville, *Mem.*, VIII, 293–4.

[61] P. 257. Stanmore, *Herbert*, II, 273–4.

[62] P. 258. Palmerston to Victoria, Jan. 31, 1860, *Windsor MSS.* A. 28 ; same to same, Apr. 4, 1860, *Windsor MSS.* E. 49.

[63] P. 258. Stanmore, *Herbert*, II, 238.

[64] P. 258. *Ibid.*, 248–54 ; Palmerston to Russell, Feb. 5, 1860, P.R.O., G. and D., 22 : 21 ; Guedalla, *Gladstone and Palmerston*, 123 ; B. and A., V, 168–72 ; Parker, *Graham*, II, 396–7 ; Morley, *Gladstone*, II, 44–5.

[65] P. 258. *Ibid.*, 31 ; Palmerston to Russell, March 29, 1860, P.R.O., G. and D., 22 : 21 ; Guedalla, *Gladstone and Palmerston*, 132–3.

[66] P. 259. *Ibid.*, 123.

[67] P. 259. Palmerston to Russell, May 5, 19, 1860, P.R.O., G. and D., 22 : 21.

[68] P. 259. *Ibid.*

[69] P. 259. Martin, *Prince Consort*, V, 115–18 ; Cowley, *Secrets*, 207 ; C. Greville, *Mem.*, VIII, 308 ; Palmerston to Russell, May 19, 1860, P.R.O., G. and D., 22 : 21.

[70] P. 259. Palmerston to Victoria, May 7, 1860, *Windsor MSS.* N. 23 ; Morley, *Gladstone*, II, 31 ; Q.V.L., 1st Ser., III, 509–10.

[71] P. 260. Palmerston to Lansdowne, May 17, 1860, *Bowood MSS. Cf.* Palmerston to Russell, May 19, 1860, P.R.O., G. and D., 22 : 21 ; Palmerston to Granville, May 21, 1860, P.R.O., G. and D., 29 : 19.

[72] P. 260. Fitzmaurice, I, 380 ; C. Greville, *Mem.*, VIII, 310.

[73] P. 260. Monypenny and Buckle, IV, 278–9 ; Malmesbury (3rd earl), *Mem.*, II, 228.

[74] P. 260. *Ibid.*, 227 ; C. Greville, *Mem.*, VIII, 309.

[75] P. 260. Palmerston to Russell, May 22, 1860, P.R.O., G. and D., 22 : 14.

[76] P. 261. Palmerston to Victoria, June 30, 1860, *Windsor MSS.* A. 28.

[77] P. 261. *Ibid.* ; Palmerston to Russell, June 25, 1860, P.R.O., G. and D., 22 : 21 ; Q.V.L., 1st Ser., III, 510–13 ; Morley, *Gladstone*, II, 32–4, 38–9 ; Drafts by Russell and Graham of proposed resolutions to be offered in the House of Commons, no date, *Windsor MSS.* A. 28 ; Guedalla, *Gladstone and Palmerston*, 138–40 ; Denison, 71–4 ; Vitzthum, *op. cit.*, II, 89–94.

[78] P. 261. *Hansard*, 3rd Ser., CLVIII, 1728–9.

[79] P. 261. Guedalla, *Gladstone and Palmerston*, 139–40 ; Palmerston to Victoria, July 4, 1860, *Windsor MSS.* E. 49.

[80] P. 261. Note 77, *supra*.

[81] P. 262. Dasent, *Piccadilly*, 101.

[82] P. 262. Denison, 73 ; *Hansard*, 3rd Ser., CLIX, 1383–96.

[83] P. 262. C. Greville, *Mem.*, VIII, 312 ; Vitzthum, *op. cit.*, II. 93.

[84] P. 262. Palmerston to Victoria, May 24, 1860, *Windsor MSS.* E. 49.

[85] P. 262. *Ibid.* See also Palmerston to Russell, May 27, 1860, P.R.O., G. and D., 22 : 21.

[86] P. 262. Palmerston to Victoria, June 2, July 4 (two letters), 7, 11, 1860, *Windsor MSS.* J. 29, E. 49, A. 28 ; Morley, *Gladstone*, II, 45–7 ; Argyll to Granville, June 17, 1860, P.R.O., G. and D., 29 : 18 ; Argyll, II, 164–5 ; Maxwell, *Clarendon*, II, 216 ; Guedalla, *Gladstone and Palmerston*, 136–7, 140–1.

[87] P. 263. *Ibid.*, 146–8 ; Morley, *Gladstone*, II, 47, 47 n. ; Vitzthum, *op. cit.*, II, 100–1 ; Fitzmaurice, I, 386 ; Palmerston to Victoria, July 21, 1860, *Windsor MSS.* G. 52 ; *Hansard*, 3rd Ser., CLX, 17–33.

[88] P. 263. Q.V.L., 1st Ser., III, 512–13.

[89] P. 263. Palmerston to the Queen, July 24, 1860, *Windsor MSS.* E. 49.

[90] P. 263. Fitzmaurice, I, 386.

[91] P. 263. Palmerston to Victoria, Aug. 28, 1860, *Windsor MSS.* A. 28.

[92] P. 263. Same to same, Aug. 23, 1860. See also Fitzmaurice, I, 386.

[93] P. 264. Morley, *Gladstone*, II, 47. See also C. Greville, *Mem.*, VIII, 314.

[94] P. 264. Fitzmaurice, I, 386.

[95] P. 264. Morley, *Gladstone*, II, 35.

[96] P. 264. Fitzmaurice, I, 388 ; B. and A., V, 203 ; C. Greville, *Mem.*, VIII, 312.

[97] P. 265. Palmerston to Russell, Apr. 12, May 17, 1860, P.R.O., G. and D., 22 : 21.

[98] P. 265. Palmerston to Russell, May 17, 1860, P.R.O., G. and D., 22 : 21. See also same to same, July 10, 16, 1860.

[99] P. 265. Cavour, 1st Ser., IV, 112 ; Lord J. Russell, *Later Corr.*, II, 260–2 ; Palmerston to Russell, July 15, 1860, P.R.O., G. and D., 22 : 21.

[100] P. 266. Same to same, Aug. 21, 1860. See also same to same, Aug. 14, 1860.

[101] P. 266. Palmerston to Russell, Oct. 28, 1860, P.R.O., G. and D., 22 : 21 ; Walpole, *Russell*, II, 325–7 ; Malmesbury (3rd earl), *Mem.*, II, 237–8.

[102] P. 266. Palmerston to Russell, Dec. 2, 1860, P.R.O., G. and D., 22 : 21.

[103] P. 266. Same to same, Sept. 28.

[104] P. 266. Same to same, Oct. 6.

[105] P. 267. Same to same, Dec. 25, Sept. 19.

[106] P. 267. Same to same, Sept. 21, Oct. 6 ; Maxwell, *Clarendon*, II, 229.

[107] P. 267. Palmerston to Russell, Sept. 21, 1860, P.R.O., G. and D., 22 : 21 ; Martineau, *Newcastle*, 296.

[108] P. 267. Victoria to Russell, Dec. 10, 11, 12, 16 ; Russell to Victoria, Dec. 12, 28, 31 ; Palmerston to Victoria, Dec. 15 ; Sir C. Wood to Gen. Grey, Dec. 16, 1860, *Windsor MSS.* A. 28, J. 31, J. 32 ; Palmerston to Russell, Dec. 18, 1860, P.R.O., G. and D., 22 : 21 ; Lord J. Russell, *Later Corr.*, II, 269–70.

[109] P. 267. Baxter, chs. VI–VIII.

[110] P. 268. Palmerston to Persigny, Sept. 18, 1860 (copy), P.R.O., G. and D., 22 : 21.

[111] P. 268. C.H.B.F.P., II, 451–6 ; Cavour, 1st Ser., IV, *passim*.

[112] P. 268. *Hansard*, 3rd Ser., CLX, 1586–9.

[113] P. 268. Palmerston to Victoria, Aug. 20, 1860, *Windsor MSS.* A. 28.

[114] P. 269. *Hansard*, 3rd Ser., CLX, 1587 ; Palmerston to Russell, July 20, 1860, P.R.O., G. and D., 22 : 21.

[115] P. 269. Palmerston to Russell, July 19, 1860, P.R.O., G. and D., 22 : 21.

[116] P. 269. Same to same, July 20, 1860, P.R.O., G. and D., 22 : 21.

[117] P. 269. Same to same, July 26.

[118] P. 270. Palmerston to Victoria, July 21, 1860, *Windsor MSS.* G. 52.

[119] P. 270. Palmerston to Russell, July 22, 1860, P.R.O., G. and D., 22 : 21.

[120] P. 270. Lord J. Russell, *Later Corr.*, II, 266.

[121] P. 270. Wolff, *Rambling Recollections*, II, 8–10.

[122] P. 270. Palmerston to Russell, March 10, 1861, P.R.O., G. and D., 22 : 21.

[123] P. 270. Same to same, Jan. 31, Feb. 5, 1861.

[124] P. 270. Palmerston to Russell, March 12, 1861, P.R.O., G. and D., 22 : 14.

[125] P. 271. Palmerston to Victoria, Oct. 20, Nov. 2, 1860, *Windsor MSS.* A. 28.

[126] P. 271. *Supra*, ch. XXIX, notes 86, 87.

[127] P. 271. Stanmore, *Herbert*, II, 350.

[128] P. 271. *Ibid.*, 354.

[129] P. 272. Q.V.L., 1st Ser., III, 538.

CHAPTER XXXI

[1] P. 273. *Ann. Reg.* for 1861, p. 2.

[2] P. 274. Palmerston to Russell, Sept. 19, 1863, P.R.O., G. and D., 22 : 22 ; Stanmore, *Herbert*, II, 428–9.

[3] P. 275. *Ibid.* ; Palmerston to Russell, Feb. 18, 1861, P.R.O., G. and D., 22 : 21.

[4] P. 275. J. P. Baxter, 3rd, ' The British Government and Neutral Rights,' *Am. His. Rev.*, vol. XXXIV, no. 1 (Oct. 1928), pp. 11–12.

[5] P. 275. *Ann. Reg.*, for 1861, p. 118 ; Mathieson, *Slave Trade,* 174 ; Palmerston to Russell, Apr. 27, 1861, P.R.O., G. and D., 22 : 21.

[6] P. 275. Palmerston's memorandum, Dec. 11, 1860 ; Palmerston to Russell, Dec. 30, 1860, P.R.O., G. and D., 22 : 21.

[7] P. 275. *Ibid.* See also B. and A., V, 209.

[8] P. 276. Palmerston to Russell, Dec. 30, 1860, P.R.O., G. and D., 22 : 21.

[9] P. 276. Adams, *Great Britain and the American Civil War,* I, 130–1.

[10] P. 276. *Ibid.,* 156 n.

[11] P. 276. Palmerston to Russell, Apr. 14, 1861, P.R.O., G. and D., 22 : 21.

[12] P. 277. Cowley, *Secrets,* 241.

[13] P. 277. Vitzthum, *St. Petersburg and London,* II, 134.

[14] P. 277. Palmerston to Russell, June 10, 1861, P.R.O., G. and D., 22 : 21.

[15] P. 278. Palmerston to Russell, Jan. 20, 1861, P.R.O., G. and D., 22 : 21 ; Q.V.L., 1st Ser., III, 551.

[16] P. 278. *Ibid.,* 550–4, 554 n.

[17] P. 278. Palmerston to Russell, Jan. 21, 1861, P.R.O., G. and D., 22 : 21.

[18] P. 278. Russell to Victoria, Jan. 15, 1861, *Windsor MSS.* J. 32 ; Maxwell, *Clarendon,* II, 234.

[19] P. 278. Palmerston to Russell, Jan. 14, 1861, P.R.O., G. and D., 22 : 21 ; Lord J. Russell, *Later Corr.,* II, 278–9 ; B. and A., V, 217–18.

[20] P. 278. Palmerston to Russell, Sept. 17, 1861, P.R.O., G. and D., 22 : 21.

[21] P. 278. Q.V.L., 1st Ser., III, 563 ; Palmerston to Russell, Sept. 17, 1861, P.R.O., G. and D., 22 : 21.

[22] P. 279. Same to same, Apr. 24, 1861, P.R.O., G. and D., 22 : 14.

[23] P. 279. *Hansard,* 3rd Ser., CLXIII, 778.

[24] P. 279. Palmerston to Russell, Sept. 26, Oct. 25, Nov. 9, 1861, P.R.O., G. and D., 22 : 21 ; Lord J. Russell, *Later Corr.,* II, 278–9 ; Cowley, *Secrets,* 233–40 ; B. and A., V., 216–19.

[25] P. 279. Lord J. Russell, *Later Corr.,* II, 291.

[26] P. 280. Trevelyan, *Bright,* 293.

[27] P. 280. Palmerston to Victoria, Feb. 11, 16, 19, March 12, 13, 1861, *Windsor MSS. B.* 70 ; Palmerston to Russell, March 31, 1861, P.R.O., G. and D. 22 : 21.

[28] P. 280. Martin, *Prince Consort,* V, 238 ; Prince Albert to Palmerston, Jan. 24, 1861 (copy), *Windsor MSS.* E. 50 ; Stanmore, *Herbert,* II, 420–1.

[29] P. 280. Monypenny and Buckle, IV, 294 ; Q.V.L., 1st Ser., III, 547–8.

[30] P. 280. Martin, *Prince Consort,* V, 243.

[31] P. 280. Monypenny and Buckle, IV, 293–5 ; Martin, *Prince Consort,* V, 238–9 ; Q.V.L., 1st Ser., III, 539–40, 547–8 ; Vitzthum, *St. Petersburg and London,* II, 126–8 ; Reeve, II, 65–6 ; Prince Albert to Palmerston, Jan. 24, 1861 (copy), *Windsor MSS.* E. 50 ; Malmesbury (3rd earl), *Mem.,* II, 243–4.

[32] P. 281. Vitzthum, *op. cit.,* II, 140 ; Palmerston to Victoria, July 30, 1861, *Windsor MSS.* A. 29 ; Reeve, II, 65–6.

33 P. 281. *Ibid.* ; Vitzthum, *op. cit.*, II, 126.
34 P. 281. Monypenny and Buckle, IV, 325.
35 P. 281. Fitzmaurice, I, 407.
36 P. 282. *Ann. Reg.* for 1865, p. 39 ; Gardiner, I, 123.
37 P. 282. Guedalla, *Gladstone and Palmerston*, 160.
38 P. 282. Prince Albert to Palmerston, Jan. 24, 1861 (copy), *Windsor MSS.*
E. 50.
39 P. 283. Palmerston to Granville, Apr. 15, 1861, P.R.O., G. and D.,
29 : 24.
40 P. 283. Lord J. Russell, *Later Corr.*, II, 276.
41 P. 283. Note 42, *infra*.
42 P. 283. Palmerston to Prince Albert, Apr. 14, 1861 ; ' Substance of
correspondence between Ld. Palmerston and other Members of Govt. respecting
the Budget, 14th and 15th April, 1861,' *Windsor MSS.* A. 31 ; Palmerston to
Granville, Apr. 15, 1861, P.R.O., G. and D., 29 : 24 ; Guedalla, *Gladstone and
Palmerston*, 160–7 ; Stanmore, *Herbert*, II, 419–26 ; Morley, *Gladstone*, II, 39–40.
43 P. 285. Palmerston to Russell, May 25, 26, 1861, P.R.O., G. and D.,
22 : 21 ; B. and A., V, 215.
44 P. 285. Palmerston to Victoria, May 13, 1861, *Windsor MSS.* A. 29.
45 P. 285. Palmerston to Prince Albert, Apr. 15, 1861, *Windsor MSS.* A. 31.
46 P. 285. West, I, 279.
47 P. 285. Palmerston to Victoria, May 27, 1861, *Windsor MSS.* A. 29 ;
Palmerston to Russell, May 25, 26, 1861, P.R.O., G. and D., 22 : 21.
48 P. 285. Palmerston to Granville, May 27, 1861, P.R.O., G. and D., 29 : 18.
49 P. 286. Palmerston to Victoria, May 30, 1861, *Windsor MSS.* A. 29 ;
Hansard, 3rd Ser., CLXIII, 336–9.
50 P. 286. Scott, 178–9 ; *Hansard*, 3rd Ser., CLXIV, 511, 514, 535–7 ;
Palmerston to Victoria, July 8, 1861, *Windsor MSS.* A. 29 (partly printed in
Q.V.L., 1st Ser., III, 566 ; Kenneth Clark, *The Gothic Revival* (London, 1928) ;
Charles L. Eastlake, *A History of the Gothic Revival* (London, 1872).
51 P. 289. Palmerston to Prince Albert, Feb. 1, 1861, *Windsor MSS.* E. 50.
52 P. 289. *Ibid.*
53 P. 289. *Ibid.*
54 P. 289. Palmerston to Russell, Sept. 24, 1861, P.R.O., G. and D., 22 : 21.
55 P. 289. Guedalla, *Gladstone and Palmerston*, 181–7. See also Q.V.L.,
2nd Ser., I, 37–9.
56 P. 290. Guedalla, *Gladstone and Palmerston*, 185.
57 P. 290. *Ann. Reg.* for 1861, p. 94 ; *Hansard*, CLXIV, 3rd Ser., 1828,
1830–2. See also Palmerston to Victoria, Feb. 22, 1861, *Windsor MSS.* E. 50 ;
B. and A., V, 221.
58 P. 290. *Ann. Reg.* for 1861, p. 94.
59 P. 291. Guedalla, *Gladstone and Palmerston*, 172–4, 180.
60 P. 291. 24 & 25 Vic., c. 129.
61 P. 291. Guedalla, *Gladstone and Palmerston*, 174.
62 P. 291. Palmerston to Granville, Oct. 8, 1861, P.R.O., G. and D., 29 : 24 ;
Maxwell, *Clarendon*, II, 244.
63 P. 291. Cowley, *Secrets*, 221. See also Stanley, 235.
64 P. 292. Palmerston to Victoria, June 12, 1861, *Windsor MSS.* A. 29.
65 P. 292. Palmerston's memorandum, July 9, Aug. 3, 1861, P.R.O., G. and
D., 22 : 27.
66 P. 292. Palmerston to Russell, July 18, 1861, P.R.O., G. and D., 22 : 21.
67 P. 292. Newton, I, 48.
68 P. 293. Palmerston to Russell, Sept. 9, 1861, P.R.O., G. and D., 22 : 21.

[69] P. 293. *Ibid.*; Palmerston to Russell, Sept. 26, 1861, P.R.O., G. and D., 22 : 21; Palmerston's memorandum, Sept. 21 (?), 1861, P.R.O., G. and D., 22 : 28.

[70] P. 293. Palmerston to Russell, Oct. 6, 1861, P.R.O., G. and D. 22 : 21. See also B. and A., V, 210–11.

[71] P. 294. Walpole, *Russell*, II, 344.

[72] P. 294. B. and A., V, 218–19.

[73] P. 294. J. P. Baxter, 3rd, *loc. cit.*, pp. 15–16.

[74] P. 294. Cowley, *Secrets*, 223; Palmerston to Russell, Nov. 29, 1861 (2 letters), P.R.O., G. and D., 22 : 21.

[75] P. 294. Dasent, *Delane*, II, 36; Q.V.L., 1st Ser., III, 593–6; Br. Mus., *Add. MSS.* 38987, f. 370.

[76] P. 295. Palmerston to Russell, Dec. 1, 1861, P.R.O., G. and D., 22 : 21; Martin, *Prince Consort*, V, 349–50; Russell to Lyons, Dec. 1, 1861, private (copy); Granville to Prince Albert, Dec. 2, 1861, *Windsor MSS.* Q. 9.

[77] P. 295. Palmerston to Russell, Dec. 6, 1861, P.R.O., G. and D., 22 : 21.

[78] P. 295. Palmerston to Russell, Nov. 29 (2 letters), Dec. 6, 1861, P.R.O., G. and D., 22 : 21; Palmerston to Granville, Nov. 29, 1861, G. and D., 29 : 18 (partly printed in Fitzmaurice, I, 401).

[79] P. 295. Palmerston to Victoria, Dec. 5, 1861, *Windsor MSS.* Q. 9.

[80] P. 295. Same to same, Jan. 12, 1862, Windsor MSS. A. 31.

[81] P. 296. Prince Albert to Granville, Apr. 12; Granville to Prince Albert, Apr. 13; Sir C. Wood to Gen. Grey, Apr. 13; Gen. Grey to Sir C. Phipps, Apr. 13; Prince Albert's memorandum, Apr. 16, 1861, *Windsor* MSS. J. 33.

[82] P. 296. Russell to Victoria, July 21; Victoria to Palmerston, July 22; Palmerston to Victoria, July 23; Prince Albert to Granville, July 27; Granville to Prince Albert, July 28, 1861, *Windsor MSS.* A. 31; Palmerston to Granville, July 21, 1861, P.R.O., G. and D., 29 : 18; Palmerston to Russell, July 26, 1861, P.R.O., G. and D., 22 : 21.

[83] P. 296. Martin, *Prince Consort*, V, 355; Palmerston to Victoria, Dec. 3, 1861, *Windsor MSS.* A. 31.

[84] P. 296. Martin, *Prince Consort*, V, 359–62; Palmerston to Sir Charles Phipps, Dec. 9, 1861, *Windsor MSS.* A. 31; Hodder, III, 132; Maxwell, *Clarendon*, II, 253; Stanley, 240–1.

[85] P. 297. Fitzmaurice, I, 405.

[86] P. 297. *Ibid.*; Cowley, *Secrets*, 228; Maxwell, *Clarendon*, II, 253–4; Vitzthum, *op cit.*, II, 182.

[87] P. 297. *Ibid.*, 186, 188; Palmerston to Russell, Dec. 28, 1861, P.R.O., G. and D., 22 : 21; Q.V.L., 1st Ser., III, 606.

[88] P. 298. *Ibid.*, 2nd Ser., I, 6–7, 13–15; Cowley, *Secrets*, 230–1; Palmerston to Sir Charles Phipps, Jan. 10, 26, 1862, *Windsor MSS.* A. 31; Maxwell, *Clarendon*, II, 257; Stanley, 256.

[89] P. 298. Cook, 148.

[90] P. 299. Palmerston to Russell, Dec. 28, 1861, P.R.O., G. and D., 22 : 21.

[91] P. 299. Q.V.L., 1st Ser., III, 606.

CHAPTER XXXII

[1] P. 301. Denison, 116.

[2] P. 301. Whitty, 40.

[3] P. 301. Q.V.L., 1st Ser., III, 587–90.

[4] P. 301. Lucas, *Glenesk*, 184–5.

⁵ P. 302. Holyoake, *Sixty Years*, I, 227.
⁶ P. 302. *Quarterly Rev.*, CXIII (1863), 258.
⁷ P. 303. Palmerston to Russell, May 7, 1865 (?), P.R.O., G. and D., 22 : 23.
⁸ P. 303. Monypenny and Buckle, IV, 369 ; Q.V.L., 1st Ser., III, 529.
⁹ P. 303. *Ibid.*, 530–1.
¹⁰ P. 303. *Ann. Reg.* for 1861, *Append.*, 433–4.
¹¹ P. 304. *E.g.* Martineau, *Newcastle*, 329–30 ; Victoria to Palmerston, Oct. 28, 1862, *Windsor MSS.* A. 30.
¹² P. 304. Bishops Jacobson of Chester, Ellicott of Gloucester and Bristol, and Browne of Ely.
¹³ P. 304. Guedalla, *Gladstone and Palmerston*, 154–5.
¹⁴ P. 304. *Hansard*, 3rd Ser., CLXX, 434–6.
¹⁵ P. 304. Denison, 122–3.
¹⁶ P. 304. *Ibid.*
¹⁷ P. 304. Lord J. Russell, *Recollections*, 260–4.
¹⁸ P. 305. White, II, 70.
¹⁹ P. 305. Palmerston to Russell, Apr. 20, 1863, P.R.O., G. and D., 22 : 14.
²⁰ P. 305. MacColl, 267.
²¹ P. 305. Wolff, *Rambling Recollections*, I, 113.
²² P. 305. White, II, 116–17 ; Wolff, *op. cit.*, I, 114.
²³ P. 306. Lucas, *Glenesk*, 153.
²⁴ P. 306. Elliot, *Goschen*, I, 64–77.
²⁵ P. 307. Beust, I, 188–9 ; Prince Albert to Russell, March 18, 1860, *Windsor MSS.* C. 19 ; Fitzmaurice, I, 449–51.
²⁶ P. 307. Palmerston to Russell, Sept. 5, 1859, *Windsor MSS.* I. 31.
²⁷ P. 307. Palmerston's memorandum, Feb. 6, 1862, P.R.O., G. and D., 22 : 22.
²⁸ P. 308. Cowley, *Secrets*, 233–4.
²⁹ P. 308. Palmerston to Russell, Dec. 25, 1860, P.R.O., G. and D., 22 : 21.
³⁰ P. 308. Same to same, Sept. 7, 1863, P.R.O., G. and D., 22 : 14.
³¹ P. 308. Palmerston's memorandum, June 27, 1863, P.R.O., G. and D., 22 : 22.
³² P. 308. Palmerston to Russell, Aug. 16, 1864, P.R.O., G. and D., 22 : 15.
³³ P. 309. Martin, *Prince Consort*, V, 179–83, 179 n., 289–92 ; Maxwell, *Clarendon*, II, 246–7 ; Q.V.L., 1st Ser., III, 585–90, 587 n.
³⁴ P. 309. *State Papers*, 1861–2, LII, 119.
³⁵ P. 309. *Hansard*, 3rd Ser., CLXII, 1181–8.
³⁶ P. 310. Vitzthum, *St. Petersburg and London*, II, 145.
³⁷ P. 310. Palmerston to Russell, Oct. 27, 1861, P.R.O., G. and D., 22 : 14.
³⁸ P. 310. Same to same, May 22, 1861, P.R.O., G. and D., 22 : 21.
³⁹ P. 311. Draft to Loftus 'proposed by Lord Palmerston,' May 22, 1861 (copy), *Windsor MSS.* I. 36 ; Russell to Loftus, May 22, 1861 (no. 129), F. O., 244 : 170.
⁴⁰ P. 312. *Inter al.*, de la Gorce, *Second Empire*, IV, livres XXIII, XXV ; *Ann. Reg.* for 1861, pp. 213–19 ; for 1862, pp. 214–18 ; Adams, *Great Britain and the American Civil War*, I, 259–61 ; C.H.B.F.P., II, 506–7.
⁴¹ P. 312. Maxwell, *Clarendon*, II, 243–4.
⁴² P. 312. Palmerston to Russell, Aug. 13, Sept. 4, 17, 1861, P.R.O., G. and D., 22 : 21.
⁴³ P. 313. Same to same, Sept. 24.
⁴⁴ P. 313. Lord J. Russell, *Later Corr.*, II, 320–1.
⁴⁵ P. 313. *State Papers*, 1860–1, LI, 64.
⁴⁶ P. 314. Palmerston to Russell, Jan. 19, 1862, P.R.O., G. and D., 22 : 22.

[47] P. 314. Jordan and Pratt, 29–32.
[48] P. 314. Palmerston to Victoria, Feb. 17, 1862, *Windsor MSS.* A. 29.
[49] P. 315. *Ann. Reg.* for 1862, *Chronicle*, 207–14 ; Mathieson, *Slave Trade*, 174–5.
[50] P. 315. Palmerston to Russell, Apr. 27, 1862, P.R.O., G. and D., 22 : 22.
[51] P. 315. Same to same, Jan. 10, 15.
[52] P. 315. Same to same, Jan. 19.
[53] P. 315. Same to same, June 13.
[54] P. 316. Same to same, Jan. 10.
[55] P. 316. Adams, *op. cit.*, I, 256.
[56] P. 316. Lord J. Russell, *Later Corr.*, II, 325–6.
[57] P. 316. Adams, *op. cit.*, I, 303.
[58] P. 317. *Ibid.*, 304–5.
[59] P. 317. Palmerston to Russell, Aug. 25, 1862, P.R.O., G. and D., 22 : 22.
[60] P. 318. Morley, *Gladstone*, II, 48–50.
[61] P. 318. Guedalla, *Gladstone and Palmerston*, 206–7.
[62] P. 318. *Ibid.*, 207–8.
[63] P. 319. *Ibid.*, 208–9.
[64] P. 319. Evelyn Ashley in *National Review*, vol. XXXI (1898), pp. 536–40.
[65] P. 319. Guedalla, *Gladstone and Palmerston*, 210–14.
[66] P. 320. *Ibid.*, 215–16.
[67] P. 320. *Hansard*, 3rd Ser., CLXVI, 1421–2.
[68] P. 321. White, I, 172–3.
[69] P. 321. *Hansard*, 3rd Ser., CLXVI, 1428.
[70] P. 321. White, I, 173.
[71] P. 322. *Hansard*, 3rd Ser., CLXVI, 1429–40.
[72] P. 322. Guedalla, *Gladstone and Palmerston*, 217–19.
[73] P. 323. Denison, 117–20 ; *Hansard*, 3rd Ser., CLXVII, 293–4.
[74] P. 323. Guedalla, *Gladstone and Palmerston*, 221–8.
[75] P. 324. Denison, 119.
[76] P. 324. *Ibid.*, 120–2 ; *Ann. Reg.* for 1862, pp. 86–93 ; Monypenny and Buckle, IV, 308–10 ; Hardinge, *Carnarvon*, I, 235–7 ; *Hansard*, 3rd Ser., CLXVII, 291–394.
[77] P. 325. Palmerston to Victoria, June 3, 1862, *Windsor MSS.*, A. 30.
[78] P. 325. Palmerston to Granville, June 4, 1862, P.R.O., G. and D. 29 : 19.
[79] P. 325. Palmerston to Victoria, June 3, 1862, *Windsor MSS.* A. 30.
[80] P. 325. *Hansard*, 3rd Ser., CLXVII, 196–221.
[81] P. 326. Vitzthum, *op. cit.*, II, 203.
[82] P. 326. Palmerston to Russell, Oct. 12, 1862, P.R.O., G. and D., 22 : 22.
[83] P. 327. Palmerston to Victoria, July 14, 1862, *Windsor MSS.* A. 30.
[84] P. 327. Morley, *Gladstone*, II, 75.
[85] P. 327. Palmerston to Victoria, Aug. 6, 1862, *Windsor MSS.* A. 30 ; Adams, *op. cit.*, II, 32.
[86] P. 327. Walpole, *Russell*, II, 349 ; Adams, *op. cit.*, II, 37–8.
[87] P. 327. Walpole, *Russell*, II, 350 ; Guedalla, *Gladstone and Palmerston*, 232–3.
[88] P. 327. B. P. Thomas, ' Russo-American Relations, 1815–1867,' in *Johns Hopkins Studies*, XLVIII (1930), ch. VIII.
[89] P. 327. Palmerston to Russell, Sept. 30, 1862, P.R.O., G. and D., 22 : 14.
[90] P. 328. Adams, *op. cit.*, II, 43–4, 54–6 ; Palmerston to Russell, Oct. 3, 8, 1862, P.R.O., G. and D., 22 : 14.
[91] P. 328. Palmerston to Russell, Oct. 20, Dec. 17, 1862, P.R.O., G. and D., 22 : 14 ; Lord J. Russell, *Later Corr.*, II, 333.

NOTES

467

[92] P. 328. Maxwell, *Clarendon*, II, 267.

[93] P. 328. Adams, *op. cit.*, II, 54.

[94] P. 328. Maxwell, *Clarendon*, II, 268–9.

[95] P. 329. Palmerston to Russell, Nov. 25, 1862, P.R.O., G. and D., 22 : 14 ; Vitzthum, *op. cit.*, II, 146–7 ; Palmerston to Victoria, Oct. 25, 1859, *Windsor MSS.* A. 27.

[96] P. 330. Crampton to Malmesbury, March 16, 1859 (no. 89), P.R.O., F.O., 65 : 535 ; Erskine to Russell, Aug. 18, 1860 (no. 64), P.R.O., F.O., 65 : 554 ; Palmerston to Russell, Oct. 15, 1860, P.R.O., G. and D., 22 : 21.

[97] P. 330. Wolff, *Rambling Recollections*, II, 5.

[98] P. 331. Palmerston to Russell, Aug. 29, 1862, P.R.O., G. and D., 22 : 22.

[99] P. 331. Same to same, Sept. 21, 1860, P.R.O., G. and D., 22 : 21.

[100] P. 331. Same to same, Nov. 25, 1862, P.R.O., G. and D., 22 : 14.

[101] P. 331. Same to same, Dec. 31.

[102] P. 331. Palmerston's memorandum, Jan. 14, 1865, Br. Mus., *Add. MSS.* 38991, f. 14.

[103] P. 332. Palmerston to Russell, Dec. 13, 1860, P.R.O., G. and D., 22 : 21.

[104] P. 332. Same to same, Sept. 19, Oct. 16, Nov. 10, 1860.

[105] P. 332. Same to same, Oct. 12, 1861.

[106] P. 332. Palmerston's memorandum, Oct. 22, 1862, P.R.O., G. and D., 22 : 14.

[107] P. 332. *State Papers*, LII, 1141–8.

[108] P. 332. Palmerston to Russell, Nov. 18, 1862, P.R.O., G. and D., 22 : 22.

[109] P. 333. Same to same, Oct. 26, 1862, P.R.O., G. and D., 22 : 14.

[110] P. 334. Same to same, Nov. 6, 1862.

[111] P. 334. Same to same, Nov. 6, 27.

[112] P. 334. Same to same, Nov. 6, 25.

[113] P. 334. Same to same, Nov. 17 ; Russell to Victoria, Nov. 16, 1862, *Windsor MSS.* J. 97 ; Q.V.L., 2nd Ser., I, 48.

[114] P. 334. Palmerston to Victoria, Dec. 5, 1862 ; Russell to Victoria, Dec. 3, 1862, *Windsor MSS.* J. 97 ; Palmerston to Russell, Dec. 4, 7, 8, 1862, P.R.O., G. and D., 22 : 14.

[115] P. 335. Palmerston to Russell, Dec. 21, 1862, P.R.O., G. and D., 22 : 22.

[116] P. 335. Lord J. Russell, *Later Corr.*, II, 302.

[117] P. 335. Palmerston to Russell, March 16, 1863, P.R.O., G. and D., 22 : 14.

[118] P. 336. Same to same, Nov. 25, 1862, P.R.O., G. and D., 22 : 14.

[119] P. 336. Vitzthum, *op. cit.*, II, 204.

CHAPTER XXXIII

[1] P. 337. Fagan, *Mérimée's Letters*, I, 361–2.

[2] P. 338. Palmerston to Russell, Nov. 16, 1863, P.R.O., G. and D., 22 : 22.

[3] P. 338. Q.V.L., 2nd Ser., I, 116–17.

[4] P. 338. 'Four Years of a Reforming Administration,' in *Quarterly Rev.*, vol. CXIII (1863), pp. 253–88.

[5] P. 340. White, I, 174.

[6] P. 340. Bright, *Diaries*, 238, 240, 243, 245, 259–60, 260 n., 272 ; Cowley, *Secrets*, 253–5.

[7] P. 340. *Ibid.* ; Sir C. Phipps to Granville, Nov. 6, 1863, P.R.O., G. and D. 29 : 18 ; Fagan, *Mérimée's Letters*, I, 356–7.

[8] P. 340. Maxwell, *Clarendon*, II, 267.

[9] P. 341. Walpole, *Russell*, II, 402.

[10] P. 341. Vitzthum, *St. Petersburg and London*, II, 228.

[11] P. 341. Maxwell, *Clarendon*, II, 275 ; *Ann. Reg.* for 1863, pp. 6, 185.

[12] P. 341. *Ibid.*, 5–6.

[13] P. 341. *Ibid., Chronicle*, 53–5.

[14] P. 342. Cowley, *Secrets*, 251–2.

[15] P. 342. Palmerston to Russell, Jan. 19, 1863, P.R.O., G. and D., 22 : 14.

[16] P. 342. *Ann. Reg.* for 1863, *Chronicle*, pp. 174–6.

[17] P. 343. *Inter al.*, F. A. Golder in *Am. His. Rev.*, vol. XX, no. 4 (July 1915), pp. 801–12 ; B. P. Thomas, ' Russo-American Relations, 1815–1867,' in *Johns Hopkins Studies*, vol. XLVIII (1930), pp. 127–36 ; François Charles Roux, *Alexandre II, Gortchakoff et Napoléon III* (Paris, 1913), livre iv, chaps. 1–3 ; W. F. F. Grace in *Cam. Hist. Journ.*, vol. I, no. 1 (1923), pp. 95–102 ; de la Gorce, *Second Empire*, IV, 414–66 ; C.H.B.F.P., II, 456–64.

[18] P. 344. Grace, *loc. cit.*, 97–8.

[19] P. 344. Thomas, *loc. cit.*, 136.

[20] P. 344. Fitzmaurice, I, 446 ; Q.V.L., 2nd Ser., I, 66–70, 82–3, 102 ; Lord J. Russell, *Later Corr.*, II, 302–3.

[21] P. 345. Vitzthum, *op. cit.*, II, 213.

[22] P. 346. Palmerston to Russell, Apr. 5, May 22, 28, 31, Oct. 2 ; Palmerston's memoranda, Oct. 5, 8, 1863, P.R.O., G. and D., 22 : 14, 22.

[23] P. 346. *Hansard*, 3rd Ser., CLXXII, 1129–34.

[24] P. 346. C.H.B.F.P., II, 461–2.

[25] P. 347. Russell to Victoria, May 17, 1863, *Windsor MSS.* H. 50.

[26] P. 347. (Later docketed) ' Sketch of Despatch to Lord Napier or of Note to be presented by him, 1863 ? ' with other sheets suggesting alterations in despatches, P.R.O., G. and D., 22 : 14 ; Q.V.L., 2nd Ser., I, 82–3.

[27] P. 347. Gen. Grey to Granville, June 1, 1863, P.R.O., G. and D., 29 : 18 ; note 29, *infra*.

[28] P. 348. Q.V.L., 2nd Ser., I, 67.

[29] P. 348. *Ibid.*, 67, 69–70 ; Granville to Victoria, Gen. Grey to Victoria, and Sir C. Wood to Victoria, undated (about Feb. 24–5, 1863), *Windsor MSS.* H.49.

[30] P. 348. Palmerston's memorandum, March 2, 1863, P.R.O., G. and D., 22 : 14.

[31] P. 348. Palmerston to Russell, Feb. 23, 1863, P.R.O., G. and D., 22 : 14.

[32] P. 348. Same to same, Feb. 26, 27, 1863, P.R.O., G. and D., 22 : 22.

[33] P. 348. Palmerston's memorandum, March 2, 1863, P.R.O., G. and D., 22 : 14.

[34] P. 349. Q.V.L., 2nd Ser., I, 95–6 ; Russell to Victoria, July 31, 1863, *Windsor MSS.* H. 50 ; Palmerston to Russell, Aug. 3, 1863, P.R.O., G. and D., 22 : 22.

[35] P. 349. Golder, *loc. cit.* ; Palmerston to Russell, Oct. 19, 1863, P.R.O., G. and D., 22 : 22.

[36] P. 350. Palmerston to Russell, Sept. 14, 1863, P.R.O., G. and D., 22 : 14.

[37] P. 350. Vitzthum, *op. cit.*, II, 240.

[38] P. 350. *Ann. Reg.* for 1863, p. 208.

[39] P. 350. de la Gorce, *Second Empire*, IV, 461.

[40] P. 350. Lyall, I, 135–8.

[41] P. 351. Bloomfield, II, 171–2.

[42] P. 351. *Ann. Reg.* for 1863, pp. 210–14.

[43] P. 351. Palmerston to Russell, Nov. 8, 18, 1863, P.R.O., G. and D., 22 : 22.

44 P. 351. Same to same, Apr. 7, 1863, P.R.O., G. and D., 22 : 14.
45 P. 352. *Ann. Reg.*, for 1863, Pt. II, 352–3.
46 P. 352. Vitzthum, *op. cit.*, II, 262.
47 P. 352. Palmerston to Russell, Sept. 30, 1862, P.R.O., G. and D., 22 : 14.
48 P. 352. Same to same, Sept. 11, Dec. 13, 1863, P.R.O., G. and D., 22 : 22, 14.
49 P. 352. Q.V.L., 2nd Ser., I, 104.
50 P. 353. Palmerston to Russell, Sept. 26, 1863, P.R.O., G. and D., 22 : 22.
51 P. 353. Same to same, Feb. 18, 1863, P.R.O., G. and D., 22 : 14.
52 P. 354. *Hansard*, 3rd Ser., CLXX, 90–1.
53 P. 354. Palmerston's memoranda, June 25, Aug. 23 ; Palmerston to Russell, Aug. 23, Sept. 4, 21, Oct. 2, 1863, P.R.O., G. and D., 22 : 14, 22, 27 ; *Hansard*, 3rd Ser., CLXX, 90–4 ; Guedalla, *Gladstone and Palmerston*, 263–4, 266–7 ; Lord J. Russell, *Later Corr.*, II, 334.
54 P. 355. *Ibid.*
55 P. 355. Palmerston to Layard, Sept. 5, 1863, Br. Mus., *Add. MSS.* 38989, f. 320.
56 P. 355. Lord J. Russell, *Later Corr.*, II, 334.
57 P. 355. Palmerston to Russell, Sept. 22, 1863, P.R.O., G. and D., 22 : 22.
58 P. 356. Dasent, *Delane*, I, 325.
59 P. 356. *Ibid.*, 326–8.
60 P. 356. F.O. memorandum, without signature, docket or date, but bound with papers for 1860, handwriting unknown, P.R.O., F.O., 78 : 1556.
61 P. 356. Palmerston to Russell, Sept. 26, 1863, P.R.O., G. and D., 22 : 22.
62 P. 356. Bulwer to Russell, June 15, 1860 (no. 332), P.R.O., F.O., 78 : 1556.
63 P. 357. Dasent, *Delane*, I, 325.
64 P. 358. Reid, *Milnes*, II, 216.
65 P. 358. Colquhoun to Russell, July 17, 1861 (no. 72), F.O., 78 : 1715.
66 P. 358. Cowley to Russell, Dec. 5, 1861 (no. 1431), F.O., 78 : 1715.
67 P. 358. Bulwer to Russell, Jan. 1, 3, 1863 (nos. 1, 2), P.R.O., F.O., 78 : 1795.
68 P. 359. Hoskins, 350–63.
69 P. 359. Palmerston's suggestions for a despatch, Nov. 23, 1861, P.R.O., G. and D., 22 : 21.
70 P. 359. Palmerston to Russell, Dec. 8, 1861, P.R.O., G. and D., 22 : 21.
71 P. 359. *Ibid.*
72 P. 360. Palmerston to Victoria, July 8, 25, 1862, *Windsor MSS.* A. 30.
73 P. 360. Lucas, *Glenesk*, 150.
74 P. 360. Bulwer to Russell, Jan. 3, 1863 (no. 3), P.R.O., G. and D., 78 : 1795.
75 P. 361. Palmerston to Russell, Feb. 2, Apr. 5, June 23, 1863, P.R.O., F.O., 22 : 14, 22.
76 P. 361. Same to same, Apr. 5, 1863, P.R.O., F.O., 22 : 14.
77 P. 361. Same to same, Apr. 5, 1863 ; Oct. 24, 1864, P.R.O., G. and D., 22 : 14, 15.
78 P. 361. Same to same, Aug. 11, 1864, P.R.O., G. and D., 22 : 15.
79 P. 361. Steefel, *passim.*
80 P. 362. Palmerston to Russell, Apr. 5, 1860, P.R.O., G. and D., 22 : 21.
81 P. 362. C.H.B.F.P., II, 548 n.
82 P. 363. Q.V.L., 2nd Ser., I, 25.
83 P. 363. *Hansard*, 3rd Ser., CLXXII, 1252.
84 P. 364. *Memorandum on the Treaty of London*, by Baron Ernst Stockmar (undated) ; Palmerston to Victoria, Nov. 23, 1863, *Windsor MSS.* I, 91.

[85] P. 364. Q.V.L., 2nd Ser., I, 118–20.
[86] P. 367. Palmerston to Russell, Oct. 19, 1863, P.R.O., G. and D., 22 : 22.
[87] P. 367. *Ibid.* ; opinions of the Queen and of individual members of the cabinet, Dec. 2 (?), 1863, P.R.O., G. and D., 22 : 14 ; Q.V.L., 2nd Ser., I, 117–18, 127–9 ; Palmerston to Victoria, Nov. 23, 1863, *Windsor MSS.* I, 91.
[88] P. 367. Palmerston to Russell, Apr. 5, 1860, P.R.O., G. and D., 22 : 21.
[89] P. 367. Same to same, Nov. 23, 1860.
[90] P. 367. Same to same, Dec. 7, 1863, P.R.O., G. and D., 22 : 22.
[91] P. 368. Same to same, Apr. 5, 1860 ; Jan. 21, 24, 1861, P.R.O., G. and D., 22 : 21.
[92] P. 368. Same to same, Dec. 26, 1863, P.R.O., G. and D., 22 : 14.
[93] P. 369. Same to same, Dec. 25, 26, 1863.
[94] P. 369. Paper on the opinions of the Queen and of individual members of the cabinet on the Schleswig-Holstein question, Dec. 2 (?), 1863, P.R.O., G. and D., 22 : 14 ; Sir C. Wood to Gen. Grey, Dec. 3, and R. Morier to Gen. Grey, Dec. 5, 1863, *Windsor MSS.* I. 91 ; Morier, I, 393–5.

CHAPTER XXXIV

[1] P. 370. Elliot, *Goschen*, I, 65.
[2] P. 371. Fagan, *Mérimée's Letters*, I, 389 ; Lucas, *Glenesk*, 153, 153 n.
[3] P. 371. Guedalla, *Gladstone and Palmerston*, 286–7 ; Williams, *Gladstone*, 116 ; *Hansard*, 3rd Ser., CLXXXIII, 114–16.
[4] P. 372. Q.V.L., 2nd Ser., I, 142.
[5] P. 372. Palmerston to Russell, Jan. 4, 6, 1864, P.R.O., G. and D., 22 : 15 ; Q.V.L., 2nd Ser., I, 141 ; Palmerston's memorandum, Jan. 5, 1864 (copy), *Windsor MSS.* I, 92.
[6] P. 372. Lord J. Russell, *Later Corr.*, II, 304.
[7] P. 372. Q.V.L., 2nd Ser., I, 144–8.
[8] P. 373. Palmerston to Russell, Jan. 16, 1864, P.R.O., G. and D., 22 : 15.
[9] P. 373. Palmerston's memorandum, Jan. 24, 1864, P.R.O., G. and D., 22 : 23.
[10] P. 373. Steefel, 175.
[11] P. 374. Q.V.L., 2nd Ser., I, 117 ; memorandum of the Queen to Phipps, Jan. 5, 1864, *Windsor MSS.* I. 92.
[12] P. 374. Gen. Grey to Victoria, Jan. 4, 1864 ; Granville to Phipps, Jan. 11, 1864, *Windsor MSS.* I, 92, 93 ; Q.V.L., 2nd Ser., I, 130 ; Morley, *Gladstone*, II, 105.
[13] P. 374. *Ibid.*, 236.
[14] P. 374. *Ibid.*, 153.
[15] P. 375. Lord J. Russell, *Later Corr.*, II, 308.
[16] P. 375. Q.V.L., 2nd Ser., I, 140, 140 n.
[17] P. 375. *Ibid.*, ch. III ; *Windsor MSS.* I. 92, 93, 94, 98 ; Fitzmaurice, I, 456–73.
[18] P. 376. Q.V.L., 2nd Ser., I, 228–9.
[19] P. 376. Fitzmaurice, I, 468–9.
[20] P. 376. Victoria to Palmerston, Feb. 2, 1864, *Windsor MSS.* I. 94. *Cf.* Bloomfield, II, 162 ; Vitzthum, *St. Petersburg and London*, II, 285–6, 336–7, 340.
[21] P. 377. *Ibid.*, 286.
[22] P. 377. *Ibid.*, 341; Palmerston to Russell, Jan. 18, 1864, P.R.O., G. and D., 22 : 15.

23 P. 377.   Gen. Grey to Victoria, June 6, 1864, *Windsor MSS*. I. 98.

24 P. 377.   Empress Frederick, *Letters*, 52.

25 P. 377.   Vitzthum, *op. cit.*, II, chs. XXVIII and XXIX.

26 P. 378.   Cowley, *Secrets*, 262.

27 P. 379.   Bloomfield, II, 163–4 ; *Hansard*, 3rd Ser., CLXXIII, 217–18, 326–8.

28 P. 379.   Walpole, *Russell*, II, 389, 389 n.

29 P. 379.   Victoria to Granville, Feb. 14, 1864 (copy), *Windsor MSS*. I. 94 (printed with slight alterations in Fitzmaurice, I, 460).

30 P. 379.   B. and A., V, 247–8.

31 P. 379.   Q.V.L., 2nd Ser., I, 157 ; Gen. Grey to Victoria, Feb. 16, 1864, *Windsor MSS*. I, 94.

32 P. 380.   Q.V.L., 2nd Ser., I, 161–8.

33 P. 380.   *Ibid.*, 163 ; Steefel, 177–9, 192.

34 P. 381.   Apponyi to Rechberg, London, May 3, 1864, Vienna Archives, no. 42 C [kindly furnished by Professor Steefel] ; B. and A., V, 249–52.

35 P. 382.   Q.V.L., 2nd Ser., I, 180–3, 181 n. ; Fitzmaurice, I, 462–5 ; Walpole, *Russell*, II, 392–4.

36 P. 383.   Q.V.L., 2nd Ser., I, 186–7.

37 P. 383.   *Ibid.*

38 P. 383.   *Ibid.*, 204, 208–9, 230.

39 P. 384.   *Ibid.*, 2nd Ser., III, 299, 355, 447.

40 P. 384.   Malmesbury (3rd earl), *Mem.*, II, 327–8 ; Palmerston to Victoria, June 27, 28, 30, July 7, 1864, *Windsor MSS*. A. 32, 33, I. 99 ; Denison, 168–70 ; ' C.W.' [Charles Wood ?] to ' Charles ' [Grey ?], June 27, 1864, *Windsor MSS*. I. 98 ; *Hansard*, 3rd Ser., CLXXVI, *passim* ; Guedalla, *Gladstone and Palmerston*, 289–90 ; Morley, *Gladstone*, II, 118–20.

41 P. 385.   Palmerston to Russell, Feb. 19, 1864, P.R.O., G. and D., 22 : 23.

42 P. 385.   *Hansard*, 3rd Ser., CLXXVI, 1300.

43 P. 385.   *Ibid.*, 775–6, 1218–19.

44 P. 385.   Monypenny and Buckle, IV, 405 ; Vitzthum, *op. cit.*, II, 374.

45 P. 386.   Denison, 163.

46 P. 386.   *Ibid.*, 165–6.

47 P. 386.   Maxwell, *Clarendon*, II, 287.

48 P. 387.   Bright, *Diaries*, 269–72, 276.

49 P. 388.   Guedalla, *Gladstone and Palmerston*, 288–9.

50 P. 388.   *Ibid.*, 279–80.

51 P. 389.   *Hansard*, 3rd Ser., CLXXV, 316–25.

52 P. 389.   Guedalla, *Gladstone and Palmerston*, 281–2.

53 P. 390.   *Ibid.*   See also Morley, *Gladstone*, II, 128.

54 P. 390.   Guedalla, *Gladstone and Palmerston*, 282–3.

55 P. 391.   *The Times*, Aug. 4, 1864 ; B. and A., V, 258–9.

56 P. 392.   *The Times*, Aug. 10, 1864.

57 P. 392.   Holyoake, *Sixty Years*, II, 78.

58 P. 392.   *Ibid.*, 80.

59 P. 393.   *The Times*, Aug. 10, 1864.

60 P. 393.   *Ibid.*

61 P. 395.   Snell, 95.

62 P. 395.   *The Times*, Aug. 24, 1864.

63 P. 395.   Snell, 95.

64 P. 396.   *The Times*, Sept. 6, 22, 1864.

65 P. 396.   Morley, *Gladstone*, II, 140.

66 P. 396.   Guedalla, *Gladstone and Palmerston*, 292–6.

67 P. 397. *Ibid.*, 297–304 ; Morley, *Gladstone*, II, 139.
68 P. 398. *Ibid.* ; Guedalla, *Gladstone and Palmerston*, 305–8.
69 P. 399. *Ibid.*, 310–13.
70 P. 399. *Windsor MSS.* A. 32, 33, *passim* ; Palmerston to Russell, March 16, 1864, P.R.O., G. and D., 22 : 23.
71 P. 400. Victoria to Palmerston, Nov. 27, 1864 (draft), *Windsor MSS.* A. 33.

CHAPTER XXXV

1 P. 401. Morley, *Gladstone*, II, 140.
2 P. 402. Q.V.L., 2nd Ser., I, 248–9.
3 P. 402. Guedalla, *Gladstone and Palmerston*, 320.
4 P. 402. *Hansard*, 3rd Ser., CLXXVIII, 794.
5 P. 402. Guedalla, *Gladstone and Palmerston*, 321.
6 P. 402. Bright, *Diaries*, 269.
7 P. 402. Guedalla, *Gladstone and Palmerston*, 322–4.
8 P. 403. *Ibid.*, 321.
9 P. 403. *Ibid.*, 320–37 ; Palmerston to Russell, Apr. 5, 1865, P.R.O., G. and D., 22 : 23.
10 P. 403. Palmerston to Victoria, March 7, 1865, *Windsor MSS.* A. 33.
11 P. 404. Reeve, II, 113.
12 P. 404. Hodder, III, 187.
13 P. 404. Guedalla, *Gladstone and Palmerston*, 326–7.
14 P. 404. *Hansard*, 3rd Ser., CLXXI, 1371–7 ; CLXXVI, 85–9 ; CLXXVII, 821–7 ; CLXXVIII, 619–23.
15 P. 406. Q.V.L., 2nd Ser., I, 255–6.
16 P. 407. *Hansard*, 3rd Ser., CLXXI, 1372–5.
17 P. 408. *Ibid.*, CLXXVIII, 622–7.
18 P. 408. *The Times*, Oct. 23, 1865.
19 P. 408. *Hansard*, 3rd Ser., CLXI, 982–8 ; CLXIV, 1653–9 ; CLXXIII, 1196–8 ; CLXXVI, 1377–88 ; CLXXVII, 1369–70 ; Mathieson, *Slave Trade*, 163–91.
20 P. 408. See, *e.g.*, the extraordinary number of letters to Russell in 1863, P.R.O., G. and D., 22 : 22.
21 P. 409. *Hansard*, 3rd Ser., CLXIV, 1654 ; CLXXIII, 1197 ; CLXXVI, 1385.
22 P. 409. Du Bois, 178–91.
23 P. 410. *Hansard*, 3rd Ser., CLXXVII, 550.
24 P. 410. Palmerston to Russell, Oct. 5, 1864, P.R.O., G. and D., 22 : 15.
25 P. 410. Same to same, Dec. 9, 1860, P.R.O., G. and D., 22 : 21.
26 P. 410. Palmerston's memoranda, March 14, 1860, May 18, 1860, P.R.O., G. and D., 22 : 21 ; Palmerston to Russell, various dates, 1860–4, G. and D., 22 : 14, 15, 21, 22 ; Palmerston's memoranda, Jan. 10, June 5, 1865, and Palmerston to Layard, Dec. 27, 1864, Br. Mus., *Add. MSS.* 38990, 38991.
27 P. 410. Palmerston to Russell, Sept. 24, 1861, P.R.O., G. and D., 22 : 21.
28 P. 411. Same to same, May 5, 1863, P.R.O., G. and D., 22 : 22 ; same to same, Oct. 5, 1864, G. and D., 22 : 15.
29 P. 411. Palmerston to Layard, Dec. 27, 1864, Br. Mus., *Add. MSS.* 38990, f. 381. See also Palmerston to Russell, Aug. 13, 1863, P.R.O., G. and D., 22 : 22.
30 P. 411. Same to same, Oct. 5, 1864, P.R.O., G. and D., 22 : 15.
31 P. 411. Same to same, Dec. 9, 1860, P.R.O., G. and D., 22 : 21.

NOTES

[32] P. 412. Same to same, July 31, 1862, P.R.O., G. and D., 22 : 22.

[33] P. 412. *Hansard*, 3rd Ser., CLXXVI, 1384.

[34] P. 412. Palmerston to Russell, July 21, 1862, P.R.O., G. and D., 22 : 14 ; same to same, Aug. 13, 1862, G. and D., 22 : 22 (extract printed in B. and A., V, 227–8).

[35] P. 412. Palmerston to Russell, July 17, 1862, Aug. 3, 1863, P.R.O., G. and D., 22 : 22.

[36] P. 412. Same to same, March 14, 1860, P.R.O., G. and D., 22 : 21.

[37] P. 413. *Hansard*, 3rd Ser., CLXIV, 1657.

[38] P. 413. Palmerston to Russell, Sept. 24, 1861, P.R.O., G. and D., 22 : 21.

[39] P. 413. *Hansard*, 3rd Ser., CLXXIX, 877–8.

[40] P. 414. Hodder, III, 178–9 ; Palmerston to Russell, July 8, 1865, P.R.O., G. and D., 22 : 15.

[41] P. 414. Denison, 174, 178 ; *The Times*, May 29, July 17, *et al.*, 1865 ; Holyoake, *Sixty Years*, II, 77 ; Fagan, *Mérimée's Letters*, 54–5.

[42] P. 414. *Ibid.*, 80, 90.

[43] P. 416. *The Times*, July 12, 1865.

[44] P. 416. Snell, 99.

[45] P. 416. *The Times*, July 13, 1865.

[46] P. 416. Barrington, *Bagehot*, 389.

[47] P. 416. *Ann. Reg.* for 1865, *Chron.*, 160.

[48] P. 416. Maxwell, *Clarendon*, II, 298–9.

[49] P. 417. Hodder, III, 184–6 ; Lucas, *Glenesk*, 154 ; Reeve, II, 119–20.

[50] P. 418. Guedalla, *Gladstone and Palmerston*, 342.

[51] P. 418. *Ibid.*, 347–8.

[52] P. 418. Palmerston to Victoria, Sept. 26, 1865, *Windsor MSS.* A. 33.

[53] P. 418. Trevelyan, *Bright*, 344.

[54] P. 418. Guedalla, *Gladstone and Palmerston*, 348.

[55] P. 418. Cowley, *Secrets*, 287.

[56] P. 419. Q.V.L., 2nd Ser., I, 275–6.

[57] P. 419. Reeve, II, 120.

[58] P. 419. Maxwell, *Smith*, 128.

[59] P. 420. *The Times*, Oct. 19 to Oct. 28, 1865.

[60] P. 421. Q.V.L., 2nd Ser., I, 279.

[61] P. 422. Quoted in *The Times*, Oct. 21, 1865.

[62] P. 422. Morley, *Gladstone*, II, 153–4.

[63] P. 422. Holyoake, *Sixty Years*, II, 78 ; Lord Ronald Gower, *Reminiscences* (London, 1903), I, 186.

[64] P. 422. Hodder, III, 188.

[65] P. 422. *Ann. Reg.* for 1865, *Chron.*, p. 149.

[66] P. 423. Holyoake, *Sixty Years*, II, 78.

INDEX *

* Virtually all the references may be taken as referring directly or indirectly to Palmerston and his activities.

AALAND ISLANDS, fortification of, i. 185 ; ii. 145, 147

Abercromby, Sir Ralph, minister to Sardinia, i. 413–14

Aberdeen, 4th earl of, and the Wellington ministry, i. 65–8 ; Palmerston's feeling toward, i. 84 ; his foreign policy attacked by Palmerston, 1829–30, i. 80–8 ; dislike of the July Revolution and satisfaction in the union of the 'Holy Alliance' Powers, i. 192–3 ; denounces British policy in Spain, 1835–41, i. 214–15 ; and the slave-trade, i. 235, 239 ; and the Maine boundary dispute, i. 250 ; and the 'Opium' war, i. 278 ; and the Near Eastern crisis of 1839–41, i. 318 ; as foreign secretary, 1841–1846, i. chaps. xv.–xvi. ; Palmerston's opinion of his foreign policy, i. 329–30, 353–4 ; his concessions regarding the slave-trade, i. 241, 331–3, 353–4 ; and British influence in Spain, i. 336–7 ; criticism of his foreign policy by both parties, i. 351–2 ; attitude toward Palmerston in 1846, i. 366–8 ; and the Prussian constitution, i. 371 ; and the Spanish Marriages, i. 374–5, 382, 384 ; dislike of and opposition to Palmerston's policy in 1846–51, i. 398, 423, 434 ; his 'antiquated imbecility,' i. 443 ; and Palmerston's attitude toward Schleswig-Holstein, ii. 10 ; his alleged agreement with Guizot to oust Palmerston in 1850, ii. 24–5 ; coaches Herbert for the Don Pacifico debate, ii. 26 ; and his dislike of the revolu-

tions of 1848–9, ii. 32 ; his attitude toward Russell's Reform Bill of 1852, ii. 38 ; attempts to form a Peelite-Whig coalition in Feb. 1851, ii. 40–42 ; the formation of his ministry, ii. 64–74 ; as prime minister, ii. 74–80, chap. xxiii., 106–9 ; assists Palmerston to form his first ministry, ii. 112–15 ; and Palmerston's defeat in 1858, Derby's second ministry, and Palmerston's return to power in 1859, ii. 176–8, 180–215 ; his alleged 'hatred' of Palmerston, ii. 188 ; and the war of 1859, ii. 203 ; his disillusionment with Gladstone in 1859, ii. 209–12 ; considers Austria to be 'fighting the battle of Europe,' ii. 221. Mentioned, i. 5, 94, 417 ; ii. 43, 59, 109, 154. See also Aberdeen Act

Aberdeen Act of 1845 for suppression of the slave-trade, ii. 410–12

Adair, Sir Robert, mission to Belgium, 1831–5, i. 132, 137 ; mission to Prussia, 1835–6, i. 222–4

Adams, Charles Francis, American minister to Great Britain, ii. 294, 315–17, 326, 355

Adams, Henry, ii. 144

Admiralty, Palmerston's service at the, i. 15 ; and the slave-trade, ii. 410

Afghanistan. See Middle East

Albert, Prince of Saxe-Coburg and Gotha (later Prince Consort), his improved position after 1846, i. 371 ; and the Spanish Marriages, i. 386–7 ; reproves Palmerston for his tone to the queen of Portugal, i. 393–4 ; and

279 ; the 'lorcha *Arrow*' war, and the diplomatic opening of, ii. 167, 183 ; the expedition of 1859–60, ii. 239–42, 271–2

Chreptovitch, Count, Russian ambassador to England, ii. 162

Christina, queen dowager of Spain. *See* Spain, 1830–46

Church of England, Palmerston's support of, i. 50 ; his relations with, as home secretary, ii. 75–6 ; compulsory levy of church rates, ii. 133 ; use of ecclesiastical patronage for political purposes, ii. 134, 157, 302–304, 395 ; jurisdiction of its courts, ii. 171 ; church rates, ii. 304 ; Anglican chaplains in the gaols, ii. 304

Church of Ireland, proposed disposal of surplus revenues, i. 188–9 ; conditions in and Palmerston's views concerning, 1841–6, i. 343–8 ; Gladstone and, ii. 387 ; Palmerston's desire for its continued establishment, i. 346 ; ii. 406

Circassia, Palmerston and, i. 282–3 ; ii. 105, 149

Civil Service examinations, ii. 134, 171

Civis Romanus peroration, probable origin of, i. 276

Clanricarde, marquess of, lord privy seal, ii. 178–84

Clarendon, 4th earl of (G. W. F. Villiers), as ambassador to Spain, i. 145, 216–17 ; opposition to Palmerston, and Palmerston's suspicion of, 1839–41, i. 301–19 ; criticises Palmerston's attack on Peel's second ministry, i. 330 ; desire that Palmerston should replace Aberdeen, i. 358 ; expected by the Court to exercise a moderating influence on Palmerston, i. 370 ; comments on the Queen's desire to control foreign policy, ii. 51 ; his attitude on Palmerston's dismissal, ii. 53–4 ; and the Crimean war, ii. 80–90, 99 ; and the peace negotiations of 1855, ii. 127–8 ; and the resumption of peace negotiations, ii. 137–41, 145–6 ; and the disputes with the United States, 1855–6, ii. 141–4, 154–6 ; and the Paris peace conference, ii. 146–52 ;

and the execution of the Treaty of Paris, ii. 160–6 ; and the Indian mutiny, ii. 173–4 ; and Palmerston's defeat in 1858, Derby's second ministry, and Palmerston's return to power in 1859, ii. 176–8, 180–215 ; and the war of 1859, ii. 203–5 ; gives up the Foreign Office to Russell in 1859, ii. 216 ; his critical attitude toward Russell, ii. 221 ; explains Palmerston's attitude toward Gladstone, ii. 234 ; and the Cobden treaty, ii. 244 ; and the *Trent* affair, ii. 294. Mentioned, i. 336, 357, 382, 410, 435 ; ii. 20, 23, 27–8, 29, 71, 111–12, 113, 116, 164, 178, 180, 200–1, 247, 249, 250, 260, 277, 297, 340, 342, 378, 386

Cobden, Richard, wishes Palmerston to join the protectionists, ii. 69 ; his feeling toward Palmerston in 1855, ii. 119 ; and Palmerston's defeat in 1857, ii. 169 ; defeated in election of 1857, ii. 170 ; refuses to enter the cabinet in 1859, ii. 217–18 ; and the rivalry in naval armaments, ii. 237 ; and appropriations for defence, ii. 280 ; overtures to the Conservatives, ii. 280. Mentioned, i. 150, 284, 306, 327, 370, 402 ; ii. 25, 28, 62, 134, 257, 317–20, 410. *See also* Cobden treaty, Radicals

Cobden treaty, and Palmerston's attitude toward, ii. 243–6. Mentioned, ii. 248, 257–8, 282, 339, 340, 387, 393

Commission on National Defence, 1859, ii. 238–9

Cowley, 1st earl (H. R. C. Wellesley), and the Paris peace conference, ii. 146–52 ; and the war of 1859, ii. 203–9 ; mediates at Vienna and warns Napoleon not to go to war in 1859, ii. 208–9 ; on Anglo-French relations in 1859, ii. 235–6. Mentioned, ii. 129–30, 139, 166, 173, 245, 250, 270, 277, 327, 358

Cracow, occupation of, i. 265, 267–71, 279 ; annexation by Austria, i. 386, 389–90

Crampton, James F. T., British minister to the United States, ii. 141–144, 155–6

fear of French designs in 1860, ii.
250–1 ; war of the Druses and
Maronites and the French expedition,
1860, ii. 268–70 ; Russia and the
Balkans, 1859–65, ii. 328–35. Men-
tioned, i. 58–9, 171 ; ii. 16–19. *See
also* Balkans, Circassia, Crimean
war, Greece, Mehemet Ali, Middle
East, Paris, treaty of, Ponsonby,
Roumanian Principalities, Russia,
Serbia, Suez Canal, Turkey, Unkiar
Skelessi, Urquhart, *Vixen* episode
Easthope, Sir John, editor of the
Morning Chronicle, friendship with
Palmerston, i. 362. Mentioned, ii. 33
Edinburgh, Palmerston's visit to, in
1863, ii. 342
Education, primary, ii. 158
Egypt. *See* Eastern Question, 1832–3,
1839–41, Suez Canal
Eldon, 1st earl of (John Scott), opposes
Palmerston in 1826, i. 54. Men-
tioned, i. 21, 23, 85
Elections, Palmerston's in particular
at Cambridge (1806), i. 12–14 ; at
Horsham (1806), i. 14 ; at Cambridge (1807), i. 15 ; at Newtown
(1807), i. 16 ; at Cambridge (1811),
i. 24 ; at Cambridge (1826) and
Palmerston's definitive break with
ultra-Tory party, i. 54–5 ; (1830),
i. 90 ; Palmerston defeated at Cambridge (1831), i. 105 ; elected for
South Hants (1832), and Tiverton
(1835), i. 204 ; Tiverton (1837), i.
205–6 ; (1841), i. 316–17, 340 ;
(1847), ii. 31–2 ; (1857), ii. 169–70 ;
(1859), ii. 209–11 ; (1865), ii. 415–16
Elgin, 8th earl of, as postmaster-general,
ii. 216, 218 ; and China, 1859–60,
ii. 241–2, 271 ; death, ii. 340
Ellice, Edward ('Bear'), opposes
Palmerston's return to the Foreign
Office in 1835, i. 203–4, 359 ; opposition to Palmerston in 1839–41,
i. 306–8 ; criticises Palmerston's
attack on Peel's second ministry, i.
330–1 ; on Aberdeen's foreign
policy, i. 351 ; opposes Palmerston's
return to the Foreign Office in 1845,
i. 356–9, 365 ; death, ii. 340.
Mentioned, i. 258, 319, 370 ; ii. 58,
214

Elliot, Capt. Sir Charles, R.N., 1st
superintendent, later plenipotentiary
to China, i. 274, 278
Entente cordiale with France, first,
established, i. 107–12 ; development,
i. 192–7 ; the economic aspect, i.
195, 212 ; Duvergier de Hauranne
blames Talleyrand for its weakness,
i. 196 ; Palmerston's responsibility
for its weakness, i. 196–7 ; general
history of, chaps. vii. and ix. ; decline of, i. chap. x. ; breaks down
during the Near Eastern crisis of
1839–41, i. chap. xiv. ; revived by
Aberdeen and Guizot, i. chaps. xv.-
xvi. Mentioned, i. 267–8
Esterhazy, Prince Paul Anton, Austrian
ambassador, i. 198, 209
Euston, Earl of (George Henry Fitzroy,
later 4th duke of Grafton), i. 13, 16
Evans, Sir Delacy, military service for
the Portuguese and Spanish governments, i. 214–16
Everett, Edward, American minister
to Great Britain, i. 241

Factory legislation, i. 326–7
Ferdinand VII, king of Spain. *See*
Spain, 1830–4
Ficquelmont, Count, Austrian ambassador to Russia, on Palmerston's foreign
policy, i. 404. Mentioned, i. 268
Finland, ii. 105
Flahaut, Count, mission to England in
1831, i. 124–7. Mentioned, ii. 249–
250, 292.
Foreign Office. *See* Palmerston
Forster, William E., member for Bradford, reproves Palmerston publicly
in 1864, ii. 392–4
Fox, Charles James, Palmerston's
opinion of, i. 21
Fox, Henry Stephen, British minister
to the United States, i. 244, 253
France, Palmerston's fear of her expansionist tendencies, i. 76–7, 86–7 ;
his understanding of middle class
influence in, i. 87, 193, 311 ; dispute with the United States and
Palmerston's mediation, i. 194, 211–
212 ; Palmerston's general attitude
toward the second republic, i. 424–5 ;

INDEX

Orsini plot, and Palmerston's defeat in
1858, ii. 180–3
Otho, king of Greece. *See* Greece

PACIFICO, DON, ii. 22–8
Palmerston, 1st viscount, i. 2–3
Palmerston, 2nd viscount, i. 3–5, 8–9
Palmerston, 3rd viscount (Henry John
Temple)
PRIVATE LIFE :
ancestry and family connections,
social and political, i. 2–5 ; at
Harrow, i. 5–6 ; at Edinburgh, i.
6–8 ; succeeds his father, i. 8–9 ;
at Cambridge, i. 9–10 ; personal
characteristics, entrance into, and
attitude toward society, i. 19–20,
23–4 ; personal characteristics in
middle age and his nicknames of
' Cupid ' and ' Lord Pumicestone,'
i. 96–7 ; his marriage, i. 259–61 ;
his life when in opposition, 1841–6,
i. 324–8 ; during his third term
at the Foreign Office, 1846–51, i.
407–9 ; his life, his interests and
his remarkable vitality as prime
minister, 1855–65, ii. 117–19, 170,
192–3, 252–4, 291, 304, 321, 340–3,
390, 414 ; the deterioration of his
mental faculties from 1863, ii. 338,
345, 362, 386, 414, in general, see
chaps. xxxiii.–xxxv. ; illness at the
end of 1861, ii. 297 ; his final
illness, death and burial, ii. 417–23 ;
his enterprise and kindliness as an
Irish absentee landlord, i. 24,
46–7, 325–6, 408 ; his experience
in business, i. 47, 57, 326 ; receives
degree from Oxford, ii. 306 ;
becomes warden of the Cinque
Ports, ii. 306 ; becomes rector of
Glasgow University, ii. 341–2 ;
receives degree from University of
Edinburgh, ii. 342 ; receives
degree from Cambridge, ii. 390.
See also Palmerston, Characteristics
as a Public Man, *Visits to the
Continent*
PERSONAL CHARACTERISTICS :
his interest in racing and other
sports, i. 45 ; his kindliness, i.
45–6, ii. 391, 417–18 ; declared by

Gladstone ' incapable of enduring
anger,' ii. 298 ; geniality, ii. 305.
(*See also* Labour Legislation,
Palmerston, *his popularity, infra*) ;
his interest in art, i. 47, 327 ; his
lack of interest in religion, ii. 133 ;
his subordination of pleasure to
business, i. 191–2 ; devotion to
exercise, i. 257–8 ; his resilience
and sense of humour, i. 258–9, ii.
418. *See also* Palmerston, *Private
Life* and *Public Life, passim*
PUBLIC LIFE :
Offices, appointment as junior
lord of the Admiralty, i. 15 ;
refuses the Exchequer and the
cabinet, and becomes secretary at
War (1809), i. 17–19 ; refuses chief
secretaryship for Ireland, i. 23 ;
failure to secure advancement, i.
44–5, 50–1 ; repeated refusal of
governor-generalship of India, i.
50 ; attempt to remove him from
War Office, i. 50 ; enters the
cabinet, i. 56 ; Canning offers,
then withdraws, the Exchequer, i.
56–7 ; refuses the governorship of
Jamaica and the governor-generalship of India, i. 57 ; Goderich
offers and withdraws the Exchequer, i. 60 ; resigns from
Wellington's ministry, i. 68–72 ;
after two years in opposition makes
a junction with the Whigs and is
appointed to Foreign Office, in
1830, i. chap. iv. ; ' dismissed '
from office with the rest of ministry
Nov. 1834, i. 187 ; his return to
Foreign Office in 1835, i. 203–4 ;
goes out of office with Melbourne's
ministry in 1841, i. 322–4 ;
returns to the Foreign Office in
1846, i. 355–60, 369–70 ; dismissed in 1851, ii. chap. xxi.;
refuses lord-lieutenancy of Ireland
and a British peerage, ii. 50 ;
becomes home secretary, 1852, ii.
72–4 ; resigns from Aberdeen's
cabinet and returns in Dec.
1853, ii. 92–102 ; becomes prime
minister in 1855, ii. 106–13 ;
receives the Garter, ii. 149 ; replaced by Granville as leader in

1830, i. 165–70 ; revolt in Russia, 1863, ii. 343–52, 363. Mentioned, i. 267–71, 438–9 ; ii. 104–5, 114, 128, 137, 149, 395. *See also* Cracow

Ponsonby, 2nd baron, later viscount, ambassador to Turkey and Austria, i. 181, 183, 185, 262–3, 280–3, 312, 413, 428, 441–2, 446 ; ii. 13, 15, 18

Portfolio, The, i. 281–3

Portland, 3rd duke of, appoints Palmerston to the Admiralty, i. 15

Portugal, George Canning and, i. 57–8 ; Palmerston's defence of constitutionalism in 1828, i. 68 ; his indictment of Miguel and of Wellington's attitude toward him in 1829, i. 80–2 ; his relations with, 1830–4, i. 139–50 ; 1835–41, i. 218–19 ; and Palmerston's attempts to put down the slavetrade, i. 232–5 ; 1846–51, i. 390–7. *See also* Slave-trade

Pozzo di Borgo, Corsican-Russian diplomatist, discussion of foreign policy with Palmerston in 1829, i. 77 ; mission to central Europe, i. 173, 177–8 ; interview with Palmerston, Jan. 1833, i. 178 ; as ambassador to England, i. 209. Mentioned, i. 184, 281

Prussia, warned not to intervene in the Polish revolt of 1830, i. 167 ; insulted by Palmerston in connection with the Eastern Question, i. 183 ; his attempt in 1835 to persuade her to bring Holland to terms with Belgium, i. 222–3 ; opposition to the fortification of Belgium and resentment at Palmerston's tone, i. 223–6 ; impresses Palmerston in 1844, i. 327 ; and the Sonderbund, i. 405 ; Palmerston's interest in her leadership and her constitutional development, ii. 5–6 ; and Schleswig-Holstein, 1849, ii. 6–11 ; Palmerston's desire to establish close relations with, in 1860, ii. 251–2 ; his unfortunate relations with, 1860–3, ii. 306, 309–11 ; his view of Austro-Prussian rivalry in Germany, ii. 307–8. Mentioned, i. 267–71, 371–2, 386. *See also* Ancillon, Belgium, Bismarck, Cracow, Polish nation, Schleswig-Holstein

QUADRUPLE Alliance of 1834, i. 139–50 ; Palmerston's and Talleyrand's views of, i. 147–49. Mentioned, i. 209–19

Quebec, fortification of, ii. 401–2

RADICALS, and Palmerston's relations with (1830–41), i. 104, 167, 189–90, 205–7, 257, 280, 282–4 ; (1841–6), i. 331, 335–6 ; (1846–51), i. 396, 402, 409–10, 420, 446 ; ii. 10, 11, 21, 24–5, 28, 30–2, 36–7, 41, 43, 50, 52, 53–4 ; (1852–5), ii. 60, 64, 73, 80, 91–3, 100 ; (1855–9), ii. 119–20, 130 ; (their variety and aims), ii. 132–3 ; increase in parliamentary strength in 1857, ii. 170 ; and Palmerston's defeat in 1858, Derby's second ministry, and Palmerston's return to power in 1859, ii. 176–8, 180–215 ; and Palmerston's second ministry, ii. 257, 279–80, 282, 302, 317–26, 339, 390

Raglan, Gen., 1st baron, ii. 107, 121–5

Rechberg, Count J. B. von, Austrian foreign minister, ii. 251

Reeve, Henry, opposition to Palmerston, 1839–41, i. 305–6 ; his change of heart, i. 315 ; works against Palmerston at Paris in 1845, i. 357–60 ; reverses his attitude, i. 409. Mentioned, ii. 24, 29, 32

Richmond, 4th duke of, i. 22

Richmond, 5th duke of, resigns from Grey's ministry, i. 188. Mentioned, i. 95, 106

Robinson, Henry Crabb, i. 47

Roebuck, John Arthur, ii. 25, 108, 115, 133, 144, 155, 157, 169, 185, 188, 214–15, 285

Roman Catholic Church :

Catholic emancipation, i. 12, 15 ; Palmerston's first pronouncements on, i. 21–2, 51 ; his advocacy annoys his Cambridge constituents, i. 53, 54 ; his continuing enthusiasm for, i. 55 ; and the Canning ministry, i. 56 ; Palmerston demands pledges from Wellington concerning, i. 62–3 ; speaks in behalf of, i. 70–1 ; taken up by Wellington, i. 74 ; Palmerston's great speech on, i. 78–80

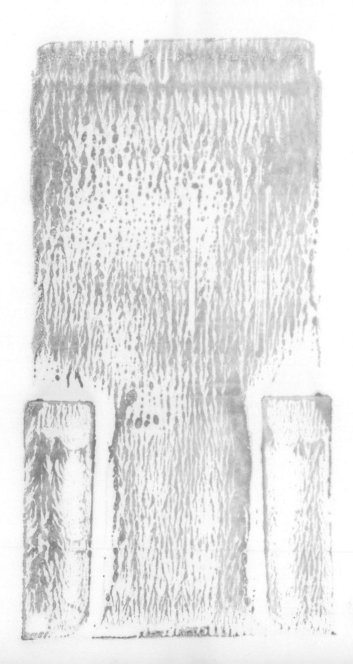